βS

Books by Allan W. Eckert

The Winning of America Series
The Frontiersmen
Wilderness Empire
The Conquerors
The Wilderness War
Gateway to Empire
Twilight of Empire

Other Books
The Writer's Digest Course in Article Writing
The Great Auk
A Time of Terror
The Silent Sky
The Writer's Digest Course in Short Story Writing
Wild Season
Bayou Backwaters
The Crossbreed
Blue Jacket
The King Snake
The Dreaming Tree
In Search of a Whale
Incident at Hawk's Hill
The Court-Martial of Daniel Boone
The Owls of North America
Tecumseh!
The Hab Theory
The Wading Birds of North America
Savage Journey
Song of the Wild
Whattizzit?
Johnny Logan: Shawnee Spy
The Dark Green Tunnel
The Wand
The Scarlet Mansion
Earth Treasures—Northeastern Quadrant
Earth Treasures—Southeastern Quadrant
Earth Treasures—Northwestern Quadrant
Earth Treasures—Southwestern Quadrant
A Sorrow in Our Heart: The Life of Tecumseh
That Dark and Bloody River: Chronicles of the Ohio River Valley
The World of Opals
Return to Hawk's Hill

Gateway to Empire

Gateway to Empire

By ALLAN W. ECKERT

Jesse Stuart Foundation
Ashland, Kentucky
2004

To my friend —
KENAN HEISE
— with appreciation.

ISBN 1-931672-27-X   ISBN 1-931672-28-8 (pbk.)

Jacket Design by Brett Nance
Original Art by John Alan Maxwell

Published by:
Jesse Stuart Foundation
1645 Winchester Avenue • P.O. Box 669
Ashland, Kentucky 41105
(606) 326-1667 • JSFBOOKS.com

The implicit obedience and respect which the followers of Tecumseh pay to him is really astonishing and more than any other circumstance bespeaks him one of those uncommon geniuses which spring up occasionally to produce revolutions and overturn the established order of things.

— WILLIAM HENRY HARRISON
Letter, August 7, 1811, to Secretary
of War William Eustis.

In my solitary walks I contemplate what a great and powerful republic will yet arise in this new world. Here, I say, will be the seat of millions yet unborn; here, the asylum of oppressed millions yet to come. How composedly I would die could I be resuscitated at that bright era of American greatness — an era which I hope will announce the tidings of death to fell superstition and dread tyranny.

— DR. ISAAC VAN VOORHIS, post
surgeon, Fort Dearborn, Chicago,
Illinois; letter to a friend, August, 1811.

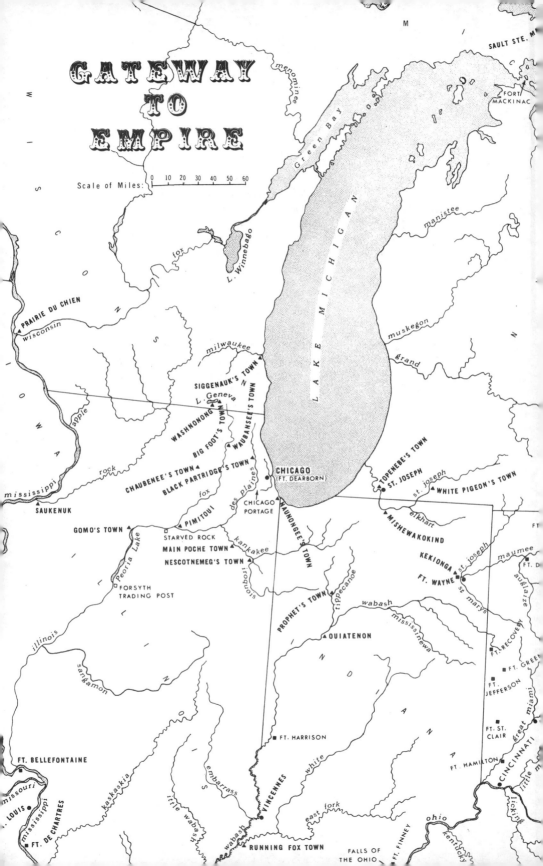

I heard the muffled beat of drum,
    The woman's wail of fife,
The Dead March played for Dearborn's men
    Just marching out of life.
        — quoted by Milo Milton Quaife
        in *Lake Michigan*, page 126.

The white race is a monster who is always hungry
and what he eats is land.
        — CHIKSIKA, brother of Tecumseh,
        March 19, 1779.

AUTHOR'S NOTE

GATEWAY *to Empire* is fact, not fiction. The incidents described here actually occurred; the dates are historically accurate; the characters, regardless of how major or how minor, actually lived the roles in which they are portrayed.

This book is meant to provide an accurate and comprehensive — yet swiftly paced and dramatic — picture of the events and people of the period it covers. It is the result of extended and intensive research through a great multitude of original documents of the times involved, including many hundreds of personal letters and notes, memoranda, general orders, diaries, legal papers, journals, deeds, military records, depositions, tribal records where they exist, governmental reports, logbooks and many other sources.

Within the text there are occasional consecutively numbered notes keyed to an Amplification Notes section at the back of the book. These notes include tangential material that provides the reader with increased understanding of events portrayed and the pinpointing of historic geography to present locales.

Since English translations of the names of Indians in many cases become derogatory or repetitive, I have endeavored, wherever practicable, to refer to these individuals by their actual Indian names. Occasionally, in cases where the Indian name involves difficulty in pronunciation, the English form is used.

As in the other volumes of this series, certain techniques normally associated with the novel form have been utilized to help provide continuity and narrative flow, but not at the expense of historical accuracy. Where dialogue is used it is actual quoted conversation from historical sources (and in such cases sometimes stilted due to the expressive forms in use at those times) or is reconstructed from historically recorded inter-changes between individuals, but not written then as dialogue. In other instances, historical fact has been utilized in the form of conversation to maintain dramatic narrative pace, but always in keeping with the character and fundamental leanings of the individual speaking the words.

As a further aid there is, at the back of the book, a chapter-by-chapter listing of the principal sources for the facts, dialogue and possibly controversial information in the text. There is also a bibliography and complete index.

Gateway to Empire is the fifth volume in the author's in-progress series entitled *The Winning of America.* Other volumes in the series are *The Frontiersmen, Wilderness Empire, The Conquerors* and *The Wilderness War.* A sixth volume is presently in progress. The individual books do not depend upon one another, yet they strongly complement each other. All of them contribute to the principal theme of the series: how the white man took North America from the Indians. Step by step this series moves across the continent, showing clearly and in the most fundamentally human terms how the land was won — through encroachment, trickery, warfare, deceit, grant, treachery, purchase, alliance, theft and treaty. In point of time, *Gateway to Empire* picks up the narrative thread where it left off in *The Conquerors,* and its time frame is largely concurrent with that of *The Frontiersmen,* but it is not necessary to have read one in order to appreciate the other.

As in past volumes of *The Winning of America* series, it is neither the intention nor desire of the author to champion either the cause of the Indians or that of the whites; there were heroes and rascals on both sides, humanity and atrocity on both sides, rights and wrongs on both sides. The facts are presented chronologically and without projection, just as they occurred, and with the greatest possible degree of accuracy. There has been a minimum of author intrusion, editorializing or moralizing. It has not been necessary. The facts speak amply for themselves and whatever conclusions are drawn must be drawn solely by the reader.

— ALLAN W. ECKERT

Everglades, Florida
June 1982

MAPS OR DIAGRAMS

Gateway to Empire

PROLOGUE

[*December 27, 1763 — Tuesday*]

THE midwife was a portly Frenchwoman whose thick ebony hair was braided into a glossy cable that normally fell below her almost nonexistent waistline. Now, however, as always on these occasions when she attended births, the braid had been coiled and perched atop her head as if it were some dark slumbering snake. The dress she wore was a gray muslin tent whose hem swept the floor, its high lace collar dull ivory in color and matched by uncommonly wide five-button cuffs snug to her wrists. A bead of perspiration on her forehead reflected tiny highlights from the four high-wick chimney lamps, attesting to the lingering nervousness she was experiencing.

As one of Quebec's most skilled midwives, Antoinette Giveaux had brought over four hundred infants into this world with never a loss after the birth and only two stillborn, over which she had no control. Her competence imbued her with such professional calm that her very presence was recognized as a soothing influence not only to the laboring mother but also to the often fearful members of the family. Nervousness seldom assailed her and in this instance she knew the cause of it was the uniformed officer who sat in a straight-backed chair along the wall, wordlessly watching as she performed her duties.

Virtually without exception, Madame Giveaux allowed no one but an assistant — usually an apprentice — to attend her at birthings. Husbands especially were prohibited, but this time there was a difference. The husband was Captain John MacKinzie, surgeon of the British Army's Sixtieth Regiment, a blunt no-nonsense Scotsman who had announced he would witness the birth of his son. Not his *child;* his son. As if already it were a *fait accompli.* With other men, other husbands, even other doctors, the midwife would almost certainly have taken exception, but there was about this man's piercing gaze and demeanor a quality of strength and stubbornness to which she acquiesced. And, true to his word, he had stayed out of the way, offering neither suggestion nor criticism, though he was himself experienced in the delivery of babies among the regimental wives.

The captain's eyes had never left her as she worked, his face devoid of expression except once when the faintest of frowns momentarily appeared as the woman on the bed, who had occasionally groaned softly with the pain of contraction, gave voice to a sharp little shriek. The sound had cut off as swiftly as it began and the captain's lady had turned her head and looked toward her husband. Antoinette Giveaux knew with certainty that the man's momentary frown was not one of concern that his wife had experienced pain, but rather one of disapproval that the laboring woman should have so lost control as to permit the sound to escape her. And in the brief glance his wife had directed toward him, there was mute apology for her transgression.

For Emily MacKinzie, this was neither her first child nor her first husband. At age seventeen, as Emily Tyne, daughter of a London carriagemaker, she had met and soon married British Army chaplain William Haliburton. Almost immediately his regiment had been ordered to America to engage in fighting the French in what the New World termed the French and Indian War but which, now that it had ended, was being referred to in the Old World as the Seven Years' War. They had had only one child born to their union — a daughter, Jane, born in New York four years ago, in January, 1759. Captain Haliburton had survived the war, but not by much. He had fought under Wolfe at the Battle of Quebec, mourned his general's death there and even the death of the gallant French commander, Montcalm, in the same battle, and was on hand on September 8, 1760, when the French capitulation, written by Sir Jeffrey Amherst, was signed by the Marquis de Vaudreuil, governor and lieutenant general of New France. With that act, Canada and all her dependencies became possessions of the British Crown. And then, only a few weeks after the death of George II, Captain Haliburton contracted a fever and within mere days had died.

The widow Haliburton, left with a daughter not quite two, remained in New York and within a year met Captain MacKinzie.[1] Though he was thirty, the Scots officer had never married and really had no anticipation of doing so. For Emily Haliburton, however, he was a means of escape from a situation to which there seemed no other solution. If she did not love him with the romantic fervor she had showered upon William, she nevertheless admired him a great deal and could envision many things worse than becoming his wife. John MacKinzie's character and physique bore many similarities; blunt, tough, filled with strength. His whole manner epitomized the qualities of a British officer of the Crown and, even though a doctor, there was little of gentleness about him. He expected a great deal of others and most of all from himself. And when they married, on the sixth day of December in 1761, he also expected much of her. To her credit, Emily Tyne Haliburton MacKinzie, attractive, soft and fair, largely lived up to his expectations except, perhaps, in the matter of stoicism. She found it most difficult to experience real pain without outcry.

The child she bore now, with only a few more muffled cries, was a son, just as her husband had known it would be; as if it hadn't had the temerity to be anything else. Not until Antoinettte Giveaux had bathed and swaddled the infant and was carrying him back to his mother did Captain John MacKinzie move or speak. He stood up, straight as he had been sitting, and in a few clipped strides intercepted the midwife. He held out his arms and, after only an instant of hesitation, Madame Giveaux passed the child to him.

"Ye've doon well," he murmured. It was both a compliment and a dismissal. He pressed gold coins of the agreed-upon fee into her hand. She bobbed her head, made the faintest suggestion of a curtsy and silently left the room, relieved to be away from this man whose very presence was so unnerving.

Captain MacKinzie looked at the tiny face in the bundle he was holding and he pulled back the cloth and inspected the body. Though earlier the babe had cried, now he was silent, though awake, his sturdy little arms and legs moving aimlessly. The officer re-covered him and then looked up. Emily was watching him closely.

"He's a fine strong laddie ye've given me, Mrs. MacKinzie," he said. Amazingly, there was a faint smile on his lips. He placed the infant in the crook of her arm and then smoothed the damp hair back from her brow. "Aye," he repeated, "a fine lad. His name is John."

And Emily MacKinzie knew that her husband was intensely proud.

[*October 28, 1765 — Monday*]

Over these past twenty months, William Forsyth had gained a whole new appreciation for the effort involved in raising a family by one's self. Even with the aid of hired help, seeing to the needs of four young sons went beyond all expectations. That was not the only reason William was remarrying today, but it was most definitely a contributing factor.

He had felt, when Isabel died a year ago February, that he might possibly marry again sometime. As the weeks expanded into months he became sure of it, just as he was sure that when it occurred it would be a marriage of convenience: a permanent contract for live-in child care without the necessity of paying a salary. Then, this past summer, he had met her, and from the beginning he was wholly enthralled. She was bright and charming and witty; a surprisingly mature, intelligent, and good-looking woman, certainly far superior to others he had encountered, who had largely been empty-headed or inextricably ensnared by their own improbable dreams. Dashing knights on white chargers did not come with four toddlers in tow.

Now, with the simple ceremony about to begin at Quebec's only Scots-Presbyterian church, William marveled at the turnings of fate which bring a man to his place in life. As a youth in Blackwater, Ireland, he had always assumed he would simply grow up to become a farrier like his father. Then the war had come and abruptly he was a twenty-year-old soldier in the service of King George II, marching behind General James Wolfe on the wilderness frontier of a different world and, ultimately, on September 13, 1759, climbing a cliff to the Plains of Abraham to help storm the French citadel called Quebec.[2]

When the war ended a year later, he settled in the city he had helped to conquer and found work as a clerk for a merchant named George Martin. In classically predictable pattern, the merchant had a lovely young daughter named Isabel, whom William married on January 2, 1761. A few months later George Martin died and, at Isabel's urgings, William Forsyth took over the business she had inherited. He poured great energies into it and the business prospered. Isabel was busy with other concerns: on December 2, exactly eleven months after they were married, she bore a son whom they named George, after her father. A year later, on the day after Christmas, a second son was born, named William, Jr.

Isabel Forsyth had found her niche; bearing babies and caring for infants seemed exactly what she was designed for and she loved it. She was perfectly content to have her husband spend progressively longer days turning the little mercantile business into a far more lucrative trade than George Martin had ever been able to develop. Then, on December 29, 1763, Isabel had borne twin sons whom they named Philip and Robert, but this time there were difficulties. The twins were sound, but Isabel hemorrhaged heavily in the aftermath of their birth. Additional hemorrhaging occurred intermittently over the weeks following and she grew ever weaker until finally, on February 21, 1764, she quietly died in her sleep.

Twenty months passed and it wasn't until several weeks after William Forsyth met the woman he was marrying today that he discovered she had lost her second husband, an army officer, only fifteen days after Isabel had died. The widow was also left with children — a five-year-old daughter and an infant son — and in the year and a half following, she cared for her two offspring alone.

The situation was prime for a union between them when William Forsyth, merchant, waited upon the young widow customer who entered his shop. The solo care of children was the basis of their first conversation and the affinity this evoked quickly evolved into much more. He fell in love and so did she and, were this not enough, it was obvious to both that the two of them together could care for the combined six children much better than either had been able to do alone.

Thus, William Forsyth, Esq., was today marrying the engaging, twice-widowed Emily Tyne Haliburton MacKinzie.

CHAPTER I

[*April 3, 1769 — Monday*]

PINI — The Turkey — was a bold youth of the Peoria tribe. Imbued with more than his share of courage, he was always somehow in the forefront of any action. Whenever the games of stick-and-bird were played, it was always he who led the field, he who produced the most points for his team, he who left behind the greatest trail of injured players to hobble homeward on broken bones. Whenever the games of war were played, it was he who demanded a leadership role and most often he got it, though more through a sense of fear in his fellows than because of loyalty or devotion.

At nineteen, Pini embodied many things admirable: he was brave and strong, his eye keen, ear sure, aim true and his resolution firm. But Pini was also many things detestable: he was cruel and he was a liar and a cheat. He was also unable to control himself when he drank, which was any time it was possible for him to get liquor. One small cup of rum would cause his zeal for aggressive action to skyrocket, with caution all but discarded and foolhardiness rampant; more than one cupful would turn him into a veritable beast feared for his brutality and carefully avoided by all until ultimate sickness and sleep restored his sensibility.

Pini yearned to be a chief; longed nearly to the point of physical pain to commit deeds so bold, so incredibly conceived and executed that he would be chosen principal chief of the Peorias — the greatest chief ever spawned by his tribe or any other. Since his fourteenth year he had waited impatiently for the special opportunity that he knew would come to him eventually. He had no idea in what form such an opportunity might present itself; only that when it came he would recognize and grasp it.

Today it had come: opportunity was a man named Pontiac, presently approaching this village of Cahokia with his two grown sons, Otussa and Kasahda, and an escort of a few other Indians.[3]

The grand council assembling here at the village today was by far the largest in Pini's memory. Even some of the elders remarked that only once or twice before in the history of the Illinois Confederacy had so large and important a council been held. While the tribes and subtribes of this confederacy had often bickered among themselves and sometimes even fought, through the years they had remained bound to one another in a common purpose — preservation of their women and children, preservation of their way of life and, perhaps most important, preservation of their territory.

This territory of the Illinois Confederacy was a vast fertile land abundant with game and fish, forests and streams and almost unbelievably expansive prairies of lush grasses which grew belly-deep to over head-tall. The soil from which they sprang was pure black loam free of rocks, clay or sand to a depth of three or four or even five feet: soil so rich that corn and melons, squash and beans and fruit grew to incomparable size and quality; so rich that more than once a warrior had thrust one end of his osage-orange bow into the ground to stand upright until he should again need it, only to return after many days and find the wood had taken root and new twigs and leaves had sprouted from the upper arm of the bow. How rich a country, how broad . . . and how coveted!

Only through their banding together, despite individual differences, had the thirteen Illinois tribes and subtribes been able to defend their land from the grasp of covetous neighboring tribes. The only tribe not of the confederacy to share the Illinois country was a small portion of the Miami tribe occupying the southwestern shore of Lake Michigan at the mouth of a stream called Checagou. The grandmother of rivers — the great Missi-Theepi — formed the western border, beyond which lurked hostile Oto, Osage, Missouri and Sioux who coveted Illinois land; to the north at Rock River and above were the Sac and Fox, the Winnebago, Menominee and Potawatomi. To the northeast, beyond the boundary formed by the great southern bulge of Lake Michigan, were the Chippewa, Ottawa, Wyandot and more Potawatomi. Eastward, beyond the boundary formed by the unpredictable Wabash River, lay the Miami, Wea, Delaware, Shawnee and Kickapoo. And to the south, well beyond the boundary created by the powerful Spaylaywitheepi — the Ohio River — were the more distant Cherokee and Creek, Choctaw and Chikasaw.

All these tribes were covetous of Illinois lands and only a combination of two things prevented their taking it: the fact that the individual tribes were too weak to assault and defeat the self-protective confederacy of the Illinois tribes, and the fact that the would-be usurpers were much too bellicose among themselves to form their own confederacy to accomplish such an end.

Then had come Pontiac. He was an Ottawa war chief who had risen from near obscurity to draw together the tribes of the upper Great Lakes and Ohio country into a confederacy to oppose the British when they moved in after defeating the French in 1760. Three years of anti-Indian policies originated by Sir Jeffrey Amherst so alienated the tribes from these new whites in their lands that Pontiac had been able to make them realize the value of a confederacy which could, upon a given signal, rise as one at various points to strike down the common foe. It was six years ago, in May, 1763, that such a signal was given. Pontiac himself led the attack against the strongest bastion of all — the fort at Detroit. Elsewhere on the frontier the British garrisons were toppled with amazing facility and in many cases the officers and men were slaughtered. During a period of six weeks, nine of the ten British frontier forts fell. Only Detroit, isolated in the wilderness, managed to hold. That bastion was kept under siege by Pontiac and his confederated warriors for one hundred fifty-three days — a tribute to Pontiac's leadership, since it was unprecedented for Indians to lay extended siege against any enemy. But finally, when expected and loosely promised help from the French failed to materialize, Pontiac was at last forced to lift the siege and withdraw from the Detroit area.[4] It was hardly a defeat for his confederacy, since though he lost eighty warriors, the British had some two thousand soldiers killed.

While he had lost a certain amount of prestige for having failed to take Detroit, Pontiac was not finished. He began coming to Illinois, endeavoring to get the Illinois Confederacy to embrace his newer plan to attack and drive out the British. Over a period of years the powerful Ottawa chief visited Illinois repeatedly. The Illinois Confederacy had remained adamant in its refusal to join him in the dangerous enterprise, not only because they doubted they could win against British might, but because they feared that during such an absence other tribes would invade their territory.

Then factors combined to make the Illinois Confederacy very nervous. First was the fact that many of their younger hot-headed warriors — such as Pini — were beginning to listen to Pontiac more carefully and be swayed by his rhetoric and his dream. Some — again like Pini — had met him, become enchanted by him, even considered him next to divine. These were the ones who were being primed to rise and follow when the Ottawa should crook his finger to them. Such a prospect was not pleasant for the elders to contemplate. It could mean a split, possibly irreparable, would occur in the Illinois Confederacy. The second matter was a personal incident involving a set-to between Pontiac and Chief Makatachinga — Black Dog — of the Peorias. The cause of their argument had never been satisfactorily explained but the upshot was that Pontiac had wound up stabbing Makatachinga in the shoulder and then threatening to return this spring with a war party to wipe out the Cahokia village.

Now this grand council of the confederated Illinois tribes was being convened and not only was it being held at Cahokia, it was under auspices of none other than Makatachinga himself. The council fire had been lighted and many hundreds of Indians had arrived — chiefs and warriors of the six principal tribes forming the inner circle and comprising the Kaskaskia, Cahokia, Michigamea, Moingwena, Tamaroa and Peoria. Beyond them, forming the outer circle, were the chiefs and warriors of the seven subtribes — the Albivi, Amonokoa, Chepoussa, Chinko, Espeminkia, Coiracoentanon and Tapouaro.

Under normal circumstances such councils might drag on for days, even weeks, as spokesman after spokesman for the various tribes and subtribes gave his own views and those of the people he represented. This time a sense of fearful urgency enshrouded them and the council moved quite swiftly to a conclusion. Makatachinga, occasionally rubbing his fingertips across the scar that was the memento of his run-in with Pontiac, proposed without mincing his words that the Ottawa war chief be eliminated when he arrived. A few of the chiefs were opposed to such a step. Although the Confederacy had something of a reputation for ambush and assassination as a policy of foreign relations, they pointed out quite logically that in this case retaliation might be the result. Such objectors were overruled by the majority, who favored the direct simplicity of Makatachinga's suggestion for ending the problem.

Pini was one of those who was at first appalled at the idea of an assassination. For years his admiration for Pontiac had grown, for here was a leader who was utterly fearless in the face of an implacable and seemingly unconquerable foe. As a matter of fact, it had been the young warrior's half-formed plan, following this council, to join Pontiac and perhaps rise to great heights himself by clinging to such an important chief. Now he was sitting in a council that had just declared a death sentence for that very man.

The matter was settled when Makatachinga spoke his final words. The burly chief stood silently before the assemblage until the murmuring dwindled away. When he spoke again, every person present heard him clearly.

"My Brothers," he said, "we are agreed that Pontiac must die. To accomplish this we might send a body of warriors against him, but this would not be wise. If we did so he would sense their mission and be prepared. Should we then try and fail, his great wrath would fall upon us and we could be dealt a blow from which we might not recover. No, Brothers, we must do as we have done before in like situations. One of us who is familiar to him must go to him with apparent friendship. When his mind is filled with ease and his weapons sheathed, then must the strike be made. I would gladly do this, but his blade has already tasted of me and thirsts for more of my blood, so this satisfaction cannot be mine. But I call on one of my own blood to avenge me and end this threat to us all in the manner to which we here have agreed. I call on one who is known to Pontiac and who has won some measure of his trust. I call on the son of my sister to so serve us. I call on Pini."

For an instant Pini was filled with confusion. He was stunned at being nominated by his uncle. Ever the opportunist, immediately he recognized the vast amount of fame that must come to him as the slayer of the great Pontiac. In an instant he shrugged aside the admiration he had harbored for the Ottawa chief. He came to his feet in a fluid movement, his hand cupping the head of the war club in his belt, his eyes gazing into those of Makatachinga.

"I will kill Pontiac," he said.

[*April 20, 1769 — Thursday*]

For the past fifteen days — beginning only two days after the council at Cahokia where he had been appointed to assassinate Pontiac — Pini had been virtually a shadow to the forty-nine-year-old Ottawa war chief. He had met Pontiac at the chief's camp a dozen miles from Cahokia, greeted him as an old and treasured friend, delighted at reinstating their friendship and, though surprised at how worn the chief looked, complimented him on his fine health. Anything Pontiac needed done, Pini saw to. He ran errands, hunted game, cooked, amused him with stories, swore eternal devotion and became at once his friend, companion, confidant, ally, bodyguard and disciple.

At first the other fourteen members of the party — Pontiac's two grown sons and three warriors each of the Chippewa, Potawatomi, Miami and Wyandot — were wary of Pini, then amused and finally resignedly tolerant toward the way Pini fawned over the war chief. They had seen this before among young warriors with visions of glory, though never before quite so flagrantly as with Pini.

The traditional weapon of assassination was the tomahawk, so Pini had made certain not to carry one when he joined the party. He had only his skinning knife and a war club. The latter was the skin of an oxtail, softened and split so that a round, fist-sized stone could be sewn into one end and the other sewn tightly around a short length of strong stick. As it dried, the hide stretched tightly around stone and handle, with a limber section of hide perhaps eight inches long separating them. Actually, it was more a makeshift mace than a war club, but an effective weapon nonetheless. Still, it was a battlefield weapon, not one that an assassin would choose.

Pini bided his time and day after day passed without his having an opportunity to be alone with Pontiac. A council was scheduled in Cahokia, where Pontiac was to expound on his new war plan and exhort the young hot-bloods to join him, and there was little reason to doubt they would do so. The days to council time dwindled with alarming speed and still Pini had no opportunity. By this morning — the day of the council — he was almost beside himself with frustration at not having been able to fulfill his mission. And it was not until the last possible moment that the opportunity finally presented itself.

Pontiac's camp was on the other side of Cahokia from where the council was to be held and to reach it, it was necessary to walk through the little town. Pontiac and his deputation, including Pini, left the camp when the sun was only an hour high. As they passed through the town, their steps carried them past the English trading post of Baynton, Wharton and Morgan. Knowing Pontiac's fondness for liquor and his inability to procure any since he had been here, the young warrior fingered the flask in his own pouch and made a decision. He stepped close to the chief and murmured that he was sure if only Pontiac and he were to stop briefly at the trading post, they could procure some rum. However, the traders would give them none if the whole party trooped in. Pini professed to be on good terms with the clerk and thought he could persuade him to part with at least enough to satisfy Pontiac.

The war chief's eyes glinted and he nodded. He motioned to his sons and the other members of the deputation, telling them to go on to the council and he would meet them there, that he and Pini had some business to take care of. The others, especially Pontiac's sons, Otussa and Kasahda, did not much care for the idea, but after a moment's hesitation they went on and Pontiac and Pini entered the post. Stacks of trade blankets, beads, vermilion in clay pots, skinning knives, copper bracelets, tobacco and other items were on display, but no liquor.

The clerk was a fragile man of about thirty who appeared older because of a greatly receded hairline. He smiled at the pair, although it was his customary smile of the lips only, the eyes remaining watchful. Pini greeted him by name, introduced Pontiac with great flair and concluded by requesting that they be provided with a gill of whiskey apiece. The clerk was neither impressed nor willing to dispense contraband liquor over the counter. He told them flatly that he had none.

Anger lighted little sparks in Pontiac's eyes and he might have had harsh words to say to the clerk, but Pini touched his arm and motioned that he follow him to the door. There he whispered to the chief to wait and returned to the clerk. He murmured to the clerk that he would be back in a few days to do some trading and, unseen to Pontiac, Pini reached into his own pouch and took out the flask of rum. He turned and strode back, smiling, and extended the flask to the Ottawa war chief. A broad grin creased Pontiac's features as he accepted it. He opened it and took several swallows, closed it and put it into his own pouch.

Now in a jovial mood, the chief turned to leave and Pini deferentially stepped back to let him pass out of the door first. On the porch he jerked the war club from his belt and followed close behind the chief. As Pontiac reached the dusty street, Pini swung the club in a broad arc and brought the heavy hide-covered rock down on the back of the man's head with all his strength. The skull crushed inward as if it were an eggshell and before Pontiac's falling body had stopped moving, Pini was upon him with his skinning knife. The blade swiftly found the heart. The war club blow was probably enough, but the knife thrust was insurance.

Pini straightened from the body, then stooped and retrieved his flask from the dead man's pouch and set off at a lope in the direction from which they had come. Several bystanders, Indian and white, stared after him, stunned at the suddenness of what had occurred. Pini's lips pulled back from his teeth in a tight grin. The deed was done. Now would come the recognition for his act.[5]

[*September 10, 1769 — Sunday*]

In the eighteen months since they were married in Philadelphia, Sarah and John Lytle had moved four times. Each time they — or at least Sarah — felt certain that at last they had found the place to put down their roots for good. Just as often one thing or another had caused John to change their minds and move on. Their latest move, only six weeks ago, had brought them here to the last real settlement of any significance on the Pennsylvania frontier aside from Pittsburgh — Lancaster.

They had hoped to build a good home and begin farming and making friends with their neighbors, but somehow the home wasn't built and they lived out of their decrepit wagon as if they were Gypsies. The ground, John found, was too rocky and the soil too lacking in nutrition for successful farming. Worst of all, the hope of making friends gradually dwindled; existence was hand to mouth and what few neighbors there were had to spend most of their time merely trying to eke out a living, with little time or inclination left over to socialize. And so, early this morning when John learned from a stranger en route from the wild country west of the Susquehanna to Wilmington that there was a new settlement forming at a place called Carlisle, some fifty miles away, he pressed the man for details.

The stranger scratched his bearded chin and spat to one side before replying. Well, he didn't know a whole hell of a lot about the place, 'cept there seemed to be some good folks thereabouts, 'specially in a place close to the Carlisle settlement called Path Valley.[6] Soil? Well, he didn't know much about what was good soil or bad, but there were trees aplenty and good water and folks there were beginning to lay out farms, so he reckoned it was pretty good land.

John Lytle thanked the man and turned back toward the wagon where Sarah was resting. The baby was due to be born during the next fortnight, but perhaps there would be time enough for them to reach Path Valley before she went into labor. They didn't have any time to waste if they were to get there, put up a cabin and get settled before winter closed it.

Lytle swung up into the wagon, anxious to tell Sarah that this time he'd found a place that could really become home for them. But before he could speak, a sharp gasp erupted from the young woman lying on the cornhusk mattress and covered by a thin blue woolen blanket, and it put John's plans in abeyance. Lord, had she begun her labor already? She had.

Fourteen hours later, just after 9 P.M., Sarah Lytle gave birth to her first child — a healthy, highly vocal little girl-child. By mutual agreement, they named her Eleanor and they were happy with her. Sarah was exhausted from her ordeal and so John sat beside her as she fell asleep. He felt very virtuous at having had the consideration not to tell her about their pending move to Carlisle. There was plenty of time for that. He would wait until tomorrow to break the news and he would further exhibit his concern by caring for her every need all that day. The day after tomorrow would be soon enough to start their journey to Path Valley.

[*September 12, 1769 — Tuesday*]

Pini was a hunted man. Haggard, hungry and with his nerve endings raw for a good solid jolt of rum, he had twice narrowly missed being caught today and the danger was not yet past.

Who could have foreseen what occurred? Who could have believed it? Instead of becoming exalted among his fellows for his great coup of slaying the powerful Pontiac, he was a fugitive, fleeing not only from the multitude of enemy Potawatomi and Kickapoo and Ottawa scouring the Illinois country, but even from his own people.

Scores of warriors of the Illinois Confederacy had been killed already and there would be more, many more. And not only warriors. The invaders were killing women and children, burning villages, destroying, leaving behind them desolation and the bleaching bones of their victims. Who would have believed it? Who could have guessed that they would have joined together as they did in a force five or six thousand strong and wreak such a sweeping vengeance upon the Illinois tribes?

Makatachinga had been among the first to die — tied to a tree and scalped while alive and then riddled by volley after volley of arrows until scarcely an inch of flesh remained from which a feathered shaft did not protrude. The Illinois warriors had resisted at first, but how does the prairie fend off the fire that sweeps across it? No more than that could they resist the invaders, and so the defenders had scattered, running, hiding, seeking shelter here or there or anywhere.

The final attempt to hold had occurred at the great rock that jutted from the earth on the south bank of the Illinois River halfway between where the Vermilion River entered from the south and the Fox River from the north. Here the remaining fighting force of one hundred fifty Illinois warriors, mostly Peorias and Cahokias, managed to reach the top and discovered that at last they had found a place where they could fend off their attackers. There were even several deep clefts where rainwater had gathered and so they did not thirst. But soon they hungered. Their meager rations quickly disappeared and there was nothing left to eat. Days turned into weeks, and dejection into desperation. Hundreds, perhaps thousands of the enemy were hidden below them, waiting; waiting as Pontiac had taught them to wait when they had lain in siege of Detroit for a period of five months.

Had the Illinois tribes been able to locate Pini, capture him and turn him over to the attackers as the murderer of the war chief, and supplemented the surrender of him with a vast array of presents to repay the northern tribes for their loss, perhaps they might have been able to buy their salvation. Scores of small parties of Illinois warriors had been sent out to find him but, wary as a hunted fox, Pini had thus far eluded them and now it was all but too late. The Potawatomi and the Kickapoo, the Ottawa and Chippewa, the Sac and Fox and Winnebago would not be satisfied until the Illinois tribes existed no more.

When first the invaders came they stopped briefly at the mouth of the Checagou River and there spoke to the new principal chief of the Miami tribe, Michikiniqua — Little Turtle. His seven villages stretched from just below the mouth of the Milwackie River on the north to just east of the mouth of the Calumet River on the south and here, along Lake Michigan's shore, they had lived in peace with the Illinois tribes, though not members of their confederacy.[7] In the council held at Checagou, the Miami were given a choice: they could ally themselves to the Illinois tribes and be wiped out just as the Illinois tribes were sure to be wiped out, or they could pack up their things, abandon their villages and leave the Illinois country forever, since very soon it would belong to the northern invaders. It did not take very much persuasion on the part of the twenty-seven-year-old Michikiniqua to convince his followers to accept the latter alternative. Within days they had moved out of the Illinois country permanently, taking up residence on the Maumee River in the Ohio country and on the upper Wabash and its tributary, the Mississinewa, in the Indiana country.

So the reign of destruction had begun and the attackers, with the Potawatomi most abundant and aggressive, methodically hunted down their enemies until the only organized resistance remaining were those seven score and ten who had isolated themselves atop the great rock along the Illinois. And at last there was nothing for the besieged to do but eventually die of starvation or attempt to slash their way through the enemy force and escape. They chose the latter course.

Not one of them escaped.[8]

And far to the south, Pini heard the sound of those who were relentlessly on his trail coming closer. His strength was all but spent and he knew he could no longer outrun them. His eyes swept the woodland around him and locked on a huge oak which years before had been shattered at its midpoint by a bolt of lightning. The tree had broken off at a hollow and immediately Pini realized that here was a haven in which he might successfully hide. Swiftly as the thought struck him he lay a false trail for a few hundred yards, then backtracked to the tree, scaled it with difficulty and lowered himself feet first into the hollow some thirty feet above the ground. He was only just in time.

The party of warriors trailing him came into view, their eyes reading the messages imparted by grasses and pebbles and earth and twigs. Pini scrunched deeper into the hollow, wriggling his whole body to slide farther inside so that no trace of him could be seen from below. When he felt he was hidden enough, he stopped, the hammering of his heart nearly smothering him.

His craftiness was a success. The war party passed, following his false trail. Then he heard them return, muttering among themselves. Again they went away and again they returned. For hours they were close by and then at last there was silence, but still Pini remained hidden, determined not to show himself until he was positive they were gone. He slept — uncomfortably, true, but he slept. When he awoke the stars were bright above him and katydids droned their monotonous melodies from all around. Beneath and not far away two raccoons squabbled, squalling and snarling and chirring at one another for a long while.

Pini knew now that he was safe and could emerge, and he bunched his muscles to climb out. He could not move. A wash of fear flooded him and he struggled harder, straining with toes and fingers to free himself but succeeding only in wedging himself more tightly.

All his life Pini had envisioned himself exalted and placed in a high position. In a way, his wish was granted. He ended his days in a high position. But death was a long time in coming.[9]

[*March 2, 1774 — Wednesday*]

In the Shawnee village called Kispoko Town, the sixteen-year-old daughter of Pucksinwah and Methotasa sat quietly in the dimness of the large wegiwa in which her family lived. Her name was Tecumapese.[10] She contributed little to the conversation taking place between her parents and brothers and the muscular young warrior who was the closest friend of her elder brother, Chiksika.[11] But while she said nothing, there was little she missed hearing or seeing and, if her color seemed heightened and her eyes even brighter than usual, there was good reason. This was a very special day for her. Outside there was a bustle of activity in the village as preparations were made for the feast tonight, and it would be during this time that she would become the wife of Chiksika's friend, Chaquiweshe.

As a rule the Shawnees were a handsome people but in many years no young woman had been raised among them who was quite so beautiful as Tecumapese. Already she was taller by inches than Methotasa — A-Turtle-Laying-Her-Eggs-in-the-Sand — and her long black hair, which Methotasa was presently braiding into a thick queue, shone as if with inner light. Her eyes were extraordinarily large and expressive, and high cheekbones lent dignity to her appearance, heightening the delicacy of her other features. Kneeling on the thickly furred bison robe before the perpetual fire, she wore a simple, ultra-soft doeskin garment which could not conceal the fullness of her breasts nor her lithe figure.

With her small hands clasped together on her lap, she stared into the low fire, rarely looking up except when Chaquiweshe spoke. In his twentieth summer, Chaqui — as he was called by those close to him — was two years older than Chiksika, but the two youths had been inseparable friends since they were very young boys. Both were well built, strong, swift of reflex and very intelligent. And Chiksika, perhaps more than anyone else present except his sister, was delighted at the prospect of Chaqui becoming related to the family through marriage.

The younger brothers of Tecumapese did not really understand the importance of this day, but they sensed the undercurrent of excitement and were more attentive to the conversation than normally. The six-year-old was named Tecumseh — The-Panther-Passing-Across — for on the night of his birth a great comet, which in Shawnee mythology was a panther, had seared its way across the heavens.[12] The remaining three boys were already famous in the tribe, for their birth three years ago in this very wegiwa was the almost unprecedented occurrence among the Shawnees of the birth of triplets. First-born of the three was Kumskaka — A-Cat-that-Flies-in-the-Air. Second was Sauwaseekau — A-Door-Opened — and the third, who from the moment of his birth was the most vocal of all, was Lowawluwaysica — He-Makes-a-Loud-Noise.

This was the family into which Chaquiweshe — The Mink — was today marrying, and he was very proud and honored. There was more than ample reason. Pucksinwah, father of Tecumapese, was not only chief of the Kispokotha sept, one of the five social divisions of the Shawnee tribe, he was also war chief of all the Shawnees and unexcelled among his people as a warrior.[13] At forty he was a very powerful man in his prime, and wherever he happened to be, his presence was a dominant factor. He was highly intelligent and articulate and his wegiwa was a focal point for the collection and dissemination of news. There was little that occurred of any moment east of the Mississippi of which he was not soon aware, and his grasp of broad situations and trends was incredible. And these days the trends were very ominous.

Since destruction of the Illinois tribes five years ago, the whole structure of Indian dominance in the Illinois country had changed, as had that of the area north of the Wabash lying between Lake Michigan and Lake Erie. Important tribal migrations had taken place and only now had these new territorial occupations taken on a degree of permanence. More of the closely united Sac and Fox Indians had migrated from the valley of the Wisconsin River to the vicinity of the mouth of the Rock River in the northwestern Illinois country on both sides of the Mississippi and now they were having problems with an influx of whites who had learned of the great lead deposits all through that area. The Winnebagoes of the Green Bay area had moved southward into the valley of the upper Rock River and into the area of the portage between the Fox and Wisconsin rivers. The Miami tribe, now under the solidly entrenched principal leadership of Michikiniqua, was firmly settled to the north of the Shawnees, joined by displaced Delawares from the east and even overlapping somewhat into Shawnee territory along the tributaries of the upper Wabash and Maumee, but there had been no belligerence between them. Kickapoo villages had been established on the Sangamon River in the central Illinois country and along the lower Wabash and its Vermilion branch.

Most of all, the Potawatomies had moved into the Illinois territory, erecting villages in abundance, streaming out of the Michigan country and establishing themselves most prevalently at the southern bend of Lake Michigan and along such streams as the Des Plaines and Checagou rivers, the Iroquois, Kankakee, Fox and Illinois rivers. The tribe still had villages in the Michigan and Indiana countries, especially along the St. Joseph River, the Elkhart, the Mississinewa and Tippecanoe branches of the Wabash, and in the Wisconsin country at the mouth of the Milwackie. Elsewhere in their former territory, however, which had been shared with Ottawas and Chippewas, they had diminished considerably. Their ties with those two tribes remained strong and many of the Ottawas migrated with them, but now there was plenty of room for all and their transplanted roots spread deeply in the new soil.

But though there was room, there was not tranquility. During these fourteen years since the British had defeated the French, Englishmen had begun penetrating far into the interior, claiming the land by right of conquest from the French and conveniently overlooking the fact that the few French who had been here had resided on the land in only a very transitory manner and only at the forbearance of the Indians, tolerated because of the goods they brought to trade for furs. The British came to trade also but, unlike the French, wherever posts were established they sank roots, claiming the land as their own and quickly considering the Indians as interlopers to be driven out. The Indians soon learned that the tiny innocuous British trading posts had a way of evolving into forts largely impervious to Indian attack.

Attracted by the security such forts offered, pioneers penetrated far into the country and established their settlements. These people were not content, as the French had been, to live in harmony with the land and its native inhabitants; instead, they felled the forests and burned the prairies, planted fences of split poles and wire, dug up vast stretches of the virgin soil and planted crops, caring little that each rainstorm which followed washed away another portion of this rich land. Far to the north the settlers thrust greedy fingers deep into the land to extract the metals they wanted, tunneling like moles to strip even the bowels of the earth of its copper and lead resources.

Over the passage of years the various tribes had become dependent upon the goods the French traders brought to them: blankets, cloth, jewelry, knives, traps, tomahawks and implements made of iron to replace crude wood and stone tools, and most of all, not only firearms that could kill at far greater distances than any bow and arrow, but liquor to heat their bellies and fire their minds. Then the French were gone and the British moved in and suddenly the goods the new traders brought were cheaper in construction but more expensive to buy; suddenly there was a great mysterious omnipotent *government* behind the traders, directing their activities and limiting them, banning the sale of liquor and thus not ending the liquor traffic but only making the commodity that much more desired and expensive.

Some of the new traders treated the Indians with fairness and respect, and those few prospered. One such was William Burnett, who began his trading out of Detroit but soon moved his headquarters to the St. Joseph River a few miles from the old French village called Petit Coeur de Cerf. The site he selected was the largest Potawatomi village in this region and its leader, Topenebe, one of the most powerful and influential of the Potawatomi chiefs.[14] Not only did Burnett and Topenebe become close friends, the trader soon married the chief's sister, Kawkeeme, and the Potawatomies accepted him as one of their own.

Another important trading site, which the French had maintained for upwards of a century, was where an entirely different St. Joseph River merged with one called the St. Marys to form the Maumee.[15] This was an important site, for it was here that a seven-mile portage began which connected the commerce of Detroit and Lake Erie to the headwaters of the Wabash and thence downstream to the Ohio and Mississippi. Many Indian trails converged at this point.

Unfortunately, for every respected and reputable British trader of the ilk of William Burnett, there were a score or more who cheated the

Indians wherever possible, who treated them at best with discourtesy and at worst with brutality and ugliness, and so the problems on the frontier began to accelerate. The Kickapoos were first to retaliate. Not being dependent upon the British traders who came among them, they therefore could afford to take offense at mistreatment. Their relationships with the Spanish west of the Mississippi, especially those headquartered at St. Louis, were very good and whatever trade goods they needed could be procured from them.[16] In addition to serving as mercenaries for the Spanish against the Osages, with whom they were having problems, the Kickapoos began attacking British traders and settlers. Cabins and posts were burned, horses and goods stolen. The newer British settlements in the area of Kaskaskia, Cahokia and Fort de Chartres were especially hard hit by the raiding Kickapoos.[17] Traders were captured and tortured, settlers were slain in their cabins, their wives and children carried into captivity and their Negro slaves either mutilated or adopted into the tribe. The pattern of retaliation for mistreatment gradually spread to the Potawatomies and Sacs, then to the Shawnees and their allies, the Miamis and Delawares. The most important avenue of entry for the British settlers into the country of these tribes was the Ohio River and attacks against the rafts of settlers descending that great stream — which the Indians called Spaylaywitheepi — became frequent. British authorities were incensed, overlooking the fact that one of the grisly pastimes the new settlers seemed to enjoy while floating downstream was shooting whatever Indians were sighted along the shores. Troops were brought into readiness to combat the threat the Indians were posing and the British military commander in America, General Thomas Gage, initiated the program when he wrote to the superintendent of Indian Affairs, Sir William Johnson:

. . . *Scarce a year passes that the Pouteatamies* [Potawatomies] *are not guilty of killing Some of the traders and of course plundering their Effects, which it becomes absolutely Necessary to put a Stop to.* . . .

Despite Indian attacks, encroachment by the whites increased. Pucksinwah was aware, for example, that British shipyards had been built at both Navy Island in the Niagara River and at Detroit, and these were turning out vessels which had now taken control of the upper Great Lakes. The latest to be launched was the forty-five-ton *Felicity*, which had slid into the water from the King's shipyard at Detroit.

Further, and perhaps most threatening of all, land speculators were coming into the Indian country, drawing together a few inconsequential village chiefs from scattered areas, grandly proclaiming them to be bona fide representatives of their people, and then, after "softening" them with liquor, buying vast tracts of land from them for very small amounts of money and trade goods.[18] None of the land deals boded good for the Indians, and Pucksinwah was becoming deeply concerned.

Many of the disturbing matters were occurring in areas far away from the Shawnees now gathered at Kispoko Town on the Scioto River, but not all of them.[19] Without any provocation, members of the tribe had been shot on the banks of the Ohio as a form of "amusement" by whites passing in rafts. There had been retaliations, of course, but killing the settlers did not bring back those whom the whites had slain. Now there was word of the Shemanese — the Long Knives — from Virginia mounting an army to come against the Shawnees and Pucksinwah knew that soon there would be a war. Then there would be few happy times, as this wedding day of his only daughter was meant to be. He shook his head and shrugged his shoulders faintly, as if to shake off the gloom that had settled over him. His expression softened as he looked across the interior of the wegiwa to where Methotasa was just tying the bottom of the braid she had woven with Tecumapese's hair. His gaze moved to Chaquiweshe and he took a step forward and placed his hand on the young man's shoulder.

"Today you become a member of our family, Chaqui," he said. "It is good. We welcome you as a son and brother and husband. Before the first deep snow of winter, Tecumapese will bear you a son."

There were exclamations and gasps of pleasure at the pronouncement, but no trace of disbelief, for it was well known and long proven that Pucksinwah, war chief of the Shawnees, was also a prophet and what he said would be, would be. In the excitement over the prediction, none noticed that behind Pucksinwah's pleasure there was a cloaked reserve, as if something else he had seen in store was much less pleasurable.

[*May 24, 1774 — Saturday*]

For a long while ten-year-old John MacKinzie stood outside the little shop in Quebec and stared at the dazzling metalwork on display within — brilliantly polished plates and platters, finely fashioned forks and spoons and knives, intricately designed jewelry with filigree like the most exquisite of lace. Although hunger pangs gripped his belly and made him weak and lightheaded, he could hardly tear his eyes from the marvelous silverwork on display. And hungry though he was, had he been given his choice of picking up a piece of bread or one of these handsomely wrought pieces of silver, he would have chosen the latter. To think that a person could learn to take raw metal and transform it with care into such lovely works of craftsmanship!

Practically without conscious volition, the boy gripped the latch and stepped inside, thrilling to the clear melodious peal of the small silver bell above the door. He stopped with his back to the portal, as if suddenly afraid to penetrate deeper into this glorious world of silver artistry. There were shelves and stands and tables upon which were breathtakingly engraved cups and bowls. Broad burnished platters reflected the interior of the shop like mirrors, and within a single long glass cabinet were a multitude of brooches, rings, necklaces, bracelets and other jewelry, along with silver-handled hair brushes, combs and mirrors. So lost was he in their beauty that when the man's voice came from nearby, John was startled.

"What d'ye need, boy?"

He turned, seeing for the first time the gnomelike white-haired man seated behind a low worktable, regarding him through squinted eyes. A heavy gray mustache flowed from beneath his nose and formed fuzzy muttonchop fringes at his jawline. Crowsfeet lines etched the outer corners of his eyes into permanent merriment, offset by an equally permanent crease that formed a deep line between the bushy white eyebrows.

"I'm hungry." The words burst from John without thought.

A faint smile tugged at the man's lips and he sat back farther in his chair, placing on the desk top the miniature brass mallet with which he had been working.

"Wrong shop," he said. He tilted his head to the right. "Two doors down from here. Breads, pies, cakes, whatever you want."

John shook his head, coloring faintly, but his eyes did not leave the man. "I have no money. I didn't come in here for food. I came because . . ." He hesitated and then moved his hand in a sweeping gesture. ". . . These things. They're beautiful. I've never seen anything so beautiful. I just . . . wanted to look."

The silversmith nodded, understanding. "They're food, too. Of a different kind. What's your name, son?"

John MacKinzie remembered what he had responded to the man on the boat when asked that question and he replied now in the same way, though more smoothly than at first.

"John Kinzie. If you are Mr. Farnham, I have a letter for you." He removed a somewhat crumpled envelope from within his shirt and held it questioningly.

"I am," said the man, extending his hand. He accepted the envelope and indicated an empty chair beside the glass case. The boy sat down and folded his hands, waiting. Farnham broke the red wax seal and began to read, and John thought about the man who had written it and the circumstances that had led up to it; the circumstances that had so recently caused him to drop the Scottish prefix to his own name.

Quebec was the city of John's birth and he loved it. And when the Forsyth family, of which he was a part, had moved to New York last September, it was a terrible blow to him. Bad enough being part of a family of which he was not terribly fond right here in Quebec; in the strangeness of New York, in a new house and attending a new school, it was suddenly detestable. There had never been much rapport between him and his half sister, Jane Haliburton, who seemed to be off in a world of her own most of the time. William Forsyth, his stepfather, was not a bad man, but neither did he inspire any great degree of adoration. He was there and he provided well, but it was always obvious that his concern was far more for his own sons than for his stepson. John's eldest stepbrother, George, was twelve now, and had little to do with him except where it came to imposing his will. Being eldest, George did the same with his own brothers, William, Jr., who was eleven, and the twins, Philip and Robert, who were John's age, ten. Of all these stepbrothers, only with Robert did John have any degree of affinity.

There had only been one occurrence of more than ordinary note for John during those years in Quebec before the move to New York. The family was reasonably well-to-do, with three excellent black slaves which John's mother always, with studied euphemism, referred to as the "house servants." Two were women — Elsie, who was Emily Forsyth's personal maid, and Salome, who was combination cook, house cleaner and overseer of the children. The third was Nero, who was pleased to refer to himself as "a gentleman's man." Surprisingly well educated — though how, when and where, John never discovered — Nero was houseman, butler, carriageman and personal valet to John's stepfather. The occurrence of note, which involved these three, was a trip taken by the entire family to the far western outpost city of Detroit. William Forsyth had heard of unlimited opportunity for the smart man with foresight enough to set up business there. Specifically, there was a hotel available for sale which, with a certain amount of repair, could be made into a very profitable business.

The hotel had turned out to be a hovel and the city was a raw settlement with all too few of the civilized niceties to which the Forsyth family was accustomed. Nevertheless, their stay in Detroit was more extensive than planned, simply because Emily Forsyth suddenly went into an early labor and delivered a son, whom they named Thomas.[20] The unexpectedly prolonged stay in Detroit had an important impact on John. Not only did it introduce him to the frontier of the upper Great Lakes and to the Indians who inhabited it and roamed the streets of Detroit so casually, it also introduced him to the matter of Indian trade. For days he and his stepbrother Robert frequented the Detroit trading post still maintained by William Burnett, whose headquarters was at a remote place far to the west, called St. Joseph.

For John it had been tremendously exciting to observe the Indians — Ottawas, Potawatomies, Chippewas, Wyandots and Miamis — as they entered the post laden with bales of furs and huge skin bags filled with the heavy brown sugar rendered from the sap of maple trees. It was fascinating to watch them sit and smoke and dicker interminably with Mr. Burnett or his agent until finally they left with the bolts of cloth, traps, skinning knives, tomahawks, gunpowder, lead, blankets and other items for which they had bargained. And John had gone away at last filled with a vision of himself as a swashbuckling figure in the Indian trade, carving a far-carrying reputation for fairness among the dangerous red men of the west.

The vision lost much of its vibrancy when they returned to Quebec and subsequently wound up moving to New York. He loathed the city with its teeming thousands and its streets abustle with carriages and drays and noisy people hawking wares of every variety. The five older boys — George, William, Jr., Philip, Robert and John — were all enrolled in the Rutledge School at Williamsburg, Long Island, just across the East River from lower Manhattan. Jane Haliburton no longer attended school; it wasn't considered necessary. Early each Monday morning the boys would be loaded into the fancy high-springed Forsyth carriage and transported to the school with Nero proudly holding the reins and snapping the buggy whip sharply in the crisp air. There the dapper black man with his perpetually dazzling smile would drop them off and not return to pick them up again until the following Saturday morning.

John because progressively more unhappy, yearned for the familiar narrow angled streets of Quebec and now began dreaming more than ever of becoming a dashing and powerful Indian trader in the wilds of Michigan or beyond. He was wise enough to realize that such a dream could not become reality unless he started with a solid foundation of money with which to buy his original supply of trade goods, with sufficient left over to transport them and himself to the west. He also realized that in his present situation at Rutledge School there was no way of acquiring the funds he needed.

Throughout fall and winter he thought and planned and dreamed, and gradually it became clear to him what he would do. He would return on his own to Quebec, find the best possible work he could and indenture himself for a period of a few years; a situation where room and board would be provided and what he earned he could salt away until the term of indenture expired, at which point he could move into the second phase of his plan.

One Monday morning at the end of April, as Nero dropped them off at school and the boys scattered to their respective classes, John raced along behind unseen and unheard, catching up with the empty carriage and hitching a ride on the trunk rack at the rear. There he clung until the carriage returned to Manhattan and was within blocks of the Forsyth home. There he leaped off and disappeared toward the North River.[21]

Before nightfall he had stowed himself away aboard a sloop bound for Albany. The fates were more than kind. Before reaching Albany he had been discovered and taken under the wing of a kindly passenger — a Mr. Henry Kilgore of Montreal, who was en route home. With a flair for the dramatic, John MacKinzie, who identified himself to Mr. Kilgore as Johnny Kinzie, launched into a bravely sorrowful tale couched in half-truths and lies. His home, he related, had originally been Quebec, but he had been taken to New York by his parents in order to better their way of life. Alas, after only a few weeks, first his father and then his mother had been stricken with a fever, lingered in weakening condition for a week and then died, both of them. What little money there was had been used for burial fees, and then he had been taken into custody to be placed into an orphanage. It was, Mr. Kilgore, a fate he could not bear. So he had run off to make his way as best he could back to the city of his birth, there to seek employment as a contributing member of society rather than a burden to an uncaring governmental system.

"You have passage to Albany, Johnny Kinzie," Henry Kilgore said slowly, after the boy had lapsed into silence, "but how will you get to Quebec from there? Have you the means to carry you through?"

John shook his head. "No sir. Enough to buy a little food, but I will get there, even if I have to walk all the way."

Henry Kilgore was taken by the youngster's pluck and he squeezed John's shoulder. "No, lad, you'll not have to walk. I have transportation arranged to Montreal and you'll accompany me. When we arrive there, I'll see to it that you are taken to Quebec."

John was moved in spite of himself and wrung his benefactor's hand warmly, promising one day to repay him for his trouble. Kilgore had waved off the offer and, true to his word, when they reached Montreal he sent John Kinzie off with a letter of introduction to George Farnham, Silversmith, who was an old friend and who, last he heard, had been considering hiring an apprentice.

So now here John MacKinzie was in this marvelous silver shop on the Grande Allee St. Louis, almost in the shadow of the great Ursuline Chapel and convent, watching as George Farnham folded the letter and placed it on the desk. The man furrowed his brow in thought for a moment and then looked over the top of his spectacles at the boy.

"Well, young man, so you wish employment?"

"Yes sir."

"What can you do?"

"Anything, sir. Anything you can teach me."

"Well now, that remains to be seen, but we'll make a trial of it. First things first. Come with me, Master John Kinzie, and we'll get you something to eat."

The boy nodded and somehow he was sure that his new name of Kinzie was the name he would use for the rest of his life.

[*December 2, 1774 — Friday*]

Tecumapese, not yet seventeen and in the final stages of her labor, sat with her back against the inner wall of the wegiwa, knees drawn up, feet firmly planted and wide apart on the blanket upon which she sat. The only person in attendance was her mother, Methotasa. Though this should have been a joyous occasion — the birth of a son, as predicted by Pucksinwah — there was little of gladness in the hearts or expressions of either woman.

The wegiwa in which they were now was not in Kispoko Town on the Scioto. They no longer lived there; no longer lived among the Kispokotha Shawnees. This was the wegiwa of Chief Black Fish of the Chalahgawtha Shawnees, located on the banks of the Little Miami River half a hundred miles west of Kispoko Town.[22] Both of these women, mother and daughter, were now the wards of Black Fish, peace chief of the Shawnee nation, in accordance to the Shawnee tradition that when a war chief died or was killed, his family automatically became wards of the peace chief and moved into his household.

Pucksinwah was dead. So, too, was Chaquiweshe, and the child to be born to Tecumapese this day would never know his father. Many others of their tribe had died as well on that point of land where the Great Kanawha flowed into the Ohio River from the south.[23] The sharply fought battle with the left wing of Lord Dunmore's army under Colonel Andrew Lewis had taken place less than two months ago — on October 10. Seventy-five militiamen had been killed and another one hundred forty-four wounded, as opposed to twenty-two Indians killed and eighteen wounded. Had the fighting continued, almost certainly it would have turned into a disastrous defeat for the whites, but the death of Pucksinwah had taken the heart out of the attacking Indians and they withdrew across the Spaylaywitheepi. Two weeks later, on the Pickaway Plains, a treaty of peace was signed between the Indians and the Virginians and the two opposing factions returned home.

Now, Kispoko Town was being called Shemeneto's Town, after the tribe's new war chief who succeeded Pucksinwah there, Chief Shemeneto — Black Snake. Following the mournful burial ceremonies for those who had fallen at the Battle of Point Pleasant, Methotasa and her daughter and five sons had moved here to Chalahgawtha. Black Fish was a good man, wise, kind and honorable, and he had been Pucksinwah's close friend for many years. There was no doubt that he would care well for his new wards, but nothing at this point could ease the pain of the two widows, and of the five sons of Pucksinwah.

The moment had come for the birth and Tecumapese, following the instructions of Methotasa — instructions handed down for generations — squatted with her feet flat to the floor and spread wide apart. Methotasa helped balance her so she would not fall with her exertions and Tecumapese delivered the baby into her own hands. She sat down again then and, even though there was not yet any milk in her breasts, placed one of her nipples into the infant's mouth for the sense of security it would provide. Methotasa, now a grandmother for the first time, gently washed the babe as her daughter held him. Neither remarked over the fact that it was a boy, as Pucksinwah had predicted. Neither had doubted for an instant that it would be.

The naming of a boy-child might, by Shawnee custom, be delayed as long as ten days, although it was not a prerequisite to wait, and there would be no need to delay in this instance. Tecumapese and Chaquiweshe had long ago decided what he would be called and the only thing that might have altered this would have been the occurrence of some significant event at the moment of birth or shortly thereafter, which would indicate that Moneto, highest deity of the Shawnees, had wished otherwise.

Except for the faintest of whimpers, the infant had made no sound during the birth and he lay in his mother's arms contentedly now with her nipple in his mouth. Since her brothers, who were waiting outside, could not know the baby was born yet, she called to them to come in and they entered gravely, eighteen-year-old Chiksika holding two of the three-year-old triplets, six-year-old Tecumseh holding the third. They stopped at the foot of her blanket.

"You are now uncles," she told them, smiling wanly, her voice faintly tremulous. "Chiksika, Tecumseh, Kumskaka, Sauwaseekau, Lowawluwaysica — this is your nephew. His name is Spemica Lawba" — Big Horn.[24]

[*April 1, 1775 — Saturday*]

The string of five horses, two of them very heavily laden packhorses, waded stirrup deep across the fording place upstream on the Great Kanawha River. They picked their way cautiously, careful of their footing on the slick rocks over which the water flowed swiftly. Each of the three lead horses had two riders and all six people were members of the same family.

Moredock McKenzie was first, his nine-year-old daughter, Margaret, astride the horse's back directly behind the saddle, her hands gripping her father's belt tightly. McKenzie was not tall but he was big in a stocky way, barrel-chested and with large hands. His upper arms and thighs filled to capacity the fabric that covered them. He wore a battered, slouchy leather hat with full brim and clenched a homemade cob pipe tightly in yellowed teeth. Frequently he looked back over his shoulder to make certain Margaret was all right. He loved all his children, but beautiful blond Margaret most of all.

On the horse directly behind, a dapple-gray, rode Moredock's wife, Erina, who was forty-four, the same age of her husband. She was a slim woman with seldom-washed chestnut-colored hair shot with gray. Before her in the saddle rode their seven-year-old, Elizabeth, a sharp-faced little girl whose resemblance to her mother was rather remarkable, except that her hair was black, like her father's.

They were followed by the two McKenzie boys astride a horse with no saddle. Seth, thirteen, perched in a disgruntled manner behind William, who was four years older. William had long ago ceased responding to Seth's whining demands to ride in front for a while and take the reins.

All six of the McKenzies were deeply weary and each step the horses took jarred them to their bones. They had been riding for five days and the words flung back over his shoulder by Moredock now, "Not much farther!" were decidedly cheering. They had no idea what the new claim looked like — only Moredock himself had seen it half a year ago. He had wanted to move immediately, but with winter coming on and a cabin to be built when they got there, common sense dictated that they wait until spring.

The piece of land in question was a fertile creek valley only a mile or so above the mouth of this big river. Moredock had first seen it last October when, as part of the Virginia militia army of Colonel Andrew Lewis, he had taken part in the Battle of Point Pleasant. He had greatly admired this land when they passed it the day before the battle, and was even more impressed with it when he inspected it more closely as they returned home just over two weeks later. With Dunmore's Treaty signed and the Indians agreeing to stay north of the Ohio River so long as the whites stayed south of it, the possible hazard of living this far forward on the frontier was greatly reduced.

As the month of March was coming to a close they packed up everything that could be loaded upon the two packhorses and simply abandoned their cabin at New River with hardly a backward glance.[25] It had not been a good choice of ground to settle on; the scenery was beautiful but the earth rocky and soil for growing good crops sparse in the extreme.

Now, as Moredock McKenzie reined up and triumphantly pointed out the land he had chosen to claim, Seth and William sighed with audible relief. The site was up the creek about a half mile from the Kanawha and out of sight of that large river. A flat shelf of rock formed a natural dockage at the water's edge, which nicely precluded getting badly muddied feet every time a boat was launched or moored. Unlike their place on New River, here there was a wide prairie flanked by deep woods, meaning very little clearing would have to be done and yet it still wouldn't be any great problem to fetch firewood.

Erina McKenzie nodded slowly as her gaze swept across the land. A clear-water spring bubbled up some thirty yards away and flowed less than a quarter mile before falling into the creek. She placed a skeletal hand on the small of her back and arched her shoulders, groaning aloud. Turning, she faced her husband and nodded again.

"Ye've chosen right this time, Moredock. How'd ye manage to do that?"

McKenzie grinned, refusing to be baited. Besides, it was seldom she approved of anything he had done and a back-handed compliment was better than none at all.

They were forerunners, the McKenzies, among the first of scores of similar families already in movement to different areas like this. Though they didn't know it, a much larger party had, on this very day, similarly ended their long trek in a direct line one hundred fifty miles southwest of the McKenzies and had already started cutting timber for the erection of a fortified station. They had come up from the south, from the North Carolina country, through the Cumberland Gap, carving a wilderness trail under the leadership of a skilled frontiersman by the name of Daniel Boone.

[*September 2, 1775 — Saturday*]

It was the better part of a year before John Kinzie — boldly signing his letter with that name, even though he knew it would not make her happy — wrote to his mother in New York and explained what had happened and that he was now an apprentice silversmith. It was an awkward letter to write and he took pains to assure her that he was quite happy to be back in Quebec, and that he had indentured himself for three years. When that period was finished, he intended to take his savings and enter the Indian trade, perhaps out of Detroit.

Her letter in return had come as swiftly as the mails could be delivered. Emily Forsyth chided him for disappearing the way he had, which had caused them unnecessary travail. Three days of searching had finally resulted in tracing him to a North River wharf, but at that point the trail petered out and they hadn't known whether he was dead or alive.

She passed along news of the family, although there was really nothing of any great moment to impart. Both she and William, she wrote, approved of his industry and commended him for his ambition. In regard to Detroit, she wrote that the possibility of William's purchasing the inn there had somewhat revived of late. They had received word that some degree of renovation had been done on the place and the price was not out of line with what they anticipated spending. Nothing was definite yet, but wouldn't it be wonderful if before too long they found themselves reunited in Detroit? In a postscript she mentioned that she was sorry he had felt it necessary to change his name from MacKinzie to Kinzie, but if that were truly his decision she would abide by it, thankful that his late father would never know.

By the time John replied and received another answer from her, she had news of greater significance to impart. The impact of two hundred seventy-three British soldiers and eight militiamen having been killed with the breaking out of hostilities at Lexington and Concord on April 19 was extreme in New York and all along the eastern seaboard. Revolutionary sentiment was high and those who were opposed to such a course — as William Forsyth was — were being branded Tories and threatened. Fearful that at best their property and goods would be confiscated and at worst their very lives might be in jeopardy, they had made the decision to move to Detroit where they would again be back within a solidly British area. The move was scheduled for May 15.

Summer passed without further word and John Kinzie was growing concerned when finally, in the forenoon today, a thick letter arrived from Detroit. Now John read it through a second time, slowly folded it and put it away in the drawer of the small table beside his bed in the back room of *George Farnham, Ltd., Silversmith.* She had told him the good news first. Though there had been a bit of initial ugliness from neighbors when they moved, no concerted steps had been taken to prevent it. Arriving in Detroit, they found it as delightfully British as before and somehow less rustic and rawboned then they had remembered. The purchase of the inn had been consummated and, with the new procedures they had inaugurated, the place was gaining a very good reputation and a marked increase in clientel. Matters had gone so well, in fact, that initial plans to find a home within Detroit proper were put aside and William had bought a very nice farm several miles east and slightly north of town, where the Detroit River opened up into Lake St. Clair. The area where their home was located was on a broad bulge of land extending into the lake. It was called Grosse Pointe.

Everyone, of course, she went on, was talking about the war between the rebel colonists and the home government and they found it deplorable that the populace had been permitted to get out of hand. News of the Battle of Breed's Hill [Bunker Hill] had just come. Rumors were everywhere and here on the frontier where things were occurring of great interest, a fair number of those rumors were turning out to be reality. It was William, of course, working at the inn, who heard most of the news and passed it on to the family. Prodigious efforts were afoot, he reported, to organize the warrior tribes as allies to the Crown. Though many of the Indians seemed not to care very much for the British, they more thoroughly disliked the Americans — as the rebellious colonists were now being called — for these were the ones who were infiltrating into their country, not to trade but rather to claim lands belonging to the Indians and settle upon them. William had heard, from good authority, that at this time the British strategy for the west was first to build a defense on the Ohio River to thwart any possible American venture in the Northwest; second, to build up a force of Indian allies capable of turning back any possible Spanish offensive from the region of St. Louis; finally, to have

British Indian agents who had won the trust of the tribes — men such as Matthew Elliott and Alexander McKee — encourage the tribes to organize raiding parties all over the frontier to terrorize American settlers. It was even whispered, though without verification, that the British commandant at Detroit would actually pay bounties to the Indians for American scalps and prisoners.

Then came the bad news. William's son George — John's eldest stepbrother — had become lost on August 6, a week before her letter was written, and hadn't been seen since. Once again their slave, Nero — their "colored servant," as she put it — was involved. It seemed that as George, now thirteen and a half, was coming home from school with two of his classmates, Henry Hay and Mark Sterling, they had met Nero on horseback going to the Common for the cows.[26] The schoolhouse was situated quite close to the old fort and everything westward of that was wild and uncultivated, with islands of open meadow where good graze grew.[27] George, Emily Forsyth went on, begged Nero to give him a ride to the Common, but Nero refused and told George he'd better go home at once. The boy refused and, along with his two friends, followed Nero for quite a distance. As the dusk deepened, Henry and Mark turned back, but George went on and that was the last anyone had seen of him. An extensive search was made for him by a large number of men from Detroit, but thus far nothing had been found and it was feared that George was dead.[28]

John's mother closed her letter with an appeal for him to join them in Detroit just as soon as he could conceivably do so. She tempted him with an offer to pay off his indenture to Mr. Farnham and buy his transportation to Detroit, but he knew he would not take her up on it.

John Kinzie had given his word and he would not break it.

[May 18, 1778 — Monday]

Moredock McKenzie was more than a little smug. While the whole western frontier was afire with Indian attacks and the supposedly civilized East was involved in extensive troop movements punctuated by harsh battles between British and Americans, his little homestead near where the Great Kanawha River emptied into the Ohio was a secure, isolated island of tranquillity. Off the beaten path, the McKenzie place stood oddly apart from the grand events of conquest and invasion that were shaping history. It was as if an invisible barrier kept them free of troubles.

" 'Tis the will of God that we are not bothered," he told his family frequently. "God led us here and He is on our side. So long as we're under His protection, no harm will come to us." But while vocally he attributed their security to the Almighty, privately he commended himself often for having chosen this location so well.

McKenzie was a stern man whose strongest credo, next to love of God, was hard work. He constantly drove himself to the point of exhaustion and enforced the same burden on his family. His word was law and, as the absolute ruler of his domain, he had achieved incredible results in the three years since their arrival here. The first year had been difficult in the extreme but, despite the hardships, the lean-to shelter they had initially built for protection from the elements had soon given way to a more secure log house. In turn, that house had been regularly improved and enlarged until now it was considerably more than merely a frontier cabin.

Constructed originally as a sturdy two-room cabin made of notched logs, the house gradually evolved through dint of enormous effort by McKenzie and his sons into its present form — a fine five-room house in which no one was cramped for space. There were three bedrooms; one for Moredock and Erina, one shared by the twenty-year-old William and sixteen-year-old Seth, and another shared by the girls, Margaret and Elizabeth, who were now respectively twelve and ten. A kitchen and a common room completed the interior and, unlike so many frontier cabins, its floor was good solid puncheon construction, not hard-packed earth. Considering that they had arrived here with all their worldly goods on two packhorses, what they possessed now was little short of amazing. There were numerous furnishings, including well-manufactured chairs and tables, dressers and mirrors, endtables and benches. There was even an expensive harpsichord with two keyboards, seven foot pedals and a hinged top — an instrument which, under Erina's skilled fingers, filled the house with lovely music of a variety this frontier had never known.

"God's gift as a reward for our labors, that's what it is!" McKenzie declared when they had suddenly come into such unusual largess on the first anniversary of their arrival here. On that day Moredock and William, attracted by the bawling of a cow and squealing of hogs, had found on the nearby Ohio River shore, about a mile upstream from the mouth of the Kanawha, a huge abandoned raft of the type becoming known as a broad-horn. Bloated bodies of four people — three men and a young woman — were on the deck. There was evidence of a considerable fight having occurred and it was obvious the raft had undergone attack by the Indians. Those aboard had all been killed and the free-drifting raft had eventually wedged against the shore here. Why the Indians had not followed up their attack with confiscation of the contents of the broad-horn was a question for which they had no answer, although they speculated that the two parties had probably killed one another.

In a partitioned pen on the broad deck of the raft were a fine milk cow and a pregnant heifer. Two other cows were dead, killed by arrows or lead balls. In another section of the pen was a huge sow with eight shoats. Were these not treasures enough, within the large structure built for humans on the raft were many other wonderful things: furnishings, clothing, utensils and cookware, flour and salt and preserved meat as well as staple supplies of all kinds, tools, coils of rope, a few guns and ammunition, some books and even a small amount of money. Included was the marvelous harpsichord. All these were things that were meant to form the foundation of a new life, probably in the Can-tuck-ee country, for the would-be settlers who had been slain. Not a scrap of identification gave any clue to who the people were and so the McKenzies merely buried them in a common grave with simple prayers.

The raft and its contents was a treasure trove beyond the wildest dreams of Moredock McKenzie and he had sent William home to fetch Seth and bring back horses for the work ahead. The distance from the homestead to the raft was not great, probably less than three miles, but it took three full days for them to free the raft from where it had wedged and float it down the Ohio to the mouth of the Kanawha, then tow it against the strong current of the Kanawha to their own little creek. Drawing it up the narrow creek a half-mile was the most difficult job of all, but it was finally accomplished. Everything aboard was put to excellent use at the McKenzie homestead and even the raft itself, when finally emptied, was dismantled and the lumber used for new construction and remodeling.

Their lean-to stable was improved and now had stalls for the horses and cows. There was a split-rail horse-lot and an adjacent pen for the hogs. The large sow, a vicious animal, had been butchered and the bacon, ham and other meat hung in the smokehouse that had been built with raft lumber. An excellent, compartmentalized three-hole privvy had also been built eighty feet from the house on the downhill side and a low spring house, covered with sod, had been constructed over the cool, constantly flowing spring. Inside were stored a variety of vegetables they had grown, and in a wooden trough within the springhouse, through which the cool waters flowed, were large-mouthed jugs filled with milk and cream, buttermilk and smooth, pale yellow butter.

In the midst of a primitive locale, the McKenzie family lived in what might almost be considered opulence. What fears they may have harbored of Indian attack being launched against them had been considerably eased last summer when, at the mouth of the Kanawha on Point Pleasant, where the battle had been fought three years previously, a small installation named Fort Randolph was built by the new United States government. It wasn't much, but McKenzie was convinced it all but precluded any Indian raiding party coming up the Kanawha with the view in mind of attacking the McKenzie homestead.

With the existence of Fort Randolph, visitors, at first rare, were becoming more frequent and the McKenzie place began gaining a reputation as a good stopover for travelers going up or down the Ohio. If for no other reason, they were welcomed for the news they brought of the outside world. All too often, however, the news was distressing.

Since the Declaration of Independence almost two years ago, frontier hostilities had increased sharply. After much counseling with the British, especially at Detroit, the Indians had almost without exception entered into an alliance with them to oppose the Americans. Attacks against boats and rafts floating down the Ohio became much more frequent and now travelers were coming downstream in great floatillas for mutual protection. Attacks against the settlements in what was now being called Kentucky were devastating and the Indians making these attacks — mostly Shawnees — were supported by detachments of British with artillery, sent out from Detroit by General Henry Hamilton. It was he who had held a massive congress at Detroit with somewhere near six thousand warriors of the Shawnee, Delaware, Miami, Potawatomi, Kickapoo, Wyandot, Ottawa and Chippewa tribes on February 26, 1777. At that meeting Hamilton had rescinded his earlier exhortation for restraint and urged them to take up the tomahawk for full-scale war. He plied them with gifts of guns and powder and lead, gave them liquor and blankets and vermilion and destroyed in their presence a peace belt being circulated by some of the pro-American Delawares. Despite all this, the tribes were still reluctant to promise full support.

That reluctance vanished last October 10.

On that day the principal chief of the Shawnees, Hokolesqua — whom the whites knew as Cornstalk — visited Fort Randolph under a flag of truce. He had arrived accompanied by his son, Elinipsico, and a subchief named Red Hawk. None of them had weapons. They had come at Hokolesqua's insistence, to give the Americans fair warning that no longer could the young hot-bloods of the tribe be restrained and that peace between the Shawnees and the Americans was herewith officially terminated. For Hokolesqua, who had signed the never-ratified peace treaty with Lord Dunmore at the Pickaway Plains, his coming to Fort Randolph was no more than a point of honor. The fort's commander, Captain Arbuckle, showed his appreciation by throwing the three Indians into a cell. A short while later a group of men led by Captain John Hall burst into the room and murdered all three of the Shawnees in a burst of gunfire. With that, all possibility of peace vanished.

Far to the east the Indians — mostly Iroquois — and British had fought a major battle in the Mohawk Valley at a place called Oriskany, at which at least a quarter of the American force involved was killed, including the American commander, General Nicholas Herkimer. All of upper New York was in a state of panic as a result.[29] The defeat of General John Burgoyne at Saratoga last October 7 was the only good news the Americans had to cling to in these desperate times, but that was a triumph far removed from this perilous frontier.

The single ray of hope for the situation here to change for the better lay in the fact that a new young commander had been named for protection of the Kentucky settlements and to carry the fight to the enemy. He was Major George Rogers Clark. Rumor had it that he was eager to lead a strong force against Detroit, but was so weak in manpower and so poorly supplied that he was planning instead to march against the weaker British posts as Kaskaskia, Cahokia and perhaps even Vincennes instead.

For Moredock McKenzie, all these matters seemed far removed. He and William and Seth were well armed and had plenty of ammunition. He had no doubt whatever that they could fight off any raiding party of Indians that came their way, although he simply could not believe it would ever come to that. Further, just to be safe, whenever he left the house for any extended time, he always left one of the boys behind to protect Erina, Margaret and Elizabeth.

That was the case today. Last night there had been a windstorm and a branch blown from a tree had smashed a section of the horse-lot rail fence. In the morning they discovered that the horses had gotten out and scattered into the woods. Leaving William behind, Moredock and Seth set out to follow and retrieve the horses, taking with them a lunch that Erina had packed, since it promised to be a difficult and possibly time-consuming chore. It was far more difficult than they had imagined it would be. Not until mid-afternoon had they been able to catch sight of the horses and it was another two hours after that before they managed to catch and halter one of the animals. That helped simplify matters and, with the elder McKenzie riding that horse, another was caught in an hour. Then, with both Moredock and Seth mounted, it was only another half hour or so before the remaining three horses were retrieved. By this time it was dusk and they were about five miles from home. Leading the three horses, they picked their way home slowly and carefully, not nearing the homestead until close to midnight.

It was the faint glow in the night sky that first caught their eye and a sick fear surged through them both.

"Oh God, Pa," Seth breathed, "it looks . . ." He couldn't finish.

The elder McKenzie's expression was grim as he dismounted. "Get down," he said. "Keep your gun ready and follow me."

They tied the horses and moved up very quietly on foot. There was almost nothing left of the stable, spring house and privvy. The walls of the house still stood, but were burning. The interior had been wholly gutted by flames. They watched from hiding for several minutes but there was no sign of anyone moving. At length Moredock leaned close and whispered in his son's ear.

"You stay here out of sight. I'm going in. Anything happens — anything at all — you get away fast, to Fort Randolph. Come if I whistle. Hear?"

Seth grunted an affirmative and his father, rifle held at ready, moved off. The elder McKenzie took his time, circling the burning house at a little distance before becoming convinced no enemies remained. At last, from a point between Seth and the house, he turned and whistled. When the boy came up to him, he squeezed his arm. Together they walked to the house and into a scene of horror.

William lay some thirty feet from the house. His clothing was gone and his body had been hacked repeatedly with a tomahawk. He was decapitated and the head, without its scalp, was a dozen feet away. Erina lay about forty feet farther away. She had been shot several times and she, too, was scalped. Incredibly, she was still alive, though unconscious. Margaret and Elizabeth were nowhere to be seen, and Moredock feared their remains would be found in the ashes of the house.

Together, gently as they could, father and son carried the woman to where the spring house had been and lay her on the ground. They bathed her as best they could and tried to make her swallow some water from the spring, but her mouth and throat would not function. For only one brief moment she became conscious and she uttered a single sentence in a raspy, croaky voice.

"They've got our girls, Moredock."

She slipped back into unconsciousness and twenty minutes later, without moving or speaking again, she died. Moredock, still crouched beside her with her hand in his, made a peculiar whimpering sound and then he stared up at Seth.

"They took my girls, Seth," he muttered. "Everything's gone and they took my girls away. Margaret. 'Liz'beth. I'll get them back," he vowed, his voice hollow and eerie against the crackling of the gradually dying flames still licking at the log walls of the house. "They're all we have left, Seth. I'll get them back if it takes the rest of my life."

Moredock McKenzie never made empty promises.

CHAPTER II

[*May 25, 1778 — Monday*]

FOR Margaret and Elizabeth McKenzie, the initial terror they had experienced at being taken captive by the band of Shawnees had passed. They had not been mistreated and even their bonds had been removed within an hour or so. With the resiliency of the very young, they had thrown off the terror and, though still fearful of what lay ahead, had adapted surprisingly well to their situation. Had they known certainly what happened to their mother and brother, the terror would have lingered, but they knew only that the two were dead. They didn't know how.

They had been the first, these two sisters, to know that Indians were anywhere nearby that day. After Seth and their father had gone off in search of the horses, they had remained in the house until the middle of the afternoon. Then, while their mother began preparing a stew in a large kettle — since it would keep well until Seth and their father returned, however long that would be — they were directed by William to slop the hogs while he saw to mending the horse-lot fence and then milked the cows.

Carrying between them a large wooden bucket into which garbage had been dumped and covered over with a layer of spoiled milk from the spring house, the girls were grabbed simultaneously from behind just as they stopped at the fence of the hog pen to dump the slops into the trough for the squalling hogs. Elizabeth's mouth had been clamped shut by a powerful hand, but Margaret's had not and her instant scream of pure terror rent the air with chilling intensity.

Both girls were picked up bodily and carried at a run toward the woods, while other garishly painted Indians rushed toward the house. Margaret had one brief glimpse of her mother at the doorway to the house, frozen in fear at the sight of her daughters being carried off, and then she was lost to sight as the abductors plunged into the woodland. The children heard shots and what might have been screaming, but then there was silence. Their two captors were joined by another pair of warriors to whom the girls were turned over. The original captors sprinted off toward the house and the girls were taken to the point beyond a stand of trees where the Kanawha River came closest to their home. Here six canoes were beached and here the girls had their wrists and ankles bound and were forced to sit on the ground.

After nearly an hour, during which time Elizabeth cried almost constantly and Margaret soothed her as best she could, the remainder of the party, heavily laden with goods they had taken from the McKenzie house, began appearing. Their appearance, frightful enough in the war paint daubed on their faces and chest in diagonal lines and whorls, was made even more horrifying by what was obviously blood staining the arms and legs of some of them. Two of the warriors howled with triumph as they came in sight of the captive girls and they shook fresh scalps in the air above their heads as they approached. There was no doubt they belonged to Erina and William McKenzie and Elizabeth became nearly hysterical. Even twelve-year-old Margaret, who was normally steady, blanched now and the tears slid down her cheeks and dribbled from her chin. The warriors stuffed the scalps into belt pouches and then helped the others load their booty into the canoes — all the weapons they had been able to find, as well as gunpowder and lead, blankets, foodstuffs and other items. One even had a copy of Shakespeare's *Hamlet* tucked in his belt.

When smoke from the direction of the house billowed into the air beyond the intervening trees, ten-year-old Elizabeth began sobbing again, but Margaret squeezed her hand and whispered seriously to her.

"Don't cry any more, 'Liz'beth. We've got to think about where we are and what's ahead. I don't think they're going to kill us or they'd've already done it. And don't think about Momma and Bill; think about Seth and Poppa. They're out there somewhere and if there's any way to do it, they'll rescue us."

Her words had carried conviction, but she was herself far from convinced of what she was saying. She looked around her at the Indians who were just finishing their loading of the canoes. There were twelve, their leader a well-built young man about twenty-two, clad in buckskin leggins and moccasins. A wide beaten-silver band was on his upper right arm and another on his left wrist. Zigzagging lines like lightning painted in vermilion and yellow ocher went down his chest and three fingertip-wide lines of blue ran horizontally across his forehead and then angled down his temples and across his cheeks. Shoulder-length black hair hung loose but was held back from his face by a yellow strip of cloth as a headband. He was the one who had initially seized Margaret. The others addressed him with considerable respect, calling him Chiksika.

The warrior who had caught Elizabeth was also muscular, but taller and thinner than Chiksika. The two men appeared to be close companions. The second man was clad only in moccasins and a loincloth, with two broad white spirals painted on his chest, each terminating at the nipple. His face was more garishly decorated than Chiksika's, painted yellow on one side and red on the other, with a white line bisecting his features from hairline to point of chin. His only ornamentation was a silver armband and he was one of the two warriors who had stuffed a scalp into his pouch — the scalp that had belonged to William. His legs and moccasins were badly stained with blood that was now dried. Chiksika addressed this man as Wasegoboah.

The other ten warriors were similarly clad and painted, though no two exactly alike, and they all appeared to be in their early twenties. Several came close to the girls and studied them intently. One even squatted and fingered Margaret's long blond hair in a speculative manner, but desisted when Chiksika spoke to him harshly. They talked and laughed a good bit among themselves, but all with an underlying anxiety to be off. Chiksika spoke some guttural words and they prepared to leave. Chiksika touched Margaret's shoulder and when she stared at him fearfully, shook his head, patted her upper arm reassuringly and smiled faintly. He picked her up easily and placed her in the middle of one of the canoes, then held the craft as another warrior got into the front. He stepped into the stern end lightly himself as he shoved it off from shore.

Margaret looked around and saw that Elizabeth was in the middle of another of the canoes, manned by Wasegoboah and a younger warrior. The others, two to a canoe, had already shoved off and were paddling. They moved quickly across the broad Kanawha and then paddled downstream very close to shore, taking advantage of cover wherever possible. In a very short time they had reached the mouth of the river and the mile-wide expanse of the Ohio — at which they pointed and said, with some relief, "Spaylaywitheepi!" — stretched before them. On the opposite point of the Kanawha's mouth — Point Pleasant — Margaret could make out the uprights of the Fort Randolph stockade, but she could see no one. Since no alarm was raised, it was evident no one had seen them, either. One of the warriors shook his fist with silent anger at the fort where their great chief Hokolesqua had been murdered.

The six canoes swept around the point and continued close to the south shore of the Ohio for half a mile before paddling diagonally across. They followed the north bank until, just at twilight, they came to where a large creek with brushy banks emptied into the Ohio.[30] They turned northward up this smaller stream and ascended about a quarter-mile to where there was a wide gravel bar. Here they were out of sight of the Ohio and this was where the canoes were beached and an overnight camp was made. Chunks of fresh meat were impaled on sharpened sticks and roasted over the fire. The rawhide strips binding Margaret and Elizabeth were cut away and the girls were each given a piece of the cooked meat on a flat section of bark. It was blackened on the outside by the fire and smoke, but it smelled very good and suddenly the children realized they were very hungry.

"What do you think this meat is, Margie?" Elizabeth whispered, pronouncing her sister's name with a hard g.

Margaret shook her head and used the back of her hand to wipe away a trickle of fat running down her chin. She was almost positive it was meat from one of their cows, but knew the thought would bother her sister, so she didn't reply. They each ate a second piece that was brought to them by the warrior named Chiksika and then, as the Indians did, drank water directly from the creek. The night air had grown chill and now it was Wasegoboah who brought them a blanket which they recognized as having been taken from their parents' bed. Elizabeth's eyes grew wide and her lips trembled, but it was not until the sisters had lain down together beneath it, their arms about one another, that she broke into muffled sobs. This time, the impact of their day suddenly crushing down upon her, Margaret joined her and the two girls cried themselves to sleep.

At dawn they were in the canoes again, slowing momentarily at the mouth of the creek while one canoe went ahead to inspect the broad expanse of the Ohio in both directions and make sure no one was in sight. Then their journey downstream resumed.

During the next four days they traveled down the Ohio until they reached a major river entering from the north, which they began ascending. This stream their captors called Sciototheepi.[31] At twilight on one of the days which followed, they came ashore on the west bank of the Sciototheepi at a large village of perhaps two hundred wegiwas. This was Shemeneto's Town and here the two little girls, holding hands and clinging close to one another, were objects of great curiosity, soon finding themselves in the center of a throng of chattering onlookers.[32] In no way mistreated, they were made comfortable in one of the wegiwas and provided with food and drink. They spent the night here and the canoes, dragged up on shore the previous evening, were exchanged in the morning for horses as a means of transportation. Before they left, however, a very powerfully built older man with ugly features strode up to where they were preparing to mount and studied the girls for a long moment without expression. From the deference paid him as he approached and the number of people who trailed behind him, it was obvious he was chief here and the warriors addressed him as Shemeneto.

Fear began welling in Margaret and her grip on Elizabeth's hand tightened until suddenly the man grinned crookedly. The features that had appeared so ugly a moment before now turned benevolent. The fear drained away quickly and the girls — Margaret first, followed by Elizabeth after a few seconds — smiled back, the older girl radiantly, the younger shly. Shemeneto laughed aloud and slapped a hand to his stomach. He pointed at Margaret's hair and said, "*Matchsquathi Kisahthoi.*" Then he pointed the same way at Elizabeth's dark hair and added, "*Matchsquathi Tebethto.*"

Their audience laughed and clapped their hands in delight, nodding in agreement. The warrior party, now with their war paint washed away and hardly so frightening in appearance as they had been previously, mounted their horses. In turn Shemeneto handed Elizabeth up to Wasegoboah and Margaret to Chiksika. With small waves of farewell, the horsemen cantered away from Shemeneto's Town, the girls not realizing that they had just encountered the chief who was among the most feared by the whites — the one they called Black Snake, war chief of the Shawnees.

For two days more they traveled a little north of due west until finally, today, from a slightly higher ground, they looked down upon an Indian village so large that both girls had gasped aloud. Here, at the junction of two streams, stood upwards of eight hundred wegiwas. Though they appeared at first to be situated haphazardly, the impression was incorrect. There were avenues of clear space running in different directions through the town like streets, most of them converging on a large central building that was fully one hundred twenty feet long by forty feet wide.

To the west, beyond the village, lay the valley of the two convergent streams, heavily bordered with woodland, but on all other sides, including the one from which they were approaching, there were expansive fields newly tilled where spikes of corn seedlings in search of sunlight were just now pushing aside little clods of brown earth. A faint haze of woodsmoke, escaping from the wegiwas, hung in the air as a blue-white mist, imparting a surrealistic sense to the scene. Dogs barked faintly, little children squealed and laughed and howled, metal clanged ringingly on metal as someone fashioned a tool or weapon or piece of jewelry.

Their approach was noted and the principal path they were following was quickly lined with spectators calling warm greetings and congratulations to the returning warriors, cheering when the two scalps were held high and waved vigorously, and craning to see the two little captives. By the time they reached the huge council house, which Chiksika pointed to for Margaret's benefit and identified as *msi-kah-mi-qui*, two or three thousand people had gathered and the din was deafening.

This was Chalahgawtha, principal village of the Shawnee tribe since the murder of Chief Hokolesqua at Fort Randolph last year. And here to greet them at the large doorway to the *msi-kah-mi-qui* was the new principal chief of the tribe, Black Fish. He was a man with extremely dark eyes and strong but kindly features, wearing a red blanket draped over his shoulders and doeskin leggins beneath. He was shod in beautifully beaded moccasins and around his neck was a string of upcurved bear claws with inch-wide cylinders of beaten silver between the claws. His graying hair hung loose, well down over his shoulders, and his voice, when he spoke in evident greeting to Chiksika, was rich in timbre.

The warriors dismounted, Chiksika and Wasegoboah lightly sliding off their horses with the girls in their arms and then standing them on the ground. A long conversation between Black Fish and most of the warriors took place then, during which a regal-looking young woman of twenty, who was holding a four-year-old by the hand, moved up close to the chief. She was followed by four boys, one about ten and the other three each about seven. Several times during the conversation, Margaret and Elizabeth heard themselves again being referred to as Matchsquathi Kisahthoi and Matchsquathi Tebethto, or even more often as simply Kisahthoi and Tebethto.

At last Black Fish turned his full attention to the girls, approached and squatted in front of them. He was amazingly graceful in his movements for a man who appeared to be in his mid-sixties. Both girls were considerably shocked when he spoke to them in English — slowly, to be sure, but quite fluently.

"You have had a difficult time and are afraid." He smiled disarmingly. "You need not fear; we will not harm you. Since your family is no more, you will have a new family here. When you have rested and eaten, you will be taken to the river by the women and there your white blood will be washed away and you will be given new clothes and adopted into a family — the family of Black Fish. Since you were taken by Chiksika's party and Chiksika is my ward, you therefore become a part of my family. You will be my adopted children. These," he swept out a hand to indicate those who stood close to him, "will be your sister and brothers.

"This one," he continued, indicating their captor, "is Chiksika, who will be your eldest brother. Your sister," he dipped his head toward the beautiful twenty-year-old, "is Tecumapese, who has with her your nephew, Spemica Lawba. This is your brother, Tecumseh, who has entered his tenth summer. And these, all of seven summers in the same birth, are your youngest brothers — Sauwaseekau, Lowawluwaysica and Kumskaka."

Margaret nodded, stood a little straighter and then made a small curtsy as her mother had taught her. "My name is Margaret McKenzie," she said and then added after a brief pause, "and I am entering my twelfth summer. This is my sister, Elizabeth, who has ten summers."

Black Fish shook his head. "No longer are those your names," he said. "I am told that Shemeneto has already given you new names. You are the fair one who smiles much, and so you are *Matchsquathi Kisahthoi*. This one," he indicated Elizabeth, "who is dark and who smiles less, is *Matchsquathi Tebethto*."

"Thank you," Margaret said politely. "They are pretty names, but I do not know their meaning."

Crinkles appeared at the corners of Black Fish's eyes as he explained. "*Matchsquathi Kisahthoi* and *Matchsquathi Tebethto*," he told them, "mean Little Sun and Little Moon."

[*June 15, 1778 — Monday*]

At the trading post, John Kinzie watched with keen interest as the Miami Indians from the Maumee River pawed through the merchandise and selected those items they wished to have in trade for the furs they had brought. Their activities, their manner of dress and ornamentation and their customs excited him. The lad was aware that they usually arrived in family groups of four or five to twenty or thirty, representing anywhere from one or two to six families; that sometimes they came individually, though not often, since the selection of trade goods seemed to be an occasion that families thoroughly enjoyed and wished to share. Only rarely, however, did they come with a chief of considerable importance. Today was one such day.

The leader of this present party of Miamis had a bearing that tended to set him apart. He was a man of medium height and build, but his eyes had a depth and penetration that young Kinzie had rarely encountered. It was as if this chief missed absolutely nothing that occurred around him. And, not understanding why it occurred, John felt a tiny shiver run through him as he studied the Indian more closely. The man was about thirty-five and clad in the most beautifully worked buckskin leggins and sleeveless pullover top that John had seen — decorated with a rainbow of tiny beads sewn into intricate geometric patterns. As with all the members of his party, he had both tomahawk and knife in his belt and he was presently examining a flintlock rifle.

John edged up to the clerk here at Burnett's Detroit Trading Post, touched the man's arm to get his attention and then tilted his head toward the chief.

"Who is that?" he asked.

"Little Turtle . . . or Michikiniqua, whichever you prefer," the clerk answered.

"He looks important."

"You might say that." The clerk smiled faintly. "He's top dog of all the Miamis. Hear tell he's killed over a hundred men in his time."

The young man nodded slowly, very impressed. Just seeing Indians like this was tremendously exciting to him and, as always, since the first encounter he had had with them here, he knew that dealing with them was what he wanted to do over anything else. He was suddenly struck with a sense of amused wonder over his own growth and change during this past year. One year ago today he had arrived at Detroit and been reunited with his family for the first time in over three years. And thinking of that, he thought as well of George Farnham in Quebec and how great a debt of gratitude he owed that wonderful old silversmith. The three years spent as Farnham's apprentice were good years and the skills John had learned from the master artisan would, he knew, be of immense value to him in his projected career.

That he had possessed a marked aptitude for metalwork in general and silverwork in particular had become immediately apparent to Farnham, and the silversmith had crammed his new apprentice with a multitude of techniques and knowledge that he had himself taken practically a lifetime to learn. Softening and stretching raw silver into fine wire, fashioning it into glittering chains, forming it by his will as well as with his mallet and pliers into burnished platters and trays and plates, working it into flatware with etched handles and into jewelry of uncommon beauty — all these and more he had learned at the side of the master silversmith. In the process, by the time his three-year term of indenture was completed, John Kinzie had become far more skilled than a great many silversmiths with decades of experience but little imagination.

Parting from George Farnham had been far more wrenching than Kinzie had anticipated, for the silversmith had become a father-figure for him as well as mentor. Most of all, they had become good friends and both had feared, when the time of departure was upon them, that they would never see one another again, although neither put the sentiment into words. It wasn't necessary.

Over his own protests, John had been paid considerably more than they had agreed upon in the beginning. Above and beyond that, Farnham had, as something of a combined bonus and parting gift for his young assistant, presented him with an ingot of pure silver weighing nearly fifteen pounds. It would help launch him into the silver trade, the old man assured him, and silversmithing might prove to be a valuable adjunct to the Indian trade he was so set on entering.

That had been an understatement considering what had occurred since their parting. A year ago this very day John Kinzie had arrived in Detroit and resumed residency with his family. After the initial excitement of his homecoming, it was all downhill and it had come as something of a shock to him to realize that he really didn't like the Forsyths very much, including even his own mother. The single exception was his half brother, Thomas Forsyth, who was now seven. Tom idolized John and, despite their difference in age, the two got along extremely well.

William Forsyth, Sr., his stepfather, had made a huge success of the inn he had purchased and it was now considered *the* place for the traveler visiting Detroit to stay. It was also a place where frequent balls were held and heavily attended, not only by the social climbers of the Detroit area, but by the officers of Fort Detroit. The commanding officer there was General Henry Hamilton, who was also lieutenant governor of Canada. As he whirled across the ballroom floor with various finely attired ladies, himself the very picture of debonair charm, it was hard to imagine that this was the same person who was supplying the Indians with the weapons and assistance necessary for them to continue and increase their savage raids against the American frontier settlements; this was the man who was paying a bounty for every American scalp that was brought to him. Though he and his officers frequently attended the balls held at Forsyth's Inn, they were rare visitors at the residence of William and Emily Forsyth.

Located at Grosse Pointe, the Forsyth estate was a lovely place, gracefully rising on the shore of Lake St. Clair, tastefully furnished and ranked among the highest for graciousness by the social elite, such as they were, of this infant metropolis of the frontier. But John Kinzie hated it. The fundamental stuffiness of the manor stifled him and he knew beyond any shadow of doubt that he would remain here only so long as absolutely necessary for him to get established on his own.

The greatest shock and. disappointment had been the change in his mother. She was a person he didn't know anymore; one he didn't really care to know. Hints of it, obvious in retrospect, had appeared in her letters to him, but he hadn't recognized them at the time. Now he found her a combination of many of the things he most disliked. She was vapid and at the same time pretentious, argumentative without basis for her opinions, which were founded on misinformation, fabrication and an unconquerable inability to admit to error. She babbled inanities almost ceaselessly and fawned over her husband virtually to the point of nausea. But, worst of all, she was stupid. Ignorance, in John's view, was forgivable, but not unremitting stupidity, and it was this of which she was profoundly guilty. John Kinzie discovered that he heartily disliked his mother and yearned for the time to come when he could free himself of her permanently. And, feeling as he did, the result was that he was at the same time filled with guilt.

Within a week of his arrival in Detroit, John had become an habitué of the Detroit branch of William Burnett's business in the Indian trade. Soon he met Burnett himself, a dour man married to the sister of the powerful Potawatomi chief named Topenebe. Burnett was among the best established and most skilled and respected of the Indian traders; skilled and respected not only by his own countrymen, but equally by the Indians with whom he dealt. At a time when cheating Indians in trade was all but endemic, William Burnett was a rock of fairness. It was that, as much as anything, that encouraged John to seek employment from Burnett.

Young Kinzie went to work for William Burnett within mere weeks of his arrival at Detroit, mostly at the Detroit post, but occasionally at the trader's principal post adjacent to Topenebe's village on the St. Joseph River, almost two hundred miles west along the Potawatomi Trail. That same trail, which John vowed to follow one day, led even farther west to the Potawatomi villages at the mouths of the Calumet, Checagou and Milwackie rivers.

From Burnett he learned the government's regulations in respect to trading with the Indians, the value of treating every Indian customer fairly. He learned who the other traders were who frequented the Lake Michigan area, from Mackinac and Green Bay to Milwackie, Checagou and St. Joseph. Some were good men who could always be trusted; others detestable and frequently dangerous. In most cases the traders were agents for fur companies, large and small; but occasionally individuals settled among the Indians and traded with them in their own villages, just as Burnett had done years before at St. Joseph.

As an example, just up the Checagou River, near where it split into a North and South branch, a French trader named Gaurie last year established a small trading post on the North Branch almost adjacent to the village of Chief Black Partridge. The Gaurie house and trading post was situated in the midst of a picket enclosure erected not so much as a protection against Indians as a protection for livestock — chickens, ducks, hogs, sheep and cattle — from marauding wolves, bobcats and occasional bears. The North Branch, as a result of Gaurie's presence there, was now becoming known as the Gaurie River.[33]

Burnett was very interested in that area and his interest fired John Kinzie's. Burnett declared that the area at the mouth of the Checagou River was strategically extremely important and would one day become one of this country's great trade centers. The reason was because the South Branch of the river provided access, via a relatively short portage, to the Des Plaines River, which flowed into the Illinois and thereby to the Mississippi, connecting the interior heartland of the country to the upper Great Lakes and thereby to the trading centers of Montreal and Quebec. All this was information which John Kinzie quietly filed away in his mind for possible future action.

As he had learned swiftly and well the trade of the silversmith from George Farnham, so now young Kinzie began rapidly absorbing the more obscure elements of Indian trade from Burnett. Before long he met Burnett's Potawatomi wife, Kawkeeme — an overflowing barrel of a woman with jolly manner that masked an unusually sharp mind. She liked John Kinzie immediately and introduced him to her famed brother.

In Topenebe, John Kinzie encountered for the first time a man possessing not only great personal magnetism and even an aura of charisma, but one with remarkably developed leadership abilities.[34] If the Potawatomi tribe had had a principal chief, as did many other tribes, chances were good that Topenebe would have filled that seat. Such, however, was not the status of the tribe. Very widely spread over the land in disparate concentrations since the destruction of the Illinois Confederacy, the Potawatomi tribe was comprised of bands which, in a general way, cooperated with one another in most matters, but which occasionally differed in matters of great importance. At the moment there were strong rifts between the pro-American, neutral, and pro-British bands. The pro-American Potawatomi faction was led by Siggenauk, whom the Americans called Blackbird, and whose village was at the mouth of the Milwackie.[35] The neutral bands were led by Chief Black Partridge at the mouth of the Checagou and Chief Windigo at Peoria Lake on the Illinois River.[36] The pro-British bands were led by Topenebe at the St. Joseph and Chief Main Poche of the Kankakee River, at the headwaters of the Illinois.[37]

John and Topenebe had an immediate affinity for one another, which quickly grew into a strong mutual friendship and respect. When merely as a matter of friendship and esteem and neither asking nor expecting anything in return, John presented him with a beautifully fashioned and brilliantly polished silver gorget upon which he had engraved a wreath of oak leaves and acorns encircling a pipe tomahawk, the effusive gratitude of Topenebe was downright embarrassing. As of that moment, Topenebe had become John's champion and protector.

Despite his easily acquired friendship with Topenebe, John Kinzie had never been particularly noted as being either garrulous or one who made friends easily and as a matter of course. To the contrary, he was inclined to be taciturn, sometimes to the point of rudeness. For this reason, there were only two people anywhere near his own age with whom he associated to any marked degree. One was his younger half brother, Thomas Forsyth. The other was a half-breed a year younger than he, named Chechepinqua — meaning Tame Rattlesnake — but much better known to both Americans and British as Alexander Robinson. He was the offspring of an Ottawa woman and a Scots trader affiliated with the British army at Mackinac.[38] Together he and Chechepinqua fished and hunted and rode through the country. The engaging half-breed was an excellent guide with a phenomenal grasp of the geography of the upper Great Lakes and an amazing ability to recognize the most subtle of landmarks. Through him John learned a very great deal about the essentially wild country between Lake Erie and Lake Michigan.

John's own fame had spread far. Scarcely an Indian of this region was not aware of his skill in silverwork. Not only did they purchase the silver jewelry he fashioned — paying him lavishly in furs which he resold at considerable profit — some were even bringing him large nuggets of raw silver from sources they would not reveal and asking him to fashion armbands, bracelets, anklebands, gorgets, headbands and other items for them from it — again, at a price the Indians themselves set, which was far more than he would have asked on his own accord.[39]

A little matter had occurred only recently that pleased John about as much as anything that had happened since his arrival here. He had been given a Potawatomi name by Chief Topenebe and practically overnight he was being addressed by this name by all the Potawatomi with whom he had contact, and by a great many of the Ottawas and Chippewas as well. The name was *Shawneeawkee* — The Silver Man.

To even the most casual of observers, it was apparent that young John Kinzie, only fourteen-and-a-half years old, was destined for great success on this frontier.

[*March 19, 1779 — Friday*]

In the ten months since their adoption into the Shawnee tribe, great changes had been wrought in Margaret and Elizabeth McKenzie. Both girls, now thirteen and eleven, spoke the language fluently, though they continued to talk to one another in English because Margaret was afraid if they did not, they would forget how.

Because of her dark hair, Elizabeth — Tebethto — was now virtually indistinguishable from other little Shawnee girls her age here at Chalah-gawtha, and only the blond hair of Margaret — Kisahthoi — marked her as being different, for in dress, actions and speech she was like the others. They wore simple doeskin pullover garments which came to their knees and, except during winter, normally went barefoot.

The girls had adapted to life with their new family extremely well and especially grew to love Tecumapese. To them she was a combination mother and older sister, and from her they had learned not only the language of the Shawnees, but the customs, social structure and history of the tribe. Very frequently they cared for her five-year-old, Spemica Lawba, who was a beautiful, well-mannered little boy with enormous dark eyes and a ready smile. He looked a great deal like a younger version of Tecumseh, who was Elizabeth's age, also polite and friendly.

They rarely saw Chiksika except when he returned from leading forays against the whites south of the Spaylaywitheepi and, though in a way they realized he was an enemy of the whites and even the leader of the party that had killed their own mother and brother, yet in some strange way they came to share the pride that swelled in Tecumapese and Tecumseh when he returned in triumph. When the accounts of exploits were related around the fire in the evening following such returns, they thrilled along with the others at the narrow escapes, the hand-to-hand combats, the incidents of uncommon bravery, the taking of scalps as symbols of victory; and they shared the sense of loss and sorrow when the death chant was sung for warriors who lost their lives in such raids.

"Why must the men fight and kill each other?" Margaret had asked at one point, several weeks earlier. "Why can't they just live peacefully with each other and share the field and woods? Surely there is enough for all."

Tecumapese smiled at her. "I often asked the same question when I was younger." She shrugged. "Sometimes I still do, but I know now that it can never be; there are too many differences between us which can never be resolved. Many times we have tried to live in peace, but even though treaties were made and hearts were in accord for this goal, it would not work."

"But why not?" Elizabeth put in. "I don't understand why not, if it is what everyone wants."

"I will answer Little Moon," Chiksika interjected. "And Little Sun," he added, glancing at Margaret. He paused, considering where to begin, and in the silence that fell a cricket chirped in a deeply shadowed corner of the wegiwa. When at last he spoke again, his young face bore an expression of grim sorrow.

"Our worlds are so different," he said. "The Indian lives with nature, accepting and using with care and restraint and love what Moneto has given to all his children. We do not drive wooden posts into the breast of the mother earth to divide her into property as the white men do, for we believe the earth belongs to all, to use wisely and well and equally. We hunt in the woods and in the prairies for the animals Moneto has placed there for our needs and we do not take more than we need.

"The whites," he continued, "cut down the forests and burn the grasses so they can plant things Moneto did not mean to be here; while they do this, animals they bring with them can wander and eat the food that belongs to the animals that Moneto meant to be here. When we allow one white man to build his cabin, soon there are two, then ten and then more until there is little room left; by then the white man has forgotten that the land is the Indians' and he has only been allowed to be there. Suddenly he looks upon the Indian as being an intruder on his land and tells the Indian he must move away to make room for more white men.

"When a white man kills an Indian in fair fight, it is called honorable, but when an Indian kills a white man in fair fight, it is called murder. When a white army battles Indians and wins, it is a great victory, but if they lose it is called a massacre and bigger armies are raised. If the Indian flees before the advance of such armies, when he tries to return he finds that white men are living where he had lived. If he tries to fight off such armies, he is killed and the land is taken anyway. When an Indian is killed, it is a great loss which leaves a gap in our people and a sorrow in our heart; when a white is killed, three or four others step up to take his place and there is no end to it. The white race is a monster who is always hungry and what he eats is land. We are now divided among ourselves as to what path we should take."

What Chiksika alluded to were the interminable councils which had been held over a period of many years to discuss the problem of white man's encroachment. The rift between the two factions among the five Shawnee septs had grown progressively wider and it was now clear that there would never be agreement. With breaking hearts the tribe had, in its last council, decided to separate permanently. More than half of the Shawnees believed with utter conviction that the only way they could survive was by agreeing to peace on the white man's terms, which meant adopting the white man's ways, laws, government and religion. The other faction was fully as adamant in its belief that Shawnee survival under such conditions would be an existence devoid of honor, dignity and self-respect and that death was preferable to this, so they advocated war.

Such war would not be long in coming. Events that had transpired just during this period that the McKenzie girls had lived with the tribe had taken grim turns for the Indians. The Virginia Assembly had just created Illinois County, with boundaries embracing the entire Northwest, from Lake Erie westward to Lake Michigan and westward beyond that to the Mississippi River, and taking in everything southward of that all the way to the Ohio River. They paid little attention to the fact that not only was this same territory being claimed as extensions of their own counties by Connecticut and Quebec, but that it was the home territory of thousands of Indians of a dozen or more tribes and subtribes.

The Kentuckians south of the Spaylaywitheepi were continuing to build strong forts and thus far had been able to resist every effort by Indians to make them leave. The peril increased enormously when a little ragtag army of one hundred seventy-five Virginians — Shemanese, as the Shawnees called them — led by the young major named George Rogers Clark had come and with devastating suddenness had captured and occupied the British posts at Kaskaskia and Cahokia on the Mississippi and Vincennes on the lower Wabash. Abruptly the Illinois and Indiana country had passed from British control to that of the dreaded Shemanese.[40]

At once Clark had held councils with the Indians, especially the Potawatomi and Kickapoo, telling them forcefully that he wished no war with them, but warning that if they supported the British, such war would be visited upon them and they would be destroyed. One of the Indians who met with Clark was Siggenauk, chief of the Potawatomies in the vicinity of the mouth of the Milwackie River, but which Clark was referring to as Milwaukee. Siggenauk departed with a pair of packhorses laden with gifts, having left behind a promise of support for the Americans and antipathy for the British. Other chiefs came also and reached agreement with Clark as Siggenauk had — Windigo of the Peoria Lake Potawatomies, Nakewoin — or Wind Striker — of the Illinois River Potawatomies, Quaquapocqua, chief of the Kickapoos from the village of Ouiatenon on the Wabash River, whom Clark presented with an American flag, and several other chiefs representing the Piankeshaw, Wea and Eel River subdivisions of the Miami tribe.[41]

Obviously, it was pointed out in the Shawnee councils, these Indians could no longer be counted on to help the Shawnees stem the white advance into their territory. Even though it was whispered that General Henry Hamilton at Detroit was preparing to counterinvade and retake what Clark had captured, the only certain thing was that more and more whites would be entering this land. And even though, for now, the whites would be fighting one another, the Shawnees knew that in the end it was the Indians who would be the losers. That knowledge only added conviction to those members of the tribe who had decided to flee before the white flood engulfed them.

Today was the day, therefore, that the Shawnee tribe split forever. Four thousand Shawnees, including twelve hundred from Chalahgawtha alone, formed a great procession and began to march westward away from the Ohio country, heading through the wilderness beyond and finally across the Mississippi to a new home in the Missouri country, where Spanish officials had granted them the right to settle. Though comprised of Shawnees from all five septs, those leaving were mainly the Thawegila, Peckuwe and Kispokotha, and leading them away was the new principal chief of that faction, Ki-kusgow-lowa of the Thawegila. He was flanked by Chief Yellow Hawk of the Peckuwe and Black Stump, the new chief of the Kispokotha. Shemeneto had stepped down in his favor, preferring to remain behind as war chief under Black Fish, to lead the remnants of the Maykujay and Chalahgawtha Shawnees.

Less than three thousand Shawnees — men, women and children — remained behind, and the moroseness that flooded them as they watched the procession leave was all but unbearable. And almost as deeply affected were the two little girls called Kisahthoi and Tebethto, who stood watching with their family.

[*March 21, 1779 — Sunday*]

The Delaware Indians, never a very powerful force to begin with, once again were choosing to flee rather than fight. Here on the White River in the Indiana country, only eighteen miles away from the post called Vincennes, Running Fox, chief of the Rabbit Clan of the Delawares, stood before his two hundred followers who were crammed into the makeshift construction that passed as a council house and addressed them soberly.

"We must leave this place forever," he told them, then stood waiting while the gasps of surprise and consternation ran their course. They had been given no preparation for this; the possibility of leaving here had never even been broached until this very moment. What could have happened? Why was it necessary that they leave? The din within the smoke-filled dimness was all but overpowering, and throughout it all there was the undercurrent of fear.

Once this clan had numbered in the thousands, when they lived far to the east along the river which bore their present name. Then they had been called Lenni Lenape — The People. But white men had come and the members of the tribe dwindled and the white men called them Delawares, as a tribute to the then governor of Virginia, Thomas West, third baron of De La Warr — better known as Lord Delaware. They had fought the menace again and again; over and over they had lost, and each time their numbers had further dwindled. A pattern became clear; they moved, they stood, they fought, they lost, and eventually they moved again. Would it not be wise, the elders reasoned, to move *before* having to fight? Would it not be best to move *before* having to lose brave young warriors in fruitless battle against an implacable and innumerable foe? The answers were clear and so they had begun the practice of moving away quickly when troubles came. The last move before now had been from their village on the Little Kanawha River before the so-called war that Lord Dunmore had waged.

Now the troubles had come again and Chief Running Fox resumed speaking. "This has become a bad land," he told them, "and the smell of death is heavy in the air. Our future is inevitable now. The white men have dug their toes into the soil of this country and the dirt can never be shaken free. They will overflow this country. Our streams will run red with blood and the skulls of brave men will grow white beneath the sun."

He spoke for hours with customary rhetoric, telling them in roundabout manner what had occasioned this development. They knew, he told them, that the young Virginia warrior named Clark had driven the British from their posts at Kaskaskia, Cahokia and nearby Vincennes. The Delawares had been greatly fearful then and had almost left, but they had learned that the Detroit warrior, General Hamilton, was coming with an army to drive out the young Clark and restore things to what they were, so they had waited. Henry Hamilton had come, as they knew, supported by Potawatomies and Kickapoos, and during the Snow Moon — December — he had taken Vincennes back and remained there with his two hundred forty soldiers and with a hundred Kickapoos forming a ring around Vincennes to protect him.

But now the unbelievable had happened. In the midst of this season when no armies move or fight because they must fight winter as well as the enemy, the young warrior Clark had led a handful of his men out of Kaskaskia and marched and waded through flooded and frozen country for two moons to reach Vincennes. His force was so much smaller than that of the British general in his fort at Vincennes as to be ridiculous. But the Kickapoos guarding that place were so awed by Clark's courage, so convinced of his invulnerability, that they would not stop him. Only a short time ago, taking Vincennes entirely by surprise, the young warrior Clark demanded and received the unconditional surrender of the British force and instantly reinstated the claim of Virginia to the entire region between the Ohio River and the Great Lakes — the Northwest. Now, as it always had before, would come the flood of white men. Now, once again, it was time to leave.

"Our land here," Running Fox concluded, "will soon be a delight only to the carrion eaters. This time we will not sink our roots until the grandmother of rivers lies a hundred days into the rising sun."

Although it did not come out in this council, there was another reason why Running Fox was ordering the migration. Runners had just brought news that a small party of Delaware warriors from this village, who had journeyed far to the east, had had a run-in with a party of Iroquois being led by an up-and-coming young Seneca named Caughna. They didn't know who he was and had killed him. Only then did they discover they might well have inspired full-scale retaliation by the entire Iroquois League to descend upon the Delawares.

Caughna had turned out to be the younger brother of one of the most powerful chiefs of the Seneca and one of the most influential voices in the greatly feared and respected Iroquois League — Chief Cornplanter.

[*July 4, 1779 — Sunday*]

Stepping from his canoe on the north bank of the Checagou River a few hundred yards upstream from its mouth at Lake Michigan, the large man grinned, his teeth gleaming whitely in contrast to the darkness of his skin. He had strong, good-looking features, very broad shoulders, and stood an inch over six feet tall. His woman, a chunky, bland-expressioned Potawatomi named Gohna, had preceded him ashore with their three-year-old son and six-year-old daughter and stood waiting patiently. Gohna always waited patiently. Had a roaring wall of water been rushing down upon them from upstream, she would have still patiently awaited her husband's command.

For Gohna, this was a coming-home. Less than a quarter-mile from here was the site where she had been living a decade ago when this dark trader beside her had first stopped at the village. During his sporadic visits over the months which followed, they had become friends of a sort. Actually, it was her father, a village chief of the Potawatomi, whom he had come to see. Gohna was incidental, at first, but she soon became an integral part of his plans.

The man was Jean Baptiste Point du Sable.[42] A clever, well-educated and quite articulate man, he was nevertheless taciturn, rarely speaking without good reason. He did not speak now, only motioned to a spot of ground nearby that appealed to him, and immediately she bade the children sit there and began unloading the bales and bundles from the canoe.

Jean Baptiste returned his gaze to the river and a trace of the initial grin returned. The faint sound of laughter came from the Potawatomi village beyond the screen of brush and trees to the northwest and he knew that soon Gohna's father would be arriving with his entourage to greet them and express his delight that they had accepted his offer to make their home on this land. As usual, Jean Baptiste would open a keg and they would drink together well into the night.

He studied the river, upstream and down. Just below where he stood, the river turned southward and angled to the lake, deflected in its eastward course by a dense sandbar twenty yards in width. With that bar removed, the man mused, the river would have a straight shoot into the lake and commerce would be improved considerably. Why could not the sand from there be removed and placed across the present river mouth, opening the one and closing the other and, in the process, creating a still-water harbor of great value?

Half a mile upstream from where he stood, Du Sable could see where the river split, half coming from the north, half from the south.[43] The North Branch was an inconsequential stream of inconsiderable length, serving no function other than to drain the area of low land between a ridge and the lake, with the water on the west side of the ridge flowing into the Des Plaines River.[44] The South Branch, on the other hand, flowed to within a few miles of the Des Plaines. A portage there, used for scores of years by Indians and traders, gave access to the larger river. The Des Plaines, in turn, converged some miles to the south with a river of similar size coming in from the southeast — the Kankakee — and these two joined to form the Illinois. The Illinois, in turn, flowed to the Mississippi only a short distance above St. Louis, giving access upstream to immensely rich fur lands, giving access downstream to New Orleans and the Gulf of Mexico, and giving access to the Missouri, entering from the west from a largely unknown and evidently tremendously important land beyond.

The Checagou Portage, therefore, was the key. Jean Baptiste Point du Sable was convinced that it needn't be merely a portage over which canoes could be easily carried. It could be changed; channels could be dug and broad roads flanking the channels could be cleared so that teams of horses

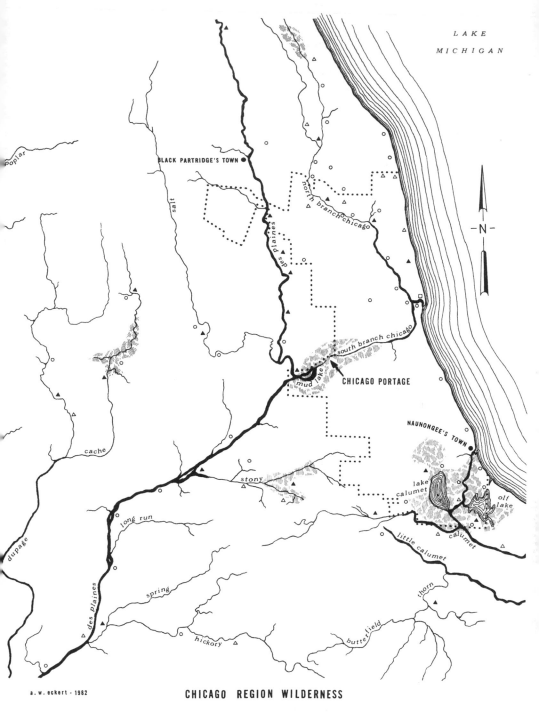

LAKE MICHIGAN

Poplar

BLACK PARTRIDGE'S TOWN ●

salt

des plaines

north branch chicago

– N –

south branch chicago

mud lake

CHICAGO PORTAGE

NAUNONGEE'S TOWN ●

cache

stony

lake calumet

olf lake

long run

little calumet

calumet

dupage

des plaines

spring

thorn

hickory

butterfield

a. w. eckert - 1982

CHICAGO REGION WILDERNESS

☐ - DU SABLE'S TRADING POST

▲ - MAJOR INDIAN VILLAGES OF THE PAST

△ - MINOR INDIAN VILLAGES OF THE PAST

○ - IMPORTANT INDIAN CAMPS OF THE PAST

····· - APPROXIMATE LIMITS OF PRESENT CHICAGO

or oxen could pull larger craft — loaded bateaux and rafts and perhaps even ships. By opening the Checagou Portage, this very place where Jean Baptiste Point du Sable was standing would become a gateway to empire, connecting the vast energies of the population of the northeast via the St. Lawrence, Lake Erie, Lake Huron and Lake Michigan to the virtually untapped resources of the unknown north and west and south of this continent west of the Mississippi.

A *gateway to empire!* Checagou, Du Sable was convinced, was destined to become a great center of commerce, where fortunes would be made. Now, as he stood looking at it, he wondered at the inability of others to grasp the concept. For a hundred years and more the French had used the portage in haphazard fashion. Jolliett and Marquette had been here, followed by LaSalle, along with his man, Henri de Tonty, and a stream of others — all *using* the portage but none ever fully recognizing its real potential and strategic significance.

Gaurie was a perfect example. The Frenchman was a trader, living on the North Branch near its mouth, just a little north of where North and South branches formed the main Chicago River. So unaware of the potential of the area that he had built his little post in a position more of service to the North Branch, which was a dead end, than the South Branch, which would have been in the path of progress and on the threshold of opportunity.

Du Sable was on that threshold, but *he* was aware of it. It had been the basis of his coming here in the first place and a motivating cause in his marriage to Gohna. Except with full accord of the Potawatomies whose land this was, his settling here and establishing a trading post was out of the question. Marrying into the tribe gave virtually automatic consent to what he had in mind. Further, since Gohna was daughter of a chief, albeit a minor one, this meant that the possibility existed Du Sable could himself be made a chief of the Potawatomi, even though he was not only not of that tribe, he had no Indian blood whatever. Du Sable's father had been French, his mother a native of Santo Domingo — the darkness of his own skin directly attributable to her.[45]

The marriage to Gohna seven years ago was not an actual wedding. As a matter of fact, it involved nothing more than paying her father a certain amount of trade goods and a horse, at which point she transferred her allegiance to him and became a largely silent shadow following him everywhere. One day, he kept telling himself, they would visit a priest somewhere, perhaps in St. Louis, and get legally married. For the time being, it wasn't convenient. Their daughter, named Susanne, was born in the late summer of 1773 and three years later Jean Baptiste, Jr. was born, both at Du Sable's trading post at Peoria Lake, where the family remained until early in 1777.

Du Sable's Indian trade was quite good and he profited, becoming rather well off, if not actually wealthy. Thus, in March of that year, he had established a new house and trading establishment, with full approval of Gohna's father and his fellow Potawatomies, on the southeastern shore of Lake Michigan near an area of immense sand dunes.[46] His selection of the location was predicated not so much on trade passing by, although the important Potawatomi Trail from Checagou to Detroit via St. Joseph did pass right by it, as it was on the fact that Gohna, who had frequently visited the dunes with her family as a child, expressed a desire to live there. Since she rarely made requests of any kind, Du Sable was agreeable to giving it a try. The post did not do badly, but neither did it do terribly well and so, after a year's trial, they moved on, establishing yet another post seventy miles by water above Detroit on the shore of the St. Clair River only three miles below the mouth of Lake Huron.[47] Here the trade was primarily with Ottawa and Chippewa tribesmen and, for the first time, he ran into difficulties. A Frenchman named François Bellecour, whom he hired as clerk to run the post when he was not there, was not above a little larceny, both from his employer and from the Indians with whom he was trading. Du Sable gave the man several warnings and, on Bellecour's promise that he would hereafter toe the mark, again left the post in his charge and headed for the mouth of the Checagou River.

Now the trader glanced toward the lake again, shading his eyes and searching the horizon. There was no sign yet of the string of bateaux that would be bringing the tools, equipment and supplies he had arranged for in Detroit in order to set up his post here. He would have been surprised if they had been visible, not expecting them for perhaps as much as two or three more days. In the meanwhile, he would select the spot where he would build his new permanent home and post.

With the arrival of Jean Baptiste Point du Sable, a seed had been planted here — a seed called Chicago.[48]

[*September 1, 1779 — Wednesday*]

Warhoyonehth, known more familiarly to the whites by two other names — Big White Man and Cornplanter — was among the most prominent of Seneca chiefs. His village, Oswaya, was located in southwestern New York at the point where Olean Creek from the north flowed into the upper Allegheny.[49] The death of his younger brother, Caughna, earlier in the year at the hands of a party of Delawares at Kittanning had occurred when Cornplanter had been in Montreal, asking the British for more weapons and ammunition to fight the Americans. He learned of it when he returned in June and a great rage and desire for vengeance filled him, but he was not able to act on it at once. Matters of war with the Americans had been a greater priority. That priority had eased now and Cornplanter had raised this party of twenty warriors who presently stood waiting his command. They had been prepared to march against the Delawares who had returned to Kittanning and eradicate them, but then word had come that not only had they fled, their whole clan — the Rabbit Clan under Chief Running Fox, which had been residing far, far to the west on a tributary of the lower Wabash — had migrated westward beyond the great river. At least for now, they were well beyond his reach. His simmering rage intensified with this frustration, Cornplanter addressed his followers briefly.

"We still go," he told them. "The rabbits have fled, but they have left in their place the Americans who wrongfully purchased the same ground. Caughna is dead. He cannot yet be avenged, but his spirit among us may be replaced by another that the Great Spirit will show us. We will go there and take such a one and return."[50]

[*September 16, 1779 — Thursday morning*]

The John Lytle family had at last settled down to stay in one place for keeps, or at least so Lytle himself had proclaimed to Sarah. She had accepted the proclamation without comment, recalling only too clearly that markedly similar comments were made when they left Philadelphia after their marriage and wound up "settling" four times in the first eighteen months. The fourth move, to Lancaster, had lasted only six weeks — until John heard from a stranger about the marvelous place called Path Valley near Carlisle and then they were off again, only two days after little Nelly had been born. Her name was Eleanor, but right from the beginning they had referred to her as Little Nelly and the nickname had stuck. Hard to believe she was nine years old already.

Path Valley *had* been nice; not really all they'd expected, but better for them than the other stops, and they'd wound up staying there for almost seven years. During that interval quite a lot had occurred and their family had enlarged. Harrison had been born in '71, two years after Little Nelly, followed by Tom the next year and then Margaret — whom the others had insisted on calling Maggie — two years later, in '74. Then word had come of the death of John's father, William, in the summer of '75 and he'd made the trip back to Philadelphia to handle the estate. His mother had died many years before and he was the only heir. He'd been stunned at the size of the estate. In addition to the home and several other nice properties, which he sold immediately, there was a sizable amount of cash, several good horses and a fine large carriage, plus five Negro slaves — three strong men, a rail-thin woman named Grace and her eight-year-old daughter, Ollie. John Lytle had left his family in Path Valley as a man of little means, barely able to eke out a living on a hardscrabble farm, and returned two months later a reasonably well-to-do gentleman.

Sarah was pleased at their good fortune and especially at the joy of having slaves to do the hard work, though she suspected that the family's change in status might well betoken another move. She was correct. John's antennae went up as he sensed about for a new and better place for them — "A place to really put down our roots this time, Sarah!" — but it was the better part of two years before he found it.

The new place — the one in which they were now living — was still farther west in Pennsylvania, about thirty-five miles up the Allegheny River from Fort Pitt, which everyone was calling Pittsburgh these days. It was quite a well built home, considering its situation on the frontier, located at the mouth of Plum Creek[51] where the smaller stream flowed into the Allegheny. The valley was fertile and especially productive of fruit such as plums, apples, peaches and pears, and the farm John purchased already had an orchard of some fifteen acres. There were neighbors, though scattered over a considerable area, and most of them were fruit growers also. Two miles up the Allegheny was a little settlement known simply as "the ford,"[52] since there was a fording place of the large river there. Three miles above that was a fair-sized town called Kittanning,[53] located on the site of an old abandoned Delaware Indian village of the same name. Local tradition had it that the Delawares who had lived there were driven out by the Iroquois because they had sold the whites a large parcel of land belonging to the Iroquois.

With the field hands to care for the orchards under John's direction and Ollie to help indoors, the new home was delightful. Unfortunately, Grace had sickened and died shortly after the Lytles' arrival, but her daughter, Ollie, skinny, energetic and very black, was, when under close supervision, becoming quite good at helping with the smaller children and with doing housework. Recently, Sarah had even been teaching her how to cook. Ollie was now twelve years old.

When over three years had passed after the birth of Margaret with no more pregnancies, Sarah had come to believe her childbearing days were over. The thought was not unpleasant. Yet, suddenly she was pregnant again and just three months ago today, on June 16, Mary had been born. Even with Ollie's assistance, having a baby around the house to care for again was more a task than Sarah had anticipated.

Now, with breakfast over, John was preparing to leave for the day with the three male slaves, Jennings, Billy and Wharf, to assist in a house-raising several miles away. Sarah wished he weren't going and was tempted to ask him not to do so. She didn't.

"When will you be home?" she asked instead.

He shrugged. "About dusk, I'd think."

"Good. I'd rather you weren't away after dark, not with all those alarms we've been having."

"Alarms be damned!" John snapped. "I'm really getting tired of hearing alarms. For the past two years every time one of our timid neighbors sees a shadow he shouts 'Injens!' and gets everyone all riled up, and every time it's been nonsense. Except for that party of friendly Delawares who stopped off at their old village site at Kittanning and camped for a couple of weeks and then left as suddenly as they came, there hasn't been an Indian seen around here for the better part of a year. I've told you over and over there's nothing to worry about."

"I suppose so," Sarah murmured, sorry she'd mentioned it. "But please be careful anyway. And for my sake, please do be home before dark."

He said he would, kissed her and all five of their children good-bye and drove off with the three black men bouncing and jostling behind him in the rear of the wagon loaded with tools and lumber. For the rest of the morning Sarah was engaged in giving the children their reading and spelling lessons and nursing Mary off and on as she did so. After this, following a light lunch, Sarah busied herself with giving Olllie another cooking lesson while six-year-old Tom and four-year-old Maggie walked hand-in-hand out to the garden to play by themselves; the older two, Little Nelly, nine, and Harrison, seven, headed for the dingle — a small hollow several hundred yards distant in the rear of the house, where some trees had recently been felled by the blacks and still lay untrimmed. They had found it was great sport to climb among the branches.

Inside the house, Sarah stood at the window and watched them go, again the faint uneasiness stirring within her. She wished she could shake it off.

[*September 16, 1779 — Thursday, 2:30 P.M.*]

"Mamma's not going to be happy when she sees how dirty your feet are, Maggie." Thomas spoke with an authority he was certain closely approximated his father's, such as when John Lytle addressed his slaves.

"Poo!" Margaret pouted her lips and wrinkled her nose with all the four-year-old disdain she could muster, which was considerable. She glanced at her shoes and socks in a cast-off pile at the edge of the cabbage patch twenty feet away, then at her own tiny feet well dusted with the soil of the garden. "I'm not a-scared."

Tom turned his head to look at her. He was lying on his back between the rows, dwarfed by the enormous cabbage heads. Margaret was sitting in the next row scooping up dirt with both hands and letting it trickle in hourglass fashion over her toes. He snorted and sat up.

"You're so brave when there's no one around to hear. How would you like me to tell Mamma what you just said?"

"Tom! You wouldn't!" She was aghast. "You promised that what we said to each other was only for us to know."

The six-year-old snickered. "Just foolin'. Didn't say I *would*, did I? Don't be such a —"

Margaret glanced up from the dirt at him to see why he had stopped. His mouth had fallen open and his face had turned the color of old ash. As she turned to see what he was staring at he lunged at her, pulling her flat to the ground and cupping his hand fiercely over her mouth, his body lying partially over hers. His excited voice became a barely audible sibilance directly at her ear.

"*Indians!* Keep quiet. Stay here and stay down!"

The frantic urgency frightened her and she flattened herself even more to the earth, eyes wide as she watched him squirm on his stomach to the end of the row. He was only an arm's length from her shoes and socks but he didn't see them. He watched intently toward the house for a brief span, then inched back to her, panting heavily, though his exertions had been slight. His face was white.

"They're between us and the house," he hissed. "They've got tomahawks. They're heading right for the house! We've got to get away and get help. Follow me, but *keep down!*"

He squirmed away rapidly toward the back fence and she followed, her silent tears turning the dust on her face into muddy tracks. They were both breathing heavily as they crawled through the rail fence into the extensive field which was a tangle of blackberry and wild raspberry. Brutal thorns scratched their arms and legs and Margaret was soon whimpering from gouged feet.

"Why didn't you get my shoes?" she sobbed accusingly. "You were right next to them."

"Shhhh. Don't talk. Just follow me."

They crawled twenty or thirty feet into the briers until they could see nothing but foliage and thorny branches. As if from miles away they heard a screaming and the voice was their mother's. They clung to one another, hands gripping so tightly it hurt, yet it wasn't tight enough. Both children were crying now. Silently.

[*September 16,* 1779 — *Thursday,* 2:32 P.M.]

Every once in a while Ollie would pause in her labors and wonder why she had to work while the other children played. All her life it had been that way and that's the way it was still. She guessed it would never change, but she wondered. Somehow, it never seemed quite fair. At twelve she was in many ways the child her years indicated, but there was a darkness in her eyes that had nothing to do with her color; a darkness that came from being deprived of childhood. A joyless dark. It wasn't that she was mistreated much. The switchings she got across the legs, mostly from not understanding what she was supposed to do or doing incorrectly what had been explained to her, were infrequent. It was just that sometimes, when Nelly and Harrison or Maggie and Tom were playing their games, it was like a deep hurt inside from wanting so much to join them. The best she could do was watch.

Ollie was watching now, from a window of the outer kitchen, which was separate from the house but attached by a roofed-over breezeway. There was a kitchen in the house, too, but that was for final cooking of good things that smelled nice. This one was for things that smelled. Hog fat was rendered into lard out here; cabbages were cooked; lye soap being made bubbled in blackened kettles; chickens were scalded and plucked; various other conglomerations were brewed or stewed, roasted or boiled, until all the stinks were rendered out and the desirable residue could be utilized in the house kitchen. Ollie liked it out here. The smells didn't bother her and this was the one place Miz Sarah seldom entered, so Ollie could sometimes stand for long minutes looking out the window at the Lytle children and not be bothered. If Miz Sarah wanted her, she wouldn't come out here. She'd just yell.

Ollie had watched Tom and Maggie enter the cabbage patch; watched for a while as they played. Then she replenished the wood in the cookstoves and stirred one of the bubbling kettles. When she looked back, they were gone. She wondered where they were and stood for a long while looking at the cabbage patch where they had been. Then she saw Tom's head poke up above the cabbages and almost immediately go out of sight again. As she mused over what they were doing, she saw the Indians.

There were ten of them, nearly as she could make out, with weapons in hand — tomahawks and knives and one with a round stone set in a curved stick. They were intent, all of them, on the door of the main house. That was all Ollie cared to see. She ducked out of sight, quick eyes searching the interior of the outer kitchen with new purpose. A large brewing tub was upside down on the floor beside the woodbox and she scurried to it, keeping very low, tilted it up and crawled beneath it. The thudding of her own heart did not drown out the screams that she knew came from Miz Sarah.

[*September 16, 1779 — Thursday*, 2:33 P.M.]

Cornplanter, Seneca chief, grunted faintly with satisfaction. No shots had yet come from the house and since half his party, which had advanced from the other side, should have been there by now, it betokened complete surprise. His own ten men were hidden in shrubbery and behind trees close by, cautioned by a movement of his hand to stay out of sight.

What had occasioned the order were the two children — a boy and a girl — whom they had spied playing among the branches of some felled trees. If the children saw them coming, either they would race screaming toward the house or they would scurry into the tangle of branches in which they were playing and be difficult to capture.

The boy and girl inadvertently made things easier. They stopped climbing and dodging in and out of the branches and sat together on the trunk of one, facing toward the house which was several hundred yards distant and only barely visible through the brush. Moving up with utter silence, Cornplanter approached to within three feet of them without being detected. The children were engaged in a discussion and oblivious to their surroundings.

Cornplanter's hand shot out and clamped on the upper arms of both children. They started violently, screamed and struggled, but could not break the grip of the powerful Indian. Others of his warriors rushed forward until they were surrounded and only then did Cornplanter release them. They stood shuddering and inarticulate with fright. The chief looked at them closely and a small smile touched his lips. They were what he wanted and he had already determined which would be adopted into his household to fill the place of the slain Caughna.

He raised a hand toward the children, palm forward. He did not know much English but what he knew was sufficient for the moment. He shook his head faintly and addressed his remark toward the boy, who seemed the more terrified.

"No 'fraid," he said. "No hurt. Come."

With the warriors still forming a cordon around them, he led Eleanor and Harrison Lytle away from the house and deeper into the woods, moving on a widely circuitous route toward the point where, later, as agreed upon, they would rendezvous with the other half of his party.

[*September 16, 1779 — Thursday, sunset*]

For Sarah Lytle, being herded along as she was with a long rawhide tether around her neck and three-month-old Mary whimpering in her arms was something out of a nightmare. She couldn't believe this was happening, yet knew it was. Her legs hurt and her back ached from the unaccustomed strain of carrying Mary so far and for so long. It seemed to her they would never get to the top of the hill they were climbing, but at last they did and the walking became a little easier along the crest. Below them lay Plum Creek valley, looking warm and safe in the sunset, and again, as had occurred a dozen times or more already, tears blurred her vision, but she made no sound.

Panic almost choked her as she thought of the children, wondering if they were safe or if, perhaps, they were already dead. And what about John? Had they waylaid him along the road somewhere? A shudder wracked her frame as she thought again of how it all began for her and though she tried to force it out of her thoughts, it came back with indelible clarity.

She had just placed Mary into her crib again, the baby sleeping peacefully after having nursed, and walked from the bedroom into the parlor to take advantage of the respite of having no one around by completing some more of the embroidery project she had been working on. Ollie was still in the outer kitchen, so far as she knew, and probably wasting time as she always did. Well, she wasn't going out there after her, but she'd certainly tell John about it. He'd probably agree with her that the lazy little slave was overdue for another switching. She picked up her embroidery from the small basket and was studying her stitches when there was a slight sound at the door. Thinking it was one of the children, she smiled and looked up, but the smile vanished and a shrill scream burst from her throat. The embroidery had fallen to the floor.

The frighteningly painted, bare-chested Indian standing just inside the door glanced about quickly to see if anyone else were there. As he did so, Sarah stopped screaming and ran toward the fireplace, where a flintlock rifle was on pegs over the mantle. The Indian lunged to intercept her and, as more Indians poured in both front and back doors, she dodged the outstretched arms and, screaming in terror again, raced to the bedroom. She slammed the door behind her and tried to hold it closed but could not against the heavy thrusts on the other side. It flew open, sending her reeling, and, catching her balance, she snatched up Mary from the crib and clutched the baby to her breast.

The warrior approaching her, as well as the others crowding into the bedroom, all had weapons in their hands and at that moment Sarah was sure she had reached her final moment. She was still shrieking but didn't even realize it until the warrior smacked her face with his open palm in a blow that momentarily dazed her. The screaming cut off and was replaced by the muffled crying of Mary in her arms.

They had forced her back into the parlor then and kept her under guard there as they searched every room for other people and, finding none, began to ransack. In a far recess of her mind, Sarah wondered why they had not brought Ollie out with them when they emerged from the outer kitchen and then immediately thought to herself, Oh, well, of course, they've killed her, and she looked to see which of the intruders was stained with blood, but could see none. The Indians gorged themselves on the available food, put apples from a large basket into their pouches, smashed some dishes and took the two rifles they found, along with the powderhorns and lead ball pouches. One stuffed the contents of a small jewelry box into his pouch and others were pulling out drawers and dumping them as they searched for anything they could use. They seemed nervous and one of their number kept going to the door and looking out, then speaking to the others harshly.

At length they tied the long strip of rawhide cord around her neck and practically jerked her off her feet to make her start walking. She was certain they would fire the house, but their nervousness had increased and they seemed unwilling to linger and equally unwilling to raise a large smoke that might bring pursuit on their trail immediately. Sarah looked around fearfully now that she was outside, expecting to see other Indians with Margaret and Tom or with Nelly and Harrison, but none of the children was to be seen. The horrifying thought struck her that since the children had been outside, they had probably been caught and killed before the Indians even entered the house. The fact that she did not see their bodies did little to assuage her fears.

They marched toward the hills, moving swiftly while in the open but then taking a more reasonable pace once the woodland was reached. Sarah tired quickly, but every time she slowed the tether was jerked and soon the skin of her neck was raw and the muscles hurt. She had never realized before how heavy Mary was to carry for any length of time and she wished desperately that they could stop and rest.

Now, with the glow of sunset spreading over Plum Creek valley, she looked down from the ridge and, though she could not see the Lytle place, she did see the house of old Mr. Prescutt, one of their neighbors, and even thought she saw him moving about outside, casually doing his late chores. How near she was to help and safety; how near . . . and how very, very far.

[September 16, 1779 — Thursday, dusk]

Afraid to show themselves, Thomas and Margaret Lytle lay amid the briers for a very long time. The screaming they had heard coming from the house had ended with ominous abruptness but neither of them spoke of it, fearful of what it meant. They held one another, comforted to a degree in sharing their plight, and it was not until late in the afternoon that Tom suggested they better move on and try to find help.

They stood up and looked around. All was quiet and they could see no sign of life at the house. The temptation to go there was great, but in their minds they could see the Indians hidden inside the structure, waiting for someone to come. So they moved in the other direction, directly across the brier field. In only a short distance Margaret was in trouble. The briers tore at her bare feet and she whimpered and cried. Thomas stopped and took off his shoes and socks and put them on her feet, but when she tried to walk the shoes kept slipping off and so he finally put them back on his own bare feet and Margaret continued to wear the socks. They helped a little.

The two small children remained certain that they were in imminent danger of being killed; that the Indians were at this moment trailing them and would soon catch up. As most children had, they were brought up with the stories of the torture and other horrors far worse than mere death that the Indians inflicted upon their victims and so their fear gave the two more stamina than they realized they had. Nevertheless, Margaret finally gave out and slumped in a sobbing heap on the ground. The brier field was finally behind them, but now what were they to do?

"Maggie, come on! We've *got* to keep going." Tom was very insistent. The four-year-old shook her head. "I can't."

Thomas considered this dilemma and finally came up with a solution that to his six-year-old mind seemed quite reasonable. "Well," he said, "I can't just leave you here to be killed by the Indians. I'll have to kill you myself." There was no levity in his voice.

"Oh, no, Tom, please! Don't kill me. I don't think the Indians will find us."

"Yes they will, Maggie, and you know what they do to people. I could kill you so much more nicely than they would!"

Against her protests, he continued trying to persuade her that she must submit to his killing her and he even began looking around for a large enough stick with which to brain her. His efforts, along with the brief rest, gave Margaret the strength and determination to get back on her feet and she promised she would neither complain nor falter if he would help her move along with him.

Tom agreed and they set out again, he with his arm around her and carefully picking the easiest places to walk. They entered a strand of woodland, emerged on the opposite side and saw to their joy that they were in a pasture and there were cows there. They recognized them as animals belonging to a neighbor called by everyone Granny Myers — an old widow woman who lived quite a fair distance from the Lytle place. The problem was, the children did not know in which direction from here.

Margaret was close to tears again, holding them back with only the greatest of effort, when Tom came up with a solution. "I know!" he said suddenly. "We'll hide here where we can watch the cows and when they head for home at sunset, we'll follow them."

The plan worked perfectly. Some short while before sunset the cows ceased their grazing and began moving off in single file. Margaret and Tom followed, having no trouble keeping up, but the sun had already set when they finally saw the old woman's house. Exultantly, they moved directly to it as rapidly as they could, but their joy was short-lived. No one was at home and the doors were locked.

Margaret sniffled, no longer able to contain the tears dribbling down her cheeks. "I guess you'll just have to kill me, Tom. I can't go on anymore."

The boy hugged her and told her not to worry, that it was no longer necessary for him to kill her and that they would find a place here to spend the night. They walked around the house and on one side of it found an old bedstead. Looking around and seeing no one, they crawled beneath it. Exhausted, thirsty, hungry and still terribly afraid, they finally fell asleep with their arms locked around one another.

[*September 16, 1779 — Thursday,* 9:00 P.M.]

The initial terror for Eleanor and Harrison Lytle had passed, though a pervading dread still plagued them. After leaving the downed trees with their captors, it had been made clear to them that they must make no sound. A knife held with the blade close to Harrison's throat put the message across very well, leaving them with no mistaken idea as to what would occur if they shouted for help or tried to escape. For a long while they traveled in complete silence but then, toward sunset, caution relaxed somewhat and the Indians talked to one another and frequently laughed.

Cornplanter remained close to the children and at nightfall he called a halt for rest. They sat on the ground and the Indians dug into their pouches and ate pieces of dark leathery-appearing material. Cornplanter handed each of the children a strip and began eating one himself. Harrison smelled it, wrinkling his nose and murmuring, "Ugh!" Eleanor, however, nibbled at a corner of hers, mused over the taste of it and then nodded, pleased.

"It's good," she told her brother. "It really is. Try it."

Encouraged, Harrison took a bite with difficulty and chewed in an exaggerated manner, but then smiled and admitted it was all right. The material was a smoke-cured dried meat, probably venison, which softened at being chewed and became remarkably flavorful.

They were sitting close to one another, slightly apart from the Indians, aware that each of the warriors was either holding a weapon or had one close at hand, prepared for instant defense in case of surprise by any party of whites who may have followed. The seven-year-old boy and nine-year-old girl looked at one another and abruptly the enormity of their situation descended on them with devastating impact and both burst into tears.

Cornplanter rose from where he was seated by the other Indians and walked to them. He squatted before them and placed one large hand on Harrison's shoulder, the other on Eleanor's. His expression gentled and though he neither smiled nor spoke, the despair being experienced by the two evaporated. Somehow both of them knew now that, come what may, they would not be harmed. He stayed with them a short while longer, gave them each another strip of the dried meat and a handful of parched corn. He then used his knife to cut bundles of the long grasses growing around the fringe of their campsite and spread them for the children to lie upon, which they did.

Around an hour later there was something of a commotion and both children, who had been dozing, sat erect. The hooting of an owl in the distance had been repeated by one of the warriors in the camp and now they were hallooing back and forth. Cornplanter's men took defensive postures, weapons in hand, in case of trick, but then relaxed when the other detachment of ten warriors strode into the camp.

"*Mamma!*"

The word burst simultaneously from Eleanor and Harrison when the arriving party's captive stepped into the firelight, still carrying Mary in her arms and her attitude one of total exhaustion. She jerked at their voices and peered across the fire as they leaped up and ran toward her.

"Nelly! Harrison! Oh, praise God, you're alive!"

Sarah burst into tears and dropped to her knees and the children rushed up and hugged her, kissed her cheeks and patted her. Eleanor took the infant from her and rocked Mary in her arms to sooth the crying which had begun. They helped their mother back to her feet and led her to their grassy bed where she gratefully lay upon her back. No, no one knew what had happened to Maggie and Tom; no one had seen anything of the slave girl, Ollie, though Sarah was sure she was dead; no one knew anything about whether or not John Lytle had been ambushed on his return home.

Cornplanter brought more dried meat and parched corn and gave it to the children's mother, along with an apple for each of them. Sarah ate the jerky gratefully and turned her back to the Indians so as to nurse the infant Mary at the same time, doing her best to hide what she was doing for fear that the Indians would become aroused at the sight of her bare breast and sexually assault her. They did not. The Senecas were talking animatedly among themselves, some of them showing off to others the guns or jewelry or other items taken from the Lytle house. All too soon for the captives, however, Cornplanter held up a hand to stop the talking and gave an order. Immediately the warriors prepared for departure.

By this time Eleanor and Harrison were reasonably well rested, but their mother was not. As the march resumed, Eleanor carried Mary for a while, but she was not able to do so for long. Harrison tried it and lasted for even less time, so Sarah, fatigued beyond anything she had ever before experienced, took the child back and carried her in her arms as before. Within a mile she was stumbling frequently and barely able to keep her balance, once even falling to her knees. Cornplanter was leading the party, which was traveling two abreast, and the captives were near the center of the line. One of the warriors directly behind them, seeing the difficulty Sarah Lytle was having, touched her shoulder and when she turned, held out his arms. Hesitant at first, then greatly relieved at his offer, she placed Mary in his arms.

He walked directly behind them for a while, carrying the infant, but then gradually fell back until he was at the rear of the line. With total unexpectedness he stripped away the swaddling, gripped Mary tightly by her ankles, swung her around in one complete circle and then, with all his strength, slammed her head into a tree, crushing her skull.

[*September 16, 1779 — Thursday, midnight*]

A sick dread mantled John Lytle as, with the several neighbors who were now accompanying him, he urged his horse the remaining mile toward Granny Myers's place. The past hours had been a horror for him and the night was far from finished.

It had been late dusk when he and his three slaves, Wharf, Jennings and Billy, arrived at the Lytle house, aware as soon as they had come in sight of it that something was wrong. No warm lantern glow shone in the windows, no lantern had been hung outside on the hitch-rail post for them and, as they came closer, they could see that the front door was well open. They had approached cautiously, Lytle with his rifle at ready and each of the slaves with a length of wood as a club. All was quiet and no one seemed to be about. When at last they called and the calls went unanswered, Lytle entered and found a lantern, which he lighted.

Smashed crockery, scattered clothing, turned-over furnishings and missing weapons mutely told the tale. A close search of the grounds outside for bodies that might be there revealed only a multitude of footprints, many of them made by moccasined feet. That was when John Lytle began frantically making the rounds to neighbors, raising the alarm and seeking to find if anyone knew anything concerning the whereabouts of his family. No one did, but the men were eager to help in finding out. The search continued until finally they arrived at the cabin of an invalid settler between Plum Creek valley and the ford on the Allegheny. Here they discovered the frightened Ollie, who told them all she could about what happened. It wasn't much.

Ollie said that while she was working in the outer kitchen, she'd heard Miz Sarah scream, she being alone in the house with Mary, the other children gone outdoors to play. Ollie said she'd started for the house to help Miz Sarah with whatever was wrong, but then she saw an Indian pass by the window. He hadn't seen her and there were so many of them screeching and hollering that she crawled under a brewing tub and stayed there. After a bit the screaming stopped and then some of the Indians came into the outer kitchen and looked around, but they didn't see Ollie. Her eyes grew large and round as she continued her tale. Still later she saw them going away, Miz Sarah with them, carrying Mary. No sir, far as she knew, no one was killed, but then, she didn't know about the children because they were out. After another bit, the slave girl went on, when everything was quiet for a while, she came out from hiding and lit out in the direction opposite that in which the Indians had gone, which was how come she'd wound up here at the ford rather than at one of the neighbors' at Plum Creek valley.

The search went on, finally working its way in the other direction from the Lytle house, toward old Granny Myers's place. Now, their horses blowing and stamping, they reined up in the front yard of the darkened place and called in a chorus of voices. No one replied and someone said he'd heard Granny had gone up to Kittanning for a few days. John Lytle dismounted, checked both doors of the house and found them locked, and the party moved on.

Somewhere they had to find *something.*

[*September 16, 1779 — Thursday, midnight*]

In the dark refuge beneath the old bedstead alongside Granny Myers's house, Thomas Lytle hit his head painfully when he jerked erect out of his sleep at the sounds filling the night. His sister was still asleep and he quickly reached over and covered her mouth and shook her awake.

"Maggie!" he whispered urgently. "Don't talk. Don't scream. Don't start crying. The Indians have come back. Keep still!"

The sounds were muffled — horses stamping their feet, huffing and blowing and nickering. And then the Indians were yelling in a chorus of voices and after a little while they heard one rattle the locked doors of the house and even come walking stealthily past where they lay hidden, but he hadn't stopped. In a little while they heard the horses canter off.

Thomas removed his hand from Margaret's mouth, sighing with relief as he did so. "We did it again," he whispered exultantly. "Maggie, we escaped again!"

The four-year-old's voice in response sounded peculiar. "I'm so glad," she said. "But, Tom, Mamma's going to be mad at me. I wet myself."

Then she remembered her mother's screams and began to cry again.

[*September 17, 1779 — Friday*]

The search through the remainder of the night carried John Lytle and his neighbors to every house in the immediate vicinity without any other information being gained. It was about five o'clock in the morning when Lytle remembered that there was still one place they hadn't checked — the cabin of old Henry Prescutt, far up Plum Creek valley. They set out for it at once and got there in less than an hour.

Prescutt, a veteran of the French and Indian War, who had, along with a friend named Daniel Boone, been a wagoneer at the defeat of General Edward Braddock on the banks of the Monongahela twenty-four years ago, was in the open doorway of his cabin with an old musket in his hands when they rode up. Suspicious at first, he relaxed when he recognized them. Telling him briefly what they knew, Lytle asked if he could shed any light on the situation. Prescutt nodded.

"A little, mebbe." He pointed a gnarled finger toward a distant ridge just becoming visible in the dawn. "Seen a party of Injens — mebbe ten, twelve — jest at sunset yestiddy. Senecas, from the looks of 'em. Single file, headin' north, movin' along right smart. Had a white woman with 'em, they did." He looked at Lytle. "Reckon that'd've been your missus."

"How'd you know it was a *white* woman?" Lytle demanded. "Why not a squaw?"

Prescutt gave him a withering glance and spat a stream of tobacco juice onto the ground. "Squaws carry their young'uns on their backs," he said. "Got more sense than t'carry 'em in their arms, like this *white* woman was doin'."

There was nothing further to be gained here. Lytle had already made up his mind. He'd head back home, get some supplies and go down the Allegheny the thirty-five miles to Fort Pitt. Maybe he could convince the commandant to mount a rescue mission. He didn't know what else he could do.

Their route back to the Lytle place took them again past Granny Myers's place. This time as they approached, two small children came running toward them, their shadows extending far before them in the morning sunlight.

"*Poppa! Poppa!*"

Lytle leaped from his horse and swooped Thomas and Margaret up into his arms, unable to speak at first because he was so choked with emotion. The children wailed with relief and joy and clung to his neck fiercely, afraid they might suddenly awaken and find this reunion was all a dream.

Much later, with the story of Margaret and Thomas pieced together, with their care and the care of the Lytle slaves and property seen to, John Lytle mounted a fresh horse and set off down the east bank of the Allegheny for Pittsburgh.[54]

[*October 31, 1779 — Sunday*]

Through these difficult days and weeks it had become clear to Sarah Lytle and her children, Harrison and Eleanor, that their treatment at the hands of their Seneca captors might have been much worse had it not been that Chief Cornplanter had selected one of them to replace his slain younger brother. Because of that, because of the adoption into the tribe of the one who had been selected, the other two were treated with kindness and compassion, though not with the devotion showered upon the one who had been selected.

The journey on foot to Oswaya, Cornplanter's village at the mouth of Olean Creek on the upper Allegheny River, had been very difficult for Sarah and the children and took many days. Even though it was obvious that Cornplanter held his warriors at a much slower pace than they usually traveled, it was all the Lytles could do to keep up.

The horror of the death of three-month-old Mary had lain heavily on all of them, especially Sarah. Only by steeling herself through tremendous effort and showing as little emotion about it as possible, believing that if she became hysterical, the same or a similar fate might lie in store for Eleanor, Harrison and herself, was she able to plod on as if plodding interminably through a nightmare. Some small satisfaction was gleaned from the fact that Cornplanter, when he learned of Mary's death, castigated the guilty warrior with a tirade of angry words they could not understand but which seemed to devastate the warrior. He was not permitted to finish the journey with them, but sent off to travel home by a different route. With his limited command of English, Cornplanter tried to explain that the act had been without his knowledge or approval and it was obvious that he was sincerely regretful about it.

After a while the days blended into one another: days of rising at dawn and marching with only brief pauses until darkness, then sleeping on the ground for what always seemed much too short a time before rising again, still exhausted from yesterday, to continue the march. Their route carried them eastward along a faint Indian trail which eventually merged into a somewhat broader trail running northeast and southwest.[55] This they followed northeast for about another twenty miles before striking yet a broader trail heading — with minor detours to accommodate the topography — practically due north for many miles until they came to the headwaters of a creek Cornplanter identified as Tunungwant.[56] Then they followed Tunungwant Creek to its junction with the upper Allegheny River.[57] Another dozen miles upstream on the Allegheny, which was relatively small here, took them to the mouth of Olean Creek and the site of Cornplanter's village, Oswaya.

Here there were about threescore dwellings constructed of bent sapling frameworks lashed together and covered with hides. In the center of the village was a large, long, quonset structure which was the council house. Beside it was a quonset dwelling slightly larger than the rest — the lodge of Cornplanter. Only now did it become clear who it was that Cornplanter had selected to replace his brother, Caughna.

The Indians of the village flocked around them as they arrived but, except for greeting them and giving them a brief account of what had occurred, Cornplanter did not dally. Instead, he took the three captives directly to a smaller lodge close to his own and led them inside. Here a robust elderly woman, known simply as Old Queen, sat on a blanket and plucked haphazardly at a peculiar stringed instrument. Twangy, melodious notes filled the dim abode, but when she looked up and saw them, she ceased playing. This was the mother of Caughna and Cornplanter, as well as widow of Nungona, who had been head chief here.

Cornplanter dipped his head respectfully to her and arranged the three weary captives so they stood directly before her. He then stood behind

Eleanor and placed his hands gently on the nine-year-old's shoulders. He spoke then, in the Iroquoian Seneca dialect, and, though none of the captives understood, the meaning became clear.

"My mother," he said, "I bring you this child to supply the place of my brother, Caughna, who was killed by the Lenape. She shall dwell in my lodge and be to me a sister." He glanced at Sarah Lytle and seven-year-old Harrison, then back at Old Queen. "Take the white woman, who is mother of this one," he indicated Eleanor, "and her boy-child and treat them kindly. Our father at the Fort of Niagara, Colonel Johnson, will buy them from us for many horses and guns."[58]

With remarkable alacrity, considering her bulk and age, Old Queen rose smoothly to her feet and stepped to the captives. They regarded her fearfully but without moving, as one after the other she lay the gnarled palms of her hands against their cheeks, cupping their faces and looking at each intently for a moment. When finished, she stepped back to her blanket but remained standing.

"At first I wondered," she told Cornplanter, "but I have seen now what you saw and I know you have chosen correctly. What will your new sister be called?"

"I have thought on that," Cornplanter replied. "She reminds me of how I felt when first I saw on the blue waters of the great lake above us the white-winged vessel of the white man. My new sister, therefore, will be known as The-Ship-Under-Full-Sail."

Old Queen had smiled her approval and took Sarah and Harrison into her care as Cornplanter led Eleanor to his lodge and introduced her to his wife, named Etomeh. At first Eleanor was deeply afraid that she had been permanently separated from her own mother and brother, but such was not the case. They were given surprising freedom in the days and weeks which followed and, though living in separate abodes, saw much of each other. The conditions were primitive, but far from unbearable. They were in no manner mistreated and The-Ship-Under-Full-Sail was given very special deference. Nevertheless, Eleanor very much missed her father, having always felt so much nearer to him than to her mother. She often imagined him heroically riding in and rescuing them.

Although Sarah seemed incapable of understanding any of the Seneca words, her two children learned an extensive vocabulary in an amazingly short time. Their sentence structure was practically nonexistent, but by saying key words and gesticulating in their own approximation of sign language, they could get their meaning across quite adequately. None had any idea, of course, how long they would be kept here or if, in fact, they would ever again see white civilization.

That matter was settled today. In the forenoon there was a considerable stir in Oswaya and soon there appeared a party of a dozen armed white men on horseback approaching under a white flag. There were also two heavily laden packhorses. The strangers were stopped a fair distance from the village by Cornplanter and his wary warriors and a long discussion took place, with one of the horsemen evidently acting as interpreter. It was not possible, because of distance, for Sarah, Eleanor and Harrison to see who the men were, but it was obvious they were whites and so their hopes for rescue soared.

After a long while one of the whites turned over the two loaded pack-horses to Cornplanter's men. Then the chief and this man left the others and came walking briskly toward the village. They were still quite a distance away when Eleanor recognized the man as her father, let out a squeal and raced toward him, followed at once by Harrison and then their mother. It was as Eleanor had imagined it so often — her father, whom she loved so deeply, rescuing them from this horrible plight. It was a joyful reunion for them, although there was a peculiar reservation in John Lytle's manner they did not at first understand.

The elder Lytle was shocked and angered at learning of Mary's death but he kept himself well under control. Their flag of truce was being honored for the moment, he said, but they were still a small party greatly outnumbered and must at all costs avoid antagonizing these Senecas. After assuring them that little Maggie and Thomas were all right, he told them of his journey to Fort Pitt and the arranging of this rescue party. It had been deemed worse than useless to attempt coming in numbers to attack the Indians and take back the captives by force. The only alternative was to pay the Indians a ransom for their release, which was probably what they wanted. Lytle had paid for all the goods that were brought and they had set out up the Allegheny, not really knowing where to look except that the most likely place would be in the country of the Senecas. They had visited four or five villages without learning anything worthwhile before finally reaching one where they were told that Cornplanter had not long ago brought three captives to Oswaya.

The talk Lytle had had with Cornplanter, through a Fort Pitt interpreter, had not been easy. Cornplanter was eager to get a ransom, but what they had brought to pay him — blankets, paints, food, trinkets, knives, cord, cloth and other goods — were not what he wanted. Cornplanter told them he had expected to sell the captives to Colonel Johnson at Fort Niagara and to receive guns and horses as payment. The chief was in a position to demand whatever he wanted and they knew it. They had finally agreed to give him all the goods they had brought, *plus* the two packhorses, *plus* half of the guns they had with them. Not until Lytle had given his word to the other men of his party that he would personally replace each of the lost weapons did they agree.

"So, it's been settled," he told Sarah. "We'll be leaving for home right away — you and I and Harrison."

"*Poppa!*" There was anguish in Eleanor's voice. "What about me? Aren't you going to take me, too? Poppa?"

He turned to her and folded her in his arms, stroking her hair and kissing the top of her head. "I can't, Nelly," he whispered hoarsely. "He won't let me. He says you are not a captive, that you are his little sister, a member of his family, and he will not give you up."

Sarah had paled and started to speak but John shook his head and went on. "Listen to me now. We know where you are and we're not giving up. We'll get you back, I promise. We can't do it now, today. It's just not possible. But, honey, we will get you back. You've got to believe that. I'll go to their agent, Colonel Johnson. I don't care if he is British. I'll go to him and somehow we'll get him to help us get you back. Nelly, look at me." He placed his hand under her chin and tilted the tearstained face up. "I promise you, I won't rest until you're home with us again. And you *will* be freed."

It was a terrible time for all of them, but most of all for Eleanor. For long minutes she clung to her mother, her face buried between Sarah Lytle's breasts, her sobbing muffled but intense. Sarah kissed her and held her tight, her own tears such that she could not speak for a while, but she also knew it was the only way. With considerable effort she regained control of herself, so Eleanor would be no more panicked than she already was. At last she disengaged her little girl and held her at arm's length and smiled at her.

"We love you, darling," she said. "We'll keep on trying to get you back, no matter what. I won't be happy until you're back with us again, right where you belong. Don't give up hope."

They had talked only a little longer, saying their sad goodbyes and now, hardly able to see them through her tears, the nine-year-old stood at the edge of the village, watching as the distant party of whites that included her father, mother and brother moved out of sight on the trail that led through the forest.

Cornplanter came up beside her, squatted so that their heads were on the same level and put his arm about her waist. He spoke softly for a considerable while and though she could not understand everything, she recognized enough of it to know he was saying that she was very dear to him and that she should not be sad; that The-Ship-Under-Full-Sail would come to love her life here in this village so much that she would never want to return to the life she had once had with the whites.

But Eleanor Lytle had never before felt so alone, so devastated, so abandoned as she did at this moment and all she wanted now was to die.

CHAPTER III

[*April 28, 1780 — Friday*]

JOHN KINZIE squinted as he inspected the perfectly arced bend he had just formed in a thin strand of silver wire as part of a filigree and nodded with satisfaction. He placed it on the desk, rubbed his eyes with both hands, and then leaned back in his chair, stretching expansively. He was weary, but it was the tiredness of honest labor and he felt good. He smiled faintly as he reflected upon how far he had come. In his seventeenth year, he was now an Indian trader wholly on his own. Few had come along who had prepared for it better than he, yet it was still no easy step. Learning to converse reasonably well in several Indian dialects was only a small part of it.

It had not taken him long at all to discover that there was fierce competition in the field. Established traders generally resented new blood entering their domain and infringing upon what they considered their exclusive territories. Their attitude, combined with distinct dangers inherent in attempting to deal with races of people whose social values, religion and regard for life were alien to so-called civilized ways of life made entering the Indian trade extremely hazardous for any young would-be trader. Those who were not forced out by the established traders through threat, harassment and even outright physical violence, stood a good chance of being killed by the very people with whom they wished to trade.

Such hazards notwithstanding, John Kinzie was slipping into his new profession with surprising facility. There were three good reasons: his own careful preparation before making the plunge, his strength of character and consideration for others, and his pronounced skill in silverwork. Unlike other young men who aspired to become traders, Kinzie had not let the ambition plunge him recklessly into a field in which he had little knowledge. Instead, virtually since his arrival in Detroit, he had imbued himself in what the Indian trade was all about, what it entailed, what its pitfalls were and how best to utilize existing conditions to his own benefit. Those who failed in their efforts to enter the trade — and there were a multitude who fell into this category — failed mainly because of their own ignorance. Kinzie was too shrewd to allow this to happen to him.

Deceptively simple in its concept, the fur trade was a complex business because it dealt closely with the vagaries of individual human behavior. To attempt to enter the trade without understanding what it was and *why* it existed was foolishness. When the French first penetrated into the country of the upper Great Lakes, the Indians they encountered lived an extremely primitive life-style. Except for copper and lead, they had little knowledge of metals and how they could be used. Their weapons were made largely of stone and bone, wood and feathers and sinews. Laboriously chipped flints provided arrowheads, spearheads, axes and crude knives. Fishhooks and needles were carved from bone. Traps were mere deadfalls made of precariously balanced logs over triggers baited with food, or animal sinews designed to form snares by which unsuspecting passing animals could be caught. Survival was difficult and existence very simply a process of filling bellies, keeping warm, fighting off enemies, and procreating. All this was done by using the bounty that nature had provided and, difficult though it was, the Indians were self-sufficient and it was a good life.

Then came the French and abruptly these extremely primitive societies were exposed to considerably advanced technology and goods. Iron was introduced and fish hooks made of this material were infinitely superior to those formed of bone. Knives and hatchets made of steel were better, had uniformly sharp edges and were lighter, more easily carried and used, and provided greater versatility. Steel traps were incredibly effective as compared to deadfalls and snares. Guns — both as weapons and as tools of the hunt — reached out to down foe or food in a manner and at a distance no arrow or spear could match. Hardly surprising, then, that the first men to bring such goods were regarded as virtual deities. The comment of one Potawatomi chief in the Green Bay area to a Frenchman who brought such marvelous goods was typical of the reaction inspired among all the Indians.

"You are a god," he told the explorer. "Because you have brought us the gift of iron, praised be the sun, who has instructed you and sent you among us."

In an instant of time the Indians leaped from a primitive life to a far more modern one; from an existence of daily struggle merely to keep alive to one of comparative ease and far greater comfort. When they hadn't known it, they were content, but once having known it, they could no longer be content without it. What the white man brought which appeared to be a great gift was, in fact, an unbreakable shackle called dependence. Unable to produce such advanced goods of their own, the Indians could only buy them with whatever they had in abundance that the white man desired; and what the white man wanted at first more than anything else was furs.

The Indians had long hunted and trapped animals in a moderate way, utilizing their meat as food, their skins with the hair on for warmth, and their skins with the hair off for leather used in a variety of ways. The white man was not particularly interested in the leather, which he could manufacture with greater facility from his domestic animals, but he was intensely interested in the furs which had long ago become virtually extinct in Europe. Fortunes were waiting to be made by the enterprising individuals who could provide for the ladies of France and England and other countries the exquisite furs of beaver and mink, muskrat and marten, otter, ermine, skunk, fox, wolf, bear, bison, lynx, wolverine and others.

So trade had begun and prospered and the history of a continent became predicated upon its vagaries. Wars were fought and governments rose and fell in the struggle to control Indian trade. More and more goods were manufactured to meet the needs and desires of the Indians and with each such new item the Indian became more dependent upon the white men who, in many cases, he had grown to depise. When dependence on the goods a government could provide bound a tribe to that government, then pressures could be applied to force the tribe to do the government's will. The elements of continued trade became more involved and demanded more than any of its native beneficiaries had ever envisioned. What it boiled down to was this: "Fight on our side as allies and we will give you even more and better goods. Refuse and you will no longer receive weapons and ammunition, blankets and trinkets and paints." And on the other side another government would counter: "Abandon those other whites and become *our* allies and we will give you even more and even better goods than they have offered." So the Indians began to sell their might and their skill at wilderness warfare as well as their furs. But the basis of it all remained the matter of Indian trade.

The majority of traders were honest men, keenly interested in a profit, of course, but reasonably willing to earn it fairly. A certain percentage, however, were unscrupulous in their dealings, taking outrageous advantage of the Indians. These were the ones who sullied the reputations of reputable traders. It was not so much that the Indians did not recognize when they were being cheated or were too stupid to know or care. In most cases they were themselves sharp traders who were not easily deceived, outbargained or defrauded under normal conditions. Early on, however, the traders discovered their point of greatest vulnerability; the means by which theft was simplified, cheating became child's play and almost any unscrupulous act could be committed with impunity. The key was liquor. Beyond anyone's expectations, the Indians had a predilection for liquor that approached obsessiveness. With certain procedures they had long made their own fermented brews and used them during their feasts and for ritualistic purposes, but rarely, because of difficulty of preparation and limited availability, with excessiveness. Introduction of the white man's rum and wine and ale changed that. Rum in particular set their minds afire and befuddled them. It became traditional that trading with the Indians involved the consumption of great quantities of the liquor. It was in the matter of timing where the fair trader differed from the unscrupulous one. The former concluded the matters of trade before providing the liquor; the latter bestowed the liquor first with jovial largess and with easily predictable results.

All this and more formed the education of young John Kinzie before he entered the trade on his own. He learned not only from other well-established traders, such as William Burnett, Peter Drouilliard, John Edgar, Alexander Henry and Peter Loramie, but from the Indians themselves. He visited every trading post he could, from Mackinac in the north to St. Joseph in the west and Loramie's Store in the south, on the upper waters of the Great Miami River in the Ohio country.[59] He listened. It was one of Kinzie's most valuable assets, this ability to listen and then to evaluate. He listened to the complaints of the traders as they articulated their problems and to their gloatings as they boasted of their successes, learning without their realizing that they were teaching him the elements of trade, good and bad. He listened to the Indians and did not make the mistake of blandly sloughing off their complaints as unimportant. He took heed of what they wanted and what they felt was fair exchange. When the time had come, finally, that he was ready to enter the trade on his own, he was probably better prepared than almost any of his predecessors had been.

In addition to this sort of preparation, he possessed a skill that no other trader who had previously come among these Indians could boast. He was a very gifted silversmith, able to take raw silver stock received from the east or from the Indians themselves and, through what seemed to be magic, transform it into the sort of silver ornamentation most desired by the Indians — broad armbands and legbands, bracelets and brooches, necklaces and pendants, earbobs and nosebobs and rings of beaten and burnished silver.

He quickly established two different posts on the same waterway — the Maumee River, often called the Miami-of-the-Lake. The first of the two was near the principal village of the Miami tribe, Kekionga, close to the point of land called the French Store, where the Maumee River was formed by the confluence of the St. Marys River from the southeast and the St. Joseph from the northeast. This was not the same St. Joseph River where Burnett had his trading post and Topenebe's village was located. For differentiation, that one was sometimes called the St. Joseph-of-the-Lake, since it emptied into the southeastern quadrant of Lake Michigan. The one meeting the St. Marys was a much smaller stream, but the two together, in forming the Maumee, created a significant river that flowed a hundred miles east-by-northeast to enter Lake Erie at its southwestern-most corner.

For a hundred years or more Kekionga and the French Store had been a center of trade for the Indians — first with the French, now with the British and with the Americans on the sidelines more than eager for their opportunity.[60] It was located about one hundred fifty miles southwest of Detroit by water, but boat travel between the two was limited because of a stretch of treacherous rapids about a dozen miles up from the river's mouth. To this post came primarily the Miami and Potawatomi Indians, along with a certain number of Shawnees and Ottawas. It was here that John Kinzie became better acquainted with the principal chief of the Miamis, Michikiniqua — Little Turtle.

The other post, also on the Maumee, was located some fifty miles closer to Detroit, at the point where a river called the Auglaize entered from the south.[61] The Auglaize, so named by the French because of the good glaz-ing clay which made up its shores and bed, was in Shawnee territory. Here Kinzie dealt mainly with Shawnees and Ottawas.

Impressed with Kinzie's honesty in his dealings with them and his understanding of their problems and needs, the Indians were soon flocking to the two trading posts and the young trader's fortunes increased signifi-cantly. Too late, other traders realized that this brash boy approaching seventeen was someone with whom to contend in the Indian trade and they now regretted having talked with him, explaining the trade and dis-cussing their problems. By the time they realized he was putting their revelations to good use in competition with them, it was too late — John Kinzie was firmly entrenched in the trade and determined that nothing was going to make him lose the important toehold he had gained.

Now, leaning forward to pick up the silver filigree he was creating, the enterprising young man was pleased with himself, pleased with his trade and inordinately pleased with the fact that he was now becoming known to Indians all over this whole territory by the name the Potawatomies had given him — Shawneeawkee. The Silver Man.[62]

[May 10, 1780 — Wednesday]

After her eight months with the Senecas in the village of Oswaya, The-Ship-Under-Full-Sail was scarcely recognizable any longer as a girl who was white. She rarely thought of herself anymore as Eleanor Lytle, primarily because early in her captivity, she had deliberately refused to dwell on thoughts of that former life. To think of it, to remember her family and home, caused such great pain that it was all but unbearable.

Eleanor Lytle was a survivor, so she had put the past into a sealed compartment of her own mind and smoothly adapted to her life as a member of Cornplanter's family. She had become extremely fond of Old Queen, to whom she owed her newly acquired fluency in the Seneca tongue. For endless hours over these days and weeks and months, Old Queen had tutored The-Ship-Under-Full-Sail not only in the Seneca language, but in the history of the tribe and its important position in the Iroquois League, which was also known as the Six Nations. The Iroquois were likened to a long-house, as they termed each village's council-house. The Mohawks, being farthest east, were considered guardians of the eastern door, while the Senecas, farthest west, were guardians of the western door. In between were the other four tribes — Cayuga, Onondaga, Oneida and Tuscarora — mostly with villages around the long narrow finger lakes of New York.

Now, clad in the simple dress of other girls her age in this village, The-Ship-Under-Full-Sail was practically indistinguishable from them. She chatted with them as if she had been born to the language, joined them in their games and brought her own special talents to the dances they performed. As deeply fond of Old Queen as she was, Eleanor had come to love Cornplanter truly as if he were her elder brother. The chief's wife, Etomeh, was another matter. From the outset, Etomeh had bitterly resented the captive white girl's adoption into the family. It was a problem apt to come to a head one day, but at the moment something else was of much greater concern to The-Ship-Under-Full-Sail.

Today, for the first time since late last October, the girl's newfound stability was threatened. An hour ago, while The-Ship-Under-Full-Sail was bringing two water-filled skin bags from the river to Cornplanter's lodge, she observed a white man in fine clothing talking with the chief. Both were looking at her and, suddenly shy, The-Ship-Under-Full-Sail had vanished with her load inside the lodge. She busied herself there, vaguely bothered by the white man's presence. She became even more concerned a few moments later when the pair entered the house, sat together on mats and talked in low tones. At length Cornplanter called to her and asked her to come and stand before them. Reluctantly, she did so.

"This man with me," Cornplanter said, "is our good friend, Colonel Johnson, son of the great Warraghiyagey."

The white man was Sir John Johnson, British Indian agent who had assumed his post on the death of his extremely influential Indian supervisor father, Sir William Johnson, whom the Mohawks had adopted and named Warraghiyagey. Sir John bowed his head slightly toward the girl and smiled at her pleasantly.

"Hello," he said, speaking in English. "You are Eleanor Lytle, sometimes called Nelly?"

She blanched and shook her head. "I am," she said in the Seneca tongue, "The-Ship-Under-Full-Sail, sister of Chief Cornplanter."

The man laughed with genuine delight. "I could believe that, even on close inspection, had I not been informed otherwise." His response was still in English. "I have come here at the request of your father, John Lytle, of the Plum Creek valley settlement. Though he lives as an American there, he assures me that his sentiments are British and I must admit to a belief in his sincerity. He has asked me to interpose on your behalf, to seek your relief from captivity here." He chuckled. "I must admit, you hardly correspond to the picture one conjures up at the term 'captive.' "

"Oswaya is my home," she replied. "Cornplanter is my brother and Old Queen is my mother."

Cornplanter smiled and glanced at the Indian agent with a look that said, "I told you so."

Not at all disconcerted, Johnson continued speaking to the girl. "Your father has authorized me to offer Chief Cornplanter many splendid presents for your release. Guns. Horses. Supplies. The chief tells me you are his sister and he does not wish to accept, but that if you wish this, he will agree."

For an instant she wavered and the door in her mind opened a crack. What was visible filled her eyes with tears and she swiftly slammed it shut and shook her head. She did not like this man, intuitively mistrusted him and feared that what he was saying was not true. She could not bear a reoccurrence of the heartache she had experienced before when her father and mother and brother had left this village without her. The door in her mind clanged shut.

"I am Cornplanter's sister," she reiterated. "I will not leave him."

[*June 30, 1780 — Friday*]

The two McKenzie girls living in the lodge of Chiksika and Tecumapese at Chalahgawtha had adapted very well to Indian life. In the two years that had passed since they were captured, they had learned the Shawnee language so well that it was as if they had been born to it. But even though they answered to the names Kisahthoi and Tebethto, the sisters always referred to one another by their true names, Margaret and Elizabeth.

Now, imbued with Shawnee ways and understanding the problems besetting the tribe, they could not help but sympathize with them and experience a sense of guilt for feeling a real antagonism toward their own white people for what they were doing. Their respect for Chief Black Fish had been deep, bordering on reverence, and at his death last year they had experienced, along with the rest of the villagers, a great grief which was a long time in becoming dulled. Chalahgawtha had been attacked last July by an army of Kentuckians. Chalahgawtha had been burned and during the battle Chief Black Fish had been wounded severely. A lead ball had smashed his hip socket. He lingered a long while, gradually weakening, and finally died three months after the battle. His place as principal chief had been taken by Catahecassa — Black Hoof.

Under Catahecassa's direction, Chalahgawtha had been rebuilt, but no one believed it would ever again be so grand a place as it once was. And the mourning for Black Fish remained very strong.[63]

Chiksika had constructed a new wegiwa into which Tecumapese and their brothers moved, along with Kisahthoi and Tebethto. The captive sisters had developed a great devotion for Chiksika and Tecumapese and truly felt they were their older brother and sister. Chiksika was now one of Chalahgawtha's foremost warriors, having won many honors for the extraordinary courage he displayed in skirmishes with the Kentuckians — sometimes leading war parties of his own, other times taking part in much larger forays organized in conjunction with detachments of British from Detroit, such as the one by Captain Byrd, just concluded.

The sisters felt a very special closeness to Tecumseh, though not only because he was closer to their age. Two years younger than Margaret, he and Elizabeth were both twelve, although in many respects he seemed much older. He was a very handsome boy, lean and muscular and with eyes that had a searching quality that was sometimes disconcerting. His memory was phenomenal and he seemed never to forget anything said or done in his presence. He was always asking questions of Chiksika, Tecumapese, Wasegoboah and others, yet not always receiving satisfactory answers, since many of his questions dealt not only with tribal traditions and beliefs, but with even more abstract concepts and philosophies. He yearned for answers that no one in the tribe seemed able to provide. Little wonder that few thought of him as being only twelve.

Tecumseh very much liked Kisahthoi and Tebethto, always treating them in the most gentle and kindly manner, and it was quite obvious that he adored Tecumapese. It was with Chiksika, however, that he exhibited his greatest devotion, admiration and respect: Chiksika, who explained as best he could the meanings of life and death and all in between; Chiksika, who taught him how to read signs with such skill that he could determine with accuracy who or what had passed a certain place, how long ago, where it was going and where it had been and, very often, the physical condition of the man or animal. It was Chiksika who taught Tecumseh an all-encompassing love of nature and respect for life; who imbued him with the virtues of honesty, compassion, integrity and justice.

The triplets, on the other hand, were simply tolerated by the two girls, as younger brothers often are. They were nine now, active in their games and other recreations. Kumskaka had become a chubby boy, jolly of nature and abundantly filled with good humor. He was the comedian of the family and often the wegiwa rocked with laughter at his outrageous antics and expressions. Of an opposite nature, Sauwaseekau was a somber boy who only rarely smiled and who almost never laughed aloud. He took things very seriously at all times, yet he displayed no particular aptitude for anything and rarely contributed to the conversational sessions around the fire. He exhibited a special willingness to do things for the third of the triplets, Lowawluwaysica, but this may have been a form of atonement. A year and a half ago, while the boys had been playing hunter with their little bows and arrows, one of the missiles Sauwaseekau shot accidentally struck Lowawluwaysica in the right eye, punctured the eyeball and permanently blinded him in that eye. Since then the eyelid had shrunk into the empty eye socket and his appearance was distressing. A surly boy before the accident, Lowawluwaysica became even more ugly-natured afterwards and he took outrageous advantage of his brother's willingness to atone. The one-eyed boy was scrawny in build, shrill of voice, highly excitable and mostly disliked by other people. Perhaps for this reason Tecumseh and Chiksika went out of their way to treat him with special kindness and include him in things wherever possible.

Spemica Lawba, Tecumapese's five-year-old son, was everyone's favorite. Energetic, good-natured, a quick learner and amazingly smart for his age, he was taller than other boys the same age and among the elders of the village there was a general belief that great things were in store for him as a man. Kisahthoi and Tebethto became greatly attached to him and cared for him often.

In the past two months the family had been increased by two members — one through marriage, the other through adoption. The former, a nephew of the late Chief Black Fish, was a new husband for Tecumapese and father for Spemica Lawba. His name was Wasegoboah — Stand Firm — and he had been a friend of the family for many years; he and Chiksika had been close companions since childhood.[64] They had fought side by side in their first battle of any significance — the Battle of Point Pleasant, in which Pucksinwah had died in Chiksika's arms and Chaquiweshe, Tecumapese's husband, had also been killed. A brave, stalwart young man, Wasegoboah was the same age as Chiksika — twenty-four. It was during the feast of the Planting Moon last month that Wasegoboah and Tecumapese had faced one another in the double row of dancers, bowed and murmured to one another and finally raced off hand in hand at the conclusion of the dance. It was a match approved of by all.

The new member of the family by adoption had arrived here only eight days ago as a result of the extensive campaign just concluded against the Kentuckians. Kisahthoi and Tebethto had watched wide-eyed as the war party from the north had arrived here a few days after the wedding of Wasegoboah and Tecumapese. It was the largest army the girls had ever seen and everyone in Chalahgawtha was tremendously excited. There were thirteen hundred British in the force — a hundred regulars of the Eighth Regiment, gaudy in their scarlet coats, and seventy green-coated rangers of the Canada militia. Led by Captain Henry Byrd under orders from Fort Detroit's commander, Major Arent Schuyler De Peyster, they had marched out of Detroit with several hundred warriors to attack the Kentucky settlements. Many more Indians joined them as they passed through various villages en route. Helping Byrd in controlling the Indians and inducing others to join them were the three Girty brothers, Simon, James and Thomas, along with the Detroit Indian agent, Captain Alexander McKee. The force had come south by boat and it was an incredible flotilla that had crossed the upper end of Lake Erie and ascended the Maumee, portaging around the Rapids and then camping for two days in the area adjacent to John Kinzie's new trading post at the mouth of the Auglaize. From there they had ascended the Auglaize to its headwaters, then portaged to the upper waters of the Great Miami River. At a place where, within a mile, two other rivers of significance joined the Great Miami, they beached their craft and marched overland the fifteen miles eastward to Chalahgawtha for the final rendezvous and battle planning.[65] By this time the Indians accompanying the party had increased to about half a thousand and included Potawatomies, Delawares, Shawnees, Ottawas, Chippewas, Wyandots, Miamis and Kickapoos, all thirsting for this opportunity to rain devastation upon the Kentucky settlements. Captain Byrd had brought along some small artillery and the Indians were sure they would be successful in their campaign. And so they were. Chiksika and Wasegoboah were included among the warriors collected at Chalahgawtha. Moving back to the boats on the Great Miami, the force moved downstream to the Ohio, then up that stream to the mouth of the Licking on the south shore. They went up the Licking and struck Ruddell's Station, killing a number of residents and taking four hundred seventy prisoners.[66]

Stephen Ruddell, an engaging twelve-year-old, was one of the prisoners. Captured by Chiksika, he was brought to Chalahgawtha and immediately put through the ritual required of males adopted into the tribe. He had to run a quarter-mile gauntlet between a double row of the village inhabitants, who swung switches and sticks at him as he passed. Many a prisoner had died in such gauntlet runs, but young Ruddell was very fleet and amazingly agile. The gauntlet line ended at the entrance to the *msi-kah-mi-qui* and Ruddell arrived there panting and grinning, having received only half a dozen minor blows. It was a marvelous performance and the boy was cheered by the entire populace. He was then taken to the Little Miami River where he was stripped and bathed. Coarse sand was vigorously rubbed over his body until he turned a bright pink. This was the ritual washing away of his white blood. He was then adopted into the family of his captor and Chiksika had the honor of naming him.

"He was as difficult to hit in the gauntlet line as it would be to catch a fish by hand in the river," Chiksika said. "Therefore, his new name is Sinnanatha" — Big Fish.

Because they were the same age, Tecumseh and Sinnanatha immediately became close friends and in these past few days they had taken to spending long hours together, sometimes by themselves and sometimes with Kisahthoi and Tebethto. The object was to learn each other's language. Sinnanatha was stunned when he learned the sisters were adopted captives because, despite Kisahthoi's blond hair, he had thought them truly to be Shawnee.

The girls were amused and teased him, but they entered into the mutual language training program with enthusiasm. The rules they set up for themselves were simple but highly effective. While they were all together — or even when only Tecumseh and Sinnanatha were together — the sisters were allowed to speak either English or Shawnee, but Tecumseh was permitted to speak only in English and Sinnanatha only in the Shawnee. The result was often hilarious at first, but it was amazing how swiftly both youths began assimilating each other's tongue.

Today, Kisahthoi, Tebethto and Sinnanatha arrived first beneath the big oak that had become their classroom and before Tecumseh arrived the three had a brief discussion in English. They spoke of their respective backgrounds and what life with the Shawnees was like. Just as Tecumseh started toward them from the wegiwa, Kisahthoi abruptly reverted for a moment to being Margaret McKenzie. Her eyes filled with tears as she spoke.

"Elizabeth and I are not unhappy here. We love the family we have been adopted into. But we're always lonely for our real family. We know our mother and older brother are dead, but our father and younger brother may still be alive. If they are, one day we will be reunited. We love them very much and miss them terribly. We love our father more than anyone else in the world and one day he will come and take us away with him. It is all we live for and it *will* happen. We don't know when, but someday, when the conditions are just right, if he has not yet come to get us and take us home, we will simply walk away from here and become Elizabeth and Margaret McKenzie again, and then *we* will search for *him*."

The words seemed to hang in the air, mesmerizing, and then the spell was broken as Tecumseh arrived and took his position with them and the day's lessons began.

[*August 16, 1780 — Wednesday*]

There was a heaviness in the hearts of the Shawnees now, manifested most in the Chalahgawtha sept and especially in Chief Catahecassa himself. Despite his shortness of stature — he was only a shadow over five and a half feet tall — he was a very distinguished looking man; yet, in recent weeks he had aged considerably and looked much older than his fifty-four years.

He sat astride his horse a dozen yards from the escort of chiefs and warriors, staring across the valley to where Chalahgawtha had been. Now it was a scene of devastation worse than the first time. Once again Chalahgawtha had been destroyed and, though he knew they would rebuild it, there would eventually come another destruction and then another and more until at last there remained no heart in the Shawnees to build again. When that time came — and Catahecassa feared it would not be long in coming — it would signal the beginning of the end.

The principal Shawnee chief was not a coward, but neither was he prone to self-delusion. He had fought against Braddock as a young man in 1755 and since that time there had scarcely been a battle involving the Shawnees in which he had not participated. Three times he had been wounded and survived. Once he had been captured and escaped. A score or more scalps had been lifted under his knife, attesting to his fierceness as a fighter. But as if it were a vital fluid he was losing, Catahecassa could feel the will to continue this struggle oozing away from him.

Nearly a year and a half ago the Shawnees had split, with the greater portion of the tribe moving west of the Missitheepi — the great-grandmother of rivers. At that time he had stayed behind to continue the fight to preserve this territory against the encroachment of the Shemanese, because at that time he truly believed that somehow the barrier formed by the Spaylaywitheepi would help hold them back. It had not. The triumph the Shawnees had shared in the destruction of Ruddell's Station was very short-lived. Almost immediately the Shemanese had mounted another powerful force — a thousand mounted men under Clark — and crossed the river to march against Chalahgawtha again.

Warning had come early enough for Catahecassa to take steps to save his people, but only at great cost. The evening that Simon Girty and his companion, Red Snake, a Kispokotha warrior, had thundered into Chalahgawtha on lathered horses with word of Clark's approach had been a bad time. All of the village's treasure, amounting to upwards of a ton of silver in the form of armbands, wristbands, medallions, rings, plates and crude bars of raw stock, were brought together and bound in small raw-hide bundles. All this and more — kettles, utensils, guns needing repair and a multitude of other heavy things — were similarly wrapped and the whole lot was carried bundle by bundle to the big spring in the marsh below the village and dumped in. They settled on the bottom of the dark water, twenty feet or more in depth, safe from confiscation from the approaching enemy until the Shawnees should come back to claim these possessions again when it was safe.[67]

The old people, the women and children were then sent north in a group to take refuge in Mackachack, principal village of the Maykujay sept under ancient Chief Moluntha. Catahecassa and his warriors moved up the Little Miami River only as far as Peckuwe Town — the southernmost village of the Peckuwe sept — only twelve miles from Chalahgawtha.[68] Here, with the warriors of Peckuwe they would make a stand against Clark's army. So they had, but the result was disaster. Clark's force soundly defeated them and many warriors were killed. The remainder had fled northward. Satisfied at his victory, Clark had retreated, pausing only long enough at Chalahgawtha to destroy it.

Staring now at the hundreds of piles of ash residue of every structure in the village, Catahecassa's shoulders slumped and despair was a cloak wrapped about him. Not satisfied with the burning of the village itself, Clark's men had spread out and cut down the corn — hundreds of acres of it, just now coming into full ear. That corn was to be the basis of subsistence for the Chalahgawthas over the coming winter. Now it was gone and, though they would survive, it would be a hard time.

A subchief, Red Horse, pulled away from the others and approached Catahecassa now, reining to a stop a few feet away. "Do we return here?" he asked. "Do we rebuild Chalahgawtha?"

The chief nodded slowly, his face set in grim lines. "They will come to destroy it again," he murmured, "but we will rebuild." He was silent for a space and when he spoke again, Red Horse knew he spoke only to himself and he frowned at the pain he saw in his chief.

"Where does my responsibility lie?" Catahecassa asked softly. "What do I offer my people? Death? That is all they will find here. Retreat? The Shemanese will only follow. Peace with the Shemanese? What, then, about honor? Shall we have it with such an end? Is it possible? If it is, should we then not grasp it before all is lost? Perhaps, but not now."

Catahecassa had answered himself, yet he knew in his heart that one day, to save his people, he would have to throw down his hatchet until its head was forever buried and then grasp the hand of the Shemanese in peace.

And in that knowledge, the heart of Catahecassa grew cold.

[*September 21, 1780 — Thursday*]

Alexander McKee, British Indian agent at Detroit, was very pleased with the way the council here at Sandusky Bay was concluding. He had accomplished precisely what he had meant to put across to the assembled

Potawatomies, Ottawas, Wyandots, Miamis and Shawnees. Twelve days ago the council had begun with the Indians disgruntled, to say the least. Their suspicions were strong that the British and Americans were involved in negotiations concerning Indian lands; secret negotiations which purposely kept them in the dark while their lands were being divided among strangers. They were most unhappy about the situation and it had taken some strong convincing by McKee to set their minds easier.

"It is true," he told them, "that the war between the British and the rebellious Americans is ending, and it is true that in the city of Paris across the great water these two are signing peace documents. It is not true, however, that your friends the British are turning their backs on you, as some of you here believe. The treaty being made in Paris is not meant to deprive you of any extent of country, of which the right of soil belongs to you and is in yourselves as sole proprietors. It is important that you realize that your great father, the King, still acknowledges your happiness by his protection. He encourages you in your usual intercourse with trade and will continue to provide you with those things you need. You will receive guns and ammunition, knives and tomahawks, blankets and tobacco and hooks and whatever else you wish. The trading posts at the French Store and on the Maumee and St. Joseph and elsewhere will still provide your wants and you will still receive gifts from your great father, the King, at Niagara and Mackinac and here at Detroit. You have not been forsaken nor forgotten. You are still the children of your great father, the King, who loves you."

To the assembled tribesmen, it was only their due. So far as they were concerned, they had won the war with the Americans here in the west. Great damage had been inflicted upon the Kentucky settlements and the Shemanese were still south of the Ohio River. That the Americans were making claims to their lands was ridiculous, since the Indians had never given either the French or British title to any of the lands — only the right to use them in a limited way to carry on the trade. There was no land to be won by right of conquest.

For the assembled Indians, the war had made one thing very clear: their support, if to be given to anyone, should be given to the British. The Americans, like the British, brought goods to them, but it was more than ordinary trade that they wanted. They expected to purchase lands from them and when they were refused, they took the lands anyway and defied the Indians to do anything about it. So now, despite the fact that the British and Americans were making peace, there was still a division between them and if the Indians were to support anyone hereafter, it would be the British.

What clinched this tacit agreement was what McKee had just told them in a very roundabout way. The war might be temporarily over between the

British and Americans, but it *would* come again. In the meanwhile, the British would continue to supply the Indians with guns and ammunition, with scalping knives and tomahawks, so that they could continue their harassment of those who would enter their country to steal their lands. And the implication McKee gave was clear: when the time was right, the British would rise up and help their red brothers drive out the Americans.

[*September 21, 1780 — Thursday*]

Eleanor — Little Nelly — Lytle had, over this past year, become so inbued with life among the Senecas generally, and more specifically as a member of Cornplanter's household, that it was with real difficulty that she could think of herself by her true name. The-Ship-Under-Full-Sail was who she considered herself to be; that painful period when she had longed for home and yearned to be rescued was far in the past.

She was now all but indistinguishable from the other ten-year-olds of the village. Chattering and laughing with them, joining in their games and activities, she was as much one of them as if she had been born to the situation. She performed her given chores cheerfully and well and had become the joy of the Cornplanter household to all but one. Etomeh, Cornplanter's wife, had never adjusted to the little girl's presence under her roof. Her treatment of the interloper was terrible. When Cornplanter became aware of it, as eventually he had, he subjected Etomeh to a severe scolding and warned her to leave The-Ship-Under-Full-Sail alone or suffer the consequences.

That only increased Etomeh's resentment of the girl's presence, strengthening her will to make life difficult for the white girl wherever possible to do so without being detected by either her husband or his mother. Since Cornplanter was often away for long periods to attend councils at Niagara with the British or councils of the Iroquois League at Onondaga, or occasionally participating in hit-and-run raids against the whites, Etomeh had plenty of latitude for her mistreatment of Eleanor.[69]

Old Queen, who was virtually as powerful in this village of Oswaya as Cornplanter himself, rarely left her lodge these days and so she was mostly unaware of the continued mistreatment.

The-Ship-Under-Full-Sail tried every way she knew to make friends with Etomeh, but it was an exercise in futility. Eventually she stopped trying and merely endured the situation, endeavoring to stay out of Etomeh's way whenever possible. It was not until a few days ago, when Eleanor was stricken with a severe fever, that Etomeh's attitude appeared to change. She was suddenly very solicitous of the girl's well-being. Both she and Old Queen, who bestirred herself from her own lodge to help, saw to every need of the little girl and there was no doubt that The-Ship-Under-Full-Sail was terribly ill.

Also visiting numerous times each day was the closest friend Eleanor had made among the children, a boy about her own age, named Stenga. At length, apparently aggravated by his popping in and out, Etomeh ordered him away and told him not to come back until The-Ship-Under-Full-Sail was well again. As soon as he was gone, Etomeh told her little patient to sleep and when she woke there would be a concoction ready for her that would take away the illness. Eleanor slept for several hours and was awakened by Etomeh's return with a bowl of the brew she had prepared. She stopped at the mat upon which The-Ship-Under-Full-Sail lay and extended the bowl toward her.

"Drink, my sister," she told her, smiling warmly and with concern. She placed one hand on the girl's brow for a moment and continued: "What I have brought will drive this fever far from you."

Eleanor raised herself to one elbow, groaning faintly, and was about to comply when she caught a glimpse of Stenga peeping in, unseen by Etomeh. He appeared very nervous and the expression on his face was so intense that it alarmed the girl. With no word having passed between them, she suddenly knew that she must not drink what Etomeh had prepared. As quickly as she thought about it, Eleanor forced herself into a spasm of trembling and lay back down with a little mournful sound.

"Just . . . set it down beside me, Etomeh. I'll drink your medicine as soon as this fit of fever passes."

Etomeh frowned faintly, then smiled and nodded. She busied herself about the lodge for a few minutes, glancing occasionally at The-Ship-Under-Full-Sail, and finally went to another lodge close by where she had prepared the mixture. As soon as she was out of sight, Stenga popped into the room, words bubbling from him urgently.

"Don't drink this," he told her, kneeling beside the mat. "Etomeh has only been waiting for an opportunity like this to get rid of you."

"Are you sure?" Eleanor croaked. "She's been so good to me lately."

"No! She is bad. I know she has treated you better since you fell sick, but she really hates you. I was afraid for you and I have been watching her all morning. I followed her out into the woods. I watched while she gathered up all the deadliest of plants and roots and carried them into the other lodge. When she came out, she carried this bowl, and I know what she gave you was made of those plants."

The-Ship-Under-Full-Sail paled and shuddered. She placed her hand on Stenga's arm. "Thank you, Stenga. You may have saved my life. Quickly now, take this bowl and carry it to my mother's lodge. Tell Old Queen what you told me."

Stenga bobbed his head, picked up the bowl in both hands and went to the door with it. He looked outside carefully and did not see Etomeh and so moved rapidly to Old Queen's lodge. A quarter-hour later Old Queen herself was at the door, two of the men of the village with her. The old woman's face was grim and she directed the men to pick up The-Ship-Under-Full-Sail and carry her to her lodge.

Outside, a cluster of squaws had formed a ring around Etomeh and were screaming invectives at her. They were very excited and it appeared for a while that they would do her bodily harm, but at last they withdrew and from that time on, no one spoke to Etomeh at all.

In Old Queen's lodge, Eleanor listened as her adopted mother told her that the medicine was carefully studied by herself first, then by the village's medicine man, whom she had summoned. Eventually they had forced some of the concoction down the throat of a dog and the animal had quickly gone into convulsions and died. Together, Old Queen and the medicine man determined that the brew in the bowl contained the juices and mashed pulp of many very dangerous leaves, roots and fruits. The major ingredient was material rendered from the May-apple, one of the more deadly poisons known to the Senecas.

Over the past two days The-Ship-Under-Full-Sail was kept in Old Queen's lodge and a guard placed over her to protect her while they awaited Cornplanter's return. Then, this morning, the chief and his war party returned. He saw at once the changes that had been made and his expression became questioning, but it was not until after the exploits of the war party's raid were recounted and the warriors had dispersed to their own lodges that he received the story in full.

Cornplanter's expression grew very dark as he listened to his mother. When Old Queen finished, he ordered that Etomeh be brought here to him. Then he turned to The-Ship-Under-Full-Sail on her mat and took her hand. This was the first day she had felt any better, the fever having broken during the previous night. She smiled weakly at him.

"You never need fear anything like this will ever happen again," he told her. He turned to Stenga who stood nearby and walked to him. He spoke as he placed his hand on the boy's shoulder. "You have been a man, my son. I am proud of you and have plans for you that you will like."

At that point Etomeh was brought in and caused to stand before her husband. She shot one quick malicious glance at The-Ship-Under-Full-Sail and then turned her gaze to the floor between herself and Cornplanter. When the man spoke, his words were cold, implacable. He turned so that his back was toward her and he was facing toward the east.

"I divorce you," he said loudly. He turned a quarter-turn, facing north, and repeated the words. Turning a half-turn, he faced to the south and said the words again. At last he faced her directly, looking toward the west, and repeated them a final time: "I divorce you."

His expression remained stern. "Etomeh," he said, "you have disgraced us all with your behavior. Your heart is a shriveled apple and for what you have done you should be killed, but because of our years together, even though you have borne me no sons or daughters, I will not order this. Instead, I have divorced you, and now I give you your punishment: a small house, large enough only for you, will be built on the edge of Oswaya, where the cornfield begins. From this day forward no one will speak to you and you will spend your days in that field, hoeing the corn for our village. If you do your job well, you will be provided with enough to maintain you through the winter. If you do not, you will receive nothing and winter will take you. Should you ever again attempt to harm The-Ship-Under-Full-Sail, you will be executed. I am done with you now. Go!"

[*September 23, 1783 — Tuesday*]

The War of the Revolution was over!

On this day, in the city of Paris, American and British officials signed the documents officially bringing to a close a war that had bathed the American frontier in blood and forced the British to recognize the United States as a free and independent nation.

The signing — following the signing of a preliminary treaty drawn up last November 30 — did officially end the hostilities between British and Americans, but in no way did it end the resentments that existed. The hatreds remained and the American frontier continued to be a very dangerous place. The Indians could not quite understand why so powerful a nation as the British had given up, nor did they fully understand the ramifications of the Treaty of Paris.

The final three years of the war had resolved little on the frontier. George Rogers Clark, without support of any consequence from either Virginia or the provisional United States government, had been forced to put aside his dream of marching through the wilderness and taking Detroit and he had drawn most of his troops from the Illinois country. The Indians swung more and more to support of the British and the Ohio and Kentucky countries became arenas for strife and horror. With British support, the Indians struck in Kentucky and badly defeated the Americans at a place called Blue Licks. In retaliation, a thousand Kentuckians under Clark and Benjamin Logan penetrated the Ohio country and destroyed seven Shawnee villages including, once again, Chalahgawtha — just as the principal chief, Catahecassa, had known would occur. That attack caused more of the Shawnees to migrate west of the Mississippi and those who remained behind to move farther north to the upper Shawnee villages, more out of reach from forays across the Ohio by Kentuckians. It had become clear that there was little likelihood of driving the Americans out of Kentucky, but hope remained that the Spaylaywitheepi — the Ohio River — would remain a boundary between them. It might have been, had it not been for John Adams. At the drawing up of boundaries in the preliminaries for peace, British Commissioner Oswald proposed that the Ohio River be the border between British possession and American. With the exception of one man, the American commissioners were amenable to this. Not Adams. He violently opposed accepting the Ohio River as boundary and held out for a line in the north which bisected the Great Lakes, excepting Lake Michigan, and, for the western boundary, the Mississippi River. He won his point.

Now the official treaty was signed in Paris and the Americans naturally expected immediate evacuation of such British posts on now–United States soil as Niagara, Detroit and Mackinac. That was a premature expectation, due to an innocent-appearing little clause in the treaty. Those areas in question, in and around the forts, were still well populated with British subjects, both civilian and military, and one could not reasonably expect them to be instantly evacuated. In the treaty, therefore, the British agreed to abandon these places "in due time and with all convenient speed."

In reality, the British had no intention of giving them up until forced to do so.

In the Seneca village of Oswaya at the mouth of Olean Creek on the upper Allegheny River, Eleanor Lytle was entering her fourth year of captivity, though she never thought of it as such anymore. And hundreds of miles southwest of there, living now in the Shawnee village called Moluntha's Town, following the destruction of Chalahgawtha, were Margaret and Elizabeth McKenzie — Kisahthoi and Tebethto. The girls were now well into their fifth year of captivity among the Shawnees. They, too, were reasonably content with their lot, although hardly a day went by when Margaret did not think of her father. In her mind he had become synonymous with love and security, the end of all ills. One day he would come for them. Margaret had absolute belief in this and Elizabeth, who usually let Margaret do her thinking for her, agreed. When he did, everything would be wonderful again — forever.

[*November 20, 1783 — Thursday*]

Once again the existence of Eleanor Lytle — The-Ship-Under-Full-Sail — was in upheaval. It had begun about six weeks ago when the Feast of the Harvest was in progress at Oswaya, following the gathering of the corn and pumpkins and other vegetables, most of which were now carefully stored away for use throughout the winter.

Everyone in the village was in a gala mood, with the single exception of Etomeh, who still lived in isolation in a tiny hut at the edge of the cornfield. In the village itself, in the clear ground before the council longhouse, a dance was in progress. The music came from different-sized drums, rattles made of gourds with pebbles inside, pipes made of different-sized willow twigs to produce different notes, and the spidery fingers of Old Queen plucking at her stringed instrument. The musical strains blended to form a weird but stirring background to the stamping, shuffling feet of the dancers and the occasional chants that erupted from the men.

Among the prettiest of the maidens involved in the dancing was The-Ship-Under-Full-Sail. In over four years with the Senecas she had changed a great deal. At fourteen she was now quite tall and lithe, her body already developing the breasts of a woman and her manner a sometimes amusing combination of childishness and womanliness. The womanly sense was considerably enhanced that festive day by what she was wearing. As many of the other girls and women were, she was clad in other than Indian garb. She had accepted the clothes from Cornplanter with little cries of joy, unconcerned that they had been taken in a raid on some distant white settlement. It was the first time in a very long time that she wore such clothing and it excited her to feel again the swish of woven cloth fabric against her skin. Little wonder she had eagerly anticipated that dance at the Feast of the Harvest.

As she had danced with the others, a petticoat of deep blue broadcloth swirled about her legs, festooned at the hem with gay little colored ribbons. Her blouse was of black silk, with three vertical rows of silver brooches, one from each shoulder to waistline comprised of inch-wide discs attached close together in a strand. The center row, from throat to waist, were larger discs, two inches or more in diameter. They clinked together cheerfully as she moved. She wore several strands of white-and-lavender mussel-shell wampum around her neck and her hair had been gathered and clubbed behind, decorated with beads of many colors. Beneath her petticoat she wore leggins made of scarlet cloth and on her tiny feet were doeskin moccasins interlaced with designs made of porcupine quills. Her movements were fluidly graceful and a delight to behold. Cornplanter was watching her admiringly when the white man rode into the village.

It was Sir John Johnson, now British Superintendent-General of Indian Affairs in North America, and he was received with the respect, consideration and friendship that had always been bestowed on him when he visited here. He greeted Cornplanter warmly and stood with him for some time, observing the swirling gaiety about them. Then the two men retired to Cornplanter's quarters where they remained for an extended conference in private.

Later in the evening, as they sat around the fire in his lodge, Cornplanter had explained to Old Queen and The-Ship-Under-Full-Sail the reasons for Sir John's visit. He spoke softly, matter-of-factly, and with little expression on his face.

"Our white brother came here for two reasons," he told them. "A large council is to be held at Fort George, the new fort of our British brothers across the mouth of the river from Fort Niagara. He wishes me to attend with my warriors and I have told him I will." He was silent for a long while as he filled his stained clay pipe with kinnikinnick from a soft pouch. After lighting the Indian tobacco with a glowing stick from the fire, he continued:

"He wishes me to bring along The-Ship-Under-Full-Sail."

The girl's mouth opened in surprise and she could feel the color drain from her face. "But why, big brother? I have nothing to do with him. Surely you would not sell me to him?"

"No! You are my sister. I could not sell you, no more than I could sell she who sits with us." He let his glance flick momentarily to Old Queen who was quietly smoking her own pipe. "Our brother, Sir John, told me that for many seasons he has been visited at times by the man and woman who were once the blood of The-Ship-Under-Full-Sail. They have pleaded with him to buy you back from me and he has always said to them that it is not possible, because he knows you are my sister. But he invited them to attend the Grand Council soon to be held. He was sure I would be there and he asked me to bring you along, so that at least these people could see you one final time."

The-Ship-Under-Full-Sail was trembling and there seemed to be a roaring in her ears. "I am afraid, big brother. I do not want to go. Let me stay here with our mother."

Cornplanter shook his head. "No, you will go, but you need have no fear. I made Sir John give two promises before I would agree. First, that no effort will be made to reclaim you, either by him or by those who were once your people; second, that no proposition of any kind, no gift of any value, be offered to me to part with you. He agreed, so I have promised him we will come."

The days since then had been a welter of confused emotions for the girl. Memories crowded back which she had long ago set aside with the determination never to revive and they warred with the happiness she had come to know as a member of Cornplanter's family. As the day had approached for them to leave Oswaya, she still did not wish to go and at the final moment she appealed to Old Queen to intercede for her with Cornplanter. The old woman cupped Eleanor's face with gnarled hands and smiled and there was such tenderness in her touch, such an inner beauty in her ancient eyes, that the girl could not keep tears from springing into her own.

"You must go," Old Queen said, "not only because it is the will and word of my son and your brother, but because it is something you must do if you are to have peace in your own heart. You have kept hidden what you were, but it is merely hidden, not gone. Only after you have seen these people and spoken to them of how you feel now for me, for your brother, for our people here and for our village, only then will that which is hidden be set free and lose its hold upon you. Or perhaps," she added, "you will come to know that it cannot be lost. That is something only the Great Spirit can determine and what he wishes is what will be. For my part, you are my daughter and I love you with the same love that I held for Caughna, whom you replaced. In your absence now I will go to the woods alone and I will talk with the Great Spirit and ask that you remain safe and return home."

They left the village not long after that, Cornplanter and The-Ship-Under-Full-Sail in the lead, followed by a column of mounted subchiefs and warriors, heading northwestward on a light trail that led to a stream which Cornplanter called Cattaraugus. There the trail turned north and came to the south shore of Lake Erie at the mouth of Buffalo Creek. Lake Erie narrowed down to become the Niagara River and they followed the east bank downstream, past the great island which split the stream, past the thunderous falls which caused the very earth to vibrate and astounded the girl, past the great whirlpool which awed her greatly, and finally to old Fort Niagara at the mouth of the river where it entered Lake Ontario. It had been a journey of about one hundred miles and very tiring, yet The-Ship-Under-Full-Sail would gladly have turned around without rest and ridden back the whole distance if Cornplanter would have allowed it. He would not.

Immediately upon their appearance, boats were sent across from the other side and they could see a crowd of men in uniform and women in dresses and bonnets on the far side. Many hundreds of Indians were in view on the other side, their camps already established and the majority of them gathered close to Fort George where the council fire was to be lighted. Cornplanter stood silently, holding the girl's hand, awaiting the arrival of the boats. When they reached the shore and the deputy Indian agent who was aboard greeted him warmly and invited him aboard, Cornplanter acknowledged the greeting and then turned and spoke to his own men.

"Stand here with the horses and wait until I return."

"Our horses are tired," spoke up a subchief. "They should be taken across in the horse-boat and be taken care of."

"No," Cornplanter said firmly, "let them wait."

He helped the girl into the boat and climbed in himself. The six soldiers at the oars bent to their task of ferrying them to the west side against the strong current. The chief and the girl stood close together all the way across, still hand in hand. She was wearing her beautiful soft doeskin garb covered by a long cape of muskrat pelts draped over her shoulders, tied at the neck and belted at the waist. As they neared the grassy bank of the opposite shore she heard, among the confusion of voices of soldiers and their wives, a voice from her past.

"Nelly! *Nelly!*"

She saw them then, older, grayer, changed a little, perhaps, but unmistakable — John and Sarah Lytle. She felt as if she were in a dream and as the boat touched shore and was quickly drawn slightly farther aground, she let Cornplanter lead her. Dazed, she vaguely felt his strong arms lift her high and set her feet on the grass.

The crowd of soldiers and their ladies had formed a sort of half-circle twenty feet or so from where the boat came ashore and now, as the girl stood there uncertainly, Sarah Lytle detached herself from the half-circle and took hesitant steps toward her. A pace or so behind, John Lytle followed.

The older woman suddenly stretched her arms forward and her emotional utterance of the girl's name caused something to break in The-Ship-Under-Full-Sail. The fourteen-year-old leaped forward toward Sarah Lytle with an inarticulate cry that finally evolved into "Mamma . . . *Mamma!*" as they reached one another and fell into each other's arms. They were crying, all three of them, the father stretching his arms wide to embrace wife and daughter and so choked with emotion he could not speak.

A fourth person cried as well. Large silent tears streamed down Cornplanter's craggy cheeks and he turned and stepped back into the boat.

"I will go back across," he told the agent.

"But the council is almost ready to begin. Sir John wants you to be present."

Cornplanter shook his head, his eyes still on the girl and her parents, now with the wives of the soldiers and some of the soldiers themselves clustered about them, patting their backs and shoulders, laughing and crying and sharing their joy. "I cannot attend," he said. "Tell Sir John I am sorry to leave. The mother must have her child. The child needs her mother. The-Ship-Under-Full-Sail is no more. Tell him. He will understand."

Later this evening, following the joyful reunion with her siblings — Harrison, Tom and Maggie, who had been waiting at the fort in the quarters of one of the officers — Eleanor Lytle related her experiences of living with the Senecas as the daughter of Old Queen and the sister of Cornplanter. She was distressed that Cornplanter had left without a farewell, but finally agreed with her parents that it was probably best. Besides, John and Sarah were still distinctly apprehensive that Cornplanter might have a change of heart and come back to try to reclaim her.

They were not, they told Eleanor, returning to the Plum Creek valley. Rather, they were leaving in the morning for Detroit aboard one of the King's ships. Eleanor's father had purchased a piece of land east and slightly north of Detroit at a place called Grosse Pointe, where their nearest neighbors would be a fairly wealthy family named Forsyth, who owned Detroit's most popular inn.[70]

[*December 10, 1783 — Wednesday*]

Although the bitter wind whipping across the face of Lake Erie swirled the tiny particles of snow into stinging bits, the man who stood on the shore did not seem to notice. This was Lake Erie's northern shore, about twelve miles east of the mouth of the Detroit River, and the man smiled tightly. Despite the cold, a warm glow suffused through him.

"I'm standing on my own property." Though he spoke aloud, his words were almost inaudible, so he shouted even more loudly: "Two hundred acres, fronting right on the water, and it's mine!"

His name was Daniel McKillip and, having served with merit in the British army for the past seven years, he was one of a large number of disbanded British soldiers, Tories and German mercenaries being permitted to establish claims on this stretch of Canadian shoreline as reward for services. Because he had been among the first to apply, McKillip was able to choose one of the best lots. The area had been divided into long narrow lots, each fronting on the lake, each containing two hundred acres and the whole area being referred to now by the designation of New Settlement. Ten miles east of the Detroit River's mouth a town had been laid out on paper as a marketplace and educational center for the community that would develop here of those who claimed their bounties. McKillip had been told that the town, when eventually built, would be called Colchester.

A very brave, intelligent young man of twenty-four, McKillip had entered the army in 1776 as a private and a year later became a sergeant in the renowned corps called Butler's Rangers. So valorous was his conduct that he was commissioned a lieutenant in 1779 and then last year, while stationed at Detroit, promoted to captain.

Now, standing on the lakefront only a little over a mile east of where the Colchester settlement would be built, Daniel McKillip considered himself a very lucky man. Already he had plans for starting an apple orchard and vineyard . . . and a family, as soon as he found himself a wife.

[*March 23, 1785 — Wednesday*]

Gradually, sometimes broadly but more often almost imperceptibly, the northwestern frontier was changing. New traders were appearing to take the places of those who had emptied their hidden gold pots and departed — some to retire in the civilized climes of London, Quebec, Paris or New York, others to see adventure farther west in lands only vaguely known. Little tendrils of exploration wormed their way so far west that reports, believed reliable, were circulating about the great blue western ocean lying beyond vast prairies, tremendous mountains, endless deserts, and beyond even more mountains. For the world of trade, that great western shore could be the long-sought avenue for unimaginably rich trade with the Orient.

The explorations were private, not governmental; the explorers were often individuals or groups of only two or three men rather than organized military or commercial expeditions. Everything was based on hearsay and everything was simultaneously suspect and exciting. Beyond all else, everything in the great western unknown was dangerous.

With disturbing regularity, those individuals who set out to find their fortunes or found their private little empires or fulfill their dreams of adventure were never again seen. Real danger existed in numberless forms, not only in that western, essentially unknown land beyond the Mississippi, but in the somewhat more familiar though still highly unstable area that lay north of the Ohio River and west of the frontier borders of New York and Pennsylvania — in that vast expanse of Indian country known commonly as the Northwest. Deep within that wilderness, established traders — mostly British — strengthened their posts and their ties with the Indians.

Jean Baptiste Point du Sable was continuing with his efforts to make his trading post at the mouth of the Chicago River one of the finest private operations of its kind anywhere. A hundred miles away, on the St. Joseph River, trader William Burnett continued to quietly operate his own post, striving to remain at peace with the various tribes and anyone else who came along.

Young John Kinzie — Shawneeawkee — was now very well established at his posts on the Maumee River — near Kekionga at the French Store, now often called Miamitown, and farther downstream at the mouth of the Auglaize. Highly thought of by all the Indians with whom he traded, he still performed craftsmanship in silver for upwards of a dozen tribes, while at the same time training his half brother, Thomas Forsyth, in the Indian trade.

As much as the Northwest was an attraction to such individual traders, so it was, too, for the infant government of the United States. Though the Americans had won this sprawling expanse of territory from the British in the war only recently concluded, it was a prize barely controlled and practically unoccupied by Americans. That was a situation being remedied step by painful step, through treaty and through treachery, as frequently through the shaking of weapons as through the shaking of hands. Insidiously, boundaries were changing and white occupancy spreading. For a ludicrously short while a large area, which included Chicago, was proposed as a new state in the United States — to be called Assenisipia. It was a dream that died almost at its inception. Yet, not all efforts by the new government at expansion were quite so transitory.

On October 27, 1784, the second Treaty of Fort Stanwix was concluded.[71] By the terms of this treaty, the once powerful Iroquois — the Six Nations — ceded to the United States all their claims to territory west of the New York and Pennsylvania boundaries. And just two months ago, the Ottawas, Delawares, Chippewas and Wyandots ceded to the United States all their lands in the Ohio country except for a reserved tract between the Cuyahoga and Tuscarawas Rivers — a treaty in which the Shawnees did not participate, though much of the land in question was theirs. As if to add insult to the injury, the United States planted its first permanent fort north of the Ohio River — an important little toehold located at the mouth of the Muskingum River and called Fort Harmar.

Land disputes between Indians and the United States increased, as did the hostilities that had never wholly been laid to rest. In their confusion and anger, the Indians turned for help to the British at Detroit, Mackinac, Niagara and other locations, repudiating their treaties and land cessions with the Americans and claiming they were fraudulently obtained. The British cautiously supported them. American encroachment was beginning to seriously undermine the Crown's fur trade and they knew that it was greatly to their benefit to retain the loyalty of the tribes. They were forced to maintain a delicate posture. They were not yet ready for another war with their rebellious offspring and so, while they could promise supplies to the Indians, and deliver them, they could not promise active military support. And while they strongly urged the tribes, especially the Shawnees, to stand fast in their determination to keep the Americans south of the Ohio River, at the same time they urged that the tribes restrain themselves from taking the offensive and thus provoke the Americans into another war which might too soon involve the British themselves.

The whole Northwest seemed to be in a state of flux — changing here and there in little ways but at the same time with the three principal forces involved — Americans, Indians and British — poised in their respective positions, waiting to spring upon the adversary's greatest point of vulnerability. Practically everyone was waiting, waiting.

All were convinced that the waiting would soon be at an end.

[April 4, 1786 — Tuesday]

Today, in the parlor of the Lytle house at Grosse Pointe, just east and slightly north of Detroit, Eleanor Lytle and Daniel McKillip were married.

The house was crowded with guests and outside a score or more carriages were parked, tended by black slaves clad in their finest, the horses standing quietly in their traces, occasionally stamping or snorting. Although the newlyweds were just over ten years apart in age, everyone present considered it a marvelous match. The twenty-seven-year-old Captain McKillip was uncommonly handsome and could very properly be called dashing in his dress uniform. Eleanor, at sixteen, was stunning. She wore the gorgeous ivory lace gown her mother had worn when Sarah and John Lytle were married in Philadelphia eighteen years ago. She was a very beautiful young woman.

A half-dozen skilled fiddlers had been employed for the occasion and immediately following the ceremony everyone trooped out onto the lawn — kept well cropped by a small flock of sheep — and the dancing had begun, led by the bride and groom. Tables sagged with the weight of food heaped on them, including roasted chicken and ducks and turkey and a huge haunch of beef, along with a variety of breads and pies and other delicacies. There was fine Madeira in abundance and a full keg of rum beside a half-keg of excellent brandy, all on a table at which clusters of men hovered, joking and laughing.

The couple had met at a ball held at the fort in Detroit last September 10. It had been Eleanor's sixteenth birthday and the first ball she had ever attended. Even before the music began, she had been a magnet attracting the unattached young men, officers and civilians alike. The first invitation to dance had come from the young man she had just married today. Throughout the whole evening he had monopolized her, much to the disgruntlement of the others, and before the ball was over both of them knew, without the words being spoken, that they would marry.

Though he lived a fair distance away at New Settlement, Daniel Mc-Killip was often in Detroit and he called frequently at the Lytle home to court this young woman with whom he had so suddenly and so over-whelmingly fallen in love. McKillip had built a good house on his New Settlement property and had planted over a hundred seedling apple trees which were doing very well, but which were still a few years away from becoming fruit-bearing. The vineyard he had started was doing especially well; the substantial crop of plump grapes harvested last year had sold at a good price to a Detroit winemaker. Nevertheless, Dan McKillip had soon recognized that the farming life was not really what he wanted. The seven years he had spent in His Majesty's service had molded him into a fine officer and so eventually he had reenlisted at Detroit on a limited service basis — still residing at New Settlement, still farming to a degree, but reporting at regular intervals for military duties at Detroit.

Now, with the festivities still in full swing, the bride and groom bade farewell to the guests generally and her family in particular. Sarah Lytle wept openly at the parting and even John Lytle had tears in his eyes when he and his eldest daughter hugged and kissed. He shook McKillip's hand and then embraced him as well.

"You take care of my daughter, Captain McKillip," he said with exaggerated gravity. "I had to rescue her once already. Hate to have to do it again."

They all laughed and in succession Eleanor embraced fourteen-year-old Harrison, thirteen-year-old Thomas and eleven-year-old Maggie, inviting them all to come and visit at New Settlement, where they would sit and eat grapes and fish in the lake for bass and perch and where they could wander along the beautiful shoreline to their heart's content.

Then they were off, the back of the carriage piled high with baggage and gifts and a long string of old shoes bumping along and kicking up dust behind. Captain and Mrs. Daniel McKillip were beginning a wonderful life together and they were extremely happy.

[*September 14, 1786 — Thursday*]

Throughout much of the Northwest a situation of peace continued to exist but in recent months it had become progressively less solid and there was a growing contingent who were predicting that it could not last much longer. The problem triggering these rumblings of war were those which existed in the Ohio country, in Kentucky and along the bloody Ohio River that separated them. Despite formalized peace between the British and Americans, and despite continuing American efforts to effect peace treaties with the tribes, the difficulties not only continued between Kentuckians and the Shawnees, they were increasing. Attacks along the Ohio River remained frequent and it was a matter of tremendous risk for anyone, Indian or white, to travel on that watercourse.

At the mouth of the Muskingum River, not only was Fort Harmar still in existence, a community named Marietta was growing around it. In addition, a land firm — the Ohio Company — had set up headquarters there for the purpose of surveying and selling to would-be settlers lands that belonged to the Shawnees. The greatest fear being harbored by both the Shawnees and Miamis stemmed from the rumors that had reached them which claimed that the United States government was already in the process, on paper, of setting aside vast tracts of land in the Ohio country to bestow on former soldiers as bounties for their service during the Revolutionary War.

What seemed to the Indians to be part of the problem they faced was that the Kentuckians had such far greater mobility because of their vast number of horses. Shawnee and Miami war parties moved through the wilderness largely on foot or in canoes, whereas the Kentuckians could, at hardly more than a moment's notice, mount large bodies of men to pursue and destroy. So vulnerable had the Shawnees become that following the last destruction of Chalahgawtha, the town had not been rebuilt and the Shawnees from there had moved northward to Mackachack and other villages of the Maykujay sept of the Shawnees, located on the upper waters of the Mad River.

A strong alliance developed between the Shawnees and their new close neighbors, the Miamis, on the headwaters of the Wabash. The Miamis were reported to have somewhere in the vicinity of five thousand warriors and many of their raiding parties were penetrating Kentucky with the sole

PARTITIONING OF OHIO

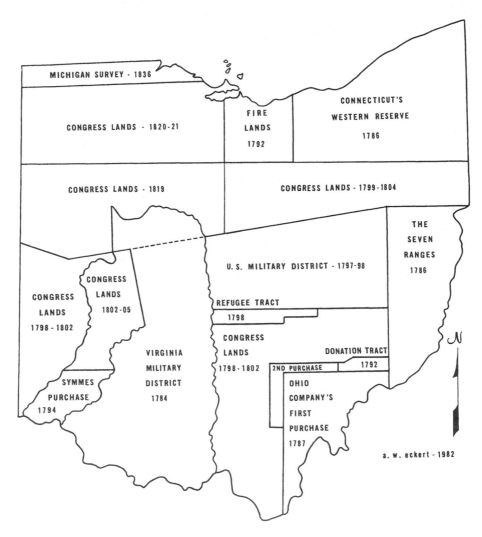

MICHIGAN SURVEY - 1836

CONGRESS LANDS - 1820-21

FIRE LANDS 1792

CONNECTICUT'S WESTERN RESERVE 1786

CONGRESS LANDS - 1819

CONGRESS LANDS - 1799-1804

THE SEVEN RANGES 1786

CONGRESS LANDS 1802-05

CONGRESS LANDS 1798 - 1802

U. S. MILITARY DISTRICT - 1797-98

REFUGEE TRACT 1798

CONGRESS LANDS 1798-1802

DONATION TRACT 1792

2ND PURCHASE

VIRGINIA MILITARY DISTRICT 1784

SYMMES PURCHASE 1794

OHIO COMPANY'S FIRST PURCHASE 1787

a. w. eckert - 1982

NOTE: THE DOTTED LINE WHICH APPEARS IN THE UPPER VIRGINIA MILITARY DISTRICT AND
THE CONTINUING SOLID LINES TO THE EASTERN AND WESTERN BORDERS OF THE STATE
INDICATE THE ORIGINAL INDIAN/WHITE BOUNDARY LINE ESTABLISHED BY GENERAL
ANTHONY WAYNE IN THE GREENVILLE TREATY OF 1795.

object being to steal horses from the Shemanese. By the beginning of July, over five hundred horses had been taken from Kentucky this year alone. In the two and a half months since then, the figure had nearly doubled and the Kentuckians were furious.

Many of the more daring Miami raids were being led by Michikiniqua — Little Turtle — who, these days, was being accompanied by a red-headed youth of sixteen. The lad had been given to Michikiniqua as a mark of respect by the Wea Chief Gaviahatte. His true name was William Wells but, due to his hair color, he had been renamed Apekonit — Wild Carrot. Because of his deceptively ingenuous manner, the boy had been singularly successful in luring travelers on the Ohio River to shore by pretending to be a white settler's boy in distress. As soon as the boats reached shore to help him, they would be attacked by Michikiniqua's warriors waiting in ambush. The boy himself would then join in the attack on the whites and so outstanding was his courage that lately he was also being called Epiconyare — the Brave One.

In the over two years since his capture and adoption into the Miami tribe, William Wells had almost forgotten his own family name and background. The attacks in which he participated became more and more frequent. In a pattern only too familiar over these past years, an appeal was sent to General George Rogers Clark to raise and lead an expedition of mounted men against the Miamis on the Wabash, not only to regain their horses but to destroy villages, crops and as many Indians as possible. Clark accepted the challenge and quickly raised seven hundred mounted men. His second in command for the mission was one of Kentucky's foremost settlers, Benjamin Logan, general of the militia.

Today, well into Shawnee territory, Clark halted his march and held a meeting with Logan. "Ben," he said, "the spies have just brought word that a lot of Maykujay Shawnees are moving northwest to join up with the Wabash confederacy. We're going to have to do something to show them this isn't a good idea and draw them back to the Maykujay towns. I want you to leave right away, tonight. Go back to Kentucky and raise as large a force as you can. We've got most of the militia here right now, so you're going to have to call for volunteers. But if you don't get enough response, start drafting men. As soon as you have five hundred or more, move against those towns to the north and destroy them. I don't need to tell you that the faster this is done, the better."

Logan nodded and in less than an hour was on his way at a smart canter back to Kentucky.

[*September 29, 1786 — Friday*]

There had been no need for General Benjamin Logan to issue a draft in order to mount the force he needed. The Kentuckians reserved a special hatred for the Shawnees and while many had been reluctant to join Clark's force to travel far up to the headwaters of the Wabash against Michikiniqua's Miamis and their Potawatomi allies, they flocked to Logan's call for volunteers to go against the Shawnees.

Today, in an assemblage of a size never before witnessed here, Logan's force of seven hundred ninety men had rendezvoused on the south shore of the Ohio River at Limestone.[72] Five hundred of these men brought along their own weapons, ammunition, horses and supplies and the remainder were provided with government mounts brought mainly from Louisville and Lexington. Half a hundred cattle had been gathered to be herded along at the rear of the march to provide the army with meat. For days the women being left behind had been baking; hoe-cake, johnny-cake and parched corn were in abundance. Gallon-sized pouches of finely ground corn meal combined with maple sugar would, when mixed with water, make a thick beverage rich in energy.

Since the preparations of organizing and packing had taken until late in the afternoon today, the men expected that camp would be made and the crossing of the Ohio River would be begun in the morning, but they had underestimated the drive of their commander.

"Boys," Logan shouted, standing high in the saddle, "let's get across starting right now. We've got a job to do."

The men roared their approval and immediately the march began.

[October 17, 1786 — Tuesday]

The town of Mackachack now vied with Wapakoneta for honors as the largest Shawnee village in the Ohio country. It had grown considerably since the influx of their kin from Chalahgawtha following its final evacuation and destruction, along with the destruction of Peckuwe. These days Mackachack boasted upwards of seven hundred wegiwas and a total population approaching twenty-three hundred, of which over five hundred were warriors. Most of the men were gone today, however, having left two weeks before to side with their allies, the Miamis and Potawatomies, in opposing the army of General Clark now bearing down on them.

Remaining in the village were the women and children and old people, along with only eight or ten able warriors. And Moluntha. No one was quite sure how old Chief Moluntha was, but he had been principal chief of the Maykujays since well before the French and Indian War, which was over thirty years ago, and everyone knew that he had not become principal chief until he was at least fifty years old. He was by far the oldest and most venerable of all the Shawnees.

In the large wegiwa that housed the family into which they had been adopted, the two young women known as Kisahthoi and Tebethto were seated side by side on a mat, cutting and sewing pieces of buckskin into garments. It was difficult work but they enjoyed it and passed the time chatting between themselves or with Tecumapese who was cooking round loaves of corn-meal bread. Nearby sat her twelve-year-old son, Spemica Lawba, busy using a sharp stone to smooth the length of osage wood he was making into a bow.

The sisters looked at one another and smiled. How grown up the boy was getting and what a fine warrior he would become. They had been amused at his distress at not being able to accompany the men on their mission against Clark. Even the fifteen-year-old triplets, Sauwaseekau, Lowawluwaysica and Kumskaka had been allowed to accompany Chiksika, Wasegoboah, Tecumseh and Sinnanatha, and he felt he should have been given the opportunity as well. Spemica Lawba had great faith in his own abilities.

The sun had risen only a little more than an hour ago and Mackachack was still very quiet. Some of the women passed to and fro to the creek for water and some worked outside at various jobs, but the big job of continuing to harvest the corn from their extensive fields around the village had not yet begun for the day. When the call for that was sounded, most would drop whatever it was they were doing and join together in the community effort.

Kisahthoi, at twenty, had developed into a mature young woman of strong stature, considerably taller than most of the women of the village and with an athletic build. Her long blond hair was worn in two queues which fell on either side of her ample breasts and both she and her sister almost always wore the sort of clothing she had on now — a simple short-sleeved deerskin pullover garment that fell just below the knee in length. As usual, her small feet were clad in comfortable moccasins.

Tebethto, darker and shorter than her sister, was more delicate in physique. She, too, wore her long hair in queues, but often tied them together behind her or coiled them atop her head. She was still of a more subdued personality than Kisahthoi, but whatever their physical and personality differences, the two remained very close.

They rarely talked anymore about the life they had had as the McKenzie sisters on the Kanawha River eight years ago. They thought of themselves as Shawnees, most of the time, and were reasonably content with their lot, having come to the conclusion that one day each would marry a warrior of the tribe and have her own family. But Kisahthoi still dreamed of her father at intervals and in these dreams she was still Margaret and her sister was Elizabeth.

Abruptly a dog began a furious barking outside and then others joined in until there was quite a din. They could hear voices and a few shouts and for an instant the occupants of the wegiwa stared at one another. Then they leaped to their feet and rushed outside. The same thing was occurring elsewhere, with everyone looking out over a prairie to the south. A white man was approaching at a trot, holding aloft a kerchief cloth on a stick. Already the few warriors left in the village were moving out to meet him and a sense of tension lay heavy in the air.

The warriors surrounded the arrival and began attempting to question him, but obviously could not understand or be understood. In a few minutes one of the warriors, whose name was Anequoi — The Squirrel — came running back and did not stop until he reached Tecumapese.

"It is one of the Shemanese," he said, "with much to say, but we cannot understand. Spemica Lawba," he pointed at the boy, "has learned much of their tongue from Sinnanatha. We need him to come with us and tell us what the man is saying."

Tecumapese nodded and her son sprinted away at once with the warrior, leaving Kisahthoi and Tebethto to wonder why they had not been asked, since they understood English far better than Spemica Lawba. They watched as their adopted nephew reached the circle of warriors and saw him talking with the white man, who was gesticulating now and then. He was obviously agitated and in a short time another of the warriors, Wapeake — Cold Earth — moved surreptitiously behind and, without warning, buried his tomahawk in the man's head. They scalped him, left him to lie where he had fallen and returned at a trot to the village, going immediately to Chief Moluntha. After a little while, during which time there was a rising hubbub in the village, Spemica Lawba returned to his wegiwa, excited.

"He was a bad man," he explained to the women. "He was part of an army coming here. The Shemanese. He ran away from them two nights ago and came here. He wanted silver for telling us. He was a bad man."[73]

The boy went on to tell them that Moluntha had ordered everything be gathered up and packed for removal at once. The old chief estimated that since the dead man had deserted the army two evenings ago and had evidently come here as rapidly as he could, the army of Shemanese, which would of necessity travel more slowly, could not possibly arrive before tomorrow. But to be safe, he ordered that Mackachack be totally abandoned before today's sun was straight up. Unfortunately, Moluntha supposed that because the dead man had been on foot, so too was the whole army. He also reckoned without realizing the speed with which Benjamin Logan moved his force.

At ten A.M., with horrifying speed and suddenness, the army of General Logan broke from cover in three wings and galloped to the attack with blood-curdling screams, brandishing swords and rifles. There was almost no resistance; a few scattered shots from here and there and a few warriors making a courageous stand in the face of overwhelming odds, not in an effort to win but in the vain hope of holding back the army just long enough for the women and children to escape. As for the latter, they fled screaming from the wegiwas, scattering as if they were covies of quail bursting from cover.

At their wegiwa, Kisahthoi and Tebethto were momentarily paralyzed. Spemica Lawba had disappeared and Tecumapese, shrieking his name, plunged into the heavy cover near the creek bank. The sisters found their legs and, hand in hand, fled as swiftly as they had ever run, managing to reach the cover of a nearby island of woods without being seen. On the far side they hid in an erosion gully, wedging themselves out of sight beneath an overhang of earth bound together by the interlaced roots of prairie grasses.

In Mackachack itself, the little resistance was swiftly overcome. The handful of able warriors, including Wapeake and Anequoi, were killed in the first onslaught. Some of the women held their ground and tried to fight, but they were cut down easily by slashing swords. Colonel Thomas Kennedy, leading the right wing, spurred his horse after a group of eight fleeing squaws, his finely honed Scotch broadsword raised high. As he overtook a heavyset middle-aged woman named Sathea, he clove her skull with his blow and nearly lost his weapon as she collapsed. Bracing a boot against her head, he jerked the blade free and regained his balance, then galloped after the other seven, chopping down six in succession. The dead squaws included seventeen-year-old Tima, who had just gotten married to a warrior named Petoui three days before the war party had ridden out toward the Wabash. The final woman, Karalo, wife of subchief Red Horse, stopped, whirled about and held up a hand to fend off the blow. Kennedy's blade chopped off all four fingers of that hand and laid open a gash on her scalp, but did not kill her. Other groups of squaws and children now ceased fleeing and fell to their knees screaming *"Mat-tah tshi! Mat-tah tshi!"* — Do not kill us!

As the raiders swept in, Spemica Lawba snatched up a tomahawk and sped toward the wegiwa of Chief Moluntha. He heard Tecumapese scream his name and looked back in time to see her plunge into the fringe of brush at the creek bank. As he neared the chief's lodge in the center of Mackachack, he heard a horseman coming at a gallop and stepped into a doorway out of sight. Almost at the same time he heard the voice of Moluntha shouting *"Bahd-ler! Bahd-ler!"* and realized the horseman was the great Shemanese warrior who had once been a prisoner of the Shawnees.[74]

Moluntha was surrendering! Identifying himself to the man called Bahd-ler, he offered to surrender himself and his three wives to the frontiersman.[75] Bahd-ler accepted Moluntha's tomahawk and then ordered a group of eight privates who had galloped up to form a protective ring around the chief and his wives while he went to bring Ben Logan here. In

a few minutes the pair returned, General Logan well mounted on a chestnut mare. They dismounted and the circle of soldiers opened to let them
enter. Moluntha smiled toothlessly and extended his skeletal hand in
greeting. Both Bahd-ler and Logan shook his hand. In creditable English,
the Shawnee chief addressed them:

"Moluntha surrenders himself and his wives into the hands of the great
white chief, Logan."

From hiding, Spemica Lawba saw the Shemanese general smile and
nod. "You will not be harmed," he said. "Nor will your wives." He
reached into an inner pocket and took out a piece of paper upon which he
wrote an official protection. He handed it to Moluntha and then questioned him briefly, in a kindly manner. Moluntha told him that all the
Maykujay towns, including Wapatomica, were practically deserted, the
warriors having gone to fight Clark. It was what Logan had anticipated.
He nodded, ordered the privates to surround the old chief and his wives
again, keeping them prisoners but not harming them, and then moved off
with Bahd-ler.

Minutes later Captain Hugh McGary and Privates Ignatius Ross and
William Lytle rode up and dismounted. Using his rank to enter the circle,
McGary questioned Moluntha briefly, discovered he had been at the Blue
Licks battle and, before anyone could stop him, jerked out his tomahawk
in rage and buried it in the old chief's head in a tremendous blow.
Moluntha was killed instantly, the official protection paper still clenched
in his hand.

Hardly had the chief fallen than two things occurred. Logan returned
and reined up, having witnessed everything from a short distance away,
and Spemica Lawba burst from the nearby wegiwa doorway with a shriek
of fury, racing to attack McGary. Some of the guards in the circle, initially
taken so by surprise, were already leaping on the captain and struggling to
restrain him. Spemica Lawba's progress was blocked by Ross, who
snatched the boy around the waist as he passed. The private hardly anticipated what came next. With surprising agility and strength, Spemica
Lawba wrenched himself out of his grip, spun and swung his own tomahawk in a vicious arc. So extremely close was the blow that Ross felt the
sharp edge slice through one of his eyebrows without breaking the skin.
Ross jerked back violently, stumbling and falling on his back. Instantly
Spemica Lawba launched himself onto the man, landing with bent knees
in his solar plexus, driving out Ross's wind with a great whoosh. Pinning
the private's arms with his knees, the Shawnee boy raised his tomahawk
again for the final blow. All this had happened with such incredible swift-
ness as to be stunning. Only Lytle's quick reaction — snatching the boy's
wrist — saved the life of his friend.

William Lytle jerked the boy away viciously, yanking the tomahawk out of his hand at the same time. The boy spun, fell, rolled over and was back on his feet in a crouch, knife in hand, all in one movement. By this time the others had shaken off their paralysis of surprise and two more of the privates grabbed the boy's arms and held him. He continued struggling violently, kicking toward their groins, biting toward their hands, butting with his head. The scalping knife was still clenched in his hand.

General Logan dismounted and walked toward the boy, stopping in front of him. "Release him," he said. The privates looked at one another uncertainly and Logan's nostrils flaired. "I said *release him!*"

They let go of his arms and immediately Spemica Lawba was back in his crouch, knife held menacingly. Logan was watching him closely and then, surprisingly, he held out his hand, palm up. "Son," he said softly, "I don't know if you can understand the words, but I hope you'll understand the meaning." He smiled genuinely. "Let me have the knife."

The boy looked at him unflinchingly for a long moment and then straightened from his crouch. He dipped his head in acquiescence, flipped the knife so the blade was in his hand and then he placed the haft into Logan's palm. Logan's smile widened and now it was he who dipped his head toward the boy. "Thank you. Please wait here."

He turned, strode a few steps to where Captain McGary was being held and verbally chastised him in coldly furious words, relieving him of his command and ordering him placed under arrest to stand trial later.[76]

The battle, meanwhile, if such it could be called, had ended and the prisoners were rounded up. Twenty-two Indians had been killed, including ten warriors. The remainder were squaws and old men. Three of Logan's soldiers were dead.

Thirty-three prisoners were brought together, mostly women and a few children. Obviously, many times that number had escaped as the attack broke out but no immediate effort was made to pursue them. General Logan ordered that thirty-two of the captives be returned with the army to Danville, to be held captive for possible later prisoner exchange. The single exception was the boy, Spemica Lawba, whom Logan retained under his special protection.

The remainder of the campaign was carried out wholly without resistance. Those who had escaped from Mackachack had quickly spread out to the other towns, warning them, so all were abandoned quickly. Logan reassembled his army and sent detachments to the other towns with orders to destroy all crops and burn the villages. They spread out and accomplished their mission before the day was done, destroying a total of thirteen villages: Mackachack, Moluntha's Town, Mingo Town, Wapatomica, Mamacomink, Kispoko, Puckshanoses, McKee's Town, Waccachalla, Pecowick, Buckangehela's Town, Blue Jacket's Town and the newest one, another village that was named Chalahgawtha. Hundreds of acres of corn were destroyed and the total plunder found in the villages amounted in valuation to $2,200, which was equally divided among the men.

Before the army pulled out, General Logan took the young Spemica Lawba aside. He indicated the boy should sit on a log and then sat beside him. In silence the general filled his pipe, lighted it and puffed for a short while. Spemica Lawba watched him closely, masking all expression. At last Logan spoke.

"Son," he said, "I have a strong feeling you speak English. Is that correct?"

For a long moment Spemica Lawba did not reply and then he nodded. "Speak some," he said. "Understand more."

"Good. You're a very brave lad. I would like to help you. Since you are now a prisoner, you must remain with us. You have a choice, however. You may go with them," he tilted his head toward the assembled prisoners some distance away, "and share whatever their lot will be. Or, if you wish to do so, you may remain with me and I will take care of you."

Again Spemica Lawba did not reply immediately and the silence stretched out for so long a time that Logan finally added, "Did you understand what I said?"

"Yes, I understood. I will go with you."

"Excellent." Logan smiled broadly. "I would like very much to adopt you and teach you about your new life. You will be my son. Just as it is the custom among your people to adopt certain captives and give them Shawnee names, so I will adopt you and give you an English name."

A flicker of interest came into the boy's eyes. "What name?"

"What is your name now?"

"Spemica Lawba. It means Big Horn."

The Kentucky general nodded and sucked on his pipestem a few times. Little puffs of blue-white smoke drifted up and away. "From now on," he said at length, "as a member of my family, you will be known by the name of Johnny Logan."

"John-ny Logan." The boy savored the name on his tongue. Then he smiled.

[*October 28, 1786 — Saturday*]

The sisters were exhausted and very hungry. They had not eaten well for days. A few nuts and berries they had found in their wanderings had formed the whole of their subsistence and now they were getting concerned. The realization had come to them on the third or fourth day that they were lost in this wilderness of forests, prairies and marshes, but at first it had not bothered them greatly. Somewhere to the north, they knew, was Detroit. If they could get there, everything would be fine. Detroit was civilization. People. *White* people. And so they had continued walking, heading generally north. Now it had become horrifyingly clear to them that not only were they lost, there was a strong possibility they might die out here in the middle of nowhere. The nights were cold, fireless; though they cuddled together and covered themselves with leaves for warmth, each morning it had taken them longer to get up and continue moving. The memory of the attack upon Mackachack still burned vividly in their mind's eye and they would never forget the screams.

Kisahthoi and Tebethto had remained hidden under the creek bank where they had taken refuge, staying there all through that day and the night which followed, then well into the next day. Not until the army of Shemanese had ridden off with the prisoners being herded among them had the two young women crept from hiding and peered fearfully through the screen of shrubbery at the still-smoldering remains of the village. A few bodies were visible on the ground, but no living soul was in sight.

"We always thought a time would come when we could just walk away, 'Liz'beth," the elder sister whispered. It was the first time in a very long while that she had addressed her sister by her true name.

"And now it's come, Margie," the dark-haired girl whispered back, completing the comment. "What do we do now?"

"We try to get to safety, that's what."

"We could've surrendered to the soldiers," Elizabeth McKenzie pointed out. "They were white, like us."

Margaret McKenzie shook her head. "We're *not* white, 'Liz'beth. We haven't been for years. We've been Shawnees. That's how they would've seen us and they'd probably have killed us like they did Sathea and the others." She shook her head again. "No, we've got to head north, not south. Toward where Detroit is. We can get there if we just keep heading that way. Let's go."

So they had moved off toward the north, without water, food or protection from the elements. Over the first few days they saw several small groups of Indians at a distance, but hid from them, having agreed they would not return to the Indian life if they didn't have to. But now, suffering from hunger and exposure, they began to wish they had let the Indians find them.

Abruptly they broke through a screen of woodland and found before them a broad river. A gravel bar was along the shore here and they walked out onto it. There was no sign of life except for a deer standing in the shallows on the opposite side, who eyed them a moment and then leaped away, disappearing in the woods. Elizabeth collapsed and suddenly she was crying, her face buried in her hands. Like her sister, she was a mass of scratches from the briers they had encountered and her hair was an impossible tangle.

Margaret dropped beside her younger sister and put her arms around her, intending to comfort Elizabeth but then finding she was crying herself and could not stop. They sat there for a long while after their tears had ceased, despair flooding them, still hugging one another. It came, therefore, as a considerable shock when a voice called out from nearby.

"Hello!"

A canoe with two men was bearing down on them from upstream. The man in the stern was an Ottawa of about forty. The man in the bow was in his early twenties, clad in buckskin but obviously a white man. The canoe slid up onto the gravel bar and the younger man stepped out, drawing the light craft higher from the water before turning to them.

He approached, smiling in a friendly manner, and they saw that he had a strong countenance and assured bearing. He was, in fact, a very good-looking man. They came to their feet slowly, their mouths still agape, and stood mutely before him as he came to a stop a few feet away.

"Thought at first you were Indians," he said, a wide grin exposing his even white teeth. He pointed at Margaret. "Until I saw your hair. Permit me to introduce myself. My name is John Kinzie."

[*November 1, 1786 — Wednesday*]

At eighteen, Tecumseh could well have been chosen as a model exemplifying what a young warrior should be. He was of medium height and weight, with erect posture and graceful carriage. His physique was admirable, smoothly muscled and proportionately ideal, and he was exceptionally agile. His forehead was broad and his nose strongly formed but not over-large. It was his eyes that were his most dominant feature, able to change from gentle warmth to bright points of controlled anger, from sparkling gaiety to deep sorrow, from compassion to iron implacability. But though physically he was perhaps an epitome of a young brave, mentally he was far beyond most of those with whom he came into contact. His mind was quick, incisive, questioning, retentive, facile and inventive; a mind that set him apart.

Tecumseh was, among the young Shawnees, the foremost hunter — again, not because of great physical prowess on his part but because he used his mind to overcome obstacles which others attempted either to batter down with brute strength or simply turned away from. If there were questions to be asked, it was Tecumseh who would ask them. Initially it was his elder brother and sister, Chiksika and Tecumapese, who answered his continuing flow of questions: Chiksika in matters of warfare and politics, religion, tribal tradition and history; Tecumapese in matters of the heart, family, love and care, compassion and beauty and self-possession.

There came a time, however, when neither Chiksika nor Tecumapese could any longer satisfy the questings of his mind. They could not explain why Moneto, if he loved his red children, allowed them to suffer so at the hands of the white men. They had no answers for what they could do — what *Indians* could do, individually and collectively — to curtail and turn back the evils the whites brought to their beautiful land, the wanton destruction of game, felling of forests, burning of prairies. They could not supply a reason beyond simple Shawnee tradition for why a Kispokotha or Maykujay or Peckuwe could not become principal chief of the tribe, that such station was reserved only for those who were of the Thawegila or Chalahgawtha septs. And most certainly they could only shrug and remain mute when he asked why, if the greatest peril facing Indians was white man, the Indians did not unite in a self-protective front to ward them off. Why was it that Menominee fought Fox and Chippewa fought Sioux and Sac fought Osage? Were they not, first of all, *Indians?* Were they not all children of Moneto?

The matters of the weeks just past troubled him greatly and there was no one to whom he could turn for answers. With what wonderful courage and purpose they had mounted and ridden off from the Maykujay villages toward the Wabash; with what fine hopes they had headed toward a confederation of Miamis, Potawatomies, Ottawas, Delawares and Wyandots to form a united front against the great white warrior, Clark; with what shame did they arrive to find that instead of waging war, the man named Clark was speaking to them, humoring them, coddling them, convincing them of the foolishness of fighting for their rights, convincing them that the whites wished no more land and no more strife with their red brothers. Tecumseh was not much more than a boy and had no voice whatever in councils and no right to speak, but he watched and listened aghast as the Indians declared for peace. First, and undoubtedly most important, it was the powerful and influential Miami War Chief, Michikiniqua, who acquiesced to the proposals of George Rogers Clark. Immediately the chief had been supported by the Miami subtribes — the Weas and Eel Rivers and Piankeshaws. The remaining Delawares and their kin, the Muncies, fell in with it. With that, the movement had become a landslide, and even the more bellicose chiefs of the Potawatomies — Mtamins, Nescotnemeg, Topenebe, Main Poche and Black Partridge — had agreed to the proposals. By the time the Shawnees arrived, it was all over. Clark and his army had departed in peace and headed back toward Kentucky on the Wabash trail via Vincennes and the unstable confederation of tribes broke apart and scattered back to their own territories, so deep in the Northwest that they had little to fear from incursions of the whites, well protected by the buffer zone inhabited by the Shawnees. But for the Shawnees there was no buffer zone and they were within easy reach of the deadly Shemanese.

So the Shawnee warriors had turned around and headed dejectedly back toward their own villages, only to find them destroyed when they arrived, their wives and children prisoners of the whites. Or dead. Or missing, as were their adopted sisters, Kisahthoi and Tebethto. A great rage burned in their breasts then, but now they were a small red island in the path of a great white torrent, and so they moved farther north again, to the limits of their territory in the north, from the Wapatomica villages northward until they were all but pressed up against the neighboring Miamis to the north-west and the Wyandots and Ottawas to the northeast.

The death of Moluntha in such barbaric, dishonorable manner filled them with fury and at the same time they sang the praises of the nephew of Tecumseh and Chiksika, the boy Spemica Lawba, who had faced the whole army of eight hundred with only a tomahawk and scalping knife. But Spemica Lawba, too, was gone and Tecumapese, having escaped and then returned, was grief-stricken at the loss of her son. Whether the boy still lived or not, no one knew for sure.

And now, sitting in gloomy council with the chiefs of the tribe, required by tradition to keep his peace and bow to the wisdom of the elders, Tecumseh heard the words of Catahecassa and Shemeneto and the new chief of the Maykujays and second war chief under Shemeneto, Weh-yeh-pih-ehr-sehn-wah — Blue Jacket. But they said only the words that had been said so many times before and there was little hope in them.

Tecumseh held his peace with great effort of will, but he knew that the time would soon come when he could no longer do so. Somehow, some way, there was a means by which the advance of the white man could not only be checked, but he could be driven back and the lands he had taken from the Shawnees and other Indians returned to them.

There had to be a way!

[*March 10, 1787 — Saturday*]

Spemica Lawba, now well into his thirteenth year, had never before felt so confused, so torn within himself. He clutched the gunwale of the boat in which he and other Shawnees, mostly women, were being rowed across the Spaylaywitheepi, from the place the whites called Limestone to the north bank of the river directly opposite. For five months he had lived in the household of Benjamin Logan and had been accepted by the whole family as their son and brother, Johnny Logan. He had learned their ways, eaten at their table, slept beneath their roof, polished his English to sur-prising fluency and been taught in a variety of other subjects he previously had not known. Most of all, he had grown to love the whole family generally and the genial, paternal Benjamin Logan most of all.

Then came this day — the day of the prisoner exchange — and Spemica Lawba had to keep reminding himself that he was going back to his own people, back to his true family. But he was not a prisoner! Why must he return? Why could he not, as he so deeply wished to do, stay another year or so here and go back to the Shawnees when it was his own decision to go back?

A great sense of guilt filled him, for he knew he should be overjoyed to be returning to his mother and to his uncles and the others. He *was* overjoyed and eager to be reunited with them once more, but at the same time he was deeply saddened at being forced to leave the Logan family, remembering with real inner pain the parting just a few minutes ago on the Kentucky shore from his adopted father.

"Johnny," the man had told him, squatting before him and holding his shoulders in a warm grip, "we love you very much. I hope you know that. In losing you today, we are losing a son. I wish you could stay, but the terms of the prisoner exchange require that all Indians be given up by us, just as all whites must be given up by the Shawnees. But we won't forget you and we hope that in better times we will see you again. This is your home, always. You may come any time you wish and stay for however long you wish."

Spemica Lawba's eyes had filled with tears and he prayed that they would not spill over his eyelids and trickle down his cheeks. It was some time before he could respond, but at last he said, "I love you, too. I will not forget you, ever. Now I will become Spemica Lawba again, but I will never harm you in any way. That is my promise."

Ben Logan nodded and reached into the pouch he wore. From within he extracted a knife — the very weapon that this youth had surrendered to him at Mackachack. "This," he said, handing it to him, "belongs to you."

Spemica Lawba looked at it and then slowly slid it into his belt. His lower lip was trembling as he looked up at the man. They embraced then and neither could any longer check the tears. When they pulled apart, the youth took the big man's hand in both of his. "To my white father," he said softly, "I will always be Johnny Logan, and I will never raise my hand against him or his army."

Now, as the boat scraped ashore on the north bank of the Spaylay-witheepi, he thought again of the promise he had made and he knew he would keep it. And he prayed to Moneto that the time would never come when his opposing loyalties would be put to the test.

CHAPTER IV

[*April 1, 1787 — Sunday*]

THE small frame building that was Detroit's Grace Episcopal Church could seat only fifty people at capacity, but on this day it was far from full. Morning services had concluded over an hour ago and it was still several hours before the evening service began. Less than a dozen people were in the church early this afternoon, including the Reverend Mr. Philip Morehouse, who was performing the ceremony.

The man and woman being married were, respectively, twenty-three and twenty years old. Their names were John Kinzie and Margaret McKenzie. The only relative of the bride on hand was her eighteen-year-old sister, Elizabeth, who was being escorted by the groom's new business partner, a rangy newcomer to Detroit from Montreal, John Clark. Kinzie's half brother, Thomas Forsyth, was on hand — a lean young man with dark, deep-set eyes and pleasant manner, who had been born in this city during a visit of his parents sixteen years ago. They were here too, the parents: William Forsyth appearing very prosperous in his well cut, expensive suit of clothes, Emily Forsyth looking frail and older than her years beside him. Kinzie had little to do with either his mother or stepfather these days. He shared practically no rapport with the latter and his mother had become a waspish wisp of a woman who disapproved of practically everything, including her son's choice for a wife. Emily Forsyth had been quite ill these past months, which had done little to improve her normal acerbity.

As the Reverend Mr. Morehouse pronounced the couple man and wife and they kissed, only one set of eyes in the little church was wet. These were the eyes of Elizabeth McKenzie. The emotion that evoked them was not happiness for her sister but, rather, sorrow for herself. She, like her sister, had fallen in love with John Kinzie shortly after he rescued them from the gravel bar on the south bank of the Maumee River and took them to Detroit with him. Margaret had been first to declare that love and, in so doing, established a priority claim without even knowing she had done so. Elizabeth had never mentioned to her sister how she felt and only one person in the church had any inkling of it. This was the man seated beside her, John Clark. And since Clark was himself smitten with Elizabeth, he was determined to console her as best he could.

[*December 31, 1787 — Monday*]

Administration of its vast holdings was, for the infant United States, a matter of some complexity. Where the former colonies were concerned, there was little difficulty, since boundaries were reasonably well established and the business of converting a colony under the leadership of an appointed governor to a state under an elected governor posed no great problem. Where tremendous expanses of wilderness territory were concerned, however, it was somewhat a knottier problem. Here was a domain close to ten times larger than England, extending from the Alleghenies westward to the Mississippi River and from the Great Lakes to Spanish Florida, most of it still essential wilderness and inhabited by native tribes that, as past experience had proven, could be hostile.

True, settlers were pouring into that wilderness in ever-increasing numbers, despite the hazards to be encountered, and so the new government had taken steps to divide that great territory into manageable sizes. With a wisdom beyond its years, the young government provided that whenever there were five thousand free males of full age in a specific region of territory, the people there should be authorized to elect representatives to a territorial legislature. These men, when chosen, were then empowered to nominate ten freeholders of five hundred acres each, from whom the President of the United States would then appoint five to constitute a legislative council. The representatives were to serve two years in office, the councilmen five. Such territories, when established, were to be only temporary governments. As soon as a particular area in one was sufficiently populated and settled, application could be made for entry into the Union as a state, as a full and equal partner of the original thirteen colonies presently in the process of officially becoming states.

Delaware had become the first state on December 7, followed five days later by Pennsylvania and, six days after that, by New Jersey. Next year there would be others. For the great wilderness territories, however, it was a first tentative step toward self-government within the nation. In perhaps its most far-reaching legislation thus far, the Congress enacted the Ordinance of 1787 to implement its policy. In doing so, it created the Northwest Territory and, with an eye to the future, in Article V provided that not less than three states nor more than five should eventually be organized from this Territory, guaranteeing that each such division would, upon achieving a free white population of sixty thousand people, be admitted as a state to the Union. If only three states were to be formed within the Northwest Territory, these would be named Ohio, Indiana and Illinois, with the Ohio River their southern borders and extending to Canada in the north. But Congress could, the Ordinance went on, ". . . at its future discretion, form either one or two additional states," — to be called Michigan and Wisconsin — "in that part of the said territory lying north of an east and west line drawn through the southerly bend or extreme of Lake Michigan."

The westernmost state, Illinois, was to be bounded on the west by the Mississippi River, on the south by the Ohio and on the east by the Wabash River upstream to Vincennes and then on a line due northward from there to the Canadian border. The middle state, Indiana, would border Illinois on the west, have the Ohio as its southern border, and on the east a line drawn due north from the western point of the mouth of the Great Miami River to the Canadian border. The easternmost state, Ohio, would consist of the remaining land east of the Indiana line to the north and west of the Ohio River and Pennsylvania border to the Canadian border.

The Ordinance of 1787 was more than one merely establishing boundaries of a territory and providing for its possible future division into states. It established as well the first commonwealth in the world whose organic law recognized every man as free and equal. Wherever posted, including at strategic localities along the frontier border, the unique and amazing document became for many weeks the single most important topic of discussion. Among other matters, it provided for the appointment of a governor, judges and other territorial offices for establishing both criminal and civil laws, for the surveying of the territory into counties, the formation of a General Assembly and the election of an authorized delegate to Congress with the right to debate but not vote during the temporary government. The Ordinance delved even deeper into the rights of individuals within the territory, proclaiming that no man could legally be molested because of his religion or his mode of worship; it provided the benefits of the writs of habeas corpus and of trial by jury; that "Religion, morality and knowledge being necessary to good government and the happiness of mankind, schools and the means of education shall forever be encouraged." Finally, adding emphasis to the credo of "every man free and equal," the Ordinance declared total prohibition throughout the Northwest Territory of either involuntary servitude or slavery. The latter was a matter that raised the ire of many, such as the Kinzies, who had recently acquired some Negro slaves, and the Forsyths, who had always owned slaves — usually Negro, but often Indian and occasionally even Caucasian — and who had no intention of giving them up.[77]

The issue of slavery prohibition was one of two portions of the Ordinance that most angered the people already on the frontier. The second was Article III, Section 14, dealing with the native inhabitants of the Northwest Territory, which declared:

. . . The utmost good faith shall always be observed towards the Indians; their lands and properties shall never be taken from them without their consent; and in their property, rights and liberty they shall never be invaded or disturbed, unless in just and lawful wars authorized by Congress; but laws founded in justice and humanity shall, from time to time, be made, for preventing wrongs being done to them, and for preserving peace and friendship with them. . . .

What bothered the settlers so much was that the Ordinance in this area, as stated, seemed to give the Indians *carte blanche* in penetrating white settlements and wreaking havoc — especially by crossing the Ohio River — and then retreating to an inviolate sanctuary north of the river where retaliatory raids were now prohibited. No longer could the Kentuckians, for example, legally mount expeditions to penetrate into the Ohio, Indiana and Illinois countries to strike the Indians . . . and perhaps stake out claims to be made when the area became safer for that sort of project. That such claims might be made was no pipe dream, as evidenced by the fact that almost immediately a new land office was established. It was situated at the Falls of the Ohio — Louisville — and its official purpose was for the reception of locations and surveys made *north* of the Ohio River.

There was peace of sorts in the Northwest Territory at the close of this year, but no one was betting on how long it would last. The Indians viewed with some degree of alarm the various points of strength the Shemanese were developing in the Ohio Valley. The tiny settlement long called Limestone was incorporated and renamed Maysville. On the north bank of the Ohio at the mouth of the Muskingum, Fort Harmar was well established. Were this not enough, just east of the fort construction was beginning on a very strong two-story walled fortification being called Campus Martius. Also on the north bank of the Ohio, Fort Finney had been built directly across from Louisville. There was equally a strong rumor circulating that Brigadier General Josiah Harmar, newly promoted from colonel, was gathering troops at Fort Harmar and planning to march — as an official United States Army — against the Shawnees when the weather warmed, to wipe them out for good. But that was merely a rumor at this moment and official government position was along a different vein.

The United States government was in a delicate position right now in regard to the Indians and their lands in the Northwest Territory. The government was only too well aware of its own weaknesses, but nowhere nearly well enough informed as to the strength of the Indian tribes. Certain messages had been received by Congress from the tribes which renounced previous treaties as unfairly drawn and illegal because of having been consummated oftentimes with mere village chiefs having no right to speak for and commit their own tribes, much less others. They indicated that they did not wish war and that they might be willing to discuss the cession of some small areas of land north of the Ohio River, but at the same time wrote ominously of the consequences should the United States government fail to keep settlers and surveyors south of the river until and unless any such cessions were completed.

Since the United States, by reason of the Treaty of Paris, already considered itself owner of the land upon which the Indians were resident, it had no desire to reopen negotiations for the same land, but neither was it prepared — either economically or in manpower — for another Indian war. Secretary of War Henry Knox put it into words for Congress, saying, "In the present embarrassed state of public affairs and entire deficiency of funds, an Indian war of any considerable extent and duration would most exceedingly distress the United States. The great distance by land which the supplies and stores must be transported would render the expense intolerable."

In the midst of all this the Shawnee brothers, Chiksika and Tecumseh, headed west, taking advantage of the respite in hostilities with the whites to visit friends they had made in an earlier trip west and to explore new and different places. No real objective was set for the trip, no specific place to reach and visit after which they would turn around and return. They planned to go wherever the whim carried them and stay however long they cared to stay. With them went a party of ten other young men of the tribe, most of them, like Tecumseh, only nineteen or twenty years old, and Chiksika, at thirty-one, their leader.

They traveled first to the upper Wabash, visiting with the Miamis on the Mississinewa and other Wabash tributaries, staying for over a month with Michikiniqua and his adopted son, Apekonit, known to the whites as Chief Little Turtle and William Wells. For Michikiniqua they had great respect and they were especially impressed with his ideas for a stronger confederacy of tribes to be formed to present a united defensive front to the encroaching whites. For the red-headed Apekonit, also known as Epiconyare, they had less respect. Despite his thirteen years with the Miamis, he always seemed to grow nervous when war with the Shemanese was discussed. His eyes would blink rapidly — a habit of his, whenever he was agitated — and he would retreat into himself almost to the point of rudeness. It was Tecumseh who, as they left Michikiniqua's village and resumed their westward journey, said to Chiksika, "Although he is Michikiniqua's adopted son and they are very close, one day we will find that Apekonit is our enemy and all that he has learned about us and our ways will be turned against us."

From the upper Wabash they traveled into the Illinois country, staying here and there during the spring with the Potawatomies and renewing associations of many years' duration. It was at the Potawatomi village of Pimitoui that a youth of about sixteen became entranced by Chiksika and Tecumseh.[78] A very powerfully built young man, he clung with great concentration to every word the brothers uttered, begging them for more stories of their past battles with the Shemanese — whom his own people called Chemokemon — when they fell silent, urging them on to greater details when they told of their journeys together. Uncommonly strong, he was not especially tall, only about five feet nine inches, but he weighed at least two hundred pounds and there seemed not to be an ounce of fat on his frame.[79] His face was round and friendly and he laughed often. He was not a Potawatomi by birth; his mother was a Seneca and his father an Ottawa named Opawana. His name was Chaubenee.[80]

Born in an Ottawa village near Detroit, Chaubenee was brought to the Illinois country at an early age by his parents, to live here at Pimitoui under Chief Spotka. Opawana, who had fought beside Pontiac at the siege of Detroit, several times accompanied him to the Illinois country. He had helped avenge the death of Pontiac at the hands of the Illinois Confederacy. He had liked the area and, years later, came back to live here, not at all discomfited by the fact that Pimitoui was a Potawatomi village. Chaubenee was now thought of more as Potawatomi than as Ottawa and, should he marry a Potawatomi woman — which was likely, since he was in love with Canoku, daughter of Chief Spotka — he would then actually become a Potawatomi. Chaubenee had a brother named Mukonse — Little Bear — who was two or three years younger than he and who also became an instant admirer of Chiksika and Tecumseh, though not with quite the hero-worship evinced by Chaubenee.

When, in May, the Shawnees left Pimitoui, still heading west, Chaubenee begged to be permitted to go along, but the decision went against him. "You have not thought on it enough yet, Chaubenee," Chiksika told him. "There are many hardships we will face, especially over the winter, and we may aid our friends, the Sacs, against the Osages. If so, there would be grave danger. Think on it longer and when we return, if then you are still of a mind to follow us, you may."

So they had left the disappointed youth behind and moved on, stopping here and there until at last they reached Saukenuk, the principal Sac village on the Rock River very close to its mouth at the Mississippi. Saukenuk was where they were now and where they were apt to stay for many months to come, since this winter, though scarce begun, was already one of the coldest and snowiest in anyone's memory.

"It is just as well, Chiksika," Tecumseh confided to his brother now, "that no attacks on the Osages have been planned this season by the Sacs. You would want to go, I know, but I could not. I *would* not. And because I would not, I would be thought of as a coward."

"I would not think of you as a coward, little brother," Chiksika replied slowly. "Not for that or anything else. I know you too well for that. But I think you have a reason beyond what others might think. Will you share it with me?"

Tecumseh nodded. "I will join any tribe fighting against the whites, who are our great enemy," he said, "but I will not put my hand to the killing of Indians by Indians, no matter of what tribe. We are a people and should not kill each other. If we do not realize that, how can we ever hope to stand against the white men?"

[*October 27, 1788 — Monday*]

Jean Baptiste Point du Sable was disappointed in the lack of growth in the Chicago area. The efforts he had poured into making his trading post here one of the most complete anywhere on the frontier had been prodigious and were not yet over. In addition to the post itself and his house adjacent to it on the north bank of the Chicago River, he had built a number of outbuildings, including stables, chicken houses, hog houses, storage sheds and the like. He had fenced areas for horse yards and hog yards and cattle yards, and his garden was large and productive. The trading post was indisputably one of the best equipped anywhere and a favorite rendezvous point of the Indians and other traders. He had prospered extremely in his trade and was a rather wealthy man and yet, despite this success, the disappointment was growing. Where were the settlers? Why did *they* not come, instead of just Indians and traders? Why didn't this area called Chicago expand into the important commercial metropolis he had so long envisioned?

A few French traders had come and stayed for a while and gone. Even Gaurie, who had lived for fourteen years near the mouth of the North Branch of the Chicago River, had one day pulled up stakes for no known reason and disappeared toward the west. Somehow, Chicago couldn't seem to hold people and Du Sable knew that the basis for its lack of permanent growth had to be the conflict between the white powers. Chicago was in a sort of no-man's-land, too far away from the active frontiers for it to be safely occupied and maintained by the British out of Detroit or the Americans out of Kentucky or the Spanish out of St. Louis.

Though disappointed, Du Sable was not giving up. He reasoned with himself that development was simply coming more slowly than he had anticipated and he forced himself to be patient. It would come eventually, he knew. The Chicago Portage was still there and it remained as important as it had ever been. One day it would come into its own.

Du Sable did not travel much these days, content to remain at home and continue improving his property, so the fact that he had undertaken this present journey to Cahokia was noteworthy. He was doing what he had long promised himself he would one day do — he was marrying Gohna, with whom he had lived for sixteen years.

The ceremony was a very simple one by a priest of the Catholic Church and attended only by a few acquaintances from the St. Louis and Cahokia areas, along with Du Sable and Gohna's children, Susanne, who was now approaching her sixteenth birthday, and Jean Baptiste Jr., who was twelve. Both children were also baptized at this time, immediately following the wedding.

For Susanne, the trip had special importance. In these few days of their stay, she had met a young French merchant of Cahokia and the mutual attraction was immediately apparent. His name was Jean Baptiste Pelletier and he was bright, engaging, industrious and very good-looking, with slightly sharp features and a thin black moustache. Because of him, the day of the wedding had become the most eventful day of Susanne du Sable's life. Not only were her parents married this day, and she and her brother baptized, but just before their departure for home, Jean Baptiste Pelletier had taken her aside, put his arms around her and kissed her. It was the first romantic kiss Susanne had ever received and her legs became weak and she clung to him tightly, as much to keep from collapsing as because she wanted to do so anyway.

"Soon," the young man murmured in her ear, "I will come to see this Chicago place where you live. If I like it, I will stay there and I will marry you. If I don't like it, I will go away, but I will take you with me and marry you. No matter what else happens, you will be my wife. Do you have anything to say to that?"

Her cheeks flushed and heart leaping within her breast, Susanne leaned back and nodded. "Hurry," she said.

[*April 13, 1789 — Monday*]

Tecumseh was greatly changed. He had left the Maykujay Shawnee villages with Chiksika a year ago as an enthusiastic youth, bubbling with excitement and soaking up experiences and impressions of people and their ways as if he were a sponge of limitless capacity. But in these months of traveling, many things had occurred. Now, here in the southern region of the Tennessee Territory, he had put aside his youthfulness forever and become a man. He had experienced joy and laughter, but he had also experienced physical pain and great emotional anguish and it had tempered him.

The many months spent among the Sacs and Foxes brought him a new understanding of a culture differing in many respects from his own. He had soon begun to realize that while societies differed from place to place, sometimes considerably, people themselves were basically similar, irrespective of tribe or race or the way they worshipped. They were all humans and they all had human desires and needs that were essentially alike, differing only in degree from one individual to another. Each had cravings to love and be loved, fears to overcome, ambitions to attempt to fulfill, and basic human values to be nurtured.

They had been welcomed by the Sacs and settled down in Saukenuk for a long stay among them. Their arrival had been in early May, just as the men had returned from their winter hunts. The various families busied themselves opening the caches where, the previous fall, they had buried food and supplies in packages made of bark. Here, in holes carefully concealed by being covered over with sod to blend in with the rest of the prairie, they had stored the dried seeds — corn, beans, squash, melons and others — that would be the basis of the gardens and fields they would soon again be planting. They ground some of the corn into meal and roasted some of the seeds of pumpkins and sunflowers and squash. Great kettles of stew in which these and other ingredients were tossed, along with large quantities of jerked and dried meats from their hunting, bubbled constantly over the fires in the lodges and the families relaxed, gorging themselves and smoking their pipes as they alternately told their own stories and listened to the stories of others, boasting of their hunts or their raids into enemy country, imbibing the liquor procured from their Indian agent or passing traders.

Soon the women had trooped out with their hoes to the gardens and fields, planting vegetables that would be harvested in the fall to again keep them in food over the next winter ahead. Most of the fields went unprotected, but sometimes a garden area would be enclosed within a flimsy fencing of sapling poles to help keep out the deer and bison and occasional elk.

Feasting and dancing followed the planting — a sort of going-away party, since immediately afterwards the tribe once again broke up. The men — including the Shawnees who were their guests — headed through the Iowa country to the area of Council Bluffs where hunting was good for elk and bison and where the excitement of the hunt was spiced with elements of danger from possible attack by raiding parties of Osages. During this absence of the men, the women remained in the home territory, fishing and sun-drying or smoking their catch, gathering bark for the construction of storage bags in which to bury food and supplies to sustain them over the winter and into the following spring. Great armloads of flag reeds were gathered and endless hours spent in weaving the mats upon which they would sleep and eat. Some of the parties of men traveled up the Mississippi to the region of Apple River where their mines were located and here they dug and smelted lead ore. The methods were crude, but by mid-July they would have from three to four thousand pounds of pure metal to use as barter with the traders.

Converging on the home villages again, the Sacs and Foxes engaged in a series of feasts and dances, participated in wedding ceremonies, repaired bows and guns, made arrow shafts, chipped flint heads for arrows and spears, cultivated the crops and attended councils. Horse racing was very popular, as was the violent game of lacrosse, played on a grassy field upwards of three hundred yards in length — a sport of modified mayhem where blood flowed freely, eyes were blackened, teeth knocked out, arms or legs broken. The Sacs and Foxes were great gamblers and Chiksika and Tecumseh and their fellow Shawnees watched closely, intrigued not only by the intensity of the sport but by the fervor of the betting, where almost anything could be a prize—guns, bows, arrows, tomahawks, horses, blankets, even liquor. The most furiously played games were those involving teams of Winnebago, Potawatomi, Menominee and Chippewa players, where team fervor became nationalistic and passions remained high.

At last had come harvest time, at which everyone worked in gathering and cleaning the crops for various uses or storage, with the youngsters employed in gathering all the crab apples they could find, then stringing them to dry and be stored for winter usage. Following the harvest feast, largest and most boisterous feast of the year, a full tribal council was called and hunting areas allotted for the approaching winter. A date was set for departure and in the time remaining before then, new holes were dug for caching of the foods and supplies to be left behind.

In early September the village crier walked back and forth calling out that this was the day of departure. Horses and canoes were loaded with traps and guns and supplies and the various parties set off in different directions. The Shawnee guests elected to go with a party heading for the country of the Dakotah Sioux, spending weeks on horseback, pursuing the bison in a thunder of confusion, stalking the elk and pronghorn, and all the while keeping alert for war parties of Sioux.

As the bitterest of winter set in, hunting ceased and trapping began, using steel traps purchased from the traders as well as deadfalls and snares of their own construction. The days were spent in checking their traps, baiting and resetting them, removing their catches, skinning the mink and beaver and otter they caught and, finally, toward the end of winter, congregating with their catch at the trading posts to barter for the guns and goods and liquor they needed and wanted.

It was as this trading was in progress that Chiksika and his party bade their hosts farewell and set off eastwardly, stopping by the village of Wabasha, chief of the woodland Sioux on the upper Mississippi, just downstream from where the Chippewa River entered from the east.[81]

They were greeted warmly, treated well, presented with gifts of food and invited to return.

From Wabasha they followed the Mississippi downstream to Prairie du Chien at the mouth of the Wisconsin, visiting briefly with the Winnebagoes gathered there for late winter trading, then moved eastward again to the mouth of the Milwackie at Lake Michigan where Chief Siggenauk of the Potawatomi had his villages. Again they were received with honors and spent enjoyable hours in the lodge of the chief, listening to his stories and his urging that the Shawnees make peace with the Americans for all time, since he was sure it was they who would eventually become the power in this country.[82]

The ride down the southwestern Lake Michigan shoreline to Chicago was a delight and they spent three days there, trading at Du Sable's well-supplied post and visiting with Potawatomi Chief Black Partridge in his village close by. He was a pleasant chief who almost always wore a gold crescent dangling from his nostrils. At their departure they moved southward across the Chicago Portage to the Des Plaines River and then down to the junction with the Kankakee, where the Illinois was formed, and then down a little from there finally to come once again to Pimitoui. Chaubenee was on hand to greet them, wild with excitement at their return, full of questions about what they had done, where they had gone, what they had seen.

"Where are you going now?" he asked, during a pause in the conversation.

"We will go to see our friends, the Cherokees, far to the south," Chiksika replied. He studied the youth and smiled. "Last year when we were here you wished to go with us and I told you to think on it more. Have you done this?"

Chaubenee nodded gravely. "I still wish to go with you."

"Then you will."

As easily as that it was settled and in the morning they rode out on the trail heading south, Chaubenee happily astride the horse given to him by his elderly father, Opawana. Though Chaubenee greatly liked both of the brothers, it was to Tecumseh that he was most drawn, possibly because they were closer in age, possibly because there was about Tecumseh a personal magnetism that was all but overpowering, yet most difficult to assess. Wherever Tecumseh happened to be, Chaubenee was nearly certain to be close at hand. At one point, as they were nearing the Ohio River, moving along casually and talking as they rode, Chiksika remarked on how much Tecumseh had changed in the past few years.

"There are great things in store for you, little brother," he said. "I see you as becoming a very important man."

Tecumseh grinned. Chiksika was almost as widely noted for his prophetic abilities as had been their father, Pucksinwah. Tecumseh, too, had prophetic skill, though not yet so much recognized for it as was Chiksika. Nevertheless, he now shook his head and spoke banteringly. "Chiksika, I think you are talking more about what you might like than what will actually be."

"You still doubt what I tell you will be?"

"Not always." Tecumseh grinned. "Only sometimes."

"Then let me tell you something else that will be and see if you will doubt this, also. Today we will reach the Spaylaywitheepi and camp there. Tomorrow we will cross. Two days after that, even though you are a better hunter than any of us here, you will fall from your horse as you chase a buffalo and you will break your hip."

"Better my hip than my head," Tecumseh countered. "But this time, Chiksika, you are no prophet. You see, now that I am warned, I will see to it that it will not happen."

"We'll see, little brother."

The little party had laughed about it and then promptly forgot the conversation until their third day in Kentucky. They had encountered the small herd of woodland buffalo unexpectedly and the animals snorted and thundered off, with the Indians in instant pursuit. At full gallop, Tecumseh nocked an arrow in his bow and drew up beside the largest bull of the herd, prepared to shoot the arrow into his heart. But the great beast lunged, bumped Tecumseh's horse with his huge shoulder and threw the horse off stride. The horse stumbled, pitching Tecumseh high into the air, and he had landed wrenchingly on a large rock. There was a sharp pop followed by excruciating pain and even as he lay there writhing, Tecumseh remembered the prediction and felt a surge of admiration for his brother. Chaubenee was sorry for Tecumseh and considerably impressed by Chiksika.

For two months they camped while Tecumseh recovered and it was only during this week that they had been able to resume their journey and reach the Cherokee villages. Not surprisingly, the Cherokees were having problems of their own with encroaching whites and in recent months there had been several hot skirmishes. They were, in fact, preparing a raid for tomorrow against a new little settlement not far distant from which considerable trouble had been emanating.

"We will help you," Chiksika said. "Are we not your guests? Have we not eaten from your cookpot with you?"

Preparations were begun immediately and it was as Tecumseh and the seventeen-year-old Chaubenee were working beside one another that Chiksika had come up to them and placed a hand on Tecumseh's shoulder. His expression was very sober.

"Something has come to me," he said, "that I would rather not share with you, but must. Little brother, what I say now will come to be." A presentiment of his own chilled Tecumseh's heart, but he only nodded. Chiksika continued: "Just as our father knew that he should die in that battle with the Shemanese where the Kanawha and Spaylaywitheepi meet, so I know that I will die tomorrow during our little battle. When the sun is at its highest, then will a bullet from the whites strike me here," he placed a fingertip to his forehead, "and my life will be ended. But do not let them falter. Lead them on with attack at once and they will emerge victorious."

Tecumseh and Chaubenee were both stunned and Chaubenee began to speak but Chiksika held up a hand, cutting him off. He continued to speak softly but with intensity. "Tecumseh, you must carry on for our people and become for them a chief. You will do this, I know. I have looked ahead and seen you not as the leader of the Shawnees, but as the greatest and most powerful leader ever known. I have seen you journey to far lands — to where we have gone together and far beyond — and I have watched you bring together under your hand a confederation of Indian nations such as has never before been known."

So upset was Tecumseh that he could not speak, but he vowed in his heart to stay by his brother's side throughout the engagement. This he did and the fight, begun in late forenoon, was a hot one. Three times the Cherokees charged, supported by the Shawnees under Chiksika, and three times they had been forced to take cover, but each time they had taken their toll of the white defenders.

The Cherokee chief had no desire to sacrifice his men, but he was also sure the flimsy fortification would fall to them with one more charge. Pulling up well out of effective range of the guns of the whites, he assembled his force behind him for the final charge. At this moment Chiksika reached out and placed a hand over Tecumseh's and squeezed it. He indicated a straight hickory sapling and then the sun above it. There was almost no shadow of the tree's trunk, since the sun was at its zenith.

"Happy am I," Chiksika said softly, "to fall in battle and not die in a wegiwa like an old squaw."

The two brothers, riding side by side, with Chaubenee directly behind them, moved to join the others. There was a heavy thunking sound and Tecumseh spun in his saddle to see Chiksika beginning to fall, a hole nearly the diameter of his thumb in the middle of his brother's forehead. Then came the sound of the distant shot which, though fired from far beyond any effective range, had accidentally found its mark.

Tecumseh caught Chiksika before he fell, then lowered him to Chaubenee, who had leaped from his horse. Tecumseh raised his war club — the weapon Chiksika had given him as a gift long ago — and shouted to the Cherokees to follow him in the final attack. They would not. Shocked at what had happened, they considered it a bad omen and began to withdraw.

Tecumseh dismounted and knelt beside his brother. Shaking off the effort of Chaubenee to help, he picked up the man, cradling him in his arms. His cheeks were wet and he did not hear what Chaubenee was saying, nor feel Chaubenee's hand on his back. All he felt was a monumental heaviness in his own heart.

[*December 31, 1789 — Thursday*]

Gradually, in many ways all but imperceptibly, the Northwest Territory was changing, just as the new nation itself was evolving into a body more sure of itself, more confident in its strengths, less fearful of its own weaknesses.

During last year and this, nine more former colonies fulfilled ratification requirements and became bona fide states of the Union, joining the three that had gained statehood in 1787. Georgia became the fourth state when the year 1787 was only two days old, followed exactly a week later by Connecticut. On February 6, Massachusetts had become the sixth state, with Maryland the seventh on April 28 and South Carolina the eighth on May 23. Two more joined the statehood ranking within a week of each other in June — New Hampshire on the twenty-first and Virginia on the twenty-fifth. A month later, on July 26, New York became the eleventh state. This year, on November 21, North Carolina became the twelfth state. Only Rhode Island, of the original thirteen colonies, did not yet have statehood, but it was evident she soon would.[83]

A quiet little invasion was occurring in the Ohio Valley, which did not go unnoticed by the tribes, especially the Shawnees. During this year no less than twenty thousand settlers floated down the Ohio River, many of them filtering into the existing Kentucky settlements, others starting new ones. There was a sudden upsurge of killings along the river, both of Indians and whites. Tempers were on edge and Kentuckians remained furious at the prohibition of their penetrating the Ohio country.

The First Congress under the Federal Constitution — replacing the Congress of the Confederation of States — gave the Ohio Territory a permanent status among the states of the Republic, thereby opening the door to eventual statehood. At Federal Hall in New York City, fifty-seven-year-old George Washington was inaugurated on April 30 as first President of the United States, with John Adams as his Vice-President. Congress appointed General Arthur St. Clair as governor of the Northwest Territory and St. Clair, acting on the basis of land acquired by the Fort Harmar Treaty, immediately proclaimed the formation of Washington County, taking in all of the Ohio Territory from the Pennsylvania border on the east to the Scioto River on the west, Lake Erie on the north and the Ohio River on the south.

A chink in the Indians' defense of the Ohio country now existed and many of the settlers streaming down the Ohio were lodging their boats on the north bank instead of the south. That chink had developed through the Fort Harmar Treaty, which was signed on January 9. The Indians had at first been cool to attending any treaty session by the Americans, but gradually the word spread among the tribes that there would be a large distribution of gifts to those Indians attending, so they came. Almost all those who signed the treaty were minor village chiefs without authority to negotiate for their nations on any level — a fact of which the United States officials were well aware but chose to ignore. Among the tribes alleged to be represented were the Senecas, Potawatomies, Sacs, Foxes, Chippewas, Ottawas, Delawares and Wyandots — an odd combination, considering that the treaty was being held on, and was negotiating for, lands owned by the Shawnees, who were not in attendance.

Having been lured to Fort Harmar through promises of presents, the attending Indians hoped to convince the Shemanese to make major concessions, but the Americans were all but inflexible in their position. They wanted the Ohio lands and they meant to have them. The Indians sighed and signed the treaty, primarily to get the presents — which were less than anticipated — and knowing full well that the agreement would be repudiated by the confederation of tribes as soon as they learned of it.

Some of the Indians spurned the gifts and were furious over what had taken place, realizing now that the United States had exploited tribal jealousies to its own advantage. The United States had gained some land, true, but they also now found the Potawatomies and certain other tribes much more willing to support the Shawnees and Miamis in their opposition to American penetration of the Ohio country.

Blandly ignoring the danger signals, the United States now opened certain Ohio lands to settlement with instant results. Settlers flocked to establish themselves at the Marietta settlement adjacent to Fort Harmar and already lands were being sold in the Scioto Purchase and the Symmes Purchase of southcentral and southwestern Ohio.

Everyone was on a downhill spiral with no way to change course — and at the bottom of that spiral lay war. It was no longer a matter of nervous whispers about what would happen *if* war came, but rather what was going to occur *when* it took place. No one was quite sure but it was daily more obvious that a war could not be avoided. In preparation for that inevitability, President Washington ordered the construction of a strong fort in the Symmes Purchase, along the north bank of the Ohio River where the settlement of Losantiville was presently being laid out.[84] General Josiah Harmar dispatched one hundred forty men from Fort Harmar for that purpose in June and now, with the installation completed and named Fort Washington, Harmar himself arrived with an army of three hundred men and took command, intent upon launching an expedition against the Indians as soon as practicable. He had received orders from General St. Clair to do this. St. Clair had merely relayed the orders he had received from President Washington. The President himself had acted on authorization by the Congress, which had learned from intelligence received that, to date, over fifteen hundred settlers had been slain and scalped by the Indians.

Congress was disturbed by only one thing in agreeing that war should be carried to the Indians: they feared that the British still occupying Detroit and other posts in the Northwest Territory might interpret the strike as being directed against them. They directed the President assure the British otherwise, and Washington directed St. Clair to see to it, unaware that the British at Detroit were again paying the Indians $50 for each American scalp and $100 for every living American prisoner. St. Clair completed his explanatory letter to the Detroit commander by writing:

. . . *The expedition about to be undertaken is not intended against the post you have the honor to command, nor any other place at present in possession of the troops of his Britannic Majesty, but is on foot with the sole design of humbling and chastizing some of the savage tribes, whose depredations have become intolerable and whose cruelties have of late become an outrage, not only to the people of America, but on humanity.*

[June 20, 1790 — Sunday]

John Kinzie was not particularly happy. Life with Margaret was not what he had anticipated. They fought frequently over the most piddling of matters and, when the angry words were finished, days might pass before another word was spoken between them.

The first six months together had been very good, apart from the fact that all she wanted to talk about was trying to find her father. He offered to help as much as he could, checking with everyone who passed to find out if any had ever encountered a Moredock McKenzie, but no one ever had. Then she had the dream — a nightmare in which she saw her father captured by Shawnees, tied to a tree and quartered while still alive. It convinced her that he was, in fact, dead and that further searching would be pointless. She had gone into a deep depression from which nothing — not even the discovery that she was pregnant — could lift her.

When their son was born, almost two years ago on July 6, John had wanted to name the boy after himself, but Margaret wouldn't hear of it. "He's my son!" she snapped. "I bore him and I'll name him. He's going to be called William and that's the end of it."

So, William it was, and the unknowing infant had become a divisor in their lives. Margaret not only would not let John hold him, more often than not she would not even let him near the child. As a result, John

turned to spending more and more of his time at his Maumee River
trading posts or en route between them and Detroit. His life was a routine
of relaying to Montreal the goods traded for with the Indians and vice
versa; a routine of bartering and bookkeeping. He enjoyed the trade but
even that enjoyment tended to pall now and then and at such times he
often left everything to the care of his partner, John Clark, and simply
rode off, allegedly to inspect possible new sites for the establishment of
more posts, but on a more realistic level, just to be alone.

John Kinzie became something of a collector and disseminator of news
and there was little occurring in the Northwest of which he was not soon
apprised, most of which concerned him a great deal. That the Indians who
had been taking a stance of neutrality or even antipathy for the British
were now leaning toward them and away from the Americans was the
only good news. At the same time, it was said that American General
Harmar was becoming progressively less patient with the tribes and was
gearing for an invasion against Kekionga. If that occurred, not only would
trade be interrupted, Kinzie's post close to the Miami village might be in
real danger of destruction.

Equally chilling in a more subtle way, Governor Arthur St. Clair had
established another county in the Ohio country and named it after Alexander Hamilton. The boundaries of Hamilton County on east and west
were the Little Miami River and Great Miami River, to a line drawn due
east from the Standing Stone Forks of the Great Miami. It included the
sites of where Chalahgawtha and Peckuwe and other important Shawnee
towns had stood and was one more galling development to irritate the
Shawnees. St. Clair had come to the little settlement on the Ohio River
called Losantiville, where Fort Washington was located, and renamed it
Cincinnati.

The presidential directive that Indians were not to be pursued north of
the Ohio, not even when being chased after their raids, was making it
easier for the Shawnees and Miamis to make their hit-and-run attacks into
the Kentucky area and already this year close to one hundred settlers
had been killed in such forays. St. Clair had gotten word that the British at
Detroit were planning to intensify their activities among the tribes of the
Northwest Territory and so this past spring he made one last attempt at
conciliation. He sent Antoine Gamelin, a Frenchman of a fur-trading
family, to the upper Wabash to negotiate. Gamelin, arriving there on April
11, received very cold treatment. The Frenchman delivered St. Clair's
message of goodwill and peace to the council, comprised mainly of
Kickapoos, and expected a friendly response. Instead, their spokesman's
reply was bitterly denunciatory.

"You come here," he said, "supposedly with a message of peace and
goodwill, when below us the Shemanese are already establishing them-

selves north of the river, where they have no right to be. You come here without even having brought a draught of milk from the great white chief of the Long Knives.[85] You come to negotiate and you bring no presents, but you have been among us before and you should know a bearer of speeches should never be with empty hands."

For hours Gamelin was subjected to the verbal abuses and then finally allowed to return to St. Clair with the answer, which boiled down to the fact that the council could not talk of peace, the young men of the tribes continued to leave for war and there was no way they could be stopped. Thus, St. Clair was preparing for an offensive to be led by Josiah Harmar.

At the same time, tribal relations with the British were warming considerably and at a treaty held at Detroit, the Potawatomies, Chippewas, Ottawas and Hurons of that area ceded to the British a gift of land they were no longer using — a large portion of the Ontario Peninsula from the Thames River westward along Lake St. Clair to the Detroit River and southward to Lake Erie.[86]

Attacks on boat traffic on the Ohio River were stepped up until such traffic had almost ceased about a month ago, so dangerous had the journey become. What few parties persisted in coming downstream joined together in huge flotillas of rafts, combining manpower and munitions for mutual protection.

For Kinzie there were other matters of a threatening nature happening in the matter of trade. More traders were becoming established in Detroit and sending out their men to erect temporary posts and deal with the Indians, which cut into his trade. Worse yet, many were unscrupulous in their dealings with the Indians. On rare occasions the Indians turned the tables when they were bilked. Such an incident had occurred early last summer. The previous year, a group of Potawatomies doing business with trader François LaFerte had been traded what they were told were bracelets, armbands, necklaces and other jewelry of pure silver, in exchange for much of their entire winter's catch of fur. Within a few weeks the thin plating of silver had worn off and all that remained were ornaments of cheap copper. When the cheated Indians angrily sent a deputation to LaFerte to complain, he merely laughed at them and told them it was their own fault, they should have been more careful. So this year, the matter seemingly forgotten, the Potawatomies had come again after the spring sugar-making. They brought thirty dozen large skin bags bulging with maple sugar, each weighing about fifty pounds — the total weight coming to eighteen thousand pounds. The efforts of the entire tribe, the Potawatomies told him. They traded for traps, blankets, gunpowder, lead and other supplies worth a great deal of money, though still considerably less than that amount of sugar was worth. Again LaFerte chortled at his knack of pulling the wool over the Indians' eyes. But not too long after the deal had been concluded, LaFerte contracted to sell it all to the British mess sergeant at Fort Detroit. The sergeant, on orders from his commander, took the entire shipment, only to discover that in each bag the top two inches was maple sugar but beneath that was coarse sand. Payment to LaFerte was cancelled and he went bankrupt as a result.

At times, trading could be hazardous and not all who attempted it were successful. Two black men had appeared at Mackinac intent upon becoming traders and they set out looking for a site to establish a post, traveling westward along the north bend of Lake Michigan. They finally chose a point of land just a little upstream from the mouth of the Menominee River where it empties into the western edge of Green Bay. There were several Menominee villages close by and these Indians were curious and a little suspicious of the men whose skins were so dark. Anticipating this and prepared to act on the superstitions that the blacks had heard were so rampant in the tribe, the two would-be traders engaged in magical tricks in an effort to impress them, pretending they were powerful medicine men in contact with the Great Spirit. The Menominees were duly impressed by their sleight-of-hand feats and disappearing acts until one of the more elaborate tricks they were attempting with several volunteer children from among the Indians badly backfired. Three of the children were killed and two others injured. Within an hour the heads of both blacks were raised on poles in the center of one of the villages.

What most impressed John Kinzie on his travels was the post that had been developed at Chicago by Jean Baptiste Point du Sable. This was the third or fourth time Kinzie had met Du Sable, but it was his first visit to the Chicago site, the other meetings having occurred at Burnett's post on the St. Joseph or in Detroit.

Du Sable was no longer the only trader at the Chicago site, as he had been since the departure of Gaurie. Only a month ago a Frenchman with a part-Potawatomi wife had settled here. His name was Antoine Ouilmette and he had been working on a little house only a few hundred yards east and north of Du Sable's post.[87] He wanted to farm a little and trade a little and Du Sable had welcomed him, considering him the vanguard of settlers who would come here and build this area into a great center of trade.

John Kinzie studied the Chicago area with an eye to its potential and he was most impressed. Even while he visited at Du Sable's post, a large flotilla of canoes came through under the leadership of Hugh Heward, clerk of another Detroit trader, William Robertson. En route to St. Louis, he had arrived unannounced, yet Du Sable was quite capable of meeting the party's unexpected demands. He fed Heward and his crew of Canadian boatmen, exchanged peroques for canoes, provided the party with a large supply of flour, bread and pork and aided them in crossing the

Chicago Portage, receiving for his troubles a handsome fee. Recognizing at once the potential of the Chicago Portage and equally the ideal location of Du Sable's post, Kinzie became intrigued with the idea of possibly buying it one day.

The problem was, however, that a thinly masked hostility existed between Kinzie and Du Sable. Neither man liked the other and though, as now, their meetings were cordial enough, there was always an undercurrent of ill feeling between them. It may have stemmed from the fact that John Kinzie considered Du Sable a black because of his dark skin and half San Domingan blood; or, the ill feelings may have stemmed from the fact that Kinzie himself now owned slaves and Du Sable took offense at this. Whatever the cause, the bad feelings existed and John Kinzie was sure that Du Sable, even if he were willing to sell — which evidently he was not — wouldn't sell to him. In that he was quite correct. So the two men discussed news of the trade, Indians, politics, war, drank toasts to one another's health and laughed sardonically over the fact that the Americans had just created a new county, named Knox, which included this very Chicago area, and finally bade one another goodbye.[88]

As John Kinzie rode off along the trail which followed the lake shore toward Burnett's post in the St. Joseph, he reconsidered what he had seen at the Chicago site and became more convinced that one way or another, he would one day own Du Sable's post.

[*August 20, 1790 — Friday*]

In the well over two years that Chaubenee had been with Tecumseh, his initial adulation had in no way diminished. If anything, it had grown stronger, with no disillusionment caused by familiarity. They had grown to be fast friends, almost brothers, bound together in part through the sharing of Chiksika's untimely death. Chaubenee, now nineteen, was perhaps an inch taller than when they met, but still relatively short; a stocky individual of amazing strength, quick mind and almost perpetual good humor.

What Chaubenee felt for Tecumseh exceeded mere friendship. He adored the twenty-two-year-old and had become something of a disciple to him, just as the other Shawnees in their little party had. It was not a misplaced fidelity by any means. Tecumseh's abilities, strength of character, courage and wisdom had rapidly resulted in his becoming the talk of the Cherokee nation. His taking over leadership of the remaining Shawnees — and Chaubenee — in his little band following Chiksika's death was so natural that it had not been necessary to formalize the process with a vote of confidence. The confidence had long ago been instilled in them all. Who else among them could possibly have offered so much? Yet, it was Tecumseh himself who was unsure of his ability to become the leader Chiksika had predicted he would be. If, in fact, it were true, then he would have to test himself and become satisfied that he was worthy of such responsibility.

With Chaubenee constantly at his side, he began a period of pitting himself against staggering odds. He always assessed the enemy's strengths and weaknesses with phenomenal speed and accuracy, directing his followers in fighting in a manner that gave them the greatest margin for success and the least for jeopardy. Time after time, in connection with the Cherokees, he attacked forces far superior in manpower and weaponry; time after time he emerged victorious. To the Cherokees, it was a revelation. They considered themselves the best fighters in the world, yet now they stood in awe of this handsome young Shawnee and his companions, before whom powerful enemies fled in terror or were slain. Even though most of the Cherokee chiefs were much older and far more experienced in warfare than he, they soon quite willingly fell in behind him, seeing in him something more than any of them possessed — an intangible, indescribable aura that set him apart as a man to follow anywhere at any time, even against seemingly invincible odds.

The Cherokee women were enormously smitten by him and quite a few made it clear that they loved him and wished to become his wife. There were none that he loved but, because it was expected of him and Chaubenee and the other Shawnees in their band, he accepted the gift of a lovely Cherokee maiden to cook for him, attend his needs and satisfy his carnal cravings. Except for the ritual of marriage, she was his wife in every respect. It was a rather pleasant preoccupation, but he did not love her as she loved him. He treated her with gentle kindness, while at the same time impressing upon her that the day would come when he would ride off permanently and he would not be taking her with him.

Chaubenee followed his lead, remaining true in his heart to Canoku back in Pimitoui, yet enjoying his cohabitation with the maiden who had been presented to him. She cared for him a great deal, saw to his every need and comfort and twice, when he was slightly wounded in battle, nursed him back to fitness. His foremost devotion, however, was reserved for Tecumseh.

The fame of the young Shawnee warrior quickly spread through the southern tribes and deputations of Chickasaws, Choctaws and Creeks came to see this incredible person, sometimes even to follow him into battle and come away marveling at his abilities and fearlessness and further spreading the word of him. There was little occasion to embellish their tales, for it was not necessary. Here Tecumseh led a party consisting of only Chaubenee, two of the Shawnees and two Cherokees against a well-armed mounted party of sixteen whites, slaying all but two who escaped to carry the news to the whites of this new demon chief who advanced and won when every circumstance dictated he should suffer terrible defeat. There he charged down upon a party of eight men, his fierce shrieks and hideously painted features momentarily paralyzing them with fear; four of them falling in succession to his solo attack before the others dropped unused weapons and fled in abject panic. He helped to lead the stinging defeat of a large force of whites on Lookout Mountain and another time he led Chaubenee and his band of Shawnees, with only one Cherokee along, in a fierce rush against a new settlement, killing every man, destroying the buildings and taking more than twenty women and children prisoners. Tecumseh had never killed or hurt a woman or a child and even went far out of his way to make certain that others fighting with him did not do so.

At least half a dozen times Chaubenee's life had been saved by Tecumseh's uncanny knack for assessing any situation in an instant and acting immediately in a manner geared to swing the scales of advantage in his own favor. Three different times his camp was attacked at night by surprise and each time he not only fought back with such ferocity that his attackers retreated, but not once was any man in his command injured.

So Tecumseh's fame and prowess had grown — and Chaubenee's along with his. Indians clamored to be included in his attack force. But now Tecumseh's thoughts turned to home. They had been gone for a very long time and he had proven himself to his own satisfaction. They had said their farewells, promising someday to return for a visit, and headed north again. They passed the place where they had buried Chiksika and they came at last to the point where the Spaylaywitheepi poured its great volume of water into the Mississippi. Here they parted from Chaubenee.

The two men stood, gripping each other's wrists, the eyes of both damp at the parting. "We will meet again, Chaubenee," Tecumseh said. "I tell you this not as a hope, but as a truth, for I know it will come to be. There is much for us together in the future."

Chaubenee nodded, pleased to hear this but nonetheless distressed at the parting. "I will always follow you, Tecumseh," he vowed. "When you call, wherever I am and no matter where you are, I will come at once. What you wish me to do, I will do without question. You are now and you will always be, my chief as well as my friend."

[October 22, 1790 — Friday]

The jubilation which swept through the combined Indian forces was like nothing they had ever experienced before. The victory over the much more powerful force of General Harmar was complete and perhaps now the Americans had been taught a lesson that would make them consider twice before ever again invading the Indian territory with an army.

Word had come of Harmar's force of over fourteen hundred men gathered at Fort Washington and runners were sent to all the tribes calling for a council to be held at the French Store — now being called Miamitown — near Kekionga. This was the site of the trading post of Shawneeawkee — John Kinzie — but the trader was not there at the moment. He was in Detroit attending the wedding of his partner, John Clark, to his sister-in-law, Elizabeth McKenzie.

The area adjacent to Shawneeawkee's trading post was a favorite place of assembly for the Indians. They gathered at the call, but the total number of Shawnees, Miamis and Potawatomies was disappointingly small — just over one hundred twenty warriors. Michikiniqua of the Miamis and Blue Jacket of the Shawnees had been selected as co-leaders of the Indian force but, even so, the Indians were fearful. How could so few possibly oppose so many who were so much better armed? Then a detachment of Sacs and Foxes showed up, raising the total number of Indians to one hundred fifty. That made the odds only a little more than nine to one against the Indians.

Some of the Miami and Shawnee families living in the area of the rebuilt Maykujay and Wapatomica towns were taken to the headwaters of the Elkhart River for safety, but many remained behind, reluctant to leave now because of the corn and other vegetables being harvested. Among those who left was Michikiniqua's daughter, Wanagapeth — A-Sweet-Breeze — who was now the wife of his adopted son, Apekonit — William Wells — who had elected to stay and fight beside Michikiniqua. So then, with decided nervousness filling them, the warriors on hand settled back to wait and watch as General Harmar's army approached.

They watched as the American force approached Miamitown, watched as it entered and destroyed not only Kekionga but several other abandoned villages as well, watched as they destroyed some fifteen thousand bushels of corn that they had worked so hard to harvest, along with much of the vegetable crop. They watched as the army looted and then burned John Kinzie's trading post at Miamitown, the American soldiers not caring that it was a British citizen's post and orders had forbidden destruction of British property. They watched and they waited, biding their time, looking for that moment when the much larger force might become vulnerable; watched and waited for Josiah Harmar to make a mistake. And eventually they were rewarded.

Harmar had stupidly and unnecessarily split his force and sent out a detachment. The Indians struck it hard, killing twenty-two. When the American survivors reached the main army and reported, it was expected that Harmar would immediately launch a counterattack. Instead, he retreated. At last, bowing to the angry demands of his own men, he consented to allow another detachment to leave the army, to return to the site of the first attack to bury the dead. It was another mistake that the Indians quickly parlayed into a second victory even better than the first. Michikiniqua and Blue Jacket swept down upon them in so ferocious an assault that the detachment under Colonel John Hardin could not recover. What little resistance they formed was quickly beaten down and the survivors fled back to the main army with the news. Again the army expected General Harmar would lead a massive retaliatory assault, but the commander's backbone had turned to jelly and he ordered an immediate retreat to Fort Washington, leaving behind a total of one hundred eighty-three men dead.[89]

Only a few warriors had been killed in the two encounters, but during the ransacking and destruction of the villages prior to the attacks, the army had found an eleven-year-old Shawnee girl in hiding and took her away as a captive. She was a Maykujay whose name was Pskipahcah Ouiskelotha — The Bluebird.[90]

Jubilantly the triumphant Indians gathered up and divided among themselves the supplies, weapons and ammunition that had been left behind by the retreating army, along with a large number of packhorses. The taste of victory was in the mouths of the warriors and it was a taste to be savored.

[*October 30, 1790 — Saturday*]

The little Indian girl clung to the officer, finding some security in burying her face in his chest. He was the enemy, but he had treated her kindly, fed her, cared for her, protected her from any harm from the other soldiers throughout the dreadful ride south. Now the defeated army was approaching a huge settlement which he pointed to and said, "Cincinnati," but she did not know the word.

Pskipahcah Ouiskelotha was desperately afraid. She envisioned being tied to a post and burned or run through with a sword or having her head chopped off. She thought it was only a matter of time and she tried to be brave, but the fear remained strong within her and she trembled. The man felt it and brought his horse to a stop, gripped her and held her a little away from him so he could see her face. He smiled and there was no menace in his voice.

"I don't know your name yet, little girl," Colonel John Hardin said softly, "but I'll soon find out. I know you can't understand me, but maybe you can get the feel of what I'm saying. You're afraid, but you don't have to be. No one will hurt you. You are one of the prettiest little girls I have ever seen anywhere. I am taking you to my home where you will meet my wife and my children, and they will love you and welcome you. You will live with us, become our daughter and sister, and our family will be your family. No one will ever hurt you."

She buried her face against his chest again and he chuckled and put his horse in motion. She had no idea what the words he had spoken to her meant, but they sounded friendly and he looked friendly. Was this, she wondered, how they treated their prisoners before killing them? Pskipah-cah Ouiskelotha was still very much afraid.

[*November 1, 1790 — Monday*]

Tecumseh, with his sixteen-year-old nephew, Spemica Lawba, seated beside him in the wegiwa, pulled the blanket closer around his shoulders to ward off the chill. His long stay in the south had made him unaccustomed to the biting cold of northern Ohio. He relighted his pipe with a glowing stick and continued listening as Blue Jacket recounted the victory over General Harmar and his Shemanese. It had, indeed, been a fine victory and Tecumseh commended the Maykujay chief on his leadership.

Blue Jacket smiled, acknowledging the compliment with pleasure. He, too, lighted a pipe and then he faced Tecumseh again, his countenance serious. "I have my own thoughts about it, but I would like to have yours, Tecumseh," he said. "Do you think they will come again?"

Peripherally, Tecumseh saw that his nephew was looking at him intently, but he kept his eyes on Blue Jacket. "I think, Weh-yeh-pih-ehr-sehn-wah," he said slowly, "that not only will they return, they will come with a larger and much stronger army than before, and perhaps a better leader."

"I hope they don't," Spemica Lawba blurted, then dropped his eyes for having the temerity to speak without being recognized.

"We all hope they don't," Blue Jacket responded dryly, "but our reasons may differ from yours. Would it be because you lived with them for some time that you now wish they would not attack again?"

The youth raised his head and looked at the chief directly, a faintly smoldering defiance in his eyes. "I do not hate them," he said. "I wish they would stay where they are and we where we are and that there could be peace between us. They are not all bad people."

"No people," Tecumseh put in, faintly amused, "are all bad; just as none are all good. From what you have told us, the General Logan who took you was a good man. I do not know if he wishes to have our land, but the Shemanese mostly do and we must oppose this."

Spemica Lawba nodded miserably. "I understand that, but I do not wish to fight against General Logan. I have told him I would never do so."

"It was a promise you should not have made," Blue Jacket said, an edge to his words.

"But one," Tecumseh said, speaking to the chief, "that a person of honor would have made; that you would have made, Blue Jacket, or I, under similar circumstances." He turned his gaze to his nephew. "I hope the time may never come when you will encounter him in war."

There was a small lapse in the conversation and then Tecumseh spoke again, this time to Blue Jacket. "You leave in the morning?"

The Maykujay chief nodded. "I will meet with the Detroit Commandant, Major Smith. If we are to successfully oppose the next army the Shemanese send against us, we will need help from the British."

[November 10, 1790 — Wednesday]

Great honor had attended Chaubenee on his arrival back in Pimitoui. Not only his own village turned out to honor him, but groups of Potawatomies from other villages far distant. Two days after his return he had married Canoku. A week after that the great feast in his honor was held. Black Partridge and a band from Chicago came, as did young Chief Gomo from Peoria Lake and Nescotnemeg from the Kankakee River. A huge feast was prepared in Chaubenee's honor. Word of his exploits among the Cherokees had long preceded him and the vastly expanded respect bestowed upon him now was extremely gratifying.

Today a council was being held and speaker after speaker had risen to extol the courage of their son who had gone away a boy and returned not just a man, but as a warrior among warriors. Hanokula, elderly chief of the village, was last to speak. So crippled was he with the ailments of old age that he had to lean upon his staff as he spoke and his voice was a croaky whisper.

"I have always been a warrior," he said. "In my youth I won great honors and excelled beyond those with whom I lived and for this I was finally made a chief. At that time I said that when a warrior rose among us who was as I was then, to him I would give over my chieftainship. This one," he pointed a long, bony finger at Chaubenee, "is such a one — not only as I was then, but even more. From this day forward, he is your chief."

Chaubenee was thunderstruck, having had no inkling that this would occur. Born an Ottawa he was now, at nineteen, the youngest village chief any Potawatomi village had ever had. He rose and expressed his gratitude to Hanokula and then spoke at length of what had happened during his absence from Pimitoui. And what he spoke of most was a Shawnee warrior whose name was Tecumseh.

[November 14, 1790 — Sunday]

Major John Smith, commanding officer of His Majesty's post at Detroit, studied the tall Indian who had addressed him. Blue Jacket, he had been informed, was believed to be a white who had been adopted by the Shawnees as a youth and had risen to become a powerful chief in the nation. Although he had to admit the Shawnee's command of English was marvelous, Smith discounted the story.[91]

Blue Jacket had appealed to him very convincingly for help in the large engagement to come next year with the Americans. The chief did not equivocate in his comments, nor cloak his thoughts in the metaphoric phraseology so common to Indian orators. The words he spoke were, in fact, disconcertingly direct.

"Whether or not you are willing to admit it, Major," Blue Jacket had said, "you are dependent upon us for the continuance of the trade you enjoy in the Northwest. We, the Shawnees, are closest to the Americans and bear the brunt of every incursion into the Ohio country. The Miamis are next and they are under Michikiniqua — the one you call Little Turtle — and they sometimes help us fend the Shemanese off. The Potawatomies are next, but they are far from the Americans. They have suffered few losses to them and are only halfway in their help to us. Some bands support us, such as those near Detroit and those on the St. Joseph, but others prefer to remain aloof. We continue to ask their help but do not know if we will get it. Whether or not we do, help from you must be given or the British — and their trade — will be eliminated from the Northwest."

Major Smith was impressed. The same thoughts in different words had been relayed to him by a committee of the merchants and traders of Detroit. Theirs was a business which depended on Northwest commerce and which brought to British coffers annually over one hundred fifty thousand pounds sterling. Already two trading posts — Peter Loramie's and John Kinzie's — had been lost to the Americans. Kinzie still had another post at the mouth of the Auglaize, but the losses had occurred and they *were* important. The recent invasion by General Harmar's army — despite the fact that he had been defeated and forced to retreat back to the Ohio River — had tremendously alarmed the Detroit traders. Now, here was this Shawnee chief underlining the problems which lay ahead if British help were not provided.

"You have given us some guns and ammunition," Blue Jacket had continued, "and supplies of food and blankets and fabric. But what we need most is support by men. Armies! Give us soldiers and officers and artillery. Support us, just as you wish us to support your interests in our territory. This I can say," he was frowning as he concluded, "if you do not help us, then we will be forced to abandon our homes and withdraw beyond the Mississippi."

Now, with Blue Jacket standing before him awaiting his response, John Smith tried to find the proper words. He had no authority to commit British forces to such an end, yet was painfully aware of the need to do so; just as he was painfully aware that if he did, it could easily provoke a new war with the Americans and, on a personally more important level, be the ruination of Major John Smith's military career.

"Chief Blue Jacket," he said at last, "you must protect the barrier between the white and red people and you must not forsake the trade that links us together in amity and interest. I have the utmost sympathy for the position and needs of the Shawnees in this matter and I commend you for the brilliant defense you made of your country. I will give you whatever support it is in my power to give and I will relay your words to your great father, the King, for his consideration and direction. You have stated your right to the country you are defending. You are the best judges of the rights by which you hold your lands. Your country, you say, has not been given away. You cannot then be blameable in being unanimous to defend it."

Blue Jacket frowned even more deeply, not entirely sure what Major Smith was saying . . . or not saying. "Your words," he said slowly, "circle like soaring birds which never land. I will try to catch them and take them back for my people to hear. I will take the weapons and ammunition you have given us and those they will understand. We will wait to see what *your* great father, the King, has to say. And we expect he will help his Indian children as they have helped him."

[*December 6, 1790 — Monday*]

John Kinzie knew, without knowing how he knew, that he would never recover from what had happened to him today.

Early this morning he and Margaret had risen and bathed — even though they had taken their usual weekly baths on Saturday — and dressed in their finest. They had spoken little to one another during their preparations, but that was not unusual; they rarely spoke much to one another these days. Somehow their conversation, however pleasantly begun, always degenerated to an argument and it was simpler not to converse much at all. After eating the breakfast prepared by the black cook, Athena, and leaving two-and-a-half-year-old William in her care, they got into the carriage that had been readied for them by Henry, Athena's husband, and headed for Grosse Pointe.

As a rule, John did not care much for weddings and parties and avoided them if he could, but he had given his word that he would attend today, so attend he would. And, after all, William Forsyth, Jr., was his stepbrother and it would have been a serious breach of etiquette to refuse to attend without good reason.

The air was sparkling clear and bright this morning, the temperature well above freezing, and, as they moved into the outskirts of Detroit, Henry's whip snapped cheerily, putting the horse into a smart trot.

They pulled up in front of the gracious Forsyth home at ten o'clock, among the last of the guests to arrive. John's mother, Emily Forsyth, met them at the front door, welcomed John with a lukewarm hug and pecking kiss on the cheek and condescended to give Margaret a frosty smile and briefly touched her hand. Behind her stood John's stepfather, William Forsyth, Sr., who stepped forward and greeted both with considerably more cordiality than his wife had shown. At fifty-one he looked hale and prosperous and was obviously pleased at the prospect of his son's wedding to be performed in this house, scheduled to begin within the hour.

John handed the black houseman a carefully wrapped package to place on a table with the other wedding gifts. Inside was a tray he had made of heavy silver, its rim a lacy filigree of intricate craftsmanship, the handles perfectly matching sections of highly polished elk antler and the name *Forsyth* in exquisite script engraved in the center of the highly burnished surface. On the back side, in very small letters, was his usual signature block — a hollow rectangle within which was engraved: *J. Kinzie — Shawneeawkee—1790.*

"Come along," John's stepfather told them, moving between them and linking arms with both. "I want to introduce you to the lady who will soon be the newest member of the Forsyth family."

The large drawing room to which he led them was crowded with guests in splendid array. Included among them was John's partner, John Clark, and his pregnant wife, Elizabeth, John's sister-in-law. Many of the guests greeted the Kinzies as they threaded their way through the milling people to where William Jr. stood with his bride-to-be. She was a lovely girl of sixteen, wearing a beautiful gown of antique ivory lace — the same gown her mother had worn when she was married and which, nearly five years ago, her sister had worn for her wedding in the house of the bride's parents, hardly half a mile from here.

William Sr. gave the bride-to-be a courtly bow and took her hand. "Maggie," he said, "I'd like you to meet my stepson, John Kinzie, and his wife, Margaret." He turned to them. "Margaret . . . John . . . this is Maggie Lytle. Actually, another Margaret."

Margaret Kinzie took the girl's hand and squeezed it, smiling. "Welcome to the family, dear. You look lovely." She turned her gaze to her husband's stepbrother and nodded. "Hello, Will. Congratulations. She's just beautiful."

John took her hand and kissed the back of it and grinned. "I echo those sentiments," he said sincerely. "Will, you have my congratulations and best wishes." He shook his stepbrother's hand warmly.

"Thank you," Maggie said. She was blushing and bore little resemblance now to the child of four who had crept barefoot through the brier field with her brother Tom to escape the Senecas. "I've heard about you from Will," she continued, "and it's a pleasure to meet you at last. Both of you. I'd like to introduce you to my family." She turned to the cluster of people standing to one side. "My parents," she said, "Sarah and John Lytle, who live just a short distance from here. My brothers, Harrison and Tom. And this is my sister, Nelly — Eleanor — and her husband, Captain Dan McKillip, from New Settlement."

In turn as they had been introduced, the Kinzies shook hands and murmured pleasantries. As they came to the McKillips, John automatically bowed and kissed her hand and then looked fully into the face of Eleanor Lytle McKillip. Without warning his ears were ringing and his heart was thudding at an accelerated pace. His expression froze in the smile he wore and a small part of his mind was warning that he was making a complete ass of himself, but evidently no one else noticed. Eleanor McKillip was the most strikingly beautiful woman he had ever seen and the impact of meeting her eyes was as if he had been hit with a club. His body continued to function, he greeted her pleasantly and shook hands with her officer husband, but his mind was in turmoil. No one, ever before, had affected him this way and he was simultaneously confused, excited, stunned and enthralled. He wanted nothing more than merely to stand and gaze at her but that, of course, was not possible.

The rest of the morning's activities were wholly a blur to him. The wedding went off well and the luncheon reception which followed was a gala affair with music and dancing and laughter. And somehow, during the course of it all, he found himself dancing with Eleanor, cursing himself for his clumsiness, wanting desperately to talk but not knowing what to say, heady with the feel of her in his arms and the scent of her hair in his nostrils.

As they danced she told him about the McKillip property at New Settlement, where her husband eventually expected to spend his days as a gentleman farmer following retirement from His Majesty's service, and where he would grow grapes and apples and peaches. She indicated, with a slight movement of her head, the black woman who was their slave, now sitting quietly in a chair near the door, holding the little bundle of bunting which contained Margaret, six-month-old daughter of the McKillips. She asked Kinzie about himself and his life as a trader, but John Kinzie hardly heard a word she was saying and found himself all but tongue-tied. Eventually, he heard himself say something, he didn't even know what, and saw her throw back her head in bubbling laughter that thrilled him. He found it interesting that she had been a captive of the Senecas for so long and found himself telling her about Margaret's captivity among the Shawnees, though he didn't wish to be talking about Margaret at all. It was as he was talking to her that she looked him full in the face and he realized that he had made a mistake a little while ago; he had thought no one had noticed how he was feeling when he first met Eleanor. Now he knew someone else had. Her eyes locked with his for a moment; just one brief, fleeting moment, but it was enough. What he felt so powerfully within himself, he saw reflected in her.

Then they were apart and it was over. But John Kinzie knew it was not over, that something had changed and that he would never really be the same again. And somehow he felt that she, too, was experiencing this.

In mid-afternoon the bride and groom, clad now in common dress, climbed into their carriage and left amid the calls of well-wishers, heading first for Detroit where the ferry would carry them across the river to Sandwich.[92] This was where they would set up housekeeping in the little cottage he had bought. The pause now, however, would be brief; simply to drop off the wedding gifts and pack some luggage for the trip east on the carriage road across the Ontario Peninsula and, ultimately, to the great falls of the Niagara River.

The guests dispersed in their own carriages then and John Kinzie caught a fleeting glimpse of Captain and Mrs. McKillip, their slave woman and the baby behind them, moving away in a carriage drawn by a matched pair of well-groomed high-stepping carriage horses. Less than half an hour later, having said their goodbyes to the family, John and Margaret set off for the return home, lapsing again into the silence of toleration. John was still full of thoughts of Eleanor McKillip and now facing the futility of it. She was married — evidently happily — and he was married and they each had a child. There was no way their futures could ever intermingle.

Back at the Forsyth house, as the servants were cleaning up, William Forsyth, Sr. decided he was not feeling especially well. He attributed it to the excitement of the day and to eating too much rich food and drinking too many brandies. He told Emily he was going to take a little nap and went upstairs to the bedroom, kicked off his shoes and stretched out fully clad atop the bed.

He closed his eyes and quietly died.

And just at this moment, two hundred eighty miles west at Chicago, another pair of newlyweds had just reached their destination. Susanne and Jean Baptiste Pelletier stepped out of their canoe on the north bank of the Chicago River and walked to the house of her father, where they would live in their own quarters upstairs. They were met at the door and effusively welcomed by the bride's mother and father, Gohna and Jean Baptiste Point du Sable.

[*June 2, 1791 — Thursday*]

"Well, Ann, we made it."

John Whistler, thirty-three, could hear the relief in his own voice and felt a wash of embarrassment at it. But, by damn, it *was* a hazardous trip down the Ohio and the fact that Cincinnati was now directly before them on the north shore and they had floated all the way down from Fort Pitt without having seen one Indian made no difference. He was sure that had he been alone, the possibility of danger would have been of little concern, but with Ann in his care and their ten-year-old William standing here with them, it was another matter.

He was unalterably determined that when they marched out against the tribes under General St. Clair's banner, he would not take them along. A good many of the officers — and ordinary soldiers as well — would be letting their families follow along behind, as was customary, but he was opposed to this on a number of counts. To begin with, while permitted, it was generally discouraged. Second, he did not like the idea of Ann and the children traveling in the company of the unattached women who were professional campfollowers. Third, Ann was pregnant again and that could cause problems. Finally, despite the confidence normally exhibited by an army at the outset of its expedition, there was always the possibility that they could suffer a disastrous attack by the enemy and, if so, the women and children following could be in grave jeopardy.

"You'll probably think this is silly," Ann replied, "but I'm impressed. I really like the looks of it."

The town beyond the pier they were approaching was neatly laid out in squares, with wide streets along which people were strolling and carriages rolled. Rows of storefronts were visible, along with at least a couple of churches. While many of the buildings were of log construction, a surprising number were built of red brick, giving an essence of solidity that reminded them of Hagerstown. At the wharves, huge rafts were being loaded or unloaded. Hogs squealed and cattle bellowed and here and there children raced through the streets playing their games and laughing. And looming as the largest single structure of all was their destination: the massive, palisaded installation called Fort Washington.

Whistler slipped his arm about Ann's waist and hugged her close to him. "We've come a long way to get here, Annie. A long way." He knew she thought he meant the journey down the Ohio, along which several score of travelers had been killed by Indians just since river travel had opened this past spring. Actually, he was thinking back a great deal further than that, remembering the chain of events since boyhood that had brought him here as an officer in an army he had once fought.

Born in Ireland to Jane and Ralph Whistler in 1758, John had spent his first seventeen years in the countryside close to Ulster, working interminably as a young boy in the rolling fields of flax, harvesting the tall, blue-flowered plants, stripping away the leaves and soaking and then beating the long stems to free the silken bast fibers for the mills at Ulster, where they would be spun into fine linen thread. It was a grueling, depressing existence, from which he vowed he would escape at the first opportunity. That opportunity came with the revolution of the Crown's colonies in America. In 1776, at the age of eighteen, he had left home and enlisted in the army. A year later, as part of General John Burgoyne's army, he was surrendered to the Americans at Saratoga and confined as prisoner of war for over two years.

Finally paroled as part of a prisoner exchange, with the proviso that he nevermore serve in the British army during this war against the United States, he was shipped with a large number of other prisoners to London in 1780. Footloose and twenty-two, he roamed about in the largest and most exciting metropolis he had ever seen, vaguely planning to go back to Ulster one of these days to visit his parents. He never did. Instead, he had met Ann Bishop, eighteen-year-old daughter of a baronet, Sir Edward Bishop, and they had fallen in love. Sir Edward violently opposed the match and so they had simply eloped and, with Ann's funds, bought passage to the United States.

Eventually they took up residence in Hagerstown, Maryland, became American citizens and settled down to a quiet life there. John had worked at a variety of jobs to support himself and his rapidly growing family — William was born in the summer of '81, the first of their present six children — but he wasn't happy at that time. His service in the British army had whetted his appetite for a military life. The Indian War in the Northwest intrigued him and he talked long hours with Ann before she agreed to his idea of enlisting in the American army, but only if he took her and the children with him to whatever post he was assigned. She would not tolerate being left behind.

So here they were, on the heels of General Harmar's disgraceful defeat, arriving at his newly assigned post, Fort Washington, and eager for the expedition being planned by St. Clair. They were only part of the hundreds of soldiers and their families who were assembling at the frontier outpost. No longer was there any hope of peace with the tribes; now the only answer was to crush them, since all attempts at negotiation with them this past spring had failed and the Indians, being well supplied with British goods, had grown intolerably arrogant.

At last, with river attacks again on the increase, Congress had — practically coincident with Vermont becoming the fourteenth state on March 4 — appropriated over $300,000 to finance another Indian campaign. At once President Washington, through Secretary of War Henry Knox, ordered St. Clair to build up a large force. As soon as it was ready — tentatively by August 1 — he was to lead them northward from Fort Washington, stopping at intervals to build a series of intermediate posts until a final strong installation was erected at the head of the Maumee River at Miamitown, where Harmar's force had burned the British trading post and destroyed the villages and crops and then was ignominiously defeated by a mere handful of the Indians under Little Turtle and Blue Jacket.

"Right over there," one of the boatmen said importantly, coming up to the Whistlers as they stood at the rail, "only two months ago, they was a party of Potawatomies come an' kilt a couple fellers jest come from Fort Pitt like we done." He was pointing across the Ohio to the mouth of the Licking River. "K'n you imagine that? Right there, in broad daylight, practic'ly under ol' St. Clair's nose. That's how bold these goddamn red niggers has got! 'Bout time Congress got up off its ass — 'scuse me, ma'am — an' *done* somethin'." He spat a stream of brown juice into the muddy water below.

"*That* close?" Ann's voice squeaked and she was immediately angry at herself. Little William's eyes grew round and he murmured "Gee!" His father frowned, glad the other children were in the cabin, but the boatman was undaunted.

"Yep," he went on, "done kilt 'em an' took their sculps an' off they went in them bitsy boats o' theirs an' they wa'n't no way anybody was gonna ketch 'em. St. Clair, he sent out a squad after 'em, but they mought jest as well've stayed ho—" He broke off as the boat thumped against the pier, then tossed them a wave and ran to his duties.

Half an hour later, Ensign John Whistler stepped up to a desk in the small room, snapped a salute with military precision at the somewhat corpulent individual who sat behind it and said, "General St. Clair, sir! Ensign John Whistler reporting for duty."

[*July 29, 1791 — Friday*]

Eleanor McKillip seldom had an opportunity to visit her sister since Maggie married Will Forsyth. In fact, this was only the second time and both young women were taking full advantage of it, happily gossiping and bringing one another up to date on all the news either of them knew, while Eleanor's year-old daughter, Margaret, slept soundly on the bed in an adjoining room. Little Margaret had been named after Eleanor's sister, but they never referred to her by the nickname of Maggie. The little house here in Sandwich was snug and bright and it was so good being with Maggie again. Will was in Detroit, taking care of the inn he had inherited, and Maggie complained lightly about never seeing enough of him these days.

At twenty-one, Eleanor was a truly stunning young woman, her complexion glowing and flawless, her dark hair nearly waist-length and falling in soft natural waves. She laughed frequently, exposing a set of very white, almost perfect teeth, one of the upper incisors slightly at an angle to the other. The calico bodice she wore stretched tautly over full breasts and bunched at her narrow waist, while the ankle-length dark blue skirt flaired over full hips and hid long, well-shaped legs.

There was a considerable difference between the sisters, at least physically. Though they were much alike in temperament and their rippling laughter nearly identical, Maggie was inches shorter and had become plump. She had laughed and put both hands on her stomach and shook her head when Eleanor asked if she were pregnant. "No, Nelly, I'm not. I'm just getting fat from good living. Are you?"

"Heavens, no! Though not that Dan hasn't been working at it. One of these days, I suppose. Can't say I'm all that sure that I really want to have another baby."

"Oh, Nelly!" Maggie was shocked. "Of course you do. What a silly thing to say. Little Margaret," she inclined her head toward the bedroom, "has got to have a brother or sister to play with."

Eleanor shook her head. "Not so silly. Dan says it looks like we're shaping up for war again. The Indians are demanding that they be reinforced with troops from Detroit. If that happens, Dan's pretty sure he'll have to go. I wouldn't like that very much. It certainly wouldn't be any time to have a baby."

"But how could we do that?" Maggie protested. "I mean reinforce the Indians. Wouldn't that mean war with the United States?"

Eleanor shrugged. "Dan thinks so, but evidently the higher-ups don't. Dan says their thinking is that if they send troops with the Indians in a sort of advisory capacity, it'll satisfy the Indians into thinking they are getting help from the British army, but at the same time will not constitute an aggressive act against the Americans." The words were parroted, as if she had heard them often enough to store them verbatim in her memory. She shrugged again and her lips turned downward. "It's all so stupid," she added. "Grown men playing at their intrigues and marching about like little lead soldiers, as if it were all nothing but games. Ugh!" She reached into the little basket on the table between them and extracted a flat biscuit and nibbled at it. "Enough on that," she sighed. "I get very tired of it all. Tell me what else is new." She seemed to be hoping for something specific, unspoken.

Maggie put a finger to her chin and thought for a moment, then abruptly brightened. "Oh, I know! Remember Elizabeth Clark?" When Eleanor looked blank, the younger sister went on. "She was at my wedding. The one with the dark hair? Oh, you remember — the one who had been a captive of the Shawnees for so many years. Margaret Kinzie's sister. Remember?"

Eleanor McKillip nodded slowly, not really remembering Elizabeth Clark, but certainly remembering Margaret Kinzie . . . and her husband. "Oh, yes, I guess both the sisters were captives."

"Those are the ones! Anyway, Elizabeth is married to John Kinzie's partner, John Clark. They had a baby girl born last spring sometime. They named her Elizabeth, too. But the funny thing is, that was only four or five months ago and already she's pregnant again. Or at least she thinks she is. I saw her last week when Will and I went into Detroit together and stopped off at Kinzie's trading post."

Eleanor couldn't help herself. "Did you see John Kinzie?"

Maggie shook her head while biting into a biscuit, then talked around the food. "No, he was off in the wilds somewhere with Tom. Way out toward that Chicago place, I think."

"Tom?"

"Tom Forsyth. Where in the world are you, Nelly? Tom is Will's half brother. My half brother-in-law, if there is such a thing. John Kinzie's half brother, too." She hadn't seemed to notice Eleanor's particular interest and rattled on. "Anyway, John's been training Tom in the trade for the past few years and now he's taken him on as a full partner. So now it's Kinzie, Clark and Forsyth, Fur Traders."

"How long will they be gone?"

For the first time Maggie looked at her sister with a speculative glint in her eye. "My, when did you get so interested in the fur trade? Or is it silversmithing?" She giggled and, when Eleanor didn't respond, continued. "I don't know. A long time, I guess. Since John had his store at Miami-town burned down by the Americans, he's been considering starting two or three other posts more out of their reach. At least that's what Will says. He may start one way over west on the St. Joseph where Mr. Burnett has his post. Chicago's another place he's considering, and then another one way south of there at some place called Peoria Lake or Lake Peoria or something like that. I guess the idea is to put Tom in charge of one of the new posts when it's finished."

They continued talking about other things then, Eleanor refraining from any further mention of John Kinzie. But she didn't refrain from thinking about him.

[*September 1, 1791 — Thursday*]

This was the day of the big meeting and little Rebekah Wells was tremendously excited.[93] Imagine, meeting an uncle she had never met before; an uncle everyone thought was dead until just a month or so ago, and now here he was coming to meet them!

It had all begun when her father had been on the return of the little expedition up the Wabash with General Charles Scott. Colonel Samuel Wells was one of his principal officers and they had moved swiftly up the river from Vincennes in a mounted force, prepared to flee instantly if they encountered a superior force, but equally prepared to wreak havoc on any small parties of Indians encountered.

The principal targets had been several Indian towns — Kickapoo, Potawatomi and Miami — in the vicinity of the mouth of the Tippecanoe River, one hundred forty miles upstream from Vincennes. The largest of these was the village called Kithtippecanoe. They had been fortunate. Most of the warriors were away when the strike was made; the villages, including Kithtippecanoe, were destroyed and fifty-eight women and children were rounded up as captives and marched away under guard a day ahead of the army, toward Cincinnati. One of those captured at Kithtippecanoe was Wanagapeth, daughter of Michikiniqua and wife of the red-headed warrior called Apekonit, adopted son of that chief.

Almost immediately a deputation of Miamis bearing a white flag overtook the column. They were a party of chiefs of the Wea and Piankeshaw subtribes of the Miami and the man who was with them to act as interpreter was Apekonit.[94] They wished to sue for peace, no longer willing to butt their heads under the banner of Michikiniqua against the Americans. They came now with Michikiniqua's blessing; he would not force them to fight if their hearts did not will them to do so, and he even sent his adopted son to act as a go-between for them with the Americans. They would need somebody who knew the Miamis intimately, yet could speak English, and Apekonit was the logical choice. Neither Apekonit nor Michikiniqua knew yet of the capture of Wanagapeth.

As the peace conference was in session, Colonel Samuel Wells had begun to take particular notice of this interpreter. Obviously, he was Indian, despite the red hair; yet there was such a paradoxically strange familiarity about him. General Scott had wound up agreeing to the peace the Piankeshaws and Weas sued for, advising that they return to their villages and remain at peace, not raising the tomahawk again with the tribes who would encourage them to join against the Americans. Throughout the tedious speeches, to which Colonel Wells was now giving scant attention, he studied the interpreter. Apekonit's red hair, his manner of speech, his gesticulations all were so nigglingly familiar. The man seemed to be in his early twenties, but still Colonel Wells could not draw the connection. Then, at one point where this emissary sent by Little Turtle felt the Indians were being exploited, he had become excited. His voice had become somewhat shrill in controlled anger, a vein pulsed at his temple and he blinked his eyes rapidly — a singular reaction. And, abruptly, Samuel Wells *knew*. He could scarcely believe it and immediately upon conclusion of the council he approached Apekonit off to the side.

"You are Apekonit, son of Little Turtle?"

The Indian looked at him levelly. "Son of Michikiniqua, yes," he said, "the one you call Little Turtle."

"Are you his adopted son?"

Apekonit stared at him a long moment and then bobbed his head. "I am. Michikiniqua has been my father since I was a little boy. Before him, my adopted father was Gaviahatte — the one whom you call the Porcupine."

"And before that? You *are* white, aren't you?"

The reply came even more slowly this time. "I am Indian. Miami. I once was white but my white blood was washed away."

Samuel Wells scrubbed at his chin with the back of his hand and then took the plunge. "Was your name," he asked softly, "William Wells?"

The subtle arrogance in Apekonit's mien oozed away and he blinked rapidly, as he always had when nervous or excited. He licked his lips and looked more closely at the white man, staring at him. "Yes," he said.

"And I," said the white man, "am Samuel Wells. I am your older brother, William. I thought . . . we all thought you were dead."[95]

The two men had talked long into the night and, though Apekonit believed with part of his mind that what the man said was true, another part argued that this was merely a trick. The white man was insisting he come to Louisville and meet his family — his wife, Mary, and his little daughter, Rebekah — but it might be no more than a ruse to take him unaware and hold him captive for bargaining with Michikiniqua.

At last he stood up and looked directly at the white man who claimed to be his brother. "I go now," he said, "back to my father. But one thing first. If you are my white brother, then you know that there were other brothers. What were their names?"

Samuel Wells stood up. "Hayden, Carty and Jonathan," he replied.

"Does Jonathan still live?"

"Yes. He is still in Kentucky, near where you were captured as a boy. He is married and has children."

"Then I will say this: you could have heard these things from others. I do not yet accept that you are my brother, but you may be. I will know when I see the one called Jonathan. I will come to the Spaylaywitheepi at the falls on the first day of your month of September. I will not come alone. I will have warriors to protect me if this should be a Shemanese trick. I will remain on the north bank. You will come across with the one you say is our brother Jonathan. Then I will know. That is all I have to say."

He turned and was gone in the darkness. Now it was the morning of the day he said he would come to the north bank of the Ohio. The family had listened in awe and delight to Samuel's account and Rebekah demanded, as only a determined little girl can of her father, to be taken along to the meeting. At first she had been refused: only her father and Uncle Jonathan would go. But she had worn him down at last and now she was in the boat nearing the north bank, just below the Falls. Far to their right, a mile or more distant, they could just barely make out Fort Finney, but no people were visible there. Downstream to their left the broad gravel bank ended in a tangled jungle of trees and as they scraped ashore and Uncle Jonathan dropped his oar to leap out and pull the boat farther onto the gravel, a party of about twenty horsemen emerged from the trees,

Apekonit in the fore. All were well armed with rifles and tomahawks.

The Indians stopped and, at a signal from Apekonit, remained in place as he came forward and dropped lightly from his horse a dozen feet from the Wells party. Rebekah looked at him, then at her father and uncle, then back at the Indian. She had promised she would be quiet and not speak unless spoken to, but if Rebekah Wells was anything, she was a head-strong little girl. Now she abruptly broke away from the two men and clattered over the stones toward the man in buckskins.

"Uncle William! *Uncle William!* It's really you!"

She gripped him with both arms around the waist, squeezing hard, and Apekonit stood there a moment taken wholly aback. The two white men were as stunned as he. The immediate shock passed and Apekonit placed his hand on the little girl's head and gently stroked her hair. Just as gently he disengaged her grip, took her by the hand and led her back to the two men. He stood regarding them, pointedly ignoring their out-stretched hands. He gave the faintest of nods of recognition to Samuel and then turned his eyes on the younger man.

Jonathan Wells, at twenty-four, was an obese individual with genial features, but his smile was not reflected in Apekonit's expression. The adopted son of Michikiniqua addressed him flatly.

"You call yourself Jonathan Wells?"

"Aye."

"I had a brother once named Jonathan. He and I and my older brother," he glanced at Samuel, "used to swim in a pond near a town. What was the town and what was it about the pond that attracted us?"

Jonathan smiled. "The town was Jacob's Creek," he replied, "in Penn-sylvania. We lived on the edge of it — the western edge — and if we walked about a mile farther we came to the pond. It had rocky edges and was clear and a good place to swim, but what we liked most about it was a big willow tree with two branches that stretched far out over the water. We would walk out on them and jump from one branch to another, even though we had been warned not to do this. Sometimes we would jump back and forth together and try to make each other fall into the water below, which often happened."

Apekonit nodded, still expressionless. His voice remained flat. "One day my brother Jonathan did something that made me angry. I don't remember what. I only remember that I picked up a rock and threw it at him. He tried to duck away but it hit him here," he put his hand to the back of his head, "and hurt him. It made a deep cut and he bled a lot and I was punished when we took him home."

"Ayc," Jonathan said, "I remember it."

"Remembering is not enough," Apekonit said shortly. "Turn around. Show me the back of your head."

Jonathan paused, then did as bade. Apekonit stepped forward and parted the hair on the back of the man's head. A white, crescent-shaped scar was there and now Apekonit stepped back and he was smiling. He squatted, placed an arm around Rebekah's waist and looked at Samuel. "I am glad to know that such a pretty little girl is my brother's daughter."

They talked for a while longer, Samuel and Jonathan urging him to come back to the white world lost to him seven years before, but he shook his head. "I am William Wells," he admitted, "and your brother, but I have an Indian father named Michikiniqua and his daughter is my wife. Her name is Wanagapeth — what you would call A-Sweet-Breeze. She was among the women and children," he added, points of anger flickering in his eyes, "who were captured at Kithtippecanoe by your brave army, who attacked when the warriors were absent. I must get her back before anything is decided. It would be hard for me to turn my back to her or to Michikiniqua or to my adopted people."

He kissed Rebekah on the cheek and stood up. In succession he shook hands and hugged his brothers, then moved back and leaped up onto his horse. He raised his hand, palm forward. "We are not finished," he told them. "I will come back to visit from time to time. Goodbye, Samuel. Goodbye, Jonathan. Goodbye, Rebekah." He was blinking.

He dropped his arm and spun his horse around and clattered back across the rocks to the other warriors. He did not pause when he reached them, but swept past with a high-pitched yell. They fell in behind him and in a moment the forest had swallowed them.

[*August 24, 1791 — Wednesday*]

Ever since the British had conquered Canada from the French some three decades ago, the territory as far west as Montreal had been known as Canada East, and the portion above the Great Lakes and beyond as Canada West. Today that was changed, as the area above the Great Lakes and westward would hereafter be called the Province of Upper Canada, while that bordering the St. Lawrence to the Atlantic would be Lower Canada.

The Indians of the Great Lakes cared little about what the British called the territory, but they were keenly interested in the man who was newly appointed as lieutenant governor of Upper Canada — a highly self-assured British officer of the Revolution, thirty-nine-year-old John Graves Simcoe. Their interest was intensified by the fact that he seemed to be a man who was concerned about their welfare and who was prepared to help them.

Actually, his devotion was exclusively to the Crown and he was much more interested in how the Indians could help the British in the west than vice versa. Simcoe was convinced that his government expected an early

renewal of the war with the Americans that had been curtailed by the
Treaty of Paris. He was quite equally convinced that the real objective of
the Americans in the west was Detroit and that the only way to defend
that strategically important post was to erect an advance post between it
and the Americans, who he believed would be invading from the south.
The most ideal location for that post, he reasoned, would be on the
Maumee River a short distance up from Lake Erie near the foot of the
extensive rapids. He therefore ordered construction of a strong fortification there, named after the tribe at its headwaters and after the fact that
the Indians called the river the Miami-of-the-Lake. The new post would
be called Fort Miami.[96]

The Indians were overjoyed, certain this meant the British planned to
provide them with active support in the major confrontation shaping up
against the large force General St. Clair was preparing at Cincinnati. John
Graves Simcoe made no effort to disabuse them of their misconception.

[September 30, 1791 — Friday]

There had never been a moment of doubt in the mind of William Henry
Harrison that he was going to go very far in his lifetime. He was filled with
a great ambition to do important things; had been filled with this ambition,
in fact, since earliest boyhood. That he had been born into a wealthy
family and was the son of an extremely influential man was no liability
and he did not hesitate a moment to take advantage of it whenever it
could serve him.

Young Harrison had set his sights on a military career — a decision
that had caused Benjamin Harrison no small amount of concern, since he
envisioned his son becoming a doctor. Even when the elder Harrison had
first married Elizabeth Bassett and long before William's birth of February 9, 1773, he talked of how his son would one day be a great physician.
He had always been quite certain he would father a son. William had
learned early to muffle his militaristic ambitions, since Benjamin Harrison
was a forceful man, but he felt that a day would come when he would
have to have a showdown with his father. In the fall of 1787, William had
dutifully entered Hampden-Sidney College, remaining there until last year
when he entered medical school in Philadelphia. But then earlier this year,
Benjamin Harrison had died and the unpleasant prospect of a confrontation in regard to career was permanently averted.

Young William had no compunction whatever about using his father's
influence and the wealth he had inherited to get what he wanted. A close
friend of George Washington, the elder Harrison had been a member of
the Virginia legislature for thirty-three years and of the Continental Congress for four. He had been one of the signers of the Declaration of
Independence and governor of Virginia for two years. So William left

school immediately, presented himself to President Washington and asked to be given a commission in the army of the United States. The boon was granted.

Now, everything was a matter of haste. A major expedition was shaping up at Fort Washington far off on the Northwest frontier and William was afire with the need to be part of it, so he could begin at once to prove his abilities. He knew that when he presented himself to General St. Clair as a presidentially appointed ensign of the United States Tenth Regiment, his career would be well and truly launched.

CHAPTER V

[*October 22, 1791 — Saturday*]

TECUMSEH was no less brilliant as a spy than he had proven himself to be as a warrior. For several weeks, working out of a secluded camp in the hills a few miles away from Cincinnati, he had watched the buildup of American military forces at Fort Washington. He had with him a party of eight warriors, including his good friend Wasegoboah, husband of his sister, Tecumapese. But the other seven served not so much as spies as they did runners, bearing the intelligence Tecumseh and Wasegoboah uncovered to the leaders of the newly strengthened Indian confederacy, Michikiniqua and Blue Jacket.

Wasegoboah ranged about the outskirts of this large settlement on the Spaylaywitheepi, keeping out of sight but noting all movements of troops, especially those coming downriver as reinforcements. Tecumseh's task was far more dangerous. Donning Shemanese clothing taken in previous raids, with his long hair concealed beneath a wide-brimmed leather hat, day after day he would suddenly appear casually walking down the streets of Cincinnati. Wasegoboah had wanted to accompany him, but Tecumseh had gently refused him.

"I understand English," he told his friend. "I speak it quite well, thanks to Sinnanatha, and can even read it. You have almost no knowledge of it. What would you do if stopped and questioned by the Shemanese? No, my friend, your task is to watch along the edges and it is no less important than my own."

So Tecumseh walked at random throughout the fledgling city, pausing as the citizens did, to read notices posted on walls, responding with "Good morning," or "Good afternoon," to passersby who greeted him. On four different occasions he actually entered the walls of Fort Washington. The first of these times his heart had been hammering wildly as he approached the sentries at the wide-open gate. Soldiers and citizens had been passing back and forth through the portal in fair numbers and he simply fell in a few feet behind a small group of citizens who were entering. The nervousness he felt so strongly was not apparent in his actions or expression. One of the guards gave him a searching glance and he smiled broadly at the man, tossed a careless wave in his direction and murmured, "Scout." The guard had returned the smile and waved him in. Moving from point to point within the fort as if he were on specific errands, Tecumseh inspected the entire installation closely. He paused to read the General Orders that had been posted, briefly watched soldiers being drilled on the parade ground and developed the habit of stopping to tie a shoe or pretend to read a paper in his hand close to wherever men were engaged in conversation, in an effort to eavesdrop.

By his fourth entry into Fort Washington, the gate sentries had become so accustomed to his comings and goings that they scarcely paid any attention to him. The amount of information he gathered, both visually and through eavesdropping, was amazing and every two or three days a runner would be dispatched from the secluded camp to carry the new intelligence to Blue Jacket and Michikiniqua.

St. Clair, Tecumseh learned, had expected to have all his supplies and three thousand men ready to march by the first of August, but not half the expected troops had arrived and no one was able to discover why supplies supposed to have been forwarded from Fort Pitt had been so badly delayed. Time after time a date was set for the march to begin and as often it had been deferred to a later date in the hope that supplies and troops would arrive. St. Clair became increasingly short-tempered as days became weeks without his requisitions being filled. He knew he could delay only so long and then would have to begin the march or be hamstrung by the winter season.

At last he could afford to wait no longer. On September 17 he formed his men and led them northward, leaving orders with the skeleton garrison left behind to forward troops and supplies by forced marches as soon as they arrived. Tecumseh, cheering along with the spectator citizens as the troops marched out of Cincinnati, closely noted numbers and weapons of the army. St. Clair had not only expected three thousand troops, fully four-fifths of them were to have been regular U.S. Army troops. Instead, he was leaving with only seven hundred ten regular officers and soldiers, plus six hundred ninety militiamen drafted largely from Kentucky. The latter moved along grudgingly, on hand only because the law required them to be and having little confidence in their commanding officer, who had virtually no experience in Indian fighting. In addition to the fourteen hundred troops, some four hundred civilians tagged along behind, mainly wives and children of the soldiers, along with a large number of prostitutes who always followed such a force.

Tecumseh slipped away, returned to his camp and alerted his warriors to leave. Fortunately, Wasegoboah was in camp and so they mounted their horses, sent an express off with the news of the march having commenced, and then flanked the army, pacing it but keeping out of sight. Twenty-three miles north of Cincinnati, at the crossing of the Great Miami River, St. Clair called a halt and, in keeping with his orders from the war department, ordered the erection of an installation to be called Fort Hamilton.[97]

Morale degenerated and discontent increased in the army, largely because St. Clair was adamant in his refusal to share the inadequate food supplies of the army with the camp followers. When the fort was completed and named, St. Clair set the army in motion again, leaving twenty men to garrison the new installation. At this point almost half of the camp followers lost their taste for the venture and started back to Cincinnati.

It was during last night and this morning that events occurred which thrilled Tecumseh and caused a considerable change of plans. Early in the morning yesterday, the army had stopped forty-four miles north of Fort Hamilton and St. Clair had ordered the construction of a second fort close to where two inconsequential little streams merged.[98] No man was considered exempt from the work, including officers and including even St. Clair himself. With thirteen hundred eighty men cutting timbers, trimming them, digging, sinking palings and other necessary work, a serviceable little fortification was completed by nightfall. It was named Fort Jefferson.

During the night, Tecumseh and his party watched — with a faint apprehension at first, which quickly changed to elation — as three hundred of the militia quietly arose in a carefully planned maneuver, slipped out of camp and hastened away at top speed in the direction they had come. It was obvious they were deserting. To make matters even better, when St. Clair discovered the desertion in the morning, he was furious and ordered a detachment of one hundred forty regulars under Major John Hamtramck to pursue them. Thus, with twenty men left to garrison Fort Hamilton, another twenty to garrison Fort Jefferson, three hundred deserted and one hundred forty in pursuit of the deserters, St. Clair's original strength of fourteen hundred men had now dwindled to a total of nine hundred twenty.

So important was this occurrence that Tecumseh ordered his men to continue their surveillance and mounted his fine black horse. "This time," he told them, "I will carry the news!"

[*November 2, 1791 — Wednesday*]

Ensign William Henry Harrison was deeply chagrined and dejected. Newly arrived at Fort Washington, he had been politely informed that General St. Clair had marched his army north fifteen days before his arrival. By this time he was no doubt at or very near the head of the Maumee and probably giving the Indians the worst whipping they had ever received.

He began asking questions and quickly ascertained that not only had the army left at less than half the expected strength, but with supplies so short that almost immediately the whole army had been put on half-rations. Supplies and reinforcements supposed to have come and been forwarded had still not shown up. Worst of all, a company of regulars under Major Hamtramck had returned to Fort Washington less than a week ago in pursuit of some three hundred militiamen who had deserted. The deserters, Hamtramck had reported, skirted Fort Hamilton on their return and evidently broke up and scattered as they neared Cincinnati. Efforts were now being made in Kentucky to round them up.

William Henry Harrison did a rapid calculation in his head, considered the state of St. Clair's army and felt a shiver run up his back. A deep sense of foreboding swept through him and suddenly he was very relieved that he had arrived too late to be included in the expedition.

[*November 4, 1791 — Friday*]

Dawn.

Chaubenee crouched behind the fallen tree and shivered. It was cold and a heavy snow covered the ground, but neither of these was the cause of his trembling. It was excitement — the most overwhelming excitement he had ever experienced — that made his nerve endings feel electric. Beside him crouched Tecumseh, his head cocked to one side, awaiting the signal. Wasegoboah was just beyond him and there were others — so many others! Never before had so many Indians of so many different tribal affiliations assembled under single leadership to attack the whites and he was proud to be a part of it, proud to be a chief who could lead his own warriors into an encounter so fraught with the potential for victory.

Chaubenee remembered with utmost clarity when the party of runners from Michikiniqua and Blue Jacket had come to his own village of Pimitoui with the urgent call for chiefs and warriors to assemble in the Ohio country on the Maumee River at the mouth of the Auglaize. There was word that there would be extensive support from the British and that the force of Indians to oppose the Americans would not be one numbering in the hundreds, but in the *thousands!* Similar parties of runners, they had been told, were at this moment on identical missions to every village within three hundred miles or more.

So he had arrived at the mouth of the Auglaize with his forty warriors, and others had come from all directions — Ottawas and Chippewas from as far away as Mackinac; Winnebagoes from the valley of the Wisconsin River; Sacs and Foxes from the Mississippi; Potawatomies from Milwaukie, Chicago, Peoria Lake, the Kankakee and St. Joseph and Elkhart Rivers; Miamis, Weas, Piankeshaws and Eel Rivers from the upper Wabash and Mississinewa and Maumee valleys; Kickapoos from the southern and central Illinois country and the lower Wabash; Delawares

from scattered villages in central and northern Indiana Territory; Shaw-
nees from the valleys of the Great Miami, Mad, Auglaize and Maumee
Rivers; Wyandots from the Sandusky River; even some Mohawks and
Senecas from western New York.

The greatest council most of them had ever known — comprised of
over three thousand Indians — assembled within sight of the Shawneeawkee Trading Post and, to aid the Indians, John Kinzie donated gratis
most of the supplies he had on hand. The council reaffirmed Michikiniqua
as principal chief of the combined Indian forces, with Blue Jacket as
second in command. Under the leadership of these two, other noted chiefs
would command their own warriors: Tarhe — the Crane — with his
Wyandots; Topenebe, Mtamins, Gomo, Chaubenee, Main Poche, Black
Partridge and even Siggenauk with their respective Potawatomies; Pipe
with the Delawares; Kasahda and Otussa with the Ottawas . . . and the
roster went on and on.

Agents of the British had come as well, from their new post called Fort
Miami, at the foot of the Maumee Rapids — Simon Girty, Alexander
McKee, Matthew Elliott and others. There were arms and ammunition,
they said, in the King's Store there, and a strong garrison of soldiers. The
impression was strongly given that these would be made available to their
red brothers, but somehow they never really said it. No one seemed to
notice. Speeches had been given by the various chiefs and strategy
planned. It was felt that the Americans under St. Clair should be allowed
to reach the headwaters of the Maumee, where Miamitown had been, and
then the Indians would fall upon them. But now Tecumseh had changed
that.

Michikiniqua, now nearly fifty, rose from where he had been seated
with Apekonit, close to the council fire. Both still harbored a great anger
and sorrow that Wanagapeth remained a captive of the Americans.
Michikiniqua held up both arms and a hush fell over the assemblage.

"My brothers!" he said, his strong voice ringing clear in the crisp air.
"Our British brother, Simon Girty, told us a short while ago that he has
seen many armies of brave warriors before, but never one so large nor so
courageous. To that I would add, never one so determined to crush the
whites who invade our lands and take away our women and children!"

A roar of approval had swept the crowd and Little Turtle waited for
silence to settle upon them again before continuing. "In these weeks past
we have sent out eyes to watch the movements of the Shemanese chief
called St. Clair. Because of the courage and skill of the young Shawnee
warrior, Tecumseh, son of Pucksinwah, we have known each move of the
Shemancsc and their strengths and weaknesses. The protective hand of the
Great Spirit had covered Tecumseh, for he walked among them, read their
words and listened to their secret meetings without detection. He sent

runners flying to us with all he learned and we have been able to plan to meet the enemy. Now he has flown to us himself with the best words yet brought. He sits among us now, there," he pointed toward the Shawnee contingent, "with his chiefs Catahecassa and Weh-yeh-pih-ehr-sehn-wah, and I would ask him now to stand before you and tell you what he has learned and what we should now do, with which I am in full agreement."

Michikiniqua turned and walked toward the Shawnees and Tecumseh, seated between Black Hoof and Blue Jacket, came lithely to his feet and met him. The Miami chief gripped his hand and wrist with his own hands and Tecumseh accepted the honor with pleasure. He escorted Little Turtle back to his seat beside Apekonit and then faced the largest audience he had ever addressed — the first major council he had ever addressed.

There was an aura of strength in his bearing and power in his words as he spoke and his listeners seemed transfixed. Chaubenee, seated with his own contingent of Potawatomies, had felt it many times before and once again he experienced that overwhelming surge of admiration and respect this twenty-three-year-old Shawnee evoked. Others who had never seen nor heard of him before seemed similarly affected.

"Brothers! I bring news that will be short in the telling, but immensely important in its meaning. The Shemanese general, St. Clair, was preparing to bring a force against us of three thousand soldiers, both Blue Coats and soldiers from across the Spaylaywitheepi. But his chiefs far to the east have failed him and when he left Fort Washington, where the Spaylay-witheepi makes its northern bend, he had less than half the soldiers planned. His supplies failed to reach him and so he marched with only half enough and his men are hungry and discouraged. He built two forts and had to leave men to guard them. Then, in the middle of the night, three hundred of his white chickens flew away and so he sent nearly half that many Blue Coats to chase them and bring them back and continued his own march north. He is now very weak, with just over nine hundred men — only a third part of the number of warriors assembled here."

He paused as an excited murmur rippled through the crowd, then spoke again as it died. "Brothers! The Blue Coats he sent to chase those who fled from him may come back. The hundreds of other soldiers he has expected may arrive at Fort Washington with the supplies and all these may be sent on to him. But they could not reach him as quickly as we! They move slowly, even when in haste, and if we ride against him now — this day! — we will find him still weak, still hungry and without defense in the place where the Wabash can be leaped across by a horse. We cannot afford to wait until they reach the place where the warriors under Michikiniqua and Weh-yeh-pih-ehr-sehn-wah defeated them during the last harvest moon. By then his belly may be filled and his weak arms strengthened. No! Brothers, we must move to cut him off, *now!*"

The Indians leaped to their feet, shrieking war cries and roaring approval to what Tecumseh had said. There was a little more talk, from both Blue Jacket and Little Turtle, but not much. Within four hours, their faces garishly painted in red and white, yellow and black, the entire Indian force set out.

Snow had fallen yesterday and today and most of the Indians had wrapped themselves in blankets and heavy buffalo coats atop their usual winter garments. Later yesterday they had arrived within three miles of the Wabash headwaters and here they pitched a cold camp, without fire and without food. The fast was upon them now and they would not eat again until the battle had been fought. But confidence filled their bellies and the fever of war heated their blood and warmed them.

The Indian spies still under Wasegoboah came in soon after camp was established and their news was good. St. Clair's army had seen no relief since Tecumseh had left. They had continued the march north, moving slowly in the growing chill, then slowed even more by the snowfall. This very afternoon as the sun was setting they had ground to a halt on the south bank of the Wabash where it was narrow enough for a horse to leap across.[99] It was precisely the place where Tecumseh had said they would find the army and this was the first time most of the warriors had experienced Tecumseh's prophetic ability. They were greatly impressed, even awed.

Wasegoboah reported that where the army had bogged down, something strange had happened. Always before whenever the American armies had stopped for the night in dangerous territory, they had immediately erected breastworks of logs and branches as a protection in case of attack. This time they had not done so. They had not even moved what wagons they had with them into a line behind which they could take cover. The wagons merely stood where they had stopped, in helter-skelter pattern. The soldiers had literally dropped in their tracks, entirely fatigued. Some built small fires, but most merely curled up to sleep, their bellies empty. Again — another ripple of wonder spread through the Indian encampment — Tecumseh's prediction had come to pass: the army of Shemanese was weak and hungry and *without defense!*

So auspicious were the signs that many of the warriors, especially the Sacs, Winnebagoes and Kickapoos, wished to leap to the attack immediately, but Michikiniqua and Weh-yeh-pih-ehr-sehn-wah stayed them. "We must wait," Blue Jacket said, "until the dawn. We are so many that if we try to attack them in the dark of night, we will hurt one another even as we try to hurt the enemy. Beyond this, at the dawn the Shemanese will be coldest and in least command of their wits and their confusion will become our ally."

So now they were in position and waiting about a quarter-mile from the

Shemanese and Chaubenee trembled again in anticipation. As he had done a dozen times or more already, he checked his weapons again. His flintlock rifle was primed and ready and the butts of two flintlock pistols projected from his waistband. A tomahawk was firm against his right hip and a scalping knife in its sheath at the left. He glanced over at Tecumseh and smiled when he saw that the only weapons the Shawnee carried were the war club and scalping knife given to him by Chiksika so long ago. Yet, Chaubenee was sure that in what lay ahead, Tecumseh would probably down far more enemies than he.

Chaubenee's smile grew more wistful as he thought of Canoku in their lodge at Pimitoui. He wished he could feel the warmth of her closeness beside him now, yearned to bury his face between her breasts and feel the firm swell of them against his cheeks, the smooth flesh of her body beneath his hands. Somehow he knew that she, too, was awake this night; that she, too, knew that something very important for her man was in the offing.

Two hours before dawn they became aware of an advance guard of sentries moving toward them and hunched down even more. It seemed they would turn and go back toward the camp as they had once before earlier this night, but then something happened. There was a brief rattle of gunfire from the whites, firing toward a spot where no Indians were positioned. The firing ceased and the whites clustered together a moment, but there was no answering fire. It seemed that they decided they had been firing at shadows, for their postures relaxed and they turned and retraced their trail in the snow, resuming their patrol.

A detachment of three Ottawa scouts sent out to spy upon the camp came in an hour later and reported that there was movement among the Shemanese. Their general was walking among them, long-knife in hand and shouting commands, and the men were rising. Still the Indians held their place. At last the naked trees began to etch crooked black lines against the growing mean gray of approaching daylight in the east.

"HAAAaaaaaahhh!"

The shriek of Michikiniqua's voice broke the eerie stillness far to the left and was instantly echoed by a similar cry from Blue Jacket on their right. In that moment the entire Indian force erupted in a cacophony of hideous cries and plunged to the attack. The forward guard of the Americans, encountered first and totally demoralized, scarcely without firing a shot dropped their weapons and fled in panic to the camp, plunging across the narrow Wabash and screaming with pure terror. Their panic was a contagion that within instants infected the whole army, crashing it into a state of fatal confusion.

As the charging Indians neared the stream, the Americans rallied enough to check them momentarily with a hot fire, but not for long. The

American commander was screaming for the artillery to open fire, but the powder was defective and only two cannon fired, neither of which did any serious damage to the attackers. Immediately the Indians attacked the artillery with their greatest firepower, flintlocks firing in a staccato din lasting several minutes. As it died away, all the artillerymen had been killed or were dying.

Chaubenee stayed as near Tecumseh as he could, determined to protect him from any danger approaching unseen. He had difficulty keeping up. The young Shawnee was an incredible fighting machine, downing soldier after soldier with his club, leaping with abandon from one clash to another in vicious hand-to-hand battle. The thuds of clubs against flesh, the cries of the injured and dying, the frenzied screams of the horses and the overpowering din of thousands of screeching Indians was a crescendo beyond mere description. Chaubenee had become separated from Tecumseh and devoted his whole attention to killing others and keeping himself alive.

St. Clair's army was in terrible straits and the problems intensified with each passing moment. There were eight cannon, but not only was the cannon powder so defective it would hardly ignite, it had been packed in mislabeled kegs marked "For the Infantry." Boxes marked "Flints" were found to contain gunlocks. Confusion and panic grew and men ran in circles, crying, or stood slack-jawed and paralyzed with fear, watching death approach. Not only soldiers were being killed. The wives and children and prostitutes that had been following the army were cut down as they tried to flee, no more than a handful of the over two hundred escaping. The snow became a scarlet slush and bodies were everywhere.

Ensign John Whistler, in the midst of defending himself, caught a glimpse of the slaughter of camp followers and murmured a brief prayer of thanks that he had not allowed Annie and the children to come along. Even as he thought this, a tomahawk swung at his head missed its mark and laid open his shoulder to the bone, wedging there. As the Indian struggled to jerk it loose, the officer brought his pistol up under the man's chin and fired. John Whistler didn't even look as the man went down, only surged away as best he could, the tomahawk still embedded in his shoulder.

The red-haired Apekonit had been given the responsibility by Michikiniqua to take a detachment of three hundred warriors and silence the eight cannon. It was his attack that had been so effective and all the big guns were now in his possession. He triumphantly carried the news back to Michikiniqua and then stayed within a few feet of his adopted father, despite the difficulty it involved, twice killing soldiers who would surely have slain the Indian commander had he not been there. With prearranged calls, Michikiniqua and Blue Jacket — the latter coated with blood, but not a drop of it his own — drew the Indians into another attack force, simultaneously hitting the rear and both flanks of the army and mowing down whole windrows of soldiers.

Of the British who accompanied the Indian force, only Simon Girty took part in the actual fighting, clad and painted like an Indian and unrecognizable as anything else by the Americans. Already half-a-dozen men had fallen to his gun and tomahawk.

For over three hours the battle had been fought. The whites remaining who were capable of fighting clustered near their commander in the midst of their encampment, desperately trying to hide behind overturned wagons, dead horses or even the bodies of their own companions. There was now only one hope remaining. St. Clair, hobbling painfully about on gout-ridden legs, gave the order for retreat and the whole of the surviving whites capable of doing so rushed en masse and broke through the line of Indians who had cut off their rear. They dropped their rifles and threw off their greatcoats to make better speed and ran with the breath of the devil at their heels. Wounded companions were left behind, still vainly trying to hold their own.

Under orders of Michikiniqua, who had his runners pass the word, "You must be satisfied — you have killed enough," the Indians did not pursue. Together Blue Jacket and Little Turtle held the warriors at the scene of battle and gradually the din faded. Sporadic shots and screams of the dying being tomahawked continued for a considerable while, but by noon it was all over. No living enemy whites were left on the field and those who fled had long since disappeared.

The scalping began in earnest then. Some of the warriors had scalped their foes as they downed them but others, such as Tecumseh and Chaubenee, had merely struck and struck again. A horde of squaws who had accompanied the warriors and remained hidden in the woods during the battle emerged now and joined in the business of scalping and gathering up weapons and supplies that had belonged to the dead or were discarded by those who fled. The bodies were stripped of shoes and clothing and left naked and bare-skulled on the stained snow. The eight cannon, too large to be taken away in the deep snow, were carefully submerged in a deep hole in the Wabash for safekeeping and later recovery for possible use against their former owners.

Michikiniqua ordered a careful search for any dead or wounded Indians. A total of sixty-six were found dead and tenderly wrapped in shrouding made of the army's abandoned tent canvas. They were tied to horses to be brought back to their villages or to a burial place away from here. Oddly, only nine Indians had been wounded. Of these, only one seemed likely to die.

By mid-afternoon they were moving off, horses staggering under the weight of the plunder they were carrying. Late in the day, as the dull gray that had persisted deepened into a gloomy twilight, a new snowfall began, mercifully coating the red mire with fresh white and covering the ghastly, grotesquely contorted bodies of eight hundred thirty-two dead American soldiers and camp followers.[100]

[*January 10, 1792 — Wednesday*]

On the whole, John Kinzie tried to steer clear of politics and his nationalism was only moderate at best. His primary wish was simply to be left alone to conduct his Indian trade in his own quiet way. Yet the swirl of politics and nationalism had a way of enveloping him and causing problems.

Now, for the first time, he was really angry with British authority. In donating virtually all his supplies to the Indians at his Auglaize post prior to their march against the Americans under St. Clair, he had cut deeply into his own capital. At that time he had entered into discussions with both Alexander McKee and Matthew Elliott. Both had implied that if he gave the supplies to the Indians, he would be reimbursed by the Crown from the King's Store out of Detroit. Simon Girty had gone even further, declaring that not only would Kinzie get back what he had given the Indians, he would almost surely be substantially rewarded as well; the British Indian department would almost certainly make restitution to him for the destruction of his post at Miamitown.

When he had received an invitation to a special festivity to be held at the fort in Detroit today, John Kinzie was all but positive that he would at this time be given the restitution and reimbursement he felt he deserved. He went alone, knowing that Margaret would not want to go, not only because she was caring for their daughter, Elizabeth, born six months ago and named after Margaret's sister, but because Margaret had become very reclusive of late. Besides, since he expected the invitation to the fort was at least partially business, it would only bore her. As he had walked to the fort, he brought his thoughts into order concerning how much he thought he was due for the supplies he had given to the Indians at his Auglaize post. He didn't care if there were a reward for his act; he hadn't done it for reward. But he certainly expected to be recompensed for his losses.

He was not.

As a matter of fact, his losses had not even been mentioned and when he brought them up at last to the Detroit commander, he was curtly informed that his losses, both through the destruction of his post at Miamitown by Harmar and his donation of supplies to the Indian allies of the Crown, had been his own concern and the British government was neither responsible nor liable for any damage or restitution.

Kinzie accepted the ultimatum with outward calm, but inwardly he seethed, the anger smoldering behind his eyes over the injustice. He made a promise to himself that it would be a very cold day in hell before he would again attempt to aid British authority in any way. The resentment he had long smothered over the restrictions on trade imposed by the Crown and to which he was forced to accede now rose and galled him. He felt, for the first time, a wash of sympathy for those traders who operated in opposition to government trade regulations.

The festivities at the fort were mildly interesting. A large number of Indians had come and — sprinkling salt on John Kinzie's wounds — received a substantial quantity of gifts from the Crown for their tremendous victory over St. Clair only a couple of months ago. One highlight of the affair was presentation to the various chiefs of large brass medals on which were depicted profiles of King George on the obverse and the clasped hands of an Indian and British officer on the reverse. Especial recognition was bestowed upon Little Turtle and Blue Jacket for their signal leadership of the Indian forces against the Americans. Both chiefs were commissioned brigadier generals in His Majesty's service. Numerous speeches were delivered in which details of the great victory were recounted, along with descriptions of the sudden sharp increase of depredations by the Indians along the American frontier.

While these matters were of some interest to John Kinzie, they were hardly sufficient to mitigate the feelings of incense that still swirled within him. But there was one matter that made the whole day worthwhile. Among the invited guests to the affair was Captain Daniel McKillip, resplendent in his scarlet coat, gold epaulets, white breeches and shiny black boots. More important to the trader was the presence of the captain's lady, linked to his arm, clad in a royal blue dress over a host of petticoats, a fine beaver shawl wrapped about her and a dainty parasol held over her right shoulder and softening the glare of the sun on her classic features. As the couple passed near the trader, for just an instant — the space of three heartbeats — their eyes met. No special glance, no demure lower of the eyes, yet something — some wholly indefinable *something* — passing between them at that moment, gone so quickly that in retrospect only a minute later, Kinzie questioned in his own mind that it had been there. She was the most beautiful woman he had ever seen. She remained in his thoughts for a long while but it was not until considerably later that an impression received at the time but not consciously recognized then came back to him. The front of her blue dress had been notably mounded at the mid-point and it came to him that Eleanor McKillip was pregnant again. And John Kinzie was both amused and mildly chagrined at the ridiculous little charge of resentment that arose in him.

[*June 1, 1792 — Friday*]

While a court of inquiry had cleared Governor-General Arthur St. Clair of any responsibility in the matter of his terrible defeat by the Indians, it was significant that even after he was exonorated, command of the military in the Northwest Territory was placed by President Washington into the hands of a very able American officer of the Revolution — General Anthony Wayne.

From the young nation's new capital, Washington, District of Columbia — established only last year and relieving New York of that honor — the President, through his Secretary of War, instructed Wayne to carefully build up a strong army which would, once and for all, remove the Indian menace from the Northwestern frontier. The President was confident that if it could be done at all, then the man to do it was "Mad Anthony" Wayne — so nicknamed by his troops for his seeming rash courage. It gave an erroneous impression; Wayne was many things — courageous, sagacious, an excellent strategist. However, he was not rash.

At just about the same time, in Kentucky, now overrun with hit-and-run Indian attacks as an aftermath of the St. Clair defeat, a long and bitter political struggle had finally ended as a constitution was framed in Danville, modeled after the Constitution of the United States. And today Kentucky became the fifteenth state of the United States. In Lexington, the large log building widely known as the Sheaf of Wheat Tavern became the temporary statehouse and the new legislature was meeting here for its first session. A strong frontiersman-settler-politician was chosen by common consent as the state's first governor and his name was Isaac Shelby.

[*August 12, 1792* — *Sunday*]

Two months apart to the day, two babies — a boy and a girl — were born that were of more than passing note to John Kinzie. The first was the second child and first son of his business partner and his sister-in-law, John and Elizabeth McKenzie Clark, born on June 12 in their little house right next door to the Kinzie mansion in Detroit.[101]

The parents were very happy about having a son and gratefully accepted from the Kinzies their gift of a beautiful scroll-engraved silver cup fashioned by the man the Indians called Shawneeawkee. A space had been left within the intertwining wreaths for the addition of the name of the newborn and the silversmith-trader was both honored and pleased when they told him that this new son would be christened John Kinzie Clark.

The second birth occurred today — a healthy girl of almost nine pounds born to Daniel and Eleanor Lytle McKillip. They named her Jeanette.

[*September 30, 1792* — *Sunday*]

Colonel John Hardin was very pleased with himself, since today it seemed evident that he was on the threshold of accomplishing what all the previous American emissaries sent among the Indians had failed to do, and to accomplish in a very quiet way what the armies of both General Harmar and General St. Clair had been unable to enforce.

The two Shawnees who were now guiding him had been of great help, especially the young man whose Indian name he could not pronounce but who spoke enough English to make it understood that he was Little Blue Jacket, son of the powerful Shawnee war chief, Blue Jacket. The other man, a rather sour-faced, taciturn individual whose name translated into something like Whirling Dust — which Hardin further deduced probably meant Tornado — had hardly said ten words since their meeting, yet he had been very helpful in attending to Hardin's comfort when camp was made this evening.

"Tomorrow," Little Blue Jacket had said a short while ago as he turned in beside his older companion, "when sun straight up, we reach village of Catahecassa."

Hardin leaned back on bedding that had been unrolled on a matting of soft grasses opposite the fire from the two recumbent Shawnees. He stretched mightily and linked his fingers behind his head, staring straight up at the night sky liberally studded with stars. He wondered, with a wistful smile, if his wife, far to the south of here in Kentucky, were looking at these same stars. Thinking of his wife, he thought also of his son, Thomas, and his adopted daughter, Bluebird.

"Pskipahcah Ouiskelotha," he whispered aloud, then chuckled. That was the one Shawnee name he could pronounce and he said it again, slowly, phonetically, enjoying the way the syllables rolled off his tongue. "Puh-skip-uh-kah . . . Whis-kee-low-tha." What a nice name it was and what a darling girl. How well she had adapted herself to living with the Hardin family. He smiled mentally as he thought of how well Tom and Bluebird got along together. He toyed for a moment with the idea that as they grew older they might fall in love and marry, but immediately rejected that. No, he thought, it's more of a close brother-sister relationship and I guess it always will be. Anyway, Tom's so taken with Ben Logan's daughter there's probably not much doubt he'll eventually marry her. But Bluebird had brought such beauty and laughter to their lives!

Thought of Bluebird and how she had come into his family as a result of his participation in the Harmar campaign two years ago reminded him of his present mission. President Washington had personally commissioned him to take a peace proposal to the Shawnees. A similar peace proposal had been arranged with the Miamis on the Wabash some months ago by General Rufus Putnam at Vincennes, with William Wells acting as interpreter. The Miami women and children who were prisoners of the Americans were released at that time, including Wanagapeth, to the great joy and relief of William Wells. It was not known to very many, but part of the concession made by Wells to gain their release included divulging to

Putnam the location of the eight cannon from St. Clair's defeated army. He had done so in confidence and Putnam had secretly sent a detachment that had recovered them. A peace of sorts had then been signed, though the Miamis made it clear that they would not be in accord with white settlement north of the Spaylaywitheepi.

Since that time, the Americans had been relying heavily on Wells as both interpreter and go-between for further peace negotiations with Michikiniqua and the Kekionga Miamis and nearby Delawares. Wells was to report the results of his dangerous mission to Putnam at Marietta. For the risks he was taking, especially if it came out that he had been the one who enabled the Americans to recover their cannons, Wells was paid three hundred dollars and promised a further bonus of two hundred dollars if he could convince the hostile tribes to negotiate for peace. And Wells, it was rumored, was now very seriously considering renouncing his affiliations with the Miamis and returning to life among the whites.

Thinking about these things, Hardin gave a faint grunt. Now it was his responsibility to try to set up a similar treaty of peace with the Shawnees. True, Anthony Wayne was building up his army to crush them, if necessary, but if peace could be brought about diplomatically, how much better it would be.

So he had ridden north out of Cincinnati alone and had finally come here, only a few hours' ride from the Shawnee capital and its principal chief, Black Hoof — Catahecassa. The two warriors had approached him this morning, giving signs of peace when they saw his white flag attached to the saddle. He had talked to them — or at least to Little Blue Jacket — for a long time. He had finally made the young warrior understand and was excited when the Shawnee said Catahecassa had longed to have peace with the Americans and he was sure a treaty could be entered into immediately upon their arrival tomorrow. He grinned again as he considered what a coup it would be to return with news of a solid peace.

Hardin turned on his side, his back to the dying fire, and closed his eyes. In a few moments he was asleep. He would have been surprised had he known that the surly warrior he thought of as Tornado had immediately recognized him on their meeting as the Shemanese officer who had carried off Pskipahcah Ouiskelotha, daughter of his brother. But John Hardin never knew that, just as he never knew which of the two warriors rose silently during the night and buried a tomahawk to the hilt in his temple.[102]

[*April 21, 1793 — Sunday*]

A pall of depression that he could not seem to shake clung over John Kinzie. He knew the cause was the situation existing between Margaret and him, but he was wholly at a loss in respect to what he might do to correct it. It wasn't the sort of thing he was inclined to discuss with anyone else.

Except to visit her sister, Elizabeth Clark, next door, these days Margaret Kinzie almost never left their large home and no matter how much John tried to spark her interest in outside matters and help her come out of the shell into which she had retreated, nothing helped. His very presence seemed to aggravate her condition rather than alleviate it. He suspected that his frequent absences, often for weeks at a time, were at the root of the problem, but he couldn't help that. The very nature of his profession dictated that he often be away. Time and again he had invited her to accompany him, but she always refused, saying she'd had enough of Indians and the wilderness to last her a lifetime.

As the result of a great deal of hard work, John Kinzie had managed to recoup the losses suffered with the burning of his post by General Harmar at Miamitown and because of his own generosity to the Indians at the Auglaize post prior to their expedition against St. Clair. He did not take too seriously the comment made to him by at least half-a-dozen chiefs independently that for his faith in them, for his help to them when no one else seemed to care, they would never forget him and they would do everything in their power to help him. Actually, he did not feel that there was all that much they could do that would be of help to him apart from continuing to be customers at his trading posts. But, he had recovered financially now and he and Margaret were certainly more than comfortable. Certainly the slaves he had bought as house-servants freed her of any complaint she may have had concerning the drudgery of running a household. All that didn't seem to matter and he really didn't know what to do about her.

For her own part, Margaret Kinzie had little conception of just how hard her husband worked. She simply didn't care. Though only twenty-seven, she had become a harsh and bitter woman who looked nearly twice her age and was filled with hatred. She hated John's work, hated being a trader's wife, hated the Indian guests who often dropped by to see him, hated his frequent absences in the wilderness and hated it even more when he was at home. Their life together was without love and most of the time without even cordiality. Theirs was an existence of mutual toleration punctuated by fierce outbursts of childish anger on her part and, at such times, moody withdrawal on his.

The birth, two years ago, of their second child, Elizabeth, had changed nothing between them. Margaret had immediately become just as fanatically possessive of little Elizabeth as she was of their firstborn, William, who was now five years old and virtually a stranger to John. She did not want him anywhere near them and railed about his having a bad influence on them because of his contact with the Indians. At first he brushed aside her ridiculous objections and tried to get closer to the children — after all, they were his as much as hers — but she carried on to such extremes at those times that nowadays he kept his distance, trying to maintain a semblance of peace in their home and hoping that somehow her strange behavior would eventually pass. It did not.

Margaret Kinzie became most abusive of all to her husband when he came home from his trips with, as she distastefully put it, "the stink of red niggers all over you." With no basis for such a position, apart from the fact that she had heard other fur traders did it, she accused John of fornicating with Indian women whenever he was gone. No amount of denial on his part, however truthful, was acceptable to her. The result was that their sex life was no joy to either and participated in solely to relieve the carnal pressures he experienced, when he could no longer stand her refusals.

Today their third child was born, earlier than expected. John had left the house early and went to the wharf to supervise the loading of three bateaux destined for Montreal with a cargo of fine furs packed in bales. Now, in the middle of the afternoon, he learned of it when a boy sent by the midwife pressed a note into his hand. Returning home at once, he took the stairs two at a time and entered Margaret's bedroom to see her and his newest offspring. His wife was dozing, the new baby asleep beside her and mostly hidden by swaddling.

Elizabeth Clark was sitting in a chair beside the bed and she smiled nervously as John approached. He put an index finger to his lips and she nodded. She rose, tiptoed from the room, silently mouthing the words "It's a boy" as she passed him, and closed the door gently behind her.

John stood by the bed for a long while and then leaned over quietly and began to lift the flap of swaddling to see his new son's face. Though he made no sound whatever, Margaret's eyes snapped open and impaled him with malevolent glare. Instantly she jerked the infant away and screamed, "Get out!" The baby woke squalling at the rough handling and John Kinzie stared at her angrily, then spun around and left the room without a word. He grimly vowed, while descending the stairs, that never again would he cohabit with her.

Elizabeth was in the front hall, peering out at the street through the curtained door glass. She turned to face him as he reached the foot of the stairs. He thought she must surely have heared Margaret's outburst, and perhaps she had, but nothing in her expression verified this. She merely smiled brightly and her voice was light.

"His name is James," she said.

"How nice," he replied dryly. "Give him my regards as soon as he understands English." He walked past her and left the house.

[*June 22, 1793 — Saturday*]

"Father, I must speak with you."

Michikiniqua, seated in his lodge with members of his family, looked up at Apekonit, a smile forming on his lips as he saw that it was his adopted son who had just entered, but the expression as quickly fading when he saw the intensity with which he was being regarded. The younger man had only recently returned from a month-long sojourn with the Americans while serving as interpreter in the continuing peace negotiations.

"My son is troubled," Michikiniqua said. "Come, sit beside me and say what is in your heart. Has the new sun brought you ill news?"

Apekonit glanced at the others in the lodge — Michikiniqua's wife, her sister and her sister's husband and their children. He shook his head. "I ask that you come with me to the Big Elm."

Michikiniqua's brows drew together. This was evidently more serious than he imagined. The Big Elm, on the north bank of the Maumee two miles below the rebuilt village of Kekionga, was a place of special significance. The great old tree — no one had ever seen a larger elm — was over five feet in diameter and, towering one hundred twenty feet above the high bank from which it grew, was a notable landmark. On the grassy knoll beneath, councils of great importance had been held for a century or more, along with feasts and weddings . . . and meetings of more than ordinary importance between individuals. Without a word the principal chief of the Miamis rose and followed Apekonit to a canoe beached on the river bank.

They spoke no word to one another during the short trip downstream, nor as they ascended the high bank to the base of the tree. The new leaves above them had not yet reached full size, but still the lofty dome of the great tree formed a large canopy that rustled in the light breeze, as if the individual leaves whispered to one another of secret things overheard in the past and about to be imparted now.

The two men sat cross-legged on the grass facing one another and Apekonit waited with ingrained patience as his Indian father methodically opened his pouch, extracted pipe and kinnikinnick.[103] As the chief packed his long-stemmed, elaborately carved pipe, Apekonit gathered some dried grasses and tiny twigs within arm's reach, made a small pile of them atop a very dry punky material from his own pouch and struck a fire with flint and steel. In a few moments he held a burning stick to the bowl of Michikiniqua's pipe and then they simply sat quietly, sharing the pipe until it had burned out.

The reunion he had had with Samuel and Jonathan had preyed upon Apekonit's mind considerably and he had been very troubled in his own heart. He was amazed at the amount of affection he felt for his niece,

Rebekah. And now, after having worked diligently as interpreter and sometimes spy and informer for the Americans at Fort Washington and Fort Harmar, he had had ample opportunity to weigh matters in a new light. He was not a stupid man and it was very apparent to him that, despite the Indian victories over Harmar and St. Clair, it was only a matter of time until the whites overran and destroyed the Indians who had been opposing them. He had been offered full-time employment as interpreter and guide and the possibility had even been held out that he might become the American Indian agent to the Wabash and Maumee valley tribes, at a substantial salary. It was very tempting.

Apekonit had spent much of his month away from the tribe as a guest in the home of his brother Samuel, at Louisville, becoming more fully reacquainted with his family. Memories had been invoked which had long been buried, bringing to mind childhood scenes and pleasures. He found himself enjoying the way the white people cherished memories of past things and laid plans for the future; mental exercises that rarely found fertile soil in the minds of the Miamis.[104] Content though Wanagapeth might appear to be with her life, he wished more for her than being a beast of burden, which he realized fully now was the life of a Miami squaw almost without exception. Furthermore, he wished more for his two sons and two daughters than they could get here. He wanted them to be able to experience the order of civilized society rather than the chaotic and largely lawless and wild democracy of the Indians that was so often subject to wars, which he felt so strongly these days were the result of a craving for bloody conflict common to wild men and wild beasts. By being able to raise them in a comfortable, civilized manner for the present, but with substantial goals for the future, as he put it to himself in his thoughts, existence in such a white society would allow them to "lay up something for old age." He wanted to establish a farm and bring up his children there with the benefits of white society so that when he and Wanagapeth finally wore out with old age, they would have brought up children who would tenderly close their parents' eyes and lay them to rest. Apart from the tribe, he might be better able to eventually bring these desires to fruition.

Some of these thoughts Apekonit wanted to express to Michikiniqua now, yet he knew he would not truly be able to make Michikiniqua understand how he felt. His thoughts were interrupted by a killdeer running about on the gravel bank of the river uttering a startlingly loud *b'DEEEeee! b'DEEEee!* in the quiet morning air and, far above them, a circling hawk adding a series of its own slightly raucous high-pitched whistlings. Michikiniqua tapped the kinnikinnick residue out of his pipe's bowl and then sat with his hands folded in his lap, his eyes on the younger man. He was ready now to listen and the nod he gave was all but imperceptible.

"Father," Apekonit took the plunge, "today I leave you forever."

Michikiniqua's jaw set a little tighter but he said nothing. There was pain in his adopted son's eyes and voice as he continued:

"Many summers ago as a little white boy I was plucked from Kentucky by Gaviahatte and brought to my life among the Miamis. I have loved these people and there," he pointed to the waters of the Maumee rushing past the gravel bar below them, "was where later on my white blood was washed away and you adopted me as your son, as Gaviahatte had done before that. Since then you have been my father and I have loved you — and still love you — but now it is time for me to return to the people into whose world I was born.

"I have been brought to this," he went on, responding to Michikiniqua's unspoken question, "not because I no longer like my life among the Miamis and not because the Mad General is building a great army to come against us. Nor is it because I fear for myself or for Wanagapeth and my children. I do this because the visions have come in my sleep and told me that this is what I must do. You have watched me on three occasions leave our village to go to the Spaylaywitheepi at the Falls, once with our warriors behind me, twice alone. I have crossed the river and walked among the Shemanese and I have slept in the house of my white brother. Part of the reason I have done this has been the hope that through what I am able to do, I could help bring permanent peace between your people here and my people there. In some of this you have supported me and have even damaged your own reputation by advocating to the tribes that we sue for peace and learn to live in tranquillity with the whites.

"You were here," he went on, "when one moon past, the daughter of my brother returned here with me so that I could show her our way of life. Her name, as I told you then, was Rebekah and though she was only of twelve years, she feared you not when she stood before you, as you know. Our warriors escorted her home again when her stay here was finished and before she left she begged me to return to my own natural family. She is very dear to me and that is yet another reason for what I do now."

He paused and licked his lips, his eyes overbright and blinking rapidly. "When I take up my life with the Shemanese, I must not do so only part way. This you know. Their struggles must be my struggles, their enemies my enemies, their wars my wars. I must share their defeats and their victories, just as I have shared yours, without reservation. I must help them where I am able to help them, and I will be able to help them much because of what I have learned in my Indian life. This," for the first time his voice cracked a little, "makes me an enemy."

In Apekonit's long pause which came now, Michikiniqua spoke quietly. "What of my daughter and your wife, Wanagapeth, and your children, who are my grandchildren?"

The younger man shook his head. "They will remain here for now. I have given A-Sweet-Breeze her choice of coming with me or staying here with you and she has chosen to stay. Your grandchildren will stay with her and they will become your children. In this I am saddened, but so it must be. One day there may again be peace and then I will be able to return for little times to sleep again in your lodge and visit with you and with them and perhaps provide better lives for them than I can now. In whatever ways it will be possible for me to do it, I will help my Miami brothers and if peace should come, you and they will find my help of great value. But it is as I have said: I am now an enemy."

William Wells — for now he was no longer Apekonit — stood up and Michikiniqua also came to his feet. The chief put both arms forward, palms facing the sky, and Wells stepped closer, placed his own wrists in his former father's hands, gripping his wrists in return. They stood that way in silence for fully two minutes and during that time the cheeks of both men became wet. Then Wells broke their grip, stepped back and pointed up through the canopy of the great elm.

"My father, we have long been friends. I now leave you to go to my own people. You and I will remain friends until the sun sends his light straight down on top of the Big Elm. From that time we will be enemies and if you want to kill me then, you may. And if I want to kill you, I may. And if we want to remain true in our hearts to one another, even though we are on different sides, that, too, we may do. Goodbye, my father . . . my friend."

He turned and strode through the grass down the knoll and melted into the woods beyond without looking back. Long after he was gone and the *b'DEEEeee! b'DEEEeee!* of the killdeer came again from the gravel bank, Michikiniqua remained motionless, looking at the place where last he saw his adopted son.

[*July 1, 1794 — Tuesday*]

Preparation.

The year just past had been one of preparation by just about everyone, laced with skirmishes here and there which kept the pot boiling and convinced everybody that a major battle must soon be fought. But goad him as they might, the Indians could not get General Anthony Wayne to attack until he was ready. And now, at last, he was as ready as he could be. By the end of this month he planned to strike the Indians on the Maumee River.

In addition to a year of preparation, it had been a year of changes, sometimes broad but more often subtle and seemingly of little importance when they occurred. Each in its own right contributed sparks to an already highly volatile situation. Wayne's pace was geared to what it was possible for him to do with the force at hand as it was building.

At the strong recommendation of General Putnam, Wayne had hired

William Wells as interpreter, adviser and spy and very quickly came to rely upon him and respect his advice as fully as Putnam had done. Wells earnestly warned him that the Miami, Shawnee, Delaware and Potawatomi Indians were leaguing themselves more closely than before and were being supplied well with arms and ammunition by the British at Detroit. The former Miami warrior said he was convinced that full-scale war would soon break out on the entire frontier, from Canada to Georgia, with the aim of the Indians being to wholly destroy the white inhabitants of the frontier.

General Wayne listened to Wells's counsel and he strengthened Fort Hamilton and built an interim fortification between there and Fort Jefferson, naming it Fort St. Clair.[105] Then, moving on to a location five miles north of Fort Jefferson, he built a very strong fortification named Fort Greenville.[106] From here he sent out a detachment to bury the remains of the Americans killed at St. Clair's defeat two years previously and to build a fort on the site. The detachment collected and buried more than six hundred human skulls and many bones, although quite a few of the bones were scattered and gone. The fort was built, equipped with a small garrison and named Fort Recovery.[107]

It was about then that, as Wells had predicted would happen, Wayne was informed by the War Department of an American peace mission that had met with the Indians first at Niagara and then at Detroit; that the negotiations had broken down and he was given permission to attack the Indians. But Wayne was not yet ready. Winter was upon them and to attack then would be risky at best, so he put his army into winter quarters at Fort Greenville and continued to drill his men and get further reinforcements.

Michikiniqua led a party of Indians in harassment raids between Cincinnati and Fort Greenville, hoping to lure Wayne out, but the American general refused to take the bait. Even when Michikiniqua wiped out a supply train of fourteen men under Lieutenant John Lowry at a place called the Forty Foot Pitch at Ludlow's Springs, seven miles east of Fort St. Clair, Wayne, acting on Wells's advice, refused to expose his troops in retaliation and now, for the first time, Michikiniqua grew worried. He called a council of the confederated chiefs and addressed them very seriously, suggesting they reconsider making peace with the Americans. With victories behind them over Generals Harmar and St. Clair, the chiefs were shocked at Michikiniqua's words and accused him of cowardice. He hadn't even taken offense, but merely shook his head and continued.

"Yes," he told them, "it is as you say: we have beaten the enemy twice under separate commanders. But hear me! We cannot expect the same good fortune always. The Americans are now led by a chief who never sleeps. The night and day are alike to him and during all the time that he has been marching on our villages, notwithstanding the watchfulness of our young men, we have never been able to surprise him. There is something whispers to me that it would be prudent to listen to his offers of peace."

The chiefs would not have it and they deposed him, naming Blue Jacket of the Shawnees as sole commander of their force and with Pinequa — Turkey Foot — of the Potawatomies as his second in command. But things did not go terribly well for them. A force of a thousand Indians assembled at Kinzie's post at the mouth of the Auglaize, marched against Fort Recovery and fought a hard battle there. Though they killed fifty Americans and took three hundred horses, all of them knew they should have carried the place by storm very easily, with virtually no loss to themselves. That had not occurred and now their confidence was shaken.

One part of the reason why the Indians had been unable to surprise Wayne and wipe him out as they had St. Clair was the fact that "Mad Anthony" Wayne almost constantly had companies of spies going and coming, keeping him apprised of what was happening and acting accordingly. And the most dependable of these spies was twenty-four-year-old William Wells. Wayne kept close watch on him, at first to be sure the man was not a double agent and, later, because he was so impressed with the skill of Wells, not only in spying but in carrying out delicate and often very dangerous missions. Now, because of the fine service he had been rendering, William Wells was given the rank of captain by Wayne and placed in charge of the spy company, which was to report only to General Wayne himself. Wells immediately returned to Kekionga and convinced Wanagapeth to let him take her and the children to Louisville where they could stay with the family of his brother Samuel until the danger was past. With this seen to, he returned to Wayne at Fort Greenville and set up his spy company. It was a company whose authorized strength was sixty men, but which normally consisted of only twenty to thirty men chosen carefully by Wells for their knowledge of the Indians. Most, like himself, had at one time or another lived among the Indians.[108] It was Wells, in fact, who had alerted Wayne to the advance of the enemy against Fort Recovery and it was through the subsequent use there by the Americans of the artillery that Wells had helped them recover from the Wabash River that a much greater disaster had been prevented. It was Wells, too, who brought word of the completion by the British of Fort Miami at the foot of the Maumee Rapids, from which the Indians were being provisioned from the King's Store; and it was he who reported the sharp increase of British agitation among the Indians to make war on the Americans and their promises — sometimes implied but lately more overt — of solid British support when they should do so.

It was all intelligence Wayne was only too glad to receive, but the matter of Fort Miami was just one more headache in a string of events that was making things difficult. A large number of his reinforcements had reached Fort Washington and were just on the point of marching to join him when the Cincinnati garrison was struck by a smallpox epidemic that killed quite a few men and incapacitated about a third of the force. Yet Wayne did not despair. He trained his troops in war maneuvers practically every day, drilling them mercilessly and, though they grumbled a lot, he now had as fine a force of American fighting men as had ever been seen in the Northwest.

William Wells had been one of the definite pluses and Wayne's reliance on the man increased almost daily. Another asset for the general had been the appointment of a sharp young officer at Fort Washington as his aide-de-camp. He was an ensign who had proven himself a good leader during the construction of Fort St. Clair, which he oversaw. The new aide was William Henry Harrison.

[July 21, 1794 — Monday]

Until a fortnight ago, Jean Baptiste Point du Sable could not help but gloat over the sudden and rather unexplainable increase in white population near his trading post on the Chicago River. Since the ice broke up this past spring, upwards of thirty new arrivals had reached the Chicago area and decided to settle. Most were traders or in some way involved with the trade. A few sought employment from Du Sable as laborers, helping to move goods and boats across the Chicago Portage. He was sure that his dream of Chicago becoming an extremely important trading center was finally becoming reality.

Then, a couple of weeks ago, an epidemic of smallpox broke out and spread with great rapidity among the whites and Indians alike, mowing people down as wheat before a scythe. Even Potawatomi villages on the Illinois and Kankakee Rivers were hit. Somehow the Du Sable family was not stricken, but they were among the very few who were not. Before the epidemic had run its course, a dozen of the new arrivals died and no less than fifty of Black Partridge's Potawatomies had expired. The Chicago area had become a place of fear and mourning.

Now, at last, it seemed to be over. No more people were dying and some who had been stricken were recovering, but Chicago's brief term as a burgeoning settlement was short-lived. Once again the Du Sable and Ouilmette families were the only whites who remained. For the first time since his arrival here fifteen years ago, Du Sable felt thoroughly frustrated and his previously unshakable dream began to dim.

[July 28, 1794 — Monday]

The waiting was over.

The men were calling it "Bright Monday" and spirits were as high in

Wayne's army as they had ever been since the construction of Fort Green-ville. It had taken two full years for General Anthony Wayne to bring his army to strength, to change a motley collection of grizzled frontiersmen, nervous settlers and overeager youths into a well-disciplined fighting force, to make sure his supplies were plentiful and his supply line was strong. Now all that was behind. With the arrival of the sixteen hundred mounted Kentucky volunteers under General Charles Scott, the time for waiting and preparing was past.

Part of the reason for moving now stemmed from a successful spy patrol carried out by Captain William Wells and two of his men — Nicholas Miller and Robert McClellan — down the Auglaize River. A few miles from the mouth of the Auglaize, they caught a glimpse of smoke from a camp fire. Carefully they had crept up and found three Shawnees cooking their dinner. At a signal from Wells, the three men shot simultaneously. Two bullets struck the same Shawnee and killed him. The second man of the trio was struck by the third bullet and he, too, was killed. The third man immediately threw up his hands and surrendered, yelling *"Mat-tah tsi! Mat-tah tsi!"* — No kill! No kill! They rushed in and McClellan reached the Indian first and subdued him. Wells and Miller, who paused to scalp the two dead warriors, joined them and abruptly Miller burst into laughter. To the surpise of the others he threw his arms about the prisoner and lifted him clear of the ground in a great hug. It was his brother, Christian, who immediately threw in with them, vowing he was finished with the Indians. They took him to General Wayne and Christian Miller provided a great deal of extremely valuable information regarding the Indians' strength and encampments and the involvement of the British in their activities. Following the questioning, and with the approval of the commanding general, Wells made Christian Miller a member of his spy company.

So now, with the intelligence from Wells and Christian Miller in mind, Mad Anthony Wayne today mounted his horse and began to lead his thirty-five hundred well-armed, well-fed, combat-ready troops on their invasion into Indian territory, making diversive movements to left and right to confound the enemy. A halt was scheduled along the way to construct another intermediate fort on the upper Great Miami River where the old trading post of Peter Loramie had been located, and it amused Wayne to name it Fort Loramie, but the destination was the Maumee River. They would strike it at the mouth of the Auglaize where, according to Christian Miller, John Kinzie still had a trading post. That place, he said, was a primary assembly point for the Indians. General Wayne was determined to wipe it out and replace it with a strong American post. After that they could move down the Maumee to the foot of the rapids and ask the British at the new Fort Miami just what the hell they were doing there and by what right did they dare to erect a British post in United States territory?

And maybe — just maybe — the British there would be fools enough to oppose the American army.

[*August 1, 1794 — Friday*]

Colonel Richard England, in his headquarters at Detroit, sat behind his desk and studied the officer who stood at rigid attention before him. The captain was a good man, steady, reliable, a family man with devoted wife and children, capable of following orders to the letter and certainly discreet enough to carry out the mission now in mind which could not be entrusted to an officer who was in any degree rash or innovative. Now Colonel England leaned forward and smiled faintly at the officer.

"One more time, Captain," he said, "let me quickly go over what your verbal orders are, above and beyond the written orders you have already received. You will leave Detroit immediately with your detachment of one hundred men and march to the Maumee River. En route, you will make it a point to pass through or near the Indian villages along the way. At each you will pause briefly, present your respects, mine and His Majesty's, to the chief and give him the gifts of powder, lead, blankets, tobacco and vermilion as stipulated in the written orders.

"At the same time," the Detroit commander continued, "you will do all in your power, without actually saying it in so many words, to convince each chief that the force you are leading is destined to give them active military support in their campaign against General Wayne. You will equally give the impression that your company of men is only the first of many others that are to follow. You will impress upon the Indians that His Majesty expects the same strength and determination of them that they exhibited in their defeat of General St. Clair. You will commiserate with them over the fact that they have been forced to set Little Turtle aside, since he has chosen to become frightened at the prospect of meeting General Wayne in battle, but add that His Majesty has great confidence in Blue Jacket, upon whom he has conferred the rank of brigadier general."

Colonel England paused, twirling between his fingers the quill pen he had picked up from the surface of the desk. "Upon arrival at Fort Miami at the Maumee Rapids, you will immediately combine your own detachment with the existing garrison, send out word for the chiefs of the vicinity to assemble and you will then parade your combined force before them in a demonstration of strength. You are authorized to fire one round from each piece of artillery so as to stress the power you have on hand.

"Finally," he concluded, "you will supply their needs from the King's Store at Fort Miami and you may imply that regular troops from the fort will follow after them and support them in their clash with the Americans.

But," his tone of voice became stern, *"under no circumstances whatever are any of His Majesty's troops to march against General Wayne's army. Questions?"*

"No sir," the officer replied crisply.

"Excellent. You'll leave immediately. Dismissed."

"Yes sir! Thank you, sir." Captain Daniel McKillip backed up a few steps, gave his commander a smart salute, did an about-face and exited.

[*August 6, 1794 — Wednesday*]

Not entirely certain of the destination of General Wayne's army, John Kinzie was also not entirely sure what he should do. Some reports brought in by the Indian spies watching Wayne's movements said the Americans were en route to the head of the Maumee where they had destroyed Kinzie's trading post four years ago. Other reports said he was heading for the Maumee Rapids and was going to hit British Fort Miami. Yet another report — and the most disturbing so far as the trader was concerned — was that he would reach the Maumee right here at the mouth of the Auglaize.

Just in case the final report was correct, the trader gave orders to the men working for him. They, along with a dozen or more Potawatomies who were glad to lend help in exchange for some goods, loaded all his stores, supplies and equipment into seven bateaux. Then he waited nervously.

The wait was not long. The huge young Potawatomi chief named Chaubenee arrived only minutes ago with definite word that Wayne's army had camped on the Auglaize last night only six miles upstream from here, and was at this moment moving downstream with surprising speed. Chaubenee told Shawneeawkee to go at once if he wished to escape at all. With a sigh, John Kinzie shook his friend's hand, gave his boatmen the signal and began descending the Maumee. At the same time, also at Chaubenee's warning, the Indians were evacuating their own village only a few hundred yards away. There was a grim silence about the way it was all occurring.

The seven bateaux now were just over a mile downstream, with John Kinzie in the lead boat, when one of the boatmen two boats behind gave a loud shout.

"Mr. Kinzie, look!"

The trader turned and looked back in the direction the boatman was pointing. A heavy smudge of smoke was rising above the trees back in the direction of the trading post. Kinzie groaned. For the second time a post of his on the Maumee was being destroyed and now he vowed that he would not establish another along this river. At least this time, thanks to Chaubenee's timely warning, he had saved his goods. His initial plan, upon leaving the mouth of the Auglaize, had been to go down to the foot of the rapids and stop off at Fort Miami, but now he changed his mind. He'd had quite enough of this treacherous river valley. He cupped his mouth and called loudly enough for all his boatmen to hear:

"We're not stopping at the fort. We're moving directly to Detroit."

The boatmen cheered.

[August 12, 1794 — Tuesday]

From their hiding place beneath a tree that had fallen, wedged against another and formed a sort of natural lean-to, William Wells and his fellow spy, Robert McClellan, watched closely as the tableau unfolded less than a hundred yards away in the final rays of the sunset. Wells felt dizzy from pain and the loss of blood and he held his left wrist, where the rifle ball had gone through. Even though he'd plugged the hole well with a wad of buzzard feathers carried in a pouch for just that purpose and then coated it over with a handful of mud, blood still seeped from the wound and the initial numbness had gone, leaving waves of pain surging up his arm.

McClellan was, if anything, in worse shape than he. The ball he'd taken had ripped through his upper arm, shattering the humerus in its passage, four inches below the shoulder joint. He was in severe pain and had stuffed a rag into his own mouth to prevent an inadvertent groan from giving them away.

Some three hundred Indians, mainly Potawatomies, Wyandots and Ottawas, were in the clearing being observed by the spies and at this moment they were tying William May to a large tree. Until half an hour ago, May had been one of two spies in Wells's party. In the midst of their efforts to escape the Indians pursuing them, May had foolishly decided he would surrender. A renegade, May had been a Kentucky settler until he found the work too hard, at which time he had deserted the whites and joined the Shawnees. Then, when things became too hot for the Shawnees, he had deserted them and signed up with Wayne for spy duty.

Wells shook his head. May was such a fool. He should have known that, once adopted, if he turned his back on the Indians and they caught him again, there would be no hope. The Indians reserved very special punishments for such people. It was the reason why Wells himself took such inordinate precautions against being recaptured.

His mind moved back swiftly over what had occurred to get them into this precarious situation. When he had arrived with Wayne's force at the mouth of the Auglaize they had, not surprisingly, found the trading post and village abandoned. Wayne had immediately ordered everything burned and at the same time the construction of a strong fortification begun on the point of land where the Auglaize flowed into the Maumee. It would be a very strong fort and at one point, standing with General Charles Scott, Wayne had grunted in approval at the work going on in the construction of pickets, blockhouses, fascines and ditches.

"When it is finished," he had exclaimed, "I defy the English, Indians and all the devils in Hell to take it!"

"Then call it Fort Defiance," Scott had remarked, and Wayne did so.[109]

That evening he'd called in Wells and told him to take some men, reconnoiter down toward the Rapids, get a good idea of the Indian strength and what British support they had, if any, then report back. If it were possible to catch and bring back a prisoner or two for questioning, Wayne had added, so much the better.

With him, Wells had taken Robert McClellan, William May, Dodson Thorp and Christopher Miller. The remainder of the spy company were out on missions of their own under Lieutenant Nicholas Miller. The Wells party reached the vicinity of Fort Miami undetected, but were cautious about approaching too closely even though all five of them were in Indian garb. About a thousand Indians of various tribes were already assembled there, with more arriving all the time. Blue Jacket was at their head and Wells recognized many others — Tecumseh, Main Poche, Topenebe, Chaubenee, Tarhe, Catahecassa, Mtamins, Buckangehela. He was relieved to note that Michikiniqua and his Miamis were not on hand, which tended to confirm the story he had gotten from the two captives that the Miami chief had refused to lead the Indians against Wayne and had been deposed.

Taking the captives had been merely a lucky break for Wells and his men. En route back to Fort Defiance with their intelligence, they had encountered a Shawnee Indian and his wife returning toward the Indian encampment with information they had spied out on Wayne's force. They caught them easily, bound their wrists behind them, gagged them with strips of cloth and were herding them back to Wayne when, about twenty miles from Fort Defiance, they'd stumbled upon the larger party of Indians. Leaving the two captives with Dodson Thorp, who was to continue with them to Fort Defiance, while Christian Miller was to wait for them at a distance so he wouldn't be seen and recognized, Wells took May and McClellan and boldly rode in, dismounted and joined the Indian party at the fire. The Indians were discussing an attack plan against Wayne's force and accepted the new arrivals in a friendly manner, even to the point of discussing plans with them. Abruptly one of the Shawnee warriors, who had been repeatedly glancing at one of the newcomers, recognized him as William May. He murmured his discovery to a companion and Wells, next to them, overheard. Immediately Wells shouted, "They know us! Shoot!" All three shot at once, each killing a man, and the camp was instantly in bedlam. Wells and his two spies, wielding tomahawks, fought their way into the adjoining woodland, in a barrage of rifle fire. That was when Wells and McClellan had been hit.

That was also when May decided to surrender himself, even though they had momentarily outdistanced pursuit. There was no time for discussion. If that was what May wanted to do, they couldn't prevent it. Wells had been tempted to kill him, but evidently May divined his intention and plunged off into the brush toward the Indians. A shot would have given away their position so they let him go and rushed on. In a few minutes they had reached Christian Miller. He wanted to help them but Wells ordered him to ride to the fort and come back with help to escort them in. Miller nodded and galloped off. Wells and McClellan continued afoot until their pain forced them to take refuge beneath the leaning tree, to rest for a short while before continuing. They were on the far side of a broad clearing in which stood a lone oak tree on a slight knoll. There was no sound of pursuit, so the two had alternately dozed and jerked awake for the next hour. Then the Indians had quite abruptly appeared on the far side of the clearing and with them stumbled William May, stripped of all clothing and his hands bound behind him. He was being cuffed and kicked and shoved as they walked and they could hear his wails as he begged for his life.

Now the Indians had finished tying May to the tree and, with dusk gathering, they stepped back some sixty or seventy feet. A large red circle had been painted on May's bare chest and, while the others watched, about fifty of the Indians spread out in a semi-circle facing the captive and raised their flintlocks. As May strained at his bonds and screeched imploringly, a sharp command was given and the fifty rifles barked simultaneously. The effect was devastating; hardly any more damage could have been done to the man had he taken a cannonball full in the breast.

The Indians shrieked and howled and raced up on the dead man now hanging limply from his bonds. They scalped him and then began a macabre series of rushes past the body, striking at it with tomahawks and knives. Wells shuddered and caught McClellan's eye.

"You able to go on?" he whispered.

McClellan nodded and, wheezing with their pain, the pair slipped quietly away in the darkening woods as the yells of the Indians from the clearing behind continued.

Not more than ten miles away, in the final moments of twilight, the company of British soldiers under command of Captain Daniel McKillip was approaching Fort Miami. Some miles back they had missed the trail where they were to have turned and so, instead of approaching the fort directly, they had mistakenly passed it by, not realizing their error until they encountered the Maumee River about a mile upstream from the fort.

At once they had turned and marched back downstream along the north bank and now, in military formation, they emerged from the woodland into the clearing where Fort Miami was located. Sentries from the fort, on perimeter patrol, were stunned to see what appeared to be an army emerging from the woods in that direction. The only armed force that way was the American army under Wayne, and that's what they took these precisely ranked shadowy figures to be.

Four of the five sentries immediately raced toward the fort to give the alarm. The fifth sentry ran to the fort, too, but not before dropping to one knee, taking aim and sending a single shot in the direction of the advancing troops. That single lead ball sped through the air and struck Captain Daniel McKillip in the hollow of the throat just below the Adam's apple and tore through his spine at about the third or fourth cervical. He was dead before his body hit the ground.

Fifty miles away on a straight line to the northeast, at New Settlement on the north shore of Lake Erie, at this very moment Eleanor McKillip, pregnant with her fourth child, checked on the baby, six-month-old Jeffrey, and found he was still sleeping soundly in his cradle. She tucked the coverlet around him and then returned her attention to the other children. Four-year-old Margaret sat at her place at the table, her eyes dancing with excitement, even though the celebration was not hers. It was Jeanette's, who was seated in a hand-made highchair at the table. Before her was a small cake Eleanor had baked this afternoon for the celebration.

Today was Jeanette McKillip's second birthday.

[*August 13, 1794 — Wednesday*]

For many years Captain William Caldwell had been one of the more influential British officers among the Indians. Perhaps not quite so revered by them as were Colonel Alexander McKee and Captain Matthew Elliott, but certainly very close to that. Unlike McKee and Elliott, who stayed with the Indians for long periods, Caldwell served more as a liaison between the Crown and the Indian leaders and had frequently led regular British forces beside them against the enemy. In New York he had often led parties of Senecas and other Iroquois tribes against the Americans during the earlier part of the Revolution and, later on, had led similar forces, augmented by British regulars, of Shawnees in attacks against the Kentucky settlements.

It was in the Detroit area fifteen years ago that Caldwell had met and married a Potawatomi woman of remarkable beauty and intelligence.[110] Close to a year after their marriage, their only child had been born — a son known by four different names. His Potawatomi name was Tequitoh, which translated into Straight Tree. It was a good name for him because he was now a tall, straight, sinewy youth of very fine features. Yet, he was rarely referred to by either of these names anymore. To his father and to the whites in the area of Detroit, he was called Billy Caldwell, after his father. But even more than that, he was called Sauganash, especially by his contemporaries. It was the name he liked most and he rarely thought of himself except by that name. It meant The Englishman.[111]

Sauganash was not only a good-looking lad, he was also very bright. Recognizing this, William Caldwell had enrolled him at an early age in the Jesuit schools of Detroit and now, at age fourteen, Sauganash was competent in mathematics, was quite at home with several Indian dialects, and was both fluent and literate in English and French. Virtually all who knew him were certain that Sauganash would go a long way.

Today he was an extremely disappointed young man. His father was leaving, under orders of Colonel England, with yet another reinforcement for the Maumee — the third to be sent. First had been Captain Daniel McKillip with a company of a hundred men. Then it had been Captain Matthew Elliott with two hundred Ottawas and a train of packhorses loaded with food and other supplies. Now Captain Caldwell was being sent with fifty-three men of the Detroit militia and eight hundred Chippewas newly arrived from the Mackinac area. Caldwell's militiamen were to report to Fort Miami and the Chippewas were slated to join the Indian forces already at the Maumee under Blue Jacket to help oppose General Wayne.

Sauganash wanted desperately to go along for his inauguration into battle, but his father hugged him and refused. He kissed the young man on the forehead and said, "Soon enough you'll be tasting warfare, Billy, but not yet." Within minutes after that, the officer had led his detachment away.

And just at this time in Fort Miami, Colonel Alexander McKee dipped the nib of his quill into the ink pot and addressed the sheet of paper before him to Colonel England in Detroit. He wrote:

Rapids, August 13th, '94

SIR —

I was honored last night with your letter of the 11th, and am extremely glad to find you are making such exertions to supply the Indians with provisions.

Captain Elliott arrived yesterday; what he has brought will greatly relieve us, having been obliged all day yesterday to take the corn and flour which the traders had there.

Scouts are sent to view the situation of the army, and we now muster 1,000 Indians. All the lake Indians from Sagana [Saginaw] downward should not lose one moment in joining their brethren, as every accession of strength is an addition to their spirits.

I remain, Sir,

Yr. Obednt. Svt.
A. McKEE

[*August 20, 1794 — Wednesday*]

Part of what made General Anthony Wayne an excellent soldier was his ability to take the advice of subordinates when those subordinates, even if not of the military, knew what they were talking about. It was largely this reliance on skilled advice that stood Wayne in good stead now.

When William Wells and Robert McClellan arrived back at Fort Defiance in a very weakened condition, escorted by the company sent out to help them, Wayne listened carefully to the report of the captain of his spies. The general then told Wells that final endeavors to negotiate a settlement with the Indians had failed and there was no recourse now but to attack. It was at that point that Wells gave him the advice that had proven so invaluable.

"General," he had said, between grimaces of pain, "when you march down there, the Indians are going to take cover in a place they call Fallen Timbers. Tornado went through a big woods there a few years ago and knocked down most of the trees. They're all tangled together and it's a hell of a place to have to attack into. What you should do is get yourself into position to attack, make your camp and get 'em to think you're going to hit 'em early the next morning. But don't. Wait until the morning after that."

Wayne frowned, not understanding the reasoning behind the peculiar instructions, and Wells grinned mirthlessly. "Ain't as mysterious as you might think," he explained. "Soon as you camp the evening before, the Indians're going to start preparing. They'll paint up and they'll have a war dance; they'll abstain from sex with their women, they'll do some praying to the Great Spirit and they'll start their fast. They don't like food in their bellies when they're heading into battle, so they won't eat. They might even start the fast soon as they know for sure you're on the march toward 'em. Thing is, they'll be expecting to fight the next morning, but you'll stay put and they'll be getting hungrier all the time. They won't eat that whole day, waiting for you to strike. Then they'll go the whole night again, still without food — maybe thirty-forty hours before you hit. It'll weaken 'em, an' it'll help you."

It made sense and General Wayne followed the advice. Leaving only a small force at Fort Defiance, he began his march down the Maumee on August 15, taking his time. On the afternoon of August 18, the army stopped within striking distance of Fallen Timbers and camped. The Indians, already fasting preparatory to battle, now did precisely as Wells had said they would, painting, war dancing and praying in addition to the fast, fully expecting to meet the enemy the next morning. But throughout the nineteenth, Wayne kept his force at the new fortified camp he had made called Fort Deposit, where the heavy baggage was to remain when the order to attack was given.

Fallen Timbers was only two miles upstream from British Fort Miami and a number of runners were sent at irregular intervals to the fort — Tecumseh among them — as messengers from Blue Jacket, to ask when the soldiers were going to join them behind the breastworks of fallen trees. The replies were consistently evasive. The Indians were told to have patience and not to worry, that support was there and would be available when it really became necessary. Throughout the night of the eighteenth, all the next day and into the night of the nineteenth they waited and now, as William Wells had known it would, their resolve had begun to ebb. This was especially true when a fierce thunderstorm came up during the night, drenching the Indians who crouched behind the fallen trees waiting for the soldiers who were dry and relatively comfortable in their tents. In small groups at first, then in increasingly larger parties, Indians left the Fallen Timbers area and went to the British fort to get the hot soup and rum that were being provided. By early this morning, the force at Fallen Timbers had dwindled from around two thousand to fewer than thirteen hundred warriors, and that was when Wayne struck. And William Henry Harrison, close to his general at all times, received a priceless lesson in leading an army in Indian warfare.

The American army began its advance in open columns, with rear and flanks protected by detachments of mounted Kentuckians. As they reached Fallen Timbers, the mounted force retired to the main army and Wayne quickly deployed the whole for action. The infantry was drawn up in two lines and raced forward at his command in a bayonet charge, while the cavalry spurred around in a circuitous route in an effort to cut off the Indians' retreat. A fierce but surprisingly brief battle broke out. So swiftly was the Indians' resistance broken, however, that even before the cavalry could get around them, they were fleeing toward Fort Miami.

Blue Jacket strove to keep them together and retreated with them to the fort, but now they found on their arrival that the gates of Fort Miami were closed against them, sanctuary within was denied and the fort's commander, Major William Campbell, called over the pickets that they could not actually fight the Americans, since Great Britain and America were not at war.

"My orders," he told them self-consciously, "instruct me to do no more than safeguard the integrity of this post."

Blue Jacket was stunned and Tecumseh was beside himself with fury at the treachery implicit in the British actions, his rage fueled all the more by the fact that his brother, Sauwaseekau, one of the triplets, had been killed in the initial fighting. The King's soldiers were, in essence, throwing their Indian allies to the wolves. For the Indians, their world had collapsed at their feet, and in full view of the British who stayed closeted behind their fortifications. It was a scene that Tecumseh knew would never be erased from his memory. The Indians swiftly dispersed.

The Battle of Fallen Timbers was over, but not without painful cost to both sides. Forty-four American soldiers had been killed and eighty-nine wounded. The Indians lost, in killed and wounded, about the same number.[112] While the losses were very nearly identical for both sides, there was no doubt whatever in anyone's mind who had won. For the first time, without reservation, the Indians realized that the Americans were now the dominant force in this country and the knowledge was appalling.

[*August 10, 1795 — Monday*]

Peace, at last!

Peace with the British in a treaty negotiated by John Jay in Paris and, more immediately important to the Northwest frontier, peace with the Indian tribes in a treaty made at Fort Greenville — the strongest and most binding treaty the United States government had ever made with the tribes.

A collective sigh of relief seemed to wheeze from Indians and whites alike as now very clear boundaries had been drawn and no one was in doubt as to their location and no one could infringe on the rights of another. Or could they? Amity existed as it never had before between Indians and whites and pipes had been smoked and peace belts exchanged hands and all wars were over forever. Or were they?

It hadn't been altogether easy getting to this point and only the determined, patient efforts of General Anthony Wayne and his brilliant aide-de-camp, Lieutenant William Henry Harrison, had made it possible. That, plus the invaluable aid provided by Captain William Wells as Indian liaison. It had taken them ten days short of a year, following the Battle of Fallen Timbers, to reach this point, but now it had been accomplished and almost everyone marveled at the accomplishment.

Immediately following the Battle of Fallen Timbers and dispersal of the Indians, Wayne had sent out detachments to destroy all the Indian villages, along with all their crops. At the same time he oversaw the destruction of the homes and posts of British traders, such as Alexander McKee, within sight of Fort Miami. To Major William Campbell, commander of Fort Miami, Wayne sent a terse note demanding to know why the British were here, why they had intruded, why they had built Fort Miami on United States territory and ordering that they leave. Campbell responded with carefully chosen words, knowing his situation was ticklish to say the least and wishing, at all costs, to avoid outright conflict with the Americans.[113]

"I am here with my garrison at Fort Miami," Campbell replied, "solely at the orders of my government. It is not my wish to occupy territory belonging to the United States, but I am only where I have been ordered to be. As soon as I am ordered to do so by my superiors, I will immediately abandon this post. I request with the utmost urgency that you,

General Wayne, will not proceed to extremities until our respective governments are consulted."

Wayne considered this and agreed, then put his army into motion, moving back up the Maumee River. At Fort Defiance he stopped and had the new post strengthened even more, then continued up the Maumee to Miamitown, where the Maumee was formed by the St. Joseph and St. Marys Rivers. On the move upstream, all the way from Fort Miami, detachments ranged ten miles out on either side of the river, destroying all Indian villages and crops. At the Miamitown site, where so many years before French traders had operated and the place had been known then as the French Store, and where more recently John Kinzie's post had been destroyed and General Harmar's army defeated, Wayne now ordered erection of the strongest American fort beyond Fort Washington.

He named it Fort Wayne. It was provided with a large garrison and named as its unofficial Indian agent, interpreter and justice of the peace was William Wells, who was still recuperating from the bullet wound in his left wrist. In a short while Wells established his own farm close to the fort and was joined there by his wife, Wanagapeth and their four children. Somewhat later came, for General Wayne, the more delicate matter of sending emissaries to each of the tribes with proposals for peace, pointing out tellingly to all that, as had been proven by what occurred at Fort Miami, ". . . the British have neither the power nor the inclination to protect you."

Again, Wayne chose William Wells as his principal emissary in the matter of inviting the chiefs and their delegations to meet with him in preliminary talks at Fort Greenville, to which he was now repairing to take up winter quarters. Wells was aided by select members of his spy company and they set out on their mission, at the same time with instructions to arrest any army deserters encountered. Their flags of truce were honored wherever they went.

Wayne himself arrived at Fort Greenville on November 2, 1794, three months and six days after initially leaving it on his move against the enemy. The Indians came. Throughout the winter delegation after delegation of chiefs arrived and agreed to preliminary peace terms and promised to attend the great peace council that was to convene at Fort Greenville the following June.

Some of the chiefs still wanted to continue the war and British agitation that they do so was strong, but an incident occurred that struck deeply to the superstitious beliefs of many of the Indians. For years their greatest friend among the British, their liaison with the Crown and the man who helped them most had been Colonel Alexander McKee. One day, several months after the Battle of Fallen Timbers, McKee was in his cabin dressing. As he stooped over to put on his trousers, his pet deer abruptly charged and struck him in the bare behind with its antlers. It might have been merely a funny, if painful, occurrence, except that one of the tines of the antlers punctured McKee's femoral artery and he quickly bled to death.[114] The Indians considered this to be a very strong omen in favor of the Americans and against the British. Abruptly they became much more inclined to negotiate.

Only a very few of the Indians steadfastly refused to have anything to do with the negotiations. Among these was Tecumseh, who left the Shawnee tribe with a small band of his own followers and established a village on Deer Creek in the Ohio country. Though he could not forget the closed gates of British Fort Miami when the Indians needed help so badly, at the same time he was convinced that in such a treaty as Wayne proposed, the Indians would be forced to cede even more land, in the continuing pattern of treaties with the Americans.

Not all was peaceful. Scattered outbreaks of violence, usually followed by retaliation, occurred throughout the Northwest Territory, especially in the area of the southern Illinois country. The Kickapoos attacked groups of settlers here and there, wiping out the family of Samuel Chew, destroying another settler and his wife and their thirteen Negro slaves, and attacking individuals wherever they encountered them. A band of Kickapoos believed to be responsible for the attacks — though they weren't — were captured by Americans near Kaskaskia and taken away toward Cahokia for trial and incarceration there, but the procession was waylaid by an angry mob of whites near Belleville and the captive Indians were killed. This caused Governor St. Clair to issue a proclamation against any white person entering Indian territory to insult, injure or kill any Indian; a ruling which did very little to increase St. Clair's popularity.

Still the chiefs came to see Wayne at Fort Greenville for preliminary talks and agreed to convene there in force in June. With most of the tribes such agreement was not difficult, but with the Potawatomies it was. This was a tribe without any central form of government. Each of its branches — in fact, even many individual villages — acted autonomously and so the chiefs of each branch, or even individual village chiefs, had to be negotiated with specifically, which was not easy.[115]

But at last, on June 15, 1795, the council fire had been lighted at Fort Greenville and negotiations begun. General Wayne had sole power to negotiate for the United States, but he received very explicit instruction from President Washington and the new Secretary of War, Timothy Pickering, in regard to what he was to get from the Indians — the foremost consideration being very large cessions of land.

Anthony Wayne kept iron control over the proceedings at all times, allowing plenty of opportunity for discussion concerning the proposals, distributing food and supplies amply to the Indians, but withholding liquor and keeping a sharp guard alerted to nip in the bud any semblance of disturbance. A case in point was the Detroit half-breed trader John Askin, who showed up in a bellicose mood and immediately set about visiting the chiefs on his own, exciting and agitating them, breeding discontent and fomenting trouble. Harkening to the concern of William Wells over this development, Wayne took care of the problem neatly, with the help of William Henry Harrison. Askin was quietly arrested, spirited away and kept in close confinement until the treaty negotiations were concluded.

The first of the Indians to arrive reached Greenville in early June and others straggled in at intervals, with the last of the delegations — the Shawnees — finally arriving July 31, six weeks after negotiations had begun. Eleven hundred thirty· Indians were on hand, representing twelve tribes, and step by tedious step the provisions of the Greenville Treaty were hammered out.

Anthony Wayne proved to be nonpareil as a United States treaty commissioner, acting always with gentle, courteous firmness with the Indians, keeping in mind at all times the official United States policy at this treaty to reduce tensions. He was meticulous in following instructions relayed from the President and the War Department which told him that, unlike earlier commissioners, he was *not* to assert that lands east of the Mississippi were fully and absolutely the property of the United States in consequence of the 1783 Treaty of Paris with the British. Instead, he admitted to the chiefs that the tribes were to have free and exclusive use of all lands not specifically ceded by them to the United States. At the same time he told them that the tribes must acknowledge, in their signing of the treaty, that they were under the sole protection of the United States and that the United States alone had exclusive right to preemption of such land in subsequent treaties. He assured them as well that the treaty said that if any white man should unjustly kill an Indian, that man should be apprehended by the whites and turned over to the Indians for punishment, and vice versa. The chiefs all considered this a fine idea.[116]

Wampum belts passed back and forth between the participants as an important part of the transactions occurring. Although such belts were valuable, they were not a form a currency, as many Easterners thought. Rather, they were a form of record keeping developed among the tribes through the centuries and used to impress indelibly the desired points embodied in the message of the speaker delivering them. Most often made from tubular shell beads strung into strings a foot and a half in length, the individual strands of the belt were skillfully woven together to form intricate variations of color and design, each significant in its own right and each imparting a special message. Even seasoned frontiersmen and traders who had been among the Indians for many years found it uncanny how an Indian could glance at such a belt and then recite verbatim the terms of a treaty or words of an agreement, as if he were reading from a printed page. Sometimes the strands woven together would form a belt as long as ten or twelve feet, but most often they were only four or five inches wide and about three to four feet long. And though the belts were originally constructed from freshwater or ocean shell pieces drilled through in a laborious process with a slender flint drill rolled between the palms, a revolution in wampum belt construction had occurred when traders began stocking variously colored glass beads. Easterners were fond of snickering over the passion of the Indians for beads, thinking them to be enthralled over the beads as trinkets. Such was rarely the case, since they were seldom used for ornamentation. Theirs was as important a function in Indian record keeping as were paper and pen to the whites, and so beads became enormously profitable trade items carried by the traders.

Many such belts passed between the participants at the Greenville Treaty, their configuration and colors of extreme importance. The Indians almost always negotiated in terms of metaphors and so it was most important for Wayne to know — as he did through the help of such interpreters at the treaty proceedings as Captain William Wells, Sterling Estrich, Spemica Lawba and others — the precise meanings. Where color was concerned, a black wampum belt signified war talk, while white was one of peace, prosperity and health. Violet signified tragedy, death, sorrow and disaster and sometimes also war. To make the message plainer, stick figures would be woven into the belt or there would be geometric designs of various types — diamond shapes, stars, hexagons, parallel lines, squares, wavy lines, intersecting line patterns and the like, each with its own special significance.

To every new group of Indians to arrive, General Wayne made a presentation of a white peace belt, which was gravely received and the message thereon carefully studied. Metaphoric expressions transferred to beaded wampum belts required extreme care in preparation, lest any wrong idea be relayed. For the Indian, making war meant lifting the hatchet and making peace meant burying this hatchet, so designs signifying these acts were woven in specially selected colors. Other metaphors could similarly be expressed in the belts — kindling the council fire meant deliberation and negotiation; covering the bones of the dead meant receiving — or giving — reparation and forgiveness for those killed; a state of disaster or war was signified by a black cloud, just as brilliant sunshine or an unobstructed path between two nations signified peace. A black bird sewn into the design represented bad news; a white or yellow bird, good news. The Indian speakers rarely spoke without various lengths of wampum draped over arms or shoulders, to which they referred frequently as their speech progressed and the speaker refreshed his memory on the points to be made.

The process of making this Greenville Treaty was slow and often tedious in the extreme, but no one rushed it. Every chief who wished to speak was given the opportunity to do so at whatever length he chose. So the days moved into weeks. For fifty-five days the speeches went on, from both sides. The Treaty of Greenville was officially signed on August 3, followed by some supplementary councils held from then until today when at last they, too, were over; when the signing of everything was completed and the council officially ended.[117]

To each of the principal chiefs who participated, such as Black Partridge of the Chicago Potawatomies, General Wayne personally presented a large brass medallion on one side of which was a profile of George Washington and on the other side were full figures of Indian and American shaking hands. The medallions were each strung on a loop of brass chain for wearing around the neck, if the owner so chose.

One of the requests made of Wayne, which he granted gladly, came from Michikiniqua. Little Turtle asked that his former adopted son, Apekonit — also known as Epiconyare and now Captain William Wells — be appointed at Fort Wayne to the office of Indian agent to the Miamis and protector of their rights and the rights of other tribes, for he knew their ways and they trusted him. However, not everyone on either side approved of the appointment. William Henry Harrison did not fully trust Wells, believing his conflict of interests — since he was still married to the daughter of Michikiniqua — was not in the best interest of the United States. Chaubenee, Blue Jacket and Tecumseh detested him as a turncoat.

The cession of Indian lands to the United States was the crux of the entire treaty. In trade for land, the Indian tribes purchased peace and annuities — a peace they felt assured would be lasting; they also purchased the right to their own territory within the new boundaries — a right they felt assured would never be infringed upon.

Wayne had begun by stating that the new treaty being made here at Greenville was to be based in large measure, with some revisions to be explained, on the boundary lines established by the Treaty of Fort McIntosh on January 21, 1785. The biggest single land cession involved the Ohio Territory. Although the Indians would retain the privilege of hunting and fishing throughout the entire Ohio area, there was a definite dividing line between Indian and white territories established in this treaty and he read it carefully to them, explaining it in detail, so they would fully understand its significance:

The general boundary line between the lands of the United States and the lands of the said Indian tribes shall begin at the mouth of the Cuyahoga River and run thence up the same to the Portage between that and the Tuscarawas branch of the Muskingum, thence down that branch to the crossing place above Fort Laurens, thence westerly to a fork of that branch of the Great Miami River running into the Ohio, at or near which stood Loramie's store, and where commenced the portage between the Miami of the Ohio and St. Mary's River, which is a branch of the Miami [Maumee] which runs into Lake Erie; thence a westerly course to Fort Recovery, which stands on a branch of the Wabash; thence southerly in a direct line to the Ohio, so as to intersect that river opposite the mouth of the Kentucke or Cuttawa River.

With those words, the Americans gained cession to more than half of the Ohio Territory without restriction. In addition, Wayne told them, the United States would require the cession of sixteen tracts of land *within* the Indian territory for government reservations. It was here that Wayne did a little improvising, for he had been authorized to negotiate for only ten such tracts. The Indians never questioned the additional six. Each of the tracts was considered important in the extreme to the United States, not only for opening the Indian trade to Americans, but for the establishment of forts within the Indian territories to keep the red men in check and to regulate the trade in such a manner as to eventually force out British trade altogether — reasons which the Indians understood not at all.

With that maneuver, Chicago and the Chicago Portage became officially recognized by the United States for the first time. One of the tracts, twelve miles square, was located at the mouth of the Illinois River just above St. Louis. Another, six miles square, was located at the mouth of the Chicago River and was considered one of the most strategic localities of all the cessions. To make sure there were no errors as to location and purpose, Wayne was careful to read and explain the passages covering this particular tract. It was, according to the treaty:

. . . one piece of land six miles square at the mouth of Chicago River, emptying into the southwest end of Lake Michigan, where a fort formerly stood . . . and stipulated that the Indians should allow a free passage to the people of the United States, from the mouth of the Chicago to the commencement of the portage between that river and the Illinois, and down the Illinois to the Mississippi.[118]

By the terms of the treaty completed today, the Indians ceded to the United States an area of territory comprising some twenty-five thousand square miles, exclusive of the sixteen isolated tracts within the Indians' territory. For these cessions of such unbelievable economic value, both strategically and territorially, the United States agreed to pay, in goods, the value of $1,666 for each of the twelve tribes here represented, plus an additional annuity of $825 worth of goods to each of the tribes. It was one of the best land deals yet consummated for the young United States

— and one of the worst the Indians had ever suffered. When averaged out, it meant that the United States was paying one cent for every six acres!

Some of the chiefs objected, but not enough of them. The Indians were tired of war, tired of disputed boundaries, tired of being caught in the pincer of two opposing white powers. The majority prevailed. Perhaps, they said hopefully, now they could hunt and fish in peace. Perhaps now they could have peaceful trade. Perhaps now they could raise their crops and their families in peace. Perhaps.

Then again, perhaps not.[119]

[*December 31, 1795 — Thursday*]

Nine days ago, when President George Washington publicly proclaimed that the United States Senate had ratified the Treaty of Greenville after thirteen days of deliberation, a sense of jubilation swept through the United States and, with it, a collective sigh of relief. To those in the East it signified that all problems with the hostile Indians in the Northwest Territory had now been successfully terminated and that what had once been a perilous frontier had become the open heartland of a strong young nation, rich in land and resources and prime for exploitation. People who had never even considered entering such country while the element of danger existed suddenly thronged westward and the spread of settlement down the Ohio Valley swelled from a moderate flow to a veritable torrent.

South of the Greenville Treaty line, which virtually bisected Ohio from east to west, Easterners flooded into the country and made their claims on land their government had set aside for settlement as reward for services in the Revolutionary War. Land speculators did phenomenal business and a countryside that was practically devoid of whites only a few short months ago was now teeming with them.

Now there was time for the wonderfully mundane matters of clearing land and tilling fields, putting out crops and building homes. Now there was time for weddings that had been deferred and the renewal of acquaintanceships that had been broken apart and the erection of civilization in the form of churches and schools, stores and villages and cities. William Henry Harrison, for his faithful services to General Anthony Wayne, had been promoted to captain and appointed commanding officer of Fort Washington in Cincinnati, and the Ohio River town itself was rapidly taking on the dignity and strength of a small city, boasting blacksmiths, bakers, merchants of all types, nearly a hundred cabins and even ten fine large frame homes, and a population exceeding five hundred. And the new Fort Washington commander, after something of a whirlwind courtship, married Anna Symmes, daughter of one of Ohio's most powerful land speculators, Judge Benjamin Symmes.

That there were lingering resentments among many of the native inhabitants was of little moment to most of the new settlers, who felt ridiculously secure in the newly established peace, as if by the mere signing of documents, all troubles were forever ended. There were those, however, who were just as certain that not only were fundamental problems not resolved, but that the frontier had experienced only a small taste of the problems that could — and probably would — arise.

Among these were the handful of Indians who traveled to the village of Tecumseh on Deer Creek in Ohio shortly after the treaty was signed. They included Blue Jacket and Shemeneto, Chaubenee, Spemica Lawba and young Sauganash. Already assembled within Tecumseh's large wegiwa were his friend and sister's husband, Wasegoboah, along with the two remaining brothers of the triplets, Kumskaka and Lowawluwaysica. Those who came had arrived specifically to tell Tecumseh and his party of the Greenville Treaty details — their first inkling that the very land on which their village was located here at Deer Creek was no longer even Indian land and that they were, in essence, trespassers on United States property.

Tecumseh was downcast and those on hand listened carefully to what he had to say, considering his opinion very important. His prestige had risen greatly among the Indians and his refusal to attend the Greenville Treaty had suddenly brought considerable attention to him, especially among younger warriors of many tribes. That refusal also very nearly had the effect of torpedoing the proceedings. Only the fact that the principal chief of the Shawnees, Catahecassa, adamantly refused to support Tecumseh's position had prevented the possibility. Catahecassa had signed the Greenville documents, as he had realized for many years that one day such a signing would be inevitable if he were to save the remnants of his people. The matters of pride and dignity and self-esteem were put aside and Tecumseh, unable to tolerate this, had voluntarily separated himself from his own people and moved, with a small number of his followers, here to Deer Creek where they had established a little village. Now, even his right to be here had been signed away and there was bitterness and pain in his eyes.

"My people and I will remain here until our corn is harvested," he said, "and then we will move away."

"But to where, Uncle?" asked Spemica Lawba. "Catahecassa cannot allow you to return to our villages now. He says this would raise ill feelings and dissension among our people."

"I would not return to the villages even were I welcome," Tecumseh said softly, "because I could not live with what is in my heart and mind and still abide by the leadership of Catahecassa. Our chief has been a good chief since the death of Black Fish, but he is weary of war and thinks he is best serving our people by ceding lands instead of lives." He shrugged. "Perhaps he is correct, but I cannot live with that. This is —

was — our land and it is here that the bones of our fathers and our fathers' fathers are buried, and if we cannot protect what is ours, what is left to us? No, Spemica Lawba," he went on, shaking his head sadly, "I will not return to our villages. I will return above the treaty line on the Great Miami, but in a village of my own making, and perhaps not for long.

"Weh-yeh-pih-ehr-sehn-wah," he said, turning his attention to Blue Jacket, "it has been good seeing you again. And you, Chaubenee, and our new young friend, Sauganash. Though the news has been painful, I thank you for bringing it." He stood and walked to the doorway of the wegiwa. A cold wind whistled beyond the heavy buffalo-hide flap. He stood for a while with his back to them and they said nothing, knowing he was not finished speaking. When he turned back to face them, his features were etched with grim lines and his voice laced with an almost chilling determination.

"Only this do I have left to say: my heart is a stone, heavy with sadness for my people; cold in the knowledge that no treaty will keep the whites out of our lands; hard with the determination to resist so long as I live and breathe. Now we are weak and many of our people are afraid. But, hear me: a single twig breaks, but the bundle of twigs is strong. Someday I will embrace our brother tribes and draw them into a bundle and together we will win our country back from the whites."

Blue Jacket studied him with a piercing stare and then finally nodded and spoke softly. "I think maybe you will."

"When you do," Chaubenee said, rising and walking to Tecumseh, "I will be where long ago I vowed always to be — at your side."

The visitors had stayed a while longer and then drifted back to their own villages. Spemica Lawba returned to the village of Wapatomica, where he now lived. He was just in time to meet an American major who had arrived for a twofold purpose. His name was Thomas Hardin and he had come to deliver up to Catahecassa certain Shawnees who had been prisoners in Kentucky, many for long periods. He also had brought a message from his father-in-law, Benjamin Logan, to Spemica Lawba. The prisoners were being surrendered in accordance with the terms of the Greenville Treaty, just as the Shawnees had already turned over their white prisoners to General Wayne. Among the prisoners Hardin surrendered was Pskipahcah Ouiskelotha — The Bluebird — now sixteen, whom his father had adopted into his family five years before, following Harmar's campaign. The message he brought from Logan was simple: tell my adopted son, Johnny Logan, that his adopted father misses him and loves him and hopes that one day we will meet again.

Spemica Lawba had felt a rush of warmth at the message and gave a similar message of his own to Hardin to relay back to Logan; but the twenty-one-year-old felt another rush of warmth at meeting Pskipahcah Ouiskelotha for the first time, though he had known of her. Nothing he had heard, however, had prepared him for her loveliness and in that very first meeting he had fallen in love with her . . . and she with him. Now, only a few months since that meeting, they were married and deeply happy together.

The distaste exhibited by Tecumseh for the Greenville Treaty, which ceded so much of the Shawnee Territory to the Americans, was not his alone. Elsewhere among the tribes there were individuals similarly incensed at the injustice of it, but equally unable to gain enough support among their own people to balk it. The Potawatomies remained the most fractioned tribe in the Northwest and dissension among them was strong. Although they had never had a central government and a principal chief and did not have one now, Topenebe certainly had great influence. Yet, others had almost as much — chiefs such as Main Poche and Siggenauk, Nescotnemeg and Sunawewonee, for example. Dissension among them had increased since the treaty, as those in the eastern areas — Onoxa on the Elkhart, Wapeme on the upper St. Joseph, Topenebe on the lower St. Joseph, Winnemac on the Mississinewa — benefited more in the treaty payments and annuities than those farther west.

Only one highly placed official in the East seemed to share the concern General Wayne voiced over the growing dissension among the Potawatomies, fearful that it might have ramifications upon the Americans. That man was Timothy Pickering, United States Secretary of War, who expressed grave concern to President Washington, believing that, considering those divisions within the tribe, too few Potawatomi chiefs had been invited to participate in the Treaty of Greenville. Further land cessions in the Northwest without negotiating with those chiefs who were still hostile, or even merely neutral, he warned, could result in strife on the frontier. Secure in the solidity of the Greenville Treaty, however, the President did not agree, feeling if negotiations were reopened with minor chiefs, it would have ramifications affecting their dealings with all other tribes.

In the midst of all this, a man sitting in a Virginia tavern unintentionally overheard two nearby patrons talking about the Greenville Treaty and the fact that as a result of it, people who had been prisoners of the Indians for years were being surrendered. Though his senses were considerably dulled from the amount of whiskey already drunk, the man abruptly became more alert. In a few minutes he lurched to his feet and walked unsteadily to their table.

"Is it true, what you're sayin'," he demanded blearily, "about the Indians surrenderin' their prisoners?"

The pair looked at him with some distaste. "It's true," replied one. "Why? Do you have relatives that are prisoners?"

"I dunno." The man shook his head as if trying to clear away the fog. "Used to have, I guess. Long time ago. Injens. Shawnees. Hit my place whilst I was away. Killed m'wife an' oldest boy an' took my girls. Over seventeen years ago, it was." He was becoming garrulous, talking more to himself than to them. "My other boy, Seth, he got killed in the Revolution. All gone. Whole fam'ly gone." Tears were running down his cheeks now as he continued. "Gone. All of 'em gone. Lef' me alone." He paused and what the other men had said struck him again and he mumbled, "Y'say the Injens gave up their pris'ners? Where?"

There was no answer. The two men had quietly left while he was rambling on and so now he wove his way back to his own table, picked up his drink and finished it. He moved unsteadily to the door and then out into the night, still mumbling to himself.

"Find 'em. That's what I gotta do now. Find my girls. Little 'Liz'beth an' Margie. I'll find 'em, by God, or my name ain't Moredock McKenzie."

CHAPTER VI

[*July 11, 1796 — Monday*]

"I, JOHN KINZIE, citizen of and resident in Detroit, do hereby solemnly swear my allegiance from this day forward to the United States of America, and do likewise swear to uphold in every respect the Constitution of the United States of America, thereby renouncing my allegiance to any other nation and sovereign thereof, so help me God."

With these words, very soberly uttered, John Kinzie this afternoon became a citizen of the United States, along with several hundred Detroit residents swearing the same oath in their own names. On the sixty-foot flagpole, the flag of the United States hung, overlooking the city and the Detroit River for the first time.[120]

The takeover of Detroit and the other British posts on United States soil — Fort Niagara at the mouth of the Niagara River, Fort Miami at the foot of the Maumee River Rapids, and Fort Mackinac on Mackinac Island — had too long been delayed.[121] By the Treaty of Paris between Great Britain and the United States in 1783, the British had agreed to abandon the posts "in due time and with all convenient speed" and that little nebulous clause had resulted in this delay of only two months short of thirteen years. In the Jay Treaty of 1794, a specific date of June 1, 1796, had finally been set by the two nations for the British to give up these posts and the Americans to take possession. However, the Americans were still not quite ready when the deadline came.

At Greenville, acting on orders from the President and relayed through Secretary of War Timothy Pickering, the ball had begun rolling with a letter written to the British commandant at Detroit, Colonel Richard England:

Head Quarters   Greenville
May 27th, 1796
Sir — Permit me to offer you my hearty congratulations, on the final ratifi-
cation of the Treaty of Amity, Commerce and navigation concluded be-

*tween our respective Countries, officially announced to me by the minister
of war, and promulged in the Gazettes which I do myself the pleasure to
enclose to you.*

*As the delivery of the Posts, held by your Royal Master's Troops, within
the limits of the United States, makes one condition of the compact, it is
my wish to concert with you, the Measures, which may be deemed expedient
to the faithful execution of this stipulation and to prevent any unnecessary
Interval, between the period of Your Evacuation, of my occupancy.*

*I stand in perfect readiness for the operation, an[d] entertaining no
doubt, that the Treaty will be fairly, fully and punctiliously executed, on
the part of his Majisty it becomes my Duty, to request information from
you of the Day, on which it may be convenient to you, to withdraw the
Troops under your Command from the Territory of the United States.*

*My aide de camp, Captain Schaumburgh, will have the honor to deliver
this letter to you, and he will receive and forward your answer to me, by
Express, to meet the advanced Corps of the Army, in the vicinity of Roche
de Bout.*[122]

With much personal respect and esteem I have the honor to be Sir

Your most obedient servant

Ja. Wilkinson[123]

Col: England of the 24th British Infantry or commanding officer at Detroit.

Wilkinson's aide, Captain Bartholomew Schaumburgh, met with a very
courteous reception from Colonel England in Detroit and the transfer of
the post was scheduled for "early July." On June 25, Schaumburgh, with
the help of the Detroit commander, was able to charter from Detroit
traders two small ships of about sixteen tons burden, named *Weasel* and
Swan. The vessels, each with a crew of three, returned him to Fort Miami
at the Maumee Rapids where, by that time, the American force had
gathered. He then joined the detachment under Captain Moses Porter,
which boarded the little ships on June 29 and left again for Detroit.

With the meticulous primping of a maiden for her first ball, Captain
Porter prepared himself aboard the *Weasel* for his appearance at Detroit.
A large crowd of somewhat apprehensive Detroit citizens and Indians
watched with sober expressions as the vessels came to dock at the King's
Wharf and Captain Porter was a striking figure as he was first to dis-
embark. He had clad himself in his dress uniform as an officer of the
artillery — with shiny black knee-high boots, brilliant white breeches, a
striking blue coat with lapels, cuffs and collar of scarlet, impressive gold
epaulets on his shoulders and the whole topped off by a fine cocked hat,
its large black plume tipped with brilliant red. He also wore his ceremonial sword with golden hilt in a burnished silver scabbard.

This was the same outfit in which he appeared today, with Captain
Schaumburgh beside him also resplendently uniformed, at exactly noon, to

take official possession of Detroit for the United States of America. Colonel England had assembled his own troops in their finest and he, in his scarlet, gold and white garb officially surrendered Detroit — both fort and city.[124] The Detroit River now became in fact what it had been on paper for so many years — the official international boundary between British Canada and the United States. Most important, for the first time the United States gained both rule of and entry to Lake Erie, Lake Huron, Lake Michigan and Lake Superior. Detroit was only a small part of it. A similar ceremony was occurring at Fort Niagara, where Captain Roger H. Sheaffe of the British Fifth Regiment of Foot surrendered that important installation to the Americans and moved his force to Fort Erie and Fort George, on either end of the Niagara River — Fort Erie directly across the river from the little community of Buffalo, Fort George directly across the river's mouth on Lake Ontario from Fort Niagara.

A third British post on American territory was also turned over to the Americans this same day — Fort Miami at the Maumee Rapids — and a fourth and very significant turnover was scheduled to take place as soon as the Americans at Detroit could send a detachment for that purpose. This would be the taking over of Fort Mackinac on Mackinac Island — the location from which the fur trade of Lake Superior and Lake Michigan was controlled.

Without delay, Captain Schaumburgh purchased from the evacuating British their fifty-ton sloop, *Detroit*, making it the first ship of American ownership on the Great Lakes. It was in this vessel that the troops would be transported north for the takeover of Fort Mackinac. The face of the Great Lakes frontier was changing and everyone was aware of it, especially the Indians. Despite the continuing, well-hidden anti-American agitation among them by some of the British traders, it was now quite clear to the tribes that the Americans were the dominant white force in this region. It also intensified their inner fears. As certain of their chiefs had warned would occur, the Americans were wasting no time in sinking their roots in the territory and, like persistent weeds, once the roots were down it was almost impossible to dislodge them.

Among the troops to arrive at Detroit was Lieutenant John Whistler. He, like others who had never been here before, was astonished at the sight Detroit presented, with its well-constructed buildings and wharves, the sailing ships and trading posts and the bustle of its commerce and other civilized activity. Almost from first glance he fell in love with it and knew that as soon as it became possible for him to do so, he would send for Ann and their children to leave Cincinnati and join him here permanently.

John Kinzie and other traders at Detroit and elsewhere — especially those who had elected not to renounce British citizenship in favor of

American — were very concerned over what effect the American occupation of these posts would have on the fur trade, but for the moment they needn't have been. The Jay Treaty stipulated that British fur traders would still be allowed free passage into American territory and continuation of the activities they carried on there in the trade. There were those who argued that this was most unwise, since some of the British traders were still covertly fomenting unrest among the Indians, with full knowledge and approval of the British superintendent of Indian affairs at Niagara, William Claus.

With the oaths of allegiance repeated by the assemblage of Detroit citizens, the gathering began breaking up and Kinzie strolled back toward his trading post with his half brother and partner, Thomas Forsyth. John was thoughtful and walked quietly for a while, considering plans for the future in light of today's events.

"Tom," he said at last, "how would you like to set up and operate on your own, as part of the partnership?"

The younger man, lean, dark and alert, looked at his half brother speculatively, guessing what was coming. "You know the answer to that. Are you talking about Peoria Lake?"

The two had only recently returned from a trip that had carried them into the Illinois country, first to Du Sable's post at Chicago, then across the Chicago Portage and to Peoria Lake on the Illinois River. There was an old French post still standing in the area, used sporadically by passing traders, but no post of a substantial nature that was properly operated. Since both men were fluent in the Potawatomi tongue, Thomas even more than John, and Peoria Lake was in the heart of the Prairie Potawatomi country, they considered the location ideal for the establishment of a new post. The Peoria Lake Potawatomies had more or less stayed neutral during the recent Indian war, so whether the post turned out to be British or American did not appear to be a stumbling block. Everything had depended upon what kind of a reception they might receive from the Indians. As it turned out, their reception had been better than either had anticipated, with the Indians showing genuine warmth toward them and eager to have a well-operated post among them — expecially since Shawneeawkee was involved in it.

"Yes, Peoria Lake," John replied, nodding. "If you want to take it on, I'd like you to establish a post there. We've had our losses on the Maumee and this is a new start for us."

"What about Du Sable?"

"What about him? We'll be in competition with him somewhat, but not enough to cause problems. Besides, we both know he's not happy and I think one of these days he's going to sell out. When he does, I mean to make sure it's to me. If we can get control of the whole system —

Chicago, the portage, the Illinois all the way down to St. Louis, we'll have an operation beyond anything we've anticipated."

"Du Sable won't sell to you," Thomas pointed out. "Or to me."

"Not knowingly," John agreed, "but who says he has to know?"

Tom grinned. "When do you want me to start?"

"How soon can you be ready to go?"

Both men laughed.

[*October 3, 1796 — Monday*]

The bearded man who sat at the table in the Three Oaks Tavern in St. Louis studied the much younger man who had just entered, noting with careful eye the assurance with which he carried himself and the way his eyes quickly flicked across those inside. He had the look about him of a man skilled in woodland ways — the sort of individual the bearded man always sought out wherever he went. He watched until the younger man walked to the bar and ordered rum, then stood and walked slowly over to him. He pushed the slouchy leather hat back farther on his head and smiled as the man glanced at him.

"Evenin'," he said. "Mind if I ask you a question or two?"

There was an immediate wariness in the younger man's eyes but he murmured in agreement. "Ask whatever you like," he added. "Whether or not you get answered, that's another matter."

"Fair enough. You know the Injens?"

"Some."

"Shawnees?"

"No. Potawatomies."

"Trader?"

"Yes. Again, with Potawatomies, mostly."

"Where?"

The younger man frowned. Still holding his drink in his left hand, he turned so that his right hand fell close to the knife in his belt. "You're going somewhere with those questions, friend," he said evenly, "but I don't know where and I don't much care for being questioned without knowing why. Or who's doing the questioning."

The bearded man was immediately apologetic. "I'm sorry. Meant no offense. I'm looking for a couple of girls. My girls. They was taken by the Indians. Tryin' to find 'em. Thought maybe you mought could help."

The younger man finished off his drink and set his glass on the bar. Immediately the bearded man signaled the barkeep and ordered another of the same for each of them. "Care to sit at my table?" he asked, after the drinks came and he had paid for them. The younger man shrugged and followed him to the table, sitting down opposite him.

"Problem is," the older man went on, "they been gone a long time." He scratched his beard, took a swallow from his glass and grimaced. "Mebbe even dead by now," he added, though it was obvious he didn't believe that. He squinted across the table. "Ye're younger than I took ye t'be at first. Too young, I 'spect. How old are you?"

"Twenty-five."

"Damn! Not much chance you'd know."

"Try me. When were the girls taken? Where? Tell me about it."

"Long, long time ago. On the Kanawha, up the Ohio. Long time ago. Hell, you was only — let's see — 'bout seven then, I reckon. Younger'n they was. Shawnees took 'em. Killed my wife an' oldest boy."

The trader shook his head. "Haven't really had much to do with the Shawnees," he said. "Been up around Detroit and now getting started at Peoria L——" He cut himself off abruptly as a thought struck him. When he spoke again, he was more intent. "How old are they now? What were their names?"

"Let's see, eighteen years ago it was, in '78. They was twelve an' ten then, so they'd be thirty an' twenty-eight now. Margie, she's the oldest. 'Liz'beth's the other."

"Would that be Margaret and Elizabeth?" At the older man's nod he went on. "Margaret with light hair, Elizabeth dark?"

The older man sucked in his breath and his face became very white against the darkness of his beard. His large hand clenched around his glass shook and some of the rum slopped over the rim and dripped from his fingers. He didn't notice.

"You know 'em?" The whispered words were almost inaudible.

"It's possible. What's your name? . . . their last name?"

"McKenzie. Margaret and Elizabeth McKenzie. My name's Moredock."

The young trader grinned abruptly and leaned back in his chair, shaking his head and chuckling. "I don't believe it," he said. "I just don't believe it." He reached his hand out across the table and the older man, after bare hesitation, shook it.

"Mr. McKenzie, my name's Forsyth. Tom Forsyth. I have a half brother named John Kinzie. We're partners in the trade. We have a third partner, too, name of John Clark. They call him 'Indian' Clark. Both of them married girls who had been captives of the Shawnees. Their names were McKenzie. Now they're Margaret Kinzie and Elizabeth Clark. They both have children and Elizabeth's expecting another next month."

Moredock McKenzie was momentarily speechless, stunned. All these years; all these endless miles of searching since he learned of the Greenville Treaty. And now suddenly, and so simply, it was over. His shoulders began heaving and he buried his face in his hands. Forsyth, faintly embarrassed at the man's emotion, waited quietly. At length McKenzie lifted his shaggy head.

"Where?" he asked hoarsely. "Where are they? Can you take me to them? I'll pay you."

Forsyth shook his head. "No need to pay me anything. Be glad to take you. They're in Detroit. I'm heading there soon and you can come along, if you like. Have to talk to some people here, first, and pick up some supplies, but then I'll be going up the Illinois to my post at Peoria Lake. New place we're just starting. Have to stay there a week or so, maybe a little longer, but then I'll be heading for Detroit. You could go on ahead of me if you didn't want to wait, but it might be dangerous if you don't know Potawatomi and can't talk to them. I should finish up my business and be in Detroit by the end of December, if that suits you."

"Suits me fine," Moredock McKenzie said. He held out his hand and once again the men shook.

[*October 8, 1796 — Saturday*]

At ten o'clock this morning, Jean Baptiste Point du Sable became a grandfather for the first time.

Susanne Pelletier's baby — an eight-pound girl — was born in the Pelletier cabin adjacent to the Du Sable trading post main building on a morning when the fog was so heavy that even the Chicago River, eighty feet away, was hidden. It was Susanne's parents, working together, who delivered the baby while both Susanne's husband and her twenty-year-old brother waited at the post, trading with a small group of Potawatomies who had just arrived from the Fox River.

Even though the infant's lusty squalling was muted by the fog, Jean Baptiste Pelletier heard it at the post and came running, leaving his brother-in-law to handle the Indian customers. Pelletier rushed into the bedroom to see Susanne and the baby and was immediately and simultaneously proud and happy, excited and ebullient, anxious to hold the tiny girl, yet fearful of doing so.

"Susanne and I," he announced to his in-laws, Du Sable and Gohna, "we have talked about what to name the baby if it turned out to be a girl. We will call her after my mother — Eulalie." He smacked his forehead with his palm as a thought struck him. "*Dieu!* If only Father Badin had come a month later, we could have baptized her!"

The priest he spoke of, the Reverend Father Stephen D. Badin, was the first clergyman of any kind to pass through since Du Sable had been at Chicago. He had arrived at the end of the first week in September and stayed several days as a guest of the Du Sables. A young, soft-spoken man, he had been ordained in Baltimore only three years before — the first Catholic priest to be ordained in the United States — and was en route from Detroit to Cahokia, his first parish.

"Now," Jean Baptiste Pelletier went on, "we will have to wait for next time we go there or to Detroit to have her baptized."[125]

It was a joyful day for the family and all throughout the afternoon a procession of Potawatomies from Black Partridge's village came to view the new arrival and murmur their approval. Everyone was very happy. Everyone, that is, with the exception of the grandfather.

Jean Baptiste Point du Sable smiled and murmured approval along with the others, genuinely pleased at the birth of Eulalie, but inwardly his mood was gloomy as the persistent fog outside. His dreams seemed to be at a standstill and he was unable to account for it. Changes — momentous changes — were occurring all around them and yet it was as if the small-pox that had struck here so hard in July two years ago still hung in the air and people were shunning the place. Antoine Ouilmette and his family were still here, true, but where were the others? Even passing strangers were extremely few and almost always quickly hurried on their way, as if anxious to leave Chicago behind without delay.

There was peace now and Chicago had been specifically mentioned in the Greenville Treaty as a location ceded by the Indians to the Americans. Hopes were raised high in Du Sable's family when they heard this; wouldn't that mean establishment of an American post here? And when that occurred, surely there would be a great influx of people, military and civilian alike. Also, just recently the Northwest Territory's Knox County had been split and Chicago was in Wayne County, of which Detroit was county seat.[126] But where were the people Du Sable had expected to arrive following such developments? They had not materialized and Jean Baptiste du Sable was becoming very discouraged with his venture at Chicago.

[*November 30, 1796 — Wednesday*]

The grand banquet room was dominated by the T-shaped table beneath an impressive crystal chandelier sparkling with the reflected light of the flames of half a hundred or more candles. Fine china, crystal and silver were in place for each of the fifty-six guests and a large staff of black servants in crisp black suits, dark ties and white gloves stood ready. The large double-doors opened on the stroke of eight o'clock and the host, clad in a beautifully made suit, ruffled cuffs and collar, strode in at the head of the others and took his place in the seat of honor, having first seated his lady on his right.

The host was the sixty-four-year-old President of the United States, George Washington, and the guests who filed in behind and were shown to their places were a decidedly colorful assemblage. To the President's left sat the new Secretary of War, James McHenry, and his wife, and on either side of these four important people were the top echelon of the United States government and their wives — cabinet members, military aides, a few senators and congressmen, advisers and department heads.

Although the guests of honor had been in Philadelphia for over a week and were properly amazed at all the trappings of a more sophisticated civilization than they had ever before seen, this final banquet given to them by the President was little short of awe-inspiring. Trip after trip was made by the servants in and out of the room, wheeling dainty carts of delicacies and carrying huge platters upon which were huge roasted turkeys and suckling pigs and large baked fish of several varieties. There were fruits in wide array and salads and perfectly prepared vergetables, decanters of Madeira and port and fine brandies.

The guests were fourteen Indians of the Northwest Territory — important chiefs among their own people — brought here for the twofold purpose of subtly showing them the might of the United States and the futility of attempting to oppose such power, as well as to cement the bonds of the new peace established with the Greenville Treaty last year. Among the chiefs of the Shawnees, Potawatomies, Miamis, Ottawas and Chippewas gathered here were Catahecassa — Black Hoof — and Weh-yeh-pih-ehr-sehn-wah — Blue Jacket — of the Shawnees. No one among the whites present realized that Blue Jacket was himself not only a white man, but a Virginian, just as the President was; a white man who had risen to become the second most powerful chief in the tribe into which he had been adopted. Onoxa was here, too, better known to the whites as Five Medals, chief of the Potawatomi villages on the Elkhart River of the northern Indiana Territory, along with his fellow powerful tribesman from the southwestern Michigan country, Topenebe. They, along with all the other chiefs, were clad in their very finest ceremonial garb and extremely colorful in their feathers and interlaced porcupine quills, beaded designs and silver and brass ornamentation.

Only one among them, Michikiniqua, had ever visited the Great White Father of the Americans before, and so he was looked upon by the others as a model for their comportment. They sipped from their glasses as did he and ate with the silver utensils as he demonstrated, showing their appreciation for the repast with great rolling belches that at times seemed to cause the delicate crystal drops of the chandelier to quiver. Also in the party, acting as interpreters, were Captain William Wells and Christopher Miller.[127]

Wells, seated beside Michikiniqua, chuckled to himself. He was feeling very good, certain his exposure here could only be advantageous in his projected career of service to the United States government. He had already seen a copy of the letter General Wayne had written from Detroit to Secretary of War McHenry, lauding the services Wells had performed. Wayne had written of Wells that for his services and because of the disabling of Wells's arm in the line of duty, he should be awarded a very liberal pension. It had inspired the desired effect. On his arrival here a few days ago, he had been awarded a lifetime pension of twenty dollars per month, which was generous indeed.

Wells chuckled again, thinking with pleasure of the future that was opening up for him — remembering the pleasant episodes of yesterday when he and Michikiniqua had met in private audience with George Washington. The President had personally thanked Wells for his services and presented several gifts to the Miami chief, among which was a beautiful ceremonial sword.

"This is given," Washington said with a smile, as he handed the highly burnished weapon to Michikiniqua, "as tangible proof of my esteem and friendship for Chief Little Turtle."

The special treatment afforded Michikiniqua had quickly established him as a celebrity. The famed artist, Gilbert Stuart, made arrangements for him to sit for his portrait to be painted; he was presented with a superb matched pair of pistols by the Polish patriot, General Thaddeus Kosciusko, who advised him, through Wells, to "Use them against the first man who ever comes to subjugate you." On that day, too, Michikiniqua became the first Indian ever to receive an inoculation against smallpox — a gift of Dr. Benjamin Rush.

Wells had managed to get a few minutes alone with James McHenry and not too subtly discussed the possibility of an official appointment for himself in the Indian Department. Though the Secretary of War was noncommittal, Wells came away from the meeting feeling encouraged and hopeful that the position would be his.

Now the presidential banquet was all but concluded. The ladies in attendance had followed Martha Washington to the parlor and as soon as they were gone, the men lighted pipes and cigars. As they smoked, the Indians listened closely as William Wells and Christopher Miller skillfully interpreted the words of the white leader. He spoke to them of the Greenville Treaty, saying it was the best thing that had ever occurred between white man and red. The British, he admitted, had long been friends of the Indians and had provided them with what they needed. Now, he went on, they could no longer do so and, though remaining glib in their promises of support and surreptitiously continuing to agitate in an effort to stir anti-American feelings among the tribes, they could not back up their words with actions.

Witness, George Washington pointed out, the deceitful and callous way they had turned their backs on their supposed red friends when the Indians needed help so desperately at the Battle of Fallen Timbers. And witness what had occurred since then. Detachments from General Wayne at Detroit had moved north and taken over the very important Fort Mackinac and the British had withdrawn from there to St. Joseph Island over forty miles away. Now the Redcoats were ensconced there in a pitiful little post that could provide little of any real benefit to the Indians. And had not the civilian residents of Mackinac become American citizens? Witness that the powerful posts of Detroit and Niagara had been meekly surrendered and the British had withdrawn to Forts George and Erie on the Niagara River and Fort Malden on Canadian territory near the mouth of the Detroit River.[128] And the citizens living at or near these posts had also renounced British citizenship and become Americans.

Look closely at the strength and power of the United States, the President cautioned, for here there was both benevolence and determination. What had only a short while ago been thirteen weak colonies — the Thirteen Fires, as the tribes had called them — had now become sixteen strong states, with the admittance of Tennessee as the sixteenth this past summer, and there would be many more. Ever more settlers were moving into the newly acquired territory of the United States and they wanted to live in peace with their Indian neighbors, and not be forced to carry war to them. Just this past autumn over a thousand large boats of the type called broad-horns had floated down the Ohio, bringing a multitude of new settlers, and on the south shore of Lake Erie a new city had just been laid out and called Cleveland.[129]

"I remind you of the promises of peace you made at the Greenville Treaty," Washington went on, "and ask that you adhere to them, that the links in the chain of peace that now binds us together may ever remain bright. It has been explained to me in detail that times are hard for you and that your bellies pinch for want of food and that there are not skins enough to keep you warm in winter, and for this I have great sympathy. We wish to help you, but in order to do so, it now becomes important for you to change your system of life."

There was a murmuring among the Indians as these words were interpreted and meaningful glances passed among them. A sense of tension developed and, though he was keenly aware of it, George Washington went on as if he were not.

"Always before you have been hunters and you have lived by the animals you could kill for food and the furs of animals you could trade for what you need. But now the animals for food have become very scarce and you often go hungry and the animals whose fur you need have also become scarce and they no longer support you. I recommend that you give up hunting in the favor of farming. We will help you in this and send among you men who are expert in the raising of crops. They will teach you our methods and the little gardens you have now that are not enough to support you will become great fields of grain and vegetables and orchards of fruit trees."

Several of the Indian chiefs seemed interested in the idea, but the majority were not and their expressions hardened. Washington noted this as well and he shook his head. "You must open your minds and your hearts to new ways," he said firmly, "for there is no returning to the old ways. You have learned of the death, only a fortnight ago, of General

Wayne and this has planted a seed of false hope in some of your minds.[130] Do not make the mistake of thinking this has left us weak and leaderless, for we are a strong country and have many strong leaders to take his place."

The President paused to take a sip of water from the glass before him, waited until the slight murmuring ceased and then went on.

"I am aware that in the past certain white men have perpetrated crimes against you, but I give you my word that this will occur no more or, if it should happen, those guilty will be harshly punished. But just as we will live up to the agreements of the Greenville Treaty and not permit our people to mistreat you, so must you live up to those agreements and turn over to us for punishment any Indians guilty of crimes against the white people. Only with such agreements can we continue to live in peace."

He paused and his shoulders seemed to sag a little and his voice was a touch more weary when he continued. "This will be the last meeting you will ever have with me as President. My people have asked me to lead them for yet another term in office, but I will not do so. So in my place the people have chosen John Adams as their next President and I know he will treat you with the fairness and concern that you wish."

He picked up the small glass of brandy before him and held it up. Others of the whites on hand were also picking up theirs and waiting, so the Indians did likewise. George Washington smiled. "I bid you farewell," he told them, "and I now offer a final toast: May our Indian brothers enjoy now to the fullest the peace that exists between us and may they prosper in happiness."

There were cries of "Hear! Hear!" and the toast was drunk, but more than half the Indian chiefs on hand set their glasses down without drinking.

[April 5, 1797 — Wednesday]

The figure standing by himself at the end of the municipal wharf at Detroit and clenching his hat by the brim with both hands seemed oblivious to the strong south wind that tousled his hair and whipped at his clothing, flapping his trouser legs and the tail of his frock coat. It was a raw morning, with the low overcast swirling and seething, reflecting the inner feelings of the man, though his face was set in expressionless lines. Only the eyes, as cold and steely gray as the clouds, showed the pain that gripped him now as they remained locked on the ship rapidly disappearing downstream.

A shudder touched John Kinzie, as much caused by the inner chill as the outer. The parting had been traumatic and, though he had shown it least of the twelve people involved, he had felt it most — still felt it most. There was a sense of relief, true, but with it a feeling of irrevocable loss and the thought struck him, I never expected I'd really feel this way.

He remembered when he had run away as a boy from New York and returned on his own to Quebec and became an apprentice silversmith. He had been alone then, but it was a different kind of aloneness. This was another matter and it had all happened so quickly. He was glad he had been almost two hundred miles away on the St. Joseph River and not in the Detroit area when Margaret's father had arrived, brought here from St. Louis by Tom Forsyth; that he had not, in fact, gotten home until the man had been here a fortnight and by then everything had been pretty much settled.

Moredock McKenzie had arrived in Detroit, Kinzie learned, on the last day of December and had been taken at once to the Kinzie house. From what Tom told him later, the reunion between the sixty-one-year-old Mc-Kenzie and his thirty-year-old daughter had been extremely emotional and was repeated a little later when they went to see Elizabeth Clark. There had been voluminous tears and hugs and touchings and long long hours of talk as they brought each other up to date on what had happened to them during their greatly extended separation. The sisters learned that their brother, Seth, had fallen at the Battle of Princeton and since then their father had more or less drifted, always asking people wherever he went about whether they had encountered or heard of the two sisters named Margaret and Elizabeth who were prisoners of the Shawnees; and, finally, of how he had learned of the Greenville Treaty and the fact that prisoners were being released and he had again begun searching in earnest.

For their part, the girls told him of the attack on their Kanawha River homestead, of the death of their mother and older brother, William, of their journey into Shawnee territory with their captors and of their subsequent adoption into the family of Black Fish, whose wards were the children of Pucksinwah. They told of the attacks against Chalahgawtha by the Kentuckians and of its destruction three different times and, finally, they told their father of how they had simply walked away when Mackachack had been attacked, made their way to the Maumee River and were rescued by John Kinzie, whom Margaret had soon married. That had been followed by Elizabeth's marriage to Kinzie's partner, John Clark. Then had come the children — William, Elizabeth and James to Margaret, now respectively eight, five and four years old. Elizabeth and John Clark had had four — Elizabeth, who was five, John K., four, and the twins, Andrew and Mary, born just last November 2.

Moredock McKenzie's announced intention to his daughters, shortly after his arrival, was to take them back to Virginia with him. It didn't take a great deal of coaxing to convince them that this was what they wanted, too. Though John Kinzie was not there, John Clark was and Elizabeth began putting pressure on him at once. By the time Margaret's husband returned from the St. Joseph River, where he had been working out the details of establishing a new post there, Clark had agreed to go with Elizabeth and Margaret and the seven children.

John Kinzie steadfastly refused. He was a trader. The Indian trade was his profession, his life, and he was not going to turn his back on it; especially not now, with his newest post just established. For days and weeks the talks went on with neither side budging. It was Margaret who finally said the word both had had in mind for some time — divorce. Whatever love had existed between them in the beginning had long since evaporated and, because of Margaret's protective hovering and ill temper, John hardly knew his own children. They settled matters fairly quickly after that, though not entirely painlessly. For John Kinzie, it became simply a matter of buying his way out of the marriage — a bargain, he felt, at any price. He also bought out Clark's share of their partnership. To Margaret he gave a substantial sum of money, silver jewelry of considerable value which he had crafted and all the slaves except two — Henry and Athena — whom he retained to care for his Detroit residence property.[131]

Now he was more than ever glad that he had extablished the new post not very far from where William Burnett had his on the St. Joseph. It was still a very small post, but John Kinzie was convinced it would grow rapidly, especially now that he could devote more time to it without the obligation of having to return to Detroit at fairly regular intervals. He would have more opportunity to cement the growing friendship between himself and the influential chief, Topenebe, whose village was only a stone's throw from the new post. Also, it had been good to renew his relationship with Burnett, whom he considered to be among the shrewdest of Indian traders anywhere and whose ability to deal with the Indians in a manner both profitable to himself and highly satisfactory to the Indians was phenomenal. Yes, he had high hopes for the new St. Joseph post.

With something of a start, John Kinzie realized that the ship carrying the Clarks and Moredock McKenzie and his two daughters and seven grandchildren had passed from sight. Little whitecaps were kicking up on the surface of the Detroit River and the temperature was dropping. His mood of gloom over this day's occurrences returned and he bent his head into the wind and began walking back toward his empty house.

His was not the only dark mood, bred of loneliness and depression in Detroit this day. Not more than ten minutes after he left the wharf, a much smaller boat — a large bateau fixed with a ragged sail — hove into view, pushed along briskly against the Detroit River's strong current by the raw south wind. In its center seat, surrounded by household goods and baggage, sat a woman dressed entirely in black, including a heavy veil that effectively masked her features. Beside her sat a child of seven, her daughter, cheeks reddened by the wind. They were en route to Grosse Pointe, where arrangements had been made for them to take up residence with the little girl's grandparents and her Uncle Tom.

As they passed Sandwich, on the east side of the river opposite Detroit, the woman turned her head and was able to see the house where her sister lived. She sighed. How was it possible, she wondered, that for one sister life was a constant delight and an existence seemingly never touched by tragedy at all, while for another — herself — life was one tragedy after another? Eleanor McKillip shook her head and sighed again, hugging little Margaret closer against her. She pointed out the house of Margaret and Will Forsyth to her daugher.

"Look, darling, that's where Aunt Maggie lives. We'll be much closer to her now than before, so we'll be able to visit more often."

"Can we stop there now?" Margaret asked. She liked her Aunt Maggie a great deal.

"No, dear, not today. She'd be very busy with little Robert." Maggie had given birth to her first son last October and they'd named him Robert A. Forsyth. Eleanor gave a little shrug and continued. "Anyway, we have a big day ahead of us just getting our things moved into grandmother's and grandfather's house. But we'll come back here soon, I promise."

The little girl seemed content with that and they lapsed into silence again. A shiver ran through Eleanor and she thought, Thank you, God, for sparing this one at least. With the thought came a resurgence of memory of the past few months and the heavy depression settled over her again. Instead of slumping with the weight of it, however, she sat even taller and held her head high. This was the way of Eleanor Lytle McKillip.

She thought briefly of Daniel and of the utter pointlessness of his death, accidentally killed as he had been by the overeager sentry at Fort Miami three years ago. Then, seven months later, on March 6 of 1795, had come the birth of their son, George. Without the two blacks they owned to help out on the place, there was no way she could have made it alone at such a time or afterward. With a brand-new baby at that time, plus the other children — Margaret, then almost five, Jeanette, close to three, and Jeffrey, not quite one — plus the New Settlement property to care for, the burden then was tremendous, yet she had been loath to give up the place. It had been Daniel's dream and, as such, it had become hers as well and she was determined to continue with it. That determination finally died last month, when the dread cholera struck.

For some reason, she and Margaret had not been touched by it, but none of the other children had been spared. Jeffrey, nearly three, had contracted it first and was severely wracked by the fever. Within a matter of less than twelve hours from the first onslaught of the disease, he died. It seemed the others would be spared but then, almost simultaneously, both Jeanette, four and a half, and George, just before his second birthday, had been afflicted. Both had died very nearly as swiftly as had Jeffrey.

The days afterward had become a blur for Eleanor. She vaguely remembered the burial ceremony — three little graves in a row — and the selling of the New Settlement property, along with the two blacks, to a Detroit merchant, and then the packing up of the few personal belongings she and Margaret were taking along with them, but the details were not clear. Now, with the raw wind at their backs, kicking up small whitecaps around the bateau, they were heading for Grosse Pointe to begin a new life with Sarah and John Lytle and Eleanor's unmarried brother, Tom.

The sale of the house and most of its furnishings, along with the blacks, had brought in enough money that she knew they would have no financial concerns for a while. She still had Margaret and there were her parents and Tom and even her sister Maggie, so she certainly wasn't alone. Yet, once again — just as it had struck her so many years ago when her parents had been forced to leave her with the Senecas — Eleanor saw little ahead except a future that was very bleak. Outwardly she gave no evidence of it, but deep inside she was very afraid.

[*December 16, 1797 — Saturday*]

Inside his snug house standing at almost the exact site where John Kinzie had once had his trading post and, long before that, another trading post had existed called the French Store, William Wells leaned back in his chair and smiled at Michikiniqua, who sat across the table from him.

"Well, father," he said in the Miami tongue, "it is good to be home again."

Michikiniqua nodded, puffing contentedly on his pipe. "We have done what we set out to accomplish," he agreed. He looked up and smiled as his daughter handed him a mug of steaming rum. "Thank you, Wanagapeth." He sipped from it carefully and murmured appreciatively as the warm liquor bloomed in his stomach. He was silent a moment, reflecting, and then shook his head faintly. "There are still troubles to come. Not soon, I think, but they will come again, Apekonit."

William frowned. "How so? You don't think the President will honor his promise?"

"He will honor it, but for some it will make no difference, since it is not what they want. For our Miamis, yes; they will take to farming well, but not the Potawatomies, despite the eagerness of Topenebe and Onoxa to try. They are hunters and warriors. They will not lay aside their traps and guns to push a plow. They move about a great deal and they will not be content remaining in one place to watch things grow. You will not —" He broke off as the heavy booming of the evening cannon from Fort Wayne, across the river from them, caused the windows of the cabin to rattle briefly. They heard the slaves murmuring in their temporary quarters in another part of the house. He continued his comment: "— have an easy job of it in performing your new duties."

William Wells did not respond. He smiled faintly as Wanagapeth set another mug of hot rum on the table before him and he touched his wife's arm in a little gesture of appreciation. She smiled back, glad to have him safely home again from the long trip, yearning to be snuggled close in his arms in their bed again but patient, as always, for that time to come. They had been apart a long time and for the moment it was a pleasure enough to have him — and her father — close again. They had arrived here only a couple of hours ago and she had immediately filled their bellies with food. Soon enough, she knew, it would be her time to be filled, perhaps to begin their fourth child. The other three, Etonah, Penezaquah and Tonon — who had been baptized James, Rebekah and William Wayne — were at this moment asleep in the loft.

William thought about Michikiniqua's last comment, hoping the Miami principal chief who had once been his adopted father was wrong, yet knowing in his heart that he was probably correct. He lighted his own pipe and thought about their just completed trip to the capital and their successful visit with President Adams. It had been their second trip together to see the United States President and the third presidential trip for Michikiniqua. A certain amount of concern had filled them both before their arrival there over what sort of man the new President would be and what sort of reception would await them. They needn't have worried. The meeting had been very friendly and, with William interpreting, the President and Miami chief had talked well into the night. At the conclusion of the meeting, John Adams had spoken warmly to William.

"I find Chief Little Turtle," he said, glancing at Michikiniqua, who stood across the room from them, gazing from the window, "to be quite a remarkable man. I only wish all the chiefs who visit here were so wise and so reasonable. I want his stay here in the capital to be comfortable and happy. Equally important, I want him to be contented after he returns home."

The President meant what he said. Part of that contentment was providing the Miami people and other tribes of the Northwest with farming implements and agricultural experts to instruct them in the fundamentals of successful farming. Another part of keeping Michikiniqua content was the official appointment of Captain William Wells as deputy Indian agent and interpreter at Fort Wayne; an appointment the President authorized before their departure, at a salary to William of three hundred dollars annually. His appointment as agent fell under the Trade and Intercourse Act of 1793, by which the President was authorized to "appoint temporary agents, to reside among the Indians."

William and Michikiniqua did not go directly to Fort Wayne from the capital. Instead, they had gone first to Pittsburgh, procured a large canoe from a shipwright in the very shadow of Fort Pitt, and paddled down the

Ohio River to Louisville. There, at Beargrass, they visited for a week with Samuel Wells and Michikiniqua was treated with great deference. It was the first time the Miami chief had met William's eldest brother and they struck it off well together from the beginning.

It was good, too, to see Rebekah again. At sixteen she was developing into an uncommonly pretty girl with light chestnut hair, deep blue eyes and a most engaging smile. She wore her prettiest frocks each day they were there and completely won Michikiniqua with her lightness and charm and her admirable efforts to speak to him in his own tongue, with instruction from her Uncle William. Michikiniqua gravely invited her to come and visit as a very special guest any time she chose and Rebekah assured him she very probably would. It was after her, of course, that William had named his daughter.

From Samuel, William procured six good slaves — four men and two women — as well as a small herd of hogs, a heifer and a bullock, a large quantity of corn for planting and over a score of seedling apple trees. As a result, the journey overland from Louisville to Fort Wayne took longer than expected, but at last they had arrived here today. Tomorrow morning Michikiniqua would return to his people and Captain William Wells would begin his official duties as deputy Indian agent and interpreter at Fort Wayne, as well as gentleman farmer here on his acreage. With peace still prevailing in the land under the terms of the Greenville Treaty, everything augured well for the future.

Nevertheless, what Michikiniqua had said a few minutes ago remained in his mind, underlining his own concern.

[*February 11, 1798 — Sunday*]

The newlyweds had taken their time on the journey through the wild country of southern Michigan. They had left Detroit on January 31, eight days after exchanging marriage vows before Magistrate William Harffy. The simple ceremony had been what both of them had wanted and the days in Detroit following the wedding had had a twofold purpose: first, to allow time to fully know one another and consummate the love that had developed between them over the past six months — but a love, both agreed, which had its inception many years before, when they had first met. The second reason had been to get outfitted for the journey westward — packing the materials that were now reaching their destination on the backs of the eight packhorses in their string.

It had not been a time of year conducive to pleasant travel; the snow was hock-deep to the horses in many places and the temperature had not risen above freezing since before they left Detroit. But they had bundled themselves accordingly, traveled in easy stages and rarely more than fifteen miles in a day, stopping early enough to make a very comfortable

camp for the night. Neither of them ever remembered enjoying themselves
so much. They had laughed with the abandon of little children, threw
snowballs at each other, built snowmen and snowwomen together, and
marveled together at the wonder of simple things and even more at the
intensity of their love for one another.

Now, as they caught sight of their destination ahead, the man called a
halt, kneed his horse to a stop beside hers and took her in his arms. The
kiss was tender and warm and when they pulled a little apart, they found
to their surprise that huge soft flakes of snow had begun falling, drifting
featherlike to the mantle of white already on the ground, catching and
clinging onto the woman's long eyelashes, emphasizing the sparkle of her
eyes and color in her cheeks.

"Beautiful!" he murmured, his face only inches from hers, and it was
not clear whether he referred to the snow or to his bride. "I love you,
Eleanor Kinzie."

"And I you, John Kinzie," she replied. Their eyes remained locked.

Behind them the horses snorted, their hooves making muffled thuds as
they stamped in the snow. Echoing their impatience, a small voice came
from the heavily bundled figure on the horse directly behind theirs.

"Hey! It's snowing again. Let's go."

The couple looked back, smiling, and Eleanor nodded to her daughter.
"You're absolutely right, Margaret. We're on our way."

The Kinzies chirped their horses into a walk again toward the distant
trading post on the bank of the frozen St. Joseph River and Margaret
McKillip, grinning, followed. She was seven-and-a-half now and surprisingly tall and mature for her age. Behind her, the lead ropes for the
packhorses attached to their saddles, John Kinzie's two slaves, Athena
and Henry, put their horses into a walk and followed. They, too, were
smiling broadly.

The post John had developed here a year ago and steadily improved
ever since was impressive. Close to a small creek which entered the St.
Joseph River at this point, it was a few hundred yards from the cabin of
the old retired French trader, Joseph Bertrand, and his wife, Nancy, who
was the sister of William Burnett. The Kinzie trading post was a large
square building with full veranda. Beside it was the residence — a sizable
cabin now, but John was already planning a larger, more comfortable
house. Beyond that cabin was a smaller one, where Athena and Henry
would have their quarters, and each cabin had its own well-built privy
ten yards behind. A stable shed and pole-fenced lot for the horses was a
short distance from the smaller cabin, to one side. Numerous bundles of
hay were packed into the loft space of the shed as fodder for the horses,
safe from the weather.[132]

Eleanor glanced at John as they approached the complex of structures. "I'm impressed," she said. "I had no idea you'd done so much."

"Actually," John laughed, "I didn't do much of it myself. I hired some workers to do it and mainly just supervised. But I'm glad you're impressed. I've been bringing things for the insides every time I've come and with what we've brought now, we should be pretty well established."

Eleanor pointed to a very small cabin several hundred feet away, a whisp of blue-white smoke curling from its chimney, and asked about it. John explained that it was the quarters of his clerk, Jean — also known as Jack — Lalime.[133] She would be meeting him later. Considerably farther off, beyond Lalime's cabin, vaguely visible through the snowfall, was another quite substantial building at the edge of a large Potawatomi village. The village of over two hundred wigwams was Topenebe's and the house adjacent to it near the river belonged to William Burnett and his Potawatomi wife, Kawkeeme, to whom he had been married for twenty-eight years. She was the sister of Topenebe and had borne all four of Burnett's children.[134]

Close to Topenebe's village were the ruins of old Fort St. Joseph, originally built by the French when this site was an important link in the French fur trade. "At that time," John told her, "they called this whole area right here by the name of *Parc aux Vaches*, meaning cow pasture. Not," he amended quickly, "cows as we're accustomed to them. It referred to the buffalo cows that were here by the thousands. They were all over in this part of the country, from Lake Erie westward, and I gather this used to be a favorite place for the cows to give birth to their calves. No one's seen any buffalo around here in years."

The Kinzie party stopped in the complex of buildings and everyone helped with the unloading of the packhorses, carrying bales, bundles, furnishings and other items into the houses and trading post. As they worked, John reflected on the twists of fortune that had brought him and Eleanor together. Less than two months after the final separation from Margaret, he had gone to Sandwich to visit his stepbrother, William Forsyth, in respect to some business. It was the first time in years he had visited the Forsyth house, since he and Will shared a somewhat less than fraternal relationship. It so happened that he had been there only half an hour when Will's sister-in-law arrived to visit Maggie. It was, of course, Eleanor.

The same odd passage of electricity that occurred between them at their first meeting — on the occasion of Will and Maggie's wedding, December 6, 1790 — happened again and what had been meant to be only the briefest possible visit for John extended throughout the afternoon and well into the night. The fact that John was no longer married and that Eleanor McKillip was a widow was excruciatingly clear to both. The meeting had opened a communication between them which grew in the subsequent weeks and became a love such as neither had ever before experienced. The upshot had been their marriage on January 23, only nineteen days ago.

Although John Kinzie retained ownership of the Kinzie mansion in Detroit, now they were here at the St. Joseph and this would be their permanent residence, at least for a few years. It was a much more central point for Kinzie's business affairs than Detroit had been, especially since his partner, Thomas Forsyth, was operating their post at Peoria Lake. And Kinzie's long-range plans still included possible establishment of posts at such locations as Milwaukee, Chicago and the point where the Des Plaines and Kankakee converged to form the Illinois River.

Now, with everything unloaded, John gave Eleanor and Margaret a more thorough inspection of the trading post and a closer look at the sort of goods he handled regularly. One whole corner of the building was devoted to John's silverwork — a little shop within a shop, with work-benches, hammers, tongs, silver bars and plates and wires, heavy iron crucibles in which to melt the precious metal, pliers and snips and a variety of other tools for pounding, flattening, shaping, trimming, molding and otherwise working the malleable metal. A collection of finished silver pieces were on shelves and in drawers — ear-bobs, brooches, armbands, bracelets, anklets, necklaces, combs, breastplates, gorgets, platters and plates and flatware — and other pieces of silver work in progress were here and there on the benches.

In the rear center of the post, throwing out a surprising amount of heat, was a large iron stove of the type invented by Benjamin Franklin half a century before. A well-used bench and several chairs were in a semicircle at this point and here was the sociability post within the post, the place where pipes and drinks and conversation were shared when business was completed and where a great many people had spent a great many pleasant hours. One chair, in fact, was reserved exclusively for Topenebe, who spent a great deal of time here.

But it was the merchandise which made this post the attraction it had become to people for hundreds of miles. Long tables filled with such merchandise stood in parallel rows from front to back of the store on either side of the stove and the walls were all fitted with shelves crammed with an astounding array of goods, with little semblance of order, though John knew unfailingly where every item was located. Here there were steel sheath knives, tomahawks, axes and hatchets, along with steel traps and fine-braided wire for snares; there were bolts of cloth, clay pipes and cob pipes, fish hooks, cords for making wampum belts, sticks of twist tobacco, shredded tobacco in tins, chewing tobacco and snuff of various qualities and flavors; there were small flasks of brandy and large jugs and kegs of rum, directly flaunting the poorly enforced regulations on the liquor trade; there were mirrors, framed and unframed, small and large, round and oval, square and rectangular; there were ornaments and gewgaws, cheap jewelry and expensive, colored beads for wampum, and medals of various sizes in silver, brass, copper and bronze; there were rolls of bark, canvas sails and caulking gum; there were ribbons of various lengths and widths and colors and materials, flags of different nations and flags of unusual design without meaning; there were quills and ink and packets of paper; there were feathers and plumes from peacocks and ostriches and egrets, from eagles, turkeys and swans and a variety of other fowl, some dyed and some in natural colors; there were needles and scissors, cotton, silk and linen thread and large balls of string and twine; there were six different weights, sizes and colors of woolen blankets, one of the foremost items of trade on the frontiers; there were boots and shoes and slippers; there was broadcloth and Irish linen, calico striped cotton material and flannel; there were handkerchiefs and scarves of fine silk or plain cotton; there were bins of dried beans and peas, corn, wild rice, oats, wheat and barley, barrels of pickles and brined pork and beef and containers of sugar, salt, pepper, flour, lard; there were long-bladed butcher knives and short-bladed paring knives, clasp knives and oiled honing belts and whetstones; there were shirts of calico and plain cotton or frilled; there were hats of all kinds and sizes, fancy and common, decorated and plain; there were kettles and pots and pans of iron and brass, copper and tin; there were kegs of gunpowder — set well away from the stove — and bullet-molds, lead bars and lead balls, gunworms and gun-flints, ramrods, fine rifles and excellent muskets for important chiefs or ordinary muskets for warriors; there were cedar arrow shafts and hickory spear shafts and osage bow shafts; there were fire-making kits of flint and steel and punky material; there were iron harpoon heads, bar iron, files and molten cloth, hammers, tongs, rosin and charcoal; there were tanned hides with and without the hair or fur; there were metal and wood containers of a variety of shapes and sizes for a multitude of purposes; there were tallow candles and lanterns and glass-chimney hurricane lamps; there was the fine cotton material called swanskin and a much coarser cotton cloth known as onasburg; there were elegant scarlet coats and jackets with brass buttons and golden epaulets for distinguished chiefs, and there were ordinary woolen coats and jackets — usually brown or green — for warriors; there were combs carved from ivory or tortoiseshell, horn or basswood; there was a wide variety of clothing for men and women, boys and girls, and there were obsolete uniforms — French, British and American; there was borax and soap, perfumes and scented oils, and there were nostrums of many kinds — patent medicines packaged in boxes and phials and bottles; there were even books on a special shelf — Shakespeare, Plato, Aristotle,

John Donne, Izaak Walton, John Milton, Samuel Pepys, Jonathan Swift, Joseph Addison, Alexander Pope, Benjamin Franklin and, of course, the Bible. And outside, stacked against the back wall of the trading post, there were half-a-dozen bark canoes and two small bateaux. In the pens beyond were hogs, sheep and poultry. Smokehouses were hung with hams and venison and bear meat and beef; sometimes with elk and moose, turkey, grouse, ducks, geese and swans. Hen houses with nest-boxes provided eggs. And in the stable yard were horses for sale or for hire — for riding, plowing, pack-use or other work. One other building was behind the post — a log storehouse fifteen feet square in which were kept the items taken in trade from the Indian customers — bales of fur skins, kegs of bear oil, dried meats and dried fish, and skin sacks filled with rich brown maple sugar.

The John Kinzie trading post was a wonderland of goods, yet lacking in many things that were still on order or still needed to be ordered from the East — special condiments and utensils and apparel and medications and tools — all the hundreds of items required to make a trading post success-ful. Eleanor and Margaret were enthralled with the variety and had seen only a portion of it when the door suddenly opened and two men strode in, closing it quickly behind them to prevent loss of the warmth inside. They stamped snow from their feet on the thick black bearskin lying on the puncheon floor for that purpose and, as visitors almost always did first of all, they sniffed the air, filling nostrils and lungs with that delightful aroma encountered nowhere else except within a well-stocked trading post: the combination of scents of good leather and perfumes, freshly ground coffee beans, pickling brines, fur skins, waxes and tallows, dried fruits and — wafting up from the fruit cellar beneath the floor — apples, pears, cabbages, corn, potatoes, beans, nuts and other items of food; the scents of lamp oil and green wood and, pervading all, the scent of wood-smoke from the Ben Franklin stove.

The two men greeted John Kinzie heartily, one of them a heavy-set man of medium height with poorly trimmed dark hair shot with gray and bushy mustache and eyebrows to match. He wore a disreputable ankle-length greatcoat of much-stained dark gray wool and his feet were clad in heavy outer moccasins. His face was fleshy and the small dark eyes porcine, yet not repugnant. He appeared to be in his late fifties and, despite his un-kempt appearance, he swept off his wolfskin cap and made a courtly bow to Eleanor and Margaret when John introduced them. This was William Burnett.

The second man was tall and craggy, clad in leggins and wrapped about with a heavy green woolen blanket. His eyes were large, dark, faintly almond-shaped, couched above unusually prominent cheekbones. On his head he wore a broad red band, from the rear of which projected five eagle feathers, two pointing upward and three down. He was an impressive figure and even before the introduction, Eleanor knew it had to be the prominent Potawatomi chief, Topenebe.

The chief stretched out his arm toward her, hand held palm down. Not knowing how to respond, Eleanor reached out and placed her hand against his, palm up. It seemed to take Topenebe by surprise and the corners of his mouth twitched.

"You . . . are . . . welcome," he said in deep, measured pace.

"Thank you," said Eleanor, dipping slightly and withdrawing her hand.

John Kinzie and William Burnett were grinning. "Topenebe only knows two English sentences," the latter chuckled. " 'You are welcome' and 'You go away now.' Looks like you've evoked the favorable one. Well, you *are* welcome here. Been a long time since a lady such as yourself graced this area. We've been looking forward to meeting you ever since John first told us about you last fall. We hope your stay here will be long and happy."

The two men then turned their attention to little Margaret, gravely shook her hand and welcomed her, and John Kinzie laughed aloud. Normally Margaret McKillip was garrulous and very outgoing, but on this occasion, more than merely shy, she was nonplussed. She'd seen Indians before, but Topenebe was the first she had actually met and her gaze was locked on him. Finally she looked away and spoke to the older trader.

"Mr. Burnett, you said he doesn't speak English except a little. Will you ask him a question for me?" When Burnett nodded, she went on. "Will you ask him to tell me what the name Topenebe means and how he got it?"

"I can probably tell you that myself, little lady," Burnett said, "but I'll relay the question so he can answer in his own words." He turned and broke into a brief guttural monologue to the Potawatomi chief. As he finished, Topenebe threw back his head and laughed aloud. He spoke to her in his own tongue, watching her closely and, when he finished, he kept his eyes on her as Burnett interpreted.

"My name, Topenebe, means 'He-Who-Sits-Quietly,' or sometimes just 'Sits-Quietly.' It was given to me by my parents because I did not cry as most other babies did, I just sat quietly. I still most often do so."

"Then, Mr. Burnett, please tell him for me that I like his name and I like him."

Topenebe listened as Burnett spoke to him again, replied briefly and lapsed into silence with a small smile on his lips. Burnett turned back to Margaret. "He says, 'I am glad for what you have said. You are my friend.' And I have to add this, little lady," Burnett continued, speaking for himself, "That's the first time I've ever known Topenebe to call someone a friend on such short acquaintance. Looks as if you've made an important conquest. It'll never hurt you to have Topenebe's friendship."

John Kinzie broke out a flask of whiskey and glasses and all but Margaret drank. They then conversed for a long while, sharing the various items of news they had learned. The most important, so far as John Kinzie was concerned, was Burnett's having heard rumors that the United States was planning to establish a garrison at Chicago, probably in a year or two. If so, the area was sure to become a much more important trading center than it had been since Du Sable had initially established himself there.

"I intend getting in on that, if it's true, John," Burnett said. "I've written to Parker, Girard and Ogilvay — my Montreal supplier — that I expect to be ordering a great deal of goods for there. I've already built a little house at Chicago. Not trading yet, but ready for when the time comes." He raised a speculative eyebrow toward the younger trader. "You still figuring on setting up there, too? I'd have no objection if you did, y'know."

"I'm considering it," John replied noncommittally, but his pulse had quickened and he knew without doubt that once it was positive the United States was establishing a garrison there, he would buy out Jean Baptiste Point du Sable if he had to cash in everything he owned to do so.

[May 8, 1798 — Tuesday]

Spemica Lawba sat in his uncle's lodge on the Whitewater River and looked across the fire at him. Tecumseh had changed a great deal since Spemica Lawba had last seen him at the Deer Creek village shortly after the tribes had signed the Greenville Treaty. He was still a very striking individual but, at age thirty, the quality of boyishness was gone and what remained was quiet manly strength. Sorrows and disappointments had begun to etch lines of character on his face, his gaze was more penetrating than ever before, the jut of his chin more firm and his whole carriage one of greater self-assurance. The entire effect was considerably heightened now by the firelight flickering before him.

To Tecumseh's left sat his brothers Kumskaka and Lowawluwaysica and to his right, his sister — Spemica Lawba's mother — Tecumapese. Beside her was her husband, Wasegoboah. It had been a happy moment for Spemica Lawba to be reunited with all of them again and over their meal they had talked of many things in common in their pasts and equally of the many things that they had done individually since last they met. But then dinner was finished and the pipes were smoked and now it was time, as all present knew, for Spemica Lawba to state his purpose in coming. It was Tecumseh who spoke first.

"My heart wants to believe," he said slowly, a touch of wistfulness in his voice, "that you have come to join us, but my mind says this is not so and that you wish only for us to return to Wapatomica and live again under Catahecassa."

Spemica Lawba shifted uneasily. He grunted an assent, adding, "As always, your mind sees the truth. I have been sent by our chief to ask that you and those who follow you return to your people." He let his eyes slide across those who were present.

"Catahecassa is *your* chief, nephew!" Lowawluwaysica spoke up harshly, the empty eyesocket deep with shadow and his unpleasant features combining in a macabre mask. "He is no longer ours. We are no longer Shawnees. We —"

Tecumseh raised a hand and cut him off, his lips tightening. He turned back to Spemica Lawba. "The words of your uncle are sharply spoken," he said, "but they are nevertheless true. You know that all of us here — and those others who have followed us — cannot agree with Catahecassa that the Greenville Treaty is binding upon us all and that we must bury the hatchet forever. I had always respected Catahecassa, always admired him, and so it came as a hard blow to learn that he really believes the Shemanese will live up to the agreement. It is why we drifted apart; why others clung to me who felt as I did, that our troubles with the Shemanese are not ended. They want ever more of what is ours, and we wish to have returned that of ours which the Shemanese have already taken. How does one come to agreement with they who have burned our villages, killed and imprisoned our people, driven us off our ancestral lands and driven wedges among us to divide us? How does one come to agreement with they who sit at this moment on land stolen from us? We cannot. We step aside now because we are weak, but such will not always be. One day we will be in a position to negotiate from strength, not from weakness, and when that time comes we will rightfully reclaim that which was taken away."

He lapsed into silence and for a considerable period no one spoke. Spemica Lawba was on the verge of doing so but then held his tongue as his mother began to speak softly, a great sadness in her voice. "Tecumseh does not always speak what is in his heart," Tecumapese said, "if he feels it serves no good purpose, but since I am your mother, I will speak what he has left unsaid. It is a difficult enough burden to bear for me — for us! — to know that you have chosen to remain with Catahecassa on the Maumee rather than with us, who are your first blood. It is much worse, much more difficult to understand, when little birds whisper in our ears that you serve with and for the Shemanese; that you carry the words of the soldier Harrison at Fort Washington as his messenger; that you have become the friend of the one who was known as Apekonit, who turned away from his father, Michikiniqua, to aid the Shemanese. These things are true?"

Her twenty-four-year-old son nodded, eyes downcast. In a moment he looked up at her and misery was evident in his expression. But there was defiance, too. "It is true. But not *all* the Shemanese are bad. Many, such as he who gave me the name of Johnny Logan, are good men, who wish nothing to which they are not entitled." He transferred his gaze to Tecumseh. "See what has happened to us. Once we were so strong that the Shemanese begged us for favors. Now, while they have increased to a strength we never knew, we have weakened steadily. More than half our people are separated and live now far west of the Missitheepi. Those who remain see the choices they have only too clearly: oppose the Shemanese and die . . . to no purpose; or else accept the terms of the agreement we have made with them, even though they be not the best for us, and live with them, accepting what little there is for us to accept, rather than lose everything. *That* is what Catahecassa has asked me to express to you." His tone became imploring. "Tecumseh, for your sake and for the sake of our tribe which needs your strength, come back to us."

Tecumseh shook his head. "It is not possible, Spemica Lawba," he said gently. "We are where we are. Our course is set. By ourselves we cannot hope to recover what we have lost, what others have lost and are still losing; others are beginning to feel that which has pierced us for so long. Some are beginning to listen. Soon many others will do so, also, and when they do, then will we begin to have the *strength* to talk with the Shemanese."

"So you will remain here until then?"

Again Tecumseh shook his head. "We leave here soon," he said. "We have been asked by Buckangehela, chief of the Delawares, to come and reside among his people on the White River, to the north and west of here. They have opened their hearts and arms to us, as our own Shawnees will not. They ask us to come and live with them, hunt with them, reside in peace with them. They have asked us, should the time come when it be necessary, if we will lead them against any enemy who might threaten them. We have told them that we will."

[*December 31, 1798 — Monday*]

As Captain William Henry Harrison removed the uniform of his rank at Fort Washington for the last time, he felt no qualms over the loss of his commission as an officer in the United States Army, nor for losing his command of this post at Cincinnati. Much more important opportunities were knocking and Harrison had always been skilled at recognizing such times.

During the early summer the free male population of the Ohio Territory had exceeded five thousand and not long afterward — on August 20 — Governor St. Clair had created Ohio's sixth county and named it Ross, after James Ross, former unsuccessful gubernatorial candidate of the Federalists in Pennsylvania. Those two matters marked a milestone. Their occurrence set Ohio Territory teetering on the brink of eligibility for statehood, according to the Ordinance of 1787. The establishment of only two more counties would fulfill the requirement and that goal was all but foreordained.

The opportunity that knocked for Harrison was an offer he recently received for him to resign his commission and Fort Washington command in favor of becoming Secretary of the Northwest Territory under St. Clair. Without an instant's hesitation, he accepted, at the same time significantly enhancing his chances of becoming the Northwest Territory's first delegate to Congress. Though he was not entirely certain where all this would lead him, William Henry Harrison was sure of two things: it would have to be a great deal better than being commander of an army post on the frontier, and it was merely the beginning of tremendous potential for personal advancement.

[December 31, 1799 — Tuesday]

The 1700s passed out of existence with a deceptive tranquillity still blanketing the Northwest Territory. United States citizens on the frontier breathed something of a collective sigh of relief in the realization that the peace consummated by Anthony Wayne was now in its fifth year. Those who had been pessimistic, gloomily forecasting a quick resumption of hostilities by the Indians, were now forced to draw in their horns a bit and admit that, well, maybe there *was* a permanent peace in the land.

There was a sense of comfort in the "normality" of events that were occurring throughout the United States. In Ohio, the first meeting of the Territorial Legislature was appointed on September 16, with the two houses organized for business eight days later. The governor, Arthur St. Clair, orated extensively and Dr. Edward Tiffin was first chosen to the Territorial Legislature and then unanimously elected as its speaker. And just as the astute young William Henry Harrison anticipated would occur, he was elected as delegate to Congress by the slimmest possible margin; the twenty-six-year-old Secretary of the Territory squeaked by with eleven of the twenty-one votes.

At Chicago, Jean Baptiste Point du Sable's daughter, Susanne, and her husband, Jean Baptiste Pelletier, finally got around to doing what they had been so long promising themselves they would do. With their daughter, Eulalie, they traveled all the way to Cahokia on the Mississippi, just below St. Louis, and there, on October 7, the day before her third birthday, Eulalie Pelletier finally received her Christian baptism.

Well to the northeast, at Detroit, painfully realizing its lack of strength on the Great Lakes, the United States government finally launched a brand-new brig and a new schooner from the River Rouge shipyard in October. The schooner was a sleek sailing vessel of ninety tons christened the *Tracy*, after Connecticut's Senator Uriah Tracy who happened to be visiting in Detroit at the time of her launching. The second — and more important — craft in the budding United States fleet on the Great Lakes, launched at nearly the same time as the *Tracy*, was the 150-ton U.S. brig *Adams*, named after the President — a very sturdy vessel whose cost was in the vicinity of fifty thousand dollars.

At Fort Wayne, the farm of Indian agent William Wells was prospering due to the efforts of his slaves who cared for it, but there was a signal lack of interest in such agricultural pursuits among the Indians of the area and Wells began to have strong doubts that the agricultural assistance programs for the Indians presently being developed by the government were going to be the success that many were anticipating. On the whole, the Indians were eager for the harvest that came from the fields, but almost totally disinterested in the spring-to-fall farming procedures which allowed such a harvest to occur.

At the St. Joseph River, the bond of friendship between the John Kinzie family and Chief Topenebe grew ever stronger and Shawneeawkee's new trading post there prospered amazingly. Despite William Burnett's optimism of the year before that very soon the United States would build a fort at Chicago, no such fort had yet been built and, so far as anyone could determine, none was even planned. It was a disappointment to Burnett who, to John Kinzie's quiet relief, abandoned his plan of establishing a trading post there. Even more to Kinzie's liking was the report he had received that because the government had failed to establish a post at Chicago as rumor had projected it would, Jean Baptiste Point du Sable had gone into a deep depression and was finally convinced that his long-cherished dream of Chicago becoming a major trading center was still, and would always be, nothing more than a dream. Du Sable let the news slip that he was ready to sell out — for the right price and to the right person.

John Kinzie was under no illusions: he very much wanted Du Sable's post and he could gather the "right price" that Du Sable wanted, but he also knew that because of the long-standing nebulous sense of antipathy that existed between them, Du Sable would never knowingly sell to him. So, in an acceptably devious manner, he called in his clerk, Jack Lalime, and spent long hours instructing him in how he should approach Du Sable with an offer to buy the establishment, apparently on his own so far as Du Sable was concerned, but actually with Kinzie's money and as Kinzie's agent. John Kinzie had long believed in his own heart that, one way or another, he would someday own the Du Sable trading post at Chicago. Now, at last, it was all looking very probable instead of merely an outside possibility.

Everything seemed peaceful, but there were warning signals if one were attuned to them. Some of the Indians were becoming restless. The annuities established for the Potawatomies by the terms of the Greenville Treaty were being paid, it was true, but only to those branches of the Potawatomi tribe closest to the frontier — at St. Joseph, Fort Wayne, the Elkhart River villages, on the upper Wabash and on the Tippecanoe. But the Potawatomi branches on the Iroquois, the Kankakee, Peoria Lake and the Illinois, on the Des Plaines and the Fox, on Lake Geneva and at the mouth of the Chicago and Milwackie Rivers were receiving nothing and they were becoming very unhappy with the arrangement. They, along with scattered factions of the Kickapoos, Ottawas, Chippewas and Shawnees, were beginning to lean far more to help from the British at Amherstburg than to the Americans.

There was yet one more important division among the tribes and at the core of it was an influential thirty-two-year-old warrior of proven courage and sagacity, who advocated that the Indians of all tribes remain wholly aloof from *any* whites — American, British, Spanish, French or whomever. For the first time, that warrior had this year spoken publicly at a council held north of the new town of Urbana in the Ohio country, expressing his feelings in stirring words which drove deeply into the minds and hearts of his red listeners from various tribes. The uncommon eloquence of the warrior at this council greatly enhanced his stature and influence among the tribes. At the same time, those among the white settlers sharp enough to perceive something ominous developing here were becoming very nervous indeed. This was not simply a tribal council where one tribe expressed itself in terms geared for that tribe alone or possibly including its closest allies. This council was an intertribal affair, attended in temporary neutrality by chiefs and warriors from many tribes, no few of which were normally hostile to one another. The eloquent speaker had his greatest impact on the younger, more hot-blooded warriors in attendance, who clung to his words in fascination. To his right sat his good friend, a twenty-eight-year-old chief who was born of an Ottawa father and Seneca mother but who was now Potawatomi through marriage and whose name was Chaubenee. To the speaker's left sat a younger warrior, just twenty-one, born of an English father and a Potawatomi mother and his name was Tequitoh, better known as Sauganash. Both had become adoring followers of the speaker, who had been born a Shawnee.

His name was Tecumseh.

Unlike most previous Indian orators, who depended upon great gesticulation and no little degree of showmanship to put across their points, Tecumseh stood almost still as he spoke. He did not bellow out his words, yet his rich voice carried clearly to all in attendance. For his listeners, accustomed to involved rhetoric accompanied by a ranting and often raving delivery, the simplicity of his speaking caught them off guard and drove home with phenomenal impact, holding them spellbound. His talk on this occasion had lasted for over an hour as he drew a stark verbal comparison of what this beautiful country had been before the coming of the Shemanese and what it was now.

"My brothers," he concluded, "how can our people continue to deceive themselves with their foolish belief in the supposed strength of the white chief Wayne's treaty signed at his fort of Greenville? The only difference between this treaty and the hundreds before it is the boundary line. Each time we have been told, 'This, Indian brother, is the last treaty; the one that will be honored by red men and white alike for all time.' Such lies make the vomit burn in my throat. This is *not* the last treaty. There will be another. And another after that. And others to follow. And each time it will be the Indians, your people and mine, who will be pushed back, not the whites. At this very moment an hour's easy ride to the south is the newest of the white settlements. The cold spring there that has always flowed for us now satisfies the whites living in the fourteen cabins they have built by it. Soon other whites will come and build. And will all of these be content to stay behind Wayne's boundary? On my tongue is the harsh laughter of mockery. Think on this, brothers. Put aside your anger. Put aside your fear. Put aside your vain hopes. Think without prejudice of what I have said here and it will become clear to you as it is to me why the very leaves of the forest drop tears of pity on us as we walk beneath. And after you think on it, remember this: any child can snap with ease the single hair from the horse's tail, but not the strongest man, nor the wildest stallion, can break the rope woven of those same hairs."

CHAPTER VII

[*March 12, 1800 — Wednesday*]

JEAN BAPTISTE POINT DU SABLE stood on the north bank of the Chicago River and took a long final look at the residue of what had once been his glorious dream. It was, he knew, the last time he would ever see it. Not being inclined to twist the knife already in his heart, he was determined never to return.

The three medium-sized bateaux loaded with his family and personal possessions were snugged to shore. Ready to shove off as soon as he stepped aboard and gave the word were the eighteen French Canadian voyageurs he had hired in addition to his own six employees to aid in the transportation, especially across the Chicago Portage. Standing beside Du Sable on the shore was the man to whom he had just sold his substantial property here at Chicago, Jack Lalime.[135] Close to them was Du Sable's friend and neighbor, Antoine Ouilmette, along with his family. Four other men were here as well, having accompanied Lalime to Chicago from the St. Joseph. The two standing nearby had come for the avowed purpose of acting as witnesses to the transaction and to sign the bill of sale as such. They were William Burnett and John Kinzie. The other two, presently inside the post, were alleged employees of Lalime, who would remain and tend the post for the time being.

A hundred feet or so distant stood a cluster of blanket-clad Potawatomies, with Chief Black Partridge at their head, to watch the departure of the Du Sables, and Chief Topenebe, who had accompanied the traders from St. Joseph to Chicago, stood with him. The two had been close friends for many years. Nearby was Black Partridge's younger brother, Mkedepoke, chief of a small village on the Fox River some forty-five miles from here. Jean Baptiste and his wife, Gohna, had already said their farewells to the Indians, who now merely waited in expressionless silence for the departure, sorry to see the Du Sables leave after all these years and wondering what sort of treatment they might expect from the new trader, Lalime, whom they knew not at all. What Topenebe told them about Lalime was not at all encouraging. At one point the powerful St. Joseph Potawatomi fingered his tomahawk while watching Lalime and murmured to Black Partridge, "It would not surprise me if one day that man forced me to lift his scalp." Nevertheless, he reassured Black Partridge by informing him that it was actually the Shawneeawkee who would become owner of Du Sable's post. Lalime would only be a temporary caretaker.

Lalime was a very short, rough, swarthy man with a heavy moustache and dark brows over narrow eyes. Married to a Potawatomi woman from Michigan named Nokenoqua, he was a man who laughed a great deal, but usually without much humor, a half-breed born some thirty years before near Mackinac, the son of an Englishman and a Chippewa woman, raised in both cultures and never really belonging to either. His education was mediocre, gained largely at Jesuit mission schools, and he was neither terribly bright nor overly ambitious. Yet there was about him a native shrewdness that elevated him somewhat over the Canadian voyageur companions among whom he grew up. He had a good ear for language and spoke fluently in the various regional dialects of the Chippewa, Ottawa, Potawatomi and Menominee tribes. He was also relatively conversant in the Winnebago, Sac, Miami and Shawnee tongues. He was not quite so honest as he might have been in his dealings with the Indians, which was primarily the reason why, even though he could manage to survive in the work, he would never excel as a trader. He greatly disliked shouldering responsibility and so most often worked at jobs — such as clerk or interpreter — where his duties were clear and essentially simple.

Until now, Jack Lalime had never been troubled very much by ambition, content to flow with the currents of whatever authority existed where he happened to be. Yet, in today's purchase of the Du Sable property in his name but actually for John Kinzie, he was surprised by the strong flame of ambition that had been ignited within him. In the inspection of the property and its setting, he saw at once how it was situated as the hub of six major Indian trails, as well as being at the strategically located Lake Michigan entry to the Chicago Portage that connected the Great Lakes with the Mississippi.[136] Lalime saw as well what Du Sable, Burnett and John Kinzie had recognized long before — the amazing potential of the site. Of the four, however, only Kinzie and Lalime remained optimistic about the United States government eventually building a post here. Du Sable and Burnett had grown weary of waiting for that dream to become a reality. Now Lalime was suddenly finding himself regretting that he had agreed to act, unbeknownst to Du Sable, as Kinzie's agent in this transaction. Although he successfully masked his feelings, a strong resentment was welling in him that it was Kinzie rather than himself who would own this valuable property. The fact that even had it been available to him as an individual, there was no way he could have amassed the finances to purchase it, was of little consequence to Lalime. He was jealous of the wealth of John Kinzie — wealth, he reasoned, which he had helped his employer to accumulate. The purchase price was six thousand French livres, each livre equivalent to about one pound of pure silver.

John Kinzie had become filled with excitement during the tour of the property, when he and Burnett accompanied Lalime and Du Sable. It was better by far than he anticipated and, while at this point it was still no more than an investment for the future, there was no doubt whatever in his mind that the property was worth considerably more than the purchase price and its potential was enormous. The bill of sale, written in French, still clenched in Lalime's hand, listed the principal assets of the property being purchased and Du Sable had ticked them off one by one as they made their inspection. The "mansion," as it was described on the bill, was a comfortable wooden house having eight hundred eighty square feet of living area on the ground floor, plus a loft nearly as large. The building itself had dimensions of twenty-two by forty feet. That was only the beginning.

There were two very well built barns, the larger measuring twenty-eight by forty feet and the smaller, twenty-four by thirty. There was also a fine horse-mill for the grinding of flour, equipped with two large millstones — the structure measuring twenty-four by thirty-six feet. There was more. In addition to an excellent bakehouse with dimensions of eighteen by twenty feet, there was a smokehouse, a poultry house, a dairy and a well-equipped workshop. There was also an uncompleted building — a horse stable — with all the sawn lumber stacked nearly ready for the barn to be finished.

The tools, equipment and furnishings that came with the purchase were no less impressive and valuable. The residence contained a lovely four-by-eight-foot French cabinet constructed of solid black walnut, highly polished and fronted with four heavy leaded-glass doors. There were a few tables and chairs and beds and, in the kitchen, wash tubs, wash stands, dry sinks and eleven copper kettles. A wide array of tools and equipment was in the outbuildings. Small items — kegs of nails, hand planes, files, rasps, hatchets and other minor hand tools — were not separately listed, but among the major items catalogued were eight long-handled axes, both single and double-bitted, and a number of excellent saws, including a large ripsaw, a plank saw, a seven-inch crosscut, a cooper's saw and several ordinary hand saws. There was a fully equipped kit of carpenter's tools, seven scythes, eight sickles, a plow and three carts. In the adjacent pens and barns there were two excellent mules, a herd of twenty-nine fully grown milk cows and one bull, plus two fine calves recently born. There

were also forty-four egg-producing hens and twenty-eight hogs, of which
seven or eight of the sows were nearly ready to drop new litters. All in
all, it was much more than John Kinzie had expected and he was delighted.

Now, on the riverbank, Du Sable shook hands with Jack Lalime a final
time, wished him success in his new enterprise here, and stepped into the
first bateau. He took a seat beside Gohna and nodded to his principal
clerk who, in turn, shouted an order. The three bateaux were immediately
thrust out from shore into the sluggish current.[137] The bateaux were
bulky, high-sided, ungainly craft designed for the freighting of goods. Yet,
as the voyageurs dipped their oars, these graceless scows suddenly came to
life and slipped through the water with surprising speed and smoothness.

The voyageurs were a wild-appearing lot, most with unkempt black hair
and beards and each, without exception, wearing a peculiar conical cap
which flopped over to one side and was tassled at the end. The caps were
of different colors — most of them scarlet, but here and there an engagee
was wearing one of bright yellow or orange, blue or green. Their shirts
were, almost without exception, heavy red flannel that was well stained
with dirt, grease and sweat. Though the temperature today was in the low
forties, few of the men wore coats, not wishing their movements to be
hampered and knowing that their labors at the oars would soon generate
heat enough to make them very comfortable. A few wore grubby leather
vests over their shirts.

Less than a dozen yards from the point of embarkation, the boatmen
broke into song, the pace of the music timed to the dipping of the oars.
The melody, sung in French, had a sweet, haunting quality. Though the
sound softened with distance, even after the three boats had turned left a
quarter-mile upstream and passed from sight as they headed up the South
Branch toward the portage, the song could faintly be heard. It was always
the way of the voyageurs, whether in bateau or canoe, to ceaselessly sing
their songs — lovely, lonely, poignant songs that almost always had love
as their theme.

John Kinzie emerged from the trading post, having gone inside to give
his two men their instructions as the bateaux were moving away. He
walked back to the shore where William Burnett and Jack Lalime still
stood. He reached out casually, relieved Lalime of the bill of sale and then
canted his head toward the canoe beached on the shoreline close by.

"Well," he said, "let's head for Detroit and get this sale recorded."[138]

[*January 1, 1801 — Thursday*]

It was highly significant that at the very instant the Nineteenth Century
began this morning at one second after midnight, one of the most important discussions ever held in North America to this time was occurring in
an Indian wegiwa on the White River, less than twenty-five miles west of

Fort Greenville.[139] The wegiwa, situated on a little knoll a few yards from the river, was set somewhat apart from the score of others in the Delaware village. In those other lodges were upwards of one hundred Delaware and Shawnee Indians, peacefully sleeping and wholly unaware of the momentous meeting taking place here.

The night was clear and bright and very cold. The heavy cloud cover of yesterday had vanished and the knee-deep blanket of snow it had deposited surrounded the wegiwa, stark against the naked dark woodland beyond. A heavy buffalo-skin flap, rolled down from the top and securely tied along sides and bottom, sealed the lone entry to the wegiwa and the only visible movement outside was a faintly wavering column of smoke rising almost straight upward in the quiet night air from the peak of the structure. There were, in the pleasantly warm interior of this small lodge constructed of flimsy wooden poles covered with skins, six men and one woman.

To be included in this meeting was, so far as Chaubenee was concerned, a tremendous honor. The Potawatomi village chief was almost thirty and an impressive figure. His stocky body possessed phenomenal physical strength and, though his features were rounded, almost cherubic, there was about him an unmistakable aura of self-assurance and power. Chaubenee had come here at the express invitation of Tecumseh, as had Roundhead, second chief of the Wyandots under Tarhe.

For longer than any of them could remember, the Wyandots — a branch of the Hurons long separated from the mother tribe — had been the most revered of all the Great Lakes tribes. Where the chiefs of other tribes might be addressed in intertribal congresses by familial terms such as brother, nephew, uncle or even father, only the Wyandot chiefs were ever addressed as grandfather — a term of great respect. That even the whites were cognizant of the ranking of the Wyandots among these tribes was clearly evident when, at the conclusion of the Greenville Treaty, the official records for all the Indians involved had been placed by General Wayne in the care of Tarhe — the Crane — who was principal chief of the Wyandots.

Roundhead was here for this meeting because although he had attended the Greenville Treaty negotiations, he had been one of the few important chiefs in attendance who had refused to sign the treaty. As Tecumseh did, Roundhead viewed the treaty as only one more of a long line of treaties that shoved the Indian–white boundary farther west and north and established an interval of peace for only so long as it took the whites to quickly populate the new territory acquired. As was becoming more obvious with the passage of each moon, the Greenville Treaty was little different. The peace it established in 1795 had lasted longer, true, but the encroachment of the whites had swiftly followed and the territory they had acquired was becoming filled. When the treaty was first signed, the permanent population of whites north of the Spaylaywitheepi in the Ohio country — primarily at Marietta and Cincinnati, protected respectively by Fort Harmar and Fort Washington — was not much more than eight hundred. Now, five and a half years later, the population of whites in the Ohio country exceeded forty-five *thousand*. It took no great visionary to realize that the tendrils of insidious white infiltration would soon again be worming their way into the Indian territory. In the past year the stage had been set for it, which was the reason this meeting was presently being held.

It was because Roundhead felt as Tecumseh did — as well as because of the considerable influence he held among the Northwestern tribes — that he had been invited to participate in this very private council. Nevertheless, despite his high station, it was apparent that Roundhead felt great deference to Tecumseh — a self-exiled Shawnee who was not even a chief, although there were many who already considered him as such.

The remaining members of this little group who were bringing in the new century with such quiet auspiciousness were related. Along with Chaubenee and Roundhead, they sat upon the thick warmth of multiple buffalo rugs on the floor around the small fire. Directly opposite the doorway sat Tecumseh, who was thirty-three and who clearly dominated the group. Chaubenee and Roundhead sat to his left and beyond them was one of Tecumseh's triplet brothers, Kumskaka. The latter was a quiet individual who bore a vague resemblance to their elder brother, Chiksika, who had been killed so long ago in the Tennessee country. Although he had never excelled as a warrior or leader, he was unalterably devoted to Tecumseh and had become, of his own choice, something of an official bodyguard to him.

To Tecumseh's right sat Tecumapese. Though ten years older than Tecumseh, she was still a remarkably handsome woman, her features firm, unblemished and so cleanly chiseled she might have been a masterpiece sculpted beneath the skilled hands of a Michelangelo. Her intelligence and sensitivity were such that she had become the only person from whom Tecumseh would unreservedly accept advice and counsel. Beside her sat Wasegoboah, not only her husband but, with the possible exception of Chaubenee, Tecumseh's closest friend. It had become axiomatic that wherever Tecumseh was, there too would be found Wasegoboah — a pillar of strength and dependability upon whom Tecumseh relied without reservation.

The final member of the group sat to Wasegoboah's right. The remaining survivor of the triplets, Lowawluwaysica, was only a month away from being thirty. He resembled no one in the wegiwa, not even his own triplet brother, Kumskaka. Though not really thin, his features were hatchetlike, the nose sharply beaked, the cheekbones high and protuberant and the cheeks themselves hollow. Perceptibly bucktoothed, his features seemed to have been carelessly tossed together with peculiar asymmetry. One of his ears had a lobe half again as long as the other and his thin lips crooked up on the right, down on the left. Over his empty right eyesocket he had only recently begun to wear a black eye patch presented to him by a trader.

In character, Lowawluwaysica was nervous and usually irritable. His rare, explosive laughter — more often elicited from someone else's discomfort than because of humor — was a shrill, grating cackle. He was swift to take offense at imagined slights and susceptible to bursts of blind rage. Tecumseh was everything he was not and, perhaps for this reason among others, Lowawluwaysica idolized his older brother, became abject under his scowl and heaven-borne beneath his smile.

Long before Lowawluwaysica had left the Shawnees with Tecumseh, he had taken to tribal medicine, attempting to learn from the skilled Shawnee medicine men the secrets of curing sickness and invoking spirits. Such secrets were closely guarded and at this, as at most other things to which he had turned his hand, he was less than mediocre. Yet, he had managed to pick up enough of their simpler skills that when he left the tribe, he proclaimed himself the medicine man of the village Tecumseh established and was rarely seen anywhere without his mysterious pouch filled with herbs and bones and symbolic bits of material. He had memorized many of the healing chants and had even, from all appearances, effected a few cures. He longed for renown in his own right and, secretly convinced in his own heart that he would never acquire it, he clung closer to his brother and basked in the reflected glow of Tecumseh's growing fame.

The private council in the wegiwa had begun after darkness had fallen last night, after bellies had been filled, bladders emptied and pipes smoked. Then Tecumseh began to speak. It was not an oration, but rather a quiet conversation. Very soon his six listeners realized that what they were hearing might well affect the remainder of their lives.

Tecumseh touched on the occurrences of the past year that directly or indirectly affected them all, most of them ominous in their portent. Nine moons ago, in March, Connecticut had ceded its Western Reserve to the United States government and immediately there was a commencement of the allocation of lands to satisfy land bounty warrants issued to American soldiers who had fought in the Revolution. At that time the new United States had not had the funds to pay the soldiers, and so land had been promised instead. Now those promises were being fulfilled. By April a thousand new settlers had poured into what had been the Western Reserve south of Lake Erie. Sawmills had been built and seven hundred miles of new roads had been cut through virgin land. On the tenth of that month, the Americans had established another frontier fort, well above the

Greenville Treaty line near the mouth of the Maumee and named it Fort Industry.[140]

A short while later, the soldier who had commanded Fort Washington and then became Secretary of the Northwest Territory and one of its two delegates to Congress — William Henry Harrison — had risen in Congress Hall and introduced a bill proposing that Congress divide the Northwest Territory into two parts — one to be the Ohio Territory, which was now on the brink of statehood; the other to be the remainder to the west and north. On May 7, 1800, the division had occurred and the new boundary was drawn from the mouth of the Kentucky River to Fort Recovery and then directly north to the Canadian territorial line. Everything westward to the Mississippi River was now the Indiana Territory, with the seat of government at Vincennes on the Wabash. President John Adams had then appointed a governor to this vast Indiana Territory, giving that individual such powers as had never before been bestowed upon any individual, civilian or military, since the organization of the nation, making of him a virtual king of the territory, responsible only to the President and even that to a relatively minor degree. That chosen individual was able at will to enact any law and he held within his grasp the power of life and death over anyone within the territory, Indian or white. And, Tecumseh pointed out gravely, that individual had been given the power to treat with the Indians in any manner he saw fit on behalf of the United States. Amazingly, the appointee — a tall, slender, gaunt man with brooding eyes and somber countenance beneath a shock of unruly rusty-colored hair — was only twenty-seven years old. His name was William Henry Harrison.

Even as he spoke the name, there was a tightening of Tecumseh's expression, as if he were containing only with great effort a vast hatred for this man; a hatred laced with a wariness that seemed to border on fear. Tecumseh's listeners glanced at one another wonderingly. How was it that such a reaction could occur in him at the mere mention of the young white man's name? What was there about him, seen by Tecumseh, that was hidden from them? They did not know, but an ominous chill touched them all as Tecumseh went on.

"All during the past summer," he said, "and into the fall and winter and even now, this Harrison has been establishing himself at Vincennes, building a great house such as this land has never seen, from which he intends to run our lives — mine, yours, the lives of all Indians." His voice became lower, abruptly filled with a huskiness that shocked them. "He is aided by many, but three in particular who can do us great harm. One of these," he glanced to his left, "is a village chief of your own Potawatomi tribe, Chaubenee. His name is Winnemac and his lips are always at the ear of Harrison. Harrison listens! He learned this from the soldier he served at Fallen Timbers — General Wayne; learned to listen and to heed the advice of those who have been more intimate with the enemy than he. In this he admits humility and in that humility there is great strength. Few leaders ever acquire such ability, but those who do accomplish many things."

Chaubenee nodded. "I know Winnemac," he said, "though not well. I have heard more of him than I know of my own witness. I am told that he considers himself to be more than he is; that he craves power over all the Potawatomi, which he will never get, not so long as we have such chiefs as Topenebe, Onoxa, Pinequa, Gomo, Siggenauk and Black Partridge."

"And Chaubenee," Tecumseh reminded softly, smiling.

"You said three could do us harm, Brother," interjected Lowawluwaysica. "Who are the other two?"

A fleeting frown passed across Tecumseh's face as he looked at his one-eyed brother, then stared into the dying fire. As if it were a command, Lowawluwaysica scrambled to his feet and moved into a shadowed recess of the wegiwa, returning in a moment with a small armload of medium-sized branch sections and a dry, barkless log about the length of his lower leg. He quickly positioned the branch sections across the coals and then lay the log atop them and resumed his seat. In a moment the branches burst into flame and licked at the log, brightening the interior. Still, Tecumseh looked into the fire wordlessly, as if seeking a vision. Lowawluwaysica fidgeted and seemed about to speak again, but held his tongue as Tecumseh went on.

"Another is he who was once white, then Indian, now white again; he whom we knew as Apekonit or sometimes Epiconyare" — there was contempt in his voice as he spat out the word, for Epiconyare meant brave and loyal —"but who is now William Wells. He learned much from his father, Michikiniqua, and from the Miamis until he began to be afraid of their future and returned to the protection of the whites. He knows about us and our ways and now he, too, tells Harrison much and performs many tasks for him which he pretends are for our benefit."

He paused again and when, after a moment, he did not continue, Tecumapese rolled her eyes toward him and spoke the words he seemed reluctant to say.

"And the third," she said tonelessly, "is my son and your nephew, Spemica Lawba."

Tecumseh nodded. "Yes. Because of the kindness of one man among the Shemanese, he has turned his heart toward them. He remains in Wapatomica with Catahecassa and Pskipahcah Ouiskelotha and the children she has borne him, but he journeys often to Vincennes and Harrison has already come to rely heavily on him for many things, among which is convincing Catahecassa that he must keep the Shawnees quiet and in place." Bitterness laced the words.

"Harrison sees too clearly for one with eyes so young," he went on, "and his eyes are set upon even more distant things which will affect all of us."

For the first time since the pipes had been finished, Roundhead spoke up. "Your eyes are as clear, Tecumseh, and they see farther and deeper. If they did not, we would not be here this night. Since you came to this village you have been thinking, and before that you thought on the Whitewater River, and even before that, at Deer Creek, it is said that you thought deeply." He grunted, sure of his ground, picked up a tiny section of twig from the matted brown hair of the buffalo skin beneath him and flicked it into the fire. "All of these thoughts of yours have now come together. Now it is time for them to become words for our ears. Will you give them to us?"

Tecumseh smiled at him. "You know my heart very well, Grandfather." The smile vanished as rapidly as it had appeared. "Yes, it is time for thoughts to become words. I have a plan. I have thought on it for many seasons. I have altered it many times to fit conditions as they have changed. Now there is little more changing that can be done and as the thoughts become words, the words must then become actions."

He came to his feet in a fluid movement, the blanket which had been over his shoulders falling softly at his heels. He wore heavy buckskin leggins and a long-sleeved shirt of the same material which, untucked, fell nearly to his knees. Thick, high-topped elkhide moccasins encased his feet and were laced with rawhide up his calves. A necklace of down-curved bear claws separated by inch-long cylinders of silver hung around his neck — a gift from Michikiniqua a decade ago following St. Clair's defeat; the claws being trophies of Michikiniqua's hunts and symbols of strength, and the silver dividers having been purchased from Shawneeawkee — the English silversmith and trader named John Kinzie — when he had his trading post on the Maumee.

A change had come over Tecumseh. It was something sensed rather than seen, and all who were present felt it strongly. He did not look at any of them, nor at the fire. His gaze was steady and straight ahead but what he saw was not within the wegiwa. And when he spoke, it was with a different timbre, filled with vision and hope and at times crackling with contained excitement that affected them all.

"What I see," he began, "may take ten or twelve summers of great effort to bring about, but I can do it. I *will* do so! Should my plan ripen into success — and it *must!* — the Shemanese will be driven back, not only across the Spaylaywitheepi, but even beyond the mountains which first greet the morning sun.

"Given equal arms and equal numbers, there is no force of white men which can stand before us. How many times have mere handfuls of Indians driven back white forces that were greatly superior? How few times have we ourselves been defeated by them, and then only through their greater numbers and stronger weapons? The victory over the general called Harmar showed what a small force of Indians could do to a larger Shemanese army. The victory over the general called St. Clair showed what a large Indian force could do to a smaller Shemanese army, even though it had cannons and better rifles and had only to hold and defend, not attack.

"Beginning in the Wet Moon," he went on, referring to April, "I will begin drawing the tribes together, but not in a confederation. Past confederations, such as those that were formed under Pontiac and Thayendanegea and even Michikiniqua, eventually failed. There were two reasons: their leadership eventually fell apart and the confederacies were not united strongly enough in the first instance to overcome the tribal hatreds that existed among them."

Tecumseh shook his head faintly. "No. They were doomed from the beginning. That is not what I will make. Mine will be a union not of five or six tribes loosely brought together to fight a common enemy. That is not enough. I will do much more. With the help of Moneto and the gifts he has given me — the abilities to see and speak and convince — I will ride far and visit many. I will take my time and convince the tribes of the necessity of joining together without hatred between them to gnaw at them and eventually destroy them. I will tell them these things in such a manner that they will stamp their feet and clap their hands and shout, and they will chafe at any delay in forming the union. One by one I will draw together and interweave in a single force the warriors of fifty or more different tribes. When at last we confront the whites, it will not be with just a few thousand warriors. No! It will be with a single unified body of *fifty thousand* warriors!"

His listeners caught their breaths at the vision and the grip of Wasegoboah's hand on his wife's elbow nearly paralyzed her arm. Chaubenee's eyes were glinting and Roundhead's mouth had fallen open. Kumskaka stared at his older brother rapturously and Lowawluwaysica was literally trembling with his excitement, his small teeth glinting in a savage grin.

"With such a force," Tecumseh continued, "we may have no need greater than showing ourselves to gain what we wish. I hope we will not *have* to fight. No more Indians must be killed needlessly. White leaders will recognize our power and for once it will be *they* who must give in to our terms. And *our* demands will be that they withdraw from our country and return eastward of the mountains. If possible, we will avoid war, but if it comes to war, we will not turn aside!

"The travels I made with Chiksika as a boy and later as a young man," he went on, the fervor of his talk lessening slightly, "showed me the strength of the various tribes. They are strong, very strong, all of them . . .

as individuals! Against the whites, as individual tribes, they are neverthe-less too weak. Even in small confederations, with each still retaining its own tribal form and its own leadership, they could not oppose the whites for long, though they were stronger and could hold their own for a while. But in the union I foresee, where they will be joined all under a single strong leadership against the most deadly foe in any of our histories, that enemy will be swept away as the autumn leaves before the wind that springs from the west!

"I will start my unification of the Indians with fifty tribes. There are more than that, many more, and once they see the value of the strength of our union, they will all hasten to join us. From the northeast there will be the Iroquois — Mohawks, Oneidas, Cayugas, Onondagas, Senecas, and their nephews, the Tuscarawas. From our own country there will be Wyandots and Potawatomies and Delawares, Miamis and the children of the Miamis — Weas and Eel Rivers and Piankeshaws. And there will be our own Shawnees, who will see at last the values to which they are now blinded. From the north I will collect the Hurons and Ottawas and Chip-pewas, and the children of the Chippewas, the Mississaugies. From the northwest, the Menominees and Winnebagoes, the Mandans and Dako-tahs. In the west I will draw together the Sacs and their brothers, the Foxes, and from beyond the Mississippi, the Iowas and Sioux, the Chey-enne, the Poncas and Pawnees and Omahas, the Otos and Missouries, the Osages and Kansas and Ouichitas.

"That is not all!" He lifted an arm arrow-straight and pointed. "From the southwest will come the Quapaws and Yazoos, the Caddos and Hasinais and Kitchais and Tawakonias." He moved his arm. "From the south, our good friends the Cherokees, and their neighbors, the Choctaws and Chickasaws, the Alabamas and Biloxies and Upper Creeks. And from the southeast, those warriors who remain of the Santees and Catawbas, and the Lower Creeks and their brothers, the Seminoles."

Lowawluwaysica had suddenly frowned and opened his mouth to speak, but Tecumseh slashed his extended arm sideways through the air and cut him off. "Think not that they will not come. They will! With the gift of prophecy that Moneto has given me — as he gave it to my father and to my brother who died in my arms — I will give them more than merely words. I will give them signs in which to believe. I will call upon their honor, their pride, their religion, their superstitions. Every argument, every force I can bring to bear, I will do so without hesitation.

"You here will help me," he said, his gaze sweeping across them, his burning eyes holding them transfixed. "Each of you will have a contribu-tion to give to make this plan ripen and come to fruit. Each of you will pass along to your own people and to others the *need* for them to join us if they are to survive. Roundhead will do it with his influence and his strength, Chaubenee with his passion, Wasegoboah and Tecumapese and Kumskaka with their persuasion and conviction that it remains our *only* course for survival, and Lowawluwaysica will put to good use his obvious talents — his ability to agitate, to anger, to stir to a fury against the Shemanese the thoughts of every Indian.

"We will form a new village and it will not be the village of a tribe nor of several tribes. It will be a village of *Indians!* We will not be Shawnees nor Potawatomies nor Wyandots nor Cherokees nor Sioux. We will be *Indians,* all of us! It will happen, but it will not happen easily nor quickly. As I told you in the beginning, it will take ten or twelve years of very great effort to bring about. But I tell you again, it *will* happen. With some of the tribes we will have to move slowly, carefully, gradually gaining their confidence, their respect, their willingness to follow. With other tribes it will go swiftly, with only a word or two needed for the war belts to begin circulating and the tomahawks to be struck into the war posts.

"Now," he added, his voice dropping, "what is most important of all: while this is going on, *they must not show it!* They must abide by their treaties at all costs. They must, when the time comes — as come it will! — overlook infringement of their rights by the whites. They must profess a peaceable intent in all things until we are ready. If there is any possibility of accomplishing our aims without warfare, then this must be the course we follow. But, war or not, it will be done. And the facts of what we are doing must be kept from the whites. No outsider must ever be allowed to sit in on the councils and those who might feel they have a right to sit in but are against us — those such as Spemica Lawba and Winnemac and William Wells — must be denied.

"We ourselves, all of us, must faithfully, honestly and forever bury whatever past insults and hostilities and animosities have risen between us and each of us, as individuals, must treat every other, regardless of his tribe, as no less than a fellow Indian fighting at his side for the same cause.

"In the village we will establish, and for the new race of *Indians* we will create, we must set up strong guides and codes that will enable us to reach the important goal we seek. We must absolutely cease the drinking of alcohol in any form. Though our pipes may still be filled with kinni-kinnick, we must stop our smoking of the tall green weed which brings strange dreams and weaknesses that could defeat us. We must, politely but firmly, break whatever alliances presently exist between us and the whites — be they Americans, British, French or Spanish. We must encourage our Indians to accept from the whites anything of value they wish to offer in the form of gratuities or annuities, but they must join no white force to fight another white force, for in that direction lies ruin. With past alliances, Indians have been used, manipulated like tools, to promote only the welfare of one white faction over another. Let the whites fight among themselves if they wish. It will weaken them. But let not any Indian bind himself to any white man or white cause or white ideal.

"There will be occasions when we must temporarily swallow our pride, and this will be one of the greater difficulties to overcome. At such times, if necessary, we must fall back when the Shemanese nudge us. We must turn our cheeks and pretend to be rabbits and under no pretext must we take up the hatchet against the whites until — and unless! — there is no other choice, and then not until I myself give the sign. Later I will say what this sign will be, but I tell you now that it will be a sign that will come to all of the tribes on the same day and at the same time.

"Finally," he concluded, "when the period of waiting and building and growing is over, we will demand the return of our lands. With such a great unified force to give power to our demand, there is every reason to hope and believe the whites will leave our lands peaceably. But if they will not, then I will give the signal. If and when this unmistakable sign is given, our irresistible wave of warriors will wash across the face of the land to drown every white man who has not the sense to flee east of the mountains of the east."

[*June 26, 1801 — Friday*]

Captain John Whistler, company commander in the United States First Infantry at Detroit, completed his perusal of the company's morning report, signed it with his usual flourish and then leaned back in his chair and stretched, feeling a succession of his vertebrae popping as he did so and enjoying the sensation. There were a few other military paperwork chores he had to complete before the day was finished, but he decided to put them off until the afternoon.

He packed his pipe slowly, tamping the tobacco into the bowl with the tip of his little finger. From his desk drawer he removed a slender sliver of wood several inches long from a box of similar pieces and leaned forward, holding the tip of it over the highly polished hurricane lamp that had been illuminating his work. The heat over the mouth of the glass chimney was so intense that the wood almost immediately darkened, began to smoke and then burst into a small flame. He withdrew it and used it to light the pipe, relishing the aroma and taste of the tobacco. He rarely smoked anywhere except here in his office, since Annie objected to the smell and mess at home and the pipe and pouch were too bulky to carry about in his uniform pockets.

The pipe made little wheezing sounds as he drew on it and he made a mental note to clean it thoroughly when he was finished with this smoke. With the stem clenched in his teeth, he reached into the drawer again and withdrew the letter he had received in the mail earlier this morning. He sighed as he finished reading it again. It was a testy dun for a bill long overdue — one of many he had not yet paid, simply because he hadn't the funds. John Whistler was almost chronically in debt and it irked him, since he was a man who liked to pay his bills on time.

"When is this government going to get around to paying its officers?" he muttered glumly. It had been nearly two years since he had received a full pay, and even then the payment had been for a lieutenant, though he had been promoted to captain on July 1, four years ago. The back pay due him would come eventually, he knew, and it would make a wonderful sum to have when received, but he could certainly use it now. It was unfitting, he felt, for a captain of the United States Army to have to find odd jobs to do on his time off in order to support his family. If it hadn't been for the handwork Ann did at home, he didn't know what they would do. The debts continued to pile up, even though the older children still at home helped to bring in some money, too, at times.

He sighed again, knowing it was no picnic for Ann and once more murmuring a little prayer of thanks that she still had not become pregnant again. Not that she couldn't be, since she was only thirty-nine now, but he truly hoped she had borne her last. Thinking of the children brought him around to thoughts of William, their eldest, who had been gone for over four years now, doing who-knew-what in New York. He was a poor correspondent and they'd received only one letter from him, about six months after he left here. In that one he had mentioned that he was thinking about a military career.

Taking a fresh sheet of paper from the drawer, Captain Whistler set his pipe aside and dipped the quill into the inkpot. He addressed the letter to the creditor who had just dunned him and, in beautifully calligraphic strokes, explained about his pay being held for so long, that the due bill would be paid as soon as he received his money, and apologizing for whatever inconvenience he was causing. He concluded:

. . . *I hope you will not think I complain against my government for detaining my pay. No, but necessity forces me to make the real statement to satisfy my creditor.*

He signed and blotted the page, folded it and placed it in an envelope and sealed it with a dollop of wax. He picked up his pipe and relighted it, smiling now as he thought of the little celebration scheduled for tonight. Annie was baking a cake today and this evening it would be in the center of their table with a large candle in the middle. Today was the first birthday of their last-born, George Washington Whistler.[141]

"Corporal!" he called, picking up the envelope. The door opened and a young, gawky noncommissioned officer entered. He handed him the letter and asked him to post it and the corporal bobbed his head.

"Yes sir," he said. "Sir, the new lieutenant just arrived and is reporting in."

Captain Whistler smiled. "Well, at last. Send him in."

The corporal nodded again and went out. A moment later an enormous young man in crisp new uniform came in and strode to the desk. He was easily a couple of inches over six feet in height, very athletic in build and weighed about two hundred fifty pounds. His heels clicked together smartly and he gave his new commanding officer a snappy salute.

"Sir," he said, "Second Lieutenant William Whistler reporting for duty!"[142]

They looked at one another for several seconds and then the captain leaped from his chair and enfolded his son in a great hug. The celebration tonight would be better than any of them had anticipated.

[*August 5, 1801 — Thursday*]

Nowhere else in the Northwest Territory had such an impressive and expansive residence been erected than the huge mansion located in the wilderness settlement of Vincennes. Its thirteen huge rooms were well appointed with the very best of furnishings and accoutrements, from finely made overstuffed sofas and chairs to huge mirrors and chandeliers and the very finest imported rugs over burnished hardwood floors. A great curving staircase in the entry parlor swept graciously to the second floor, its balustrade hand-carved and exquisite. There were four very large fireplaces which terminated in four proud chimneys jutting straight up nine feet above the highest level of the mansard roof. A beautiful, hand-polished mahogany piano graced the drawing room for the use of the owner's lady, Anna, and a large staff of uniformed slaves — the men in black trousers, black jackets and white shirts with ruffles, the women in black dresses with white collars, cuffs and hems — kept the many items of silver and brass highly polished and the carved mantels and doors and bannister uprights free of dust.

This was the mansion of William Henry Harrison, the new governor of the equally new Indiana Territory, and because the woodlands surrounding its meticulously landscaped gardens were abundant with ruffed grouse, he had named it Grouseland. Anticipating many councils to be held here in the future, Harrison had had a large council ground laid out, with here and there extensive arbors constructed for cooling shade, to be aided by the grapevines planted at their corners and already climbing the uprights.

That there would be many Indian councils, Harrison had no doubt. With every passing week tensions had been rising in the Northwest, especially in the Indiana Territory. Once again bands of Indians were roving, stealing horses, killing livestock, shooting at — and often hitting

— settlers as they cleared their fields or laid out new roads. Their wilderness was changing and they were upset. No longer was game abundant as it had once been; the buffalo had disappeared, as had the elk. The few deer remaining were wary and hard to hunt successfully. The beaver were largely gone and the mink, muskrat, fox and otter had become so scarce as to make trapping them ordinarily unprofitable. Woodlands were being felled to provide lumber for the construction of houses and fences; grasslands were being burned away to facilitate the bite of the plow in virgin soil.

There were troubles ahead and Governor Harrison knew it. He received reports regularly from a large, well-scattered force of spies, representative of whom were Johnny Logan — Spemica Lawba — and Christopher Miller in the Auglaize-Maumee area, William Wells in the area of Fort Wayne, Thomas Forsyth in the area of Peoria Lake, Jack Lalime at Chicago, Cornelius Washburn on the Mississippi near the mouth of the Illinois and Shadrach Bond well downstream from there in the area of Cahokia and Kaskaskia.

Only a year ago the Louisiana Territory had passed back into the hands of France from Spain and interesting negotiations were occurring in that respect, with the remote possibility of everything beyond the Mississippi opening up to the United States. In the East, John Adams's term as President had concluded last March and the new President was a brilliant and ambitious man named Thomas Jefferson, who was meeting at intervals with representatives of France regarding the trans-Mississippi west.

Changes were occurring throughout the Northwest, sometimes gradually, sometimes swiftly, but always inexorably and with each change more of the wilderness became civilized, more of the Indian inhabitants shrank back from the encroaching whites. Just last May the United States government had begun to bring into the market and offer for sale a wide tract of Ohio wilderness south of the military bounty lands and east of the Scioto River, and only last month a land office had been newly established at the Steubenville settlement for sales of that portion of Ohio called the Seven Ranges. At Cincinnati, a crowd of hundreds had only recently stood on the banks of the Ohio and cheered mightily as an oceangoing vessel weighing one hundred tons, built at the shipyard in Marietta, passed on its maiden voyage downstream to New Orleans. It was more than merely a ship; it was a symbol of the white progress and increasing domination in this raw country.

William Henry Harrison was concerned about a growing problem throughout the territory. Liquor had always been an important trade commodity on the frontier, even though various regulations controlling or prohibiting such traffic had been enacted from time to time. Now, with their land being eaten away from around them, the Indians were turning more and more to liquor as a solace, with the resultant drunkenness and violence it inspired.

Topenebe, Keesas and a few of the other more responsible chiefs of the Potawatomi complained bitterly about the increase of liquor in their country and its effect upon their warriors. Some tried to limit the traffic in it, but were largely unsuccessful. Others — Onoxa, for example — gave lip service to prohibition of liquor while at the same time being strongly addicted to it themselves. And a new horde of American traders was discovering what British traders had long known — that the Indians had a particular weakness for liquor and, when under its influence, would gladly sign away almost anything for promise of more.

Keesas, the Potawatomi chief nearest on the middle Wabash to Vincennes, viewed with alarm the increase of whites in that area and the mansion called Grouseland had become symbolic of the nature of the Americans to establish a sense of permanence for themselves on the very edge of the frontier. Keesas was aware that Harrison was within his rights in building Grouseland at Vincennes, but there were clear dangers inherent in its presence. It was attracting many other settlers. Keesas had been one of the chiefs at the Greenville Treaty who had ceded a tract of land to the Americans in the Vincennes area, but the borders of the cession were only vaguely drawn and Keesas was very concerned — with justification — that the whites would encroach even farther onto lands the Potawatomies still considered their own.

The only seeming bright spot William Henry Harrison saw in this developing picture came in reports from his spies, who told of a Shawnee medicine man who had begun to preach a doctrine of abstinence from liquor to whatever Indians would listen to him and, surprisingly, quite a few were beginning to. The Shawnee was an ugly, one-eyed man whose name was Lowawluwaysica who was getting known as The Prophet, and this was the first time Harrison had ever heard of him. But the governor expected little help from that quarter; the reports of his spies went on to say that though Lowawluwaysica was proclaiming loudly against the use of liquor, he was himself addicted to its use and was very frequently intoxicated.

[*September 17, 1802 — Friday*]

As always, William Wells was impressed with Grouseland. The mansion was so out of place in this wilderness that it was all but laughable. No one, however, was laughing about it. Events of great moment had been occurring here, not the least of which was the meeting Governor Harrison was having with a delegation of chiefs of the Northwestern tribes.

Topenebe was here, accompanied by his two close white friends, William Burnett and John Kinzie, along with Onoxa, Magaago, Winnemac and Keesas, representing the Potawatomies. Wells himself had come with Michikiniqua, whose meeting with President Jefferson in Washington last January — his fourth presidential meeting — had directly resulted in this council. In that meeting, Michikiniqua, Onoxa and Winnemac had asked the President and his Secretary of War, Henry Dearborn, for assistance in four matters. First was the distribution of annuities, which were of poor quality and had, heretofore, been made at Detroit, with the result that Potawatomi branches farther away were getting little or nothing. The same was true for other tribes. The Miami chief requested that Fort Wayne, more centrally located to the Indians, be made the new distribution center and that William Wells be named as agent in charge of the distribution. Second, he reiterated the need for help in getting Indian people launched into the new system of agriculture if, indeed, this was to replace hunting and trapping as a basis of the Indian economy. Third, that steps be taken to quiet the Kickapoos and Sacs who were increasing their hostilities in the Illinois country and causing new frictions that might well erupt into another Indian war. Finally, he pleaded that the government suppress the growing trade in liquor which, he concluded, ". . . is a fatal poison among the tribes."

Michikiniqua's requests met with a very favorable response from both the President and Secretary of War. Because it would not only help mollify the tribes, be more just in application and — especially! — since it would tend to help keep the Indians away from the subversive influence of the British at Fort Malden, they agreed to move the annuity distribution center to Fort Wayne under supervision of William Wells and, equally, to instruct Governor Harrison to make efforts to curtail the liquor sales and cool down the Kickapoos and Sacs. They also discussed the possibility of the government establishing an official government store at Fort Wayne, to be called an Indian Factory — an operation to compete with the private fur traders. Such a factory system was already being tried in the South among the Cherokees and Creeks with considerable success. The government agent in charge of such a post was being called the factor. In respect to the request for aid with agriculture, well beyond what had already been done, President Jefferson was especially agreeable.

"We shall with pleasure," he told Michikiniqua and the others, "see your people become disposed to cultivate the earth, to raise herds of the useful animals and to spin and weave for their food and clothing. These resources are certain. They will never disappoint you, while those of hunting may fail and expose your women and children to the miseries of cold and hunger. We will, with pleasure, furnish you with implements for the most necessary art, and with persons who will instruct you in how to make use of them."

Now Governor Harrison, acting under the President's orders, had called this meeting and it was going quite well. Part of the matter being discussed was the influx of whites in the Vincennes area and the need to define more precisely boundaries of that tract. Harrison spoke slowly and calmly, allowing William Wells and other interpreters ample time to relay with exactness what he was saying.

"According to the terms of the Greenville Treaty, to which all of you have put your hands," he said, "the Vincennes Tract set aside for the United States government stretched along both sides of the Wabash in a band six miles wide from the mouth of the White River to the place called Point Coupee, some forty miles upstream, eighteen miles above Vincennes.[143] Any Potawatomi claims to this tract of land are without foundation," he continued, "since the nearest of your villages are at Keesas' town."[144]

The assembled chiefs agreed to this and signed a formal and binding cession of the land in question to augment the Greenville Treaty. Then Governor Harrison went on to other matters. "The government," he said, "has been most concerned about the unprovoked attacks by some Indians" — he glanced at the Kickapoo contingent, but did not name them —"and in an effort to curtail this, a company of government troops is now being stationed at Kaskaskia. What the Indians there and elsewhere need to consider is that not only is the government agreeable to helping the tribes in the matter of learning proper methods of agriculture, there are private religious organizations who are also willing to help in whatever way they can — the Quakers, the Shakers and the Moravians, to name a few."

The governor now became more pointed in directing his remarks to the Kickapoos in attendance. "You must," he told them sternly, "bury the tomahawk and fire your arrows only at the buffalo, the bear and the deer, which are provided by the Great Spirit for your use, but spare your fellow man. Such killings will avail you nothing and will only undermine the good feelings your Great Father Jefferson in Washington now holds for you."

He ignored the frowns and murmur of protest from those assembled, who knew there were no buffalo left and few bear and the deer were all but unhuntable. It was why so many angry settlers in the Illinois country were complaining that Kickapoo hunters were "shooting deer with bells on their necks."

"The President," he went on, "wishes for the chiefs of the tribes in this country to assemble their scattered warriors and take them to situations best adapted to cultivation and there to form new towns and villages. When this is done, you will be furnished with horses, cattle, hogs and implements."

The murmuring continued and Harrison addressed himself to it. "It is true," he said, "that the game which affords you subsistence is yearly becoming more scarce and in a short time you will be left without resources and your wives and children will in vain ask you for food. There is nothing so pleasing to God as to see His children employed in the cultivation of the earth. The experiment of farming has been tried with your brothers, the Cherokees and Creeks. This has had a most happy effect on their population and all their wegiwas are filled with children. Let me entreat you to make the experiment, for the sake of the rising generation."

The talks continued for hours, with the Indians receiving a few small concessions here and there to soothe them and the United States government more firmly entrenching itself not only in the wilderness of the Indiana Territory, but in the lives of its native inhabitants. When at last the council ended, there were few smiles on the faces of the departing chiefs. Although they were not quite sure how, they were certain they had been manipulated, perhaps even cheated, but they didn't know what to do. William Henry Harrison was a different cut of white man — one with whom they did not yet know how to deal.

The seriousness with which Michikiniqua viewed the situation was reflected in his taciturnity on the journey back to Fort Wayne. And William Wells, as much confused as any of the chiefs about which way to turn now, rode with equal silence, anxious only to get back to his farm at Fort Wayne — to his wife, Wanagapeth, and their four children.

[December 25, 1802 — Saturday]

Ann Whistler opened her eyes and looked directly into those of her husband. The sleep had worked wonders for her and she smiled. Immediately the concerned expression on John's face was supplanted by an answering smile.

"Is it still the same day?" she whispered. At his nod she reached out with her free hand and touched her fingertips to his cheek, liking the feel of the faint stubble. "Then, merry Christmas, darling. I forgot to say it before. I'm sorry."

He put his finger to her lips to hush her. "Nothing to apologize for. You've had a busy time. How is she?" His eyes traveled to the little bundle beside her.

Ann dropped her hand from his cheek and lifted a flap of the swaddling to expose head and shoulders of the tiny infant born a few hours earlier. "Still sleeping." She let the flap drop softly and her smile widened. "What'll we name her?"

"How about Quietus?" He was still smiling but there was a trace of seriousness in his eyes.

"Quietus indeed! Silly man. Let's call her Caroline, after my aunt. Is that all right with you?"

"Caroline it is," he agreed. "Good name." But Captain John Whistler, still struggling with debts, offered up a silent prayer that there would be no more children for him and Ann.

Fifteen was more than enough.[145]

[*February 21, 1803 — Thursday*]

The public image of President Thomas Jefferson was almost universally one of a man of sterling character, high morality and humanity exemplary in the highest degree; a man of extreme intelligence and altruism. That image would quickly have become tarnished if the public could have read the words flowing from his pen at this moment to William Henry Harrison:

Our system is to live in perpetual peace with the Indians, to cultivate an affectionate attachment for them by everything just and liberal which we can do for them within the bounds of reason and by giving them effectual protection against wrongs from our own people. When they withdraw themselves to the culture of a small piece of land, they will perceive how useless to them are the extensive forests and will be willing to pare them off in exchange for necessaries for their farms and families. To promote this we shall push our trading houses, and be glad to see the good and influential individuals among them in debt, because we observe that when these debts go beyond what the individual can pay, they become willing to lop them off by a cession of lands. But should any tribe refuse the proferred hand and take up the hatchet, it will be driven across the Mississippi and the whole of its lands confiscated.

[*June 1, 1803 — Wednesday*]

Captain John Whistler was weary, infinitely weary. It seemed to him that he had been in perpetual motion ever since mid-March and, in a way, he had been. Now he had returned to Detroit at last and would shortly be reunited with Annie and the children. He'd already sent word to the house with a private to let her know he had returned safely and would be there soon. First, however, he had to make his report to Colonel Hamtramck.

At the fort he walked with some stiffness to headquarters and presented himself to the sergeant in the outer office of the Detroit commander. "Is the commanding officer in, Sergeant?" he asked.

"Yes sir, Captain Whistler, he is." The sergeant smiled. "Glad you're back safely, sir. Must've been a helluva trip."

"It was," Whistler agreed. "Thanks. Would you please tell Colonel Hamtramck I'm here to report?"

"Colonel Hamtramck?" The sergeant paused in mid-stride and then turned back slowly. "But sir, Colonel Hamtramck is —" he paused and then went on apologetically. "I'm sorry, sir, I guess there's no way you could've known. Colonel Hamtramck died a few weeks ago. Captain Pike's in command now."

John Whistler's mouth fell open. "How?" he asked. "I mean, was it a fever?"

The sergeant shook his head. "No sir. His heart. It just gave out on him one day."

"And Zeb Pike's the new C.O.?"

"Yes sir."

The captain nodded. "All right. Tell him I'm here, please."

In a moment the sergeant was back, followed by Captain Zebulon Pike, who had been senior among company commanders of the First Infantry.[146] They exchanged salutes and then shook hands warmly. The two had known each other for a long time and, while never very close, had always been friendly with one another. Pike led the way back to his office and brought out a bottle of Madeira from a small cabinet, filled two squat crystal wine glasses and they drank to one another's health.

"Sit down and relax, John," Pike said, indicating a chair near the desk. He sat in his own behind it. "I want to hear all about your expedition, but first let me fill you in on what's occurred since you left. Obviously, you know that the colonel died."

"The sergeant just told me. I hadn't known till then."

Pike opened a hinged box on the desk and offered Whistler a cigar, then took one himself. When both were lighted he went on. "Very unexpected. Just keeled over and was gone. As second in command, I took over. It's permanent now, confirmed yesterday in dispatches from General Dearborn."

Secretary of War Henry Dearborn, he went on, had ordered him to continue operation of Detroit as Hamtramck had, including the matter that had sent Captain Whistler on his expedition.[147] "More of that in a moment," he added, "but first let me go on. Some pretty grand things've happened. You haven't heard about the Louisiana Territory yet?"

Whistler shook his head. "What about it?" He sipped his wine.

"It's ours now." Pike grinned, pleased at Whistler's surprise. "All the way from the Red River to Canada," he added, "and way west. It's damned near doubled the size of the United States."[148] He chortled, thinking of it in personal terms. "Think of it! A territory that size, essentially unexplored, and someone's going to have to lead expeditions to open it up. There's advancement there, John. Real advancement!" He held up his glass as if this comment were a toast of itself and Whistler drank with him. "I understand," Pike said, "General Wilkinson's the number one choice as territorial governor.[149] What a plum!

"Let's see now," he went on, "What else has happened? We've had a number of official councils with the Indians here, trying to neutralize their affection for the bloody British over there at Amherstburg." He tilted his head toward the east. "Mark my words, we're going to have trouble with 'em again eventually and if we do it'll be because John Bull's behind it. Anyway, Jouett's been handling the talks here. You know him, of course."

It wasn't a question, but John Whistler nodded anyway. Charles Jouett had been appointed Indian agent at Detroit by President Jefferson just about a year ago and he and John Whistler had struck up an acquaintance. Whistler had attended the wedding last January 22, when Jouett had married a Detroit girl, Eliza Dodemead.

Pike and Whistler leaned forward simultaneously and tapped ashes from their cigars in the large ashtray on the desk. Pike refilled their glasses and went on. "The only other thing of any significance, I guess, is that Ohio's a state now. The seventeenth. Edward Tiffin — he's a prominent physician there — was elected governor."

The Detroit commander picked up his drink and leaned back in his chair. "All right," he said, "that's the major news from this end. Now it's your turn. I've familiarized myself with all the correspondence and orders pursuant to your expedition, so you can take it from the time you left here."

"Yes sir." Captain Whistler placed his glass on the edge of the desk and tapped his cigar against the ashtray again, using the time to organize his thoughts. Colonel Hamtramck had received a letter from Inspector General Cushing, dictated by Secretary of War Dearborn on March 14, stating that the government now deemed it important to establish a permanent military post at Chicago on the land ceded to the United States by the Greenville Treaty. Hamtramck was ordered to detach an officer and six men to make a preliminary investigation of the situation at Chicago and of the route there from Detroit. The party was to proceed by land to the mouth of the St. Joseph River, marking a trail and noting suitable campsites for the company of soldiers which would ultimately be sent. The officer Hamtramck selected was to make inquiries concerning to what extent traders on the St. Joseph could supply the needs of the army, both en route and when garrisoned at Chicago, and he was also to select a site at St. Joseph for the temporary encampment of the company until preparations could be made for its reception at Chicago. Hamtramck had chosen John Whistler for the mission.

Captain Whistler gave his report now to Captain Pike in a clear, concise manner. The journey to Chicago by land had essentially been over the well-marked Indian trail called the Sac Trail by some and Potawatomi Trail by others. It was a relatively easy march of somewhat over three hundred miles. They had stopped for several days at St. Joseph and met with two of the foremost traders of the area, William Burnett and John Kinzie. Burnett admitted that at one time he had been interested in establishing a post at Chicago, but was no longer inclined to do so, as he was getting too old and considering retiring from the trade.

John Kinzie, on the other hand, Whistler reported, was eager to do business with the government and was prepared to provide the passing troops with just about anything they required. "Not only that," Whistler added, "he indicated that he has a special interest in the Chicago area and is prepared to establish his own post there. Although he did not say so directly, he gave me to believe that he had already taken steps in this direction by having one of his clerks, a Mr. Jack Lalime, occupy a post already at the Chicago site and hold it until Kinzie himself arrives there, at which time Lalime is to turn it over to him."

The detachment, Captain Whistler went on, followed the Indian trail to the mouth of the St. Joseph and then the Lake Michigan shoreline around its southernmost bend to the mouth of the Chicago River. "We found Mr. Lalime situated in a rather substantial post on the north bank of the river near its mouth," he said. "The ground in the area is quite low and marshy and inclined to frequent flooding. However, directly across the river from Lalime's place, on the south bank, there is some advantageously situated high ground which would be an ideal location for the establishment of the fort. It would command the mouth of the river and the Chicago Portage and is the nucleus for all the major Indian trails of the area. The river presents a navigation problem. At the point where the fort could be built, it is only a few hundred yards from the lake, but there is quite a substantial sandbar closing its direct flow into the lake. It — the river, that is — takes a sharp southward turn at this point, runs parallel to the lake shore for a quarter mile, more or less, and finally empties into the lake over a shallow sandy area. Even at times of high water, it is not navigable to large ships, although the removal of the sandbar impeding the flow near the proposed fort site would give immediate and direct access to the lake. The area is inhabited by Potawatomies in several villages. They seem peaceably inclined and indicate a positive disposition towards the establishment of a fort at the point mentioned. There are a few buildings, the only ones of a truly substantial nature being those of Lalime and a less significant trader named Antoine Ouilmette, who also lives on the north bank. Two other French traders — Pierre Le Mai and Louis Pettle — live there off and on in poorly built cabins, one of which belongs to Mr. Burnett of St. Joseph, but which has been let fall into disrepair. The ground is very fertile and there is, adjacent to the proposed fort location, a substantial area of prairie that would be very suitable for a post vegetable garden. The Indians grow considerable crops of corn in the fields beyond that. Timber for construction of the proposed fort is not available anywhere near the proposed fort site, but I was assured by Monsieur Ouilmette that a few miles to the north along the lake shore there are extensive

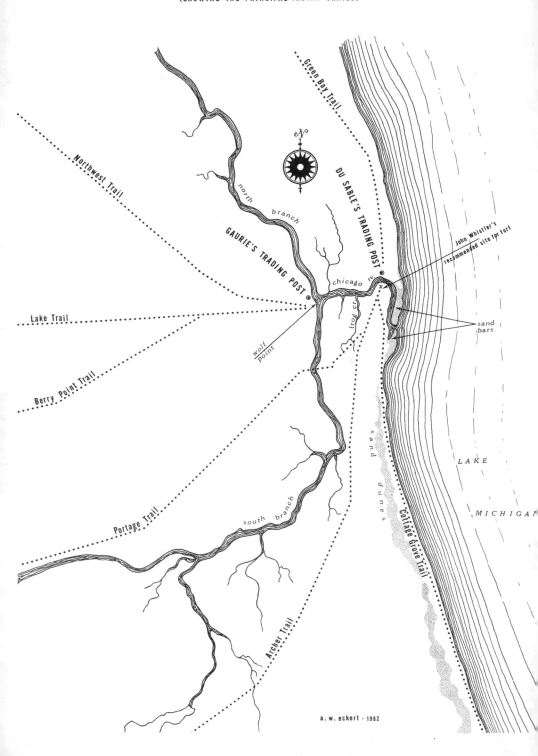

CHICAGO IN DEVELOPMENT

JUNE — 1803

(SHOWING THE PRINCIPAL INDIAN TRAILS)

Green Bay Trail

Northwest Trail

DU SABLE'S TRADING POST

GAURIE'S TRADING POST

north branch

John Whistler's recommended site for fort

chicago riv.

frog cr.

Lake Trail

wolf point

sand bars

Berry Point Trail

Portage Trail

south branch

sand dunes

LAKE

MICHIGAN

Cottage Grove Trail

Archer Trail

a. w. eckert - 1982

forests of oak, hickory, maple and elm, and timber cut there could readily be rafted directly to the fort site." He paused. "I believe that's it, sir."

"In regard to a ship harbor," Captain Pike said, snubbing out his cigar, "how will it be managed if supplies to maintain the fort are sent by ship?"

"Until a satisfactory harbor can be built, sir, ships will have to anchor offshore and the material brought in by smaller boats."

"Hmmm, that *is* a drawback," Pike murmured, then smiled, "but not one that cannot be overcome. My congratulations, Captain, on an excellent report." He picked up the quill pen lying on the desk and twirled it between his fingers. "Now are you aware that in the original correspondence, the Secretary of War directed that should the overland route be found practicable for a company with packhorses carrying provisions and light baggage, Colonel Hamtramck was to dispatch it under, as he termed it, 'a discreet, judicious captain' to go at once to the Chicago site and erect a fort? Tools, equipment, field pieces and ammunition are to be sent by ship. That captain to become permanent commander of the new fort."

John Whistler suddenly felt a knot in his stomach as he divined what was coming. He began to speak, but Pike cut him off with a flick of the feather. "I know of no one better in whom to place that responsibility, Captain Whistler, than you."

"Sir," the subordinate captain said quickly, coming to his feet, "I wish you would reconsider."

Pike stood also, his expression hardening. "Do I understand you wish to disqualify yourself, Captain? On what grounds?"

"Purely personal, sir," Captain Whistler replied, feeling his neck growing warm. "My family is here, and our home. I would not wish to be separated from them."

"There is no reason why you should be, Captain. The government will provide for their transportation with you to Chicago."

Whistler shook his head. "I have fifteen children, Captain Pike. Not all at home now, that's true, but those who are cannot be expected to travel so far on horseback. Some are very young."

"Insufficient reason, Captain," Pike said firmly. "You and your family will be given leave to travel from here in the ship carrying the equipment. I will appoint a lieutenant to lead the company overland to rendezvous with you at the mouth of the St. Joseph and you can continue to Chicago together from that point. You may consider that an order. You'll have plenty of time to make arrangements while we prepare here for the project. I want the detachment to leave here within six weeks — no later than July 14. Understood?" It was a dismissal.

"Yes sir." Whistler came to attention and saluted his commander, about-faced and began to leave the office, anger seething in him. Annie's pleasure at his return was now going to be significantly dampened, to say nothing of what Sarah's reaction would be. Their fourth daughter, Sarah, had only recently become engaged to James Abbott, Detroit trader.

"Captain."

Whistler stopped at the door and looked back. "Sir?"

"The West is opening up and Chicago could be an important part of it," Captain Pike said. "This may be considerably more of an opportunity than you realize at the moment."

"I'll try to think of it as such, Captain," Whistler said tightly, the sarcasm not too well masked.

"Incidentally, Captain Whistler," Pike added, stopping him again as he turned to leave, "you'll be naming the new installation at Chicago Fort Dearborn."

[June 7, 1803 — Tuesday]

Indian Agent William Wells shifted uncomfortably at the accusing look he was receiving from Michikiniqua, knowing his former adopted father was entirely correct in his assessment that the government of the United States was suddenly looming as a greater threat to the Northwestern tribes than most of the Indians realized.

"You promised you would do all in your power to protect your Miami brothers," Michikiniqua said sternly as they stood in the shadow of Fort Wayne and watched the departure of the Indians who had assembled here several days ago for the signing of the new treaty. "Why have you not protected us?"

"I *have* protected you as best I could under the circumstances, Father," Wells replied, blinking rapidly. "No one else could have done as much. But what is, is. I cannot change it. I can only hope to make it more bearable for you."

"Your land," Michikiniqua said coldly, pointing toward the Wells farm across the river, "came from the white government. The money you are paid comes from the whites. Your interest, therefore, lies there. Whatever loyalty you retain for us, who are your brothers, is secondary."

Wells sighed. "You, my father," he replied quietly, "attended the council with Governor Harrison at Vincennes nine moons ago where these things were discussed and you agreed to them then. Now you have changed your mind, refused to sign the treaty and are angered that it has been signed despite your refusal."

"What I agreed to, Apekonit, at the place called Grouseland, is not what was presented here. It *seems* the same to those who do not look closely, but not to he whose eye is careful. And who was here to sign it? Only a few of the Miamis, Weas and Piankeshaws who are most deeply concerned, but a great many of the Potawatomies who are far removed and who do not care." The bitterness in his voice was strong.

"The changes, as I pointed out to you so carefully," Wells replied patiently, "were very slight and of little difference to the Vincennes Tract boundaries that you agreed to."

"It is not the slight change in boundaries that upsets me most. It is the fact that this new treaty is clearly designated as only the first of a number of treaties to follow, each of which, when signed, takes more away from us and opens it to new floods of white settlers. It is the beginning of our end here."

Michikiniqua turned and strode away, Wells watching him go, sorry for him, knowing he was correct, wishing he had been able to help more. The strictures of his office, however, were such that he could not appear to be agent of the Indians to the government, when the opposite was true.

"Michikiniqua is still upset?"

Wells spun around at the unexpected voice and saw it was the Potawatomi village chief, Winnemac, who had come up behind. He regarded the Indian sourly, disliking him, considering him no more than an opportunist ever alert to fill his own pockets at anyone else's expense.

"It is easy," Wells replied pointedly, "to sell lands that one neither owns nor occupies, but a hard thing to bear when one sees his own lands eaten away."

"He has been paid," Winnemac sneered. "And when more is sold, he will be paid more."

"Perhaps no more will be sold," the Indian agent replied, but not believing it.

"We both know better, don't we, Apekonit? I have just left Governor Harrison in the fort and he is already preparing for more. And there will be more. The other chiefs who signed the treaty here with me have agreed." He turned and walked away, oblivious of the hatred burning in Wells's breast for him.[150]

[*July 14, 1803 — Thursday*]

Captain John Whistler shook hands in turn with Captain Zebulon Pike and Second Lieutenant James Swearingen, then stepped back and first saluted Pike, then returned Swearingen's salute. This was the official departure of the detachment under orders from the Secretary of War. The three men stood at the foot of the Detroit wharf, where the ninety-ton U.S. schooner *Tracy* was moored, her sails still furled, her deck lined with waiting seamen and Captain Whistler's family. It was just now 5:30 A.M., the air calm and sweet with the scent of dawn still lingering.

"Good luck, Captain," the Detroit commander said.

Whistler smiled. "Thank you, Captain Pike." He turned to the lieutenant and nodded. "Have a safe trip. I'll see you at the rendezvous in about a month."

"Yes sir." James Strode Swearingen, twenty-one-year-old artillery officer who had volunteered for this duty, grinned broadly. "We'll be there, sir." He turned and walked purposefully to his waiting sixty-seven men. Captain Whistler watched him a moment and then strode out onto the wharf and up the gangplank to the deck of the *Tracy*. Ann met him there, seven-month-old Caroline in her arms, and walked with him toward the bow. They passed the bulky figure of Captain Dorr, master of the *Tracy*, and John Whistler tossed him a casual salute. "Ready whenever you are, Captain," he said.

Dorr nodded. "Breeze beginning to pick up," he murmured. "In our favor, too. Give it another few minutes and we may be able to use the sails after all."

At the bow rail the Whistlers were joined by their son and daughter-in-law. William was to be second in command when Fort Dearborn was finished. He and his wife had been married just a little over a year and yet Mary Julia Fearson Whistler had only just now turned sixteen. She was a pretty girl, daughter of a British lake captain. She and William had been married in the month of May by a Congregational minister, the Reverend Mr. David Bacon, missionary to the Indians, who was visiting Detroit at the time.[151] Now, pretending to give John a kiss on the cheek, Ann whispered, "She still looks like such a baby!" John agreed with his eyes and then looked at his son.

"Well, William," he said, "looks like we're on our way. God knows into what, but it certainly won't be anything like Detroit."

Second Lieutenant William Whistler, natty in his fresh uniform, squeezed his young wife's arm, having predicted to her earlier almost exactly what his father would say as they departed. "That's right," he agreed, "but maybe it'll be even better."

John Whistler didn't respond. He was looking shoreward, where Lieutenant Swearingen had formed up his men and put them in motion toward the west. They would be following the trail Captain Whistler had marked last spring, moving by land to the St. Joseph with their train of packhorses carrying baggage and provisions. After a brief stay there, they would move down the St. Joseph to Lake Michigan and rendezvous there with the *Tracy* which, in addition to the Whistler family, was carrying the artillery and ammunition as well as the tools and a crew of civilian carpenters and laborers to aid in the construction of Fort Dearborn. The *Tracy* would traverse Lake St. Clair, travel up the river of the same name to Lake Huron and then continue northward to the Straits of Mackinac, with a brief stopover at Fort Mackinac to deliver dispatches. Then the schooner would round the tip of Lower Michigan and follow the east shore of Lake Michigan southward to the rendezvous with Lieutenant Swearingen.

The calm of the river surface had broken into well-defined wavelets with the freshening breeze and behind them they could hear Captain Dorr shouting his orders to cast off. A crew of seamen were suddenly active, scurrying about to release the ship from her moorings and hoist the sails. Ann Whistler adjusted the sleeping Caroline more comfortably in her arms and leaned her head against John.

"Reminds me," she said softly, "of our first voyage."

"First and only," the captain said, putting his arm about her waist, "until now, assuming we don't count that float down the Ohio River as a voyage. Twenty-three years and an ocean away and two scared kids eloping to America. Where'd we ever get the nerve?"

She smiled up at him. "Who needed nerve? We only needed each other. That's all we've ever required."

"Mamma! Mamma! Are we sailing now?"

They turned to see three-year-old George Washington Whistler, his hand firmly held by his older sister, Sarah, whom he was all but towing toward the group. Sarah's eyes were red and swollen from crying. John snatched his son up from her grip, holding him high so he could see the widening gap between the *Tracy* and the wharf. They waved at the small crowd of civilians and soldiers standing on shore.

"Yes, we're on our way, George," his father said.

On the wharf a youth of about eighteen was leaping up and down and waving frantically. He finally broke away from the others and ran along the shoreline, still waving and yelling, the words "Sarah! Sarah!" coming to them faintly. It was James Abbott.

The sixteen-year-old girl caught sight of him through her tears, shrieked and waved in return until he was lost from view, then burst into tears again and fled to the cabin.

"Poor baby," Ann said. "The course of true love —"

"— never did run smooth," John finished the quotation for her. "Well, let's go see if we can cheer her up."

[*July 27, 1803 — Wednesday*]

Even as the United States Army detachment under Lieutenant Swearingen moved out of sight downstream from St. Joseph, John Kinzie's mind was working at high speed, calculating the difficulties that would be involved in uprooting his entire operation here and moving it to Chicago, as he had long planned. There was no longer any doubt whatever in his mind that he would make the move. The question was, exactly when? He had no intention of doing so without Eleanor, but she wouldn't be back here for about another month. Nor was he inclined, even then, to have her undertake the journey at that time. He sighed. It wasn't exactly what he wanted to do, but perhaps it would be better if they waited for spring. It would be too tough making a go of it in Chicago next winter if they tried to start later this fall. The last thing he wanted to do was get Eleanor into a situation that was so difficult she'd be soured on the whole thing very quickly.

Thinking of her made him feel good. A son! She'd given him a son and they'd named him John Harris Kinzie. He laughed aloud when he realized that though he'd never even seen the infant yet, he felt closer to this baby than he ever had to any of the three his first wife had borne. The baby had come a little sooner than expected. Eleanor had been wanting for a long while to visit her sister, Maggie, in Sandwich and felt sure she could get there, have a nice visit and be back long before the baby came. It had not worked out that way at all. On July 7, the day after her arrival in the town across the river from Detroit with thirteen-year-old Margaret in tow, she'd gone into labor and right there in Maggie and Will Forsyth's house, less than eight hours later, John Harris Kinzie had been born.

They'd sent word to her husband immediately, saying mother and son were doing just fine and if John could get away and come for her, that would be wonderful, but it wasn't essential if he were involved in something important. In fact, wrote Will, it was quite all right with them if Eleanor stayed for a month or two. After all, Will argued somewhat acerbically in his scrawling hand, she really deserved something of a vacation and a reacquaintance with a somewhat more civilized form of life than she'd had there in St. Joseph for the past five years.

John Kinzie was inclined to agree; the more so when the same messenger who brought the letter reported that a sizable army detachment was being readied at Detroit to march to Chicago and was planning to stop and purchase some equipment when it reached St. Joseph. So he'd written back, telling Eleanor to rest, enjoy herself, take care of their new son and he would come to get her about the first of September. Then, together over the winter, they could take their time about getting everything packed and ready for the major move to Chicago. It would make little if any difference at all to the Indians, since the majority of the trade John Kinzie had now was from Potawatomies west and southwest of St. Joseph, and Sacs who stopped en route to or from their visits with the British at Amherstburg. The move to Chicago would, if anything, increase rather than lessen his business with these tribes and he might begin picking up some of the Winnebago trade as well.

The detachment under Lieutenant Swearingen had arrived about noon two days ago, eleven days out of Detroit. They were in good spirits and the commander had given his men the liberty, after checking with the trader, to browse in the Kinzie Trading Post and buy whatever personal items they wanted and could afford. It had turned out to be quite a significant day and a half of cash buying.

Lieutenant Swearingen bought a good bit of material on government credit for army use, including the purchase of two medium-sized bateaux. These two craft had been loaded with the company's baggage and, early this morning, the young officer had set his men in motion again for the rendezvous point at the mouth of the St. Joseph. Seventeen of his men rowed the two bateaux and the remainder, led by Swearingen, kept pace with them, marching along the river trail.

John Kinzie and Topenebe had watched them go and then strolled together back to Kinzie's post where, as a sort of celebration, John opened a bottle of brandy and poured for both of them. Topenebe talked about the Quakers who had arrived at Fort Wayne and begun to show the Indians under Michikiniqua and the Potawatomies under Onoxa their methods of successful farming. The chiefs themselves had been interested, swayed as they had been by the glowing prospects the whites had painted of what a boon it would be for the tribes to begin large-scale cultivation of the land. But already there was disappointment. A model farm had been set up on the Wabash and the followers of the two chiefs watched curiously as the land was cleared and then plowed and the seeds planted in long neat rows, but they refused to help. They were hunters, not farmers. They would be happy to share in the rewards when the crops were harvested, as the Quakers promised them they would, but had no intention of contributing toward that goal. They looked with suspicion and some anger at the way the whites quickly changed the face of the land and came to the conclusion that it was bad; if the Great Spirit had wished such things to grow there, he would have made them grow naturally.

"I had once hoped that our people could learn how to make the land give up food to us," Topenebe said, sipping from his brandy glass, "but I see now that this will not be. To try to replace our traditional hunting with farming is, to them, only a different way for the white man to come into their country and change it. And cows and pigs do not take the place of buffalo and elk and deer for us. Our people will not —"

He broke off and turned around as the door to the trading post opened and a short man entered. Both were surprised to see that it was Jean Lalime. There was an aura of contained excitement in the little man's manner as he greeted the two and then told John Kinzie that he had merely stopped by while en route to Detroit. He had met the Swearingen detachment downstream and talked with them briefly, greatly pleased that they were actually going to build a fort ". . . across the river from my post. I met the other officer, Captain Whistler, when he came earlier looking for a place to build it. At that time he told me — and the lieutenant I just met agreed — that the new fort would need a suttler and there was no reason why I could not suttle for them."

With studied nonchalance he went on to say that he had temporarily closed up the store at Chicago and was now heading for Detroit ". . . to make arrangements with the merchants there to supply my post with goods of value to the military." There was a peculiar arrogance in his manner and John Kinzie frowned and held up a hand.

"Twice," he commented, "you have referred to the Chicago establishment as your post, in a manner which suggests you actually feel it *is* your post. I remind you that you are my *agent* at the Chicago store and that is all. As for becoming suttler to the fort, it is my own intention to become just that when Mrs. Kinzie and I arrive next spring to take over the situation there."

"You can't," Lalime said tightly, drawing himself up to his full five feet four inches. "It is *my* post. I am legal owner on the bill of sale."

John Kinzie scowled, hardly believing what he was hearing. "Whatever you're trying to pull here, Lalime, it won't work. You acted only as my agent and with my money in the purchase of that post from Du Sable."

Topenebe had been looking back and forth between the men, not understanding the words but clearly reading the heat rising between them. He held up a hand. "Speak in my tongue," he demanded.

John nodded and repeated in Potawatomi what Lalime had said and his own response. Topenebe's features hardened as he listened and then he spoke quietly to Lalime.

"When you worked in the trade at Mackinac, you were not always fair in your dealings with the Indians and eventually they drove you away. You came here and you were not fair with us here and we were glad to see you go away. Now you are at Chicago and I am told by Black Partridge that his people are not happy with how you are trading with them. Beware."

John Kinzie strode to a desk and brought out paper and quill. "You agreed," he told Lalime, still speaking in Potawatomi, "when you acted as my agent in the purchase of Du Sable's post, to run it as I wished it run, to treat the Indians fairly and to sign the post over to me on my demand." He dipped the quill and wrote swiftly on the sheet, blotted it and then straightened. "I now make that demand. This," he tapped the paper with a forefinger, "states that the Chicago post is now and always has been, since its purchase from Du Sable, mine. Sign it."

Lalime shook his head. "It's legally recorded in my name, remember? It's my post." His hand was resting on the tomahawk in his belt. His nostrils flaired above the thick black moustache and his narrowed eyes were locked on John, so he was unprepared for Topenebe's swift movement.

The Potawatomi chief took a quick step forward and his hands shot out. One gripped the wrist of the hand poised on the tomahawk and pinned the arm at his side. The other gripped Lalime's long hair and twisted, jerking his head backward and pulling him off balance. Before he could recover he was pulled down, with the small of his back across Topenebe's knee and the chief's face hovering over his.

"You lie!" the Potawatomi hissed. "I do not care what the papers say. You forget I was there. I saw. I heard. You have gotten away with cheating the Indians in small ways. You will not get away with cheating my friend in a big way. Do you wish Nokenoqua to sing the death song for her husband? You will sign Shawneeawkee's paper now or, I promise you, what I hold in my hand," he jerked the hair savagely, "will hang in my lodge this night!"

Topenebe pulled Lalime's hand away from the tomahawk and he snatched the weapon out of the man's belt, then thrust him away. Lalime rolled over on the floor and came to his feet in a crouch in the same movement. His eyes were filled with fear as he looked from Topenebe to Kinzie and then back to Topenebe again. The Potawatomi stared at him scornfully and merely tilted his head toward his trader friend.

Lalime straightened slowly, careful in his actions, and moved to the desk. He signed the paper with such force that on the final stroke the point of the quill collapsed and caused a blot. It made no difference. Kinzie didn't even look at it.

"Get out," he said flatly. "Don't come back. You're no longer working for me and you're through in Chicago."

Lalime glared at him and then walked quickly toward the door. Topenebe flicked his wrist and Lalime's tomahawk sped through the air and buried itself on the inside of the door just as Lalime reached it. The man stopped, facing the door, body taut.

"Take your toy with you," Topenebe said, his tone of voice mocking. "If you ever see me again, be prepared to use it. If you can."

Lalime reached out and wrenched the tomahawk free and returned it to his belt, still facing away from them. Then he opened the door and turned on the threshold. He didn't look at the Potawatomi, only at the trader.

"We'll see whether or not I'm through in Chicago," he said in English, his words hardly more than a raspy whisper. "One of these days, Kinzie, I'll kill you."

Then he was gone.

[*August 17, 1803 — Wednesday*]

"Well, Annie, there's our new home." Captain John Whistler spoke in a voice that was distinctly lacking in ebullience. He and his wife stood at the bow of the ninety-ton *Tracy*, now at anchor a quarter mile from shore.

Lake Michigan was incredibly blue under the afternoon sun and the sand beaches gleamed brightly under the rays, the line of the shore broken only by the mouth of the Chicago River. The shore was alive with people, not only the soldiers unloading goods brought from the ship, but some two thousand Potawatomi Indians who had come to see the ship and watch the unloading activity. Many had never seen any boat larger than a bateau and this "great canoe with wings" filled them with wonder.

Beyond the shallow river mouth and a short distance upstream, where the bateaux were being unloaded, the soldiers were clearly visible on the higher ground, eight feet above the river level. Already, though only a few trips had been made back and forth by the bateaux to the *Tracy*, much material was stacked up on the shore. The river was ninety feet wide at its mouth and, except for the shallow water over the sandbar at the entry, was eighteen feet deep. Beyond the high ground where the fort was to be situated were a few haphazard cornfields of the Indians and beyond them were great stretches of prairie. Near the riverbanks there were trees, mostly willows and cottonwoods. Opposite the fort site, on the north bank of the river, several houses were visible in addition to the extensive trading post, with some woodlands beyond. Rolling sand dunes rimmed the shoreline to the south, with scattered pine trees among them.

"It *is* a pretty area," Ann Whistler replied hesitantly. "Maybe we'll really come to like it here."

"Maybe. Whether we do or not, it's going to be home for a while." Her husband faced her. "I'm going to have to go ashore to oversee things and get camp set up. Soon as the cargo's all ashore, you and the children can come in if you want to. Or you can stay aboard until I come back this evening and we'll all go in together tomorrow morning."

"I think we'll stay aboard for now and get our things packed up and ready," she said. "You'll be back about dusk?"

He nodded and kissed her and then moved back amidships to step aboard the loaded bateau just ready to put off. Twenty yards from the *Tracy* he looked back and saw her still at the rail. He returned her wave and sat down, his eyes on shore. He could make out Lieutenant Swearingen giving instructions and was pleased to see that he had posted a guard over the materials already brought ashore and stacked up. The lieutenant was a good man and he wished he would be staying here instead of going back to Detroit in a few days with the *Tracy*. The schooner's skipper, Captain Dorr, was anxious to be away as soon as possible, fearful of remaining here in unprotected anchorage should a gale rise.

The journey from Detroit to Mackinac and then back down the east shore of Lake Michigan to the mouth of the St. Joseph had taken twenty-nine days. For the children, who'd never been on a sailing ship, it was exciting and they'd stood by the rails almost all the way, watching the shoreline slip past. Even Sarah, a few days out of Detroit, had emerged enough from her sorrow at having to part from James Abbott to join the others on deck.

The *Tracy* had anchored at the mouth of the St. Joseph on August 12 and Captain Whistler, accompanied by William, had immediately gone to shore to confer with Lieutenant Swearingen, who was camped there, waiting. His overland detachment had arrived there on July 28 and Swearingen computed that they had thus far marched two hundred seventy-two miles from Detroit.[152] With the lake extremely rough, they had remained in camp here going over their plans throughout the next two days. At 5:15 A.M. on August 15, they'd resumed the journey. Riding in the bateaux, the Whistlers — father and son — set the pace, with Swearingen and the majority of the company marching on shore on one side and the *Tracy* farther out in deeper water on the other. From the mouth of the St. Joseph to the mouth of the Chicago it was ninety miles and they had reached their destination at two o'clock this afternoon.

Among the large crowd of Indians watching with unfeigned interest as the Whistlers stepped out of the bateau at the fort site were two Frenchmen and two half-breeds, all with Indian or part-Indian wives. The Frenchmen — actually French Canadians — were Antoine Ouilmette and Louis Pettell, while the two half-breeds were a furtive, unkempt man named Pierre Le Mai and a dapper, sharp-faced young man named Jean Baptiste LaGeuness. They welcomed the newcomers and offered their services if needed. Ouilmette, Pettle and Le Mai had carried on desultory trade with the Indians for some years here and elsewhere. LeGueness, on the other hand, was only about twenty and new to the business. He had applied some months ago to Governor Harrison for a license which would give him status and legality under American law as a bona fide licensed trader, but had not yet received his authorization, so he had been working for Ouilmette while waiting. Ouilmette, who seemed to be their unofficial spokesman, said that the trading post across the river was closed for the time being since its owner, Jean Lalime, had gone to Detroit. Ouilmette and LaGueness were keeping an eye on the place and expected that Lalime would return in a few weeks.

"I remember him from when I was here in May," Captain Whistler said noncommittally. He had not been impressed with Lalime then, nor was he overly impressed with these three men now. Ouilmette, of only average height, appeared to him to be little more than a half-starved Indian and Pettell, a short, sallow man, wore a rather vacant expression.[153] Le Mai, on the other hand, was tall and gaunt with strange eyes — a man, Captain Whistler decided, that it might not be a good idea to let get behind your back.

Ouilmette then beckoned to an impressive Indian who wore a shiny gold ornament dangling from his nostrils and a large brass medallion on a thong about his neck. It hung on his bare chest and as he came to a stop near them, John Whistler recognized it as one of the medallions that had been given to the various treaty-signing chiefs at the Greenville Treaty. He was a powerfully built man with direct gaze and strong features.

"This is Black Partridge, Captain," Ouilmette said. "He is chief of all the Potawatomies here. His village is over there 'bout a mile." He pointed vaguely northwest. The French Canadian spoke a flurry of words to the chief and then Black Partridge smiled in what appeared to be a friendly manner and extended his hand to the commander. The grasp was firm, but Captain Whistler noted that the Indian chief's eyes were not reflecting his smile; they were hooded, calculating, weighing the measure of this white officer.

"I have little English," Black Partridge said. "American chief welcome. White warriors," he swung his arm in a gesture that took in the Swearingen detachment, "welcome, too. All friends; all peace." He tried to find the correct words for something else and, failing, frowned and then spoke to Ouilmette.

"He wonders how long you're planning on camping here, Captain," the trader said innocently, and Whistler was abruptly quite sure the chief was well aware that their intention was to build a permanent fort and that he was not in the least pleased at the prospect. Nevertheless, he smiled and explained patiently as Ouilmette interpreted.

"We are not here just to camp. We are here permanently. This land was ceded to us by you and other chiefs, as you remember," he let his eyes drop to the chief's medallion, "at the treaty you signed with General Wayne at Greenville. We intend to begin at once to build a fort here, which we will occupy. I am pleased to accept your friendship and your offer of peace. We offer you the same and you and your people are always welcome here." The chief's expression did not change and yet, just for an instant, John Whistler thought he detected a contained animosity and he resolved to keep a close eye on Black Partridge and his warriors.

At that moment Lieutenant Swearingen came up to them and reported that he had given instructions to the men to pitch their tents at the southeastern area of the fort site. Murmuring his approval, Captain Whistler introduced Swearingen and his own son to the chief. They all shook hands gravely and exchanged friendly greetings. He then gave Swearingen orders to have a squad scout northward along the lake shore toward the timberland to select a site for felling trees for lumber as soon as the unloading of the *Tracy* was completed.

Swearingen nodded. "Yes sir. I'll put Private James Corbin on it. He's had a good bit of experience at that; used to run a lumber mill for his father in New Jersey."

"Excellent," the captain said. "I want that fort raised as soon as possible."

The lieutenant saluted and returned at once to his men and John Whistler watched him go, hoping now that the urgency in his voice had not been transmitted to the Potawatomi chief. He glanced at the Indian and saw no indication that it had. Nevertheless, he decided to keep his men on alert at all times until the fort was completed. His own instructions had been not to erect the sort of fort that could withstand attack from a force with a battery of artillery, but rather just a small stockade with blockhouses — one that could hold, if necessary, against direct attack by Indians. From the present attitude of Black Partridge, there seemed little likelihood of that, but one never knew.

Black Partridge again spoke in his own tongue and when he was finished, Ouilmette turned to the commander. "The chief would like to know, Captain Whistler, what you will call your fort when it is built."

"Fort Dearborn," he replied, and suddenly he liked the sound of the name coming from his mouth.

[*August 21, 1803 — Sunday*]

John Harris Kinzie, forty-five days old, stared with bright, uncomprehending eyes at the camp fire burning heartily a few feet away. He was snug in his little papoose board that had been carried all day — except for those intervals when they had paused so he could nurse — on the shoulders of François Tuffult, one of John Kinzie's French Canadian engagees from the Detroit post. Now that papoose board was propped against a tree where the infant could watch the flames while his mother was otherwise occupied.

An hour ago they had stopped to camp for the night and, after she had fed her new son, Eleanor Kinzie prepared a meal for herself, thirteen-year-old Margaret and François. The first cool front of the late summer had moved down from the north today, portent of approaching autumn and the radiant heat of the cooking fire felt surprisingly good.

Margaret McKillip set down her empty plate and yawned hugely. Eleanor reached out and rubbed her daughter's nape. "Tired, honey?" The girl nodded and Eleanor smiled. "Me, too. I feel as if I could sleep a week and it still wouldn't be enough. Well, we should be home around noon tomorrow."

They could have waited in Sandwich for John to arrive, since he was planning to be in Detroit around the first of September, but both Eleanor and Margaret were anxious to get home again, so they'd decided to head for St. Joseph and surprise John with an earlier look at his new son than he anticipated. Thinking of her husband, a surge of warmth flooded Eleanor and she looked across the fire at the engagee.

"Let's get an early start in the morning, François. I want to —"

The fire popped loudly, interrupting her. As if it were occurring in a slow-motion dream, they watched a large ember glowing bright red burst from the fire and arc into the growing darkness like a meteor. It sped directly toward the papoose board, struck little John Harris Kinzie on the side of his chin and then ricocheted into his garment, lodging between the fabric and the tender skin at the side of his neck.

Instantly the infant began to cry and his little arms thrashed ineffectually. Just as quickly the three at the fire were on their feet and Eleanor was first to reach him. She tore at the garment, sickened by the sweetish stench of the burning flesh, but it was still several seconds more before she could expose the still-glowing coal, grasp it and hurl it away, her own fingers painfully burned in the process.

They gently rubbed soothing bear oil on the burn, but it was quite severe and the baby cried for a long while.[154] And throughout the night, Eleanor Kinzie sat up, holding him, comforting him and at frequent intervals nursing him. It was a very long night.

[*August 23, 1803 — Tuesday*]

In just the six days since their arrival here at Chicago, Captain John Whistler had learned more about the temperament of the Potawatomies than he had learned about any Indians during his entire tours of duty at Fort Wayne and Detroit. For the first time he was dealing with them directly and it was easy for him to see now why those who came inexperienced among the Indians were apt to have troubles.

During the initial days following his meeting of Chief Black Partridge, he had viewed the Indians in the usual way — that is, thinking of them as essentially ignorant savages who squatted about their fires thinking of no more than filling their bellies and making war. They were, in his mind, peculiarly dissociated from the human race, or at least from the *civilized* human race. What did they know of love and compassion, of introspection and humor and grief and ambition? Weren't they merely primitives, with no thought beyond today, without comprehension of art and music and dance, without the graces of gentleness and virtue and fundamental kindness, and without respect for human life?

His education concerning Indians had undergone a massive revision in these days, beginning subtly during the first five days, but crashing home all at once after that. In those first days of directing the establishment of a tent camp for his company and initiating the construction of the fort the Potawatomies were much in evidence. They watched with great interest everything that was going on and, not yet knowing them well and fearful of theft, Captain Whistler had stationed guards over their supplies. It was true that the Indians looked covetously at the neat stacking of provisions and goods that were intended to last the garrison for a year, as these were brought ashore in bateaux from the *Tracy*. Yet, though he stationed the guards, somehow he realized it was not necessary, that there would have been no pilferage even had the items been wholly unattended.

John Whistler, with the hesitant approval of Antoine Ouilmette, had moved his family into the Lalime Trading Post residence on the north side of the river, directly across from where his men were under canvas. He kept a permanent guard of three men at the house during his absence. The commander assured Ouilmette he would vacate the premises upon Lalime's return and pay the trader a rental fee for his use of it. He also borrowed oxen from the herd of the absent trader, to use in the difficult job of hauling timber from where it was cut, on the north shore, to the rafts in the lake and then from the Chicago River landing to where they would be used in construction of the fort. The trading post's sawmill was an unexpected boon put to good use immediately. Two canoes were borrowed for the family's use in crossing the river to the fort site.

The Whistler family was reasonably well ensconced in their new quarters when, on the fifth morning after their arrival, August 22, Lieutenant Swearingen bade them farewell and, in accordance with his orders from Captain Pike, reboarded the now cargoless schooner *Tracy* and departed with it for Mackinac and Detroit, carrying with him a preliminary report from Captain Whistler to his commander.[155]

On the same day of the *Tracy*'s departure, later in the afternoon, they had their first white visitor. He was British and his name was Thomas G. Anderson. For several years he had been trading among the Winnebagoes, Sacs, Foxes and Potawatomies and for the past two years had made the mouth of the Milwaukee River his headquarters, adjacent to the village of Potawatomi Chief Siggenauk, whom he called Blackbird. Two days before, he had received word from an Indian runner that the Americans had arrived at Chicago to establish a fort. Since he was here as a trader under license by the United States government, he decided that it would be politic to pay his respects without delay. On the following morning he had mounted his black stallion named Keegekah — Swift-Goer — and followed the Green Bay Indian Trail and the hard-packed sand of the Lake Michigan shoreline southward to Chicago.

Though Thomas G. Anderson, clad in the usual garb of the trader, at first glance appeared to be simply another uncouth wilderness rover, that illusion was put to rest immediately. He had presented himself to Captain Whistler at once on his arrival and his education, breeding and excellent manners were immediately evident. Within a few minutes, taken by the charm of his first guest, who told him that though Milwaukee was his headquarters, his home base was Mackinac, John Whistler invited him to dinner with his family and Anderson accepted. He excused himself, promising to arrive at seven in the evening, and repaired to Ouilmette's house to freshen up and rest for several hours.

A few minutes before seven, Anderson, freshly shaved and clean, clad in a beautiful pair of soft doeskin trousers and spotless white linen shirt, presented himself at the door of the trading post residence. It opened directly into the dining room where, at the large, neatly set table, were three ladies. They were wearing lovely gowns suitable for the attendance of a banquet, ruffled and frilled and laced, bright in their gay colors. Ann

Whistler greeted him graciously and introduced him in turn to her daughter, Sarah — the sixteen-year-old very pretty in a robin's-egg-blue dress with long skirt and short sleeves — and her daughter-in-law, also sixteen, Julia Fearson Whistler, whose high-necked gown was a deep burnt-orange and, though full, could not disguise the shapeliness of the wearer. Ann, wearing an emerald floor-length dress with snug bodice and flaired skirt, seated him to the left of her place at the foot of the table, to the right of Sarah and across from Julia. The table itself was neatly set with fine china plates having a light floral pattern of rosebuds and foliage in the center and a thin band of gold at the rim. Sparkling goblets for wine were at each place, while serviceable silverplate flatware flanked the plates. On each service plate was a slice of bread from a freshly baked loaf. Two four-stemmed silver candelabra graced the table, one near either end and another pair, each with five candles in stairstep mode, were situated on a sideboard along one wall. Two bottles of burgundy were also on the sideboard. A long rectangular mirror hung horizontally on the wall behind the candelabra enhanced the illumination and the room was bright and cheery, pleasantly pungent with the scent of tallow.

The four engaged immediately in animated conversation — the trader eager for news from Detroit and the women anxious to know more about what to expect in this wilderness locale. In a moment a door opened and the two Whistler officers entered, beaming, both wearing their dress uniforms. Young William came first, carrying a platter upon which were neatly arranged rows of boiled vegetables — carrots, potatoes, summer squash and green beans. John followed with an even larger platter holding a pre-sliced roast of beef much too large for only six people. It was surrounded by a halo of fresh green onions.

There were more greetings and the commander introduced his son as soon as the platters were put down. The two officers took their seats — the captain at the head of the table and the lieutenant beside his wife. In the family tradition they all joined hands and bowed their heads as the host offered a brief grace.

"I must admit," Anderson said, immediately following, "that I have not felt this civilized in years, nor so charmed by such lovely ladies."

"Hear! Hear!" said William, and they all laughed.

John had raised a finger to get attention and was on the point of saying something when the door burst open and a half-dozen Indians rushed in, led by Black Partridge. All were garishly painted on the faces and bare chests and their scalps bristled with ornamental feathers. Some wore necklaces of bear claws or rattlesnake rattles and others carried deer antlers which they clattered together noisily. Some shook long-necked dry gourds filled with pebbles, adding to the din of the shrieks and howls which left their throats. None was in any way armed, though in those first moments no one at the table realized it.

The three women screamed, scrambled up and out of the room and the two officers leaped to their feet, prepared to grapple with the foe. Anderson stayed them when he thrust out both arms in an imperative gesture and hissed, "Sit down!" Slowly the men settled into their chairs again, still very tense, baffled by what was occurring.

The Potawatomies leaped and pranced around the table for more than a minute, noting but paying no attention to Ann who had reappeared at the doorway to the inner room with a rifle held at ready, restrained from shooting only by the fact that, incomprehensibly, her husband and son and their guest were still seated at the table. As the warriors circled, they snatched the slices of bread from the service plates and devoured them. Finally they stopped. As they studied the expressions of the still-stunned Whistlers, a ripple of laughter spread through them, led by Black Partridge. It grew in great bellowing guffaws until they were holding their sides with it and leaning against the walls and doors to keep themselves upright.

Struggling to contain his own laughter, Anderson spoke apologetically to his host. "It's just a joke," he explained. "A prank. They wanted to scare hell out of you and are tickled that they did."

"Rotten joke!" William growled. "I've a mind to —"

"Be quiet!" Anderson interjected quickly. "Don't show anger. It's a test as much as it is a joke." He spoke to John again. "Go along with it."

John Whistler saw that although Black Partridge was still laughing, the chief was watching him closely. His own lips turned up and he chuckled, then broke into laughter, at first forced but then becoming genuine with relief. His son grinned sheepishly and then he, too, laughed and Anderson joined them in it, the three rocking back and forth with merriment in their chairs. Ann continued to stare at them from the doorway, totally bewildered. Between his gasps of laughter, John spoke to her.

"Ann, what gun is that you have?"

"The one that was leaning against your chair. The first one I could find."

"Good! Good!" He roared with laughter again, tilting far back in his chair until suddenly it tipped over. The laughter bloomed anew and then abruptly died and an eerie silence filled the room. John had turned a backward somersault and -come to his feet in one liquid movement, snatched the rifle from Ann's grip and leveled it at the center of Black Partridge's chest. The tension was at a high peak and the Indians were frozen in place, some in half-crouches. John Whistler's finger squeezed the trigger and the cocked flint leaped forward and struck the pan with a tiny spray of sparks but the rifle, which he knew was unloaded, did not fire.

"Bang!" John said, then burst into laughter again, handing the weapon back to his wife.

Black Partridge slowly relaxed and the ferocity of his expression faded.

His lips twitched and then he, too, howled with laughter at the counter-joke played on him, his nose ring bobbing and flashing in the candlelight. Gales of laughter erupted again and the tension was gone permanently. Thomas Anderson moved closer to the captain and, between laughs, murmured with new respect in his voice, "Don't know how you came up with that idea so fast, but you sure scored high with the chief."

The trader then turned to Black Partridge and shook a finger at him with mock severity. "You should be ashamed of yourself," he said in the Potawatomi tongue, "frightening these good people."

"The Big Knife chief," Black Partridge replied, chuckling still, "overcame his surprise very well. Tell him I think he is a good warrior and that his woman is very brave." When Anderson did so, he went on, pointing at the table, his eyes twinkling. "Tell him also that if I were holding a feast in my village, I would have invited him."

John Whistler listened to Anderson's repetition of the comment in English and nodded, more serious now. "I should have done the same. My table is your table, Chief Black Partridge. I now correct my error and ask that you and your brave men sit and eat with us."

The chief nodded when Anderson interpreted and a long low bench and other chairs were brought in. While this was going on, Captain Whistler spoke to Ann in an undertone. "Where are the girls?"

"Still under the bed, I think."

He grinned. "Tell them they can come out now."

The remainder of the evening had gone well and, though not enough food had been prepared for them all, they made do with what was available. Much later the Indians left after warm handshakes with the three men. The following morning there were two freshly killed deer on their doorstep. Thomas Anderson mounted up for his return to Milwaukee, after accepting the thanks of Captain Whistler for his invaluable guidance the night before.

"I hate to think what the consequences might have been had my guard been outside the house last night when the Indians burst in," the commander commented.

Anderson grinned down at him from the back of Keegekah. "You don't understand 'em yet, Captain. Black Partridge did it *because* your guard wasn't there. Think about that." Then he reined away and was gone.

Since that event Captain John Whistler, despite continuing work at the fort site, had visited Black Partridge's village three times — twice alone and once with his family for an Indian feast. What he learned was a revelation. Instead of the stoicism he had expected, there was lightness and gaiety. There was great respect, almost reverence, for parents and the aged. There was a deep, abiding love and respect for nature and an ingrained revulsion for wasting anything nature provided. The dances, when understood, expressed profound feelings of love and thankfulness. Their pride of heritage was intense and their sensitivity to slight or to insult keenly pitched. And John Whistler began to wonder, as only very select individuals had wondered before him, why the Americans and the Indians could not live together in peace, always. In the very asking of the question of himself, he answered it: Because we constantly take from them, move ourselves onto their lands and disrupt their way of life, and I am a part of that. The knowledge saddened him, but it also made him grow.

Today, with the fort only beginning to take shape with the erection of the stockade outer wall posts with sharpened ends, the second white visitor approached. They thought at first he was an Indian for, though he was wearing some of the garb of a white man, he rode his horse bareback, flowed smoothly with the movements of his mount and was leading a dozen warriors. The warriors were Miamis. Their leader was William Wells.

The Indian agent from Fort Wayne, whom Captain Whistler had met on several occasions before, both at Fort Wayne and at Detroit, murmured approval as his eyes moved across the work in progress.

"You'll have a good fort when it's finished, Captain," he commented. "You've chosen the most ideal spot for it here."[156]

He went on to explain that he had been dispatched here by Governor Harrison to issue a trading license to one Jean Baptiste LaGeuness. A messenger was sent to Ouilmette's house at once and LaGueness returned with him to the trading post where the little ceremony was to take place.

There were two copies of the same document on a table there, both with three signature blanks on the bottom, one of which was already signed by William Henry Harrison. William Wells took a small Bible from his pouch, placed it on the table beside the documents and told LaGueness to put his left hand on it, raise the right and repeat an oath. LaGueness, grinning, did so.

"I, Jean Baptiste LaGueness, citizen of the British Empire, resident of Quebec, temporary resident of Chicago, do hereby swear that I will abide by the Indian trade regulations of the United States of America; that I will treat the Indians fairly with whom I trade under this license; that I will forbear from providing such Indians with alcoholic liquors in any form; that I will forbear from providing such Indians with any weapons of war or sustenance of any kind in the event of hostilities between such Indians and the United States of America; and that I will not subvert said Indians with whom I trade, either overtly or covertly, against the United States or in favor of any other nation; and that I further understand any failure on my part to abide by this oath signed by me this day will result in the permanent suspension of said trading license and expulsion from all States and Territories of the United States Government. This I swear, so help me God."

Jean Baptiste LaGueness then signed the appropriate blank and at the bottom William Wells wrote:

This license for Indian Trade within the boundaries of the United States of America is issued by order of William Henry Harrison, Governor of the Indian Territory and Superintendent of Indian Affairs, through William Wells, Agent at Indian Affairs, Chicago, August the 30th, 1803.

After the ceremony was completed, John Whistler and William Wells sat for a long while discussing news of the frontier: the total failure of the agriculture program with the Indians; the inability of the United States government to enforce liquor controls regarding sales to the Indians; the Sac Indians on the Mississippi waging war on the Osages in Missouri and killing some whites along with it; the two expeditions in the planning stages at the moment — one to go up the Missouri to its headwaters and to the ocean beyond, under Captain Meriwether Lewis and William Clark — the latter George Rogers Clark's younger brother — and another to go to the headwaters of the Mississippi under young Lieutenant Zebulon Montgomery Pike. It was from these expeditions, Wells opined, that trouble was going to generate.

"Why?" Captain Whistler asked. "Who from?"

"There's a Shawnee agitating against the Americans right now and he's getting a bigger following all the time. Somehow he's got influence with tribes all over and he's been warning 'em to expect new encroachments into their territories despite the Greenville Treaty. These expeditions'll give him just the kind of ammunition he wants."

"A Shawnee? Who? What's his name?"

"Tecumseh."

"I've never heard of him."

"Not many have, Captain, but you will. Take my word for it, you will. He's big trouble."

[*March 12, 1804 — Monday*]

Jack Lalime was not happy. He had just heard that the Kinzie family was wrapping up its affairs at St. Joseph and would soon be arriving at Chicago permanently and would reopen the trading post. A welling of anger flushed through him at the thought and his hatred for John Kinzie gnawed at his insides. There would be some satisfaction, he thought, on seeing the expression on Kinzie's face when he learned Jack Lalime was re-established at Chicago in a new position — as official Indian interpreter at Fort Dearborn — but it would not be satisfaction enough. One day, he knew, he would kill John Kinzie.

Lalime's presence back in Chicago had come about through a peculiar series of events. Following his set-to with the trader and Topenebe at St. Joseph, he had drifted northward and stayed for a while at Mackinac, then drifted again to Detroit. He was there, eking out a living at odd jobs, when the detachment left to establish Fort Dearborn at Chicago, and he was there when Lieutenant Swearingen returned with word that Captain Whistler and his company were settled at the mouth of the Chicago River and construction had begun on the new fort.

But most fortuitously of all, Jack Lalime was spending his meager pennies on ale in a tavern near the fort in Detroit when he overheard a conversation between two officers at a nearby table. One of them was Second Lieutenant James Strode Swearingen, who was telling of his journey to Chicago and the situation there. One comment had struck him most forcefully.

"One of the biggest needs Captain Whistler has right now," Swearingen said, "is a good interpreter. One's authorized, as soon as he can find the right man, but finding one's the problem. Not too many people around — white men, anyway — who can speak Potawatomi and still have American interests at heart."

The next day Lalime, along with his Potawatomi wife, Nokenoqua, had set out for Chicago, skirting St. Joseph en route, and arriving at the still-under-construction Fort Dearborn in late November. The situation there was not good at all. Captain Whistler's company was handicapped by a number of minor calamities — improper and insufficient clothing for the advancing winter season, lack of nutritious food, lack of the proper tools to properly erect the fort they were sent to build and, worst of all, suffering under recurring attacks of a "bilious fever" which usually had half the work force or more too sick to work.

Having expected Lalime ever since his arrival and still believing him to be owner of the trading post, Captain Whistler moved his family out of the post residence and into a rather wretched cabin that had been vacated by the trader Jean Baptiste LaGueness, who had packed up and left for the upper Mississippi shortly after getting his trading license. Lalime was careful not to say he owned the trading post, but neither did he disabuse the commanding officer of the notion. In fact, he displayed his greatest charm to the officer and his family, offered many helpful hints about existence here at Chicago and subtly allowed the commander to learn of his fluency in the Potawatomi tongue. John Whistler thought it was entirely his own idea when he offered Lalime the job of interpreter for Fort Dearborn. After giving the offer due consideration, Lalime accepted.

In the four months that had passed since his arrival back in Chicago, work had progressed on Fort Dearborn, but slowly. Fortunately, the winter had been a relatively mild one and work continued whenever the

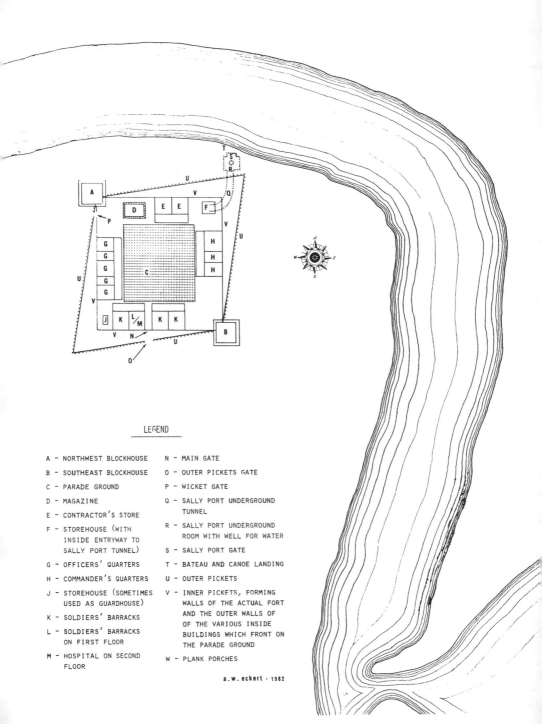

FORT DEARBORN
at Chicago

LEGEND

A – NORTHWEST BLOCKHOUSE

B – SOUTHEAST BLOCKHOUSE

C – PARADE GROUND

D – MAGAZINE

E – CONTRACTOR'S STORE

F – STOREHOUSE (WITH INSIDE ENTRYWAY TO SALLY PORT TUNNEL)

G – OFFICERS' QUARTERS

H – COMMANDER'S QUARTERS

J – STOREHOUSE (SOMETIMES USED AS GUARDHOUSE)

K – SOLDIERS' BARRACKS

L – SOLDIERS' BARRACKS ON FIRST FLOOR

M – HOSPITAL ON SECOND FLOOR

N – MAIN GATE

O – OUTER PICKETS GATE

P – WICKET GATE

Q – SALLY PORT UNDERGROUND TUNNEL

R – SALLY PORT UNDERGROUND ROOM WITH WELL FOR WATER

S – SALLY PORT GATE

T – BATEAU AND CANOE LANDING

U – OUTER PICKETS

V – INNER PICKETS, FORMING WALLS OF THE ACTUAL FORT AND THE OUTER WALLS OF OF THE VARIOUS INSIDE BUILDINGS WHICH FRONT ON THE PARADE GROUND

W – PLANK PORCHES

a.w.eckert - 1982

weather permitted. Part of the incentive had been the completion of the four log barracks for officers and men, who were heartily weary of the continuing discomforts of living out of tents. At least Fort Dearborn now *looked* like a fort, even if it wasn't completed.

Dominated by two log blockhouses guarding the northwest and southeast angles of the fort, the installation was surrounded by a stockade and cannon positioned in each of the blockhouses to enfilade the space between the main stockade wall and the outer pickets, as well as the territory surrounding the fort, from which all underbrush had been removed. In mid-winter the shingle-roofed barracks with covered galleries had been completed and the men moved in. Morale improved at once and work progressed more swiftly. It was a good fort in most respects, its two-story barracks, officers' quarters and commander's house and other structures built around the four sides of a quadrangle, their rear walls part of the stockade and their fronts facing toward the central flagstaff and parade ground. Smaller buildings within the palisades were being erected, surrounding the central parade ground. Set off by itself along the north wall, between the contractor's store and the northwest blockhouse, was a low sturdy building constructed of brick, which was the magazine. On the other side of the contractor's store was a fairly spacious storehouse building sitting by itself. Actually, it was more than a storehouse; inside was the entry to a tunnel that was eighty feet long. Called the sally port, this was an emergency exit — or entry — that traveled underground beneath the stockade wall and outer pickets to a reasonably well-concealed exit at the river's edge. A well had also been dug in the sally port as an emergency water supply in case of siege. The main gate faced directly south.

Outside the fort, to the immediate southwest, were the garrison's stables and a sort of corral for cattle. In addition to the fort's principal garden of about eight acres south and west of the fort, a smaller garden plot was located somewhat to the east between the fort entry and the mouth of the river. The garrison seemed to find nothing wrong with the fact that the earth turned over for this second garden lay directly beside a small burial ground of the Indians. In an area directly west of the fort, the ground was being prepared for the erection of a large Indian Agency House for the United States factor who would ultimately arrive, along with whatever Indian Agent was appointed to this post. Besides the meager military stores, now almost depleted, the post had its two bateaux — one of which had been converted into a sailboat — plus two rowboats, four canoes, four oxen and a wagon, all purchased from the trading post.

Jack Lalime had quickly become friends with the post surgeon, Dr. William C. Smith. Shortly after his arrival, Lalime moved into the quarters at the trading post residence vacated by the Whistlers. Before long, Smith had moved in with him for the winter. In letters to family and friends back East, the surgeon described Lalime as being "a very decent man and good companion."

Now, however, with word having arrived that the Kinzie family would be here soon to reopen the trading post and take up permanent residency, the disgruntled Lalime and his doctor friend would have to move out of their "borrowed" accommodations and Jack Lalime was not happy. In his perverted way, he blamed Kinzie for the inconvenience and discomfort that would result. It was just one more log added to his fires of resentment directed against the man who had once been his employer.

CHAPTER VIII

ALTHOUGH there was no way to prove it, John Kinzie was quite convinced that the antipathy developing between himself and Captain John Whistler was the work of Jack Lalime. Time and again in ordinary conversations with people, bits and hints of things Lalime told the Fort Dearborn commander to undermine the character and practices of the trader had filtered through to him. And, well aware of the unsavory character of Lalime, Kinzie was quite willing to believe his deduction was accurate.

Since his arrival here last May with his family, slaves and employees in seven bateaux carrying all the goods from the post he had operated at St. Joseph, great changes had been wrought in the trading post here in Chicago — now becoming widely known as Kinzie's Store. Although little of his anger showed, he was furious on his arrival at the post to see the condition in which it had been left by Lalime. The former employee had obviously showed little care for the post or the trade. He had alienated customers and he had let the post itself fall into disrepair with no effort whatever to perform the most minor maintenance, including cleaning.

Now, over the past summer, with considerable effort expended by himself, his slaves and engagees, John Kinzie had transformed the post into a better operation in every respect than it had ever been before, even under Du Sable. He had salved over the wounds Lalime had caused with the Indians and with passing fur brigades of French Canadian voyageurs working out of Mackinac. In only this short span of time, Kinzie's Store had become a place where every passing traveler stopped and quite often stayed; where such people found cordiality and family warmth; where their varied travel or trade needs could be filled uncommonly well; where they could sit and chat, passing on the news they had gathered in their travels and receiving news they had not yet heard. John Kinzie's Store had become more than merely a trading post; it was a center of society, a news post, a library, a depot for provisions, a source of manpower for crossing the Chicago Portage. It was a place where visitors whose bellies had been warmed by brandy or rum or wine would find themselves revealing things they had never intended to relate, yet secure in the knowedge that the proprietor respected confidences and identities.

The post now had seven men as regular employees, including Antoine Ouilmette. In addition, there were another dozen men on call for use in helping with the work of portaging the bateaux of the fur brigades and other travelers passing through.[157] A good string of packhorses at the post could also be used in this respect if the need arose.

Great as the changes had been in this short span at the store, they were greater by far among the Potawatomies living in the vicinity and other Indians who were attracted. Just as John Kinzie had won the respect and friendship of Indians wherever he traded before, so he won them now. He had very quickly become the favorite white man of the Indians in the area. Partly this was due to his silversmithing ability and the ornaments he continued to make for the Indians; part was due to his striving to understand the Indians and both ease their problems and anticipate their needs; part was due to his long-standing very close friendship with the powerful Topenebe. But most of all, it was simply because he always treated them fairly, never assumed a superior pose, was concerned for their welfare, never lied to them and was genuinely eager to be a friend. He had long cultivated his ability to remember names and rarely, having once met an individual, failed to address him by name the next time they met, however difficult the Indian pronounciation may have been. He also did what virtually no other trader had ever done with them before: he *listened*.

In addition to Topenebe, three other Potawatomi chiefs now became numbered among Kinzie's closest friends. One he saw very often because of the proximity of his village. That was Black Partridge. The other two, who passed through every now and then, were Chaubenee and Sauganash. Twice since Kinzie's arrival, Chaubenee had come to Chicago, and twice Kinzie had visited his village — a newly established town located at a beautiful grove of oaks projecting from the prairie at the headwaters of Indian Creek some sixty-five miles west of Chicago.[158] In the sea of prairie grasses, the grove appeared from a distance to be a great dark schooner with deep green sails.

Chaubenee was one of the most intelligent and perceptive Indians John had ever met, with a surprising grasp of concepts as well as realities. The trader and the chief, on these rare occasions, had talked together for hours that had seemed like minutes and each time they were more loath to end their discussions. It was from Chaubenee that John Kinzie first heard of

Tecumseh and his one-eyed brother, Lowawluwaysica. Though the Potawatomi did not go into extensive details, it was abundantly clear that he believed Tecumseh to be a truly great man. The trader hoped one day to be able to meet him.

It was at Chaubenee's village that John was introduced to Sauganash for the first time and won immediate favor with him for refusing to address him by the name which immediately emphasized his half-breed heritage and by which almost all other whites called him — Billy Caldwell. Kinzie considered him, too, to be an especially intelligent man and he was particularly impressed at Sauganash's ability to both read and write English and French. Their friendship had ample opportunity to develop even more when, shortly after their first meeting, Sauganash moved to Black Partridge's village.

A fourth Potawatomi chief had also developed a distinct admiration and respect for John Kinzie, though he was not quite so willing to become an actual friend of the trader in the sense that Black Partridge, Chaubenee and Sauganash had. This was Siggenauk — whom Kinzie had previously heard about under the name of Blackbird. His village was at Milwaukee and it was not long before he came to Chicago on a special trip to politely and rather formally invite the trader to establish a post there.

Now, into his fourth month here at Chicago, John had not only transformed the Chicago establishment into the finest and most prosperous post west of Detroit, he was planning subsidiary posts to be established at the mouths of both the Milwaukee and Kankakee Rivers, as well as on the Rock River and well to the south on the Sangamon. These posts, if and when built, he would place in charge of clerks in his employ. Some would be overseen by Tom Forsyth from his headquarters at Peoria Lake.

The coolness that so quickly developed between John Kinzie and the Fort Dearborn commander was almost certainly abetted by Jack Lalime, but its roots went deeper than that. Captain John Whistler was not entirely a "by-the-book" military man, but he was close to it. He demanded the utmost respect and obedience from his garrison and made the error of thinking that because he was military leader at Chicago, he was also foremost authority over the civilians living here and could dictate to them. When, early in their association, he began issuing directives to John Kinzie that were tantamount to orders, he touched a raw nerve. The first such encounter came when he "instructed" the trader that he wished him to be suttler for the fort, to help make up deficiencies of supplies under which the garrison was suffering. Kinzie had hoped for suttling privileges, but he chafed at the imperiousness of Whistler and masked his own irritation only with some effort.

"I'll be happy to do that, Captain," he responded.

"As a government installation," the officer went on, "we will expect to receive these goods at cost, for which I will sign vouchers which you, in turn, may submit to Colonel Kingsbury for payment."

Kinzie could hardly believe the temerity of the man and looked at him steadily for a long moment before replying. "Captain," he said at last, "whatever you or your men buy, you'll pay the same price as anyone else. And I'm not too keen on trying to collect debts from the United States government. I prefer cash."

Captain Whistler stiffened. "Sir," he said, "you seem to overlook the fact that this post has been established here to protect citizens such as yourself. You have a moral obligation to provide us with goods at reasonable prices."

"My goods, sir," Kinzie retorted coolly, "are *all* priced reasonably. That's why I stay in business. But my business is also to make a profit. It is not to support government troops."

The Fort Dearborn commander fumed and obliquely suggested that John Kinzie was unscrupulous, but the trader only smiled and waited patiently. At length, because he had no other choice, Captain Whistler agreed to purchase from him at his normal fair price. However, on returning to the fort he wrote a letter to Colonel Kingsbury, bitterly complaining about the delinquency of adequate military supplies being forwarded for maintaining the post. He also took the opportunity to denounce Kinzie for his stance.

Another set-to occurred between them when Captain Whistler made an ineffectual effort to cut off Kinzie's liquor trade. It was axiomatic on the frontier that a trader could not survive unless one of his principal stocks in trade was an abundant supply of liquor. In certain respects this was true and even the government recognized it. Though regulations had been made prohibiting a liquor trade, it was little more than a sop to moral groups who demanded it. The regulations were largely ignored and almost never enforced except where flagrantly abused. John Kinzie never engaged in the alcohol abuses. At least half of the liquor he imported was given away, not sold, to visitors to Kinzie's Store, both Indian and white. That which he used in trade was always sparingly distributed and never until he had personally overseen the transaction and was satisfied that the Indian with whom he was trading had first purchased sufficient necessaries for himself and his family to carry them through the winter. Oddly enough, this stricture of the liquor-purchasing ability endeared him to the Indians rather than antagonized them. They, more than anyone else, were aware of their own peculiar susceptibility to alcohol and their general lack of willpower in abstaining from it. They considered it a boon to have John Kinzie provide them with it only in sensible moderation.

That was a bit too gray an area for Captain Whistler, who much preferred the inflexibility of black-and-white rules and regulations. And so, while he was not able to abolish John Kinzie's liquor trade activities, he did manage to curtail them to some degree and force the trader to operate somewhat clandestinely in this respect. The two men were obviously thorns in one another's sides but thus far open warfare had not been declared between them. Neither was convinced it would not ultimately degenerate to that.

At the moment, Fort Dearborn was just about the most isolated post of all the American garrisons and military duty here was tantamount to exile. The only real diversions were hunting in the surrounding prairies and woodlands and fishing for yellow perch, pike, herring, walleye and black bass in Lake Michigan and farther up the Chicago River. There were no newspapers and information from the outer world was always delayed. News that reached other posts in good time arrived in Chicago weeks or sometimes even months after the fact. Visitors were few and, as a result, treated regally when they arrived, their needs attended to and their news of the outside world voraciously devoured. The nearest post was Fort Wayne and that, at best, was over a week's journey away over difficult and sometimes hazardous trails. Detroit was essentially a fortnight's trip along the Sac and Potawatomie Trails, even longer by water. The round trip to St. Louis over the Chicago Portage and Illinois River took five or six weeks under the best of conditions. The ship *Adams* was tentatively being scheduled for two or three trips annually from Buffalo to Chicago, with interim stops at Cleveland, Detroit and Mackinac, its primary purpose to bring provisions and new military personnel. It had come only once since Kinzie's arrival. That had been in mid-August when it arrived with supplies and a few soldiers in response to the needs Captain Whistler had communicated to Colonel Kingsbury. In his accompanying dispatches, the colonel had congratulated Captain Whistler on having accomplished so much at Chicago with his meager resources. However, Colonel Kingsbury could have used some of Kinzie's resourcefulness in responding to Captain Whistler's requests for supplies. The requisitions had been very badly filled: a large saw ordered for continued construction work at the fort turned out to be a whipsaw that quickly dulled to uselessness in cutting oak timber, which was the most available. No one had thought to send sharpening files along with the saw and so now it was quietly rusting in storage. Clothing had been requisitioned and there were cries of joy when bundles of clothing were unloaded from the *Adams*. The joy was short-lived. The clothing was only uniforms for sergeants and, apart from that, no invoice of it had been sent and so therefore, according to regulations — to which the commanding officer adhered — it could not be used and the men continued to wear the ragged remnants of what they had brought with them originally. A separate order, with invoice, of fifty-six suits was also unloaded and gratefully received, but Captain Whistler's garrison was now comprised of sixty-nine men, so some had to go without. The fort had two fifers as part of its musical corps, but the only fife the company owned had long ago been lost and the requisition for more had been ignored. Other requisitions had been equally ignored or improperly filled, so the post was very nearly as destitute of supplies as before the *Adams* arrived. Only in the matter of food and ammunition had the requisitions been properly met.

Never slow to act on opportunity when it presented itself, John Kinzie quickly drew up an agreement between himself and the skipper of the *Adams*. Now the trade goods Kinzie ordered from Montreal, Detroit and Mackinac would be brought to Chicago aboard the *Adams* and, on its return voyage, the ship would carry a cargo of furs from Kinzie — pelts brought to him in bales on packhorses to trade for goods — to the fur depots of the South West Fur Company and American Fur Company at Mackinac. And so Kinzie's Store prospered even more.

Construction of the fort was nearly completed and, not unpredictably, there had been a small influx of settlers since the establishment of the fort, with the promise of many more to come. Jean Baptiste Beaubien, formerly of Detroit and now with a small trading house at Milwaukee, was one of those who came and decided that before long he would return to Chicago permanently.[159] Another who came, but stayed, was Charles Lee with his wife, Martha, and their two children, Charles, Jr., seven, and Mary, four. Lee was not interested in the trade, but he became enthralled by the incredible richness of the black soil in the Chicago area and decided it would be a marvelous place to farm. In partnership with a friend, William Russell, Lee had already established just such a farm, now called Lee's Place, on the South Branch of the Chicago River four miles upstream from the fort. It was the intention of Lee and Russell to hire an overseer and some men to farm it for them.[160] However, Lee and his family built their own residence on the lake shore fairly close to Fort Dearborn and the Russells — William and Tess — built a small place near them.

Despite the 1787 Ordinance prohibiting slavery in the Northwest Territory, most people of means still owned slaves and the slave trade itself remained quite active. John Kinzie continued to buy and sell slaves when the opportunity presented itself and he had never been quite so taken by the potential of a slave as he had become in regard to a huge, enormously powerful black by the name of Jeffrey Nash.

On the trip that Kinzie had made to Detroit just a year ago, he and Tom Forsyth had seen Nash on the block, for sale. That was the trip upon which he was to pick up Eleanor and his new son, but they had arrived at St. Joseph early, with little John Harris badly burned on the neck — a wound that left as its reminder a scar that was still bright pink and very tender. The beginning-bid asking price for Nash was unusually high, but he was an exceptionally fine figure of a man and both John and Tom were strongly taken by the idea of owning him. The slave auction took place on

September 5 and the partners entered into the bidding determined not to lose. The final bid they made was higher than anyone in recent memory had paid for a slave on the Detroit block — possibly the highest ever — but they got him.

Jeffrey Nash was twenty-eight and had previously been owned by a New Orleans merchant, as were Nash's wife and young son. The merchant had fallen on hard times and so had sold Jeffrey, who was taken away from his family and shipped to Detroit for resale at a nice profit. Only seventeen days after he was purchased by Kinzie and Forsyth, the legislature of the Indiana Territory at Vincennes adopted what was called "The Control of Slaves Measure." The subjects of the measure were called slaves in the title only. Elsewhere throughout the document they were referred to as servants.

News of this action by the Indiana Territorial Legislature did not reach John Kinzie until after Tom had returned to Peoria and he and Eleanor had made the move to Chicago with Jeffrey. Though the new measure adopted by the legislature did not affect Kinzie as owner or Nash as slave, by the time the trader learned of it the report was so garbled that he became concerned that he would lose his high-priced slave unless he legally indentured him for seven years.

On May 22, only a few days after their arrival in Chicago, John Kinzie drew up the legal indenture papers and ordered Jeffrey Nash to sign them, a copy for each, which he did. It was a curious contract stating that in return for meat, drink, apparel, washing and lodging fitting for a servant, he, Jeffrey Nash, was indenturing himself to "Kinzie and Forsyth, Merchants of Chicago," for a term of seven years. By the terms of the contract he agreed, during this period, to keep their secrets and gladly obey their lawful commands; that he would not waste their goods nor lend them to others; that he would neither commit fornication nor contract matrimony; that he would not play at dice, cards nor any other unlawful game, nor haunt taverns nor other places, nor absent himself day or night from his master's service.

Now, on this eleventh day of September, a messenger had arrived at Fort Dearborn with dispatches from Vincennes. One of the documents he carried was an official notification from Governor William Henry Harrison that by his order, "John Kinzie, Trader of Chicago, is hereby appointed justice of the peace at Chicago, with all the privileges and responsibilities attending thereto."

[*December 14, 1804 — Friday*]

At his Grouseland mansion in Vincennes, the governor of the Indiana Territory broke into a broad smile as he read the dispatch just received from Washington.

He had pulled it off!

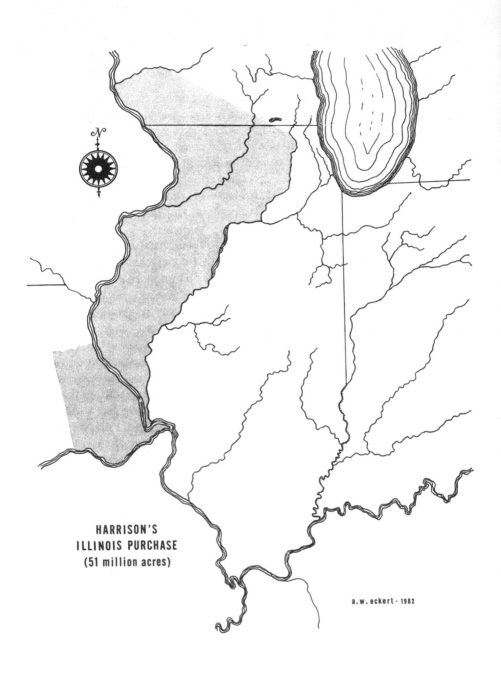

HARRISON'S
ILLINOIS PURCHASE
(51 million acres)

a.w. eckert - 1982

If William Henry Harrison experienced any remorse over what had led up to today's triumphant news, he showed no sign of it. The matter in question was a treaty he had consummated with the Sacs and Foxes at St. Louis just a little over a month ago, acting on instructions from President Thomas Jefferson and Secretary of War Henry Dearborn. Recurrent raids by the Sacs on settlers of the middle Mississippi River Valley and western Illinois had convinced the United States that the only way to end the peril was to buy the land from them so they would have no excuse for future attacks of like nature.

Arriving in St. Louis, Harrison found that his agents had done exactly as he'd ordered them to, which was to locate some Sac and Fox chiefs who might be convinced to sign a treaty ceding land to the United States. They had brought in five such chiefs.[161] It made little difference to him that only two of these chiefs had any small degree of authority among the Sacs as a tribe and that the other three were merely very insignificant village chiefs. Nor did it make any difference that none of the chiefs involved even resided in the land to be ceded and that, instead, their villages were some distance up the Missouri River.

Assisted by an Indian agent and two interpreters, Governor Harrison very quickly drew up a treaty and dangled a paltry payment before the greedy eyes of the chiefs. They immediately agreed to the terms of the treaty and signed it. One of the chiefs was a little reluctant to do so, but since he was one of the more important of the little group, he was bribed into signing by being offered the life of a relative who had been jailed for murder.[162] This seemed of little consequence to the treaty commissioners. The five chiefs signed and thus, in the eyes of the United States government, the entire populations of the Sac and Fox tribes were thereby committed to abide by the terms of the treaty. And what a treaty it was!

The terms were basically simple: the Indians were to be given an annuity of $1,000 — $400 for the Foxes and $600 for the Sacs. In addition, the five Indian signers received goods to the total value of exactly $2,234.50. For this munificent payment, the Americans received full cession of an area in the Illinois Territory which was bordered on the north by the Wisconsin River, on the east by the Fox River of Illinois (less than forty miles west of Chicago), on the southeast by the Illinois River and on the west by the Mississippi River plus a parcel running westward up the Missouri River for about one hundred miles, then north by northwest for another eighty miles, then back east to the Mississippi — the entire cession encompassing a total of fifty-one *million* acres!

As a gesture to show the great benevolence of the United States — and perhaps inhibit any immediate drastic repercussions — the treaty stated that so long as the territory ceded remained public lands of the United States, the Sacs and Foxes would be given the privilege of hunting on it and living upon it. As soon as white settlement began, however, with the land passing into private ownership, they would have to vacate.

Word of the treaty spread quickly and there was a burst of outrage from the combined Sacs and Foxes. The five chiefs who had signed the treaty, now fearful of their own lives, fled up the Missouri River to a place where, they hoped, they would be safe from the wrath of their tribes.[163]

The anger of the tribes was of no concern to Harrison or the United States government. The government position was quite loftily clear: it did not interfere in the intratribal squabbles of the Indians, content to let them settle their own differences in their own way.

Immediately following the signing, Harrison sent the treaty by express to the capital. The President submitted it to Congress without delay. The Congress acted instantly. The dispatch Governor Harrison had just received notified him that the United States Congress had just ratified the St. Louis Treaty.

For the first time in the nation's capital an exciting whisper began making the rounds: even though he was only thirty-one years old, might it not be that this remarkable young governor of the Indiana Territory was of presidential caliber?

[*December 27, 1804 — Thursday*]

Having missed the birth of his son a year and a half ago, John Kinzie was determined he was not going to miss the birth of his second child with Eleanor and so he postponed a round of trips he was going to make to his new posts at Milwaukee and the Rock River. But while John Harris Kinzie had been born several weeks earlier than expected, this pregnancy of Eleanor's dragged on and on.

The baby's birth had been anticipated in the middle of November but now, six weeks later, the infant still appeared disinclined to trigger the mechanism that would cause Eleanor's labor to begin. The delayed arrival, causing John Kinzie to remain in Chicago, also resulted in his being on hand to perform the first marriage to occur here.

The young trader of Detroit named James Abbott had corresponded faithfully with Sarah Whistler ever since she left Detroit with her father and family to establish Fort Dearborn. Though the elder Whistler had tended to believe his daughter's romance with the trader would wither due to the separation, it had not. The two became ever more determined to marry and finally, in September, the *Adams* had brought a mail pouch in which there was a letter from Abbott declaring that he was coming to get her in early November and they could either be married right there and then, or he would take her back to Detroit with him and they could be married there. However it worked out, nothing was going to prevent their being joined. And, since there was no opportunity for the Whistlers to get away in order to attend a wedding in Detroit at this time, the captain and his lady consented to having the ceremony take place at Fort Dearborn.

Much as he disliked doing so, since their relations remained rather strained, Captain Whistler formally requested John Kinzie to preside at the simple ceremony, since he was the only person nearer than Fort Wayne with the authority to do so. John had agreed and so, on the ninth day of November, he married them. And less than an hour after the ceremony, the newly married couple mounted the horses young Abbott had brought from Detroit and set off to return there and make it their permanent home.

Now, at last, only four days before the close of the year, Eleanor Kinzie went into labor and in less than ten hours gave birth to the first white child ever born in Chicago — a healthy, beautiful little ten-pounder whom they named Ellen Marion Kinzie.

[*September 22, 1805 — Sunday*]

For Chaubenee and Sauganash, who had traveled together from Illinois to Tecumseh's village on the White River, the reunion with the man to whom they had both sworn their devotion and allegiance filled them with great satisfaction. While careful to keep from the whites any hint of what was planned, these two Potawatomies had been very busy carrying Tecumseh's doctrine to various Potawatomi villages in the lower Wisconsin and Michigan country and throughout the entire Indiana Territory, which embraced the Illinois country. They had won many converts to the grandiose plan but, even so, they were unprepared for the phenomenal successes Tecumseh himself had achieved since last they saw him.

Chaubenee and Sauganash were among the very privileged few who made up a most secret inner council of which Tecumseh was unquestionably leader. They, along with other members of this elite body, listened with admiration as he told them of his travels to distant tribes over these past years. Wasegoboah was there, as he always was, husband of his leader's sister, Tecumapese, who was also part of the inner circle. Chief Roundhead of the Wyandots, resplendent as usual in his garb and ornamentation, was on hand, as well as Tecumseh's younger brothers, Lowawluwaysica and Kumskaka. Here, too, was Skesh — formerly Oskesh — a Potawatomi village chief originally recruited by Chaubenee, who had traveled far to find Tecumseh to listen to his words, and who had become as completely won over to him as Chaubenee and Sauganash had been.[164]

The group listened, mesmerized, as Tecumseh told them not only of his progress, but equally of his failures in some areas. Already he had more tribes firmly aligned behind him than any other chief had ever gathered, yet he admitted they were not enough and though he traveled incredible distances, he told them he would have to travel even farther, work even harder, if the grand plan were ever to come to fruition. There were still many Indian nations to the southwest, south and southeast with whom he had to meet and whom he had to convince to accept his precepts. This would take much time. In addition, he had no intention of ignoring the fact that there were still a half dozen or more tribes of the northeast, the far north and the northwest who had initially rejected his ideas; tribes he was convinced he could swing to his support with further visits, especially in view of the fact that at this very moment the Shemanese had exploratory expeditions inching their way to the far North and deep into the West — tangible proof of the white peril he had warned them of and undoubtedly a vanguard opening the way for a great flood of whites to follow. That must not happen and to those tribes he would return with stronger arguments and more convincing prophecies, as soon as the problems here in their own country were seen to.

It had been to Lowawluwaysica and Kumskaka that Tecumseh had left the responsibility of convincing the homeland tribes to accept his plan, while he traveled to more distant places for the same purpose. They, however, had been less than smashingly successful in their endeavors. The many predictions Tecumseh had given to Lowawluwaysica to relay to the Indians here, as if these predictions were Lowawluwaysica's own, had all come true and had brought the ugly one-eyed Shawnee some notoriety as a prophet, but it was only his own image that had improved, not Tecumseh's. Neither brother had convinced very many to swing their allegiance to their elder brother.

Part of the problem was that some important chiefs whom it was imperative to convince heartily disliked Lowawluwaysica and distrusted his motives. Among such chiefs were Michikiniqua and Catahecassa, the principal chiefs of the Miamis and their own Shawnees. Onoxa of the Elkhart River Potawatomies was another. These chiefs, all signers of the Greenville Treaty, considered Tecumseh's plan as being dishonorable, in view of that treaty, and even Tecumseh's friend and admirer, Blue Jacket, war chief of the Shawnees, was not fully convinced it was the proper thing to do. Many of the older Shawnees felt that Tecumseh was trying to usurp Catahecassa's authority and that he aspired to the post of principal chief of the tribe to which, by Shawnee law and tradition, he was not qualified.

It was not Tecumseh's idea to do this and it bothered him considerably that this notion was so prevalent and that Kumskaka and Lowawluwaysica had been so singularly unsuccessful in their efforts to disabuse them of it. How could they expect the Miamis and Potawatomies, the Wyandots and Delawares and other tribes of their own home area to pledge themselves to his amalgamation of nations if they could not convince even their own Shawnee people to do so?

In those initial meetings held following the arrival of Chaubenee and Sauganash, all attending were given their own special instructions on how to proceed in successfully putting across the importance of Tecumseh's plan. They agreed, before resuming their own individual missions, to accompany Tecumseh as he spoke to each of the chiefs personally. Although disappointed in Lowawluwaysica thus far, he felt it was because he had not given his younger brother instruction enough. Now, in the presence of all the others, he instructed Lowawluwaysica in great detail about what he was to say and even the manner in which he was to say it. Lowawluwaysica's task at this point was to convince the *people* more than the chiefs. To aid him in this end, Tecumseh provided him with a whole new set of prophecies to give them — prophecies of such significance that when they came to pass, *as they would*, the people would be convinced.

The inner council then began its rounds to the chiefs with Tecumseh and it pained Chaubenee to see that the old chiefs, especially Catahecassa and Michikiniqua, were so set in their ways, so blinded by their own importance and so fearful of losing their own positions of leadership that they gave Tecumseh and the council short shrift.

Then came an abrupt turnabout for many, just when matters seemed at their worst, as Tecumseh and his followers visited the Shawnee village of Tawa on the Auglaize River. An epidemic of severe stomach sickness was occurring on their arrival and before sunset of that day, the most esteemed of Shawnee prophets, old Penegashega, had died. At once Tecumseh and his followers held a hurried conference in private. It was to the one-eyed Lowawluwaysica, however, that Tecumseh directed his comments most specifically.

"This is a bad sickness that has struck our Shawnee brothers," he said, "and it is not yet over. More than twenty have been afflicted by it and already Penegashega has died. What is yet to come provides us with an opportunity we must not let pass by. Lowawluwaysica, I want you to assemble the warriors — all of them, including those who are sick — and you are to tell them you have had a vision. In this vision, you will say, you have seen that three more men will die of the sickness, but that by the end of five days, those others now afflicted will be well again, because you will cast the sickness from them. You will tell them that the three who are yet to die are men who are evil, men engaged in witchcraft, and they will die because you, Lowawluwaysica, will not save them because of what they are and what they do. But you will tell them that at the end of the five days, when you have cured all the others who are sick, you will summon them again to hear you, at which time you will tell them something of great importance. Do you understand?"

Lowawluwaysica nodded slowly, but there was something about his response, some slight hesitation, that caused Tecumseh to place his hand on his brother's head and look into his eye with a stare so intense, so penetrating, it was frightening. Lowawluwaysica began to tremble and tried to look away.

"Look into my eyes and do not let your own stray," Tecumseh commanded. "Hear and remember what I say to you now." He then repeated, virtually word for word, the instructions and predictions he had just given.

It all came about precisely as Tecumseh had prophesied: the three men died and the others recovered. When Lowawluwaysica then said he was ready to speak, a remarkably large crowd had assembled. Not only were the Shawnee warriors of Tawa on hand today, but during those preceding five days — as Tecumseh had known would happen — the word of what was occurring had spread to other Shawnee villages and even the villages of other tribes, so there were Delawares on hand, too, as well as Miamis and a few Ottawas and Wyandots, Chippewas and Potawatomies.

Tecumseh and his lieutenants sat together to one side as Lowawluwaysica moved slowly to the front of the assemblage and stood there quietly as the murmuring gradually died. Chaubenee, who disliked his leader's one-eyed brother and doubted his ability to carry this off, leaned toward Tecumseh and whispered.

"Will he be able to do this, Tecumseh? Can he make them believe?"

Tecumseh smiled. "Watch, my brother. Those of this village already believe, as do many who have come. Those who do not yet believe will be caught up. During the night, while you and the others slept, I stayed up with him and talked to him. He knows well now what he is to say and how he is to say it. Listen!"

"Hear me, Brothers!" Lowawluwaysica raised his hands and the last of the murmurings stilled. Chaubenee, who had never heard him speak, marveled at the power of his voice. "You have witnessed my powers of prophecy in the past," Lowawluwaysica went on. "The things I have said would be have come to pass. And you have seen the three die as I predicted they would and you have witnessed the miracles I have performed in casting out the sickness which threatened your own lives.

"You have known me by the name of Lowawluwaysica, but no longer! From this day forward I shall be known to all men as Tenskwatawa — One-with-Open-Mouth — and my mouth will be open with words which will lead you to a better life, to better health, to a better future. Penegashega the Prophet is dead. I say to you now that henceforth I am your Prophet and that there is none other who qualifies, none other who can do for you what I can do. Do I hear you say that you wish me to take this high office?"

He had begun his talk slowly, with some hesitation, as if unsure of himself, but his words had picked up pace and vibrancy and now he had become more animated, more in control. He paused after his question and

Chaubenee grinned as he watched the speaker cup a hand behind each ear in an exaggerated stance of listening. There was a roar of approval and Chaubenee saw from the corner of his eye the hand of Tecumapese reach out and squeeze the wrist of her brother.

"*That* is our little brother?" she murmured wonderingly.

The man who now called himself Tenskwatawa waited until the cries died away and then, his eye glinting and a faint smile creasing his thin lips, he began to speak again. "I am Tenskwatawa and my people call on me to serve them as Prophet. But such must first be approved by the Shawnee Council. Since those wise men are among us today and since our Prophet is dead and there is little time to waste in lengthy discussion, I call on them now, here and at this moment, to say whether or not *I* am the Shawnee Prophet!"

Tecumseh's nod was so imperceptible that it was scarcely visible, but Chaubenee saw it and knew that this was exactly as he had planned it, calculated to take the old Shawnee Council members in attendance by surprise and without opportunity to confer and gather opposition strength if such would have been their intention. It was a brilliant maneuver and Chaubenee shared the exultation that swept their little group as one by one Tenskwatawa pointed at the Shawnee Council members, called their names and demanded response. Even though there was momentary hesitation among a few, all finally nodded. Tenskwatawa was officially the new Shawnee Prophet.

Now the speaker raised his arms to still the excited talking that had risen among his listeners, then resumed speaking. At considerable length he went over the points Tecumseh had instructed him to make. He was, he told them, truly a Prophet, given to see into the future without need of such superstitious paraphernalia as bits of bone and tiny smooth stones and little pouches of fine sand to sprinkle and spread in strange designs on a piece of cured skin, such as Penegashega had needed. The use of such, he told them, was itself a form of witchcraft — evil sorcery that depended upon supplication to the Devil, Matchemenetoo, rather than the Great Spirit.

"I will lead you away from such evil beliefs!" he cried. "I tell you that those who practice such medicine are themselves possessed and will not go to the good Afterworld, nor will they ever see Moneto. Listen, my Brothers!" he thundered with increased vehemence. "On the day that Penegashega died, I went up into the clouds and the first place I came to was the dwelling of Matchemenetoo; here I saw all who had died as drunkards, with flames of fire issuing from their mouths."

A sudden whispering rippled through the crowd and Tenskwatawa smiled as he let it run its course, knowing the reason. He was himself a heavy drinker and few among them had not frequently seen him almost blind with the effects of liquor, staggering and reeling toward his wegiwa to fall on his bed-mat and sleep it away.

"Yes!" His single word exploded like a gunshot and again snatched their attention. "Yes," he repeated, "previous to this revelation I myself drank, but this has so frightened me that I will never drink again and I say to you gathered here that neither must you drink." He continued expounding in this vein for a considerable while and then abruptly switched to another topic and spoke earnestly.

"Brothers! We are Indians! We must keep our women from marrying white men. This is one of the great causes of unhappiness and the means by which white men have long tried to destroy the pure strain of Indian blood." Chaubenee glanced at Sauganash and saw that he, son of an English father and Potawatomi mother, was frowning and a muscle was twitching in his cheek. Tecumseh saw it, too, and leaned far over to pat his knee and reassure him as Tenskwatawa went on without pause. "The blood of Indian woman and white man must nevermore be allowed to mix, under threat of the most severe penalty!"

Only Tecumseh, of all those who comprised his inner circle, was not flabbergasted at the extraordinary scope and depth of the speech as it continued for over three hours, or amazed at the transformation that had occurred in the formerly inept Lowawluwaysica, who was now a very domineering speaker who called himself Tenskwatawa — The Prophet! Chaubenee, Sauganash, Roundhead, Kumskaka, Skesh, Wasegoboah, and even Tecumapese, who knew him best, listened with fascination as the one-eyed Shawnee propounded on the matters they had so often heard from Tecumseh, but which Tenskwatawa now delivered as his own and, in the process, held the entire audience spellbound. He emphasized the importance of all Indians everywhere in this land becoming one people, united to common goals — just as those people who were first of all Americans were comprised of English, French, Spanish, Irish, German and other races. He told them that the property of one Indian must become the property of all Indians; each Indian working for the common good of all. He told them that it was the duty of the young at all times to cherish and support those who were old and infirm; that new forms of dress, especially the wearing of white man's clothing, were detestable practices which had to end — no Indian should wear woolen or linen or cotton material made by whites but, instead, they must return to the ways of their fathers and dress in the skins of animals; that they must return to all the habits of their fathers and their fathers before them and, in so doing, reject the habits they had learned from the white men. Since Moneto had created the buffalo, elk, deer and other wild creatures for their use, it was wrong to eat the flesh of hogs, cattle or sheep; and it was equally wrong to eat bread made of the white man's wheat flour when their own bread was of the flour ground from Indian corn.

"You must believe," he went on in a voice filled with passion, "that the Indian race — not just this tribe or that, but the whole Indian race — is superior to any other race on earth, for this is true! Now that I am your Prophet, we have embarked on the trail that will show our superiority to the entire world. Hear what I say! No Indian who believes in the power and protectiveness of Moneto and has confidence in himself and his Indian brothers need ever look to any man of another race for help. We do not *need* help, as the whites would have us believe. They have tried every means in their power to make us dependent upon them and upon those things which they can provide for us, but the fathers of our fathers lived well without such things and so must we. We have allowed the white man to lead us away from our own beliefs and traditions. Now we must go back to them. We must return to a greater respect and admiration for Moneto and for the many gifts and blessings he has bestowed upon us all."

His voice dropped and his listeners automatically leaned forward and listened more intently so as not to miss a word of what he was saying. "The Great Spirit has revealed to me why it has been, in the past, that no matter whether we lost battles or won them, it has always been the Indian who has found himself on the side where lands and crops and lives have been lost, and the Great Spirit has shown me how all this can be changed.

"As I take on my duties as Prophet — as I begin a life of devotion to the cause and principles of the Indian people — this now I say to you: a tremendous power has been given to me by the Great Spirit to confound our enemies, to cure all diseases and to prevent death from sickness or on the battlefield. I am your Prophet — Tenskwatawa!"

The entire audience was deeply moved by what this inspired speaker was saying. Tecumseh's noddings had become more evident as the various points were made and he was both impressed and pleased with the way his little brother was mesmerizing his listeners. The only area thus far in which he had been surprised was in the change of name to Tenskwatawa, but he thought it was very timely and he fully approved.

Chaubenee, for his part, was overwhelmed by the change that had been wrought in the self-proclaimed Prophet; a change that seemed to visibly be occurring even as he spoke. Tecumseh's brother was still the unpleasant ugly man who was devoid of any of the dignity or noble characteristics the leader himself possessed so abundantly. This one-eyed man was, Chaubenee knew, still not a brave or truthful man, or one above cruelty if he could benefit by it. He had not lost his feral cunning nor his showy smartness. Yet somehow — and Chaubenee could not fathom how it had occurred — on this day the man who now called himself Tenskwatawa was possessed of powers of persuasiveness and plausibility entirely equal to those of Tecumseh himself. Perhaps, Chaubenee mused, closer to the truth than even he suspected, perhaps it was because on this day, at this time and place, Tenskwatawa had not only really believed in what he was saying, he believed in *himself*, possibly for the first time in his life.

Chaubenee still did not like Tenskwatawa, but he admitted to himself that he was greatly impressed, and he knew the others were, also. He promised himself he would use some of the Prophet's rhetoric — which was, of course, Tecumseh's initially — in his own talks to Indian groups whom he yet hoped to convince to join Tecumseh. During the body of his speech, Tenskwatawa had referred to Tecumseh frequently. Now, in his concluding remarks, he told his listeners that Tecumseh's village on the White River west of Fort Greenville was not a Shawnee village but, rather, an *Indian* village, and all who believed in him as a Prophet and Tecumseh as the leader who would lead them to greater glory than they had ever before known were welcome to come there to live. With great satisfaction, Tecumseh and the members of his inner council saw now that far more would be joining them from here than they had at first believed.

[*April 2, 1806 — Wednesday*]

"The Prophet be damned!"

A stunned silence fell over the delegation of Delaware chiefs visiting William Henry Harrison at Vincennes and immediately the governor regretted his outburst. But then he damned the man again, mentally. The Prophet! That's all he was hearing about these days and he was fed up with it. All his problems lately seemed to wind up in a spiral that terminated in some strange one-eyed Shawnee who had come out of nowhere and proclaimed himself a prophet. And what was so galling was that the stupid savages were so obviously willing to accept him as such. Wasn't it difficult enough dealing with them in matters of reality without having to get involved in their damnable superstitions? He composed himself with an effort and spoke more calmly to the delegation's spokesman, Chief Peke-tele-mund.

"The man you speak of as The Prophet, who lives in your village on the White River, has no more prophetic ability than I," he said, then waited patiently as Spemica Lawba interpreted for him. The Shawnee remained one of his most trusted spies and interpreters and as important a contact and go-between for him with Black Hoof — Catahecassa — as William Wells was with Little Turtle. And both Wells and Johnny Logan, as he preferred thinking of Spemica Lawba, were of equal value with the Delawares. Now, as the latter finished, he went on.

"You have been misled. Your people should all know of this. You say he tells you that those who deal in magic and witchcraft should be burned at the stake. By what right does he pretend to be God among you? By what foolishness do you and your chief, Buckangehela, accept what he says without proof? Are you such mindless children as that?" He shook his head sympathetically and, after a moment, pointed toward the other end of the extensive canvas-covered arbor and said in a friendlier voice, "On those tables you will find food and drink. Refresh yourselves and while you do I will write a letter to your people that you may take back with you, that they may know the truth."

He dipped his head to them and even as Spemica Lawba was still interpreting his remarks, rose from his seat and strode toward the massive brick mansion called Grouseland. He was still seething inside and determined to write a letter that, when circulated among the Indians, would put the quietus to The Prophet's growing influence once and for all. *Something* had to be done! Everything had gone so well for so long and now the situation was changing. There were rumblings of war and hostilities were rising.

The governor was convinced that The Prophet was nothing more than a pawn of the British at Amherstburg. Consistently more reports were coming in of British agitation among the tribes; their tendrils — usually in the guise of traders — stretching deep into the most remote recesses of the Northwest. Here a trader decried desecration of Indian burial grounds by the Americans; there a trader stirred up resentment over the upper Mississippi River expedition of Zebulon Pike; in another place a trader warned of the ramifications of the Lewis and Clark Expedition to the far West; everywhere the British traders stirred hatred of Harrison himself in their minds, verbally depicting him as a ravenous monster gobbling up their lands. Now this fool Shawnee Prophet had suddenly appeared and his following was swelling with alarming speed. How could there be any doubt he was being used by the British?

A year or so ago the likelihood of another war with the British would have seemed wholly implausible. Now the smell of it was in the air and war talk was everywhere as relations between Great Britain and the United States became ever more strained. Old wounds of the Revolutionary War, still not entirely healed, had begun festering anew and the aura of fear was drifting through the land with the insidiousness of a gradually developing ground fog.

Harrison was grateful that Thomas Jefferson had been reelected President and had begun his new term last year with George Clinton as his new Vice-President to replace the erratic Aaron Burr; and that Henry Dearborn had been retained as Secretary of War. Jefferson now had enough experience with the Indians that he was able to perceive a serious situation with a minimum of data. Alerted by Harrison of increasing hostility being shown by the tribes, the President had last January personally addressed the chiefs of the Potawatomies, Sacs and Foxes, saying, "Our nation is numerous and strong, but we wish to be just to all, and particularly to be kind and useful to our red children. We are establishing government factories among you as rapidly as possible to supply you with goods in exchange for the fur pelts you bring. We do this as a favor to you; for we wish no profit in this business. My Children, we are strong; we are numerous as the stars in the heavens, and we are all gunmen, yet we live in peace and friendship with all nations."

The President had then immediately ordered Harrison to make every endeavor to be particularly friendly to the Indians and try to divert their growing attachment to the British by paying them higher prices for their furs and selling goods to them at cheaper prices than the British could afford. All well and good, Harrison grumbled to himself as he entered the large double door, until the damned British had learned about it and then neatly countered by sending parties of Indians to buy supplies from the Americans and return with them to Amherstburg, where they would buy them from the Indians, thus getting them more cheaply than they could be brought from England.

The governor walked into his private office and seated himself at his expansive desk with a sigh. Well, at least the scope of his problems had eased somewhat with establishment a little over a year ago of the Michigan Territory. That took Detroit and its manifold problems of trade and Indian affairs out of his hands and put them into the hands of the man who had been appointed governor of that new territory, William Hull.

All Harrison wanted was to keep matters on an even keel as long as possible on the frontier as he continued seeking peaceful land cessions from the Indians. His success with the St. Louis Treaty had inspired him to duplicate it with minor chiefs among the Potawatomies, Miamis and other tribes in his jurisdiction. He'd been succeeding, too; nothing quite so spectacular as his fifty-one-million-acre land purchase in Illinois, of course, but significant cessions nonetheless. Much of his dealing thus far had been with Winnemac and a group of very minor chiefs whom Winnemac controlled. In very quiet little arrangements with them he had already purchased for the United States a number of pieces of Potawatomi lands that neither Winnemac nor any of the others had any authority to sell. This bothered neither Harrison nor the President, and Congress was quite eager to ratify each of these little land cession treaties almost without question, especially since the price being paid for them by the government through Harrison was ridiculously low. Such chickens were bound to come home to roost one day, he knew, but by then it would be much too late for the tribes to do anything about it. Besides, some cessions that he had gained — such as that of last December when the Piankeshaws ceded the last of their Illinois territory to him — were quite ethical transactions, as well as being legal.

Another indication that the war fever was rising among the tribes was the occurrence of two heavily attended councils held by the Indians, for Indians only, at Stony Creek in Ohio — one on February 17 and the other on March 20. Even Indians sympathetic to the whites had not been permitted to attend. Ohio had gotten into an uproar over that and Governor Tiffin had investigated. The Indians, addressed by a non-chief Shawnee named Tecumseh, assured the investigators that the council was strictly of a tribal nature and entirely innocuous. Tiffin had accepted that, but Harrison was not so sure. This Tecumseh, whoever he was, might bear watching.

More important at the moment, Harrison was disturbed over this Prophet business and was determined that the one-eyed Shawnee was not going to stampede the tribes into warfare against the United States with a lot of mystical mumblings and prophesies. He now removed fresh paper from a drawer, dipped his pen and wrote swiftly to the Delawares:

MY CHILDREN:

My heart is filled with grief, and my eyes are dissolved in tears at the news which has reached me. You have been celebrated for your wisdom above all the tribes of red people who inhabit this great island. Your fame as warriors has extended to the remotest nations, and the wisdom of your chiefs has gained you the appellation of grandfathers from all the neighboring tribes.[165] *From what cause, then, does it proceed that you have departed from the wise counsels of your fathers and covered yourselves with guilt? My Children, tread back the steps you have taken, and endeavor to regain the straight road which you have abandoned. The dark, crooked, and thorny one which you are now pursuing will certainly lead you to endless woe and misery. But who is this pretended prophet who dares to speak in the name of the great Creator? Examine him. Is he more wise and virtuous than you are yourselves, that he should be selected to convey to you the orders of your God? Demand of him some proofs at least of his being the messenger of the Deity. If God had really empowered him, He has doubtless authorized him to perform miracles that he may be known and received as a prophet. If he is really a prophet, ask of him to cause the sun to stand still or the moon to alter its course, the rivers to cease to flow, or the dead to rise from their graves. If he does these things, you may believe that he has been sent from God. He tells you that the Great Spirit commands you to punish with death those who deal in magic, and that he is authorized to point them out. Wretched delusion! Is then the Master of Life obliged to appoint mortal man to punish those who offend Him? Has He not the thunder and the power of nature at His command? And could He not sweep away from the earth a whole nation with one motion of His arm? My Children, do not believe that the great and good Creator of Mankind has directed you to destroy your own flesh; and do not doubt that if you pursue this abominable wickedness His vengeance will overtake you and crush you.*

The above is addressed to you in the name of the Seventeen Fires. I now speak to you from myself, as a friend who wishes nothing more sincerely than to see you prosperous and happy. Clear your eyes, I beseech you, from the mist which surrounds them. No longer be imposed on by the arts of an imposter. Drive him from your town, and let peace and harmony prevail amongst you. Let your poor old men and women sleep in quietness, and banish from their minds the dreadful idea of being burnt alive by their own friends and countrymen. I charge you to stop your bloody career; and if you value the friendship of your great father, the President; if you wish to preserve the good opinion of the Seventeen Fires, let me hear by the return of the bearer that you have determined to follow my advice.

Your friend and adviser,
William Henry Harrison
Governor — Indiana Territory

Harrison placed the letter in an envelope, addressed it to Chief Buckangehela at the White River village and dropped a glob of wax onto the flap, into which he pressed his official seal. He then returned to the arbor and placed the letter into the hands of Spemica Lawba.

"Go back with them to their village, Johnny," he ordered. "Hand this personally to Buckangehela. After he reads it, encourage him to show it to every other chief he can."

"Yes sir," Spemica Lawba said. He returned to the Delaware delegation and Harrison, watching him go, felt quite sure he had just demolished the influence of the man who called himself The Prophet.

[*April 28, 1806 — Monday*]

Tecumseh and Tenskwatawa heard the sound of many feet approaching their wegiwa and they moved to the doorway and stepped outside. The delegation of Indians from this village, led by Buckangehela and Peke-tele-mund stopped a dozen feet from them and Buckangehela held up the letter from Governor Harrison. He opened his mouth to speak, but Tecumseh held up a hand, stopping him.

"Who is it that I only partly see behind my Delaware friends?"

Spemica Lawba stepped forward. "I greet my uncles with respect and friendship," he said. "I came here to deliver to Chief Buckangehela and to translate for him a letter from Governor Harrison. I had looked forward to seeing you." His eyes shifted briefly beyond the brothers, then back to them. "I had also hoped to see my mother, whom I have not seen for too long."

"Tecumapese is on a journey," Tecumseh said evenly. "My eyes are glad to see you; my heart is not, since it knows you come here as the agent of one whose aim is to harm the Indians."

"Indians and whites can live in peace, Tecumseh." Spemica Lawba spoke softly, without rancor. Though he was six years younger than Tecumseh, there was a remarkable similarity in their appearance.

"You are incorrect, nephew," Tecumseh replied. "Indians and whites can *never* live in peace. They can only live close to one another *if* the Indian does what the white man wishes and moves aside when the white man stretches. All our history and that of other tribes has shown this to be true." He turned his eyes back to Buckangehela. "What has the white beaver written to you?"

Buckangehela stepped forward and handed him the letter. "Spemica Lawba will read it to you," he said.

"I will read it myself."

Tecumseh read it aloud, smoothly putting it into the Shawnee tongue. When he was finished, Tenskwatawa's expression was strained, though his brother seemed unconcerned. Tecumseh nodded to him and, the unspoken message understood, Tenskwatawa addressed the Delaware chief.

"Let the messengers rest and eat. I will retire to my place and meditate on this to see what direction, if any, I shall receive from the Great Spirit in this matter."

Tenskwatawa turned and reentered the wegiwa and Tecumseh followed him. Inside, the facade of calm dissolved and fear became naked on the face of the one-eyed man.

"What do we do, Brother?" he asked tremulously. "This could throw down all we have built."

There was sorrow in Tecumseh's reply. "After all this time, Tenskwatawa, do you still not believe that I can foretell what will occur, just as our brother Chiksika could, and our father Pucksinwah before him? How can you not believe what you, above all others, know to be true?" He sighed. "Come. Sit with me and we will prepare your reply."

Some fifty minutes later the brothers emerged and Tenskwatawa ordered that everyone in the village — the resident four hundred as well as half that many transients, plus the forty Delawares who made up the delegation — assemble at once. When they had done so, Tenskwatawa denounced the whites generally and Harrison specifically, bitterness heavy in his voice. That Harrison had termed the Delawares "grandfathers" was clear evidence that he knew not whereof he spoke and that he, Tenskwatawa, had nothing but scorn for any Indian who believed what white men said or wrote. He told them he had conferred with the Great Spirit and that the Great Spirit was angry and that he would give them a sign.

"The white beaver, Harrison," he went on, "said that you should ask me, if I am really a prophet, to cause the sun to stand still and that if I can do this, then you can believe that I have been sent from God. Those are his words, not mine! Therefore, listen now to what I have to say: Fifty days from this day there will be no cloud in the sky. Yet, when the sun has reached its highest point, at that moment will the Great Spirit take it into his hand and hide it from us. The darkness of night will thereupon cover us and the stars will shine round about us. The birds will go to roost and the night creatures will awaken and stir. Then you will know, as the white chief Harrison has said, that your Prophet has been sent to you from Moneto."

[*June 17, 1806 — Tuesday*]

In their villages throughout the Northwest a strange ritual was being repeated by the Indians. In mid-morning the men, women and children left their abodes and assembled in the open. On this beautiful bright cloudless day there was an air of expectancy over them all. This was the day, according to the runners who had spread the news to every village, that would prove whether the Shawnee who called himself Tenskwatawa was a prophet or a charlatan.

This was the fiftieth day.

At exactly noon there was a total eclipse of the sun.

In the forests and fields confused birds went to roost and nocturnal animals roused and began moving about.

In the villages there was consternation and fear and unequivocal awe for a man so great he could command even the sun.

In Fort Wayne, William Wells stepped outside the door of his house, looked up and muttered, "Damn! There'll be hell to pay now."

In Chicago, where word of Harrison's challenge and Tenskwatawa's acceptance of it had arrived only a few days before, John and Eleanor Kinzie stood in their yard silently, both keenly aware of the tremendous impact this would have on the Indians.

In Chaubenee's village on Indian Creek, sixty-five miles west of Chicago, the chief's guest, Sauganash, muttered the single word, "Tecumseh," and Chaubenee nodded, for they knew.

In Vincennes, Governor William Henry Harrison was furious at having been bested at his own game and wondering from whom Tenskwatawa had learned that a solar eclipse was to occur.

In the White River village, Tenskwatawa lifted his arms and the several hundred assembled Indians heard him cry, "Behold! Did I not prophesy truly? Darkness has shrouded the earth!"

And in his wegiwa, also in the White River village, Tecumseh sat quietly in the darkness.

[*October 22, 1806 — Wednesday*]

John Kinzie had rarely found himself so enchanted by a stranger as he was by the man who had walked into Kinzie's Store a short while ago. Certainly he'd started off on the right foot with the trader when, as his opening remark, he was extraordinarily frank.

"My name is Liberty White and I've just arrived here on foot from Detroit. I stopped off at Fort Dearborn and talked with the commanding officer. I'm afraid I don't like Captain Whistler."

He was a very tall, gangly, easygoing individual with what seemed to be several times as many teeth as he should have had. His face was so expressibly flexible that it might well have been made of rubber and he quickly endeared himself further to the Chicago trader by telling him that he had just refused an offer of work in a civilian capacity for John Whistler at the fort.

"Couldn't do that, Captain," he quoted himself as saying. "I don't care much for the military. Never liked having some men tell other men to do things that're apt to get the other men killed. Seems to me that things never do get quite so messed up as when the government's involved."

"That's hardly a sensible posture, Mr. White," John Whistler had responded, frowning. "After all, it is because of such government posts as Fort Dearborn that citizens can live safely on the frontier. And in defense, I must say that the army is always very careful *not* to lead its men into situations where they are apt to be killed."

"Funny," the newcomer had replied, "that's almost exactly what they told my father the day he marched out with the army. That was the day his company commander led them into an ambush and my father was killed."

Now John Kinzie laughed, envisioning how the encounter must have disturbed Captain Whistler, who was so accustomed to having his own way with whomever he met. The trader shook hands with the man, introduced himself and invited him to sit down. He then poured them both a brandy.

"Welcome to Chicago, Liberty White," he said. He raised his glass and sipped from it, then set it down, savoring the liquid heat. His lips quirked. "Liberty's a rather unusual name."

The long narrow man grinned, exposing the numerous horselike teeth. "Not if your father was a New England patriot and you were born in late April of 1775. I figure I'm lucky. He could've named me Lexington."

"Or Concord," John Kinzie laughed.

"Or Concord," White agreed. He went on to tell the trader that his home had been in Hopkinville, New Hampshire, and that, following the death of his father late in the Revolution, he'd gone to live with an uncle just outside the same town. There he'd remained until last year when he left to travel west for opportunity with his good friend, Aaron Greeley. The two had gone all through school together and when Greeley had gotten married and had children, to those offspring he was always Uncle Liberty. He was himself unmarried.

"About the middle of last year," he went on, after having a swallow of the brandy and lighting his pipe, "Aaron got the notion of moving way out to Detroit and asked if I wanted to come along. I had no real ties left in

Hopkinville, so why not? Aaron — he's a surveyor — got work right
away when we got there, surveying private land claims along the Detroit
River. I worked with him a while, then at a few other jobs, but didn't care
much for Detroit. 'Specially after spending a winter there. Heard about
Chicago and decided to give it a try, so here I am. Got to admit," the easy
grin was there again, "there's not a whole lot of work opportunities here,
'specially if you're an independent cuss like me and don't much like taking
orders. Kind of thought Chicago'd be a bigger settlement. Can't be more
than twenty-thirty people here, apart from the garrison."

"That's about right," John grunted sympathetically, understanding his
dilemma. "I wish I could take you on here but, actually, I have more help
right now than I really need." He paused as a thought struck him and then
looked at his visitor speculatively. "What do you know about farming?"

"Enough. My uncle was a farmer. I was a farmer's live-in nephew,
which meant, when I got older, he gave all the orders and I did all the
work. Didn't much care for that — the orders, I mean — but I like
farming."

"Think you might like to take charge of a farm here?"

"With what strictures?" White responded, interested.

"I don't know, but we'll find out after we finish our brandy."

They continued to chat and sip their drinks. John found Liberty White
an unusually easy person with whom to talk and he was pleased to tell him
about Chicago.

"You seem to fit the mold of most of those who come here," he said,
"because for those who do, it's pretty much the severing of any regular
ties with home, wherever that is. We get occasional couriers from Detroit
or Fort Wayne, and much less often from St. Louis, who bring news from
what we call the outside world. Depending on what you like or don't like,
Chicago can be one of the worst places you've ever been, or one of the
nicest. There's no real entertainment except what you figure out for yourself. I get enjoyment out of playing the fiddle and sometimes the fifers and
drummers from the fort come over and we stir things up a bit. There are a
few books to read. In the summer there's the lake for swimming and
canoeing and beautiful sand beaches to stroll on. Lots of game to hunt
and all the fishing you want. In spring and summer there are all kinds of
flowers and there are wild grapes, strawberries, cranberries, whortleber-
ries, lots of nuts — hazel, beech, hickory, walnuts. If the Indians like you,
they'll invite you to some of their dances and feasts." He paused.

"I'd hazard a guess you like it here," Liberty White said, filling the
gap.

"I do. But there are a good many who don't. Most of those at the fort
hate it, but maybe that's partly because they're not here of their own free
will. It makes a difference."

White nodded. "Do many ships come here?"

"Not many. Two, three, maybe four times a year, mostly bringing the supplies we need from Mackinac, Detroit and the East, and taking back to Mackinac whatever we have to ship, which in my case is furs. This post," he waved a hand in a careless gesture toward the shelves and tables loaded with goods, "is larger than most and carries a greater variety of goods, but the staple items are still the most important. Prices are high, compared to the East, but about as low as we can reasonably make them. Tobacco sells here for fifty cents a pound; same for butter when we make it and flour when we grind it. Whiskey, when I sell it — which I don't anywhere near so much as Captain Whistler contends — goes for fifty cents a quart. Lead shot goes for thirty-three cents a pound and gunpowder for a dollar-fifty."

Kinzie indicated the corner of the store where his workbench was located. "I do a fair amount of silverwork. Learned it as a boy in Quebec. Indians love silver ornaments, especially armbands for the men and brooches for the women."

Since the trader had been the one to bring up the matter of prices, Liberty White felt no compunction about asking what sort of price the trader placed on the silver items he made. John shrugged.

"Depends on the size and intricacy of the work," he said. "A simple armband usually goes for four 'rats, and a brooch with a little scrollwork for six."

"Rats?"

"Muskrats. Pelts. A prime muskrat pelt's worth about a dollar here, more in Mackinac. Unfortunately, I don't have as much time anymore as I'd like for the silverwork. Too many other things interfere: keeping accounts, ordering goods, visiting the branch posts, trying to figure out what people are going to want and getting the goods here when they need them. Then, too, being suttler for the fort takes a lot of time — suttling's providing goods for the soldiers and their families that the military doesn't normally requisition. At the beginning I did all the suttling myself. John Whistler didn't like that very much, so he found a way to undermine me a little. One of his sons, John Jr., was interested in becoming suttler. He's not in the military like his father or like his brother, William, who's second-in-command at the fort, but the whole idea smelled to me.[166] I told Captain Whistler I thought it might be against regulations and let him think I was going to make some inquiries about it with the government, so he backed off a little and we compromised. Now John Jr. and I are in partnership, suttling for the garrison." He grunted. "It still smells, but it's better than nothing, I suppose. I don't mind the boy; he's a bright young man. A lot easier to get along with than his father."

Liberty White finished his brandy and placed his empty glass on the table. "I take it," he said slowly, "you and Captain Whistler are not on the best of terms?"

"That might possibly be considered an understatement," John said wryly, pouring another dash of brandy into the glasses. "Actually, it's become something of a feud. It stems, I think, from a former employee of mine who's interpreter at the fort. He tends to foment problems. Name's Lalime. Jack Lalime. Whistler likes him and they have a faction who support them, just as there's one that supports me. Hardly anyone's exempt. I'm made out to be the unscrupulous, money-grabbing, Indian-exploiting trader and Whistler's made out to be the stiff-necked, by-the-book military disciplinarian. Neither side bends unless it has to and each looks for whatever ammunition it can find against the other.

"Every now and then John Whistler has to come to me for a favor, which amuses me and galls him enormously. He's had to hire me to transport goods for various military reasons and he's had to rent my boats for the contractor in order to unload the cargo that comes on the government brig, since we have no adequate harbor and wharf. What bothers him most, I guess, apart from the liquor issue, is when he's forced to ask me to advance him funds."

"Why in the world would he have to do that?" White looked surprised.

"Because all too often the government is delinquent in sending the necessary funds so he can pay the soldiers the bounty they're entitled to if they reenlist. If he can't pay them, they'll just up and leave the moment their term of enlistment expires. But it irks him terribly to have to ask me to advance him money, and the more he's irked, the hotter the feud grows. It's all really very silly." He chuckled. "At least it tends to liven things up at times. The sides used to be pretty even where the factions are concerned, but that's been changing."

The visitor was fascinated. "In whose favor?"

"Not mine!" John was rueful. "You've heard of the United States Factory System?" Liberty White shook his head, his mouth filled with brandy at the moment, and John sat back in his chair more comfortably. "The factory system is the government's way of trying to break up private control of the Indian trade and keep liquor out of the grasp of the Indians. Ostensibly it was established to weaken British influence among the tribes, but it's been tough on American traders, too. With government backing, the factories supply the Indians with superior goods at lower prices than the private traders can match. They've made some pretty significant inroads on our business, though not so much as the government expected. There were a few things it overlooked." He took another sip of his drink.

"Such as?" White prompted.

"Such as they didn't take into consideration that the Indians like dealing with traders they know and trust. They don't trust the government and they especially don't like dealing with the government factor — that's the title of the man appointed to be in charge of the factory — who usually doesn't know a damned thing about the Indians or how to deal with 'em. Even more important, the Indians don't like going to the U.S. factories because they don't stock liquor. The private traders aren't supposed to, either, but we all do. To try to prohibit it is not realistic at all."

Liberty White tugged at his earlobe thoughtfully. "Seems to me I've heard something about that," he said. "Some of the religious groups — Quakers especially — are upset about the heavy trafficking in liquor the traders do with the Indians, almost without exception, they say, to exploit them. They claim the Indians can't handle it."

"That's what they claim." John had become suddenly wary.

"And don't they say the Indians trade all their pelts for liquor instead of the supplies they and their families need, with the result that they become destitute?"

"Yes, they do," John agreed grimly, "and so far as it goes, they're basically correct. There've got to be controls on it, but total prohibition's not the answer. A lot of traders — especially the British who get licensed to trade in American territory — take terrible advantage of the Indians with liquor. Take Robert Dickson, for example. He's British, operating out of Mackinac and spending most of his time in the Upper Mississippi River country, trading with Menominees, Winnebagoes and Sioux. Good God, the amount of liquor he brings in with every shipment is staggering. I was in Mackinac a year ago June when the British sloop *Saginah* out of Sandwich came in with a cargo of goods. Dickson was one of the largest consignees and his goods on that shipment alone included ninety-five kegs of liquor. I haven't brought in that much in all the time I've been in Chicago. Now *that's* the sort of trader who gives the ethical ones a bad reputation.

"All right, let me get back on the original subject. A year ago last spring, Fort Dearborn was made an Indian agency. You probably saw the big Agency House that was built just west of the fort. Charles Jouett was appointed Indian Agent.[167] He's a big man — tall, I mean, about six feet three. Indications are he's aligning himself with the Whistler faction."

"He's what you call the factor?"

"No. More about that in a minute. Jouett's the United States Indian Agent for this district. He'd been Indian Agent at Detroit. He was treaty commissioner for the United States when the treaty was made with the Wyandots and Ottawas at Fort Industry on the Maumee River a year ago last July. As Indian Agent here, he's in charge of official government relations with the tribes south of the St. Joseph to the Illinois headwaters and westward to the Mississippi. Includes Potawatomies, Sacs, Foxes, Chippewas, Ottawas and Miamis in that area. He's assisted by an interpreter. No," he cut off the question, "not Jack Lalime, who is the fort's interpreter. Jouett's interpreter is an Ottawa half-breed named James Riley. His father's now Judge Riley of Schenectady, but he used to be a trader at Saginaw Bay, up north of Detroit. All right, Jouett, assisted by Riley, distributes presents and annuities to the tribes, holds councils with the chiefs, listens to complaints, tries to settle Indian-and-white disputes and acts as the civil arm of the government in its peacetime relations with the local tribes. There are similar agents scattered about in different areas of the country — Wells at Fort Wayne, Choteau at St. Louis, and so on."

"Well, what makes you think Jouett's in Whistler's camp?"

John Kinzie hesitated. "Admittedly, I'm not sure he is. Maybe he's just doing his job as he sees it best and I don't agree with his conclusions. Consider this: the Potawatomies in this area have never shared equally in the annuities paid to the tribe as a whole, mainly because those annuities have been distributed at Detroit. Mine was one of the voices raised in complaint to the government about that, in support of the suggestion that the Indian agency here be made distribution center for the Indians of this area, which only makes sense. The Secretary of War ordered Jouett to try it out. He did it one time, then reported back to Dearborn that it really wasn't necessary and got the annuity distributions moved back to Detroit. Black Partridge and his people here, along with Siggenauk up at Milwaukee and a lot of others, aren't happy about that at all."

"Wouldn't having the distribution center here bring you a lot more business from the Indians?" White asked the question innocently enough.

"Yes, it would. I'm trying not to believe Jouett would tamper with people's lives like that just to spite me, but the indications are there. Let me go on. After Jouett was here for a little while, another appointee came — Ebenezer Belknap, out of Connecticut, who hadn't the foggiest notion of how to deal with the Potawatomies. He was given the appointment as United States factor here.[168] He very definitely sided with the Whistler crowd, but he didn't last long. He resigned last December and we've just recently got a new factor — nice young fellow by the name of Thomas Hayward. Where he stands is anyone's guess at this point, but I get the impression he doesn't much like either Jouett or Captain Whistler."

Liberty White pursed his lips and shook his head. "Hard to imagine there's so much friction in such a small community. What's the situation with that other fellow you mentioned who used to work for you? The interpreter."

"Lalime?" The trader gave a disdainful bark of laughter. "Let me tell you something, Liberty, Jack Lalime'd gladly tear my heart out and use it for fish bait if he thought he could get away with it and had guts enough to try. He was my clerk for a while at St. Joseph and then acted as my agent in the purchase of this post from a trader named Du Sable. I put Lalime in charge here for a couple of years until I could wrap things up at St. Joseph and take over. Lalime didn't do all that well in the job, and he also got to feeling it was *his* post and decided he'd make a stab at taking over. It didn't work and he's held a grudge ever since.[169] His favorite pastime now is putting me down to anyone who'll listen, especially Captain Whistler, and causing trouble for me."

"What's he done? I mean," Liberty White amended, "what sort of trouble has he actually caused you?"

"All kinds. I'll give you just one example and then we'd better leave. Colonel Jacob Kingsbury was given orders to establish Fort Bellefontaine opposite the mouth of the Illinois River on the west bank of the Mississippi above St. Louis. As soon as the ice broke up on the lakes, Kingsbury ordered Henry Brevoort — he's skipper of the government brig, *Adams* — to convey him and his company from Mackinac to Chicago.[170] About the time they got here, I was in the process of transporting the bateaux of a couple of traders northward over the Chicago Portage from the Illinois with their winter's peltry. At my suggestion, Kingsbury and the traders got together and a deal was worked out whereby Major Brevoort would take the traders and their furs to Mackinac aboard the *Adams* on its return, and Kingsbury got their bateaux to convey his troops down the Illinois and Mississippi to St. Louis. It was a pretty good arrangement and so at the same time I worked things out with Brevoort to transport goods to me from Mackinac and take back with him the furs I was shipping to Mackinac."

"And Lalime got wind of it?"

"And Lalime got wind of it. He complained to the government that United States vessels on the lakes — and that could only mean the *Adams* — in addition to transporting government property and authorized people, were habitually conveying the goods of, as Lalime put it, 'favored private citizens and commercial enterprises.' "

"Oh oh."

"Yes. It resulted in Brevoort receiving an order directly from the Secretary of War. He showed it to me. It commanded the major to enter and clear, without the least deviation, all privately owned goods of dutiable nature that he might in the future transport aboard the *Adams*. That put an end to our arrangement. It didn't ruin me or even hurt the business very badly, but it did cause a hell of an inconvenience, especially when one realizes that most of the time the *Adams* is running around the lake with nothing in her hold."

The trader put down his glass and stood up. "Well, enough of that. Let's go see a friend of mine."

The two men left Kinzie's Store and paddled down the river in the trader's canoe, putting in to shore near the mouth of the stream. John Kinzie led his visitor along the Lake Michigan beach to a substantial log house where he introduced him to Charles Lee. Within half an hour, Lee had hired Liberty White as superintendent of his expansive farm on the South Branch of the Chicago River, four miles above the fort.

[*November 30, 1807 — Monday*]

There was the smell of cordite in the air and the smell of blood. It began on the Atlantic and flowed eastward to the halls of Parliament and westward to the remotest frontier posts. It was a smell of fear and destruction, a smell of contained frustrations and hatreds poised to break loose. It was a smell of death.

It was the smell of approaching war.

No longer was this merely the rattling of sabers and spears in the prairies and woodlands of the Northwest. No longer was it whispers of subversive activities of government agents slipping from village to village, inciting unrest and stirring war fevers. No longer was it even the very quiet but very significant melding together of scattered bands and villages and tribes of Indians into a single-minded coalition of raw strength and purpose under a still largely unknown Shawnee named Tecumseh, who was not even a chief.

The abrupt change had come about as the result of two incidents far apart and neither on the North American continent—the first in June, the second during this very month of November.

On June 22, the proud sleek American frigate *Chesapeake*, under command of Captain James Barron, slipped her mooring lines at the port of Hampton Roads, Virginia, and began a voyage. Her destination: the Mediterranean. Before the journey was even well under way, the *Chesapeake's* crew spied a British naval squadron ahead, anchored in American waters. Uneasy, Captain Barron ordered his ship's course altered to skirt the flotilla far to starboard. As the *Chesapeake* passed, one of the British ships, a fifty-ton man-of-war named the *Leopard*, weighed anchor and fell in behind. She was the flagship of Vice-Admiral George Berkeley and she was closing fast. At Barron's orders, the *Chesapeake* put on more sail and immediately the following became a pursuit. Drawing within hailing distance, an officer of the *Leopard* shouted for the *Chesapeake* to haul to, accusing her of having hired British deserters as seamen. Captain Barron refused, maintaining course and speed. Immediately the *Leopard* laid a shot across her bow. Furious, Captain Barron ignored it and ordered evasive action, but it was to no avail; the *Leopard* was far more maneuverable than the *Chesapeake*. The British man-of-war opened fire in earnest, slamming twenty-one cannon shots into the *Chesapeake* in ten minutes before Captain Barron struck his colors and surrendered. Three of his men were dead and eighteen others, including Barron himself, were wounded.

The repercussions were immediate and predictable. Thomas Jefferson darkly threatened war against the British and told the French minister in Washington, "If the British do not give us the satisfaction we demand, we will take Canada, which wants to enter the Union." A New York mob formed to protest and in the ensuing riot all but dismantled a British ship in port. Throughout the United States there were angry public meetings denouncing the British as "perfidious." John Quincy Adams enhanced his own political posture with an inflammatory speech in which he flatly stated: "No nation can be independent which suffers her citizens to be stolen from her at the discretion of the naval or military officers of another!" Jefferson immediately banned all British warships from territorial waters of the United States and issued an order temporarily prohibiting all ships presently in American ports, irrespective of national origin, from sailing to foreign destinations. In Quebec, Lieutenant Colonel Isaac Brock, commander of the British Eighth Regiment, quickly reported to his superiors in London that ". . . every American paper teems with violent and hostile resolutions against England and associations are forming in every town for the ostensible purpose of attacking these Provinces."

It took a little longer for the news to filter to the more remote western posts; but when it got there, the Indians hooted with glee and many poised themselves to ride on the back of the British lion when it attacked the American eagle in earnest. No less cognizant than John Quincy Adams of the political advantages to be gained, Governor William Henry Harrison thundered a message to the Indiana Territorial Legislature at Vincennes. "The blood rises to my cheek," he stormed, "when I reflect on the humiliating — the *disgraceful!* — scene of the crew of an American ship of war mustered on its own deck by a British lieutenant for the purpose of selecting the innocent victims of their own tyranny! . . . British agents slink through our woodlands, goading the savages to violence and murder on our frontier; for who does not know that the tomahawk and scalping knife of the savage are always employed as instruments of British vengeance? At this moment, fellow citizens, as I sincerely believe, their agents are organizing a combination amongst the Indians within our limits, for the purpose of assassination and murder. . . . This business *must* be stopped! I will no longer suffer it!"

Again Sir Isaac Brock wrote to his superiors, telling them: "It is impossible to view the late hostile measures of the American government towards England without considering a rupture between the two countries as probable to happen. I beseech you to provide the means to prepare a better trained and expanded militia and for repairs to the fortress of Quebec."

The British were poised, breaths held, waiting for the threatened counterattacks by President Jefferson, but the days turned into weeks and they did not transpire. The passion abated, the fires of war were banked, the shipping embargo lifted — a failure. The French Foreign Minister in Washington reported to his own superiors in Paris that neither President Jefferson nor United States Foreign Minister James Madison wanted war to break out.

With the cooling of tempers, matters seemed to be resuming a state of greater stabilization, but such appearances were very deceptive. Convinced that war was absolutely inevitable and Canada would be invaded by Americans, the new governor-in-chief of Canada, Sir James Craig, sent specific instructions to Indian Department Supervisor William Claus and the Indian Agent at Amherstburg, Thomas McKee, to keep the Indians in check but also to keep them strongly agitated against the Americans until their services would be required.

"You are," he ordered, "to avoid specific instructions to the Indians, but you are always to insinuate that as a matter of course we shall look for the assistance of our red brothers. It should be done with delicacy, but still in a way not to be misunderstood."

At the same time, unknown to McKee or Claus, Craig secretly reinstated former Indian Agent Matthew Elliott at Amherstburg.[171] He instructed Elliott to ". . . act as secret emissary to the various chiefs to sound them out in private, impressing upon them with delicacy and caution that England expects their aid in the event of war and being certain to remind them that the Americans are out to steal their lands."

Exacerbating the already volatile situation on the American frontier, agents moved about among the tribes purposefully to turn up the heat beneath long-simmering resentments, making nebulous speeches in public but privately promising British support when the war came. Tecumseh was already well known to them and they were impressed by the extent of his influence, yet thus far they had given him wide berth, fearful of his independence, disturbed by his disinclination to ally himself directly to the British or any other white faction, embarrassed by his not-infrequent caustic reminders to his Indian audiences of the despicable failure of the British to support them as promised at the Battle of Fallen Timbers. The agents went instead to Tenskwatawa, mistakenly believing his growing stature as The Prophet placed him at least on a level equal to his brother's, if not surpassing it. They met with him in private, urging Tenskwatawa to begin all-out war immediately on the Americans. Quaking inside over what Tecumseh's reactions would be if he knew of this, Tenskwatawa put on a stern face and refused, telling them, "My forces are not yet strong enough, but in a few years we will destroy every American!"

All these machinations, however, were well under cover and matters, so far as the general populace was aware, were on a much more even keel when, only a few days ago, the second momentous incident occurred. The British Parliament exploded a bomb of considerable significance in its normally sedate chambers with the enactment of what it ambiguously called "Orders in Council." With all the excessive verbiage put aside, this was an extreme act of reprisal against the French. Disdaining the maritime rights of neutral nations as well as American naval strength, the act flatly warned that the British fleet would seize — even on the nonterritorial waters of the open ocean — any and all ships that would dare to sail with any French port as destination.

In the midst of all this international and frontier uproar, an occurrence went largely unnoticed on the Hudson River, despite the fact that it carried the potential to alter the course of the world considerably. A Pennsylvania-born inventor who had been experimenting with a device for the past few years on the River Seine in France, now gave it the acid test in America. He placed his device — a boat called the *Clermont* — on the river at New York City and, during a five-day period beginning August 17, traveled to Albany and back, wholly independent of winds and currents.

The forty-three-year-old inventor, named Robert J. Fulton, called his creation a steamboat.

CHAPTER IX

[*July 13, 1809 — Thursday*]

*T*ECUMSEH!
The name was spoken in fearful whispers and bold cries. It spread across the land, through the forests and prairies, on the lakes and rivers, in wegiwas and hogans, in quonsets and tipis. It was repeated in log cabins and brick mansions, in open-air councils and in echoing legislative halls. It brought hope and it brought fright, it evoked anger and inspired devotion. It was on the tongues of a vast multitude who had never seen him nor heard him speak and it was on the tongues of an incredible number who had. Never before had any Indian of any tribe been so well known and at the same time so little known.

Tecumseh! A warrior. Not even a chief. A man, but not an ordinary man. A man with a vision, a dream, and a voice — a voice that could touch the masses powerfully; a voice that caused hearts to swell with pride, that filled bodies with dignity and minds with determination; a voice that instilled into cowed Indians the wonder and glory of restored belief in themselves.

He was everywhere and nowhere; a wraith, a phantom presence that appeared and was gone, only to appear somewhere else. From the vast prairied reaches of Saskatchewan to the cypressed swamps of Florida, from the cloaking pinelands of the lower St. Lawrence to the arid expanses of the land called Tejas, they knew him.

Wherever he spoke, large crowds assembled to listen. He did not shout, yet his strong words carried well to every ear. He did not coax or wheedle or beseech; he explained. He gave them his vision, his dream of one people, *Indians*, united in a powerful amalgamation which no outside power could rend asunder and before which all enemies would quail. He did not threaten, did not coerce, did not demand; he explained. He

sketched in verbal pictures the irresistible encroachment of the white man.
This was what he told them:

That the first white man came with timid contact and fawning obedience and great desire for nothing more than to be of help, often in the
form of benevolent men in flowing robes or unsmiling men in dark clothes
with white collars, sometimes in the form of sturdy men whose eyes saw
great distances ahead and who wished no more than to cross that mountain or follow this river; then came the men with sun-darkened skin,
carrying gifts of marvelous things we red men had never had, which they
would trade for the furs of the animals given so abundantly by the Great
Spirit to his red children, and soon the animals were no longer so plentiful
and the men with sun-darkened skins would move on; then would come
the men whose skins had seen little sun and with eyes that squinted and
could not look directly into the eyes of another, and these men brought
even greater gifts to us and the promise of more, in exchange for just a
little piece of land here and another little piece there, and for all these
wonderful things they held in promise all that was necessary was to make
a mark on a piece of paper; then would come the flood of men of all
kinds, bringing with them large families of women and children and
dreams somehow always bigger than capabilities, and these men said that
a tiny piece of the small piece of land belonged to them and they could do
with it as they wished and they cut down its forests and burned its grasses
and ripped open its belly with great heavy blades drawn by oxen; and then
when the little pieces of land — no longer places where we Indians could
roam and hunt and fish as we always had — were filled with the white
people and dotted with the ugly log houses in the midst of the devastation
they had created, then again would come the men in robes and the far-
seeing men and the sun-darkened men with gifts and the men with papers
to be marked and they all moved deeper and deeper into the land; and
then, when it was enough and there should be no more and we Indians
turned them back, then came the men who all dressed in the same clothes
and who all moved at the same time to the same drumbeat and who all
had harsh cold eyes and long cold swords and hard cold hearts and what
they could not get by trade or by gifts or by treaty, they then took by
blood, killing our men and taking away our women and our children and
desecrating the graves of our fathers and letting their herds of animals eat
what the wild animals needed, so there were no more of them left when it
was time to hunt them and feed our own families; and fences barred our
way and fish could no longer swim up our streams to lay their eggs, for
their way was barred by dams the whites had built to turn the wheels of
their mills and grind their flour; and when the little war would be over, it
would be of no matter who won or who lost, for it always became such
that the boundary between white man and red was farther toward the

setting sun; and always they promised — *and promise still!* — they are friends who wish only peace. Yes, we killed them, but for each who fell there were two or three or ten or one hundred who appeared to take his place and the lone warrior or the lone village or the lone tribe could not stem them; and even when two or three or five or ten tribes came together to try to hold them back, they were not enough. Yes, the tribes have warred against one another and there are great hurts that go back to times that none of us can remember, though we still war with one another over them; and this, brothers, is our weakness. Knowing our weakness, we know as well the seeds of our strength, for each of us is such a seed and our strength is all of us together, as one, for only in this way can we turn aside, turn away, stop and drive back the white flood that will forever drown us if we do not. It can be done! It should be done! Brothers, *it must be done!* This — and much more — was what Tecumseh told them.

Most were convinced; some were not. Many came with him; many more did not, but of those who did not, most stood ready to come when the sign eventually appeared that he told them would come. And to help them know the sign was near, he gave to the principal chief of each nation a bundle of red sticks of the same size; bundles that grew smaller by one stick for each month that he traveled. The chief was to discard one stick from the bundle at each moon. And when at last only one stick remained, they were to watch the skies at night and before another moon had come, a preliminary sign would appear in the darkness above. This would be the sign under which he, Tecumseh, had been born and for which he had been named. A great star, visible to all, would flash across the skies and its light would be pale green. This would be in the nature of a proof that Tecumseh was still guided by the hand of the Great Spirit. And when this sign came, the remaining red stick was to be cut into thirty pieces of equal length and each day one such piece was to be burned in the light of dawn. But when only the thirtieth piece remained, it was to be burned in the darkest deep of night. After that would come the great sign that all would recognize. It would come in another night and they would not have to stay awake to watch for it, for it would be a great and fearful groaning from deep within the earth; and their water jugs would break and their hanging pots would fall and the ground beneath them would move and shake them awake and tell them that this was the time and they must rise as one, with one will and one heart and one mind and reclaim the land that had been theirs and their father's and their father's father's before them. And those of them who were of a will to do so, those who believed in Tecumseh and in the future of the Indian nation would take up their weapons and strike out at once for the village that had only a short while ago been established where the waters of the Tippecanoe become wed with those of the great Wabash.

It was to this new Tippecanoe village that Tecumseh returned at intervals, to rest, to learn what new things had occurred, to plan and prepare for the next journey that would take him to warriors and villages and tribes as yet unconvinced. It was in March over a year ago when the delegation of chiefs and warriors of the Potawatomi and Kickapoo tribes came to Tecumseh in the White River village of the Delawares and asked him if he would establish a new village, nontribal, for all Indians, on the very site where many years before had stood the village of Kithtippecanoe, which the white man had destroyed. And so they had, and in the weeks and months that had followed, the village had grown as warriors filtered in from every direction and took their places here. Now over eight hundred were here, but for each man here, a hundred more stood ready in their own villages, watching and waiting as one by one their chief discarded the red sticks.

In his absences, Tecumseh left Tenskwatawa behind to be in charge of the village, at intervals to utter the predictions he had left with the man called The Prophet, as if they were his own. Tecumseh noted and was no little disturbed at the changes that had come over his little brother. Tenskwatawa walked now with pompous strut, wore furs and feathers and frills that set him apart, painted his face and body and limbs in grotesque ways and often removed the black patch that covered his empty eye socket and placed into the hole a round white stone upon which had been painted a hideous glaring eye. Tecumseh noted how those of the village tended to avoid his younger brother and he sensed the fear in them. When he spoke of these things to Tenskwatawa, his one-eyed brother merely smiled deferentially and explained that the superstitions of the people went deep, that they expected their Prophet to be different, not as one of them, and that what Tecumseh saw in them as fear was a vast respectful awe, which was only to be anticipated of those who were in the presence of one whom they believed to be the chosen of the Great Spirit. Tecumseh had nodded and accepted the explanation for the time being, but he was uneasy.

Twice during Tecumseh's absences, Tenskwatawa visited William Henry Harrison at Vincennes. The first time the governor believed this so-called Shawnee Prophet was the leader of the new Indian solidarity movement, of which so many whispers had been reaching him. In that meeting he found Tenskwatawa to be reasonable, with interesting ideas for the improvement of his people and wholly innocuous insofar as any potential threat to white settlement and expansion was concerned. Then he had heard increasingly of the real power behind The Prophet, the elder brother of Tenskwatawa, whose name was Tecumseh. The more he learned, the more concerned he became. At no place on the frontier was this Tecumseh unknown. From all reports, his influence had become phenomenal and there were unsettling rumors, unconfirmed, that he was preparing a great coalition of Indians to attack the whites and that he had allied himself and his followers to the British at Amherstburg. But then these fears had been unexpectedly eased when Governor Thomas Kirker of Ohio, harboring the same fears, sent him a copy of the report of a committee of Shakers. Kirker had sent members of this religious sect as a delegation to the Tippecanoe village to study it closely and see if it represented a threat to the whites. They had returned marveling at the wonder The Prophet had wrought and how impressed they had been during their stay. In part, the Shaker committee's report said:

. . . On this occasion our feelings were like Jacob's when he cried out, "Surely the Lord is in this place, and I know it not . . ."

Although these poor Shawnees have had no particular instruction but what they received from the outpouring of the Spirit, yet in point of real light and understanding, as well as behavior, they shame the Christian world. . . .

For a while it had set Governor Harrison's fears at rest, but then more and more stories came of Indian unrest and he had summoned Tenskwatawa again and questioned him about a rumored Indian surprise attack to be launched against Vincennes. The Prophet denied it vehemently, but now the governor no longer looked upon him in a favorable light. He interviewed this erstwhile Shawnee several times during the visit but when Tenskwatawa finally left, Harrison's fears had increased rather than abated. The man he really wanted to see was Tenskwatawa's brother . . . but where was Tecumseh?

Tecumseh was everywhere, striving as always to gain converts to his doctrine. Slowly — in some cases, very slowly — he was gaining ground. His greatest difficulty was stemming from the Potawatomies, despite the great energies of both Chaubenee and Sauganash in his cause. Chiefs such as Onoxa, Winnemac, Gizes and Topenebe were still actively trying to block him, not at all inclined to having their annuities and additional "presents" cut off by the Americans.

On the Kankakee River, Chief Main Poche was finally won over and it was a signal victory, for he was an extremely volatile man, jealous of his own position as chief and not pleased with the idea of throwing his forces — and himself! — behind a man who was neither a Potawatomi nor a chief. In recent months he had been wooed considerably by William Wells on behalf of the Americans generally and Governor Harrison specifically. He had accepted the gifts and presents gravely with an "I'll think it over" comment, but now it was to Tecumseh that he pledged himself, while privately averring that the one thing he would *not* do would be give up his drinking.

At Chicago, Tecumseh, accompanied by Chaubenee and Sauganash, won the wholehearted support of Black Partridge. Sauganash, who was now acting as Tecumseh's private secretary because of his education and skill with languages, strongly supported Tecumseh's stand against polygamy, a practice common among many tribes, including the Shawnee. "I have but one wife and she is all that I will ever have," Sauganash said. "She is enough! She is the sister of Chief Yellow Head and daughter of Chief Nescotnemeg. From them she has gained a temper sufficiently hot for several and her rage can be loud and strong!"

John Kinzie knew of Tecumseh's presence and the council of chiefs at Chicago and said nothing of it. Not until weeks afterward was it known in Fort Dearborn that Tecumseh had even been anywhere near, but the change in the Indians was not difficult to detect, as remarked by Indian Agent Charles Jouett in a letter to the secretary of war:

. . . Tensions in this quarter increase and the Indians in this vicinity favor war and are trying to stir up the other tribes. The tomahawk is uplifted, waiting only for a leader to direct the blow. . . .

As far away as Manitoba, John Tanner saw the Indians thronging to hear the words of a Shawnee warrior named Tecumseh. Tanner, now a trapper, had been captured by the Indians in Ohio when he was a boy, had lived with the Ottawas for many years and was now living with the Chippewas. He was not allowed to come to the village while Tecumseh was there and, afterwards, was told that the Shawnee had ridden on westward, to see the Blackfeet.

After a visit by Tecumseh to the villages on the St. Joseph, the Elkhart and the Mississinewa, both William Wells and Charles Jouett wrote to Governor Harrison, deeply concerned. The Chicago Indian Agent recommended that both Tecumseh and The Prophet be captured and imprisoned to prevent their continued rallying of the Indians in a fomentation of unrest. The governor rejected Jouett's advice with the patient explanation that doing so would, more than anything else, cause the tribes to unite and result in an outbreak of war. With William Wells he was less patient. Wells, without mincing words, suggested that Tecumseh be assassinated. Harrison, without mincing words, told Wells he was a fool.

At Peoria Lake, Tecumseh visited Chief Gomo in his village along the northern shore.[172] Gomo welcomed him, but would not commit himself to support. He had just recently visited William Clark in St. Louis and was fearful that the Americans might invade his village with troops.[173]

When Tecumseh attended a major Indian congress called by the British at Amherstburg a year ago, he listened carefully to the public words and private proposals of the florid-faced forty-year-old Francis Gore, who was lieutenant governor of Canada. Over a thousand warriors and more than one hundred chiefs had gathered and the British were amazed to see that the individual receiving the greatest respect and most attention was a mere Shawnee warrior. Here, then, was a person whose influence was so great that not to winnow his favor would be foolish. Gore's public speech to the assembly was carefully couched to restrain the Indians from declaring war on the Americans until the British themselves gave the word.

"I am sure, my Children," Gore said through the interpretation of Matthew Elliott, Thomas McKee and William Claus, "that it is quite unnecessary for 'me to call to your remembrance the faithful assurance with which the King, your Father, has so uniformly complied with all his engagements and promises made to your forefathers and yourselves in former times. Nothing is required of you in return for your Great Father's benevolence and religious regard to his promises but a renewal and faithful observance of the engagements made by your ancestors and yourselves. I will not offend you by entertaining the smallest doubt of your readiness on all occasions, when called upon, to prove your affectionate attachment for the King, your Great Father. I came not to invite you to take up the hatchet, but I wish to put you on your guard against any attempt that may be made by any enemy whatever to disturb the peace of your country."

In the private meeting that followed, Tecumseh sternly told the lieutenant governor that he did not fully trust the British and this distrust was only reinforced when British leaders such as Gore himself attempted to make the Indians believe that the British had always lived up to their promises. He bluntly pointed out that a great many chiefs and warriors had been killed at the Battle of Fallen Timbers because of the British refusal to help, as they had promised. After more talk, however, the chill between them dissipated and they parted on cordial terms. Immediately after his council ended, Lieutenant Governor Gore wrote a report to his superior, the governor-general of all Canada, Sir James Craig:

> . . . The Prophet's brother, who is stated to be his support and who appears to be a very shrewd, intelligent man, was at Amherstburg while I was there. He told Colonel Claus and Captain Elliott that they were endeavoring to collect the different Nations to form one settlement on the Wabash, about 300 miles south west of Amherstburg in order to preserve their country from all encroachment; that their intention at present is not to take part in the quarrels of white people; that if the Americans encroach upon them, they are resolved to strike — but he adds that if their father, the King, should be in earnest and appear in sufficient force, they would hold fast by him.

Today, far to the east in the nation's capital, President James Madison's new Secretary of War, William Eustis, was writing to Governor William Henry Harrison. In the incredibly obtuse belief that Indian affairs had improved along the Wabash River, Eustis ordered Harrison to call a major council of the Indians at Fort Wayne this coming fall for the purpose of obtaining another major land cession for the United States. The lands obtained at Greenville and at subsequent treaties being now nearly all settled, Eustis put forth, more room for settler expansion was needed. His order called for Harrison to:

. . . take advantage of the most favorable moment for extinguishing the Indian title to lands lying east of the Wabash. . . .

The acquisition he had in mind was three million acres of rich Indiana land, beginning at a point twenty-one miles north of Vincennes and extending northward and eastward — its northern boundary hardly more than a few miles from the village being called Prophet's Town near the mouth of the Tippecanoe.

[*September 30, 1809 — Saturday*]

Captain Nathan Heald carried on his duties here at Fort Wayne in the midst of rapidly increasing Indian tensions with an air of insouciance he did not really feel. He was worried, not so much for himself as for someone else. For the first time in his thirty-four years, Nathan Heald was deeply, completely, marvelously in love. She was, beyond any doubt whatever, the most beautiful, intelligent, witty and wonderful woman he had ever met.

Her name was Rebekah Wells.

Because of the fact that her Uncle William, who lived across the river from the fort, had been Indian Agent here for years and knew the Indians very well, she probably wasn't in any real danger, yet he couldn't help worrying about her. And thinking about her now, with all the Indians gathered here as a result of the treaty proceedings just concluded by Governor Harrison, he marveled again at how it had transpired that at such an unlikely place as a remote frontier post he should have met someone with whom to fall in love.

Nathan Heald had never seen battle. A native of Ipswich, New Hampshire, he was the son of Colonel Thomas Heald who, on April 20, 1775, had commanded the New Ipswich Company which marched before daylight to avenge the affair at Lexington and Concord — exactly five months before Nathan was born. It was not until March of 1799, when he was twenty-three, that Nathan joined the United States Army as an ensign and was assigned to recruiting duty. In just over a month he'd been promoted to second lieutenant and then stationed at a variety of posts over the years since then, performing his duties quite well and becoming a first lieutenant.

In the fall of 1806 he had been ordered to take command here at Fort

Wayne, where he arrived on January 7, 1807. Twenty-four days after his arrival, he had been promoted to captain in the First Infantry Regiment, with an ensign named Philip Ostrander as his second-in-command.[174] It was an exciting step for Heald and he quickly imbued himself with the flavor of this post, thanks to a lot of information passed along to him by the Indian Agent, William Wells. Not only had Wells told him about his life as the adopted son of Michikiniqua of the Miamis, he had also told the story of how he had come to be reunited with his family in Kentucky and subsequently Indian Agent at Fort Wayne.

By the time Captain Heald had arrived at Fort Wayne to take command, however, William Wells was no longer a happy man. Wells had hoped that when the United States Indian Factory System was put into action by the government, he would be named to the lucrative position of factor at Fort Wayne. But he hadn't been. The appointment had been given to a former law clerk and storekeeper who had failed at both jobs but who had some powerful political connections. He was an immigrant from Ireland named John Johnston and there was instant antipathy between the two.

To further undermine Wells's happiness, matters had not gone well between Governor Harrison and himself for some time, not because of Harrison's remarkable knack for gobbling up Indian territory on behalf of the United States, but because he felt the Miamis were not being paid enough. From Grouseland at Vincennes, Harrison had complained to the Secretary of War that Wells was too attached to the Miamis and was urging them to unite and protect their rights just at a time when Harrison was striving hardest to acquire more land from them for the United States. Obviously, Harrison went on, Wells was "more attached to the Indians than to the people of the United States." Without any real evidence for such accusations, Harrison accused Wells of defrauding the Indians, embezzling annuity funds and maneuvering matters so his friends got government contracts. Wells then made the mistake of going outside normal channels. He appealed to General Wilkinson, asking him to intercede in his behalf with the President. This had quite effectively alienated the Secretary of War, who warned Wells that if his attitude did not change for the better, he would be dismissed.

The friction with United States Factor Johnston went from bad to worse and Wells went into a deep depression a year ago last summer when his wife, Wanagapeth, died. Crushed by the loss of A-Sweet-Breeze, he took their two sons and three daughters to Kentucky and left them there temporarily in the care of the Wells family. He visited frequently and during one of these visits met the daughter of a well-known Kentucky family named Geiger. Her name was Mary and by the end of a year they were engaged.

Last fall, his son William Wayne Wells with him, the Indian Agent accompanied a delegation of chiefs to see the President, planning to return via Kentucky where he would wed Mary Geiger and bring her back here to Fort Wayne with him, along with his children. He was still having extreme difficulties with John Johnston, who lost no opportunity to continue the long string of character assassinations concerning Wells that he had been sending to Secretary of War Henry Dearborn. It was during this absence of Wells from Fort Wayne that Dearborn finally had enough and, as one of his final communications as Secretary of War, sent Wells a letter firing him.

Wells had returned to Fort Wayne with his new wife and old family last April 12 and was handed his letter of discharge by a very smug John Johnston.[175] Wells and his whole family were upset and though Nathan Heald commiserated with him, there was nothing that could be done. There was for Heald, however, a happy page to the whole episode. Along with his children and new wife, Wells had also brought from Kentucky his niece, Rebekah. Now she and Nathan were very deeply in love, dreading the time when Rebekah would have to go back to Kentucky and planning how to see one another when that occurred.

Although he had not met Tecumseh, Captain Heald had heard a great deal about him and was aware that the Shawnee disliked and distrusted William Wells and that Wells disliked and greatly feared Tecumseh. The Shawnee had by this time all but given up in his attempts to get the Miamis under Michikiniqua to support his grand plan. Acting at the advice of his former adopted son, Michikiniqua refused to support Tecumseh. Now, considering Wells to be a traitor, Tecumseh had nothing but scorn for the former Indian Agent. But it was Wells's fear as much as anything else that had prompted him to suggest to Harrison that Tecumseh be assassinated before it was too late. Harrison was still rankled with Wells and even the fact that Wells had convinced Michikiniqua and the Miamis, in light of the growing unrest of the tribes around them, to reaffirm their friendship and loyalty to the United States had not yet wholly restored the former Indian Agent to the governor's good graces, but he was definitely working at it.[176]

The treaty that William Henry Harrison had concluded here today was extremely important and he was pleased with himself. That it would eventually cause considerable dispute among the Indians was a foregone conclusion, but he considered that of little significance in light of what he had achieved. And Captain Nathan Heald, as an observer, was both amazed and just a bit appalled at how easily the governor had taken a massive chunk of land away from the Indians.

When Harrison had arrived here fifteen days ago, the Miamis were already on hand and during the next couple of days the Potawatomies had come straggling in. They were led by Harrison's long-time cohort in the matter of land cessions, the village chief Winnemac. No other influential chiefs were on hand. The large piece of land in question was owned essentially by the Miamis, partially by the Potawatomies. Winnemac had no authority to sell even the Potawatomi land, much less that belonging to the Miamis.

At first the Miamis balked, not at all willing to sell. A certain amount of whiskey was provided for "refreshment" and then the talks resumed. The pattern repeated itself time and again as the days passed. Winnemac moved among the minor chiefs, coaxing, coercing, imploring, and finally even threatening to make war on them. Harrison continued to talk, painting the British in the worst possible colors, blaming them for the fact that the Miamis were now in a position where selling their land was all that remained to them. At last the governor stood solemnly before them and in a voice vibrant with sincerity and tinged with reproach, he had said:

"This is the first request your new Father has ever made of you. It will be the last — he wants no more of your land. Agree to the proposition which I now make you and send on some of your wise men to take him by the hand. He will set your heart at ease. He will tell you that he will never make another proposition to you to sell your lands."[177]

And so, with the pressure from Winnemac — for which he was well paid — and from Harrison bludgeoning them and with the promise of abundant whiskey after the treaty was signed, they gave in. The documents were duly signed and a drunken revel followed . . . at which one of the Miami warriors was killed.

With the Fort Wayne Treaty signed, Governor Harrison was jubilant. Once again he had done it! The United States now owned another forty-seven hundred square miles — an area of some three million acres — and, in direct obedience to the directive he'd received from President Madison to that effect, Harrison had paid next to nothing for it. The Miamis, who received the most, would get an annuity of seven hundred dollars — less than seven dollars per square mile. Eventually, Harrison knew — and in a not too distant future at that — American settlers would pay the government two dollars per acre for this same land — a potential of six million dollars.

In his quarters, Governor Harrison had already begun triumphantly writing his report to Secretary of War Eustis:

. . . The compensation given for this cession of lands is as low as it could possibly be made. I think, upon the whole, that the bargain is a better one for the United States than any that has been made by me for lands south of the Wabash. . . . As soon as the treaty has been ratified and a sales office is opened, there will be several hundred families along this Tract. . . . If an

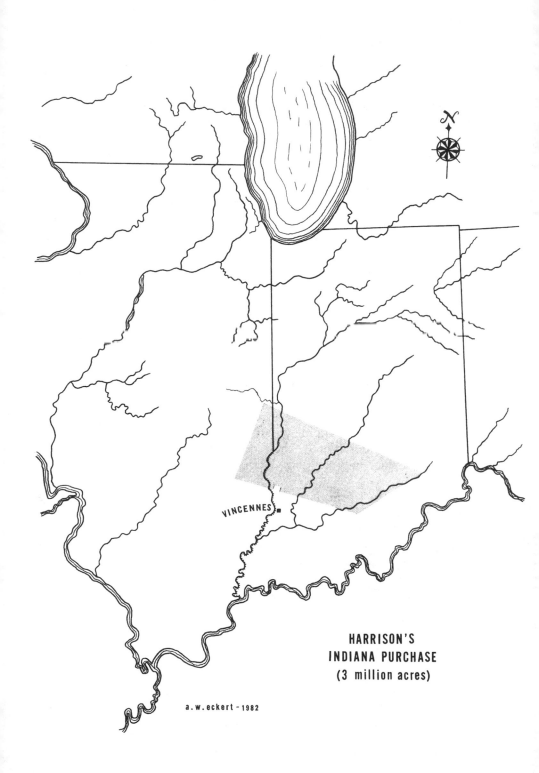

VINCENNES

**HARRISON'S
INDIANA PURCHASE
(3 million acres)**

a.w.eckert-1982

ill blood yet remains, a little attention to the influential chiefs will soon re-move it. . . .

[*June 30, 1810 — Saturday*]

The long-festering feud between the Whistler and Kinzie factions in Chi-cago, which had been simmering for six years, finally turned into white heat and exploded with reverberations heard all the way to Washington. And today, at last, the dispatches had come which would once and for all end the dispute.

Chicago had grown considerably over these years, although it was still not much more than a very small town. Dominated by Fort Dearborn, as it had been since the military first came here, there were now a number of houses on both sides of the river, although the Kinzie's trading post com-plex was still the largest and the center of activities for civilian life. At least once a week in the warmer months much of the populace gathered at the store, bringing their own picnic lunches or buying food prepared by the Kinzies' black cook, Athena. At such times, as evening approached, the much-scarred harpsichord would be rolled out onto the porch and with Eleanor at the keys, John doing a creditable job on the fiddle, a couple of fifers and a drummer from the fort, and long, lanky Liberty White coming in from the Lee Farm up the river to play his harmonica with surprising skill, music would fill the air and there would be dancing. Sometimes small groups of Potawatomies would come, standing at first in little clusters apart from the others but then, at coaxings from Shawneeawkee, finally joining in with hand-clapping in time to the music. Occasionally they would bring gourd rattles or their own skin drums and do their own shuffling, leaping, high-stepping dances to the wonderment of the on-lookers.

Though Indian tensions were high throughout much of the frontier, here at Chicago there was a quality of amity between white man and red that was pleasant and reassuring. Black Partridge was frequently here, even though he'd moved his village farther away toward the Des Plaines River. Sometimes when Black Partridge came he would be accompanied by Nescotnemeg, whose fiery-tempered daughter was the wife of Sau-ganash. Occasionally with other visiting dignitaries — Siggenauk from Milwaukee, Topenebe from St. Joseph, Chaubenee from Indian Creek, and Naunongee, the obese Potawatomi chief whose village was southeast of Chicago, around the bend of the lake a bit at the mouth of the Calumet River. Once, Chief Gomo of Peoria Lake came, accompanied by Thomas Forsyth, and brought with him two powerful chiefs of neighboring vil-lages, Mittatass and Sunawewonee. Sometimes, between afternoon pic-nicking and evening music and dance, games were played and races held, both on foot and on horseback. More often than not, the horse races were won by the Indians. In the foot races, however, no one, Indian or white, had been able to best Lieutenant William Whistler. Though twenty-nine now, he still showed no sign of losing his phenomenal speed and when he ran, no one would bet against him.

Two summers ago Tecumseh had been one of the Indians who visited Black Partridge, accompanied by a party of men which included Chaubenee and Sauganash. John Kinzie, who was visiting at Black Partridge's village at the time, was introduced with high praise by his host to Tecumseh, who had looked at him closely and then shook his hand with warmth.

"I have long heard of John Kinzie," he said, smiling, "sometimes by that name and sometimes by the name of Shawneeawkee. All Indians who speak of you have called you their friend and it is good to meet you. Chaubenee and Sauganash, who you know, have said you are to be trusted in all ways." The Shawnee's gaze was especially intense as he added, "You never need fear that you or your family will ever suffer injury from the Indians." For Kinzie it had been reassuring, but it had also convinced him, more than all the rumors he had heard, that Indian troubles were coming.

Gradually Chicago was changing. Sometimes would-be settlers would come and stay a few days and then move on. Little by little, though, the settlement was growing and the lives of its citizens intermingling. A house had been erected to the west of Kinzie's Store by a jolly, robust settler named Ezekiel Cooper. That house was closer to Wolf Point, the slightly projecting point of land on the west shore where the North Branch and South Branch joined to form the main Chicago River.[178] He was the first of the permanent Chicago settlers to die — stricken by the miasmic fever so common and so feared in this marshy region and dead within a week of its onslaught. But his widow, Mary, stayed on with her four children — three daughters and a son — and now she was being courted by Private Thomas Burns from Fort Dearborn.

Since his employment by settlers William Russell and Charles Lee as supervisor of their farm up the South Branch, Liberty White had shown his value many times over. He'd built a cabin and barn at the farm, hired itinerant French voyageurs to work for him and had turned the Lee farm into a huge success. Already he had planted an apple orchard and over twenty acres were under cultivation, the heavy loam now turned more easily by a new plow brought to Chicago on the *Adams* last May 16 and purchased through John Kinzie. Liberty White had become a prominent member of the growing community and everyone depended upon him for a variety of excellent produce — cabbage, potatoes, beans, peas, squash, pumpkins, cucumbers, watermelons, cantaloupe, corn, carrots, celery and lettuce. The deep black soil of the area was incredibly rich and Liberty White had suddenly made the people here realize that farming in this region could be a very profitable business. Recently he had even begun to experiment with milk cows in the lush grasslands adjoining the tilled acreage and this aspect of his farming looked very promising as well.

Despite his continuing problems with Captain Whistler, John Kinzie did better than ever in his trade; the pelts brought by Indians and white trappers were carefully graded and tied into bales and then hundreds of these bales each year shipped to the fur trade center at Mackinac. Kinzie's Store was now as much a general merchandise establishment for the Chicago residents and the Fort Dearborn garrison as it was an outfitting establishment for the wilderness trade. His portage service across the Chicago Portage — at the southern end of which he now had a secondary station to aid travelers coming up from the Illinois and Mississippi — was now an important operation, much of it being handled by his employee and neighbor, Antoine Ouilmette. He still did a certain amount of slave-trade business, though rarely for his own use these days. He merely acted as a middleman, buying and selling them whenever a reasonable opportunity presented itself and dutifully logging the transactions in his account books. As recently as last April 25 he had sold ". . . one negro wench, by indenture . . ." to the new clothing merchant who had settled in town, Francis Bourbonne. He still retained for his own and Eleanor's use, their devoted house servants, Henry and Athena, who had been with him now for nearly twenty years. He also still had Jeffrey Nash, who had turned out to be a decided asset with work requiring great strength and stamina. A good worker, Nash was always quiet and respectful and spent the evenings in his own tiny quarters, using the reading skills Athena had taught him, to read laboriously by candlelight the books borrowed from his master.

Fort Dearborn remained much as it had been since its completion, with a few minor improvements here and there. John Whistler, now fifty-two, still commanded, and most of the soldiers he had brought here in that summer seven years ago had reenlisted and were still part of the garrison. But there were a few new faces: counting both officers and men, the full strength of the garrison was now seventy-seven and quite a few of the army wives had joined their husbands, some with children. William Whistler remained second-in-command, but there were now two additional lieutenants — Seth Thompson and Thomas Hamilton, the latter Captain Whistler's son-in-law.

The Indian Agency adjacent to the fort continued to conduct its business under the skilled hand of Charles Jouett, who now was residing with his new wife in a house he had built on the north side of the river not far distant from the houses of Kinzie and Ouilmette. Over the Christmas and New Year holidays in 1808–09, Jouett had made a quick trip to Clark County, Kentucky, where he married a lovely girl of twenty-three, Susan Randolph Allen. Despite the cold weather and deep snow of January, the couple had mounted their horses and set off overland for Chicago, accompanied by their black slave, Joe Battles, and guided by a sharp-eyed, friendly half-breed from the Des Plaines River; a man who used the name Alexander Robinson when among the whites, but among the Potawatomies he was called Chechepinqua — Squint-Eye.[179] For many years he had been a friend of John Kinzie, having met him when he was a young man new in the trade at Detroit. They had arrived safely in Chicago, having carefully marked their trail all the way so future travelers would be able to follow it, and settled down in the little house close to the Kinzie place. It was here, last October, that their son had been born. They had named him Charles, after his father, but with a middle name in honor of the Indian Agent's good friend at Fort Dearborn, Jack Lalime — Charles Lalime Jouett.

Although the Indian Agency had remained under the same leadership in Chicago, such was not the case with the government's Indian factory, which was presently under its fourth factor. After taking over that office from the first factor, Ebenezer Belknap, Thomas Hayward had not lasted very long. He resigned in the spring of 1807 and Joseph B. Varnum had been appointed to the office. Two summers ago Varnum was transferred to Mackinac and the present factor here in Chicago was a pleasant, interesting, well-spoken man of medium height named Matthew Irwin.

The fact that Illinois had finally become an official United States Territory in its own right on February 9 last year was only one of a number of events of significance involving Chicago and Fort Dearborn and affecting the lives of John Whistler and John Kinzie.[180] Almost three years ago, Eleanor Kinzie presented her husband with another daughter, born in the autumn. They had named her Maria Indiana Kinzie. Then, just last February 8, they had another son — Robert Allen Kinzie. Shortly after that, on what was to have been a brief visit to her Aunt Maggie Forsyth at Sandwich, Eleanor's daughter, Margaret McKillip, had met and fallen in love with an officer at Detroit. So, instead of coming home as planned, she had stayed on at the Forsyth house to be near him. He was a handsome young lieutenant named Linai T. Helm. In a very short while he had proposed and eighteen-year-old Margaret had accepted. And had it not been for the savage eruption of the Kinzie-Whistler feud here in Chicago, John and Eleanor would probably have been in Detroit right now, for today was the day the young couple were being married.

The hatred that had been bubbling between John Kinzie and John Whistler began to boil over about eight months before Margaret even left Chicago and subsequently met Lieutenant Helm. It started when the post surgeon, Dr. William C. Smith, left for good and the individual appointed to succeed him arrived.

Dr. John Cooper — officially, Surgeon's Mate John Cooper — presented himself to Captain John Whistler at Fort Dearborn on the thirteenth day of June two years ago. He was a thin, almost scrawny and decidedly nervous individual with dark blond hair and a head that was disproportionately large. He had watery blue eyes and his large Adam's apple bobbed frequently. Oddly, his voice was rich and deep and because of its projection he might well have been a stage actor. He hailed from Duchess County, New York — a graduate of the Fishkill Academy in the town of Fishkill. He was bright and seemingly pleasant enough, smiled seldom but laughed often and too commonly at the wrong places. He was eighteen years old.

From the very beginning, the commanding officer and the new post doctor achieved rapprochement that was little short of remarkable, considering their difference in age. By the end of three months each considered the other the best friend he'd ever made, with the problems of one the concerns of the other. When Captain Whistler told Dr. Cooper that he was not happy with the suttler situation at the fort, the young physician was eager to help him in any way he could. The problem, Captain Whistler told him, was that his son, John Jr., had for some time been engaged in a suttling partnership with John Kinzie and was not very satisfied with the arrangement, having decided that suttling was not really what he wanted to do. He wanted out, which he could effect easily enough simply by washing his hands of the whole thing; John Kinzie would be more than glad to resume handling the whole operation. That was precisely the problem; the commanding officer did not want John Kinzie to be the exclusive suttler to the garrison, yet he could not arbitrarily terminate the privilege. There had to be cause.

"Didn't you say," Cooper queried, his brow furrowed, "that Mr. Kinzie was selling whiskey to the Indians?" At the captain's nod he went on: "All right, why not revoke his privilege on those grounds, break up the partnership, which is what your son needs to get out, and put the suttling operation into someone else's hands?"

"Whose? It can't be anyone in the military, and I don't know any other civilian here who wouldn't do the same as Kinzie's doing, or worse."

"How about me?" Cooper displayed one of his rare smiles.

The more the commanding officer thought about it, the more the idea appealed to him. More than anything else, he knew, it would infuriate John Kinzie, which would be just fine. He called in his son, explained what was under consideration and found him more than receptive to the idea. That settled it and Captain Whistler made the announcement at once. The fury of John Kinzie over the development was deeply satisfying, but the captain quickly discovered that there were a few problems he had not anticipated.

Within a short time it became obvious that in suttling to the garrison, Dr. Cooper had become overzealous and his activities had begun harming the operations of the United States Factor, Matthew Irwin, who dealt with the garrison as well as with the Indians. Irwin was no less furious than Kinzie had been and the pair quickly united in defense. They had a sudden and unexpected ally when Indian Agent Charles Jouett sided with them, not caring at all for Dr. Cooper and considering Captain Whistler's actions little short of reprehensible. He also feared it might have ramifications in Irwin's ability to properly meet the needs of the Indians.

With the Indian Agent and the Indian Factor both backing him, John Kinzie sent a letter of complaint to Whistler's superior, Colonel Jacob Kingsbury, claiming that the military — meaning Captain Whistler — was taking unfair advantage of the civilian populace — meaning John Kinzie. He questioned the ethics and the legality of Dr. Cooper acting as suttler, in that it was a conflict of interest and prohibited Factor Matthew Irwin from acting as suttler, which should be the case. He neglected to mention that the United States Factory System often failed to come through with the goods Irwin requisitioned, with the result that he had to purchase such supplies from John Kinzie.

Colonel Kingsbury wrote a stiff letter to Captain Whistler demanding an explanation. Stung by the inferred reproof, encouraged by Cooper and eagerly abetted by Jack Lalime, Whistler struck back savagely at Kinzie and the battle was joined. Kinzie, the commander retorted in his response to Kingsbury, was guilty of selling whiskey to the Indians, which was against government regulations which he, as commanding officer, was obligated to enforce. He neglected to mention that every trader in the Northwest sold whiskey in varying amounts to the Indians and that William Henry Harrison himself dispensed it with some abandon to the Indians as a handy tool in acquiring land cessions.

That launched all the participants into an extensive correspondence which grew progressively hotter and more accusatory, then leaped from the pages of correspondence to insults and even threats in personal encounters. It was the most excitement Chicago had ever known and virtually no one was exempt. Where before there had been vague lines of demarcation between the Kinzie faction and the Whistler faction, now these became painfully sharp. The principals arrayed on Captain Whistler's side included John Jr. and Lieutenant William Whistler, Lieutenant Thomas Hamilton, Dr. John Cooper and interpreter Jack Lalime. In John Kinzie's camp were Factor Matthew Irwin, Indian Agent Charles Jouett, Liberty White and a defector from the enemy camp, Lieutenant Seth Thompson. In general, the military and those connected with them sided with Captain Whistler and the settlers and traders sided with John Kinzie. Because this was such an isolated community, the feud became magnified far beyond the proportions it deserved in the year that followed.

John Kinzie countered the thrusts of Captain Whistler adroitly. He explained that while, yes, whiskey was sold at his post, this was never done with abandon, that it was never sold to an Indian before all business with that Indian was completed and the customer had fully taken care of his own and his family's needs for the coming season. Then, more often than not, the whiskey dispensed was not as a purchase but as a social gift. The trader continued:

. . . A certain amount of whiskey within sensible guidelines, to which I have always adhered, has proven for over two hundred years to be a very important part of successful commerce with the Indians. Obviously, there are those who abuse the matter, emphasizing the need for control of the use of whiskey in the trade, but not its complete abolition. I have been accused by the Fort Dearborn commander of excessive distribution of liquor to the Indians, but this is not true and never has been true in my many years of dealing with them. Enclosed is a copy of the manifest of the Adams, which was the last ship to forward supplies here, having arrived at Chicago on May 16 last. You will note that my consignment of beverages consisted solely of 7 barrels of non-fermented apple cider; whereas Dr. Cooper, whom Captain Whistler has illegally appointed suttler to the garrison, received on this same shipment, 4 barrels of whiskey.

The civilians living at Chicago are not under martial law, yet Captain Whistler and most of his officers give our people here orders as if we were subordinate soldiers. Except in matters of war, a military force has no right to set itself up as a law enforcement agency to civilians. . . .

Making good use of the information supplied by Liberty White and Lieutenant Seth Thompson, John Kinzie now fired his guns in some new directions, with some rather devastating charges against Whistler:

. . . It should further be pointed out, Sir, that a witness to the occurrence has told me that when Captain Whistler's son, John Whistler, Jr., was suttling to the garrison, the commanding officer forced his soldiers to buy goods from him and that when one private soldier refused to do so, that Captain Whistler beat that soldier to insensibility. Further, it has come to my attention that Captain Whistler, in a direct effort to thwart the legal commerce of Chicago, required his soldiers, under threat of punishment, to raise ten acres of corn for his private use, and said corn, when harvested, was privately sold by Captain Whistler in direct competition to our most prominent farmer, Mr. Liberty White, at a cost below that which Mr. White could equal if he were to profit from his efforts. In these matters and others, Captain John Whistler has defrauded the government.

The anger this caused among the Whistler faction was almost beyond belief. Whistler's son-in-law, Lieutenant Hamilton, raged with the fury of a wounded bear and immediately threatened to kill John Kinzie. Jack

Lalime was of like disposition. Captain Whistler, abruptly finding his very military career in jeopardy, wasted no time in firing off a new salvo in response to Kinzie's accusations:

. . . The malignant wretches opposed to me are guilty of defrauding the public. Lieutenant Thompson is a tool in the hands of Mr. Kinzie and Mr. Irwin, who despise him even while using him. Lieutenant Thompson is a man of low character and even Mr. Jouett some time ago repeated to me a confidence from that officer that in some past time he had run away to escape paying a debt to a landlord. And on one occasion, Sir, to which my officers will attest, Lieutenant Thompson acknowledged that he was a liar in the presence of all the gentlemen of this garrison. . . .

Even while Captain John Whistler was busy writing his reply, his adherents were taking matters into their own hands. Dr. John Cooper, furious at the charges that had been levied by John Kinzie against his friend, also wrote to Colonel Kingsbury, saying that the accusations were utterly groundless and that he would willingly give up his life to prove Captain Whistler innocent of the charges.

Jack Lalime and Thomas Hamilton were still heatedly discussing how to kill John Kinzie. Lalime favored assassination under cover of darkness, but Hamilton rejected that, deciding instead to challenge the trader to a duel. He named Dr. Cooper as his second and sent the nervous young physician to bear the challenge to Kinzie.

John Kinzie stared unbelievingly at the skinny, very nervous man who confronted him and whose Adam's apple bobbed furiously as he relayed the formal challenge to duel on Hamilton's behalf.

"You goddamned little white-livered bastard!" Kinzie growled, controlling his own fury only with great effort. "It would please me very much to accept and put both of you young fools in your grave, but if John Whistler wants me dead, he's going to have to be man enough to do it himself. Now get the hell off my property and go tell that son of a bitch Hamilton that his asinine challenge is declined."

As Cooper hastily departed, John Kinzie retired to his own quarters and wrote a report of the incident to Colonel Kingsbury, restating his accusations against the Fort Dearborn commander and demanding that Colonel Kingsbury bring Captain Whistler up on formal charges and have him court-martialed. He sent the message off by express rider and, upon receipt of it, Colonel Kingsbury, weary of the whole situation and realizing that it had now taken on a seriousness beyond his own authority, dumped the whole matter into the lap of Secretary of War William Eustis.

At last, today, on the very day that John Kinzie's stepdaughter was getting married in Detroit, the dispatches had come from Washington. The Secretary of War had found the situation to be something of a dilemma in that since all the military at Fort Dearborn were involved in the situation, it would be no easy matter to assemble a court in Chicago to hear the testimony and render judgment, and it would be impracticable and very expensive to hold court-martial proceedings in Detroit or St. Louis or elsewhere, due to the difficulty of transporting the principals to such location in order for them to testify. With Solomon-like wisdom, therefore, William Eustis neatly solved the problem by reassignment of all but one of the Fort Dearborn officers to distant posts. Only Lieutenant Seth Thompson was to remain at Fort Dearborn.

Lieutenant Thomas Hamilton was ordered to report immediately to Fort Wayne. His brother-in-law, Lieutenant William Whistler was sent at once to Fort Washington at Cincinnati. Captain John Whistler was permanently reassigned to Detroit and ordered to leave Chicago as soon as the officer who would take command of Fort Dearborn arrived. Jack Lalime was not mentioned in the dispatches. Dr. John Cooper, though not military, was technically subject to being ordered elsewhere by the Secretary of War, but he was permitted to remain at Fort Dearborn as surgeon's mate; however, under the terms of a special order, his privilege to suttle to the garrison there was revoked.

In effect, John Kinzie had won.

[*July 3, 1810 — Tuesday*]

"I don't understand it, Sauganash," Chaubenee said in an undertone to his companion. "The more cause he has for anger, the less he submits to it. If I were up there," he tilted his head toward the front of the assemblage, "I'd burn off their ears with my words."

"Which is why," Sauganash pointed out, "he is a warrior who leads and we are chiefs who follow . . . and gladly!"

The huge-chested Chaubenee and more slightly built Sauganash were seated next to one another in the assemblage that had gathered to hear Tecumseh speak. Several hundred Indians from neighboring villages had converged here at Catahecassa's Town on the Auglaize, where Tecumseh had come in one final effort to swing the neutral Shawnees to his doctrine. Actually, he had not really planned to make any further attempt to win them over, since Catahecassa, now eighty-four and highly venerated in the tribe, had made it clear at their last meeting that to his final breath, if need be, he would prevent his Shawnees from following Tecumseh on a path that must lead to war.

"We have fought enough," he had said then. "Always we have been first to suffer the bites of the white dogs. No more. We will not join the whites in their struggle against one another, and we will not join you in your struggle against them."

But then Tecumseh's old friend, Blue Jacket, had become so disenchanted with Catahecassa's unrealistically bullheaded stand and with what was happening to Indian lands that he had begun leaning strongly toward Tecumseh. When word had spread of Harrison's latest maneuver, with the help of Winnemac, in getting a cession of three million more acres of Indian lands, he was beside himself with anger and had sent word to Tecumseh to come to Catahecassa's Town to address the neutral chiefs and warriors. When he did so, Blue Jacket said, at that time Blue Jacket would himself side with Tecumseh in direct and open opposition to Catahecassa. Together they stood a good chance of swinging the scales in their own favor.

So Tecumseh had arrived here with his entourage, including Chaubenee and Sauganash, only to be devastated by the news that Weh-yeh-pih-ehr-sehn-wah — he who was known as Blue Jacket — had died a few days previously of a fever.[181] And Catahecassa, though not able to prevent the council that had convened, refused to meet in preliminary council with Tecumseh.

Now, standing before the assembled chiefs and warriors of the Shawnee, Miami, Delaware and Potawatomi tribes, Tecumseh held up a sheet of paper for all to see. "This," he told them, "is a letter Chief Catahecassa has shown me with pride. It is from the white devil, Harrison, who praises Catahecassa for his peaceful disposition." He spoke the words as if they were an epithet. Then, in an unexpected movement, he crumpled the paper and tossed it into the small council fire that burned between him and his audience. The wad of paper on the coals stretched, browned and then burst into flame. There was bitterness and sorrow in Tecumseh's voice when he spoke again.

"So much for praise from our greatest enemy! If your Governor Harrison were here, I would serve him in the same way." He let his eyes leave Catahecassa and move across the audience for a long quiet moment and the only sounds heard were the swish of the waters of the Auglaize rushing past and the distant barking of a dog behind the village. When his words came again, their brittleness was the only clue to the anger that seethed within him.

"Can you people here not see that the whites are deceiving you? For my part, I will never put any confidence in them. Look around you. How well have you been treated by them? How much have you gained by the treaties you have signed in the absence of those who wished to save our land? As to you chiefs here who sold land to the white chief Harrison, the words I have to describe you, my mouth is too ashamed to speak. Dogs and skunks have not so little mind as those who did this. If only I had been here, not one inch of our land would he have bought. And every Indian who has put his thumb to it should have his thumbs cut off!"

He looked at them with contempt and then strode through them, their bodies parting to let him pass and Chaubenee and Sauganash, Wasego-boah and Tecumapese and the others falling in behind. Following the lead of Tecumseh none of them looked back.

[*July 10, 1810 — Tuesday*]

In the huge red brick mansion called Grouseland, Governor William Henry Harrison, his stomach still churning with the anger that had flooded him upon learning the details of Tecumseh's speech at Catahecassa's Town, wrote swiftly and without pause, at no loss for what he wished to say:

William Henry Harrison, Governor and Commander-in-Chief of the Territory of Indiana, to the Shawnee Chief and the Indians assembled at Tippecanoe:

Notwithstanding the improper language which you have used towards me, I will endeavor to open your eyes to your true interests. Notwithstanding what white men have told you, I am not your personal enemy. . . . Although I must say that you are an enemy to the Seventeen Fires, and that you have used the greatest exertion to lead them [the Indians] astray. In this you have been in some manner successful; as I am told they are ready to raise the tomahawk against their father, yet their father, notwithstanding his anger at their folly, is full of goodness, and is always ready to receive into his arms those of his children who are willing to repent, acknowledge their fault, and ask his forgiveness.

There is yet but little harm done, which may be easily repaired. The chain of friendship which united the whites with the Indians may be renewed, and be as strong as ever. A great deal of that work depends on you — the destiny of those who are under your direction depends upon the choice you make of the two roads which are before you. The one is large, open, and pleasant, and leads to peace, security, and happiness; the other, on the contrary, is narrow and crooked, and leads to misery and ruin. Don't deceive yourselves; do not believe that all nations of Indians united are able to resist the force of the Seventeen Fires. I know your warriors are brave, but ours are not less so. But what can a few brave warriors do against the innumerable warriors of the Seventeen Fires? Our blue-coats are more numerous than you can count; our hunters are like the leaves of the forest, or the grains of sand on the Wabash. Do you think that the red-coats can protect you; they are not able to protect themselves. They do not think of going to war with us. If they did, you would in a few moons see our flag wave over all the forts of Canada. What reason have you to complain of the Seventeen Fires? Have they taken anything from you? Have they ever violated the treaties made with the red men? You say they have purchased lands from those who have no right to sell them. Show that this is true and the land will be instantly restored. Show us the rightful owners. I have full power to arrange this business; but if you would rather carry your complaints before your great father, the President, you shall be indulged. I will immediately take means to send you, with those chiefs you may choose, to the city where your father lives. Everything necessary shall be prepared for your journey, and means taken for your safe return.

[July 14, 1810 — Saturday]

At the Tippecanoe village, Tecumseh silently read the letter just handed to him by William Barron, special messenger from Governor Harrison. Barron, streaks of perspiration making channels on his temples and cheeks, waited nervously. He expected a great burst of anger and was nonplussed when, upon finishing, Tecumseh spoke to him calmly for several minutes, discussing quite reasonably the claim of the Indians to this land and their inability to remain friends with the United States unless the whites acknowledged this claim. He then spoke of Harrison with deceptive mildness:

". . . I remember him as a young man sitting by the side of General Wayne. I have never troubled the white people much, but now I will go to Vincennes. . . . I will arrive there in one moon with some of my principal men and probably a large number of young men who are fond of attending upon such occasions."

The time had come for giants to meet.

[July 16, 1810 — Monday]

At Fort Wayne, Captain Nathan Heald, who had a short while before welcomed Captain Oscar James Rhea to his post, now listened with sour expression and mounting anger and frustration to what the other officer had to say.

"Damn it!" he exploded at last. "I don't *want* that command!"

Rhea shrugged. He was sober today, which was something of a special occasion for him, and he had difficulty in trying to put from his mind the thoughts of the unopened bottle of whiskey in his saddlebag. "I guess you don't have a great deal of choice," he murmured.

"By God," Captain Heald went on, his nostrils pinched, "I was planning on getting married this fall."

He glared at Rhea as if it were all that officer's fault, knowing it wasn't, but not caring. Rhea had received his orders from his commander, Major Zebulon Pike at Detroit, who had gotten his orders directly from Washington. Captain James Oscar Rhea was to leave Detroit immediately for Fort Wayne and, upon arrival there, to assume command of that post from Captain Nathan Heald. Heald and his first officer, Ensign Philip Ostrander, were in turn to leave Fort Wayne at once and proceed to Chicago where Heald was to relieve Captain John Whistler of his command at Fort

Dearborn. The orders included a promotion for Ostrander, to lieutenant, since he was to be second-in-command. Captain Whistler, as soon as he completed turning over command of Fort Dearborn to Captain Heald, was to proceed immediately to Detroit in a permanent reassignment to that post.

Nathan Heald cursed aloud again. He had heard quite enough of Chicago to know it was considered the hell-hole outpost of the frontier, a place wholly lacking in the niceties. Fort Wayne was not all that special, he knew, but it had to be far and away better than Fort Dearborn. He grimly pictured what would be in store for him there — limited diet, a marshy terrain that was a breeding place for fevers that caused people to sicken and sometimes die, a place where there was absolutely no cultural stimulation. God! He wouldn't even be able to hear regularly from Rebekah.

That clinched it. "Just a moment, Captain," he told Rhea. He took out paper and pen and swiftly wrote a brief letter to Colonel Kingsbury, confirming that he had received his orders, turned command of Fort Wayne over to Captain Rhea and was now departing with Lieutenant Ostrander for Chicago. He then added that he had not had leave from his regular duties in nearly four years and was requesting in the most urgent way that he be granted extensive leave in the fall that would allow him ample time to return East to visit his parents in New England and then, on the way back to Chicago, to stop off in Louisville to marry his fiancée, Rebekah Wells. He concluded the note with a strong remark:

. . . I am sorry to have to say this, Sir, but I will resign if not given a furlough for the winter.

[August 15, 1810 — Wednesday]

"If the President does not comply with my terms," said Tecumseh to Governor Harrison at Vincennes, "I will be obliged to take the other side."

The cold implacability of the comment was indicative of the tenor of everything that had been said since Tecumseh's arrival here at Grouseland and the governor was not at all pleased with how things had gone. The very manner in which Tecumseh had shown up for this meeting, Harrison decided, was an insult. The Shawnee, bare-chested and standing in the prow of the lead canoe, had been painted with streaks and swirls of red, blue, white and yellow and the multitude of warriors in the eighty canoes following his had been similarly painted. They were expected, of course, but their appearance in such a manner had greatly excited and disturbed Captain George Floyd when they had passed his little post called Fort Knox just upstream from Vincennes.

Harrison and his commissioners had been waiting, all of them clad in their finest — the judges of the Territorial Supreme Court, his military aides, a platoon of thirteen Fort Knox soldiers under a sergeant, as an honor guard, and various civilian onlookers. They were at a portico where Harrison had had his staff set up chairs enough to accommodate the principals, but such was not to be. Leaving the majority of his men in camp at the river's edge, Tecumseh and about a score of his followers, including Chaubenee, Wasegoboah, Roundhead and Sauganash, stopped some distance away and sent word that he would prefer holding the council at a nearby grove of trees.

The governor had acquiesced. A large table was set up and chairs were brought. Harrison seated himself in a large, rather thronelike armchair and others took their places in ordinary chairs on either side of him. Spemica Lawba and Winnemac, on hand to act as interpreters and advisers, stood behind and slightly to one side of Harrison. Tecumseh refused even to look at his nephew and remained standing some twenty feet from the governor. His Indians sat on the ground behind him. The Shawnee lost no time in launching into his talk.

"Brother, I wish you to listen to me well. As I think you do not clearly understand what I before said to you, I will explain it again. Brother, since the peace was made, you have killed some of the Shawnees, Winnebagoes, Delawares and Miamis and you have taken our lands from us and I do not see how we can remain at peace if you continue to do so. You try to force the red people to do some injury. It is *you* that are pushing them on to do some mischief. You endeavor to make distinctions: you wish to prevent the Indians doing as we wish them — to unite and let them consider their lands as the common property of the whole; you take tribes aside and advise them not to come into this measure; and until our design is accomplished, we do not wish to accept your invitation to go and see the President. The reason I tell you this: you want, by your distinctions of Indian tribes in allotting to each a particular tract of land, to make them war with each other. You never see an Indian come, do you, and endeavor to make the white people do so? You are continually driving the red people; when, at last, you will drive them into the Great Lake, where they can't either stand or walk.

"Brother, you ought to know what you are doing with the Indians. Perhaps it is by direction of the President to make those distinctions. It is a very bad thing and we do not like it. Since my residence at Tippecanoe, we have endeavored to level all distinctions — to destroy village chiefs, by whom all mischief is done. It is they who sell our lands to the Americans. Our object is to let our affairs be transacted by warriors.

"Brother, this land that was sold and the goods that were given for it were only done by a few. The treaty was afterwards brought here and the

Weas were induced to give their consent, because of their small numbers. The treaty at Fort Wayne was made through the threats of Winnemac . . ." he glared at the Potawatomi village chief and Winnemac dropped his eyes, ". . . but in the future we are prepared to punish those chiefs who may come forward to propose to sell the land." Tecumseh looked back at Harrison. "If you continue to purchase them, it will produce war among the different tribes and, at last, I do not know what the consequences will be to the white people."

Tecumseh turned and caught the eye of Sauganash, who immediately stood and held aloft the letter that Harrison had sent to Tecumseh a month ago. He turned slowly in a circle with it and, when all had seen it, refolded it and sat down again. Tecumseh addressed Harrison anew.

"Brother, I was glad to hear your speech. You said if we could show you that the land was sold by people who had no right to sell, you would restore it." He pointed a level finger at Winnemac. "Those that did sell did not own it. . . .[182] These tribes set up a claim, but," he let his pointing arm swing toward the river where the rest of his warriors waited, "the tribes with me will not agree with their claim." He paused for several heartbeats and when he spoke again, there was an ominous quality in his voice. "If the land is not restored to us, you will see, when we return to our homes, how it will be settled.

"*Hear me!*" the two words came like rifle shots and Harrison mentally cursed himself for jerking in surprise. "We shall have a great council at which all the tribes will be present, when we shall show to those who sold that they had no right to the claim that they set up." Again his eyes had impaled Winnemac. "And we will see what will be done to those chiefs that did sell land to you."

Tecumseh put his clenched fist to his chest. "I am not alone in this determination; it is the determination of all the warriors and red people that listen to me. I now wish *you*," his eyes flashed to Harrison, "to listen to me. If you do not, it will appear as if you wished to kill all the chiefs that sold you the land. I tell you so because I am authorized by all the tribes to do so. *I* am the head of them all! I am a warrior and all the warriors will meet together in two or three moons from this. Then I will call for those chiefs that sold you the land and shall know what to do with them. If you do not restore the land, you will have a hand in killing them!"

Winnemac blanched in earnest now. This was no longer a vague threat and he was suddenly very much afraid. Tecumseh had paused and in the silence of the grove the whites shifted uncomfortably in their chairs and some put their heads together and began murmuring. They stopped at a gesture from Harrison, who then nodded at Tecumseh to go on.

"Brother, do not believe that I came here to get presents from you. If you offer us any, we will not take them. By our taking goods from you, you will hereafter say that with them you purchased another piece of land from us."

Despite his control, the governor felt a faint heat in his neck and cheeks and once again he was angry with himself that he had allowed the words of the Shawnee to hit home so pointedly. He was, for the first time, being struck by the impact that the man he faced here was no ordinary Indian; that here was a man of intelligence and rare power who was apt to become the greatest threat he had ever faced.

"It has been the object of both myself and brother," Tecumseh was continuing, "to prevent the lands being sold. Should you not return the land, it will occasion us to call a great council that will meet at the Huron village, where the council fire has already been lighted, at which those who sold the lands shall be called and shall suffer for their conduct."

His voice softened just a little, implicit with reasonableness. "Brother, I wish you would take pity on the red people and do what I have requested. If you will not give up the land and do cross the boundary of your present settlement, it will be very hard and produce great troubles among us. How can we have confidence in the white people? When Jesus Christ came on earth, you killed and nailed Him on a cross. You thought He was dead but you were mistaken. . . . Everything I have said to you is the truth. The Great Spirit has inspired me and I speak nothing but the truth to you."

Tecumseh studied Harrison's face but could read nothing in his expression. The Shawnee had the sudden feeling that no matter what words were used on this man, it would make no difference to him. And so, though he had planned on talking much longer, going over past treaties and the ultimate breaking thereof by the whites, he realized it was pointless and he now concluded his remarks quickly.

"Brother, I hope you will confess that you ought not to have listened to those bad birds who bring you bad news. I have declared myself freely to you and if any explanations should be required from our town, send a man who can speak to us. If you think proper to give us any presents — and we can be convinced that they are given through friendship alone — we will accept them. As we intend to hold our council at the Huron village that is near the British, we may probably make them a visit; but should they offer us powder and the tomahawk, we will take the powder and refuse the tomahawk. I wish you, Brother, to consider everything I have said as true and that it is the sentiment of all the red people that listen to me."

When Tecumseh took his place with his people, Harrison came to his feet and began to speak, denying that the Indians were one nation, saying that the Miamis had acted in their own best interest in selling the lands and that Tecumseh was not justified in attempting to dictate whether or not the Miamis sold their own land. He turned to sit down and allow time for interpretation, but Tecumseh had understood his words. It became one of the rare occasions of his life when he lost his temper. He leaped to his feet and shouted loudly in the Shawnee tongue, gesticulating savagely all the while.

"You are a liar! Everything you have said is false! The Indians have been cheated and imposed upon by you and by the Seventeen Fires. Nothing you have said, before or now, at this council can be trusted. You lie and you cheat!"

His back still to Tecumseh, Harrison was shocked at the outburst and his eyes widened as he caught a glimpse of Winnemac trying to prime his pistol without being seen. General Gibson quickly ordered Lieutenant Jennings to bring up the guard and the young officer sprinted away. Immediately the Indians sprang to their feet in a semicircle behind Tecumseh with tomahawks drawn. Harrison jerked his sword from its scabbard, a captain drew his dagger and Winnemac cocked his pistol. Time seemed balanced on razor edge and the sudden silence was broken only by the pounding of feet as Lieutenant Jennings ran up with the guard, guns ready. Only the sudden lifting of Governor Harrison's hand in unspoken command stayed them.

"What did Tecumseh say, Johnny?" the governor asked. Spemica Lawba interpreted accurately and, as he did so, Harrison's lips tightened. He stared at Tecumseh bleakly. "I will have no further communication with you," he said coldly. "You and your people may go in safety, since you have come under my protection to the council fire, but you must leave immediately."

Tecumseh withdrew at once and camped just outside Vincennes. His temper had cooled and he was upset that he had lost control. That was exactly the sort of edge Harrison was looking for to bring war down upon them and it was too soon for such a war to begin; it would damage the grand plan that had been so many years in preparation. He would have to make amends. Much as he disliked doing so, in the morning he sent a messenger to summon Spemica Lawba to him. A short while later his nephew appeared before him and looked him full in the eyes.

"Uncle?" he said.

Tecumseh barely inclined his head in recognition. "I first tell you," he said, "your mother is well. She is with Tenskwatawa and Kumskaka in our Tippecanoe village."

"I am glad she is well," the Shawnee said. He was clad in white man's shirt and trousers, but he wore moccasins and there was a knife sheathed at his belt. He said no more, waiting.

"I wish you to carry to Governor Harrison my words of regret over what took place yesterday. Tell him I ask that the council be reconvened, that I may explain to him why I acted as I did. Assure him that no direct threat was intended against the whites attending the council and that such an action will not happen again."

"I will do as you ask." The Shawnee turned to leave.

"Spemica Lawba!" When the young man stopped and looked back, Tecumseh went on. "We miss you — your mother and your uncles. It is not too late for you and Pskipahcah Ouiskelotha to return to us."

A faint smile touched Spemica Lawba. "I thank you. Pskipahcah Ouiskelotha is in the village of our chief, Catahecassa, where she cares for our two sons. She remains loyal to her chief, as do I. He *is* my chief and I will remain loyal to his wishes. Only if he should agree to join you — or you should come back to us — can we again be together."

"Catahecassa will not. I cannot."

"Then it is sad," Spemica Lawba said softly.

"Yes," Tecumseh repeated, "it is sad." Abruptly he held out his hand and, surprised, his nephew gripped it with both of his, then turned and trotted back toward Grouseland. In less than an hour a different messenger brought word that Harrison had agreed to another council. This time when Tecumseh arrived he saw that all the whites were armed, but he made no comment about it. He faced Harrison and the governor spoke without preamble.

"Do you intend to prevent the survey of the land on the Wabash?"

"I am determined that the old boundary shall continue."

As the governor looked in their direction, one by one the other chiefs rose and stated their intention to support Tecumseh, that he was their leader and they had all united as Indians. As the last chief finished, Harrison addressed Tecumseh.

"Since you have been candid in acknowledging your intentions, I would be so, too. I will send the President a faithful statement of what you have said in disputing the claim to the lands in question. I will tell you what the President's answer is when I receive it. However, I am sure the President will never admit these lands to be the property of any other than those tribes who have occupied them since the white people came to America. Since we have come to title of them by fair purchase, then I am sure that these titles will be protected and supported by the sword. I hereby adjourn this council."

Now it was the governor who had second thoughts. He considered the two councils all night long and in the morning appeared alone at Tecumseh's camp, where the Shawnee received him with politeness. Again, it was Harrison who spoke first.

"Are your intentions really as you stated them in council?"

"They are," Tecumseh replied. "It would be only with great reluctance that I would make war upon the United States, since I have no complaint against them except their purchase of Indian lands. I am anxious to be at peace with the Americans and if you will prevail upon the President to give up the land in question and agree never again to make a treaty without the consent of all the tribes, I will be your faithful ally and assist you in all your wars against the British. I know that the British are always urging us to war for their own advantages; certainly not for the good of the red man. They urge us to attack the Americans as one might set a dog to fight. I would rather be a friend of the Seventeen Fires. However, if the President does not comply with my terms, I will be obliged to take the other side."

Harrison sighed. "I will tell the President of your propositions. But again I say, there is not the least probability that he will accede to your terms."

"Well," Tecumseh said, nodding gravely, "as the great white chief is to determine the matter, I hope the Great Spirit will put sense enough in his head to induce him to direct you to give up this land. It is true, he is so far off he will not be injured by the war; he may sit in the town and drink his wine, while you and I will have to fight it out."

And Harrison could only nod.

[*September 8, 1810 — Saturday*]

Only yesterday the orders had come from headquarters granting a nine-month leave of absence to Captain Nathan Heald and he had delayed not one instant in preparing to go. The six weeks he had been here at Fort Dearborn had gone rather quickly and, in all honesty, Chicago was not quite so bad as he had envisioned. Because of the great expanse of the sparkling blue Lake Michigan and the beautiful sand beaches, it was definitely a much prettier area than Fort Wayne. The people seemed nice enough, although he had tended to remain somewhat aloof from them, especially the Kinzies. By this time he had heard all the conflicting stories about the feud that had resulted in the breaking up of the Fort Dearborn command and he was resolved to maintain an even keel with the local populace.

Privately, he had drawn some conclusions of his own. The few days he had spent with Captain Whistler before the former commander here had left with his family for Detroit gave him the impression that John Whistler was a reasonably good officer, although perhaps a bit too impressed with his own rank and status; a proud man who, having once taken a stance, found it almost impossible to admit he might have made an error. Lieutenant Seth Thompson, who was still here, was essentially inoffensive, yet he was not, in Heald's opinion, top-grade officer material and the new commander was glad that Philip Ostrander had come from Fort Wayne with him to be his second-in-command here.

In the Indian Agent, Charles Jouett, he had found a quiet, competent individual whom he liked and felt he could trust. Quite the opposite was true of the surgeon's mate, Dr. John Cooper, who had been a chronic complainer and who inspired little confidence in himself among others; a man who could treat minor injuries well enough, but who was abysmally lacking in diagnostic abilities or the treatment of diseases. Factor Matthew Irwin had turned out to be a very likeable individual who reminded Heald of a friendly puppy eager for praise and approval and whose worst fault seemed to be too close a friendship with trader John Kinzie. The interpreter, Jack Lalime, remained an enigma. He was obviously skilled in his job and an asset to the fort, but his value was somewhat tainted by an abiding hatred of Kinzie. The troops were simply the troops; no better nor worse than enlisted men Heald had encountered wherever he had been assigned. A few had recently left upon expiration of their enlistments and the strength of Fort Dearborn at present, including officers and musicians, was sixty-seven men.

Now, his necessaries packed in saddle bags on his horse waiting outside and his compass in his pocket, Captain Heald made a final check of his headquarters office. He looked up as Lieutenant Ostrander rapped on the door and stepped in. The young officer bore a sober expression and Heald immediately divined the cause.

"Cooper couldn't help?"

The lieutenant shook his head. "No sir. The fever wouldn't break and he died a few minutes ago."

"Bloody shame," Captain Heald muttered. "All right, I'll stop by on my way out." He looked around and then back at Ostrander. "It's all yours. I hope things'll run smoothly for you."

The lieutenant came to attention and saluted. "Thank you, sir. Allow me to wish you the best, too — a safe journey and congratulations."

The two officers shook hands and Captain Heald left the building. Ten minutes later, having crossed the river, he tapped gently on the door to the Indian Agent's house. It was opened by Charles Jouett, his face drawn and a deep pain in his eyes. Beyond him the officer caught a glimpse of John Kinzie and heard the soft voice of Eleanor Kinzie consoling the weeping Susan Jouett. The Jouett's son, Charles Lalime Jouett, less than a year old, had died.

"I heard," Captain Heald said quietly. "I'm sorry. Please relay my respects and sympathies to Mrs. Jouett when you feel it proper to do so. I regret I will not be here for the services. As you know, I'm leaving. Lieutenant Ostrander has taken command."

"Thank you for dropping by, Captain. I'm sure Susan will appreciate your thoughtfulness. Good luck to you. We'll look forward to your return." They shook hands and Jouett reentered the house, closing the door softly behind him.

[*December 31, 1810 — Monday*]

The decade was ending and the killings had begun.

There were only a few at first — savage, unexpected attacks on the inhabitants of lonely cabins or isolated settlements scattered here and there on the frontier along the Mississippi and in the Illinois Territory, along the Ohio and in the Indiana Territory. They were omens of things to come, almost everyone was sure, and few were the whites who still considered the peace as permanent.

Tecumseh was in constant motion among the tribes, convinced now that war was inevitable. Chaubenee and Sauganash, usually working together, sometimes accompanied Tecumseh, but more often did not. They spread his doctrines far and Tecumseh's influence and prestige rose to unprecedented heights. The Shawnee leader wished no military alliance with the British, but he knew that irrespective of how many tribes backed him, the Indians could not stand against the whites unless substantially supplied. His visit to Matthew Elliott at Amherstburg a month ago had been for that purpose and he made his position very clear to the shrewd old Indian Agent.

"I have come here," Tecumseh told him, "with the intention of informing you that we have not forgotten — we can never forget! — what passed between you Englishmen and our ancestors; and also to let you know our present determination. The warriors have taken all the chiefs and turned their faces toward you, never again to look toward the Americans. And we, the warriors, now manage the affairs of our nation; and we sit at or near the borders where the contest will begin. You, Father, have nourished us and raised us up from childhood. We are now men and think ourselves capable of defending our country, in which case you have given us active assistance and always advice. We are now determined to defend it ourselves and, after raising you on your feet, leave you behind; but," he added firmly, "expecting you will push toward us what may be necessary to supply our wants."

With Sir James Craig terminally ill at Quebec, Elliott made a lavish distribution of gifts to the Indians — weapons, gunpowder, blankets, food and other supplies — and promised there would be plenty more to come for so long as he would need it.

In the Indiana Territory, William Henry Harrison was fidgeting. He saw statehood approaching in the distant future and it could not come soon enough for him. "I am," he confided to the President, "heartily tired of living in a territory." Ever since the confrontation with Tecumseh his concern had grown that the influential Shawnee would convert even more of the Indians to his beliefs and thus, despite the promises so sincerely given to the Indians at the Fort Wayne Treaty that it would be the last cession of land the United States would seek, he now asked President Madison for authority to begin negotiations with various chiefs to secure more land before it was too late. President Madison agreed and immediately the governor summoned Chief Main Poche of the Potawatomies to Vincennes to discuss a possible cession.

Main Poche sat and listened, his congenitally deformed hand in his lap, his quick mind assimilating and analyzing the supposed friendship and presents the governor was offering in exchange for lands. And the implication was clear: since Main Poche was a powerful war chief and had certain real authority to speak for his people, such a cession — and the payment therefor — could quickly be made without the bother of having to assemble a great many other Indians to engage in interminable councillings about it. When Main Poche hesitated, the governor misread him and made a mistake. In reminding Main Poche that Indians had, of late, made attacks on isolated settlers, Harrison overlooked the fact that in large measure those who had been attacked had violated the boundaries. The governor then compounded the error by subtly threatening the Potawatomi with the might of the army.

Main Poche stood and glowered at the Indiana governor for a long, uncomfortable interval. When he spoke, the menace in his words was not feigned.

"You think us fools! Can you truly believe we do not know to the last little bit what sort of games you play with us? Do you think we do not see how you try to divide us? You try to entice us with gifts to forget our people, our lands, our heritage. You astonish me with your talk! Whenever you do wrong, there is nothing said or done; but when we do anything, you immediately take us and tie us by the neck with a rope. You say, what will become of our women and children if there is war." His nostrils flared. "On the other hand, what will become of your women and children?" He started to walk away, then stopped and swung back for a final, very meaningful comment. "It is best," he grated, "to avoid war."

Throughout the continent sabers were rattling and even the Congress of the United States was not exempt. War hawks were gaining ground in the august chambers and there was a growing number who felt the United States would not be safe so long as the British were in America. In the War Mess, Felix Grundy declared himself quite willing to receive the Canadians as brothers and added, "We shall drive the British from our continent." His friend, Henry Clay, of Kentucky, seconded the concept, nodding sagely and saying, "The conquest of Canada is in our power." A few doves were raising their voices in protest, but their cooings were largely drowned out. Virtually everyone was sure war with the British — meaning, as well, war with the Indians — was coming.

One big question remained. *When?*

[*March 15, 1811 — Friday*]

The big marquee tent outside the gates of Fort Wayne rocked in the early evening dusk with the din erupting from within it. Lanterns had been hooked on the uprights and in their flickering light a dozen Potawatomi dancers leaped and pronked and howled to the accompaniment of rattles and drums. Behind them, blankets over their shoulders and clutched tightly in front, stood the remaining thirty warriors of the party, grinning widely and evidently enjoying the performance every bit as much as their guests.

The guests, seated in chairs on the opposite side of the tent from the Indians, were Captain Oscar James Rhea and his officers from Fort Wayne, along with their ladies, all of them enthralled by the cries and wild gyrations of the primitive ceremony. Too seldom was entertainment of this sort available to them. The party of Potawatomies had come here late in the afternoon and set up their camp only a short distance from the fort. Their leader, a powerfully built chief known as Grasshopper, had come to the fort at once, explained that they were en route to a council with the Miamis on the morrow and invited the officers to come out and witness the grand dance they were going to hold to celebrate that coming council. Since it was quite chilly and the skies were threatening, Captain Rhea had ordered the erection of this large tent so the elements would not interfere and deprive the officers and their ladies of this opportunity for entertainment.

The dance ended abruptly and almost at once another began — a solo — and the star performer was none other than the one the Americans knew as Grasshopper. Clad in leggins, barefoot and bare-chested, he leaped and shrieked, slashing the air with his tomahawk in one hand and knife in the other, dancing back and forth across the circle. It was the moment for which he planned and waited, the moment when he would give the prearranged signal.

At that moment a new figure entered the tent. He was clad in fringed buckskins, his cheeks streaked with alternating narrow bands of white and black paint, his red hair tied back tightly, tomahawk and skinning knife and horse pistol in his belt. His eyes flicked across the circle to the Indians. Immediately his lips tightened and he moved with quick grace to the front and came to a stop beside one of the wives seated there.

He was William Wells.

The woman he stopped beside was about twenty-three, attractive and with long blond hair cascading over her shoulders and almost to her waist. She was a little woman with a pixielike quality about her. She was Ruthy Edwards, daughter of Colonel Thomas Hunt of the Fifth Infantry. To her right was her husband, the Fort Wayne post surgeon, Dr. Abraham Edwards. Both were old friends of Wells, since it was William Wells who, as justice of the peace, had been officiating magistrate at their wedding on June 3, 1805, right here at Fort Wayne. Now, however, Wells neither spoke nor looked at them, his eyes on the dancer.

Grasshopper had seen Wells and his eyes narrowed. He danced closer and swept the tomahawk menacingly toward them. He stopped dancing, spoke a guttural sentence to Ruthy Edwards and then turned and began walking back toward his men. Instantly Wells opened his mouth and shrieked a war cry so unearthly and frightening that officers and wives started in surprise. He leaped high into the air and came down in the circle in a crouch, picked up the jawbone of a horse that one of the dancers had dropped and began a cavorting dance of his own that was even wilder than anything the Indians had yet done. After circling several times, punctuating his movements with a series of amazing leaps and cries, he stopped and brandished the jawbone in Grasshopper's direction.

"Peesotum!" he shouted.[183]

He leaped toward the chief and, continuing to brandish the jawbone, addressed him scathingly in the Potawatomi tongue. Peesotum — the Grasshopper — blanched and backed away until he stood amid his warriors. He waited until Wells had finished and contemptuously threw the jawbone to the ground at his feet before he raised the hand still holding the tomahawk — very slowly, so his meaning would not be misconstrued — and slipped the weapon into his waistband.

Wells gave him a final scornful look, turned his back and returned to where the whites, all on their feet now, stood staring in wonder. He spoke to the commander softly, but with an intensity that alarmed them all. "Captain Rhea, get these people into the fort. _Now!_"

They moved quickly and Wells, waiting until the last had moved outside, backed out of the tent and then sprinted after them, shouting for the gates to be closed as soon as they were inside. Captain Rhea, not sure what was going on, nevertheless had presence of mind enough to order the guard on the walls doubled and the entire fort placed on alert. In the darkness outside they could hear the Indians shrieking again as they moved away. Then, still with the officers and wives clustered behind him, he demanded an explanation from Wells.

"Where are your eyes, man?" Wells retorted angrily. "Didn't you even _look_ at those blanket-wrapped bastards against the far side of the tent? My God, every one of 'em had a rifle under his blanket. All they were waiting on was the signal from Peesotum to attack. If I hadn't jumped in as I did, you'd all have been dead in the next few minutes!"

"What . . . what'd you say to Grasshopper?" Rhea asked, the color having left his face.

"I had to beat him at his own game. I challenged him, personally, to a death fight right there, the jawbone against his tomahawk. It made no difference. I'd've killed him and he knew it. It shamed him before his people. It prevented his warriors from acting. My actions required a council on their part. They figured, as I knew they would, that I'd alerted the troops outside who were ready to rush in and cut them down when I gave the signal. Once the immediate danger was over, then I shamed Peesotum even more. I told him I had killed more Indians than I had killed whites when I fought beside Chief Michikiniqua — Little Turtle. I said that I had killed one that I now supposed was Peesotum's brother, because he looked just like Peesotum, except he was a lot less ugly and he was a better warrior than Peesotum was."

"Mr. Wells?" It was Ruthy Edwards. "What was it he said to me just before all that took place?"

"He said, 'The yellow hair you wear on your head at this moment, I will be wearing on my belt before the sun comes up again.' "

The woman's eyes widened and her mouth opened in a gasp. She swayed and Dr. Edwards put his arm about her, obviously angry that Wells had frightened her.

"What now?" Captain Rhea asked, in control of himself again.

Wells shrugged. "Probably be wise to keep the alert for a day or two, but I don't think they'll attack, now that we're on to them. Peesotum . . . that's another matter. He's lost face among his warriors. He can only regain his stature in one way." He smiled bleakly. "We are now final enemies."

"Final enemies?" Rhea frowned. "What's that mean?"

"It means from this time on, he won't rest until he kills me. Or I kill him."

[*May 22, 1811 — Wednesday*]

In the seven years that he had worked for John Kinzie, there had been little physical change in Jeffrey Nash. The huge, powerful black was still a quiet, highly dependable slave who did his job admirably, kept to himself, read and studied in his little quarters and never complained about his duties; not even when, over the past several years, they had increased substantially by his being assigned most of the heavier duties of the trader's principal house servants, Henry and Athena. The latter couple, who had faithfully served John Kinzie for many years, both suffered from a crippling arthritis that had progressively left them unable to do any but the lightest of chores.

At thirty-eight, Jeffrey Nash might not have changed noticeably in a physical sense, but he had improved his own mind considerably during these years. In a sense, he had been preparing for this day — the seventh anniversary of the day that he had signed a seven-year indenture to the Kinzie-Forsyth partnership.

Now, having cleaned himself and dressed in the best of his shabby clothing, he entered the trading post to sever his relationship with John Kinzie. He found the trader engaged in conversation with the United States Indian Factor, Matthew Irwin, and stood back deferentially until noticed.

". . . and although I don't know where it stands now," Irwin was saying, "at least the Congress is finally paying attention and that's a big first step. My own feeling is that if these troubles weren't occurring with the British and Indians, there'd probably be no trouble at all getting a canal bill passed. Mr. Porter has a very influential voice in the Congress and he's piqued their interest."

John Kinzie's eyes glinted. He removed the pipe from his mouth, blew out a little puff of blue-white smoke and said, "About time, too." He glanced over at Jeffrey Nash, murmured, "Excuse me," to Irwin and addressed his slave. "What is it, Jeffrey?"

"Beg pardon, Master John. I didn't mean to interrupt. I'd like to speak to you a moment when you have time."

The trader nodded and pointed his pipe stem toward a wooden chair near where Nash stood. "Certainly. Take a seat there and we'll be done here in a little while."

As the black did so, John Kinzie turned back to Irwin. The pair had been discussing the exciting news that Peter Buell Porter had been responsible for initiating. Porter, a resident of Buffalo, was a member of the United States House of Representatives. Intrigued with the potential of Buffalo as a port and trading center, he had been advocating — with considerable success — the construction of a waterway, to be called the Erie Canal, which would connect New York City and Buffalo. That such a canal was going to be built was certain. His foresight had then carried him to Chicago last summer, where he had become excited over the possibility of building a ship canal across the Chicago Portage. Chicago, he was convinced, was truly a gateway to empire, for the construction of such a canal, linking the Mississippi Valley to the Great Lakes would also become a link for shipping directly to New York, with Buffalo the key port in the eastern Great Lakes and Chicago the key port in the west. Construction of the two canals would mean that no longer would American shipping on the lakes be limited only to the lakes themselves. The vast resources of the far West, the Mississippi Valley and the Upper Great Lakes could be shipped directly to New York City without ever even leaving the territorial waters of the United States.

"However interested Congressman Porter is in the canal idea," Kinzie said to Irwin, renewing their conversation, "I doubt he'll be able to accomplish much until these Indian problems are settled. Between Harrison and Tecumseh, we've lost an awful lot of goodwill with them. We've both seen how our relationship, even here, has degenerated. The Indians are angry. And with justification. Harrison has *got* to stop gobbling up their land. He's just driving them into the arms of the British."

"And into Tecumseh's," Irwin added. "Last report I had from Harrison, he's just learned from William Wells that Tecumseh's got at least a thousand warriors gathered together now at that damned Prophet's Town on the Tippecanoe."

Kinzie nodded, then looked up sharply. "Wells? I thought he and Harrison had had a falling out and Wells was dismissed as Indian Agent."

"He was," Irwin agreed, "but evidently he's back in Harrison's good graces again. The word is that the governor's going to have him reappointed. Anyway, Harrison sent him to the Tippecanoe to look things over and Wells came back rather shaken by what he saw. Tecumseh's got a lot more strength than any of us really know, and not just on the Tippecanoe. He's been here twice that we know of and evidently he's been just about everywhere else twice, too. There's never been such agreement between the tribes and I'm not too sure even Harrison fully realizes what that could mean. Just imagine what it'd be like if fifty or a hundred thousand — or even more! — Indians all rose at once and said to the whites, 'Get out or die!' We've got big troubles ahead, John, and though they wouldn't agree in the East, right now I think the Indians are a greater potential threat to the United States than the British."

Kinzie nodded in agreement. "Wouldn't be surprised. Look what's been happening lately. Did you send your report on Tecumseh's activities in this area to the Secretary of War?"

"Yes. And Lalime just gave me a copy of a letter he wrote." He extracted a folded paper from his inner pocket and handed it to the trader. The letter, written by the Fort Dearborn Indian interpreter, was addressed to William Clark, now governor of the Missouri Territory. It referred to the recent attack by a party of Potawatomi warriors against Kaskaskia area settlements, almost within sight of the home of Illinois Governor Ninian Edwards. Kinzie read it swiftly:

Sir —

An Indian from the Peorias passed here yesterday and has given me information that the Indians about that place have been about the settlements of Kaskaskia and Vincennes, and have stolen from fifteen to twenty horses. It appears by the information given me that the principal actors are two brothers of the wife of Main Poc. He is residing at the Peorias, or a little above it, at a place they call Prairie du Corbeau. By the express going to Fort Wayne, I will communicate this to the agent. I presume, Sir, that you will communicate this to the Governor of Kaskaskia and to General Harrison. I am, Sir, with respect,

Y'r H'ble Servt.
J. Lalime

John Kinzie handed the letter back to the Indian factor with a non-committal sound. "I don't like any of it," he said. "We're getting quite a few people here at Chicago now and if there's going to be trouble, it's the civilians who'll bear the brunt. What's Ostrander have to say? Any word from Captain Heald about when he'll get back here? What about more military being assigned to the fort?"

Irwin sighed. "Nothing I've heard about increasing Fort Dearborn's garrison. Lieutenant Ostrander's itching to get back to Fort Wayne, especially now that your son-in-law's here, along with Ronan. Expects Captain Heald to be here in the next few weeks. Maybe when he takes over we'll get some reinforcements. Can't be soon enough to suit me."

Irwin's reference to John Kinzie's son-in-law was not technically accurate, but it was close enough. Lieutenant Linai T. Helm, who had married the trader's stepdaughter, Margaret McKillip, had finally received the transfer he'd requested and he and Margaret had recently moved back to Chicago from Detroit. Part of the reason for his assignment had been the sudden death of Lieutenant Seth Thompson from a fever. Helm was now second-in-command — a role he would continue to Captain Nathan Heald when the commander returned from his extended leave and freed Ostrander to return to Fort Wayne. Ronan was another newly arrived officer — Ensign George Ronan — freshly promoted and assigned here from his cadetship at West Point. A cheerful, engaging young man, Ensign Ronan was very intellectual and already well liked by practically everyone except Eleanor Kinzie. She objected to the penetrating theological questions he raised and considered him an atheist. The intellectual discussions the young officer engaged in on a wide variety of subjects and especially with the new surgeon's mate, Dr. Isaac van Voorhis, had become the talk of both Fort Dearborn and the Chicago community.

As his predecessors had been, Van Voorhis was a very young man — only twenty. Intense, introspective and also highly intelligent, he and George Ronan had quickly become close friends. Again, the only one in Chicago who seemed not to like him was Eleanor Kinzie, and for the same reason — that he questioned the Gospel and dared to discuss his doubts openly with Ronan. Van Voorhis had arrived here last December to succeed Dr. John Cooper. The latter had finally resigned in disgust over working for the government. His depression over the breakup of the Whistler faction and the removal of his privilege to suttle to the garrison had never lifted. As soon as Van Voorhis had arrived to relieve him, he left Chicago permanently to establish a private practice in Poughkeepsie, leaving behind muttered imprecations about "that damned Kinzie family" and clutching in his hand his treasured copy of William Shenstone's *Poems*, which had been a parting gift from Captain John Whistler some months before.[184]

The peculiar thing about Van Voorhis being assigned here was not only that he was the same age as the young physician he was replacing, he and Dr. Cooper had been boyhood friends in Fishkill, New York, and classmates at the Fishkill Academy. The coincidence had created some concern among the Chicago residents that Van Voorhis would be cut from the same cloth as Cooper, but it hadn't worked out that way at all. Van Voorhis, son of a respected old Dutch family of Fishkill, was not interested in engaging in feuds with or against anyone. He had quickly gained stature in John Kinzie's estimation by spurning — as did Ensign Ronan — the attempts by Jack Lalime to keep the old feud fires burning.

"Well," Matthew Irwin said, standing and repocketing the letter, "I'd better get going. Give my regards to Eleanor and the children. I'll see you later."

Jeffrey Nash stood as they did and was still standing when John Kinzie returned from showing the Indian Factor out. The trader cocked an eyebrow and smiled faintly.

"Now, what's on your mind, Jeffrey?"

"Today's the day, Master John," the black said, his own smile a bit strained.

"The day? What day? I don't understand."

"The day my indenture to you ends, Mr. Kinzie." It was the first time he had ever addressed the trader as anything but Master John. "Seven years ago today we signed it. Today I'm a free man!" He was conscious of his own copy of the indenture papers in his inner coat pocket.

John Kinzie's smile vanished and his brows drew together. "Just what the hell are you talking about?" he demanded. "You know damned well we found out later there was no need for indenture papers to have been filled out in the first place."

"Begging your pardon, Mr. Kinzie, but the indenture papers *were* legally filled out and signed by us. The Ordinance of 1787 makes the owning of slaves in this territory illegal."

A hot anger touched the trader and he retorted sharply. "Ordinance be damned!" he growled. "No one pays any attention to that. I bought you as a slave in Detroit and you're still my slave. Nothing's changed. Nothing at all. Now get out of here and get back to work."

Nash hesitated, then meekly said, "Yes, sir, Master John," and walked out, closing the door softly behind him. He returned to his own small quarters, picked up his meager belongings wrapped in a large, ratty-looking bearskin pouch and left the room without looking back. He walked to the riverbank and got into the one-man bark canoe that had been a gift to him over a year ago from Chief Black Partridge for a favor he had done.

Jeffrey Nash pushed off from shore and paddled swiftly upstream and out of sight up the South Branch of the Chicago River, heading for the portage that would take him to the Illinois River system and then down the Mississippi to New Orleans and the wife and child he had not seen in over seven years. Irrespective of what anyone said, Jeffrey Nash now considered himself a free man and he meant to stay that way.

[*May 29, 1811 — Wednesday*]

Averaging about fifty miles per day, the three riders had completed the hazardous journey from Louisville to Chicago in six days. For the man it was no great feat, for he was accustomed to long rides on horseback, although the possibility that they might be discovered by marauding Indians had weighed heavily upon him throughout the journey. For the remarkably attractive young woman he had married on the day of their departure, the ride was a little more difficult, though she allowed little of the strain to show and her natural ebullience eased the difficulties for all. For the twenty-five-year-old black woman who rode with them, now in the sixth month of her first pregnancy and her belly lately having begun to swell noticeably, it was most difficult of all, but no word of complaint left her.

The three were Captain Nathan R. Heald and his bride, Rebekah, and the bride's devoted slave, Cicely, who had been her mistress's handmaiden for almost fifteen years. The journey had been eased in part by the quality of the horses they rode, for these were not merely ordinary riding horses. The three steeds, all geldings, were fine thoroughbreds from the herd of Colonel Samuel Wells, who raised some of the best horses in all Kentucky. A fourth horse, being used as a pack animal, was itself a better than average saddle horse which, for the first three days of the trip, was cantankerous and troublesome, as if distinctly miffed at having to undergo the indignity of being put to work at a job more fitting to a mule.

Ten days ago, Nathan Heald had arrived at Louisville for the nearly unbearably joyful reunion with his love, Rebekah Wells. His long trip by horseback from Chicago to New England last fall had been essentially uneventful, as had been his prolonged stay with his parents. Twice he had delayed his departure from them; they were elderly and, though no one put it into words, the knowledge was there that this was quite possibly the last time they would ever meet. The eventual parting had been painful and through their tears they had sent their love and good wishes to the young woman they had never met who was to become their daughter-in-law, and they loaded him down with presents for her and for him. Among these was, for him, a beautiful, gracefully curved saber with engraved silver guard just in front of the hilt, the grip of wonderfully carved ebony wood and the curved finger guards of tempered steel no less in quality than the blade itself. And among the gifts for Rebekah was an exquisite tortoise-shell comb, the top portion carved to represent the head of an eagle, with brightly polished ornamentation to represent the eyes and nostrils and silver strips rimming the edge of the proudly curved beak. The ten teeth of the comb were five inches long for firm seating when holding thick lovely hair swept up in the pompadour fashion of the day.

He had planned to spend a couple of weeks in Louisville prior to the wedding, enjoying a period of closeness with Rebekah and renewing his acquaintance with her family, but it hadn't worked out that way. On the ride southwestward from New England, when he was somewhere in the wilds of Pennsylvania, the horse he rode had slipped on a bank of shale, pitching him off into a bush. The horse fell heavily, rolling over and over down into a wooded ravine, dragging the packhorse after it. He had scrambled to the bottom and found them lying there, screaming and writhing in the pain of their broken legs, and he had had to destroy them both. Much of what he was bringing with him he had to leave behind then, hiding it in a cache he made in a huge hollow log, planning one day to come back for it if possible.[185] He had walked, then, for a long distance, carrying what he thought he could manage but gradually discarding the heavier items until he was left with very little. At last he had reached a well-used trail and subsequently purchased a worn-down old nag from a settler no longer able to ride. He continued westward until finally that horse simply rolled its eyes and died beneath him a few miles from Pittsburgh. He had walked the remaining distance into Pittsburgh and found passage on a broad-horn heading for Kentucky, arriving at the home of Samuel Wells with only three days remaining before he must begin his journey to Chicago to resume command of Fort Dearborn.

Despite the rush, the wedding had gone well, though there was a little disappointment that the bride's uncle, Captain William Wells, had been unable to attend. At the moment he was very busy performing tasks for William Henry Harrison in view of the rapidly degenerating Indian situation. In addition to the three fine thoroughbreds and one extra horse, Colonel Samuel Wells had also given them a set of solid silver, long-handled tablespoons and a similar silver soup ladle, each piece engraved with the initials N.R.H. He also presented to his daughter a lock of his own graying hair in a polished silver locket engraved with the initials S.W. Plain gold bands exchanged in the ceremony were now on their ring fingers, Rebekah having moved to her right hand the gold ring with the delicate green peridot that had been given to her by her father on her eighteenth birthday; a ring with the initials R.W. engraved on the inside.

They left on their journey the day of the wedding — May 23 — and at first had no intention of taking Cicely along with them, but the black woman begged so piteously that she was allowed to come and continue to serve her mistress. Rebekah had delicately mentioned the hardship of such a trip for Cicely in view of her condition, but Cicely sloughed aside the concerns of her mistress. Unmarried, Cicely had no ties in Louisville and she was quite prepared for whatever hardships might be entailed. She did not mention who was the father of her unborn child and it was considered too delicate a matter to question her about.

Now, the exhausting trip ending, Rebekah exclaimed in delight over the aspect of Chicago and Fort Dearborn spread out before them. The day before they had been overtaken and passed by an express rider carrying dispatches from Vincennes to Chicago but, despite this, they were unprepared for the extravagant welcome that awaited them. Alerted by the dispatch rider, the entire Fort Dearborn garrison had turned out to receive the commanding officer and his bride with the highest honors, the men in their finest uniforms, the officers proudly astride their mounts, sabers raised in salute, the fifers and drummers playing a lively air, the fort's artillery booming three times in greeting. Most of the Chicago settlers were there as well, although a notable exception was John Kinzie, who was presently in the courts of New Orleans, engaged in a legal battle to recover possession of his former slave, Jeffrey Nash. But Eleanor Kinzie was on hand along with their children, plus the whole Ouilmette family, Charles Lee and his wife, son and daughter, and the Russells, the Jouetts, the Lalimes and the Irwins and many others. Even Liberty White had paddled in from the Lee farm to be on hand for the welcome. It was a day of festivity for Chicago, the long tables loaded with a great spread of fresh vegetables and fruits and excellent cuts of meat — pork, venison and beef, with plenty of fowl, both wild and domestic.

Indians were on hand, too — a welcoming cluster of men, women and children who had arrived with their chief, Black Partridge, to greet the returning white chief of the fort and his new bride. The Potawatomies were delighted when, with her limited vocabulary in the Miami and Potawatomi tongues, she spoke to them in their own language. And there were "tame" Indians to meet as well — Nokenoqua, the pleasant-faced, somewhat chunky wife of the fort's half-breed interpreter, Jack Lalime, and their little son, named after his father; Archange, the Potawatomi half-breed wife of Antoine Ouilmette, and her sister, Sheshi, usually called Susan, who was married to French trader Pierre Buison; the half-breed Chechepinqua, called Alexander Robinson, who was working for John Kinzie as a clerk. She met the family of Jean Baptiste Mirandeau, a trader from Milwaukee who had just moved to Chicago. Mirandeau and his Ottawa wife and their five children had moved into a cabin southwest of the fort. Their eldest daughter, a thirteen-year-old named Madeline, had just moved into the Lalime home where she was being employed as housekeeper.[186]

Rebekah was very honored and pleased with everything about Chicago and she all but bubbled with her enthusiasm. "I just love it all!" she exclaimed to her husband. "It's so bright and cheerful and so . . . so *wild!* Wild lake, wild prairies, wild town, wild Indians, everything wild and I love it."

"And that," her husband replied, putting an arm about her waist and hugging her to him, "is because you're on the wild order yourself. You always have been."

Nice though their reception was, there were some ominous clouds overhanging the fort. As soon as Nathan had shown his wife and her slave into the new quarters within the fort and Rebekah and Cicely had busied themselves with unpacking and setting up their new household, he went directly to the fort commander's headquarters room to confer with Lieutenant Ostrander.

The younger officer came to attention and saluted as Captain Heald entered, then grinned and shook hands with him. "Let me say again, sir," he said, "it's good to have you back. Did you wish to take a day or so to get reacclimated before assuming command again?"

"No, thank you, Lieutenant. You're relieved of the responsibility as of this moment. If there's any brandy in the desk, let's each have a bit while you brief me on the situation here and elsewhere."

Philip Ostrander bobbed his head and immediately brought out a nearly full bottle of good French brandy and two glasses. As he poured, Captain Heald took a seat behind the desk and then accepted with thanks the drink his lieutenant handed him. He held it up and smiled.

"Cheers."

"And good health," the lieutenant added, acknowledging the toast and taking a seat in the hardbacked chair to one side. Then they got down to business. The younger officer quickly informed his commander of such occurrences since his departure as the arrival of Dr. Van Voorhis to replace Dr. Cooper, and Lieutenant Linai T. Helm as second-in-command, replacing Lieutenant Thompson, who had died; plus the arrival of Ensign George Ronan. Then came the bad news. Although the situation at Chicago remained relatively calm, that was hardly the case in practically all other quarters. Attacks on outlying settlements and isolated cabins were becoming very frequent: houses were burned, livestock slaughtered, women kidnapped and men killed and scalped. Indians of various tribes were involved, but most of the depredations were being caused by the Sacs to the west, along the Mississippi basin, and the Potawatomies elsewhere in the Illinois and Indiana Territories. On those infrequent occasions when the marauders were captured or killed, they were found to be armed with new British rifles and good, tempered-steel tomahawks manufactured in England.

"There's something big in the wind, sir," Ostrander concluded. "The Indians here — everywhere, in fact — seem to be biding their time for a general uprising. Rumor has it that there's going to be some kind of a signal given before the end of the year and when it comes, all the Indians, even the ones we consider our closest friends, are going to rise and attack. All over. Simultaneously."

Captain Nathan Heald raised an eyebrow and there was the slightest trace of a smile on his lips. "I don't mean to make light of what you're saying, Lieutenant," he said, making light of what the lieutenant was saying, "but one has to take such rumors with a good dose of salts. That's a very old rumor that's been going the rounds ever since I was stationed at Detroit, before even taking command of Fort Wayne. No one seems to question what kind of a signal it could be that could reach all the Indians at once so they could rise simultaneously to do whatever they're supposed to be planning. No," he shook his head, "I think we have a problem of unrest, to be sure, but chances of any kind of general uprising are, I suspect, merely scare stories."

"You're probably right, sir. I hope so."

"Orders call for you to repair to Fort Wayne at once," the commanding officer said, "but if you wish to take a few days to just relax a bit before leaving, you're welcome to do so."

"No, sir!" The answer was immediate. "I have to admit I've been anxious to get back and if you have nothing slated for me here, I'd like to leave as soon as possible."

"Whatever you wish. Would you mind holding off until tomorrow morning, so I can get some dispatches prepared for you to take along for relay to Vincennes, Detroit and Washington?"

"Certainly, sir. I'll come by first thing in the morning for them." He hesitated, then added, "If I may take the liberty of saying so, sir, your wife seems to be a very fine woman. My sincere congratulations on your marriage."

"She is, indeed, a fine woman, Lieutenant. Thank you. I'll see you in the morning." It was a dismissal.

Lieutenant Philip Ostrander saluted, turned on his heel and left the room.[187]

[*August 31, 1811 — Sunday*]

Young Dr. Isaac van Voorhis was not a religious man, yet neither was he irreligious in that he made light of the beliefs of others. He would never do that. Yet, it was always difficult for him to experience any sort of exalted feeling in church or chapel . . . or prayer group. On Sunday mornings like this, when the garrison prayer group met, he was assiduous in avoiding being included. Sunday mornings became, therefore, the times when he would walk and observe and absorb the sensations of his surroundings. In so doing today, he stood overlooking the whole span of the Chicago area from a slight prominence and, in a way, he saw much of the potential for glory here that its first prominent settler, Jean Baptiste Point du Sable, had detected but could not articulate. Van Voorhis, however, was a very articulate person and when now he returned to his quarters, he expressed this feeling well in a letter to a friend:

. . . In my solitary walks I contemplate what a great and powerful republic will yet arise in this new world. Here, I say, will be the seat of millions yet unborn; here, the asylum of oppressed millions yet to come. How composedly I would die could I be resuscitated at that bright era of American greatness — an era which I hope will announce the tidings of death to fell superstition and dread tyranny. . . .

[September 26, 1811 — Thursday]

William Henry Harrison, astride his huge black gelding, cantered past the nine hundred cheering troops and took his place at their head. If any doubts assailed him in respect to what he was putting into motion on this day, he gave no outward sign of it, though he was keenly aware that his entire future, both military and political, could well rest on the outcome of this expedition.

The events of the past summer on the Northwestern frontier had all contributed to this moment. The killings, the unrest, the panic sweeping like a prairie fire through the settlements, the councils with various Indians, including Tecumseh — all these and more had been closely analyzed, fitted together in the intricate pattern until now the parts had formed a whole. That whole, to Harrison, so clearly dictated what course of action must be followed, that there was no question he would do so. It was all a matter of timing, of correctly evaluating the enemy. If he had misjudged, if his timing were off, his career would be over. If, on the other hand, his conclusions were correct, what he had thus far accomplished in his career would be but a paltry first step to what lay ahead.

The bits and pieces that had brought him here and now to this critical juncture were diverse. The sharp rise of altercations between Indians and whites throughout the frontier had begun in earnest in the spring. Whites attacked Indians and Indians attacked whites and no one knew for sure what the provocation had been. In Vincennes, an Indian on an entirely peaceful visit was shot and killed by an Italian innkeeper without just cause. He was arrested and tried for murder, but so great was the antipathy of the settlers for the Indians that the jury acquitted the man practically without deliberation. On the west bank of the Mississippi in Missouri, a party of whites under a Captain Cole had been attacked and killed. Near Vincennes, two Potawatomi warriors killed two white men who, without provocation, had shot and seriously wounded two Indians. In Illinois, too close for comfort to the seat of the Illinois territorial government, a family named Cox had been attacked on Shoal Creek, the son of the family, Elijah, slain, and the daughter, Rebecca, kidnapped and fortunately rescued after being wounded in the hip. At Detroit, an Indian inspecting a rifle accidentally discharged it. The ball struck and killed a white resident. It was very clearly an accident, but the Indian was arrested and tried for murder . . . and executed. Just northeast of St. Louis, again in the Illinois Territory, two settlers named Ellis and Price were attacked while working in a cornfield. Price was killed and Ellis wounded. Settlers were becoming trigger-happy and shooting at wholly innocuous Indians and some were killed. Here and there among the Indians who were captured or killed were some found to be bearing new weapons supplied by the British. The Indians captured were questioned and gave up little information, but the little bits that they did reveal, when all considered together, brought a pattern into focus. There were still questions, to be sure, but the portent of the assimilated data was devastating. The tribes were being primed for a massive uprising so gigantic in its scope that it was staggering to contemplate. And it all hinged on a pair of Shawnee brothers.

Tecumseh and Tenskwatawa, The Prophet.

The plan, it seemed, was for Tecumseh to provide the tribes with a great sign. That sign, whatever it was, according to the bundles of red sticks the chiefs had received from Tecumseh, would take place in mid-December. When and if it occurred, tribes everywhere east of the Rocky Mountains and from the Gulf of Mexico to the Canadian wilds, would pick up their weapons and converge at the Tippecanoe village. Other whites who heard of this simply scoffed, laughing it off as ridiculous. Harrison was not among them. Ever since the successful prediction of the solar eclipse by The Prophet — a prediction Tecumseh had given to Tenskwatawa to make public, the governor was now convinced — he had studied other predictions that had been made by the Shawnee and was stunned by the virtually one hundred percent accuracy. Harrison had no idea what sort of "great sign" Tecumseh was planning to conjure up for the uprising, but he did not discount it. What he had to do, he realized, was to so badly shake the faith of the tribes in Tecumseh that when — or if — such a sign actually did come, they would not rise to follow.

The Prophet, Harrison was convinced, was nothing more than a megalomanic puppet who only occasionally held the reins of power while Tecumseh and his disciples were out convincing more tribes to convert to the "one Indian nation" ideal. If the village at Tippecanoe could be attacked, if the relatively few amalgamated Indians presently there could be enticed into battle — and defeated — it would go far toward demolishing Tecumseh's influence. But Tecumseh, Harrison knew now, was far too shrewd to be maneuvered into such a position. Tenskwatawa, however, was not. Thus, whatever was to be done had to be done while Tecumseh was absent . . . and before December.

And so, in mid-July, Harrison had engaged in another talk with Tecumseh, his senses attuned to anything that might provide him with a plan of action. And Tecumseh himself had inadvertently provided it. The council had gone badly. It helped matters not at all when Harrison, at the outset, insulted Tecumseh by referring immediately to the murders of Illinois settlers, implying that Tecumseh was vaguely responsible, and then going on in almost the same breath to complain bitterly about the size of the party Tecumseh had brought with him for this meeting instead of the "minimal number" Harrison had requested. Actually, Tecumseh's party of one hundred eighty men was distinctly "minimal" for a council of such importance, where a retinue of upwards of five hundred warriors would have been the more procedural order of things. In declaring that Tecumseh had brought "far too many" with him, Harrison had wounded the Shawnee's self-respect and dignity.

Ignoring the ominous murmurings from the assembled red men and the tightening of Tecumseh's expression, the Indiana territorial governor moved right along, promising to listen to whatever Tecumseh or other chiefs might have to say about the Wabash land purchase, but he would not negotiate about it since the matter was now in the hands of the President. He then brought up the recent matter that had so irked him — the confiscation by Tenskwatawa of a shipment of salt he had sent upriver, about which he had written in controlled fury to William Clark at St. Louis on June 19:

. . . but the most daring piece of insolence that they have yet ventured upon is that of seizing the salt destined for the tribes above them. The piroque I sent up with it returned last evening and the man who had charge of her reports that he stopped at the Prophet's village and offered him three barrels of salt intended for him, and the whole was then taken from him. If our government will submit to this insolence, it will be the means of making all the tribes treat us with contempt.

Now Harrison demanded an explanation of why the salt had been confiscated. Tecumseh, still rankled by the insults he had received already at the governor's council, replied with some degree of asperity.

"The salt that was taken was taken in my absence, just as the salt that was refused in the previous year was refused in my absence. It seems to me that it is impossible to please the governor. Last year you were angry because the salt was refused and this year you are just as much displeased because it was taken!"

A wave of anger gripped Harrison at that and, unwilling to continue in a state of mind that would make him prone to impulsiveness or error, he peremptorily adjourned the meeting until the following day. It was a bad beginning and things improved not at all the next day when the chief of the Weas, Wapawawqua — White Loon — opened with a speech clearly implying that great deceit had been employed by Harrison in the many treaties he had concluded with various Indian groups.

The governor's eyes narrowed and smoldered, but when the Wea chief finished and sat down, Harrison had regained his control and deliberately dealt Wawpawawqua a significant insult by wholly ignoring what the chief had said and going on to a different subject. Tension increased substantially and guards on both sides prepared for the eruption that now seemed inevitable. Harrison demanded of Tecumseh the surrender for trial in the white man's court of the two Potawatomi warriors who had recently killed the two white men near Vincennes. He added that if Tecumseh did this, it would show he was sincere in his profession of friendship for the United States.

"I will not deliver them up to you," Tecumseh replied. "You say the whites who died were murdered, but they were not; they were executed and brought their fate upon themselves by shooting two Wea Indians without provocation." The Shawnee paused and then went on. "I have taken great pains to unite the tribes under me and I find the whites becoming alarmed at this. Why should it be so? Has not the United States itself set the example for us by establishing a union of Seventeen Fires? We do not complain of this; why, then, should the whites feel justified in complaining when we unite? Is it not as fair for one as it is for the other?"

Again Tecumseh paused, weary of this council which was going nowhere and accomplishing nothing. He decided to conclude it and it was in his final words that he had inadvertently given William Henry Harrison the very key that the governor had been hoping for. It was a tribute to the governor's control that no hint of the surge of exultation he experienced was visible in his expression.

"We have said enough here," Tecumseh went on. "You yourself have said the heart of the problem between us is in the hands of your President. There is, then, no further point in speaking with you. Soon after this council is concluded, I will leave this country to visit the tribes to the south and ask them to become a part of our Indian nation. A great number of Indians will be coming back to settle on the Tippecanoe with us. We will make them welcome. But the land you falsely purchased on the Wabash is our finest hunting ground and we will need it to secure food for these people." Tecumseh seemed suddenly to realize his error and sought to correct it. "I hope," he added, a note of sternness strong in his voice, "that nothing will be done by the whites toward settling this hunting ground before my return next spring. At that time, when our union is complete, then I will be ready to visit the President and settle all difficulties with him."

To mask his elation, Harrison matched sternness with sternness. He pointed to the newly risen moon and his voice was harsh. "The moon you see would sooner fall to the ground than the President would suffer his people to be murdered with impunity, and I will put petticoats on my soldiers sooner than give up a country I have bought fairly from its true owners!"

The Indians under Tecumseh departed immediately after that, ascending the Wabash toward their Tippecanoe village. Harrison lost no time returning to his own quarters to consider in private the slip Tecumseh had made. The key was Tecumseh's revelation that he was soon to go away to the south again. Harrison was positive that his comment a short time after that to the effect that he would return "next spring" had been inserted strictly as a false trail for the purpose of building a sense of complacency in the whites, leading them to believe they had until next spring to prepare for whatever would occur. He knew that couldn't be true; the red sticks Tecumseh had given to the various chiefs all indicated that the sign would come in December and Tecumseh would certainly not be absent from Tippecanoe then.

Immediately Harrison had sent out spies to watch Tecumseh's moves and report to him the moment the Shawnee left for the south. Prior to this the governor had been assembling and preparing his army. At his request, the President had last May ordered Colonel Charles Boyd at Fort Pitt to take his United States Fourth Regiment to Vincennes and place them and himself under Harrison's command. Since then his army's strength had been augmented by the arrival of sixty-five seasoned Indian fighters — well-mounted volunteers from Kentucky. In late July the spies he had sent out returned with their report: Tecumseh had just departed for the south, accompanied by his secretary and aide, Billy Caldwell — Sauganash — and a select number of chiefs and warriors. As usual, he had left Tenskwatawa behind in charge of the Tippecanoe village, but this time he had also left Chaubenee and Wasegoboah to oversee Tenskwatawa's activities and make sure he made no mistakes.

It was then that William Henry Harrison launched his own final preparations for this day. He had just received a letter from Secretary of War Eustis in which the secretary relayed the President's concern about a possible outbreak of Indian war. Eustis had written:

I have been particularly instructed by the President to communicate to your excellency his earnest desire that peace may, if possible, be preserved among the Indians, and that to this end every proper measure be adopted.

But this is not intended . . . that the banditti under the Prophet should not be attacked and vanquished, provided such a measure should be rendered absolutely necessary.

Harrison replied immediately, assuring the secretary that he would obey both the letter and intent of the instructions and that only if there were justification for such an act would he march against the Indians at Tippecanoe. In that same letter of August 7, he wrote of Tecumseh with the admiration due an accomplished and very formidable enemy:

. . . The implicit obedience and respect which the followers of Tecumseh pay to him is really astonishing and more than any other circumstance bespeaks him one of those uncommon geniuses which spring up occasionally to produce revolutions and overturn the established order of things. If it were not for the vicinity of the United States, he would perhaps be the founder of an Empire that would rival in glory that of Mexico or Peru. No difficulties deter him. His activity and industry supply the want of letters. For four years he has been in constant motion. You see him today on the Wabash and in a short time you hear of him on the shores of Lake Erie, or Michigan, or the banks of the Mississippi, and wherever he goes he makes an impression favourable to his purpose. He is now upon the last round to put a finishing stroke to his work. I hope, however, before his return, that that part of the fabric which he considered complete will be demolished and even its foundations rooted up.

Then had come the period of waiting — waiting for something, *anything*, to be done by Tenskwatawa which would provide justification for Harrison putting his army into motion up the Wabash beyond the territory of the whites, beyond the territory under dispute and into the territory of the Indians. And Tenskwatawa, fool that he was, had very soon provided that justification. The Prophet had ordered a small party of warriors from the Tippecanoe village to descend the Wabash and steal horses from the settlements. They had done so and, instantly, Harrison's own grand plan was activated. Most encouraging of all had been the report of his spies that many hundreds of the estimated two thousand Indians who had been at that village had gone to their homes to visit briefly in their leader's absence, but planning to be back in force at Tecumseh's return. The spies estimated that at this time only three hundred fifty warriors remained at the Tippecanoe village.

So now, standing high in his stirrups at the head of his troops, William Henry Harrison gave the signal that, one way or another, would affect his entire future and perhaps even that of the United States, and the army of nine hundred began to move up the Wabash.

[*October 1, 1811 — Tuesday*]

"We'll miss you here, Charles," John Kinzie said, still gripping Jouett's hand. "Both you and Susan."

The former United States Indian Agent — former, as of five o'clock yesterday evening — made a small sound of agreement. "We'll miss you and Eleanor and the children, too. But," he shrugged, "Susan's tired of living so far from all society and I really can't blame her." His eyes moved across the rude settlement that was Chicago and then back to his friend. "No offense meant to you, of course, but there's really very little of a cultural nature to be enjoyed here. I have to agree with young Van Voorhis, one day it'll come, but that day's a long distance in the future and we'd rather not wait."

"Can Captain Heald handle your job well enough, in addition to his own?" John was referring to the fact that, under orders from Washington, the Fort Dearborn commander was to take over the Indian department in Chicago when the resignation of Jouett became effective at the end of September and to act as agent until another should be assigned in Jouett's place.

"Oh, I think he'll handle it adequately enough," Charles Jouett replied, "although I can't really say I'm in favor of a military commander also serving as Indian Agent. They tend to be mutually exclusive and I'm certain the Indians aren't going to care for it." He shrugged again.

John Kinzie agreed, not caring at all for the situation and wondering what kind of problems might be in store. He had never become very close to Nathan Heald, though there was no antagonism between them save for that which Jack Lalime continued trying to promote — and which, by and large, the post commander had chosen to ignore. Yet, there was a disturbing ignorance of the Indian mentality about Nathan Heald that bothered the trader; an ignorance which, under certain circumstances, might cause serious problems.

Actually, in these months since Captain Heald had returned and resumed command, he'd had little contact with the man. Much of the time Kinzie himself had been gone, trying to resolve the court case involving Jeffrey Nash. Prior to that he'd had somewhat more contact with the captain's lady than with the commanding officer himself. Because of the crippling arthritis that was making life so difficult for his own Athena, he'd talked it over with Eleanor and they had agreed it might be a good idea to see if Rebekah Heald would sell them her slave, Cicely. But the new first lady of the fort had refused even to consider selling the devoted Cicely. Although Eleanor Kinzie said she didn't care, that Rebekah Heald could certainly suit herself in the matter, a certain coolness had nevertheless developed between them since the refusal. And Cicely, during John

Kinzie's absence south, had given birth to a son, whom she had named Benjamin.

For his own part, John Kinzie was determined not to engage in another dispute with the military if it could be at all avoided and so, before leaving for New Orleans with Tom Forsyth, he had suggested to Eleanor that she keep muffled whatever resentment she might feel and that he would endeavor to find her another girl while in the South. Now, having arrived back in Chicago only the day before yesterday, he told Eleanor that not only had he not been able to procure a new slave for her down South, things had not gone well there in court. Though he still had a large, powerful slave named Black Jim for heavy work, Kinzie was loath to let Jeffrey Nash just walk away as he had done. So, Kinzie and his half brother had traced Jeffrey to New Orleans and, upon arrival there, they had instituted a legal suit to recover Nash as their property. Reunited with his own family, Jeffrey Nash had no intention of leaving them or of losing his freeman status and he countersued. The local court upheld Nash and so it was appealed to the Supreme Court of Louisiana. The claimants produced their Detroit bill of sale of September 5, 1803, as proof of ownership. The defendant immediately produced his copy of the Bill of Indenture signed by himself and the claimants. The Court gave short shrift to either document. Instead, they judged that the claimants' pretended right of property in Jeffrey Nash was invalid due to the Ordinance of 1787 which prohibited slavery in the Northwest Territory except as punishment for a crime, upon due conviction. So, in a decision that set New Orleans on its ear, the Supreme Court of Louisiana had validated the conduct of Jeffrey Nash in running away from his slavery and conclusively decided him to be a free man.

Snapping out of his momentary reverie, John Kinzie now smiled at Jouett. "You're heading for Kentucky?"

"Yes. Mercer County. Somewhere in the area of Harrodsburg."

"Good luck, then. Keep your hair on, hear?"

Charles Jouett grinned. "Oh, I intend to. I've grown rather fond of it. Thanks for the good wishes. Who knows, maybe one day Susan and I will come back here. Goodbye."[188]

John Kinzie watched him walk away with his distinctive long strides. The admonition to keep his hair on was a common one in times past and gaining in popularity again. It was not lightly given. More and more reports of Indian trouble had been coming in and scalpings were no longer something vaguely remembered from the Indian War. They were a here-and-now peril and though none had yet occurred anywhere close to Chicago, they were happening with unsettling frequency elsewhere. The trader was quite well aware of the cause and laid the blame where it belonged — primarily in the lap of William Henry Harrison and his unconscionable greed for acquiring Indian lands, and secondarily in the lap of the British traders who were fomenting antagonism against the Americans all over the frontier. His own business at distant posts had fallen off sharply because of it. He sighed, wondering where it would all end, and turned back toward his trading post.

At this moment, across the river in Fort Dearborn, closely related thoughts were in the mind of Dr. Isaac van Voorhis. He was in the midst of writing a letter to a friend in New York, but his expression of the problem and its cause was only partially correct. In his youthful naiveté and unaware that at this instant the army of William Henry Harrison was marching to invade Indian territory, he exonorated his own government from any blame in the increasing Indian problem, writing:

> . . . I cannot but notice the villainy practiced in the Indian country by British agents and traders; you hear of it at a distance, but we near the scene of action are sensible to it. They labor by every unprincipled means to instigate the Savages against the Americans, to inculcate the idea that we intend to drive the Indians beyond the Mississippi, and that in every purchase of land the Government defrauds them; and their united efforts aim too at the destruction of every trading house and the prevention of the extension of our frontier. Never till a prohibition of the entrance of all foreigners, and especially British subjects, into the country takes place, will we enjoy a lasting peace with the credulous, deluded, cannibal savages.

[November 7, 1811 — Thursday]

"Do you *dare* defy me, Chaubenee?"

The words, heavy with malevolence, rolled across the hushed assemblage of Indians standing before the large rock upon which Tenskwatawa stood. The change in the Shawnee known far and wide as The Prophet was both amazing and frightening. His pointing finger impaled the burly Potawatomi chief standing slightly apart from the mass, the only ones close to him being Tecumapese, Wasegoboah, Roundhead and Skesh. They stood rooted as Tenskwatawa went on, the pointing finger steady, the veins at his temples standing out in the fury that roiled within him.

"You are a chief in your own nation, Chaubenee, but you are no chief here. You tempt death by defying me!"

It was no idle threat. Overwhelmed by the power that had been placed in his hands by Tecumseh, Tenskwatawa had become despotic. He had largely forgotten that his power was but a reflection of Tecumseh's and in the megalomania that had grown within him, his was the *only* power. Upwards of a dozen Indians of different tribes had challenged his authority in the past. In his anger, Tenskwatawa had "predicted" the death of each and, at the hands of his growing group of adherents, especially a select handful of enforcers, his predictions had come true. The temper of the crowd now standing before him was so obviously in his favor that to defy or attempt to thwart Tenskwatawa was indeed tantamount to signing one's death warrant.

This was a side of Tenskwatawa that Tecumseh did not know; a personality Tenskwatawa had kept well hidden from his older brother whenever he was home from his journeys. Yet, enough word of it had come to Tecumseh that he suspected strongly that the power he had given to his younger brother had gone to his head and was devouring him. It was for this reason that before leaving on his present journey south, Tecumseh had instructed Chaubenee and Wasegoboah to remain behind, to keep a close watch on the increasingly unpredictable Tenskwatawa and to prevent his doing anything that would jeopardize the grand plan.

Tecumseh had called them together before leaving — Tecumapese, Wasegoboah, Chaubenee, Skesh and Roundhead — and spoke to them earnestly in private. "I am strongly tempted to take Tenskwatawa out of his seat and place there another during my absence," he had said, "but to do so would be to put in the minds of our followers a doubt that might damage the very structure of our union. 'If Tecumseh does not trust even his own brother,' they would say, 'then what is there about these two Shawnee brothers we do not know and are we not hasty in following him?' This we cannot permit. But neither can we continue to give Tenskwatawa the free hand he has enjoyed so long in my absence. You here must be my eyes and my voice while I am gone.

"I have spoken to him in strong words," Tecumseh went on. "I have explained to him that Governor Harrison remains our greatest threat, yearning for any excuse to attack us. *This must not happen!* I have told Tenskwatawa that the white chief may not *wait* for an excuse to attack and that if he makes *any* move in this direction, Tenskwatawa is to immediately order the village abandoned and move our people out of reach. If our village is destroyed, it can be rebuilt, but not the union of our people. *That*, above all else, must not be jeopardized. Do not let Tenskwatawa jeopardize it."

Then he had gone, but even Tecumseh had not fully realized the extent of the power Tenskwatawa had taken onto himself and how convinced the Indians were who came here and listened to his predictions that he was truly a prophet. And when word had come that Harrison's army was on the move toward them, Tenskwatawa had again garbed himself in outlandish costume and harangued his followers for hours, bringing them to fever pitch in their eagerness to attack the whites. Now the army had penetrated far into Indian territory and were camped less than a mile and a half from this point, poised, so Tenskwatawa had been telling his listeners, to attack. And the Indians had been clinging to his words, their lust for war like a great gorge in their throats, all but choking them.

The presence of Tenskwatawa on the great rock before them was one carefully calculated to inspire awe and fear . . . and acquiesence. He had painted a solid white circle three inches in diameter over the black, empty right eyesocket, making the eyehole all the more frightening. Wrapped turbanlike around his head was a flamboyant headpiece of scarlet satin with a tassel of frilly, red-dyed feathers protruding from the rear. A thick braid of hair hung down behind his left ear, imprisoned at its end by a silver cylinder. From his ears dangled large round, flattened silver earrings in which holes had been filed out to form a five-pointed star in one and a crescent moon in the other. Around his neck he wore a large silver gorget, atop which rested a necklace of upturned bear claws. A pair of knotted scarlet sashes attached to his sides in front, crossed over his chest in an X, passed over his shoulders and formed a similar X in back and attached to his waistcord in the rear. Tied snugly around his neck and flowing down his back to his hips was a rich cape of ermine. At least a dozen bracelets — silver, beaded and brass — encircled his wrists and the beautiful buckskin shirt and leggins were decorated with painted porcupine quills in geometric designs. On his feet he wore knee-high moccasins trimmed in ermine to match the cape.

The rain had begun shortly after midnight — a persistent, dreary, clammy rain accompanied by infrequent blue-white flashes of lightning in the distance and the ominous grumbling roll of muted thunder — but Tenskwatawa had paid no attention to it and his listeners, mesmerized by the fascinating being who addressed them, remained rooted in place.

Chaubenee, Wasegoboah and the others had listened only a little apart from the others, expecting at every moment the common sense of the audience would rise and they would back away from his wild exhortations. They *knew* they must not clash with Harrison; *knew* that their own spies had reported that the army had brought with them three powerful brass cannon. How could they even contemplate facing this? Yet, under Tenskwatawa's spell, they had.

"Ever since the army left Vincennes," Tenskwatawa had shouted to them, his voice an ugly rasp in the dank night, "my spies have watched, and we are ready for them. Now," his bracelets jangled lightly as he raised his arm and pointed toward the darkling woods, "they are before us and have made camp. Their firelights glow in the distance. They only await tomorrow's dawn to attack. That is why *we* cannot wait; why *we* must attack first, while it is still dark and they are unprepared. White men cannot fight in the dark. We must smash them before dawn!"

That was the point where Chaubenee could no longer hold back. He had stepped forward, thrust his arms above his head and shouted in a powerful booming voice filled with urgency a single word.

"*No!*"

There was a universal gasp from the assemblage, not only from surprise but at the temerity of anyone to so insult the speaker. An ugly murmuring began to rise but Chaubenee silenced it with a slashing chop of his arm and he continued angrily.

"No! We must *not* attack them! Before he left, Tecumseh warned that Harrison might lead an army against us and that if he did, we were to fall away and avoid contact. He'll be back soon. He is on his way now. We must fall back and await his orders."

"Do you *dare* defy me, Chaubenee?" The malevolence in Tenskwatawa's words was heavy in every ear. "You are a chief in your own nation, Chaubenee, but you are no chief here. You tempt death by defying me!"

The threat took Chaubenee aback. He was not afraid of Tenskwatawa nor of his henchmen, yet for a moment he hesitated and in that brief interval Wasegoboah stepped up beside him, his own anger barely under control.

"*Tenskwatawa!* You know me well. I am Wasegoboah, friend of Tecumseh and husband of your sister and his, Tecumapese. Listen to my words! I tell you now that there is great evil in your heart." The assemblage gasped and murmured anew, but he went on without pause. "When Tecumseh left last, he told me — he told *us* here"—a sweep of his arm took in the small group —"to be sure you allowed no confrontation with the whites to take place during his absence." He turned and faced the crowd more directly. "My brothers, listen to me! Chaubenee is right. We must move away, not fight. It is Tecumseh's order. They have thunderguns and better rifles. *We must not fight them!*"

The blood vessels in his temples and neck bulging alarmingly, Tenskwatawa literally shrieked his response. "You lie! You wish to take power to yourself. I will not permit it." He lifted both his arms in a widespread embrace of the gathering. "Listen! Hear me and then speak from your hearts. Am I not The Prophet?" There was silence and he went on hurriedly. "Has not all I predicted come to pass?" A few voices responded affirmatively. "If Tecumseh was to lead you in this matter, why is he not here now? Tecumseh is not here because I *sent* him away. *I* am your leader, not Tecumseh! Think on it and then tell me: who has led you? Tecumseh? No!"

From the crowd a larger scattering of response came, mingling with his own negative, and the fear that had bloomed in him began to abate. "Who," he went on quickly, tightening his grasp on them, "has given you the prophecies by which you have lived, with never an error? Tecumseh?" A heavy roar of "No!" followed his words. "Was it not The Prophet?"

The village clearing resounded with the cries of "Yes!" from several hundred throats simultaneously.

"Yes!" Tenskwatawa echoed them excitedly. "Yes! It was The

Prophet, *not* Tecumseh. It is The Prophet who has seen to your needs, who has provided you with food and clothing and shelter and weapons! It is The Prophet who has seen to your welfare and your health! It is The Prophet who speaks on your behalf to the Great Spirit! Therefore, I ask you now, whose orders will you obey?"

An unbelievable din of voices arose shouting "The Prophet! The Prophet!" At first they came as a raucous, barely understandable clamor, but gradually they took on a cadence until it became an overwhelming chant. It lasted for a long time and Tenskwatawa folded his arms across his chest and stood there basking in the adulation, immensely pleased with himself. Gradually the voices died away and he prepared to speak again.

"*Tenskwatawa!*"

Startled, he turned at the familiar voice and his good eye widened when he realized that the single word had been spoken by his sister. Her eyes were blazing, her voice tremulous with emotion.

"What are you *saying?*" she demanded. "How can you dare to so openly defy Tecumseh? Has a bad spirit entered your mind and eaten it?"

"Be silent, Tecumapese! How do you, a *woman*, take it on yourself to question the words of your chief?"

Her mouth fell open at the incredulity of it, but when she spoke her words were the cutting blows of an icy tomahawk. "My *chief!* You are my baby brother, not my chief! You are still Lowawluwaysica, not Tenskwatawa. I have seen you grow in body over the years, but your mind has not grown; it is small and mean with the meanness of a disobedient child. You are *still* a child in your mind and you know — *you know!* — that Tecumseh, who *is* our chief, would not permit you to do this."

The anger abruptly became replaced with a more conciliatory tone as she went on. "I beg you, little brother, as your sister and in the name of our brother, do not do this! Heed the wise words of Chaubenee and Wasegoboah and —"

"*Silence!*" Tenskwatawa roared. "Tecumapese, you are a squaw. Go with the squaws now, or I will order your death . . ." he measured the words with frightening finality, ". . . *and . . . you . . . will . . . die!* Go!"

Tecumapese hesitated, appearing on the verge of responding, but then she suddenly wilted, covered mouth and nose with a hand and fled at a staggering run toward her wegiwa, the darkness swiftly swallowing her. A hundred or more whisperings began at once in the crowd but they hushed as Tenskwatawa raised an arm high, then lowered it slowly, dramatically, until his finger pointed at those who opposed him.

"Chaubenee and Wasegoboah would have you believe," he said, his voice better modulated now but still far-carrying, "that you will be destroyed if you fight the white chief Harrison, but *I* tell you — as your chief and Prophet — that they lie! I have spoken with the Great Spirit. You have seen me in my trance. He has eased my fears and now he will ease yours. I call on him now to say to you what he told me."

Wasegoboah and Roundhead, Chaubenee and Skesh watched in mute frustration as Tenskwatawa outstretched his arms, lifted his face to the sky, unmindful of the rain, and spoke beseechingly. "O Great Spirit, enter my body. Assure your children through me. Strike away all their fear and bring them courage. O Great Spirit . . . *speak!*"

He continued standing in that pose for a long moment and then abruptly began shaking violently, bending double with the spasms apparently wracking him. Transfixed, the assemblage watched as he slowly straightened to what seemed far more than his normal height. His face was utterly devoid of expression and the words that left his mouth were delivered in a hollow booming quality unlike anything they had ever heard.

"Warriors of Tippecanoe! I speak to you through your chief. Listen and heed. Do not fear the enemy that has come against you. It cannot harm you. Pick up your weapons and attack them. Do not be afraid. Though at first some of you may fall, you will rise to fight again. You will strike them down for a great victory. The orders of your Prophet are to be obeyed, for he speaks my words."

Many of the listeners had fallen to their knees and cowered at the words of this apparition before them. Others stood frozen, astonished, mouths agape. As Tenskwatawa shook violently again, seeming to throw off the possession, they recovered themselves but a great sense of awe was still within them. When The Prophet spoke to them again, it was in his normal grating voice.

"Now, you yourselves have heard. The Great Spirit has spoken. Can you doubt further? You *cannot* be hurt! You *cannot* die. There can only be great victory! Go now! Paint your faces! See to your weapons! Listen for my voice! Listen for my drum! When you hear them, just before the dawn, *attack!* You cannot be hurt as long as you hear them. One half of the white chief's army is now dead. The other half is now crazy. It will be a small matter to finish them off with our tomahawks. Go!"

They dispersed, but Chaubenee and Wasegoboah and the others of their group did not go with them. They retired to the wegiwa of Wasegoboah and Tecumapese and made their own plans. There was a hollow sickness in their minds and hearts in the knowledge that they had failed Tecumseh in the one imperative he had left with them. In each of their minds was a similar thought: had they acted sooner, they might have stopped Tenskwatawa, but now it was too late and there was no stopping what had begun. All that remained was to wait and watch. Yes! They must watch Tenskwatawa and if — none of them dared to think of it as *when* — if the battle were lost, Tenskwatawa would not be allowed to vanish.

Just over three hundred united Indians of various tribes spent the next hour or so preparing themselves according to Tenskwatawa's directions, but they finished too soon and were too excited to contain. By four in the morning, hours before dawn, they had begun to creep forward toward the encamped army. Tenskwatawa, learning of it, snatched up his skin drum and raced to his high rock, not realizing he was watched and followed at every step. He sat himself atop the rock, the drum in his lap, and began to thump in an uneven cadence. In a few moments his voice came up in weird incantation and the Indians in the darkness, hearing, moved on more boldly.

A voice shrieked. A sentry shouted fearfully. A shot. More shouts and a flurry of shots. A growing uproar of voices and gunfire and the sounds of metal upon metal and terrified horses screaming. A strong stream of commands. The sounds, the smells, the taste of death.

Behind, barely audible, the chant and the drumbeat. Ahead, Indians confident in the gift of invulnerability from the Great Spirit, attacked with such self-abandon as had never before been witnessed. Even when protective cover was available, it was not used. What need? The American bullets would rebound when they struck Indian flesh; their swords would slice only empty air; the exploding balls from the great thunderguns would be only sounds and flashings, ineffectual, useless; the army was half dead, half insane, so what was there to fear?

A runner, blood streaming from the side of his neck, raced up to where Tenskwatawa sat and drummed and chanted. His voice was teetering on panic and he cried out that Indians were falling and not rising, that bullets were striking, hurting, killing; that bombs from the thunderguns were tearing away limbs from the red men who supposedly could not be hurt.

"Fight on!" Tenskwatawa replied sternly. "Fight on! It will take a little while for the prophecy to be fulfilled. I will raise my voice to encourage it."

The wounded Indian nodded and raced off again, followed by the increased volume of Tenskwatawa's eerie song and the heavier tattoo of his drumbeat. But still they fell and fell some more and at last the chant and drumbeat faltered and died. Looking this way and that, Tenskwatawa slipped down from his perch, tore away his garish costume until he wore only buckskins and moccasins and then he loped away as the first gray of morning began streaking the sky, the continuing sound of the battle becoming fainter as he fled. But he could not flee fast enough nor far enough.

He nearly wept when he all but ran into the bearlike form of Chaubenee in his path and, in trying to leap away to the side, was grasped in the powerful grips of Wasegoboah and Black Partridge.[189] Then he did in fact weep and in his frightened blubberings said there had been some mistake, some error in the preparation of his magic, some blunder in his incantations. The fault lay elsewhere, not in him; bad spirits were afoot.

"You are a coward!" Chaubenee said with utter coldness. "You are a murderer, a betrayer of all the Indians, and for what you have done, you must die."

Black Partridge grunted in agreement, adding his own judgment. "You are a liar," he told Tenskwatawa. "You are a false prophet. You told us the white people were all dead or crazy, when they were in all their senses and fought like the Devil! For this you must pay!"

But it was not the place of Tecumseh's lieutenants to kill him. What would happen to Tenskwatawa, how and when, would be for Tecumseh only to say. With those who had escaped the carnage and had not fled in panic to their own countries and villages and homes, they would take this fool who called himself a prophet to the village on Wildcat Creek, a branch of the Mississinewa, and there they would await the return of Tecumseh.

Such was the battle of Tippecanoe, small in scope, gigantic in importance. By the evidence on the field of battle, it was the Indians who had won. Of the hundred eighty-eight corpses lying there, only thirty-eight were those of Indians. Yet, in the light of the new day, Harrison's army held the ground and the united Indians had broken and fled. The victory that Harrison was at this moment preparing to proclaim was far more psychological than actual, but that was by far the more important aspect.

Only about forty of the warriors who had taken part in the fight remained with the group heading toward the Mississinewa under Chaubenee. Very widely scattered as individuals or in groups of two or three or four were somewhat over two hundred Indians, many of them wounded, heading for their distant homes, carrying with them news of the disaster at Tippecanoe; carrying with them the germ of fear and dismay that would spread to the remote villages that Tecumseh had visited; the germ that would lodge in their hearts and prey on their minds; the germ of degeneration that destroyed and devoured beyond any hope of reconstitution the foundation of a never-before-equalled amalgamation of tribes. They carried with them the germ of destruction for all tribes of Indians everywhere in North America, even those as yet untouched by the hand of the white man.

They carried with them the germ of destruction for the dream of the Shawnee named Tecumseh.

CHAPTER X

[*November 10, 1811 — Sunday*]

"TECUMSEH is coming!"

The news swept as a freshening breeze through the encampment on Wildcat Creek near where it joined the Mississinewa River and the Indians poured from the village wegiwas and from the score or more of hastily erected shelters. Very quickly a small crowd formed and waited, Tecumseh's most devoted friends and lieutenants in its van.

From the distant woodland, riding on the trail that came from the west, half a hundred men emerged with Tecumseh leading them and Sauganash beside him. They had ridden a great distance and the newly acquired weight in their hearts was a greater burden by far than any that might have been strapped to their backs. Yet, they rode erect and there was about their approach a peculiar silence that became contagious to the waiting group.

Since his departure in late July, Tecumseh had been in almost constant motion, the swing through the south carrying him to the villages of the Creeks, the Cherokees, the Choctaws and Chickasaws. At each village he had articulated his dream, his plan and the signal that soon would come and, though many stayed in their own villages with the promise of coming when the sign was given, many others had fallen in with his group and followed. Far in the south they had crossed the Mississippi and returned northward through the territory to the west, visiting the tribes and villages there, gaining new converts to the dream and new followers to the procession. They had skirted St. Louis and crossed the Mississippi to its eastern bank above the mouth of the Des Moines. They had visited the principal Sac village of Saukenuk on the Rock River near its mouth and then followed the southeastern trail leading to the Potawatomi villages on Peoria Lake and by that time they had become an army of four hundred.

As they had proceeded up the Illinois River and then along the Indian trail that led toward the Wabash where it is joined by the Tippecanoe, they encountered the wounded, frightened, angry, fleeing remnants of Tecumseh's Tippecanoe village and the news these refugees brought them had been devastating. In that first night of camping which followed, three hundred of those who had accompanied him from the south deserted Tecumseh, slipping away in the darkness to carry back to their own villages and those along the way the news of this terrible tragedy.

Tecumseh and the remains of his party passed through where the Tippecanoe battle had been fought and through the charred remains of the vast village that Harrison's army had destroyed before it left for Vincennes. They buried the mutilated bodies of the Indians still lying there and camped in grief outside where the village had been and on that night fifty more of his followers slipped away, their faith in the grand plan of Tecumseh as demolished as the village behind them. And Tecumseh could not find fault in those who had deserted him earlier and those who abandoned him then.

From survivors of the battle they learned the details of how it had come about — Tenskwatawa's firing them with the lust for war, his threats against those who demanded adherence to Tecumseh's orders, his usurpation of Tecumseh's leadership, his vision with the Great Spirit, his prophecies that there could not be death but only glory, his ultimate capture and detainment at the Wildcat Creek village off the Mississinewa.

Now, as they rode into the village and the near one hundred who waited parted to accept them, there were no words of greeting, no smiles of pleasure or relief. All took their cue from Tecumseh, whose face was set in hard lines and whose eyes smoldered with controlled fury. It was beside Chaubenee that Tecumseh reined his horse to a stop and to the brawny Potawatomi that he directed the four words that surprised no one.

"Take me to Tenskwatawa."

He slid lightly from his mount and followed Chaubenee to the council house, the others falling in behind silently. A post had been erected in the middle of the earthen floor of the expansive structure and bound to it, his wrists tied behind him with rawhide tugs, was Tenskwatawa. He cringed and a repugnant whimpering sound escaped him as he saw in the dimness that his brother had returned. Those who followed Tecumseh filed in quietly and formed themselves along the walls and none among them believed Tenskwatawa had more than mere moments to live; a belief reinforced when Tecumseh, approaching the prisoner, slid his razor-edged knife from its belt sheath.

Tenskwatawa's whimpering evolved into a mournful wail. The front of his leggins began suddenly darkening as a bladder he could no longer control discharged its contents. He slid to the ground when his knees, equally out of control, collapsed beneath his weight and his head hung, his face hidden by the scraggle of dirtied hair. It was this hair that Tecumseh reached forward and gripped, his expression now one of loathing. He jerked his brother's head back savagely, exposing the vulnerable throat and placing the edge of his blade against it. He moved it slightly and a trickle of scarlet blood slid down Tenskwatawa's neck, staining his collar. Now the wailing ceased and was replaced by a gurgling, blubbering sound. Tecumseh's voice was soft but clearly audible as its utter coldness froze the breaths in every chest.

"It would be a favor to you, Tenskwatawa, were I to let my hand have its way. But I will not kill you. That would be too easy, too honorable a fate."

He lifted the blade away from his brother's throat and cut away the bonds. Slowly, unbelievingly, still fearful, Tenskwatawa came to his feet as his older brother returned the knife to its sheath. Tecumseh's hands suddenly shot out and gripped the hair at Tenskwatawa's temples and he shook him so violently that his nose began to bleed. Tenskwatawa wailed again, certain that his scalp was being ripped away and his neck broken. Then Tecumseh threw him away. Tenskwatawa sprawled on the floor and began scrambling to escape. Instantly several warriors moved forward, jerking tomahawks or knives from their waistbands, but a harsh order from Wasegoboah stayed them.

"Stop! Do not interfere! What Tecumseh plans for his brother is his concern only. No one has more right to say what should be done," his voice became heavy with scorn, "with the one who called himself a prophet!"

Even as the warriors had moved, so had Tecumseh, gripping his brother's hair again, pinning him with one knee and jerking the head back so Tenskwatawa's eyes were forced to meet the cold glare of Tecumseh's. And when Tecumseh spoke, there was an implacability so intense in his words that even those who looked on felt stricken.

"In one day, Tenskwatawa — *in one day!* — you have destroyed what I have taken over ten summers to build and which now can never be rebuilt. In one day you have destroyed the hopes of *all* Indians. You are a liar, a cheat, a fool filled with the lust for power. You are no longer The Prophet. You are no longer my brother. You are no longer a Shawnee, nor even an Indian! You are dishonored as no man has ever before been dishonored." His voice dropped, became even more frightening. "I will not kill you, but your death begins this day and it will be years in coming, for each day you will die a little more. From this time forward you will live with scorn and disgust, with the hatred and distrust of all men. You will be without family or friends. You will be without a people and you will live the rest of your miserable life outside the villages of those you sought to rule, and who now despise you. From this day forward you will be all alone, and when at last death becomes final for you, no living creature will mourn." He paused, then thrust the head away from him. "Go! I am finished with you!"

Devastated, Tenskwatawa let his gaze move across those watching, but now they averted their eyes from him. With the attitude of a craven dog that has been severely whipped, the once Prophet slunk from the council house and disappeared outside. In the silence that filled the chamber, Tecumseh moved among his people quietly grasping their hands in turn, his features gradually softening. In this way he greeted them, embracing some — such as Tecumapese — and those who were closest to his heart.

"Tecumseh," Wasegoboah murmured, deeply moved as Tecumseh gripped his shoulders, then his hands, "our hearts are full — filled with sorrow for what has happened, filled with regret that we failed you, yet filled with joy at your return."

"Few of us are left," Chaubenee said when his turn came, "but those who stayed and those who have returned, and those who will yet come back to support you, remain loyal in every way, even unto death."

Roundhead, the Wyandot, agreed. "I vow to you, Tecumseh, from my heart, that my warriors and I will stay by you and fight beside you until, if necessary, we are no more."

"We wait only for your word," Black Partridge said next. "Whether we are with you or on the shores of Lake Michigan, you have only to whisper and we will do as you require."

When the greetings were finished, Tecumseh immediately called a council of all present. A large fire was built and when all had gathered about it, he spoke for many hours, telling them where he had gone and what had occurred, of the alliances formed and of the sure knowledge that when word of the Tippecanoe defeat reached them, many who had sworn allegiance would renege, even though the great sign would come.

"I stood upon the ashes of my own home," he told them, an emotion he could not contain making his voice tremulous, "where my own wegiwa had sent up its flames to the Great Spirit and there I summoned the spirits of the warriors who had fallen in their vain attempts to protect their homes from the grasping invader. And as I snuffed up the smell of their blood from the ground, I swore once more eternal hatred — the hatred of an avenger!"

Now he was here among them and his grief was great. And since no longer would enough tribes be united to enable Tecumseh's grand plan to succeed, they would have no recourse but to do what he had so long discoursed against; they would have to throw their weight behind the British and aid them in destroying the Americans. Perhaps many of the Indians who initially panicked when they learned of Tippecanoe would yet return to the amalgamation to unite in fighting for what was theirs, but on this they could not depend. An effort must be made to reassure those who had not wholly turned their backs, those who wavered. All those assembled here, therefore, would tomorrow mount their horses and disperse to their own villages and relate what had occurred here, assuring their own people that not all was lost; that with the union of all tribes they could still regain what had been taken from them and safeguard that which lay waiting to be taken. They were to spread the word that though The Prophet had failed them, Tecumseh would not. The great sign he had predicted would still come. All of the tribes that had received bundles of sticks had only one of these red sticks remaining. Six days from now the preliminary sign would come — the sign under which he had been born and named. It would come at night and be clearly visible to all and, when it came, the final red stick was to be cut into thirty equal lengths, each, save the last, to be burned in the light of successive dawns; the last to be burned in the midst of night. Then would come the great sign. Then, all who yet believed in Tecumseh and in the future of the Indian race were to take up their weapons and strike out at once for the new site of their convergence — the British fort called Amherstburg.

[*November 16, 1811 — Saturday*]

It was an utterly exhausted John Kinzie who brought the word to the whites at Chicago and Fort Dearborn of the Battle of Tippecanoe. In the six days since he first learned of it, he had been riding almost constantly, with but short pauses to rest and eat. The jaded horse that brought him back was ruined and very likely to die, but in view of what was occurring, that was of little moment. And now, in this dark night, things were happening of even more ominous portent and for the first time in many years, John Kinzie was afraid — not so much for himself as for his family.

He had left Chicago for Detroit on the fourth Wednesday of October — the twenty-third, it was — and had taken his time, stopping off for a pleasant visit with Topenebe at St. Joseph. There had been no hint then, other than the same general rumors of unrest, that anything significant was in the wind. At length he had moved on and was at De Charmes' Trading Post, a day's journey from Detroit, when an Ottawa runner had brought the astounding news.[190] Though the victory was Harrison's, the probability that now there would be a general uprising of the tribes was so strong that the Chicago trader immediately mounted his horse and headed back. Two thoughts were paramount in his mind — first, the protection of his own family; second, the urgent need to relay word to his traders at the branch posts to hide their stores of gunpowder and furnish none to the Indians and to alert those traders still at his headquarters who had not yet left for their wintering grounds to take no excess powder or shot with them for trading purposes.

The news he brought to Captain Heald caused the commanding officer to order an immediate alert and bring his troops to a state of preparedness for any eventuality. The captain was very nervous and uncommonly anxious to know the state of mind of Black Partridge's people in the village a few miles distant. Despite his grinding weariness, John Kinzie volunteered to go there and find out, since it could well be a grave risk for anyone from the fort, but probably would not be so for him.

And so, after alerting his family and his traders and dispatching messengers to his distant posts, he had mounted a fresh horse and, as darkness had fallen, rode out of Chicago toward Black Partridge's village. His speculation over whether or not word of the battle had reached the village was dispelled at his arrival. The coldness and suspicion with which he was greeted, when always before he had been warmly welcomed, answered the unasked query.

Above and beyond the chilly reception he received, something else was wrong here and it did not register what it was until he was shown into Black Partridge's lodge. The hairs at his nape prickled as he realized there were no fires in the village. The night air was cold, close to freezing, yet nowhere was a camp fire burning, not even here in the domicile of the chief. In all his years on the frontier, of all the scores of villages he had entered, day or night and irrespective of season, there had always been fires. The coldness that overhung the village penetrated deep into his own heart and his fears increased.

Black Partridge sat by himself on a mat, a deep shadow among the deeper shadows of the interior. He neither moved nor greeted Kinzie as the trader stopped and squatted on his heels before him. It was protocol for the chief to speak first, but John Kinzie was in no mood for customary politeness.

"Black Partridge sits in darkness, as does his village," he observed in the Potawatomi tongue. "I sense a coldness in his heart and those of his people that is colder than the night air alone brings. Is there cause for a great sorrow?"

A slight movement indicated that the blanket-wrapped chief had raised his head. For a while he remained silent. Then:

"Shawneeawkee comes to call at a time when it would be better that he remained with his family."

The remark was a distinct insult, but the trader took no affront. When he replied, his voice was even gentler than before. "Your voice tells me that you are very weary. Were you among those who fought Harrison at the Tippecanoe?"

Only a sharp indication of breath indicated how startled Black Partridge was by the remark. "As always," he responded, "Shawneeawkee sees much and hears much and knows more. Yes, I was at the Tippecanoe. Two of our warriors died there. It was very bad. But the birds of the forest whisper among themselves that it is only a beginning of worse times. You are a friend. I have eaten in your lodge and you in mine. Therefore, I will say this to you and then you must leave: we remain friends, but there is a danger for you if you remain in this country. Heed the wise bird who alights on your shoulder and tells you to take your women and children and go far into the rising sun until the great water is at your feet."

He fell silent and John was convinced he would say no more. He came to his feet and looked down at the shadowed form. "I have heard that bird," he said, "but I have brushed him away. I cannot leave. Yet, I cannot believe that I, who number Black Partridge and Topenebe among my closest friends, need fear that I and my family are in danger."

He turned and walked to the door-flap, but, as he stooped to go out, the words of Black Partridge halted him. "Shawneeawkee! You are one who has never been known to flee from shadows. But there are times when shadows have substance and are to be feared. I and my people — as is true of Topenebe and his people — would not harm our friend nor his family. Yet there are many who know you not except as a white man. From them the danger rises. Should it move toward you, I will do what it is in my power to do to keep you from harm. It may not be enough."

John Kinzie felt some of the tension leave him. "Friendship is a river that must run in two directions," he said. Then he left.

Black Partridge continued to sit quietly for almost another hour, still holding in his hand the object that had been invisible to Shawneeawkee in the darkness. Then he came to his feet with a faint groan at the ache in his muscles. As John Kinzie had, he had come far to be here among his people this night. He stepped outside and murmured to the warriors who were there and they hurried off. The chief continued to a broad clear place in the middle of the village and, still holding the object, sat down before the cold ashes of the principal village fire. New tinder and dry twigs were upon the ashes and heavier pieces of wood atop them.

In a short while his people began to converge and sit with him, ghostly silent shapes wrapped in blankets to ward off the cold. They took their places in a circle about the dead fire site. No one spoke, but all tilted their heads back and watched. There was no moon and the Great Bear and other constellations and individual stars twinkled with incredible brightness against their deep blue-black background, the air crisp and very clear, unsullied by firelight or woodsmoke.

They sat for a long while this way, unspeaking, most of them unaware that elsewhere throughout the land other chiefs sat with their people in this same way, at this same time. Waiting. Watching. In southern Canada, from the broad snow-covered prairies and the Lake-of-the-Woods to the great falls of the Niagara, they watched; in western New York and Pennsylvania, in Ohio and the Indiana Territory and elsewhere in the Illinois Territory, they watched; in the mass of land west of Lake Erie and Lake Huron and east of Lake Michigan, they watched; in the valleys of the Mississippi and Missouri from far north to far south, they watched; in the lands westward of the Mississippi and in those southward of the Ohio to the great Gulf, they watched. And each of the appointed chiefs held in his hand an object similar to that which Black Partridge was holding.

It came at last, what they were watching for, just before the midpoint of the night. A great searing ball of intense greenish-white fire sprang out of the southwest and scored the heavens at incredible speed, immeasurably awe-inspiring. And the heads of a vast multitude of Indians turned to watch its fiery progress as it swiftly approached, passed and as swiftly disappeared in the northeast. Even after it was gone they sat still, spell-bound.

At length a murmur left the chief and a warrior sprang to his feet, crouched at the fire site and struck flint to steel. Sparks in showers, smoke in tendrils, little flames that grew apace. Fire. And in the light of it, Black Partridge reached out and took up a twig of charcoal and with it he made twenty-nine lines on the red stick he had been holding for hours. And with his knife he cut through the stick along those lines. And when he was finished, he carefully picked up the thirty pieces of red wood and carried them to his lodge.

And then he prayed to the Great Spirit.

[*December 16, 1811 — Monday*]

At the middle of the night, select chiefs in widely separated villages many hundreds of miles on either side of the Mississippi from the Canadian wilds to the Gulf Coast burned the thirtieth piece of red wood from the final stick that each had cut up. Then they waited, as they had waited a month before when the great meteor had scorched the skies. But this time they did not turn their eyes skyward; they merely waited. For those far to the east the wait was two and a half hours, for those in the great plains far west of the Mississippi it was an hour less. They waited for the great sign that for years past Tecumseh had predicted would occur this night. At 2:30 A.M. it came.

The earth shook.

A massive earthquake occurred where one had never happened before in recorded history; where no one could possibly have anticipated it; where no one could possibly have predicted it would strike.

No one but Tecumseh.

The epicenter was in that area where the great Ohio River empties into the greater Mississippi River; where, within a mere matter of miles, Illinois and Kentucky, Tennessee and Arkansas and Missouri converge. Significantly, there were few humans in this immediate area and even fewer structures, so the damage to man and his possessions was slight. But the earth was torn and buckled and split in the midst of a monumental crescendo of sound beyond that which any living person in North America had ever heard. Several miles from the Mississippi along the border of Kentucky and Tennessee, a vast section of ground caved in upon itself as if some incredibly heavy invisible foot had stepped on soft earth there and crushed it down. Water from subterranean sources spurted up in fantastic volume, quickly filling the depression and creating a large lake.[191] Great bluffs overlooking the midsection of the Mississippi toppled and crashed into the phenomenally writhing, heaving waters. For a time, the Mississippi itself in this area stopped and then flowed backward. Vast expanses of lowlands flooded to great depth in some areas, while riverbeds became exposed and lifted high in others. The shock waves of the unparalleled cataclysm spread outward in swift concentrically expanding rings and the surface of the land bucked and heaved, swelled and rolled as if it had become suddenly viscous.

Within a hundred miles settlers were tossed from their beds amid the splintering crashes of their cabins being wrenched asunder; bricks crumbled and were ground into a choking dust; bridges disappeared into the roiled waters of the streams they were built to span; ravines were filled as earth slipped and slid and squeezed together; chasms were created as great splits appeared in the earth's crust and spread amid devastating roar. Birds shrieked and flapped as they were pitched from their treetop roosts into the darkness. Barns collapsed, fires broke out, cattle bellowed and horses screamed in terror as they were thrown to the ground.

In every direction of the compass phenomena caused by the earthquake occurred: in the southeast, tall palms became lashing whips while long-established lakes abruptly drained and declivities in the land became new lakes; in the south whole forests fell in a continuous din of snapping trunks and branches and new streams sprang into being where none had been before; in the southwest enormous boulders rolled down slopes on top of which they had long perched, cutting fierce swaths through trees and brush, while streams stopped and eddied or disappeared, leaving fish flopping in the drained beds; the ground shuddered and herds of bison fell, then scrambled to their feet in panic-stricken stampedes accompanied by prolonged grinding roars from deep beneath the surface; in the Great Lakes, especially Michigan and Erie, the waters danced in a frenzy and formed into huge waves that crashed destructively against the shores; in St. Louis, Detroit, Vincennes, Chicago, Kaskaskia, Cleveland, Cincinnati, Dayton, Louisville, and numerous smaller towns and settlements, varieties of damage from mild to severe occurred.

Such was the great sign of Tecumseh and, though they represented only a small percentage of those who initially promised to do so, quite a number of warriors of the widely separated tribes took up their weapons and began their journey toward the mouth of the Detroit River to join the incredible Shawnee known as Tecumseh.[192]

[*January 30, 1812 — Tuesday*]

Gradually Chicago was growing and, with the old Whistler-Kinzie feud now a thing of the past, a far more comfortable sense of community solidarity had become established. There were minor squabbles or disagreements among the inhabitants at times, but nothing of a significant nature that might cause the little society to fraction as it once had. Soldiers came and went as they were either assigned to Fort Dearborn or reassigned elsewhere or discharged. New settlers trickled in, some staying only a short while, but others putting down more permanent roots. As in most small communities, everyone's business was largely known by everyone else. Gossip was one of the principal pastimes, engaged in to greater or lesser degree by virtually everyone, and anything newsworthy that occurred or was learned via dispatch was very quickly common knowledge.

Although he knew his wife did not much care for the young officer, John Kinzie found himself liking Ensign George Ronan more all the time. Eleanor's dislike, he knew, was predicated solely on Ronan's cavalier attitude toward religion and, while the bright, engaging young man had never professed a disbelief in God, she considered him an outright atheist and, as such, refused to have anything to do with him. Nor would she allow John to entertain him in their house or in Kinzie's Store. As a result, these days John had been dropping by the fort far more often than customarily.

George Ronan was only part of his reason for doing so. He had formed a similar liking for the young doctor, Isaac van Voorhis, and often joined both of them in their discussions about politics, people, religion, the state of the world and the nation, literature, music, poetry, the volatile Indian situation in Illinois and elsewhere, the fundamental asininity of most military matters, and an almost clinical analysis of the character, abilities, failings and love life of practically everyone they knew. The surgeon's mate was another whom Eleanor objected to in a most definite manner, considering him quite as much *persona non grata* at the Kinzie place as Ensign Ronan, and for the same reason.

Yet, the stimulation John Kinzie felt when engaged in conversation with them — or, more often the case, listening to them — was a pleasure he refused to forgo. Occasionally others at the fort would join them in their little discussion group. Matthew Irwin was one of these and the Indian factor, while no match in ready wit and sharpness to either Van Voorhis or Ronan, was no slouch and often contributed penetrating observations.

Less frequently John's son-in-law, Lieutenant Helm, would join them, saying little, obviously enjoying the conversation but just as obviously made uncomfortable by it and soon drifting away. It was as if he felt there was a disloyalty inherent in listening to — much less participating in — the group discussions, especially when the Fort Dearborn commanding officer became a topic, as often occurred. For his own part, Captain Nathan Heald never joined their discussions and seemed to dislike the fact they were held, yet was unable to find any regulation prohibiting them so long as they did not interfere with regular duties.

Another who never joined the discussions was Jack Lalime, even though more often than not he was at the fort. He seemed consistently less able to control the anger that welled in him at each contact with John Kinzie and the insults and veiled threats he dropped toward his nemesis had become much less subtle in recent months. In most cases John merely ignored him, which infuriated the interpreter even more. Now and again words would pass between them and at such times Lalime would become virtually apoplectic in his fury. The grievances he harbored involving John Kinzie — whether real or imagined — were becoming obsessive and both Ronan and Van Voorhis had at separate times murmured warnings to the trader that Lalime might bear watching; that it might not be beyond him to actually try to harm John Kinzie physically. John laughed at such notions, but he nevertheless became surreptitiously more prepared for trouble when Lalime was near.

On a few occasions the droll but laconic Liberty White had joined them, mainly content to sit smoking his pipe and listening to the repartee and general discussions, but occasionally contributing a gem to the conversation, accompanied by outrageous facial expressions, that caused them to burst into gales of laughter. His employer, Charles Lee, had participated in the discussions at first, but then simply became too busy and stopped coming. His wife, Martha, had just had her third child, a daughter named Sally, with whom she was helped by her twelve-year-old, Mary. Charles Jr., now fifteen, had taken an interest in his father's farm and was working there on a fairly regular basis under the supervision of Liberty White.

In recent months George Ronan had become rather anathema to Captain Heald, not only because he had the unfortunate propensity to question orders he considered stupid or questionable, but equally because of his prevailing inability to keep gratuitous observations or suggestions to himself. Verbal reprimands were not uncommon and Ronan accepted them in poor grace, the very presence of Captain Heald having the ability to cause his bile to rise and be checked only with the greatest of difficulty. Part of the problem was that George Ronan's rank was still ensign, even though by custom he should have been put forward for promotion to lieutenant long before now, especially in view of the fact that he had been graduated from the United States Military Academy at West Point. He declared privately that he believed Captain Heald to be resentful of the fact that he was a West Pointer and accused his commander of deliberately withholding recommendation for promotion on unsubstantial grounds of "nonconformance" and "disrespectful attitudes." There seemed to be some justification in Ronan's complaint.

Good friends though the ensign and post surgeon were, it was not friendship alone that made Dr. Van Voorhis tend to agree with Ronan's unfavorable assessment of Captain Heald. Rebekah Heald was pregnant — lately becoming obviously so — and due probably in early May. Yet, because of Van Voorhis's age — only twenty-one — and the fact that he had never delivered a baby, even though he had been trained in the procedure and assisted twice, Rebekah Heald was adamant that she was not going to have him attend her for the birth. In this she was supported by her husband and, though there was no arguing with them in the matter, it rankled young Dr. Van Voorhis considerably. He had great confidence in his ability successfully to bring an infant into the world and meet emergencies, if any, with proper measures.

Ensign George Ronan was, at his own cheerful admission, an incurable gossip. He was always keenly interested in whatever was going on within his scope. But his was not a malicious form of observation and gossip. Though he was candid in his dislike for his commanding officer, he got along well with practically everyone else, military and civilian. When he passed along little details of the doings of others, it was not in a judgmental sense. He had become noted during this winter for his great skill as an ice skater and after the Chicago River had frozen solidly and ice skating races were held, it was soon obvious that no one could come anywhere near besting him. Not infrequently he would skate the four miles up the South Branch to visit Liberty White at the Lee farm and pass along whatever news he had. Quite often he would join with the Indians in their games on the ice and had one special trick with the squaws that greatly delighted them. He would grasp one of the squaws by the hands and skate in a circle until she was pulled off her feet by the centrifugal force. Then, while still going 'round and 'round in tight circles, he would move with her from one side of the river to the other until he came to a deep snowbank. There he would let her go, supposedly by accident, and she would fly into a snowdrift, squealing with laughter, sometimes to be buried clear out of sight.

Several new residents had come to Chicago in recent months, including two French families not at all unfamiliar with life on the frontier. John Kinzie knew them both, having become acquainted with them long before their move, since they hailed from the area of Milwaukee. One of these families was that of Francis LaFramboise and his wife, Madeline, along with their eighteen-year-old daughter, Josette, and her younger brothers, Claude, seventeen, Alexis, sixteen, and LaFortune, fifteen.[193] They built a small place on the south side of the river not far from Fort Dearborn and were more than pleased at the arrival of their old neighbor from Milwaukee, trader Jean Baptiste Beaubien, who built his own place close to the LaFramboise residence.

Beaubien, who had initially entered the Indian trade at Detroit and afterwards worked at it in Mackinac, had eventually set up a post at Milwaukee. He and his Ottawa wife, Mahnawbunnoqua, had two young sons; the eldest, Charles Henry, had been born at Milwaukee in 1800 and the youngest, Madore, had also been born there in 1810. When Mahnaw-bunnoqua died in the first week of January, Beaubien had immediately moved to Chicago with his sons and hired Josette LaFramboise as house-keeper and nursemaid. Josette, who had been working for Jack Lalime as assistant interpreter — her knowledge of the Winnebago and Menominee tongues far better than his — much preferred working for, and being with, Jean Baptiste Beaubien. The arrangement caused some eyebrows to lift and tongues to waggle among the ladies in the fort, but that hadn't lasted long, since only the day before yesterday, just a few weeks after the death of his Ottawa wife, Jean Baptiste married Josette, with John Kinzie officiating as justice of the peace.

John Kinzie had also officiated, last summer, at the marriage of the widow Mary Cooper — whose house was just west of Kinzie's — to Thomas Burns, who had been a private at Fort Dearborn and stayed on in Chicago as a civilian after his enlistment expired. He was a quiet, strong, good-natured man who accepted her four children — fourteen-year-old James, eight-year-old Isabella, Anne, six, and Frances, three — as if they were his own. Now Mary Burns was pregnant with his child.

A concern of late for the Kinzies here in Chicago was the absence of educational facilities for their children. A year ago John Kinzie had hired his thirteen-year-old nephew, Robert Forsyth — son of Maggie and Will — and brought him to Chicago as a tutor for seven-year-old John, but Robert had soon tired of it and went back to Sandwich. As a consequence, only a few months ago the trader had hired a newly discharged private from the fort, John Kelso, as a tutor, but that hadn't lasted long either.[194] Kelso had certainly been intelligent enough and was a fairly good teacher, working equally well with little John, now eight, and his sisters, Ellen, six, and Maria, four. The problem was that Kelso imbibed much more than Eleanor thought proper for someone teaching her children and so she had had John discharge him less than three months after he had been hired. Feeling a little guilty about that and genuinely liking Kelso, the trader found him a job as a farmhand under Liberty White out at the Lee farm, where he was still working and evidently doing quite well. A fellow worker there, whom White had also just recently hired shortly after his arrival in Chicago, was a short, stockily built, taciturn little Frenchman named DuBou. For John Kinzie, however, the problem of schooling remained and unless some sort of school could be established for his own and other children here in Chicago very soon, he and Eleanor had decided to send John and Ellen to Detroit for schooling next fall, to be joined by Maria in a couple of years and, if it came to that, by little Robert when he was old enough, though now he was only approaching his second birthday.

As much as gossip involving local people and occurrences was a mainstay in Chicago's little society, there was one matter of much more serious nature that had become the most prevalent subject of discussion: last November's Battle of Tippecanoe and the frightening rise of hostilities on the frontier since then. Dispatch riders came and went at Fort Dearborn with much greater frequency than ever before and with each new arrival came more unsettling reports of outrages — killings, scalpings, mutilations. Each time a dispatch rider galloped in, the word of his arrival swept through the community at lightning speed and within minutes a crowd would be gathered at the fort to learn what news was brought. It was rarely good:

. . . Fort Harrison, built by General Harrison's army on its march up to the Tippecanoe and still garrisoned by United States troops, was in a perpetual state of alert due to parties of hostile Indians hovering close by.[195]

. . . An attempt by a militia detachment from Kaskaskia to cut off a party of Potawatomies led by Chief Chaubenee had failed.

. . . Rebekah Heald's uncle, Captain William Wells, now reappointed as Indian Agent at Fort Wayne, reported to Governor Harrison that the Indians — including many, he was sure, who had fought at the Battle of Tippecanoe — had had the gall to appear at Fort Wayne for their annuities. Even Tecumseh, Wells added, had shown up and demanded rifles and gunpowder and, when refused, had said in a threatening manner that it didn't make any difference, he would get them from the British. Then he had given a terrible war whoop and ridden off.

. . . Captain John Whistler had been placed in temporary command of Detroit when Governor William Hull had gone to Washington to confer with the President and Secretary of War, and there were rumors that he was to be given command of the Northwestern Department of the United States Army for the war that was coming.

. . . Governor Harrison's overblown accounts of the Tippecanoe affair as a "smashing victory" had been picked up by the war hawks in Congress, supplemented by reports of the British providing the Indians the wherewithal to attack Americas throughout the frontier; and one of those war hawks — Tennessee's Felix Grundy — had taken the floor and shouted,

"America must by force redress the violated rights and honor of an injured and insulted people!"

. . . Governor Ninian Edwards of the Illinois Territory was fearful of the increasing Indian attacks and darkly warned, "We need not flatter ourselves with safety. Only by waging war against them and perpetually harassing them can we convince them that it is in their interest to sue for peace."

. . . Governor Harrison at Vincennes raised his voice in a call for "a war of extirpation."

Yet, with all that upset, here in Chicago and the surrounding area, no outrages had occurred and no threats and there were those of the populace who still clung to the hope that the reports which filtered to this outpost of civilization were blown out of proportion or that, if true, perhaps the threatened war would never materialize; or that, if war did come, somehow their very isolation here would keep them out of it. Black Partridge and his people had always been friendly, hadn't he . . . hadn't they? Even Chaubenee, whose village was fairly close and who had been here often, had never shown anything but kindness toward the whites of Chicago, and wasn't he a rather close friend of John Kinzie, just as Black Partridge was? Surely the whites in Chicago were safe, weren't they?

But there were some who were not so sure of anything and John Kinzie was one of these. He may have been the first, but certainly he was not the only one who realized that Black Partridge's people had recently been coming to the settlement much less frequently and that when they came, though they smiled and gave friendly greetings as always, there was a reserve in them, a growing coolness. And so, taking their cue from settlers elsewhere on the frontier, many of the men of Chicago, even though not having suffered outrages themselves, were now carrying rifles with them wherever they went.

[*March 22, 1812 — Sunday*]

War was now inevitable.

Too many forces had been set into motion for it *not* to occur. Too many preparations had been made; too many agents prepared; too many warriors readied; too many soldiers eager for it to occur; too many congressmen already convinced of that inevitability and poised to vote for it. The Kentucky *Gazette* had already had the indelicacy to state on its first page:

Upper and Lower Canada to the very gates of Quebec will fall into possession of the Yankees the moment the war is started, without much bloodshed, for almost the whole of Upper Canada and a great part of the Lower Province is inhabited by Americans.

The war fever infected the Indians on the frontier as well and while many of them made their plans in concert with Tecumseh, who was regaining some of his lost influence and had collected several hundred warriors at Amherstburg, there were others who did not care to wait for a formal declaration of war. Their raids became bolder, harsher and even more shocking. The massacre of the O'Neal family near Peoria Lake in the Illinois Territory was a case in point. A party of Kickapoos swooped down upon it by surprise, killed and horribly mangled the ten members of the homestead and then, after looting it of everything usable, burned every structure to the ground.

All at once the urgency had transmitted itself to the United States government. William Henry Harrison was given authorization to take command of all troops in the Indiana and Illinois territories and even to call upon Kentucky for militia assistance if necessary. A dove by nature, the scholarly little James Madison had finally become convinced that no other course but war was possible and he summoned to Washington the governor of Michigan, William Hull, and former Secretary of War Henry Dearborn, who was now the customs collector in Boston. They had come enthusiastically — Dearborn believing he was being called to be named commander-in-chief of the whole United States Army, Hull believing he would be named Secretary of War to replace the less than adequate William Eustis. Both were mistaken.

Dearborn had been called to be asked if he would command the Eastern wing of the United States Army in an invasion scheme against Canada; Hull was asked to command the Northwestern wing. If they accepted, Dearborn would have to give up his lucrative position in Boston and Hull would have to give up his governorship of Michigan. Both refused, considering the cost too high and neither imbued with patriotism enough to justify the deficiencies. They left the capital.

Now they had been recalled by the President, who was convinced that in all of America he had no better military leadership potential than Hull and Dearborn. Adjustments were made and confirmed on this day. While he would still have to relinquish his customs position in Boston, Henry Dearborn would be given the rank of major general and placed in full command of the United States Army. Hull would be allowed to keep his governorship of Michigan and, on leave of absence, be given the rank of brigadier general and command of the Northwestern army.

Dearborn would direct the war from command headquarters, to be established at Albany, New York. Simultaneous invasions of Canada were to take place — always assuming, of course, that war was actually declared — from Sackett's Harbor in eastern Lake Ontario, from Niagara, perched between Lake Ontario and Lake Erie, and from Detroit.

But first it would be necessary to get an army to Detroit. Hull's orders were issued: he was to raise a Northwestern army of twelve hundred men, assemble them at Urbana, Ohio, and cut a road northward through the wilderness one hundred seventy-five miles to Detroit. In doing so, he was to cow the Indians into neutrality, convince the British at Amherstburg that they could no longer depend on Indian support, establish the Northwestern army at Detroit and be prepared to use that city as a launching point for the invasion of Canada when — and if — the time came.

A marvelous plan — assuming that one overlooked the fact that several hundred Indians had already gathered there, with more to come, all of them burning to take the harshest possible vengeance for the theft of their lands and the destruction of the Tippecanoe village.

And overlooking the fact that their leader was Tecumseh.

[*March 23, 1812 — Monday*]

John Kinzie, at work on his accounts, looked up and smiled as Eleanor entered the house. Her hair was slightly disheveled, a wisp of it curling down her left forehead, and he felt a surge of love for her, as so often happened when she moved a certain way or looked at him with a certain expression. He marveled inwardly that he could still feel this way about her after fourteen years of marriage.

"Be with you in just a moment," he said. "I'm on the last entries here."

She nodded and returned his smile as she removed the knitted shawl and draped it across the thick wall peg on the back of the door. She loved her home here, which was very comfortable and well appointed. As compared to the other houses in Chicago, it was a veritable mansion. And she believed that she had hidden very well from John the apprehension that had welled in her — and remained — when John had told her several weeks ago of his great gamble. He had learned from one of his agents in Detroit that the Fort Dearborn garrison, which had not been paid in five months, would be paid all back wages due them early in the summer through a special order by Congress. Lack of military enlistments and reenlistments had finally made the legislators realize that if the army was to get men — and keep them — the soldiers would have to be paid. At the present moment, John was owed a great deal of money by the Fort Dearborn soldiers and their families, to whom he had been selling, as official fort suttler, considerable goods on credit. Getting low on goods himself, he had realized the wisdom of stocking up well, not only on merchandise, but also on liquor. The problem was, his own cash reserves were quite low as a result of having extended so much credit to the garrison. It had not daunted him. On the first ship of the season to reach Chicago, he had sent back to Buffalo an enormous order for supplies, including more liquor than he had ever ordered at one time. Because the cash he had was insufficient to cover the order, he had put up his subsidiary trading posts at Milwaukee, Rock River, Kankakee River and St. Joseph as collateral. Not only that, he had included their own fine property here at Chicago as part of that collateral.

"Don't worry," he had said reassuringly, cupping her face in his hands when he saw her expression, "it's really not so much a gamble as you think. Besides, just being a trader has always been a gamble. It's something we live with."

"But John," she'd said then, "it's so much! We'd lose everything if anything happened."

"What's to happen? The war everyone expects is still only that — a war everyone expects. They've been expecting it for years, ever since that *Chesapeake* and *Leopard* affair on the Atlantic. It didn't come then, when there was more justification for it than now, and it didn't come after the Tippecanoe affair. We can't go through life not doing things because war *might* be declared. That's foolish.

"Anyway," he had kissed the end of her nose, "when this shipment I've ordered comes in and the garrison is paid, we'll be very, very well off. Not only will the bills be paid for the credit I've extended, but they'll be buying everything we can possibly stock up on. We're considered pretty well off now, but when that happens, we're going to find that we're very wealthy. So don't worry."

But Eleanor Kinzie *was* worried and she thought again, as she had a hundred times or more since then, that she wished he hadn't taken such a risk. She managed to hide her thoughts now as he closed his ledger and looked up at her again.

"Getting colder out?" he asked.

She shook her head. "Not really. Very mild. I think it's warmer today than it was yesterday. We'll probably pay for it in April. Oh, look at my shoes!"

The buckle-top shoes were heavily clogged with mud and she braced herself against the door as she gingerly took off one, then the other, and put them side by side near the wall. "I'll clean them later." She paused. "Better yet," she looked around, "where's Johnny?"

Her husband shrugged. "In his room, I suppose."

"Johnny!" she called loudly.

"Coming!" There was an unnecessarily loud clatter as the boy ran in and clumped to a stop before her, grinning. She smiled, bent down and kissed his forehead and then tilted her head toward the footwear.

"How 'bout doing mother a favor and cleaning those for me while Athena and I start getting dinner ready?"

"Aw, Momma." His face fell, but as her eyebrow quirked he grinned again and bobbed his head. "All right."

"Outside, if you please," she said. Her eyes followed him as he picked up the shoes with an exaggerated show of distaste and went out onto the porch, closing the door behind him. She glanced at the Seth Thomas pendulum clock on the mantel and grimaced. "Sorry I'm so late," she murmured, heading for the kitchen where Athena was already rattling pots and pans. "Mary and I let the time get away from us." Mary Burns, their neighbor, lived about a quarter-mile west.

He followed her out to the kitchen. "How's she doing?"

"Mary? Oh, she's fine. Big as a house now. If that baby doesn't come soon, she's apt to have problems."

"No sign of labor yet?"

"No, not yet." She looked at him questioningly. "Thought you were going over to the fort."

His smile became sheepish. "Fell asleep," he admitted. "Then got involved with the accounts. Do I still have time?"

"If a couple of hours is time enough," she replied. "No more than that, though, all right?"

He lifted her hair and kissed the back of her neck. "Fine. I'll see you later."

The discussion group, if it met at all, usually met on Mondays and Thursdays. Ordinarily John had their servant, Henry, take him across and wait for him, but this afternoon the genial black man was working in Kinzie's Store, helping the trader's chief clerk, Jean Baptiste Chandonnais, take inventory. Since he did not want to interrupt that, he moved quickly by himself to the riverbank, placed a foot inside the canoe and launched it, then paddled with easy strokes to the other side where he beached it well at the Fort Dearborn landing. The Mirandeau sisters, fourteen-year-old Madeline and twelve-year-old Victoire, were playing at a sapling, reaching up to bend the little tree far over and then letting it spring back and giggling. He waved at them and went on.

It was already near sunset and so if the group were in discussion, it would probably be breaking up within another half-hour or so. He walked a little faster and did not notice the head that had been peering over the wall at him as he crossed the river and which now ducked back out of sight.

Jack Lalime's stomach churned. How much he hated that bastard, John Kinzie. He had *everything* — everything, Lalime was convinced, that was rightfully his. Home, trading post, good clothing, good food, good liquor instead of harsh rum that burned your throat raw. And money! Wealth that should be mine, Lalime thought. As so often had happened before at the mere sight of Kinzie, the hatred rose in an overwhelming flood in him. This time there was a difference. This time it didn't reach a peak and then gradually abate.

This time something in Lalime's mind snapped.

The little man raced to his quarters and rummaged in a small trunk. When he straightened, he had a pistol in his hand. He checked the load, then thrust it into his waistband and covered it with his pullover shirt. He slapped his hand to his hip, feeling the sheathed knife there — a narrow-bladed weapon that he had become quite adept at throwing.

John Kinzie was at this moment leaving the officer's barracks and moving back toward the gate, though more slowly than he had entered. At the barracks he had discovered that there was no discussion group today. Ensign George Ronan was officer of the day and presently inspecting the defenses. As the trader walked back toward the gate his eyes lifted to the parapet, expecting to see Ronan. Instead, he saw his son-in-law, Linai Helm, and lifted a hand in brief greeting to the lieutenant.[196] He was not terribly fond of his stepdaughter's husband, but Linai and Margaret got along reasonably well, so his own feelings were largely inconsequential. So long as Margaret was happy, that was all that mattered.

The trader didn't even see if his wave were returned. His attention was taken by Jack Lalime, who fell in beside him. There was a peculiar glint in the interpreter's eyes, but his expression was unreadable. John Kinzie felt his own features tighten.

"What do you want, Lalime?" He continued walking toward the gate.

The color seemed to be draining from Lalime's face and his breathing became audible. They passed out through the open main gate together and Kinzie stopped, facing him. "I asked you a question," he said flatly.

Still the smaller man did not answer. His lips were pinched and blood-less. His dark eyes bored up into Kinzie's and there was a strangeness, a wildness about them that caused the trader to take an involuntary backward step. Though the interpreter was only four inches over five feet tall, he was well built and the menace of his aspect now suddenly made him look much larger.

"I told you, Kinzie," he rasped, his voice harsh, strained. "I told you back in St. Joseph I was going to kill you some day. I am. I'm going to kill you, you son of a bitch."

Despite the more than usual oddness of Lalime's behavior, Kinzie did not take the threat seriously. It was one Lalime had made many times before. He looked at the man steadily until Lalime shifted his eyes away, then said quietly, "Get away from me, Lalime. I don't know what's bothering you now, but I don't want to know. Just leave me alone. If you keep on like this, one of these days I'm going to have to step all over you."

He shouldered his way past the interpreter and continued toward the river where his canoe was beached. Again he saw the Mirandeau girls playing where they had been before, their faces aglow in the golden light of the sunset. Almost simultaneously he heard running footfalls and a yell.

The latter came from Lieutenant Helm, looking over the top of the stockade wall, and the note of urgency in it caused Kinzie's hair to prickle.

"John, *look out!* He's got a pistol!"

Kinzie spun about, feet widespread. The sound of footfalls came from Lalime. The Mirandeau girls were watching wide-eyed as he raced to overtake the trader, the pistol in his hand pointed directly at him. The expression on the interpreter's face was maniacal and an unearthly grunting sound came from him at each step. The trader reacted instantly. Instead of fleeing, throwing himself to one side or the other, or even remaining rooted in place, he plunged toward his assailant.

John Kinzie gripped Lalime's wrist and forced his hand upward, but their combined momentum caused them to slam together with stunning impact and the trader lost his hold on the wrist. They grappled fiercely and the little interpreter turned out to be much stronger than Kinzie had anticipated, jerking himself free enough to swing the pistol in toward the trader's head. John saw it coming, had a momentary glimpse of the muzzle of the weapon pointing into his face, the hole in the end of the gun barrel in one frozen fraction of time appearing to be as large as a cannon's. He jerked his head frantically to one side just as the gun exploded with a deafening concussion not more than a few inches from him. The muzzle flash burned his skin and the ball struck him with jarring impact in the left side of his neck just above the clavicle, smashing a hole the diameter of his little finger through the thick musculature there and passing out the rear without having struck the carotid artery. Neither had the bullet struck any bones.[197]

As the searing pain tore through him, Kinzie pivoted sharply and struck Lalime's forearm with a heavy blow of his fist, numbing the interpreter's arm and sending the gun spinning away. They closed, grappling fiercely again, the trader with his arms around the interpreter and Jack Lalime now struggling to pull his knife from his sheath. They fell to the ground together, both becoming stained by the blood pouring from Kinzie's neck wound. At last Lalime got the knife free and thrust it toward the trader's body, but Kinzie managed to deflect it with his elbow and clamp his hand over Lalime's on the haft.

Now it became a struggle of pure strength and in that the smaller man was no match. The muscles of his arm abruptly gave out and the knife, thrust forward with the power of Kinzie's grip, plunged to the fingerguard near the center of Lalime's chest, narrowly missing the sternum, sliding between two ribs, and the blade penetrated the heart. For just an instant Lalime's crazed eyes opened wide and his body stiffened. Then his muscles relaxed and his head fell back, eyes still open but no longer seeing.

John Kinzie came to his feet and stared down at the crimson stain spreading on Lalime's shirt where the knife still projected. Then he turned and ran unsteadily to his canoe and shoved off into the river. Waves of pain from his wound began throbbing through his neck and shoulder, but he paddled strongly nonetheless and in moments had reached the other side. He leaped from the boat and ran to his house.

"Oh my God, John!" Eleanor stared at him as he plunged inside and slammed the door closed behind him. The amount of blood on him made her suddenly weak and she swayed slightly. The children — Johnny, Ellen and Maria — were frozen, staring at him, frightened. Athena, coming in from the kitchen, also stopped, eyes widening. He gripped Eleanor's arm and shook his head.

"Not as bad as it looks," he said. "I have to get out of here. They'll be coming for me. I've killed Jack Lalime."

Eleanor shook off her immediate shock. "Wait," she said. She ran to another room and came back in an instant with a roll of bandaging. She took his right arm and began leading him toward the back door. "Johnny," she said over her shoulder, "take care of your sisters until I get back. Listen for Robert. If he wakes up, go get him and bring him in here. Don't be afraid. Some soldiers may come from the fort. If they do, tell them your father rode away and I'll be back in a little while."

They left the house by the back door and walked quickly to the stable, John explaining as they did so what he was going to do now. They led John's horse out by the bridle and snubbed the reins close over the gelding's mane so he would not trip on them or get caught in branches. Then John slapped the horse's rump sharply and yelled and the gelding immediately leaped away at a gallop, rounded the corral corner and thundered away northward into the dusk.

"He'll come back later," John said. "Come on."

They moved off afoot at a northwestern angle, crossing the small prairie pasture enclosed by what was called a worm fence, which was simply a fencing of interlocked split rails, and entering the grove of trees beyond. Within five minutes they reached the place John was looking for. It was a little hut that he and Henry had helped Johnny build as his "woods house" and where the boy often came alone to play, pretending he was a fearless frontiersman in his isolated cabin a thousand miles from civilization. It was so small that they had to get on their hands and knees to get inside.

In the rapidly fading daylight it was very dark within the structure, but it was dry and there was even an old ragged blanket that Johnny had brought out here. Quickly, Eleanor used a piece of the bandaging to wipe away what blood she could, then placed compresses on both entry and exit wounds and bandaged it, pulling the cloth stripping snugly enough around his neck to curtail the bleeding but not enough to hamper his breathing more than a little. As she worked, John explained everything that had occurred.

"I'm not concerned about being cleared," he told her. "What bothers me right now is the immediate reaction. Lalime had a lot of drinking cronies among the enlisted men. God only knows what they'd do if they got their hands on me."

Eleanor understood what she had to do without being told. "Stay here," she whispered. "Don't leave. I've got to get back to the children and talk to whoever comes. I'll be back here later tonight with some food and things. Everything'll be all right. Don't worry."

She kissed him and then crawled out the doorway, sliding back into place the unhinged piece of wood that served as a door. Then she retraced her steps to the house, entering the back door. She touched Athena's arm reassuringly as she passed through the kitchen. The children were as she had left them, huddled together and still frightened, the room lighted by three hurricane lamps. She reassured them and looked out the front window. The dusk was very heavy now, but she could see that a boat had landed and a number of men were getting out. Her eyes fell on John's rifle hanging over the mantel and she hesitated, then quickly took it down and slid it beneath the cushions on a settee. She smoothed her dress, picked up one of the lamps and stepped out on the porch as the squad of men came up.

There were seven of them — Ensign George Ronan and Quartermaster Sergeant Hugh Griffith with five privates. Ronan was the only one without a rifle. They stopped a dozen feet from the porch and the young officer took a step or two closer. He looked faintly embarrassed.

"Good evening, Mrs. Kinzie," he said. "Would you mind asking John to step out here, please?"

She shook her head. "He's gone. He rode away and said he was going to Milwaukee until all this blew over. He told me he thought he might have killed Mr. Lalime, but that Mr. Lalime attacked him. John was unarmed when it happened."

"The Mirandeau girls witnessed the whole thing," Ronan said. He looked past her into the house, saw the empty rifle pegs above the mantel, saw the children staring out toward him. "They said he'd been shot. Excuse me for saying so, ma'am, but wouldn't he have had a difficult time riding?"

She saw that now he was looking at a smear of blood on her sleeve. "He was hurt," she admitted, "but it wasn't bad. I dressed it for him and he left."

Ensign Ronan looked at the noncommissioned officer. "Sergeant?"

"Yes sir," Griffith said. He started to walk toward the stable.

"Wait!" Eleanor came to the edge of the porch and extended the lamp. "It's dark out there. Take this."

Surprised, the sergeant accepted it and moved off with three of the privates. Ronan watched them go and then turned back toward her. He hesitated before speaking, obviously even more embarrassed than before.

"Please excuse me, Mrs. Kinzie, but would you mind if I looked around inside? It isn't," he added hastily, "that I don't believe you. I just have my orders."

"I understand. Come in if you must."

She led the way and Ensign Ronan and the remaining two privates entered the house. They looked in the various rooms in a cursory way and then walked back toward the door. The privates stepped out on the porch and Ronan paused in the doorway, facing her.

"A board of inquest will be called on this," he said. His expression softened. "I don't really know what happened. I didn't see it. But I feel sure John'll be cleared of any murder charges." His voice lowered. "I will be part of that board. I'll help however I can."

The bobbing light in the darkness indicated the others were returning from the stable. Ensign Ronan went out onto the porch and Eleanor followed him to the doorsill. Sergeant Griffith came up on the porch, saluted the officer and handed the light back to her. "Thank you, ma'am," he said. "Sir, he's not in the stables, the store or any of the outbuildings. We checked the ground by the stables. There are fresh hoofprints of a horse going fast, heading north."

"All right, Sergeant, reform the squad. We'll return to the fort."

As the men reassembled in the darkness, George Ronan touched his fingers to his hat. "Thank you for your assistance, Mrs. Kinzie." Again he lowered his voice, this time to no more than a whisper. "I hope John's all right. When you see him, please give him my respects and best wishes. I'll let you know when matters have settled and he can come in."

He turned and went off into the darkness with the men. Eleanor remained where she was until she heard them thumping into the boat and then the oars dipping before she returned inside. She swiftly instructed Athena to serve portions of the dinner she'd been preparing, gave Johnny further instructions and quickly packed a small basket with bread, wine, cheese, some meat and fruit. She bundled up some fresh clothing and a blanket, picked up a lantern with its wick turned down to the lowest possible flame and left the house by the back door.[198]

[*March 24, 1812 — Tuesday*]

The burial of Jack Lalime took place at three o'clock in the afternoon.

In the morning, while a postmortem examination was being made by Dr. Isaac van Voorhis, the grave was being dug by a detail of soldiers. However, the grave was not located in the small military cemetery adjacent to the fort.

The news of the fatal incident had spread swiftly and within an hour or

so there was no one at Chicago, military or civilian — including even
Liberty White and his employees out at the Lee farm — who had not
heard of it. Reactions varied, but the most angry were the enlisted men at
the fort, many of whom were Lalime's drinking companions. In their
fury they presented themselves to their commander and demanded that a
detachment be sent to Milwaukee to arrest John Kinzie and bring him
back to be hanged, unless he resisted and had to be killed where apprehended. Captain Nathan Heald, who was not in the habit of entertaining
demands from privates, ordered them back to their quarters and told them
no action regarding Kinzie would be taken until after the military board of
inquest had completed its investigation. By his order, that board would
view the evidence and hear the testimony of witnesses on Wednesday.

The tempers had cooled somewhat by this afternoon, although the
commander was himself quietly furious that the incident had occurred.
Not only had the life of a government employee been taken, Fort Dearborn was now without the services of a good interpreter. Aware of the bad
blood that had existed between the trader and Lalime for so many years,
Nathan Heald's anger focused on John Kinzie. All sorts of stories were
circulating — ranging from reasonable representations of what had occurred to fanciful accounts of Kinzie having waylaid Lalime to murder
him in cold blood. Captain Heald had come to no conclusion in his own
mind yet, but the anger at Kinzie was there and that resentment was the
basis for his strange order regarding where Jack Lalime was to be interred.

Now, virtually the entire population was on hand for the burial, including Eleanor Kinzie off to one side, holding two-year-old Robert in her
arms, while Johnny, Ellen and Maria pressed close to her legs. Henry and
Athena, along with Black Jim, stood quietly to one side of them.
Nokenoqua was there, too, the Indian wife of Lalime. She was softly
weeping, holding in her arms the infant Lalime had sired. She was flanked
on the left by Lalime's assistant interpreter, Josette Beaubien, who was
also crying, and on the right by their fourteen-year-old housekeeper and
nursemaid, Madeline Mirandeau. Though no one commented on the fact,
it was perhaps significant that Nokenoqua was the only Indian in attendance, though all of the Indians in the vicinity had heard of it.

Although the site chosen for the grave had created an inconvenience for
some of those who were attending, including the military, Captain Heald
had remained adamant in respect to where it should be located. He had
also ordered one of the fort's carpenters to prepare a picket fence, to be
painted white and erected so as to enclose the grave. The burial spot the
Fort Dearborn commander had chosen with colossal bad taste was on the
north side of the river across from the fort and just slightly downstream,
within direct view from the front of the Kinzie house.

Now, with three riflemen standing ready to fire a salute over the grave when he was finished, Captain Heald stepped up to the head of the grave and stopped, opened *The Book of Common Prayer* he was holding, turned to the well-thumbed pages three hundred thirty-two and three hundred thirty-three and began to read:

" 'In the midst of life, we are in death. . . . Earth to earth, ashes to ashes, dust to dust; in sure and certain hope of the Resurrection unto eternal life. . . .' "[199]

[*March 25, 1812 — Wednesday*]

It was late in the afternoon when John Kinzie heard someone coming and stiffened. Whoever it was made much more noise than Eleanor had when she slipped in and out and so, for a moment, an apprehension gripped him. Then, through one of the cracks, he saw that it was Eleanor after all and he grinned at her as she entered.

"You sounded like a plow horse coming," he chided in a bantering way.

She sniffed in mock affront. "That's a fine thing to call me! How's the neck?"

He shrugged, then winced in reaction. "Stiff. Sore. Painful. But I'll live. What's happening?"

"A lot!" She laughed lightly and kissed his cheek. "It's why I was careless about noise this time. You've been exonorated, John. They held the inquest this morning. Ensign Ronan came and told me about it after it was finished. Said I could send word to you to come home now."

A relieved breath whooshed from him and he pressed her for details. She told him what George Ronan had told her. The board of inquest had been comprised of Captain Heald, as president, and Lieutenant Helm, Ensign Ronan and Dr. Van Voorhis as members. Soldiers who had seen or talked to John when he had entered the fort that afternoon had testified, as had the Mirandeau girls, Madeline and Victoire. The Kinzie's son-in-law had also testified to how he had seen John and Lalime leave the fort together through the main gate and then of John's walking away toward the river, with Lalime a moment later pulling out a pistol that he had hidden in his clothing and running after John. All the testimony showed that John had been unarmed and was obviously acting in self-defense when Lalime had been killed by his own knife. Ensign Ronan had testified to the recovery and removal of Lalime's body into the fort and the subsequent unsuccessful call at the Kinzie house to arrest the trader. And Dr. Van Voorhis had testified clinically to the cause of death, saying that the blade of the knife had penetrated the victim's heart. A sharp clash of opinion had occurred between Captain Heald and Ensign Ronan when the commanding officer alleged that Kinzie's flight appeared to be an indication of guilt and Ronan angrily retorted that it was no more than an indication of damned good sense, since the man was quite familiar with the headstrong nature of Lalime's friends, especially when in their cups, and had wisely chosen not to expose himself to it. The upshot was the judgment, unanimously given, that John Kinzie, trader, had acted strictly in self-defense, was not guilty of murder and any and all charges against him were dropped.

"So," Eleanor said, touching his cheek gently, "you can come home now, John."

"Not just yet," he replied. "Tonight. After dark. You go back now and I'll see you then. We don't want to have people think you did not tell the truth about my going to Milwaukee. I'll come in after dark and stay out of sight for the length of time it would reasonably have taken to send someone to Milwaukee and get back here. Go on, now, I'll see you later."

Agreeing with him, she began to leave but stopped when he spoke her name.

"Two things," he said. "I didn't like Jack Lalime, but I very much regret having killed him. And concerning his grave, so long as we live here, we're going to see that it's well cared for."

She nodded and her eyes filled with tears as she crawled outside and began walking home. She was *very* proud of her husband.[200]

[March 28, 1812 — Saturday]

For all intents and purposes, much of the frontier was already at war.

Chief Main Poche and his Potawatomies, recently joined by roving bands of Kickapoos and Winnebagoes, were the principal cause of the troubles. Feeling that the crumbling of Tecumseh's amalgamation of tribes due to the Tippecanoe affair had more or less released him from his promises to sit tight and not take offensive action, Main Poche struck. He still had full intentions of being on hand with Tecumseh and the Indian force still under the Shawnee when he was needed in the country at the western end of Lake Erie, but until then he was going to take his measure of satisfaction.

Throughout March he had been hitting the settlers of central and southern Illinois Territory and some of the western Indiana Territory. With frantic haste, little blockhouses were being erected at almost every settlement in that country, where settlers, at first alarm, could gather up and retire for mutual defense. It didn't always work. Andrew Moore and his seventeen-year-old son, returning home from the little bastion grandiosely named Fort Jordan, camped along the old Massac Road where it crossed a ford of the Middle Fork of Big Muddy River. Main Poche's party found their trail, followed them up and killed them after a savage little fight.[201]

In similar raids they wiped out the Huston family at their homestead on the Wabash River to the southwest of Vincennes, the Harriman family on the Embarrass River of the Illinois Territory and the Hinton family on Driftwood Creek, a branch of the White River southeast of Vincennes. In one frightening week, the band killed fourteen settlers in the Illinois country less than a dozen miles from Vincennes.

Unafraid of the American detachments being sent out by Governors Harrison and Edwards to intercept him and his men, Main Poche nonetheless had respect for their strength and realized that sooner or later they would march against his own village. To thwart this, only last week he had ordered the village abandoned and led his people unseen past Chicago, stopping briefly to visit with Black Partridge, then continuing north and slightly west to the shores of a substantial little lake sixty miles from Chicago.[202] Here they visited for a day or two with Potawatomi Chief Mawgehset, whose village was at the far eastern end of the lake. Mawgehset perpetually wore a red handkerchief wrapped around his head in a band. A large, unusually ugly, angular individual with enormous splayed feet — for which attribute he was known to the white traders as Big Foot — Mawgehset welcomed them with liquor. He was delighted with their intention of settling close to him and helped them select a pleasant site on the south shore of the pretty glacial lake. Main Poche named his new village Washnonong.

Despite their passage close to Chicago, the band under Main Poche made no move against the settlement. And though the whites there had no inkling yet of his proximity, there was an aura of fear and suspicion prevailing in the village as a result of the rumors and reports that had filtered in about increasing Indian attacks. Those feelings were sharply augmented by the minor incident which occurred today.

There had never been any trouble in Chicago with either Black Partridge's Potawatomies northwest of Fort Dearborn, nor from the Potawatomies under Chief Naunongee, whose principal village was twelve miles south of the fort at the point where the Calumet River emptied into Lake Michigan. But today Naunongee, with one of his subchiefs, came to visit the fort, as he was accustomed to doing on infrequent occasions.

In the prairie directly south of the main gate to the fort and adjacent to the main trail paralleling the lake shore, Rebekah Heald and Margaret Helm were playing a game of battledore, laughing brightly as they batted the little feathered ball back and forth.[203] They were being observed from the sidelines by several of the soldiers' wives, plus Emmaline Clark, wife of the new settler, Samuel Clark, who had just arrived and was building a house at the fork of the Chicago River. Also there was Rebekah's slave, Cicely, holding her infant son, Benjamin. Rebekah was very distinctly showing her own pregnancy these days.

Margaret Helm, who had lived for a long time in proximity to the village of Topenebe at St. Joseph, when her name was Margaret McKillip, was quite conversant with the Potawatomi language. What she had not been able to learn from association with the Indians, she had learned from her trader stepfather, John Kinzie.

Now, as Naunongee and his companion passed close by and stopped for a moment to watch the women at play, the women waved at them and they waved back. Then Naunongee, speaking in the Potawatomi tongue, said something to his companion. Both men laughed and continued into the fort. Behind them, Margaret's face had gone white.

Rebekah saw something was wrong and came to her side at once. "Margaret, what on earth's the matter?"

"It's . . . it's what Naunongee said. He didn't know I'd understand."

"Well, in heaven's name, girl, tell me. What did he say?"

Still pale, still staring at the open gate of Fort Dearborn, Margaret Helm spoke in a strained voice. "He said, 'The white chief's wives are amusing themselves very much. It will not be long before they will be hoeing in our cornfields.' "[204]

[*April 5, 1812 — Sunday*]

Mary Burns had gone into labor as the clock was striking noon.

"It's time, Tom," she told her husband, and immediately he had sent fifteen-year-old James running to get Eleanor Kinzie, then helped Mary into bed. The moment James excitedly blurted his message at the Kinzie house, Eleanor gave some rapid instructions to Athena and Henry and then she went with the youth to his house, where they arrived in a few minutes. She took over midwifery duties with the competence for which she was noted in the community and now, at 4:30 P.M., the first lusty squallings of a newborn filled the cabin.

Her hands and the infant slightly stained with blood, she held it up, umbilical cord still convoluting downward toward its source, and showed it to the mother. Mary Burns, dark hair plastered to forehead and temples by perspiration, smiled, weak and relieved.

"It's a . . . ?"

"Oh, sorry," Eleanor said, moving her hand away that had been blocking the mother's view of the genitalia. "Girl. She's a beautiful little girl."

She lowered the infant onto a cloth and in a few moments the placenta was ejected from the mother. Eleanor expertly tied and snipped the cord and took the baby to the drysink where the large basin of tepid water that Tom had prepared was waiting. As she did so, he moved to his wife with another basin and cloths and cleaned her carefully. It was her fifth child but his first and his excitement was evident, yet he did not let it master him.

By five o'clock, Eleanor was ready to leave. She stopped at the doorway and looked back, hoping her smile masked the weariness that was filling her. "If you need anything, just send James or Isabella to fetch me," she said. The nine-year-old looked up at mention of her name and smiled shyly. "I'll send Athena over with some food in a little while. And I'll be back to give you a hand here tomorrow. I like the name you've picked for her. Catherine. It's a good name."

"Nelly," — Mary Burns was the only one in Chicago that ever called her by the old childhood nickname — "we can't thank you enough. God bless you. You're a good woman . . . a good friend. I'm happy for you that John's home from Milwaukee again and everything's been settled."

Eleanor smiled, more genuinely this time, and closed her eyes momentarily. "Thanks, Mary. So are we." Then she was gone.

[*April 6, 1812 — Monday, 9:00 A.M.*]

The party of eleven Winnebagoes from the upper Rock River stopped to prepare their meal and themselves on the little meandering stream known as Salt Creek. At this point the creek wound through a lovely glade of massive old oaks, shagbark hickories and occasional stately elms, their buds already swelling. The ground cover was a low grass newly turned to brilliant emerald in these early warming days of spring. From this place, along one of the minor Indian trails heading southeastward, they were nineteen miles away from Fort Dearborn.[205]

Their leader was a strong young subchief named Okat, who had first come into prominence among his own people several years ago when he had inadvertently blundered into a black bear which attacked him, and which he ultimately killed with his knife during a ferocious struggle. The keloid scars on his chest and back in neat parallel lines, caused by the bear's claws, and the heavier scar tissue on his left shoulder, along with his split left ear, where the bear's teeth had gripped him, were trophies he wore proudly.

At Okat's admonition, the warriors ate sparingly or not at all, as was their custom before confronting enemies. In this case the enemies were Americans — *all* Americans. Plied in their home village by strong words and strong liquor provided by a British trader, they had decided to prove their courage by moving against the settlers in the area of Chicago, determined to kill every settler they could find outside the fort.

With the light meal of jerky and parched corn and pemmican to sustain them, they set about painting one another's faces in patterns meant to strike fear into the hearts of enemies. Most of the patterns were diagonal lines or horizontal bars of ochre, vermilion and white on forehead, cheeks and chin. Okat, however, was painted in a manner that set him somewhat apart from the other ten. From just above the eyebrows to the hairline, his forehead was painted solidly from temple to temple with the brilliant red of vermilion; from his nasal septum to his chin and across each cheek to just below the earlobes and down to the jawline it was the muddy yellow of ochre. Across the center of his face, from just in front of one ear to just in front of the other, it was painted black. But what made the appearance even more hideous was the torn ear painted red and the other painted blue. Upper and lower eyelids were painted stark white so that when the eyes were open they were only rimmed with white, but when closed they were circles of pure white. The effect of the whole was no less than frightening and he was very pleased.

Of the warriors in his party, only he and his closest friend, Neckech, could speak any English — he only brokenly at best, and Neckech even less. Four of them were armed with new British rifles and the remainder carried bows and arrows. A few had war clubs. All had tomahawks and knives.

Now, with the preparations completed, Okat stood up. "We have business to see to," he said.

As one, they came to their feet and fell in behind him in single file as he led the way, more cautiously than heretofore, along the narrow winding trail leading toward Fort Dearborn.

[*April 6, 1812 — Monday, 11:30 A.M.*]

Eleanor Kinzie inspected her husband's neck with experienced eye and made a soft sound of approval. "It's healing very well," she said. "Hurt much now?"

"Only if I forget and turn my head too fast," John replied.

"Fine. Try to remember not to turn your head too fast. It's scabbing over pretty well and I think we can leave the bandages off now so it'll heal faster." She went to the kitchen and returned in a moment with the two fresh loaves of bread Athena had baked this morning, now wrapped in a cloth and under one arm, and carrying a pot of stew by the handle in the other hand. "I'm off," she said. "I'll probably stay at Mary's house until around sunset. If you need me for anything, send Henry or Athena over."

"All right." He smiled as he opened the door for her and watched as she moved purposefully off toward the Burnses' house, thinking how lucky the new parents were to have her as a neighbor.

[*April 6, 1812 — Monday, 12:20 P.M.*]

Corporal Richard Garner had easily shoved the little skiff off from the Fort Dearborn landing, hopping into the front of the boat as the bow left the shore. Four other soldiers, all privates, were with him, two at the oars and two in the rear. On the floor of the boat were five long slender poles cut from riverside willow saplings, each with lines, whiskey-cork bobbers and hooks attached. Two packs lying beside them contained a small amount of food for the outing, and a fair amount of whiskey. Several prepared torches lay there, too, next to a container of lamp oil, which they would be using on their return, since they planned to fish until dark before returning to the fort. Finally, there were several tins of dirt containing the bait they would be using — dozens of nightcrawlers they had collected from the dewy surface of the ground under lamplight last night.

Because the corporal and four privates had pulled guard duty yesterday when it was a day of rest for the remainder of the garrison, Corporal Garner had asked permission of Captain Heald to take the skiff to a particularly good fishing hole they knew of up the South Branch, a couple of miles beyond the Lee farm. Permission had been granted and now they were en route. Shortly after shoving off, the heavy wooden boat moving sluggishly to the pull of the oars, they had passed the Burns house. They knew Tom Burns well, he having been a private among them before his enlistment expired, and they'd heard of the birth of the baby girl there yesterday. Seeing Eleanor Kinzie just approaching the cabin, Corporal Garner had stood up and waved.

"Morning, Mrs. Kinzie," he called through cupped hands. "How's the new Burns baby doing?"

"Just fine," she called back. "It's a girl, you know. Fine and healthy."

"Well, give Mary and Tom our congratulations. We'll try to bring them back some fish this evening."

"I'll tell them," she responded. "They'd like that. Good luck!"

A few moments later they had reached Wolf Point, where the North and South Branches formed the main river. They turned left, up the South Branch. They saw Samuel Clark and his wife, Emmaline, at work on their new cabin on the same side of the river as the fort, but since the couple were new here and they didn't know them well, they only waved and continued upstream.

Now, after almost an hour of steady rowing, switching places at the oars now and then, they were passing the Lee farm, which was bisected by the river. On their left, along the south bank, were a number of little haystacks and, beyond them, eight or ten milk cows grazing on patches of new grass that had sprouted. To their right, on the north bank, was the house and barn and several smaller outbuildings. The house was enclosed by a split-rail fence with a gap facing the river. There was also a small wharf of heavy planking laid across oak pilings, with two canoes tied to it. In the field beyond the house two men were plowing behind two different teams of horses. One of these was the relatively new field hand whom they'd heard about but not met — the heavy-set French-Canadian named DuBou. The other man they knew very well, since he had not only been a private at the fort, he had also been a drinking companion. Like Tom

Burns, he had settled in the area following the expiration of his enlistment. He was John Kelso. Since he was too far out in the field to call to effectively, Corporal Garner put two fingers into his mouth and whistled shrilly. When Kelso looked their way, they all waved at him. He waved back.

Closer to the house, the three who had been repairing the fencing of the hog pen straightened. Two of them the men in the boat recognized immediately — the farm's supervisor, Liberty White, and fifteen-year-old Charles Lee, Jr., son of the co-owner. The other man, unfamiliar to them, was a new worker White had hired only a short time ago — a heavily mustached Frenchman named Jean Baptiste Cardin. A small white dog at his feet barked at the men in the boat and wagged its tail. The three workers also waved and immediately bent back to their labors.

"Never knew of anybody who works as hard as that Liberty White does all the time," commented one of the privates at the oars, between grunts. The fat private in the stern snorted.

"That's probably because he's never learned the wonder and glory of whiskey," said another, speaking in a broad brogue.

"Speaking of which," piped up the thin young private in the stern seat beside the fat one, "what say we uncork one of our bottled treasures in the pack?"

Corporal Garner knew his companions too well for that. He grinned and shook his head. "Not till we get where we're going," he told them. "We start guzzling it now, we're apt never to get to the fishing hole at all. Row on, boys."

[April 6, 1812 — Monday, 6:00 P.M.]

Because he enjoyed cooking, Liberty White had declared himself cook at the Lee farm as well as its supervisor, and he'd made young Charlie Lee his chief dishwasher and cleaner-upper. At the moment, White was in the midst of preparing dinner and pleased that he could provide a good substantial meal for the hungry men here who had worked hard all day. Slabs of precooked ham were sizzling in a large frying pan on the heavy iron cookstove and a pot filled with several pounds of diced potatoes and cut carrots was bubbling merrily. Five places were set at the big table, each with sturdy pewter plates and flatware. There were also five large pewter mugs, each filled to the brim with fresh milk. White insisted that each of them drink at least one mug of milk at breakfast and another at dinner, contending that it made their bones strong. There was a large bowl of butter on the table, too, the shapeless pale yellow lumps fresh from the churn, and a squat loaf of bread that he had already sliced into five thick slabs. A high-crusted dried-apple pie was resting on the sideboard.

Cardin was presently outside the door at the washstand, scrubbing his face and hands, his little white bitch, Dolly, prancing about at his feet. She rarely left his side. Kelso and DuBou, having been summoned by Charlie, had just finished unharnessing the horses and giving them fodder and were now coming toward the washstand with the youth.

"Dinner in about fifteen or twenty minutes, boys," White called out. "Come in and relax until then." He continued with his cooking, turning the meat with the point of a butcher knife and resuming his tuneless whistling. Cardin, Dolly at his feet, entered first, wearing his perpetual grin and his teeth gleaming whitely beneath the bushy black mustache. He was followed by young Charlie, who sniffed and salivated.

"Boy, does that smell good, Liberty," he said, "I'm starved!"

"Never knew you not to be," White responded. "I've even heard you smacking your lips in your sleep, which means you're either dreaming about food or women, and since you're too young for women . . ." He let the sentence trail off and DuBou and Kelso, now entering the door, joined in the laughter as Charlie flushed deeply.

They took their seats around the table, both Frenchmen lighting pipes as the supervisor continued with the preparation of their dinner. They dug at one another good-naturedly — with poor Charlie the butt of most of their ribbing — and casually discussed the weather, livestock, the rapidly approaching planting season and women. They were in the midst of talking about Corporal Garner and his friends having passed in their boat earlier in the day when, without any warning, the door was yanked open and the Indians entered.

There were eleven of them, all garishly painted, and one with a split ear stained bright red — Okat and his Winnebago warriors. They crowded in, blocking the door, and simply stood there unspeaking. So startled were the white men that they were paralyzed in their attitudes of surprise and the only movement was that made by Dolly as she slunk under the table, her tail between her legs, and crouched there making a sound that was half whine, half growl. The first of the men to recover was Liberty White.

"Easy," he said softly, conversationally, "just sit still." There were few weapons among them: a pair of flintlock rifles on pegs above the fireplace, a horse pistol in a holster hanging from a wall peg closer to the door, an old army saber, slightly rusted and with its tip broken, leaning in a corner. Only DuBou and Cardin carried sheath knives on their belts. White, at the moment, was still holding the butcher knife.

The unceremonious entry of the Indians was not a terribly uncommon event. Small parties coming from or heading to Black Partridge's village occasionally stopped by and, in their usual way, entered without knocking or otherwise announcing their presence. When they did, they stayed only a little while, passing news and hoping for a little handout of food and perhaps a swallow of whiskey, which they unfailingly received. But those were friendly Potawatomies, unpainted and smiling. These Indians were very different.

"Greetings, friends," White said casually, addressing the split-eared Okat, whom he correctly took to be their leader. "Do you speak English?"

There was no reply, no change in the generally sour expressions. A trickle of perspiration began coursing down the small of White's back. He noticed that Split-Ear was staring at the butcher knife he held and he reacted casually.

"We're just getting our dinner ready," he said lightly. Still smiling, he walked carelessly to the sideboard, carefully skirting the fireplace where the rifles were hung. He picked up the pie and walked to the table with it, where he put it down and used the knife to cut it into wedges. As he did so, he muttered in an undertone for the others to hear.

"We've got troubles here, I think. They're not Potawatomies. Maybe Winnebagoes, the way they're painted."

"Oh my God," Cardin murmured. They had all heard rumors of murders being committed recently by Winnebagoes and Sacs in the Mississippi Valley.

"If that's the case," Kelso whispered, "we'd better get away from them if we can."

White looked at him. "Get the boy away. We'll try to follow in a little while." When Kelso gave a barely perceptible nod, he straightened, placed the knife on the table beside the pie so as to allay the suspicions of the Indians and walked back to the stove. Still unmoving, the Winnebagoes watched him.

"What's your name?" he asked the split-eared Indian. He touched his own chest with a finger. "I am White."

Okat let his eyes flick across the other hands and then looked back at the supervisor. "All men here white," he said. It was not a joke.

Liberty White laughed aloud as if it were the funniest thing he'd ever heard. He wiped one eye with a finger and then glanced at the ex-soldier. "Kelso, did you and Charlie finish those chores?"

"Not yet," Kelso replied, managing to look shamefaced.

The farm manager's laughter stopped and his voice became curt. "Then, damn it, get out there and finish them! You're not getting any dinner until you do. You were hired to do a job here!"

Kelso sighed and got up, momentarily turning his back to the Indians, during which he whispered quickly to the youth. "Follow my lead. Say nothing. Do as I do." He made a motion with his hand for the boy to follow him and walked directly toward the door, Charlie at his heels. The Indians didn't move and he carelessly began shouldering his way through them. So taken by surprise were the Indians that they moved aside enough to let them pass and they were outside by the washstand before Okat shouted, "Stop!" He was at the door.

Kelso and Charlie stopped and looked back. "Where go?" Okat demanded.

Kelso pointed across the river where, in the last rays of the sunset, the cows had moved in closer among the haystacks. "Forgot to feed the cows," he said. When Okat frowned, not understanding, he spoke louder, pointing again. "Cows! Moooo! Must feed!" He scooped up a handful of grass, put it close to his mouth and made chewing movements. "Food! Must feed! We come back soon. Eat dinner!" He patted his stomach, then turned and walked toward the little wharf without another backward glance, Charlie following closely, his face drained of color. "On your life," Kelso gritted, "don't look back!"

The canoes were tiny, built for one person each. Kelso directed the boy into one and got into the other himself. They quickly shoved off and paddled the sixty or seventy feet across the stream. Beaching the boats, they walked up on shore, separated and made a little show of rounding up the cows, aware the Indians were watching them. They deliberately forced one cow to amble toward the woodland and followed, as if attempting to turn her. Twenty yards from the trees the cow broke and ran back toward the others.

"Run for it!" Kelso shouted and the pair fled to the protective cover. Safely out of sight, they circled back and peered through a screen of bushes, panting with their fear more than their exertions. Some of the Indians were still in the doorway, gesticulating and shouting in their own tongue. Then they leaped inside and there came the sound of crashing and more shouts.

Then there were shots — two in succession.

"Jesus God!" Kelso breathed. "Come on, boy, we've got to get back to the fort. *Run!*"

[*April 6, 1812 — Monday, 6:18 P.M.*]

In the dusk beginning to gather, Corporal Richard Garner looked with distaste at the dozen or so bullheads of various sizes in the bottom of the boat, some quiescent, some still flopping. "Dunno who's gonna clean 'em," he said, " 'cept I know it's not gonna be me." His voice was thick, attributable to the goodly portion of whiskey he had consumed from the two bottles, now empty, circling in a little eddy near shore.

"Well," said one of the privates, with more stridency than necessary, "sure's hell ain't gonna be m——"

"*Quiet!*" Garner's hand came up with the command. "You hear that?" There was less slur in his voice.

They all took attitudes of listening, some exaggerated, until finally the fat private broke wind very loudly and instantly the other three were convulsed with laughter.

"Damn it, I said quiet!" Garner hissed. "Thought I heard shots."

"Shots? Hell, Garner," the thin private said, hiccoughing and containing a strong urge to giggle, "who'd be huntin' 'round here?"

"I dunno," the corporal said thoughtfully."I dunno. C'mon. Let's get the hell out of here. Time to head back anyway."

They weren't in any hurry and by the time they brought in their lines and wrapped them around the poles, stowed the gear and moved the fish out from under the feet of the rowers, then untied the boat from the large willow branch overhanging the river, the dusk had deepened, though it was not yet dark. Corporal Garner, in the bow, picked up one of the premade torches from the bottom of the boat, carefully soaked it in the container of lamp oil, recapped the container and moved it away and then used his flint and steel to light the torch. It ignited with a little poof and he held it aloft. Then they started downstream.

[*April 6, 1812 — Monday, 6:20* P.M.]

Eleanor Kinzie left the Burns house with a little wave and began to hurry home, irritated with herself for getting so involved in talking with Mary that she'd let the time slip away. She'd told John she'd be home about sunset, but already the dusk was pretty heavy. The sound of excited voices came from the opposite side of the river, back toward the forks, and she could just make out the shadowy forms of two men outside the Clark house, yelling something she couldn't make out. She thought they were soldiers who might have had a little too much to drink. Even as she watched, they left the house and ran downstream along the shore directly opposite her, heading toward the fort. She was about midway between the Burns house and her own when the pair on the opposite side caught sight of her.

"Mrs. Kinzie! Is it Mrs. Kinzie?"

"Yes," she called back, stopping. "What is it?"

"*Indians!*" There was raw fear in the word but she didn't recognize the voice. As if realizing this, the man went on. "It's me, ma'am, Kelso. John Kelso. Warn the Burnses and Mr. Kinzie. They're hittin' the Lee farm. They may've killed Mr. White an' the others. You better come to the fort!"

The pair raced on and now she recognized the smaller one as Charles Lee's son. Turning, she ran back to the Burns house and threw the door open. "Tom! Douse your lights and bar the door. Indians! At the Lee place! We'll send help from the fort."

Before they could even reply, she slammed the door and ran.

[*April 6, 1812 — Monday, 6:24* P.M.]

John Kinzie was chuckling as he drew the bow across the strings of his fiddle in a lively reel, pleased that his neck wound hurt little and hardly interfered at all with his playing, pleased also at how much Johnny had improved on the harmonica and how well he could now accompany his father. Ellen was whirling before the cheerily crackling fire in her own version of a solo dance and little Maria was clapping her hands and giggling. In the high chair, Robert was pounding with a wooden spoon, though with no conception of keeping time.

As a surprise, under the stern and disapproving eyes of Athena, they had prepared dinner and the tea-table was spread and waiting for the wife and mother whose arrival they had been expecting momentarily for the past half hour or so. Athena had finally gone to join Henry in their own quarters several minutes ago. The faintest niggling of worry had begun bothering John and he glanced at the mantel clock again. He decided he'd wait another few minutes. If Eleanor weren't back by half-past, he'd go to the Burns house.

He didn't have to.

The door burst inward and Eleanor was there, gasping from the unaccustomed exertion of her run as well as from fear. "Indians!" she blurted. "The Indians!"

The fiddle clattered to the floor as the trader leaped to his feet and ran to her. "Where?" he demanded. "What's happened?"

"Coming! They're coming! They're up at Lee's farm, killing and scalping!"

John Kinzie took over. He pulled the rifle down from the mantel. "Get the children to the boats," he said. "I'll go warn the Burnses."

"I've already told them. Mary can't walk. I told them we'd send help from the fort."

"All right, then, let's get out of here." He quickly turned out the two lamps and in the dimness pulled Robert, who was crying, out of the high chair and handed him to Eleanor, then snatched up Ellen and Maria, one under each arm.

"Johnny," he said, "run over and alert Henry and Athena. And Black Jim. Chandonnais, too, if he's still in the store. Then meet us at the boats."

They left the cabin, slamming the door behind, and ran toward the river shore where their two piroques were beached.

[April 6, 1812 — Monday, 6:40 P.M.]

The alarm brought by John Kelso and Charlie Lee had turned Fort Dearborn into a madhouse. Orders were being called, women were screaming for their children to stay close and children were crying. Soldiers shouted to one another as they tumbled from the barracks, followed by more wives and children. Scattered residents from outside the fort were coming in, from both sides of the river.

Captain Nathan Heald was trying to be everywhere at once and not succeeding. At his orders, Lieutenant Helm was attempting to form his men, get the artillery crews in position and men situated and ready to slam and bar the gates of the fort as soon as the Indians should appear. The Kinzies intercepted the commanding officer as he trotted across the parade ground.

"You've got to send help for the Burns family," Eleanor told him anxiously. It was nearly full dark now.

"Mrs. Kinzie, my first duty is to protect this fort and those within it. They'll have to get here on their own. I won't order my —"

"They can't," John Kinzie interjected calmly. "Mrs. Burns can't walk. She just had a baby yesterday. There are complications. Also, they have four other children. They don't have a boat. If —"

The thudding boom of one of the cannon interrupted him, shaking the ground with its heavy concussion and startling those who had not expected it. Captain Heald had ordered it fired to alert anyone outside the fort who was still unaware of the danger.

"Sir!" It was Ensign George Ronan, who had overheard the conversation. "You don't have to order anyone to go out there. I'm volunteering. Let me take half-a-dozen men and the boat and I'll bring them in."

Captain Heald hesitated, frowning, but then nodded. "Go ahead. Take volunteers *only* from among the enlisted men. If the Indians have gotten between you and the Burns house, turn around and come back instantly. That's an order."

"Yes sir!" The junior officer raced off, forgetting to salute.

"Lieutenant Helm!" The commanding officer looked around at the shadowy figures, not seeing him. He called again and the lieutenant ran up.

"Yes sir?"

"Lookouts posted?"

"Yes sir."

"Good." The commander was much more in control of himself and the situation now. "If they sight any Indians, get those gates closed immediately, I don't care who's outside. But if you have to close them, put a guard on the sally port to let Ronan and his people in when they return. I also want you to issue rifles from our store to every man who does not have one."

"Yes sir! Do you think it's a general uprising, sir?"

"I don't know, Lieutenant, but I intend being ready for whatever it is."

A few feet away, John Kinzie, undoubtedly the most knowledgeable man in the fort in regard to Indians, was not asked for his opinion about anything.

[*April 6, 1812 — 7:10 P.M.*]

Moving as quietly as possible in the darkness, the soldiers approached the little wharf at the Lee farm. They were unarmed and frightened and the four privates wanted nothing more than to continue rowing and get back to the fort as quickly as possible. Whatever alcohol-induced fuzziness was in them had dissipated when they'd heard the muted rumble of the cannon half an hour ago. They'd stared at one another and then Corporal Garner had plunged the flaming torch into the river.

It was then that the corporal remembered earlier having heard what he thought were distant shots and he felt the gooseflesh rise on his arms and legs. "I don't know what it all means," he'd whispered to the four privates, "but it's got to be a danger signal. Indian trouble, probably. No more talking now. That's an order. Dip those oars as quietly as you can and keep in the middle of the river till we get to the Lee farm. We'll stop there and warn them, or see if they know what the trouble is."

Now they were approaching the little pier and their fear was all but dominating them. The place was in total darkness and Garner hadn't counted on that. Somehow he had thought the lights would be ablaze and they would just go right on in. Now he was sorry he'd said they would stop here and wished he could back out. Not a sound was coming from the darkened buildings.

"If you think I'm going to get out of this boat, you're crazy," one of the privates whispered.

"Shut up!" Richard Garner hissed. "I told you, no talking."

The boat slid through the darkness and bumped with muffled thud against one of the pilings. Garner quickly wrapped the bow rope around it in a loose knot. Then they sat quietly a moment and listened. Nothing. No sound of bird or insect or any living creature and the very silence compounded their fears.

"Listen to me," Garner said, whispering as softly as he could and still be heard. "You boys stay here. I'll check the house. *Stay here!* I swear to God, if you're gone when I get back here, I'll kill every one of you. I mean it!"

No one responded. They believed him. He removed his shoes and soundlessly placed them in the bottom of the boat, then eased himself up onto the wharf. Tears formed in his eyes from trying to see into the darkness and he wiped them with the heel of his hand. Then, in a half-crouch, he began moving forward. It was some twenty yards from the wharf to the house and he took his time, feeling ahead with sensitive feet for any twig which might snap and give him away. He could feel the blood throbbing in his temples and he could not stop the trembling that had come over him. He could not remember ever being so afraid and he felt an overwhelming impulse to cry.

His outstretched hand touched an obstruction before him and he felt it back and forth for a moment before identifying it to his satisfaction as the split-rail fence that enclosed the house except for the gateless opening. He didn't know which way that opening was, so he carefully started climbing over it. He hooked one leg over the top, then the other, until he was sitting on the top rail. He paused and listened, holding his breath. For an instant he thought he heard the faintest whisper of sound, perhaps the sigh of a breath, and his heartbeat increased. He continued to listen but no further sound came and he convinced himself that he had been mistaken. He leaned forward and put a foot out, feeling for the ground inside the fence. Then the top rail turned beneath him and, off balance, he pitched forward into the darkness.

He landed on his knees in the center of something soft that made a wheezing gurgle and instantly he rolled off it and crouched, fear shrieking in his mind, panic a razor's edge away. Gradually he calmed himself and when nothing occurred, he stretched out a hand. His fingers touched an arm and he froze. When there was no movement he let his hand slide up the sleeve. He reached the shoulder, the neck and then the face. There was a bushy moustache. He thought the skin of the cheek still felt warm and he reached farther. The smoothness of skin gave way to a hard sliminess and he felt the gorge rise in his throat as he realized the man lying here had been scalped. He jerked his hand away, then reached out again right away. The skin felt warm, he thought, and scalping didn't always kill. Whoever it was, he might still be alive. His hand encountered the shoulder again and he reached for the throat to feel for a pulse.

His fingers slid into a gaping gash, spongy with coagulation.

Richard Garner gasped involuntarily and jerked himself away a few feet, stomach acids searing his mouth. Still on hands and knees, he swallowed convulsively, forcing the bile down, eyes squeezed tightly closed, fighting for control. At that instant something moist and cold touched his cheek. A scream ripped from his throat and he felt a flood of warmth as his sphincter muscles failed.

Then he saw what had touched him — the nose of the little white dog that had barked at them. Jean Baptiste Cardin's dog whined and approached him, groveling, but Garner had had all he could take. He leaped to his feet, vaulted the fence and, heedless of noise, raced to the wharf, almost overshooting before he could stop. Someone was already freeing the rope from the piling and he leaped into the middle of the boat, gasping.

"Get out of here!" he cried. "*Move!*"

Actually, his men required no encouragement.

[*April 6, 1812 — Monday,* 7:20 P.M.]

The Burns family entered the main gate of Fort Dearborn, escorted by Ensign George Ronan and his squad.

After receiving permission to go after them, Ronan had swiftly found six volunteers among the enlisted men — with at least that many more willing to go if he needed them. He didn't. The fort's scow was not large enough. The seven men, rifles primed and ready, raced to the riverfront and launched the heavy wooden scow. There were places for four rowers and in a minute quadruple oars were thrusting them over the darkened waters upstream toward the Burns house.

They shouted to announce themselves when they got there so Tom Burns would not shoot them by mistake. Mary Burns, calm but very weak and not at all well, was in bed with the infant Catherine in her arms. Nine-year-old Isabella and her two smaller sisters stood huddled nearby, wide-eyed but not crying. Tom Burns, with his fifteen-year-old stepson James beside him, was deeply relieved at their arrival but worried about the lifting and carrying of Mary to the boat.

"You see," he murmured in Ronan's ear, "it's . . . well, there's a problem." He was obviously embarrassed. "It's been over a full day since Catherine was born and Mary's . . . well," his voice dropped even lower, "she's still bleeding from . . . down there. I'm afraid it'll get worse if we carry her."

Ronan squeezed his shoulder. "Don't worry. She'll be all right. You and the boy better see to the other children." He turned and issued orders to the squad and instead of attempting to carry the woman herself, they picked up the entire bedding — cornhusk mattress, coverlets and blanket — with her in the midst of all with Catherine and carried her to the boat.

With a little difficulty they got it aboard and somehow everyone squeezed in. There was not room to row properly, so the oars were used by four men as if they were paddles, while George Ronan, Tom Burns and the two other privates stood ready with their rifles. James Cooper crouched beside the bedding with his three sisters.

Now they were inside the fort and the mother and infant, still in the bedding, were being carried into one of the barracks, a cluster of soldiers' wives hovering about like clucking hens to help. The ensign, along with Tom Burns and James, strode to where a group of men had gathered around John Kelso and Charlie Lee, who were repeating their story for the fourth or fifth time. With the fort under full alert and sentries well posted, Captain Heald and Lieutenant Helm had relaxed and were listening again, perhaps for some forgotten item that might now come out.

"Look," said John Kinzie when they were finished, "I don't for a minute doubt what you saw or heard, but everyone's pretty excited here and I think we need to consider this more closely. The precautions we've taken are well advised, but I think we should bear in mind that we don't know for certain yet that anyone's even been hurt."

"Then what's happened to Liberty White and Cardin and DuBou?" Kelso demanded, bridling. "And what about those shots we heard?"

Kinzie held up a hand. "Whoa! I'm not denying the likelihood that they've been killed, but we don't *know* that. What I'm getting at is that one or more of them may be out there needing some help and maybe we ought to send out a rescue party."

"Absolutely not!" Captain Heald snapped at once. "I forbid it. No one — and I mean *no one*, military or civilian — is to leave this post tonight. We can't afford to have a party of *any* size ambushed. If things look calm in the daylight tomorrow, we'll send out a party then."

"Sir," said Ensign Ronan, "may I ask if you still have a guard manning the sally port?"

"No, not since your return." The commander appeared irritated by the ensign's question. "I considered it no longer requisite."

"But what if one of the men from Lee's farm manages to get back here and needs to get in in a hurry?"

Nathan Heald scowled, obviously not liking Ronan's observation. "I'm quite sure," he replied stiffly, "that whatever the circumstance, with covering fire by the sentries, we could get the sally port open in time to let them in. Assuming, sir," he added, "that any of them are still alive, which even Mr. Kinzie agrees is unlikely."

"Excuse me, sir," the junior officer persisted, refusing to back down, "but I think you've forgotten something else."

"What is it?" The words were bitten off sharply.

"Corporal Garner and four privates went fishing about noon today. Up the South Branch past the Lee farm. They still haven't returned."

He spoke the words softly but they hung in the air like great lead weights. Everyone waited for the superior officer's reply and, when it came, there were more than a few — including Ensign Ronan — who couldn't believe it.

"My order stands," Captain Heald grated. "No one is to leave this fort."

[*April 6, 1812 — Monday*, 11:00 P.M.]

The skiff bearing Corporal Richard Garner and the four privates slid to the shore beneath the north wall of Fort Dearborn. The men leaped out, beached the heavy craft slightly and raced for the outer sally port close to the river. They had to pound on the portal for several minutes and shout loudly before they finally gained entry.

The journey downriver from the Lee farm had not continued with the speed at which it had initially left the little wharf. After a few minutes, their immediate panic abating and only a healthy fear remaining, the corporal had again issued the order for silence, including oar-dippings as nearly noiseless as possible. That, along with the lack of a torch to light their way — they didn't dare chance that — had made their progress very slow. Several times they had stopped for ten or fifteen minutes at a stretch when they thought they heard suspicious noises.

Despite their fear, Corporal Garner was not popular in the boat due to the stench arising from his fecal-stained clothes. He wished nothing more than to divest himself of the offensive garments and toss them into the river but, fearful of making noise, he — and his companions — bore the discomfort in silence.

Having arrived at the fort, the corporal blurted out the salient details swiftly, then begged permission to take just a few minutes to get himself cleaned up, after which he would return and report in minute detail all that had occurred. The request was granted and Garner bolted away. Now he had returned and step by step, not forgetting to mention having thought he heard shots, he related everything to Captain Heald while a cluster of his men, officers and civilians, mutely listened. The fact that Corporal Garner had actually encountered the dead body of one of the men at the Lee farm — obviously Jean Cardin, since the corpse had a moustache and the little dog had remained by the body — confirmed their worst fears. No one any longer held out much hope for survivors.

Not even John Kinzie.

[April 6, 1812 — Monday, 11:30 P.M.]

The secret council of the Potawatomi chiefs being held at Black Partridge's village just outside Chicago initially had nothing whatever to do with the incident at the Lee farm. That meeting had originally been planned to be held at Topenebe's village on the St. Joseph, but so many spies had been prowling the woods in that country and such a buildup of American troops was occurring in Ohio that it was considered safer and wiser to hold it here.

Eight extremely influential Potawatomi chiefs were on hand, including Black Partridge, of course. They had arrived within an hour or so of one another, from varying directions, just about twenty-four hours ago. They came in secrecy, in the midst of night, and except for a select handful of Indians apart from those attending, no one realized they were there, not even the inhabitants of Black Partridge's village.

The meeting concerned the fate of Chicago — Fort Dearborn specifically — and was being held to correlate war plans here with those of Tecumseh, who was presently at Amherstburg conferring with the saga-

cious old Indian Agent, Matthew Elliott. Because it did involve a direct
tie-in with Tecumseh's plans, Chaubenee and Sauganash were two of those
now in Black Partridge's lodge involved in secret discussions. Topenebe
was here, saying little but the few words spoken carrying great weight, and
next to Black Partridge sat his younger brother, Chief Waubansee, whose
village was forty-five miles northwest on the Fox River.[206] Main Poche
was on hand, his new village now well established on the lake where the
village of Mawgehset — Big Foot — was located.[207] The two remaining
chiefs were those who almost fanatically despised, with few exceptions, all
Americans and had long yearned to attack and destroy Fort Dearborn,
which they considered such a threat to their country. The first was Siggenauk — Blackbird — whose village, and that of his father before him,
was at the mouth of the Milwaukee River. The other was the father-in-law
of Sauganash and brother-in-law of Main Poche, Nescotnemeg — known
to the whites as Mad Sturgeon — who was chief of the village located
where the Iroquois River emptied into the larger Kankakee River, sixty
miles from Chicago.[208]

With the exception of two hour-long breaks for meals and one four-
hour break for sleep, the secret council had been continuously in sessions.
As always, Siggenauk and Nescotnemeg were for immediate assault on
Fort Dearborn. Main Poche tended to agree with them. Black Partridge
thought that to be premature and he was backed by Waubansee and
Topenebe. Chaubenee and Sauganash had no objection to such an assault,
concerned only that it be timed to Tecumseh's movements. All of them
were in agreement that Fort Dearborn should be destroyed, along with its
American occupants.

With a few exceptions.

The principal concern was with their consistently good friend, Shawneeawkee — John Kinzie — and his family. Every one of them here had
known Kinzie for years, had accepted many favors from him and had
always been treated more than fairly by him. Several of them had been
guests in his home, just as he had often been a guest in their lodges. Not
one of them wished to see him harmed and therein lay the problem. If and
when the place were attacked, it would be by a great number of Indians,
not only from different branches of the Potawatomi tribe, but by other
tribes, too — possibly Kickapoos, Winnebagoes, Sacs.

They agreed among themselves that if and when the attack occurred,
they personally, and their principal warriors, would exert themselves in
every possible way to save the Kinzies from being killed or harmed —
accidentally or deliberately. Beyond such exertion, there was little they
could do.

Insofar as *when* Chicago should be attacked, Chaubenee and Sauganash
explained that matters were quickly moving to a head in the area of

western Lake Erie. Tecumseh's union had more or less collapsed, but he still had over two thousand warriors strongly faithful to his leadership, many of whom were collecting at Amherstburg and on the lower Maumee. At the same time, the Americans were at this moment organizing a large army under a white chief named Hull, at the towns of Dayton and Urbana in Ohio, with the intention of very soon marching north to Detroit and possibly even to invade Canada from there.

"Tecumseh has said the critical time will come in the middle of the Heat Moon," Sauganash said, referring to August. "Battles will have been fought before then between Indians and whites and he says the Indians will win them. By that time, he says, Mackinac and Detroit will no longer be in American hands, and those Americans who have not been killed or captured will have fallen far back from the frontier and be very much afraid."

"I do not wish to wait," Nescotnemeg said coldly. "The Chemokemon at the fort here are very weak now.[209] Perhaps later they will not be so weak. Now is when we should attack them."

"I agree with Nescotnemeg," Siggenauk said. "Perhaps Tecumseh is wrong. Perhaps the Americans will then have a stronger army, against which we will have to fall back. Then suddenly Chicago would become so strong with Chemokemons that perhaps we could not snatch it back from them at all."

Chaubenee bridled. "Tecumseh is not wrong! Tecumseh knows!"

"How then was it," Nescotnemeg was deceptively casual, "that he did not foresee what The Prophet would do?"

"He *did!*" Chaubenee flared. "It was *we* who failed; we who were left behind by him with specific instructions to make certain Tenskwatawa made no mistakes; we who did not realize the power Tenskwatawa had taken unto himself until it was too late and we were unable to prevent it. It was *our* misjudgment, not Tecumseh's."

Sauganash spoke up. "Chaubenee speaks the truth. If Tecumseh says that the critical time will come in the midst of the Heat Moon, so it will be. On that our plans must be built."

Then it was Topenebe's turn and as he spoke they all listened very carefully, for he was the oldest and most influential of them all. "It should be as Tecumseh wishes," he said. "We have all felt the result of not working together. That must not happen now. Siggenauk and Nescotnemeg are the most anxious to attack, so let them work it out — but in concert with what Tecumseh foresees. Let Nescotnemeg be the one who devises the plan of attack and let Siggenauk be the one who will command the Indians when the attack is made. Let all of us have our warriors follow what these two chiefs say — and let these two chiefs," there was a finality in his words, "follow Tecumseh's wish."

It had been during the midst of their talk earlier this evening that the rumble of the cannon at Fort Dearborn reached them and they were all perplexed at its cause. Black Partridge immediately dispatched three different parties of warriors to discover what had happened.

Now they knew: that a party of Winnebagoes had struck the Lee farm; that near-panic was occurring in Chicago; that the whites had all assembled in the fort for mutual defense; that the Winnebagoes had struck and run and were now moving up the Des Plaines River Trail. Black Partridge was furious, not so much that an attack had occurred, but that it had been perpetrated by Winnebagoes in his territory without his permission.

"Do I send my warriors out to kill the Winnebagoes for this?" he asked the assembled chiefs. "Do I have them captured and bring them back to be punished for their discourtesy to us? Do we reprimand them for bringing the soldiers at Fort Dearborn to alertness, when we wished rather that they remained complacent? Or do we ourselves now take up the tomahawk, not in war at this time, but for the purpose of keeping the Chemokemons within the walls where they have chosen to collect themselves, or do we cut off their lines of supply and let them become weak?"

They continued to discuss this at length and now, though no firm decision had been made, it was very clear they were leaning strongly in the direction of Black Partridge's final alternative.

[*April 6, 1812 — Monday, 11:45* P.M.]

Okat had finally called a halt. His ten followers were so weary they could hardly take another step. Part of that weariness stemmed from the large amount of plunder they were carrying — loot taken from the Lee farm. Their plan to kill everyone between them and Fort Dearborn had abruptly dissolved with the booming of the fort's cannon in the deepening dusk. They were only eleven men and however lofty the plane on which they placed their own bravery, they were not stupid. The cannon blast meant the fort had been alerted — undoubtedly by the man and boy who had crossed the river and escaped — so they had quickly bound into packs the objects they had already gathered up and fled, not even taking time to burn the buildings. Who knew how many soldiers were at that very moment coming after them? But they had left behind a war club as a message to those who came.

They had moved rapidly at first but after a couple of hours their headway slowed. Their route from the Lee farm had been almost due northwest until they encountered the Des Plaines River. At that point, after crossing the river, they had followed the River Trail northward. Now, with no sign whatever that they were being pursued, Okat had finally agreed to halt here on the west bank of the Des Plaines on the point where Buffalo Creek entered from the west.[210]

To a certain point, Okat acquiesced to their desires, but no further. When they wanted to build a camp fire, he refused to let them do so. "You are brave warriors," he told them, "but more than one brave warrior who thought himself safe and became careless has died. The men who follow me will not be permitted such carelessness."

[*April 7, 1812 — Tuesday*]

A sick, frustrated rage burned in John Kinzie and was reflected in Ensign Ronan, Dr. Van Voorhis and others of this party of soldiers and civilians who had accompanied him to the Lee farm this morning. They had arrived in five boats — twenty-two men, of whom fourteen were enlisted men. It was Captain Nathan Heald himself who was in command of the detachment.

They had approached carefully, weapons at ready, not really expecting to encounter any Indians — because John Kinzie had told them the chances of that were slight — but prepared nonetheless. The little white dog, Dolly, heard them coming and barked excitedly, but she would not leave her position next to the split-rail worm fence. Everyone of the group was gloomily aware of what they would discover on the other side of that fence.

The body of Jean Baptiste Cardin still lay where Corporal Garner had encountered it the night before, the glazed, sightless eyes staring into the sky. He had been shot once, in the back of the neck, slightly off center and almost into the shoulder. It was evident that the ball had downed him, but it had not killed him. They surmised that he had probably been shot in the house and managed to stagger out this far before falling or being knocked down. Death had been caused, as was obvious by the huge pool of coagulated blood, by his jugular having been severed. His scalp was gone, but there was little blood on his skull, indicating that the Indians had waited until he was dead before removing it. Dr. Van Voorhis had accompanied the group this morning in case a victim was still alive and needed help. Cardin was far beyond the need of any help.

So, too, was Liberty White.

They found his body inside the house. It was impossible to reconstruct what the string of events were that had occurred inside the house, but the results were most distressingly apparent. Liberty White lay in front of the fireplace. Actually, what was left of Liberty White lay there. He had been shot twice, once in the stomach and once in the chest. As with Cardin, his throat was laid open in such a severe gash that at first glance he appeared almost to be decapitated. It didn't end there. He had been stabbed ten times — nine times in the chest and once in the hip. He was scalped, but not in the customary way in which a round portion of hair was cut off the crown of the head. Instead, they had pushed the knife point in at the hairline and followed it completely around the head. The whole top por-

GATEWAY TO EMPIRE

tion of the head was bare skull, without a hair remaining. There was one further atrocity: his nose, lips and portions of his cheeks and chin had been cut off and taken away. One of the privates in the squad, Private Phelim Corbin, shuddered and was thankful that his wife, Victoria, who was four months pregnant, could not see this.

Of the Frenchman named DuBou there was no trace.[211]

In plain view on the table was a Winnebago war club, left as a sign, John Kinzie explained, that they intended to return and kill more. The detachment wrapped the bodies in blankets and took them back to the fort. They were buried, still wrapped in the same blankets, in the little cemetery adjacent to the Fort Dearborn garden.

It was not until they returned to the fort that anyone thought to ask what happened to Dolly. The little white dog had last been seen as Cardin's body was being wrapped in the blanket. No one had any idea what happened to her after that.[212]

[*April 8, 1812 — Wednesday*]

In these two days since the attack at the Lee farm, the initial panic that had swept through the Chicago populace had eased to a continuous haunting fear. Every person living in Chicago was now keenly aware of his own fundamental vulnerability should the Indians attack in force. Nevertheless, it simply wasn't feasible to maintain the entire Chicago population inside Fort Dearborn.

Captain Heald announced that the civilian population could not stay in the fort proper, but he did mitigate turning them away today by giving them permission to move into the Indian Agency House located just west of the fort. The U.S. Factor, Matthew Irwin, was given permission to move his goods inside the fort for protection and as soon as he had done so, the Chicago residents moved into the Agency House. It was a long log building with a large long room on each side, divided by a hallway down its length. The verandas at front and rear of the building were closed with planking to provide greater security and in these were cut portholes from which to fire rifles in case of attack. A schedule was established whereby every man had his turn at sentry duty, the watches being maintained day and night.

It had been early this morning that Captain Heald summoned Thomas Burns, whom he had considered being a good soldier when he was a private at Fort Dearborn. He had even offered Burns promotion to corporal if he reenlisted at that time, but Burns had refused.

"Mr. Burns," the commanding officer had begun, without preamble, "we have here a most unusual and potentially very dangerous situation. We need to make provision for the protection of the citizens of Chicago. Under my authority as commander of this post, I am establishing, as of now, a militia. In light of your past exemplary military experience, I'd like to place you in charge of this militia with the rank of sergeant. Will you accept?"

"Well . . . yes sir, I guess I will." Taken aback, Burns was not overly enthusiastic.

"Fine! Fine!" Captain Heald warmly clapped him on the back. "Now, then, I want every able-bodied male, down to and including the age of fifteen, to be part of our militia. Unfortunately, I do not have the authority to *force* anyone to serve. However, I would hope you will be able to convince all civilian males that it is their responsibility — their ethical *duty*, sir! — to enlist in that militia. I will provide arms and ammunition for the militia out of the government store. Will you please ask the men immediately." It was not a question.

Burns swallowed. "Yes, sir, I'll see to it at once."

"Thank you . . . Sergeant. Dismissed."

Burns left him and returned to the Agency House where most of the civilian men had gathered. He was decidedly unhappy about having walked into this responsibility and his attitude was not one to inspire confidence. There were about forty civilian men eligible under Captain Heald's broad qualifications. But when Tom Burns had finished talking to each of them, his militia company, including himself, had a total of only fifteen individuals.[213]

John Kinzie was not among the volunteers.

CHAPTER XI

[*May 4, 1812 — Monday*]

FOR very nearly a month Chicago had been existing under great tension, its citizens crammed into the fortified Indian Agency House, where individual family cubicles had been created by stringing ropes from one wall to another and draping blankets over them for a modicum of privacy. Without exception they all wanted to get back to their own homes, but without exception they remained huddled together for mutual defense. The Indians were seen frequently, moving about at a distance and menacing in their demeanor.

Captain Heald could not believe that Black Partridge and his people were responsible for the deaths at the Lee farm, as some of the civilians were accusing despite the fact of the Winnebago war club found at the scene. As a recognizable character, Black Partridge was someone who could be pointed at, accused. Captain Heald disagreed. Was not Black Partridge a friend of the whites in Chicago generally? Did he not have special personal friends among the whites, such as the families of John Kinzie and Antoine Ouilmette? Did he not often visit the Lee family and hold their infant daughter, Sally, on his knee? Did he not also hold a special fondness for the Lees' twelve-year-old daughter, Mary, who always called him "My own special chief" during his visits? These things being true, how then could he have allowed such an attack to occur at the Lee farm or allow its perpetrators to go unpunished?

To get answers to these questions, Heald sent the fourteen-year-old mixed-blood interpreter named Salienne to visit Black Partridge and pose the questions. Black Partridge's unsatisfactory response was simply that his people had taken no part in it.

Yet, the hostility of the Potawatomies had increased greatly in these four weeks. Under cover of darkness, warriors had slipped in and killed livestock belonging to the settlers and garrison and once, after a soldier had fired at an Indian, a tomahawk had been thrown at a sentry, missing him narrowly and burying itself in a wagon wheel beside him. Morale in the garrison sank even lower when it was discovered only yesterday that Sergeant John Crozier and his old friend, Private Nathan A. Hurtt, had deserted.[214]

All this while Rebekah Heald's pregnancy had been advancing and at last, early this morning, she had gone into labor. Unwilling to become obligated to the Kinzies in any way, the commanding officer decided against utilizing the services of Eleanor Kinzie as midwife. He was also distrustful of permitting the twenty-two-year-old Dr. Isaac Van Voorhis to help, considering him much too inexperienced. Instead, they allowed the labor to progress of its own accord. Unfortunately, it was a breech-birth and for this reason the infant became wedged at the shoulders in the midpoint of its delivery. Still they waited, hoping nature would correct the malfunction. Finally, after several hours in this condition and growing fearful at Rebekah's agony, Captain Heald summoned Dr. Van Voorhis.

The young physician arrived within minutes, took one look at the situation and realized it was already too late for the infant. With contained anger at the commander's bullheadedness and outright stupidity, he did all he could do under the circumstances, his main concern at this point to in no way further endanger Rebekah's life. The baby, a boy, was finally freed, already dead from lack of oxygen, the umbilical cord in a strangling loop about his neck. But Rebekah was saved. Immediately upon seeing to her health and comfort, the young physician took Captain Heald to another room and berated him for having allowed matters to develop as he had without seeking professional help.

Captain Heald was in no mood to accept criticism from one he considered to be no more than a boy still wet behind the ears and he ordered the doctor out. In a depressed and fatigued state, the captain retired to his desk and wrote a brief entry in his journal, indirectly placing the blame for his own failure on Isaac van Voorhis:

On the 4th of May, 1812, we had a son born dead for want of a skilled Midwife.

More than merely being unfair and unjustified, the journal entry underlined a dangerous characteristic in the makeup of a man entrusted with a command involving the lives of others: a dogged determination to abide by a decision once he had made it, irrespective of circumstances, coupled with an almost total inability to admit to his own error. It was a failing hardly calculated to inspire confidence among those who served beneath him.

[*June 18, 1812 — Thursday*]

War!

Everyone knew it had to come sometime soon, and now it had. Early today the United States formally declared war against Great Britain.

One of the reasons was the continuing policy of the Royal Navy to board American ships and impress American seamen into British service under the claim that they were deserters. Already upwards of perhaps seven thousand men had been taken in this way. And, under the British Orders in Council, meant to prevent American ships from dealing with France, about four hundred American ships had been confiscated on the Atlantic, some of these within sight of the American mainland. It was more than could be tolerated.

The ramifications of the declaration of war were as extensive as the reactions were varied. Immediately the militias were called up in the eighteen states — including Louisiana, which had become the eighteenth state only a little over two months ago, on April 30. Connecticut's governor, John Smith, whose inclinations were more on the side of the doves, pointed out at once that the Constitution provided for Congress calling out the militia to execute the laws of the Union, suppress insurrections and repel invasions, but not to support a war of America's own declaration. His voice was drowned out in the tumult of exultation. Henry Clay heard the news at the War Mess and, along with fellow hawks, leaped about in an approximation of a war dance. Here and there in the East rockets were fired, cannon exploded noisily, church bells rang and volunteers ran to join the army. Even Thomas Jefferson was inspired, writing to a friend:

. . . upon the whole I have known of no war entered into under more favorable circumstances. . . . We . . . shall strip Great Britain of all her possessions on this continent. . . .

Regular communications being poor at best in the frontier areas, no one there had any idea yet that war had been declared. Unfortunately, that also included Brigadier General William Hull and the twenty-two hundred men he was currently in the process of marching toward Detroit through a country infested with Indians and whites already engaged in an undeclared war.

Hull was so miscast as commander of war theater operations that it would have been laughable, had not the situation been so potentially disastrous. He was not particularly distressed that elections of officers among the militia, which made up the bulk of his army, had caused so much dissension that there was a grave discipline problem, or that his own regular army second-in-command, Lieutenant Colonel James Miller, was outranked by the three elected militia colonels, Duncan McArthur, James

Findley and Lewis Cass. William Hull had gathered his regulars and militia in Ohio — at Cincinnati, Dayton and Urbana — and from the beginning it had all the earmarks of a circus, complete with parades, meaningless rhetoric meant to inspire, and clownish performances. Uncaring of the possible stigma of nepotism, General Hull had immediately named his own son, Captain Abraham F. Hull, as his principal aide-de-camp, conveniently overlooking the fact that the young officer was unreliable, hotheaded, fuzzy-thinking and only occasionally sober.

In preparation for the march northward, Hull, fifty-eight and paunchy, spoke to the assembled troops in a stentorian voice intended to penetrate to the grass-root patriotism of his captive audience:

"In marching through a wilderness memorable for savage barbarity," he intoned, "you will remember the causes by which the barbarity has been heretofore excited. In viewing the ground stained with the blood of your fellow citizens, it will be impossible to suppress your feelings of indignation. Passing by the ruins of a fortress erected in our territory by a foreign nation, in times of profound peace, and for the express purpose of exciting the savages to hostility and supplying them with the means of conducting a barbarous war, must remind you of that system of oppression and injustice which that nation has continually practiced, and which the spirit of an indignant people can no longer endure."

Rousing cheers had followed and Hull, with his coterie of officers, regular and militia, reviewed the paraded troops. Captain Abraham Hull's horse, frightened by fife and drum, reared and pawed the air, nearly dumping its besotted passenger, then galloped off in the wrong direction. General Hull's horse, not to be outdone, became intractable, realized the man on its back was no rider and spun about in tight circles. Hull lost his hat, his stirrups, his balance and his dignity, dropped the reins and clung to the horse's mane in terror, somehow managing to stay on until the animal calmed down. Were that not enough, the northward march was begun with Captain Abraham Hull reeling in the saddle at the effects of his usual state of inebriation. The general's son was clad in his finest uniform as they encountered the Mad River at a fording place. Determined to show the troops the proper way to do it, Captain Hull spurred his mount into the river. But he jabbed the spurs in too hard. His steed took one great leap from the bank, landed in three feet of water and, instead of continuing to plunge across, planted all four feet solidly and stopped.

Captain Hull did not.

The commanding officer's son sailed high over the horse's head, executed a commendable but wholly unintentional mid-air somersault and landed in a sitting position in the water with just the top of his head showing and his fine cocked hat floating jauntily away with the current.

With such an inauspicious beginning as this, General William Hull had begun leading his Army of the Northwest toward Detroit. The army evinced little concern that the frontier was abroil with hostility, that all wilderness travel these days was hazardous at best and ambushes were frequent, that settlers near Fort Dearborn had recently been killed, as had others near Vincennes and Kaskaskia and elsewhere — to the number of nearly forty already this spring in the Indiana and Illinois territories. But the army had heard the speeches that imbued all listeners with something akin to invulnerability and they chose to believe them as onward they marched. The day before yesterday they had reached the headwaters of the Scioto River and here, on the south bank, they built two blockhouses, each twenty by twenty-four feet, connected by a stockade and enclosing a half-acre of ground. They named it Fort McArthur.[215] Almost at once the first casualty occurred.

It happened when one of Colonel McArthur's men, Private Peter Vassar, on guard duty, sipped too frequently from the canteen at his hip. The canteen held whiskey, not water, and made him so drowsy that he decided it would be all right to take a brief nap beneath a tree. He dreamed and the dream became a nightmare of attacking Indians. Jerking awake, he snatched up his rifle, looked wildly about and shot the first thing he saw moving. Unfortunately, that turned out to be his fellow sentry, Private Joseph England. Vassar was led away under guard to be held for court-martial and Joseph England, shot high through the left chest, survived, but was out of this campaign.[216] There were some who considered Joe England lucky, because by now there were a fair number of men in this army who had seriously begun wondering if it was a very good place to be.

And on this very day of the declaration of war . . .

    . . . while the sixty-one-year-old American Army commander-in-chief, Major General Henry Dearborn, gorged himself on rich food in a Boston restaurant;

    . . . while Governor Ninian Edwards of Illinois Territory was gloomily announcing to his constituents that "We have no security from these Indians" and that more attacks would occur;

    . . . while Tecumseh, with Chaubenee at his side, met with Main Poche at Amherstburg and then provided assembled warriors with arms and ammunition from the British, with which they could strike the approaching army of William Hull;

    . . . while the British at Amherstburg placed a reward of one hundred fifty dollars on the scalp of Tecumseh's nephew, Spemica Lawba, who was now serving as a spy for Hull's army;

    . . . while express messengers on strong horses were speedily bearing urgent messages to all British commanders in Canada, informing them of the American declaration of war . . .

. . . while all this was occurring, someone in Washington suggested that it might be a good idea to inform General Hull that war had been declared . . .

. . . and someone else agreed and wrote out the necessary advisories and orders and directed that they be dispatched to General Hull at once . . .

. . . and someone else dispatched them to General Hull in an ordinary envelope that found its way into an ordinary leather mail pouch that found its way into an ordinary mail-packet shipment bound for Cleveland and Detroit.

And, if not lost en route, as ordinary mail sometimes was, delivery of the envelope to the addressee might be accomplished . . .

. . . in due time.

[*June 30, 1812 — Tuesday*]

"Gentlemen," said Brigadier General William Hull with an unmistakable air of finality, "I have made the decision and intend to stick by it."

He eyed the group of subordinate officers with a hint of belligerence, irritated at what he felt to be another subtle attempt on their part to undermine his confidence in his own son. They had come before him only a short while ago, suggesting — courteously but firmly — that it might not be altogether prudent to let the little schooner *Cuyahoga* go off to Detroit on the mission he had ordered. And he had heard them out — as a good commander should, he told himself — before rejecting their suggestion with such finality. As they spoke, he thought about his army's arrival here, through the midst of Indian country without any problem whatsoever with the natives, and commended himself.

The army's march under his command had brought it, the day before yesterday, to the Maumee River opposite the place where eighteen years before General Wayne had humbled the Indians in the Battle of Fallen Timbers. A small village had sprung up at the foot of the Rapids and the troops were greatly cheered by the sight of civilization after so long a march through the wilderness. They had rested there a day, visiting with the American settlers who had established themselves in the fertile valley, and then had come down the Maumee to the ruins of the old British installation, Fort Miami.

Here, at the top of the navigable waters of the Maumee, they had found a trader named Captain Luther Chapin who owned the little schooner *Cuyahoga* which he plied frequently between Detroit and here. General Hull immediately thought it would be a fine idea to hire Captain Chapin to transport to Detroit aboard his schooner the army's excess baggage, entrenching tools, all the army's musical instruments and the men who played them, three soldiers' wives, and the paymaster, Lewis Dent. About thirty officers and privates, who were incapacitated because of illness and under command of Second Lieutenant George Gooding, would accompany the schooner in an open boat. Gooding's wife was also to go along, but in the schooner. And the man put in charge of packing the baggage aboard the schooner was General Hull's son.

Abraham Hull, relatively sober this day, had executed his father's orders quickly and efficiently. Then, in an effort to display his initiative, he also carefully packed in the general's trunks all of his father's papers, orders, notes, correspondence, accounts and field reports. Since it was the end of the month, he also thoughtfully included the up-to-date muster rolls for the whole army, company by company, made out this very day. All these and the remainder of the baggage put aboard the *Cuyahoga* were placed under direct charge of Assistant Quartermaster General William Beall.

It was at this juncture that the delegation of officers, with Captain James McPherson of Cincinnati as its spokesman, suggested that it was altogether possible that war had been declared by now, that the *Cuyahoga* would have to pass directly in front of the British Fort Malden at Amherstburg where the Detroit River was narrow and that there might be problems.

General Hull sniffed. "Had war been declared," he responded frostily, "I assure you I would have been informed of it by now. No, gentlemen, you are shying at shadows. The *Cuyahoga* will be awaiting us at the Detroit wharf when we arrive."

Even as Hull was discussing the matter with his officers, nearly four hundred miles to the north British agent and trader Robert Dickson and one hundred thirty-five Indians he brought from the Wisconsin country arrived at St. Joseph Island at the Straits of Mackinac and reported to the British commander, Captain Charles Roberts. They immediately began active preparations for an assault on Fort Mackinac as soon as they should learn of war being declared. Swift Menominee runners were dispatched to Amherstburg to advise of the readiness to the north; all that was needed for their attack to be launched was an order from Major General Isaac Brock to that effect.

And also, at this very moment, some twenty miles away from Hull's camp, a young Cleveland lawyer named Charles Shaler was on his horse traveling as rapidly as possible toward the Maumee, desperately hoping to intercept General Hull there. Word of the declaration of war had reached Cleveland and, along with it, an imperative message from the War Department. Finally realizing its error, the War Department urged that the ordinary letter en route to Hull be located and sped on its way by express. Much to the disapproval of the Cleveland postmaster, the Cleveland mail was pawed through but no dispatch to Hull was located. With even greater disapproval he watched as the seal on the Detroit mail packet was broken and its contents sifted through. And there it was! Immediately Shaler was on his way with it.

But Hull was on his way, too, putting his army in motion again on the final leg of the march up the west shore of Lake Erie toward Detroit, confident that the *Cuyahoga* would reach the city long before his army did.

[*June 30, 1812 — Tuesday*]

"Actually, Mr. Mirandeau," Captain Nathan Heald said, his arms at his sides but his hands turned upward in as near a manner of supplication as he could achieve, "we need every man here possible. I wish you'd reconsider and stay."

Jean Baptiste Mirandeau shook his head as he looked out through the Fort Dearborn main gate to where his family sat patiently awaiting him on their horses. The three eldest children, Madeline, fourteen, Joseph, thirteen, and Victoire, twelve, each had a packhorse tethered to his own saddle. Mirandeau's Ottawa wife, again pregnant, had two in tandem attached to hers. Their youngest, the year-old Jean Baptiste, Jr., was in a papoose board on her back and she held three-year-old Louis on the saddle blanket before her. She also held the reins of her husband's mount, to which two more packhorses were attached. Each of the seven pack animals was heavily laden with bundles, luggage and even pieces of furniture.

"Thank you, Captain," Mirandeau replied, "but there is a danger here that I wish to take my family from. Perhaps one day, when the strife has finished, perhaps then we will return." He shrugged. "Who knows?"

"The point is, sir," the Fort Dearborn commander persisted, "we need your strength here in the fort in case there should be trouble. And look at it this way, your family would be safer here with the protection of the garrison, don't you agree, Mr. Kinzie?"

John Kinzie, standing nearby, shook his head, feeling a faint stab of pain in his neck muscles, even though the wound was now almost wholly healed. "Afraid not, Captain. I agree with Mr. Mirandeau. He and his family lived in Milwaukee a long time. They know Siggenauk — Blackbird, if you prefer — and have nothing to fear from him. They'll be much safer there than here, I think." He stretched out his hand to the Frenchman. "Jean Baptiste, I'll miss you. Be careful and perhaps we'll see you up there before the end of the year."

Captain Heald frowned at Kinzie's response, having expected the Chicago trader to back him up. He looked on sourly as the old friends shook hands. It irked him that John Kinzie always seemed to be in opposition to the garrison's needs, as Heald saw them. It also irked him to have to confer with the trader at relatively regular intervals about the Indians, since no

one here knew them quite so well as he and could more accurately evaluate what was happening about them and the precariousness of the situation of the whites here. A few more minor incidents had occurred with the
Indians in these past few weeks, but nothing of great significance. Had it
not been for Kinzie, he would have told the civilians still taking refuge in
the Agency House to return to their own abodes. Kinzie, however, had
warned that it would be a dangerous thing to do so: the Indians probably
were not going to attack, but the possibility existed and, so long as it did,
they'd be safer here close to the fort. Now the officer gave up his efforts
with a sigh and also shook the Frenchman's hand.

"Good luck then, Mr. Mirandeau, to you and your family."

Mirandeau nodded, flashing his familiar broad grin, dipped his head a
final time to Kinzie and strode back to the horses. He took the reins of his
horse from his wife and mounted smoothly, then took little Louis from her
and placed the boy onto the front of his own saddle. He then led his
family away in a small, single-file train.[217]

Without another word to Kinzie, Captain Heald returned to his office
where he found Ensign Ronan awaiting him. He masked his irritation,
wishing Ronan could be reassigned to another post. The young and much-
too-bright officer grated on his nerves and it was only with concerted effort
that he was able to be civil to him. Now, expressionlessly, he returned the
West Pointer's salute in a casual manner and then listened to the efficient
end-of-the-month muster roll report.

"Our present garrison strength, sir," Ronan said, looking at the figures
he had jotted on a piece of paper, "not counting Sergeant Crozier and
Private Hurtt, who deserted last month, is sixty-eight men, including
officers, noncommissioned officers, surgeon's mate and privates. It is
broken down as follows: one captain commanding — yourself, sir; one
second lieutenant, second-in-command — Lieutenant Helm; one ensign
— myself; one surgeon's mate — Dr. Isaac van Voorhis; three sergeants,
including Isaac Holt, Otho Hayes and Quartermaster Sergeant William
Griffith; four corporals — Joseph Bowen, Richard Garner, Thomas Forth
and Rhodias Jones; four musicians, all privates, two of whom are on the
sick-list, including the bandmaster, Fifer John Smith, whose place has
temporarily been taken by drummer John Hamilton; and fifty-three other
privates, of which eighteen, in addition to the two musicians, are on the
sick list with fever. This gives us a total on-duty effective strength as of
today of forty-eight officers and men."[218]

Nathan Heald grimaced, mentally cursing the miasmic fever which almost constantly incapacitated upwards of half his garrison, thinking again,
wistfully, of his previous command at Fort Wayne where such a condition
rarely occurred. He continued to listen as George Ronan went on with
his report, listing the state of defenses, stocks of ammunition and weap-

onry and various other supplies in the government store, and present assignments of the men. He was in the midst of a report on the state of affairs with the Potawatomies in the Chicago area when a disturbance outside interrupted him. Captain Heald craned his neck to look out the window and grunted with surprise.

"Well, wonder of wonder," he said. "Evidently Washington has decided we really are here. It's Lieutenant Eastman and his escort." First Lieutenant Jonathan Eastman was district paymaster for the United States First Infantry Regiment, to which the Fort Dearborn garrison was attached. It was his duty, escorted by six heavily armed soldiers, to deliver the payroll to the various forts in his jurisdiction. "We'll finish the monthly report later, Ensign Ronan," the commander went on, dismissing him with a wave of his hand. "Please have Sergeant Griffith show the lieutenant in."

"Yes sir." Ronan saluted and left. A few minutes later Quartermaster Sergeant Griffith entered with the paymaster, who was carrying a leather saddle pouch of considerable weight. Eastman was a thirty-year-old Vermonter — a tall, thin-lipped, humorless man in full uniform. Beside the big sergeant in his somewhat soiled, mismatched uniform, the lieutenant was virtually a fashion model for a First Regiment officer. White, snug-fitting trousers were tucked into black half-boots, the midnight blue of his split-tailed coat highlighted by three-inch scarlet cuffs and upright collar, with gold embroidery and brass buttons, a large gold epaulet on each shoulder and nine horizontal embroidered gold darts on the front, in the center of each of which was a round brass button. His high round hat with a three-inch bill was black, decorated with an arc of gold braid tassled on the ends and a gold tuft projecting above the hat from the square brass foreplate medallion bearing the eagle grasping olive branch and arrows in its talons. Diagonally across his chest from right shoulder to left hip was a three-inch-wide white band in the center of which was an oval brass medallion embossed with intertwined wreath. A maroon sash was tied about his waist, in the right side of which was a pistol. His brass-hilted sword was in a scabbard slung on his left hip. He entered the commander's office stiffly and, as Sergeant Griffith took a stance of attention to one side, saluted with precise military form and placed the heavy pouch on Captain Heald's desk.

"I'm sure," the commanding officer said, smiling and returning the salute, "that your arrival has brightened everyone's day here, Lieutenant Eastman. Especially," he added wryly, "since it's been nine months since the men were last paid."

Eastman was not amused. "I deliver the garrison payrolls where and when directed, sir," he said. "Yours is not the only post where such delivery has been delinquent." He paused only a moment and then went directly to business. "You will no doubt be interested in learning, Captain Heald, that the Congress has approved an increase in the pay of privates and noncommissioned officers, effective last April." Captain Heald's expression brightened, though not so much as Sergeant Griffith's, but he said nothing and Lieutenant Eastman went on. "Privates will now receive ten dollars monthly, up from three dollars; musicians eleven-fifty, corporals fifteen and sergeants twenty-one."[219]

Sergeant Griffith's eyes widened at his own pay increase from his previous ten dollars monthly. "However," the paymaster went on, "the present payroll I have brought is on the previous basis and the back-pay retroactive payment will be made at an as yet unspecified date. The pay for officers remains the same, although an increase is expected to be approved by Congress in the near future." He touched the pouch on the commander's desk. "The payment I have brought is for your full garrison strength of seventy-two men and officers."

"We fluctuate considerably from full strength," Captain Heald pointed out, "especially among the privates. That's over a period of time, of course."

"The full payment will be deposited with you nonetheless, along with pay in advance for the next three months, for which you will be held accountable to the War Department's Finance Division. That amount, too, I'm sorry to say, is on the old pay scale, but will be made up by the retroactive back-payment to be scheduled. Therefore, what we have here, sir," he patted the pouch affectionately, "is nine months' back pay for your garrison at full strength, plus three months' advance pay — for a total of one year's pay at the old rate." He took a small notebook from his tunic pocket and consulted it briefly. "At the new pay rate," he said, "the total comes to $11,820.00. What we have here, however, is $5,800.80 — the old rate."[220]

Within an hour or so the proper papers had been signed and the garrison was paid its nine-month back-wages totaling $4,350.60. The remaining amount of three months' pay, totaling $1,450.20, Captain Heald placed in a locked chest in his own chambers, to be distributed in one three-month payment at the end of September.

Everyone was more than pleased to get paid and no individual in Chicago was more pleased at the arrival of the military paymaster than John Kinzie. In a flurry of business he collected most of the bills due him for extended credit and also quickly sold out his entire stock of liquor, plus a great quantity of other goods at a very handsome profit. He was also highly pleased with his own perspicacity in taking the gamble early last March to go deeply into debt and order such a huge shipment of merchandise and liquor from his suppliers in Buffalo. He had only recently learned that those goods had already left Black Rock at Buffalo aboard the sister ships *Erie* and *Friends' Good Will* and, if bad weather did not intervene, they were expected to arrive here at Chicago within the next week.

Yes, everything was working out very well and John Kinzie considered himself justified in feeling smug.

[*July 5, 1812 — Sunday morning*]

Events had suddenly begun to move with a momentum of their own, no longer under complete control of those who had begun them.

Charles Shaler finally reached the Maumee on July 1 with news of the American declaration of war, his horse bug-eyed and gasping with exhaustion from the forced ride from Cleveland. A detachment of twenty-five of General Hull's soldiers under Lieutenant Davidson were busily engaged in building a small blockhouse, but the general and his army were gone. So was the schooner *Cuyahoga*. Shaler groaned and, despite the exhaustion of his mount, galloped on into the night, following the army's trail.

For the army, the march was still a lark. Some envied the men who had been able to continue to Detroit from the Maumee by taking their ease aboard the *Cuyahoga* or its accompanying open boat, but most merely observed with interest this part of the country that they had never before seen, where the blue waters of Lake Erie lapped peacefully against the Michigan shore. They passed a few small Indian villages, all but abandoned now, and a few equally small French settlements where they were welcomed. This was especially true when they reached the handsome little unnamed settlement along the Raisin River. The Americans immediately dubbed it Frenchtown.[221]

Sergeant James Foster, an Ohio volunteer from Highland County in the company of Captain William Key, continued to faithfully record in his journal, as he had since the army's march began, the occurrences of this expedition, and this day had been especially fruitful with things to write about:

. . . our march was principally through a beautiful country, interspersed with French settlements. At the first of these settlements, a party of twenty-five Indians of the Tawa [Ottawa] tribe came to us with a white flag. Like the Indians at Urbana, they professed friendship and solicited permission to march with the army. Among these natives of the wilderness were four old squaws, the most hideous animals that the votaries of Vulcan have ever crowned with the emblems of ugliness. To describe the physiognomy of each would be a task for Job, indeed! One particularly attracted my attention. She was low of stature and remarkably corpulent. The numberless wrinkles on her broad bloated face were presumptive proofs that an hundred winters at least had passed by without shattering her

frame. Her large black eyes, scarcely divided by a nose — the massy side of which extended or rather rested on her cheeks and eclipsed the intervening carbuncles — could hardly be considered as fellows; with one she looked the general full in the face and with the other reviewed the army. Around her neck innumerable rows of beads were strung to which was attached a silver cross, suspended between a pair of breasts wrinkled with age and lengthened by their weight. In short, if the witch of Endore was such a squaw as this, no wonder she could "call spirits from the vasty deep!"

It was not until 2:00 A.M. on July 2 that Shaler finally rode his exhausted steed into General Hull's camp and immediately repaired to the commander's tent with the momentous news. Deeply shaken, Hull summoned his officers, instructed them to keep the news secret for the time being from their men and informed them of the declaration of war against the British. He overlooked relaying notification of the news to Fort Mackinac, Fort Dearborn and Fort Wayne as a result of his most immediate concern — the jeopardy in which the schooner *Cuyahoga* had unconsciously been placed. Now the warnings of the delegation of officers who came to him at the Maumee about the British fort at Amherstburg rose up to haunt him and he sent a party of men to locate a boat and set off after the schooner to warn it before it was too late.

It was already too late.

News of the declaration of war had reached the British at Amherstburg long before this and they were quite ready. The Fort Malden commander, Lieutenant Colonel Thomas Bligh St. George, had stationed a lookout with a powerful telescope to watch for any American ships. Early in the day the *Cuyahoga* was seen entering the Detroit River, her American flag fluttering jauntily. St. George immediately dispatched a well-seasoned twenty-nine-year-old French-Canadian, Frederic Rolette, to intercept her. Rolette, a member of the Provincial Marines, had served in sea battles under a great teacher — Horatio Nelson. He was a veteran of the battles of Trafalgar and the Nile, had been wounded five times and managed to survive. Now he immediately gathered six of his men, armed them with swords and pistols, then set out in a small boat on an interception course. Several canoes bearing traders and Tecumseh's Indians followed.

Unaware of the war in progress, the troops in the *Cuyahoga* and accompanying open boat made no effort to stop their approach, considering them a welcoming party. Lieutenant Rolette fired one shot from his pistol and boarded the *Cuyahoga* without resistance, informed Captain Chapin and his crew and passengers of the declaration of war, replaced the American flag with British colors and took his prize into Amherstburg without contest, adding the final ignominy of forcing the American band aboard to play *God Save the King* all the way to shore. Some five hundred Indians in the town crowded the shores to whoop and shriek with delight at this first evidence they had seen of the British actually warring against the Americans, as had so long been promised. Not until later did Lieutenant Colonel St. George become aware of just what a prize had been taken — when the ship was searched and all of General Hull's up-to-date rosters, war plans and correspondence were found. Yet, William Hull was not the only commander who made serious errors: Lieutenant Colonel St. George was so badly rattled by the knowledge that an American force of two thousand men was across the river from his little garrison that he completely overlooked sending word of it — or of the captured Hull papers — to his commander, General Brock, at York.[222]

Early in the morning General Hull put his army in motion again toward Detroit, now being spied upon by numerous parties of Indians under Chaubenee, Main Poche, Roundhead and even Tecumseh himself. Shaler moved along with the army and not until that evening were the troops informed of the declaration of war. At the same time, General Hull was informed that the *Cuyahoga* had been captured. He could hardly have been more adversely affected had he been struck in the stomach with a tomahawk. Confidence oozed away from him as water away from a squeezed sponge.

Only a few hours later, over three hundred miles to the north, the British commander at St. Joseph Island, Captain Charles Roberts, received news of the outbreak of war, brought from Amherstburg by canoe as speedily as possible by fur trader Toussaint Pothier of the South West Company. Roberts immediately put his men on alert, raised an additional force of one hundred forty French-Canadian voyageurs, and had his little army augmented by Robert Dickson's one hundred thirty-five Indians. All that was needed now was permission from General Brock for them to make their surprise assault on the Fort Mackinac American installation under command of Lieutenant Porter Hanks, who was still wholly ignorant of the war.

William Hull lost a good bit of time when he reached the Huron River and a bridge had to be built for the passage of his army. Here, with an air of flamboyance, he erected a large red-and-blue-striped marquee tent in the center of camp while the bridge was being built.[223] While he was doing so, Tecumseh's forces were augmented by the arrival at Amherstburg of three hundred more warriors, principally Sacs.

Today, once again in motion, Hull's army passed the large Huron village at what was called Brownstown and another a little farther along called Maguaga.[224] The latter was the village of Chief Walk-in-the-Water, who still had not agreed to follow Tecumseh's leadership and would not permit his warriors to do so. He was one of those who clung to the precepts of the principal chief of the Wyandots, Tarhe — The Crane —

and leaned toward neutrality and peace with both British and Americans. Now he and his people greeted Hull's army politely as it passed.

The army finally reached Spring Wells, at the southern edge of Detroit and from which they could see the houses of its twelve hundred inhabitants. Here they went into camp, with General Hull prepared to send a messenger on the morrow to demand the release of the *Cuyahoga*, its captain, crew, passengers and cargo . . . and, he hoped, his private papers, which might yet be undiscovered.

Just as they entered Spring Wells, Charles Shaler's horse finally dropped dead beneath him.

[*July 5, 1812 — Sunday noon*]

The job of unloading the cargo consigned to John Kinzie took most of the day yesterday and half of today. The two ships, *Friends' Good Will* and *Erie*, had arrived at Chicago about nine in the morning yesterday and, unable to enter the Chicago River because of the sandbar, anchored offshore and unloading had to be done through numerous trips by bateaux. The trader, greatly overjoyed that his large shipment of goods and liquor had arrived safely, oversaw the whole operation, pressing all his employees into the effort and even hiring Antoine Ouilmette and Louis Pettell to lend a hand. He also tried to hire John Kelso only to find that the former Fort Dearborn soldier, having escaped being killed at the Lee farm, had reenlisted in the army on May 3.

Today, just before noon, the last of the bateaux was emptied and its contents placed in Kinzie's Store. The trader had grinned at Eleanor's obvious relief and murmured, "I told you there was nothing to worry about," but his own relief was very nearly as great as hers.

A much smaller cargo had been taken on by the ships, including ninety-nine packs of fine furs from the U.S. Factory and one hundred fourteen from John Kinzie. As soon as the outward-bound cargo had been taken aboard, the ships were ready to sail and now, at the Chicago River shoreline near the fort, Kinzie shook hands with Matthew Irwin, the U.S. Factor. He was returning with the *Friends' Good Will* to Mackinac for the purpose of hiring an interpreter, since he had been struggling along without one of any real skill since the death of Jack Lalime three months ago. Both *Friends' Good Will* and *Erie* were returning together, planning to make stops at Mackinac, Detroit and Cleveland before returning to their Buffalo home port of Black Rock. The young doctor, Isaac Van Voorhis, looked on as they said farewell.

"You'll pass the word along at Mackinac that I'm looking for some more hands to hire here?" Kinzie asked.

Irwin nodded. "I hope I'll be able to find some for you," he replied. "If I can't locate any immediately, I'll ask the captain of *Friends' Good*

Will to pass the notice at Detroit. Surely you'll get someone from there."

"Thank you," John said. "Enjoy your trip and come back safely. And I hope you'll be able to find the interpreter you want there, since I was responsible for depriving you of Lalime." It was the first time since the incident last March that he had mentioned it to either of the men and there was a little embarrassed silence. Irwin broke it by turning to Van Voorhis and shaking his hand.

"Isaac," he said, "I appreciate your taking over in the factory until I return. It won't take a great deal of your time, since there's really not much to do at the moment, especially now that the government's fur packs are on their way, but whatever you do will be a big help."

The surgeon's mate grinned. "I'll see to it," he said. "I echo John's sentiments: have a good trip and stay safe. Bring back some newspapers or magazines if you can. Books, too."

"That I will," the factor said, stepping into the bateau.

They watched until the small boat crossed the choppy span of water to the larger ships and then saw the *Friends' Good Will* and *Erie* weigh anchor and spread sails which quickly became full-bellied in the offshore wind. The ships moved off swiftly and the two men strolled back toward the fort's main gate together. Before getting there, however, they stopped and watched curiously the approach of a man who was trotting up the lake trail from the south. As he came closer, John recognized him. "That's my man, Pierre LeClerc," he said. "He's supposed to be at the post at St. Joseph."

Together, Kinzie and Van Voorhis walked out to meet the arrival and intercepted him several hundred yards from the fort. A lean, wiry man, LeClerc was a half-breed French and Potawatomi, who had been one of Kinzie's most dependable clerks for years. Only a fortnight ago Kinzie had sent him to the St. Joseph post ninety miles away and he hardly expected him back so soon.

The runner slumped to the ground as they reached him and lay there gasping, gratefully accepting a drink of whiskey from the flask his employer offered him. After a few moments he had caught his breath enough to speak with some degree of coherency and told them he had run the whole distance from St. Joseph without sleep and had paused only twice to rest and eat. John Kinzie felt a churning begin in his stomach, knowing that whatever the news was that had brought LeClerc here in such a manner, it had to be bad. It was.

"War!" LeClerc puffed. "We're at war with the British!"

[*July 5, 1812 — Sunday afternoon*]

Less than two hours later and sixty miles to the south, where the Iroquois River emptied into the Kankakee, two mounted Indians trotted into view on the trail from the east and rode directly to Nescotnemeg's lodge in the middle of the Potawatomi village. Though they were Potawatomies, they were not of this village and though they did not speak, they acknowledged with waves or nods the greetings of the inhabitants. One was the influential village chief named Wapeme, better known to the whites as White Pigeon. His companion, a large younger man, was the subchief Peesotum.

Inside Nescotnemeg's lodge they were made welcome by the chief and spoke only of inconsequential matters until they had finished a pipe together. Then Wapeme said the words he knew would bring great pleasure to Nescotnemeg — Mad Sturgeon.

"I come to you directly from Tecumseh at Amherstburg," he said.

Nescotnemeg said nothing but his heart beat a little faster as he waited for Wapeme to continue. The visiting chief's village was located on the upper St. Joseph, where the Portage River from the north and Prairie River from the sourtheast emptied into the larger stream in the southern Michigan country.[225] Peesotum, no longer a village chief since his loss of face to William Wells at Fort Wayne had resulted in his ouster, had in the past year become something of a disciple to the aged Wapeme and his eyes glittered as he waited for the chief to speak further.

"Tecumseh," Wapeme went on after a pause, "has sent messengers like me to all the villages to announce that the time has come. The Americans have declared war against the British."

Nescotnemeg let a broad smile crease his features, though it was in poor taste to do so while Wapeme was still speaking. He could not help it; this was what he had been awaiting and he heard the faint hissing sound as a pent-up breath escaped him. Wapeme ignored the breach of etiquette and went on without pause.

"Main Poche is on his way here now with many kegs of gunpowder and much lead ball in sacks, but he will not stay. He will only give you what he brings and hear more of your plans and then return to Tecumseh to aid him and the British against the Americans at Detroit. Tecumseh said it was agreed as your place to plan the attack that is to be made on Fort Dearborn and that it was agreed as Siggenauk's place to lead that attack and that Black Partridge will bring his men behind you, as will his brother, Waubansee, from the Fox River and Naunongee from his village on the Calumet. Tecumseh said to tell you that the time is still the same for when that attack should be made — in the middle of the Heat Moon.

"It will be as Tecumseh has said," Nescotnemeg replied. "I will ready my warriors and I will send to Siggenauk quickly and we will meet as before at the village of Black Partridge when the time has come. This you may tell Tecumseh."

"I will tell him."

"May I speak?" Peesotum interjected. At Nescotnemeg's nod, he went on. "There is one white man I must kill, but he is not at Fort Dearborn. He is at Fort Wayne, where he shamed me and where we became final enemies. My shame will continue until I kill him. Tecumseh has said that when the affair at Chicago is finished, our feet should then take us to Fort Wayne. I ask that I be permitted to lead the attack there and that the one who was once the son of Michikiniqua and who was known as Apekonit, but who is now called Captain Wells, be reserved for my tomahawk and my knife."

Nescotnemeg looked at the large young man for a long while and then dipped his head once. "So it will be, Peesotum."

[July 17, 1812 — Friday morning]

The campaign of Brigadier General William Hull continued to be the plot of a tragi-comedy. With two thousand troops behind him, he should have swept across the Detroit River and easily crushed the paltry British opposition at Amherstburg, but he had not. Instead, his actions had become marked with indecisiveness and he vacillated for long crucial days doing little or nothing.

There were high hopes among the Americans at first, all of whom — save for their commander — were eager for the affray. But thus far it hadn't happened that way. On July 6, the day after the army's arrival at Detroit, Hull sent Colonel Lewis Cass as a messenger to the British commander at Fort Malden, Lieutenant Colonel Thomas Bligh St. George, with a politely worded demand that he give up the schooner *Cuyahoga* and the Americans taken with her . . . along with the baggage that had been aboard. In just as polite a response, St. George, although quaking at the size of the enemy force across the river, in essence told General Hull to go straight to hell and then finally realized that he had better inform General Brock of the appearance of Hull's army here. He did so, also forwarding to his commander the captured Hull papers. But, beset by mass desertions of his militia and weakly garrisoned to begin with, St. George knew there was no way he could stand against a hard onslaught by Hull. Even some of the Indian allies were having second thoughts and considering taking a neutral stance, encouraged in this direction by the Wyandot chief Walk-in-the-Water at Maguaga, across the river from Amherstburg and somewhat upstream. It was only through the strong, sometimes threatening councils held by Tecumseh, Roundhead, Chaubenee, Sauganash and Main Poche that Walk-in-the-Water was convinced to stop advocating neutrality among tribes not his own.

On the same day, July 6, Hull finally concluded he had better notify the commanders of the forts under his jurisdiction — at Mackinac, Chicago and Fort Wayne — that a state of war existed and for them to get their

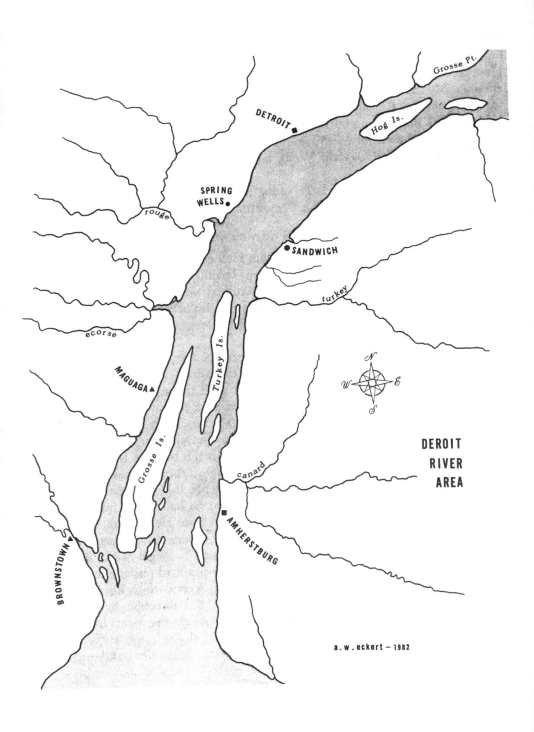

DETROIT ■

SPRING
WELLS ●

rouge

●SANDWICH

Grosse Pt.

Hog Is.

turkey

ecorse

MAGUAGA ▶

Turkey Is.

N
W ✦ E
S

BROWNSTOWN ▶

Grosse Is.

canard

■ AMHERSTBURG

DEROIT
RIVER
AREA

a.w.eckert — 1982

forts in a defensive state. Unfortunately, though he dictated the messages, he left no orders for the immediate dispatch of the notifications by express to the posts in question and so the orders continued to rest in their pouches in Detroit for the time being.

Ten days ago five pieces of artillery from the fort at Detroit were rolled into position at Spring Wells opposite Sandwich and a brief bombardment of Sandwich took place. But it quickly petered out and nothing of any significance was accomplished and, to the intense disappointment of Hull's troops, the anticipated invasion of Canada did not take place.

Just as much disappointment was occurring far to the north at St. Joseph Island, where British Captain Charles Roberts was still holding his force in readiness to attack Fort Mackinac as soon as permission came from General Brock. On July 8 a dispatch arrived, not with the desired permission but with orders to hold still and await further orders.

General Hull continued to sit on his hands day after day at Detroit. His force had been augmented by the Detroit garrison, including Captain John Whistler and his sons, Lieutenant William Whistler and Ensign John Whistler, Jr., but he still hesitated in taking the offensive. He held inconsequential councils with small groups of Indians who presented themselves, professing peaceful intentions, including Chief Walk-in-the-Water. The old brig Adams, at the Detroit shipyard, was in need of extensive repairs, so a crew was put to work on this, but the labors went slowly. Finally, after six days of the army doing virtually nothing and Hull basing his lethargy on lack of supplies, the general gave in to the growing pressure from his increasingly impatient subordinate officers. He dispatched an express to Governor Return J. Meigs at Chillicothe, Ohio, asking him to send supplies immediately, and then told his officers the army would invade. Colonel McArthur was placed with his regiment at Spring Wells as a feint, since this was the likeliest place for the invasion to occur. The feint worked well and during the night of July 11, Tecumseh set up a major ambush on the Canadian shore to hit the Americans when they crossed there.

But it was a mile above Detroit, at the lower end of Hog Island, that the actual crossing in a flotilla of small boats took place in the predawn hours of July 12, wholly without opposition.[226] Within a few hours the entire army had crossed, Sandwich had been taken, having been found all but deserted, and General Hull established his headquarters in the new brick home of Georgian architecture recently built by the French-Canadian militia colonel, Jean Baptiste Baby. No few of the American officers and men noted that General Hull was among the last to embark from the American side and when his boat touched the Canadian shore he announced grandly, "The critical moment draws near!" The ambush having failed, Tecumseh pulled his warriors back toward Fort Malden. Now,

Hull's officers were sure, the way was clear for them to strike southward toward Amherstburg immediately. Again General Hull vacillated.

On the day of the invasion, he issued a strongly worded proclamation advising the populace of Sandwich to return to their homes without fear, but also warning that any white man found fighting beside the Indians would be destroyed.[227] The next day, a force of forty men under Captain Henry Ulry was sent southward to reconnoitre toward Fort Malden. At the Turkey Creek Bridge he found where Tecumseh's Indians had lain in ambush and he returned with this news to Hull, which unsettled the general considerably. For the first time some of his field officers began to suspect the truth: that William Hull had such an incredible fear of Indians that the very mention of them could cause him to perspire and become pale. A force of twenty or thirty Indians could devastate him mentally far more than a force of enemy soldiers fifty times that large.

On July 14, when a body of Indians was reported moving away from the Detroit River area and toward the Thames River, Hull's relief was almost pathetic and he only grudgingly acquiesced to the demands of Colonel McArthur that he be allowed to pursue with a strong detachment of his own men, supported by Colonel Findley's rifle corps. While they never overtook the Indians, they did find and loot considerable stockpiles of British supplies along the Thames and confiscated enough boats to transport the captured goods back to Sandwich.[228] But time continued to pass without much happening. The same sense of lethargy, in fact, seemed to prevail among all the American commanders. Major General Dearborn, still tarrying at Boston, finally left there reluctantly, writing to Secretary of War Eustis:

. . . I have been in a very unpleasant situation, being at a loss to determine whether I ought to leave the seacoast. . . . I begin to feel I may be censured for not moving. . . .

Finally, yesterday, Colonel Lewis Cass had convinced Hull to let him advance with a force of two hundred eighty men toward Fort Malden. The detachment got within four miles of the British installation when they came to the partially destroyed bridge over the Canard River, being held at its southern end by a well-entrenched pocket of forty British regulars. Here at its mouth, the Canard River was ninety feet wide and quite deep, so Cass left a detachment of riflemen at the spot to keep the British guard pinned down and led the rest of his force up the Canard, looking for a fording place. It was five miles before they found one. Returning on the south side to hit the British bridge guard from the rear, they were within half a mile of the bridge when their forward progress was halted by an impassable feeder creek flowing into the Canard from the south. Again they had to go upstream, on the feeder creek, looking for a crossing. They found one in about a mile. But by the time they returned on the other side, the British guard had been reinforced and it was late in the day. A hot fight broke out and three times the Americans pushed the British back until it finally became too dark to fight any more. But at day's end, the crucial Canard River Bridge, still usable, was in American hands.

Sure victory was now within grasp of the Americans, requiring only a strong drive of the whole army against Fort Malden. As an added benefit, today Colonel McArthur returned to General Hull from the Thames with the spoils of his foray, including two hundred barrels of flour, four hundred new blankets, a good many captured arms and plenty of ammunition. The whole army, jubilant, eager for anything, was poised now, waiting for the order to send them into major assault against Amherstburg.

And once again Brigadier General William Hull vacillated.

[July 17, 1812 — Friday noon]

United States Factor Matthew Irwin stood on the great wooden wharf at Mackinac Island and, despite the fact that he was in the midst of the whole Fort Mackinac garrison, he could not contain the rush of emotion which flooded him and he wept uncontrollably.

How, he asked himself, could the events of these past forty-eight hours have occurred? How was it possible? The mental questions were rhetorical, for he knew — just as everyone else gathered here knew by now — how it had all transpired.

It had begun two days ago, when the *Friends' Good Will* and *Erie* arrived at these very wharves. Here, on this gemlike, craggy island in the midst of the Straits of Mackinac separating Lake Michigan from Lake Huron, was the fur trading capital of America. Here the fur barons had set up their warehouses and sorting rooms for the hundreds and thousands of bales of fur which were collected — brought by parties of Indians and fur brigades of French-Canadian voyageurs from the Canadian wilderness, from the wilds of the upper Mississippi and the little-known territory of the upper Missouri. From here at Mackinac the furs, carefully sorted and graded and rebaled, were transshipped to Buffalo and to Montreal and Quebec and eventually to New York and Europe. Here was one of the oldest and most beautiful villages in the American wilderness, with fine large homes and shops, stables and distilleries, shipyards and excellent dockage. This was where the British had reigned supreme until the summer of 1796, when they had been forced to vacate and reestablish themselves forty miles away on the less pleasant, less accessible and less strategic island called St. Joseph.

And on St. Joseph Island, at almost the same moment that Matthew Irwin was stepping down the gangplank from the *Friends' Good Will* at Mackinac, a canoe was beaching and a messenger was running to the

British commanding officer, Captain Charles Roberts, with a dispatch from General Brock — the one they had been impatiently awaiting since the last day of June. In the dispatch, Brock instructed Captain Roberts to:

. . . adopt the most prudent measures, either of offense or defense, which circumstances might point out.

The ball had been dropped in Roberts's lap; he could act at his discretion and there was no doubt what he would do. Immediately he put his forces on order to prepare themselves and their weapons for attacking Fort Mackinac. They would have the remainder of this evening and most of tomorrow, July 16, to get some rest and be ready. The invasion force would leave St. Joseph Island for the forty-mile trip to Mackinac before sunset tomorrow.

At Fort Mackinac, Matthew Irwin reported to the American commander, Lieutenant Porter Hanks, in mid-morning yesterday, after having a fine meal and a very good night's rest at the Whitefish Inn. Irwin filled the officer in on the disturbing occurrences that had taken place recently at Chicago: the death of Jack Lalime in March at the hand of John Kinzie, the early April killings and mutilations of Liberty White and Jean Baptiste Cardin at the Charles Lee farm and the disappearance of DuBou, plus the minor Indian harassments that had occurred since. It all looked very bad, they both agreed.

Lieutenant Hanks was especially concerned since his own garrison here, including officers, totaled only fifty-seven effective men of the First Artillery. Yet, if an Indian attack came — and he had noted a decided coolness among visiting Indians in recent weeks — Fort Mackinac was strong and he was confident they could easily withstand a siege.

It was because of Lalime's death, Irwin went on, that he was here, since now Fort Dearborn and the United States Factory at Chicago were without the services of an expert interpreter. Hanks felt sure Irwin would have no difficulty locating one and promised to help him in his search on the morrow.

Then, late in the afternoon, a Mackinac physician, Dr. John Day, came to Lieutenant Hanks with the disturbing news that had just come to him — that a large number of Indians gathered at St. Joseph Island were planning an immediate attack against Fort Mackinac. At once Porter Hanks made preparations, had ammunition readied in the blockhouses and called a meeting of his officers and some of Mackinac's most influential citizens to discuss the situation. Indian alarms were not uncommon here, but they were never casually sloughed off. There were some old traders here who still remembered only too clearly when, in 1763, Fort Mackinac — then on the mainland shore to the south — had been taken by surprise by the Indians and a terrible massacre had resulted.

The consensus of the present meeting was that someone who knew both the Indians and British well — someone who could go to St. Joseph Island in an ordinary manner with impunity — should be commissioned to undertake a spying mission there. The obvious choice was Michael Dousman, a prominent fur trader and agent of John Jacob Astor's South West Fur Company. A genial man, well liked and especially noted for his integrity — he had never been known to break his word once it was given — Dousman agreed to do the job. At sunset he shoved off in one of his larger canoes, paddled by a select crew from among his own employees.

Forty miles east and a little north, the British and Indian invasionary force was already in motion. Aboard the *Caledonia* was Captain Charles Roberts with his forty-five scarlet-jacketed regulars and two brass six-pounder cannon on wheels. The flotilla surrounding this flagship of sorts was impressive to say the least. Ten large bateaux carried twenty-six men each — British traders and French-Canadians, who were all militiamen — along with their rifles, ammunition and packs. Around the whole were seventy long slender war canoes, all containing at least ten warriors each and five of them containing eleven.[220] The light breeze was in their favor and the *Caledonia* skimmed along gracefully under sail, while the full complement of oarsmen in each bateau and paddlers in each canoe kept pace, stroking firmly, strongly, all of them realizing the importance of reaching Mackinac Island before dawn with their combined assault force of one thousand twenty-one men.

Michael Dousman had gone peacefully to sleep in the bottom of the canoe within an hour of his departure from Mackinac. The smooth cadence of his paddlers and gentle lapping of the waters had lulled him into a pervading drowsiness he could not shake off and so at last he had lain down on his doubled-over blanket. Now, about twelve miles from Mackinac under a clear, starry sky, he was awakened by voices and, lifting his head, was stunned to discover they were surrounded. Voices hailed him, calling him by name, and he recognized traders with whom he had associated for many years — Robert Dickson, John Askin, Toussaint Pothier, Lewis Crawford and others. They recognized him as well and he was taken aboard the *Caledonia*.

The situation was explained to him: the invasion was to be against the fort, not the town. However, once it began, who could tell what would happen? They were not desirous of seeing the townspeople or their property hurt. All knew Dousman well for his honesty and that his word was his bond. Would he voluntarily precede this flotilla, return directly to Mackinac and secretly awaken each resident in turn and tell him, for his own safety, to go to the old distillery on the west side of the island? There, they and their goods would be protected by a strong guard. He was to tell Lieutenant Hanks absolutely nothing. Awed by the size, armament and determination of the force and strongly wishing not to see neighbors and friends jeopardized, Dousman gave his word to do as directed and left, his lighter canoe skimming swiftly away toward the southwestern shore of the island, where Mackinac was located, while the assault force headed at a slower pace for the one small area of beach along the cliff-faced north shore.[230]

At 3:00 A.M. today the invasion force landed on the beach and began the difficult job of drawing the two cannon up the three-hundred-foot rise to the plateau. At the same time, townspeople warned by Michael Dousman were already beginning to gather in the old distillery. All, fearful for their own lives and property, moved silently and maintained the secrecy Dousman imposed upon them. All, that is, save one.

Dr. John Day was one of the last to be awakened by Dousman, just as the first gray light of dawn began streaking the eastern sky. He listened grimly and agreed to gather up some things and go to the distillery, but as soon as Dousman had slipped away, the doctor ran to the fort and alerted Lieutenant Hanks. Immediately the troops were roused and manned their stations, but with strict orders not to fire under any circumstance except by a direct order from the commander. Then they waited, the fort's cannon — the very same guns taken from Lord Cornwallis at Saratoga during the Revolution — pointed toward the water, whence the attacking force was expected.

They didn't have long to wait, but the approach of the invaders was from the rear, not the front. Working swiftly in the pre-dawn hours, the attackers had brought their cannon across the rocky, bushy plateau and mounted them in a position one hundred fifty feet above and behind Fort Mackinac. For all its fine defenses against attack from the landing, which was the only reasonable approach, Fort Mackinac was utterly vulnerable to artillery on the bluffs behind.

As this morning's dawn and sunrise came and passed, those inside the fort saw more and more Indians ducking about among the rocks out of range. Then, at 9:00 A.M., Captain Roberts and a small party of regulars approached the fort under a flag of truce and were admitted. Hanks was completely nonplussed when he learned that the United States and Great Britain were again at war. Until this instant, he had thought the attack was by Indians alone. There was little to negotiate and Roberts pointed out the obvious with galling calm. He pointed to the bluffs overlooking the rear of the fort and for the first time Lieutenant Hanks could see the soldiers and cannon positioned there in a commanding situation.

"Do not," Captain Roberts ordered sternly, "allow a single shot to be fired by any of your men. If one shot is fired, an absolute massacre will occur here. You are outnumbered by about eighteen to one. You have no defense whatever from our cannon on the heights. It is now nine o'clock. You have two hours to decide what your course will be. I trust you will wish to spare the unnecessary effusion of blood that resistance will occasion, not only among your garrison, but among the Mackinac citizens as well. Once the Indian forces with us begin to attack, there will be no stopping them so long as a single enemy remains alive. I will return to the heights," the British commander said, pointing again. "If surrender is the course you choose — and I strongly advise it, sir — then at eleven o'clock you will leave the fort, with no more than one other officer, and come to the heights where capitulation papers are at this time being readied."

Captain Roberts stared at Lieutenant Hanks for a long space, then spun on his heel, returned to his small escort and ascended the narrow trail to the heights. Hanks called an immediate meeting of his entire garrison and relayed the dreadful news. The alternatives left little choice: surrender or massacre. They chose surrender.

At eleven o'clock, clad in his best dress uniform and escorted by a subordinate officer, Lieutenant Porter Hanks left the front gate of the fort and climbed the trail to the top of the bluffs. There he was handed a copy of the capitulation to read and sign:

Heights above Michillimackinac
17th July, 1812
CAPITULATION

Agreed upon between Captain Charles Roberts, commanding his Britannic majesty's forces on the one part, and Lieutenant Porter Hanks, commanding the forces of the United States, on the other part.

1st. The fort of Michillimackinac shall immediately be surrendered to the British forces.

2d. The garrison shall march out with the honors of war, lay down their arms, and become prisoners of war; and shall be sent to the United States of America by his Britannic majesty, not to serve this war, until regularly exchanged; and for the due performance of this article, the officers pledge their word and honor.

3d. All the merchant vessels in the harbor, with their cargoes, shall be in possession of their respective owners.

4th. Private property shall be held sacred as far as it is in my power.

5th. All citizens of the U. States, who shall not take the oath of allegiance to his Britannic majesty, shall depart with their property from the island in one month from the date hereof.

Signed   **CHARLES ROBERTS**
Capt. commanding the forces of his Britannic majesty.

Lieutenant Hanks looked up from the paper and nodded to Captain Roberts. He was provided with a pen and directly beneath the British commander's signature he wrote:

P. HANKS
Lieut. commanding the United States troops.

Half an hour later, as the American troops left the fort and lay down their arms, Captain Roberts made an addition to the capitulation and signed it, then handed it to Hanks who read it and also signed it:

Supplement to the articles of Capitulation signed on the 17th July:
The captains and crews of the vessels Erie *and* Freegoodwill [sic], *shall be included under the second article, not to serve until regularly exchanged, for which the officers pledge their word and honor.*[231]

Fort Michillimackinac
17th July, 1812
CHARLES ROBERTS
Capt. commanding the forces of his Britannic majesty.
GRANTED P. HANKS
Lieut. commanding the United States forces.

The Indians had been spoiling for a fight and now, with that prospect averted, they complained to Robert Dickson — whom they called Mascotapah — that they had been cheated and they wanted scalps as trophies of war.[232] Dickson shook his head and explained that the Americans, once surrendered as they were, could not be killed. However, he added, undoubtedly there were spoils of war to be taken inside the fort, which would be divided among the Indians. This mollified them, especially when the goods within the fort turned out to be considerable quantities of flour, pork, salt, candles, vinegar and soap . . . along with a substantial number of guns and ammunition, plus three hundred fifty-seven gallons of whiskey. Beyond that, there was also a very large number of fur skins owned by the government, which were also distributed. The total value of the goods came to about ten thousand pounds sterling.

United States Factor Matthew Irwin, also taken into custody by the British, had watched with rage as the United States government-owned goods were distributed. A portion of these, he knew, had been destined for shipment to Chicago. Now, with land access to Fort Dearborn evidently interrupted by the Indians and water access cut off by the British here at Fort Mackinac, Fort Dearborn could no longer be supported. It was entirely on its own, but didn't know it.

That was when Matthew Irwin wept.[233]

[*July 18, 1812 — Saturday*]
Captain William Wells faced the silent, sober Miami Indians in a semicircle before him. He stood high on his toes in the cheerless light of the

setting sun and raised both arms above his head, then sank to his knees with a harsh cry. With his head bent so far back it seemed his neck must break, he opened his mouth wide and the weird, discordant, mournful death chant erupted from him.

"*Ho-eee-nuh huh huh,*" he cried, over and again, interspersed with the additional atonal phrase, "*No-tha . . . huh huh . . . nep-wah . . . huh huh.*"

Tears swept clean little tracks through the streaks of black paint on his face as they coursed down his cheeks and dripped from his chin onto his bare chest, also streaked with black, where again they caused the paint to run. His hair hung loose, wild, glinting reddish in the fading sunlight, reddish and black with the paint that had been smeared in it as well. He wore no ornamentation and his only apparel was a rawhide waistband with an old scalp hung from it on the left side. From waist to knees he was painted with drab ochre except for his genitals, which had been garishly stained with vermilion, and a diagonal slash of white across each buttock, forming an inverted V. His legs from the knees down, and his feet, were painted black. On this day he was not the white man Indian Agent known as Captain William Wells. On this day he was the Miami whose name was Apekonit.

The transformation had been incredible. Only three hours ago he had ended the council at Fort Wayne that had been scheduled for today at the direction of William Henry Harrison. Weeks ago the word had gone out that the council was to be held this day, at which time the governor would attempt to placate the Indians — especially the Potawatomies — with gifts in abundance, in an effort to woo them away from the British . . . and from Tecumseh. Whiskey had been provided and a great deal of food and there were to be gifts of blankets and clothing and even a small amount of gunpowder and lead. The council fire had been lighted and they waited. And waited. Twenty-five hundred Indians had been expected, mostly Potawatomies. Only two hundred fifty had shown up, none Potawatomies. They were Miamis, led by the severely ailing, seventy-year-old Michikiniqua, whose gout was so advanced he could not walk and had been carried here on a litter. In the midst of their waiting for the others to arrive, Michikiniqua had suddenly sat upright and his eyes blazed as he pointed a trembling finger at something none but he could see, and then fell back.

Michikiniqua — Little Turtle — was dead.

A military honor guard shot a six-gun salute over his recumbent form a little later and a visiting clergyman spoke a few words that none of the Indians understood.[234] Then, at the request of Wells, the whites left and the mourning Miamis had bathed their chief and dressed him in fine doeskin and placed him, still upon the litter, into the shallow grave they had dug at the spot where once his lodge had stood. All present knew the futility of sending away for others to come and mourn. They were with Tecumseh now and too far away. And July was a hot month.

Beside their chief in the grave they placed his rifle, fully primed, and his tomahawk and skinning knife and a war club he used when he was younger. A narrow-necked gourd filled with water that had been sweetened with maple sugar was placed beside his left hand and a pouch filled with pemmican and jerky before the right — supplies to sustain him on his journey to the afterworld. And they passed and looked at their chief and they wept.

And then had come Apekonit, and they fanned back from the grave, sat upon the ground and watched, occasionally nodding their approval, as he danced the slow, agonizing dance of the dead before the grave for many minutes until at last he raised his arms and fell to his knees.

"Ho-eee-nuh huh huh . . . ho-eee-nuh huh huh . . . No-tha . . . huh huh . . . nep-wah . . . huh huh . . . No-tha nep-wah . . . huh huh . . ."

My father is dead.

[July 26, 1812 — Sunday]

In whatever esteem Brigadier General William Hull may have been held by the men of his army early in this campaign, it had now all but ceased to exist. Murmurings of "coward" and "fool" and even "traitor" were becoming increasingly audible and it was clear that if the commander of the Northwestern Army of the United States did not do something very significant — and quickly at that — his own army might become his foe every bit as much as the British.

The campaign had become a farce. With the capture of the bridge over the Canard River, the way had become clear for an assault in force against Fort Malden at Amherstburg, only four miles south. There was no other practical way for the army to approach; no other place within ten or fifteen miles where the heavy artillery could be brought across the river without becoming hopelessly mired — artillery which could quickly shatter the British bastion and bring the Redcoats to their knees. Colonel Cass, with Captain Josiah Snelling beside him, held the position and sent expresses to General Hull in Sandwich, requesting reinforcement and orders.[235] And at the same time they wondered with great uneasiness why Captain James Brown, one of General Hull's aides, who had been with them at Hull's direct order, had slipped away toward Fort Malden under a flag of truce; and why, later, he had returned and refused to explain his actions.[236]

Then a reinforcement U.S. Fourth Regiment company had come without written orders from Hull but with the verbal directive to evacuate the position. Entreaties were urgently dispatched to Hull, requesting permission to retain possession of this vital link to Amherstburg, but Hull remained aloof, refusing to respond. The murmurings among the troops became louder and it was only with the greatest reluctance that Cass and Snelling gave up the position.

Within hours of the American withdrawal from the bridge, a strong force of British, Canadian militia and Indians moved back and occupied it, tearing down enough of its structure to render it impassable to artillery carts. They also immediately built a breastwork and battery at the south end of it and moved artillery into position. Colonel Findley, confronting General Hull at his headquarters in Sandwich, found the commanding officer nervous, irascible and disinclined to discuss the matter except inexplicably to order a detachment back *to* the bridge, but with direct orders not to cross.

On July 19 Colonel Duncan McArthur led a detachment back there and was immediately fired upon. A ball struck the colonel's horse in the forehead, killing it beneath him, and he narrowly escaped injury. Suddenly a swarm of Indians streamed across the bridge to the north side with great agility. They split into two groups, one under Tecumseh, one under Main Poche. The party under the Potawatomi chief made a frontal attack, driving the American force back, while Tecumseh's party made a wide sweep around in the woods to cut off their retreat. The Americans rallied and drove Main Poche's Indians back and one of their rifle balls struck Main Poche himself in the neck, felling him. For several minutes the chief lay there as if dead, but then he regained his senses, staggered back toward the bridge and was helped across by one of his warriors. It was a painful but not mortal wound. Only by great good fortune did the Americans manage to slip past Tecumseh's force before the trap could be closed. The detachment of Americans returned to the camp at Sandwich depressed, discouraged and greatly fatigued. General Hull remained incommunicado.

The next day, July 20, Colonel McArthur returned to the bridge with his detachment, this time bringing along a six-pounder. Again his orders were to go to the bridge, but not cross it. The British force at the southern end of the bridge was now much larger and they opened fire immediately with their own artillery. McArthur returned it with a few shots from the cannon, but it was hopeless and once again they withdrew. By this time virtually the whole American army was losing confidence in General Hull.

The shock that rippled through them was intense the next morning when, with only the flimsiest of excuse, William Hull left his camp headquarters in Sandwich and had one of the boats take him back across the river to Detroit. There was no indication given of when — or if — he would return. His only order was to place Colonel McArthur in command on the east side of the river.

Time continued to slip away and, with it, the overwhelming advantages the Americans had from the outset. British forces were being augmented now and more Indians had arrived. To get across the Canard River now to attack Fort Malden would be very costly in lives, but it was still possible and the only course of action open to them if they were to maintain the offensive. Learning of the increase in the Indian force and of a path Tecumseh was to lead his warriors out upon, Colonel McArthur ordered Major James Denny to take a detachment and set up an ambush. He did so, in the vicinity of a little settlement called Petit Cote, just north of the Canard River Bridge. But it was the Indians, led by Tecumseh and a neck-bandaged Main Poche, who surprised the Americans and, after a brief skirmish, Denny was forced to retire. The Indians pursued for two and a half miles and Denny's force, already with six dead and two wounded, was saved only by the timely arrival of some reinforcements under Robert Lucas of the Ohio Militia.[237]

At last, this morning, General Hull came back across the river, appearing a little less harried than when he left five days previously. He reestablished himself in command in the fortification dubbed Fort Gowie, that had been built around the residence of a Mr. Gowie. The general seemed on the verge of issuing an important order when a ship hove into view on the Detroit River, coming from the north under British colors. She was brought about by a shot across her bow from shore and a few minutes later a substantial group of American soldiers and citizens were disembarking. Their leader was Lieutenant Porter Hanks, who immediately informed General Hull of the surrender of Fort Mackinac.

The commander's jaw dropped and his eyes became glassy and there were those on hand who swore he swayed and they thought he would faint. He did not, but that he was tremendously shaken was clearly apparent to all. "Dear God," he murmured, not even realizing he was speaking aloud, "the whole northern hordes of Indians will be let loose upon us!"

In addition to being shaken by the news he had just received, the fear that had risen in him, almost bordering on panic, was painfully evident. As if in a daze, he turned and reeled back to his headquarters and the silence that followed him was bitter, accusing. Whatever the prospects for successful attack may have been before or still existed now, it made no difference.

In one brief moment the Army of the Northwest had ceased being on the offensive.

[*July 27, 1812 — Monday*]

Whatever wavering might have been left among the tribes of northern Illinois and southern Wisconsin to back Tecumseh dissipated with the arrival at Black Partridge's village near Chicago of Chaubenee and Sauganash. They had been sent by Tecumseh on fast horses to spread the news of the fall of Mackinac and the weakness and indecisiveness of the American army. Tecumseh had been informed of Mackinac's fall a day before the British at Amherstburg learned of it and two days before General Hull was shattered by the news. Immediately he had dispatched Chaubenee and Sauganash on their mission. Nor was that all the Potawatomi chiefs had to say: Tecumseh had been given the rank of brigadier general by the British and, highly significant, Chief Walk-in-the-Water of the Wyandots, who had so long held out for neutrality, had finally given in to Tecumseh when word of Fort Mackinac's fall had been brought to him and he had crossed the Detroit River with his warriors to fight beside the British.

Chaubenee and Sauganash were not here for a long visit. They had come not only to tell their important news but to reaffirm what Tecumseh had predicted much earlier and was still predicting — that Detroit would fall and the American Army of the Northwest would be lost at the middle of the Heat Moon, and that the attack on Fort Dearborn should be launched to coincide with that. It was Tecumseh's suggestion that Black Partridge and his people, acting with what would seem to be peaceable intent, should begin moving back into Chicago five or six days prior to that, setting up their lodges close to the fort and carrying on normal activities to allay fears.

Immediately all this information was relayed by swift riders to Siggenauk at Milwaukee, Mawgehset at Lake Geneva, the Winnebago chiefs Karamone, Mackraragah, Sansamani and Shawonoe on the upper Rock River, Wisconsin River and Apple River, as well as to Black Hawk at Saukenuk, his village at the mouth of the Rock River, to Gomo at Peoria Lake, to Nescotnemeg on the Kankakee and Naunongee on the Calumet. By tomorrow night, war dances would be occurring in all these villages.

Chaubenee and Sauganash then rode boldly into Chicago, stopping briefly at Fort Dearborn to pay their respects to a nervous Captain Nathan Heald who came out to meet them. The pair pretended not to notice the soldiers positioned too casually on the parapets with their weapons, ready to fire at once if their commanding officer should be jeopardized. Many of the Chicago residents were still taking refuge in the Agency House, but a few — those whose houses were close to the fort — had gone home. Captain Heald, knowing Sauganash could speak English well, asked about the war and what was happening, especially at Detroit, but Sauganash merely shrugged.

"We have been away from there a long while," he said, "and know nothing of it. We have heard that the white brothers are warring against one another again and this is very sad, but it is their concern, not ours.

Chaubenee's people and Black Partridge's and others are content to sit quietly in their villages and take no part in such matters. Only foolish warriors seeking honor for their courage have been doing bad things, such as the little party of young Winnebago warriors who foolishly attacked the Lee farm near here. That was very bad and Black Partridge was angry and sent people to chastise those who did this. Soon he will return here, close to the fort, with his women and children and set up lodges and resume with you the friendliness that had always been before."

"That is good," Captain Heald said, the words of Sauganash confirming what he had believed ever since the Lee farm massacre — that it was the work of an isolated band and had nothing to do with the Potawatomies of this area. "Black Partridge and his people will be welcome, as always. But there have been things since the Winnebagoes struck the Lee farm that have bothered us here: some of our livestock has been killed and shots have been fired and once a tomahawk thrown. What of that?"

Sauganash shook his head. "Those were unfortunate things done by high-spirited young men who are hard to control. They did so without the knowledge of Black Partridge and he was angry with them. No further such incidents will occur. Black Partridge said to assure you of that. It is why he is coming back here close to the fort, to ease your minds and show you that he wishes only peace and that there is nothing to fear."

They left the Fort Dearborn commander then and crossed the river to visit John Kinzie, which was the real reason for coming into Chicago. They found him at his store and greeted him with genuine friendliness, as they had for so many years. He made them very welcome, fed them a good meal and afterwards smoked with them and sipped brandy. They talked of many things, although the Indians continued to profess no recent knowledge of the war or what was occurring in the east or what the British and Tecumseh were doing.

It was Chaubenee who finally came to the point. "Shawneeawkee," he said, "Sauganash and I are your friends and we are concerned for you and your family — for their health and well-being. Only recently we heard of your having been shot and then your having killed Lalime, who shot you." He shook his head. "Lalime was an unpredictable man; he could be good, but also he could be very bad. It is best he is gone. Nevertheless, we worry about your health."

Kinzie misunderstood. He pulled back his collar to show them the bullet scar, still in angry pink. "You see," he told them, "it is healing well and there is no danger from it. Only now and then, when I move my head too fast, does it hurt."

"Still," Chaubenee persisted, "it might be wise for you and your family to take a trip for your health; you are always working very hard here. Your woman and children should have some time with you when you are not concerned with work and can devote yourself to them. Yes, it would be very wise for you to take a trip."

The trader looked at them sharply and he was silent for a little while. "Perhaps," he said at last, "my friends are right. It might be well for our health to take such a trip as you suggest. Maybe we will do it when autumn comes and traveling is more pleasant. But," he added, and his voice had hardened, "I could not leave here until at least then."

John Kinzie watched his Potawatomi friends riding off and wondered. Had they been hinting at something, as it seemed? He was not certain, but he was thankful for his friendship with them and the other Potawatomies. If something should occur here, it was better that he and his family were in their home rather than at the fort. Whatever happened, if anything, would be directed there and he was confident that his Indian friends would not permit the Kinzie family to be molested. And if something were to occur, his presence here, his influence among the Indians, might help in saving some lives.

[*July 29, 1812 — Wednesday*]

General William Hull's hand shook as he sat at the desk in his headquarters at Sandwich and wrote a letter to Secretary of War William Eustis, reporting the disastrous news of Fort Mackinac's fall and his own lack of headway here in the Detroit area — the latter issue glossed over as having been due to insufficiency of supplies. This, he assured the secretary, was only a temporary tie-up since, on July 11, he had written to Governor Meigs of Ohio urgently requesting supplies and he anticipated their arrival momentarily. As soon as they arrived, nothing would then stand in the way of assaulting Amherstburg.

The matter of Fort Mackinac, however, was having grave consequences. He said that reports had come to him of great numbers of previously unaligned Indians now swinging their support to the British. All communication to the north had been cut. A disturbing ramification of this was that now Fort Dearborn's supply line was cut. No further goods could be shipped there. That being the case, Hull paused, dipped his pen and then continued the letter:

. . . I shall immediately send an express to Fort Dearborn with orders to evacuate that post and retreat to this post or Fort Wayne, provided it can be effected with a greater prospect of safety than to remain. Captain Heald is a judicious officer, and I shall confide much to his discretion.

Hull finished the letter quickly after that, sealed it and placed it inside a pouch with the other dispatches to go east. Then he took out a fresh sheet and wrote to Nathan Heald at Chicago:

Headquarters at Sandwich
29th July, 1812

SIR: —

It is with regret I order the evacuation of your post owing to the want of provisions only a neglect of the Commandant of Fort Mackinac has occasioned.[238]

You will, therefore, destroy all arms and ammunition, but the goods of the factory you may give to the friendly Indians who may be desirous of escorting you on to Fort Wayne and to the poor and needy of your post.

I am informed this day that Mackinac and the Island of St. Joseph will be evacuated on account of the scarcity of provision and I hope in my next to give you an acct. of the Surrender of the British at Malden as I expect 600 men here by the beginning of September.[239]

Wm. Hull, Commd Gen.

Captain Nathan Heald
Commanding at Fort Dearborn

Folding the letter and placing it into an envelope, then sealing it with wax, he enclosed it with another he had already written, addressed to Captain Rhea, commander of Fort Wayne, in which he instructed Rhea to relay the letter by the swiftest possible means to Fort Dearborn and to render Captain Heald any assistance it was in his power to give. Then he called for an orderly.

"I want this dispatched immediately by express rider to Fort Wayne," he said. "I want it carried by a man who is very capable and who will be damned sure of getting it there."[240]

[*August 1, 1812 — Saturday*]

Captain Henry Brush, lawyer of Chillicothe, Ohio, and now leader of this little force of ninety-five volunteers, was under no illusions as to his own strength or vulnerability. His scouts had encountered so much Indian sign and seen so many Indian spies skulking about watching his movements that he knew he would be a fool to allow his supply train to advance much farther toward Detroit without an escort. He ordered a halt, sentries placed and then wrote a hasty note to General Hull:

Camp north of Maumee Rapids
August 1, 1812

SIR: —

Your letter of the eleventh instant was received by Governor Meigs at Chillicothe on the 18th, who immediately issued a call for your requisite supplies and volunteers. Ninety-five citizens volunteered, of whom I have been given the honor of command. Our brigade is composed of 150 pack-horses loaded with flour and other provisions and a drove of beeves number-

ing about 300 animals, which have given us many problems in the driving. We left Chillicothe on the 20th inst and today we reached and crossed the Maumee Rapids. Due to the large number of Indians hovering about us, reported by my spies, it is considered altogether too dangerous for us to continue much farther toward Detroit without a strong escort being provided by you, since Indians control the road which follows the lake shore and the British control the waters. Our intention, therefore, is to continue only as far as the French town at River Raisin and then remain at that place to await said escort. I am, Sir,

Yr mst obdt yr mst humble svt,
H. Brush — Capt., commanding
the Ohio volunteers.

BRIG. GEN. WM. HULL
Commander — Detroit

[August 2, 1812 — Sunday]

When William Wells arrived at the office of Captain Oscar James Rhea at Fort Wayne in response to the summons he had received, he found his old friend Winnemac already there. Both Winnemac and the commanding officer looked very sober. For Captain Rhea, that was a rather singular achievement. The latter wordlessly handed him the dispatch just received from General Hull and waited until Wells finished reading it before speaking.

"I know of no better team to carry the message to Captain Heald than you and Winnemac, Captain," he said. "Assuming, of course, that you'd be willing to undertake it. There could well be some jeopardy involved for you, although Winnemac here doesn't seem to think so."

Wells nodded. "There could be problems," he murmured. "In fact I'd bet on it, especially if Heald follows those orders to the letter. Obviously General Hull doesn't understand the problem."

"What do you mean?"

"Captain, if they destroy all their excess weapons and ammunition and give away all their supplies and march out of the fort, they're asking for trouble. God only knows what might happen, but it's an open invitation for an attack. I don't like it. Not at all." He shook his head. "Captain Heald's married to my niece and I know him, but not all that well. You probably know him better. What do you think his reaction will be when he gets this order?" He tapped the paper with a finger.

"I know exactly what he'll do. He'll follow it to the letter. It's an order from his commanding general, isn't it? He has no choice."

"Damn!" Wells turned to the Indian. "Winnemac, what do you think? Will Black Partridge's people give them an escort?"

Winnemac grunted sourly. "No escort," he said. "Bad birds are flying everywhere. I have been told they recently came to roost on Black Partridge's shoulder and whispered things into his ear."

"What if I brought an escort from here? Not soldiers. I mean some of the Miamis. Fifty or a hundred?"

Winnemac shrugged. "You would have a difficult time convincing any Miamis to act as escort. It would indicate they are no longer neutral, that they are on the side of the Americans. The Potawatomies — Black Partridge, Siggenauk, Topenebe, Naunongee, Nescotnemeg, Sunawewonee, others — all would be very angry."

"Maybe, but dammit, they wouldn't hit a hundred Miamis! There'd be hell to pay."

"If you could get them to go along with you," Winnemac said slowly, "they might not hit one hundred Miamis. They might not hit fifty. Less than fifty . . ." He left the sentence dangling and shrugged again.

"I'll get them," Wells said. "You're willing to go?"

"I would go. I would carry message. I would not be escort. I would not fight Potawatomi."

Wells grunted and turned to the commander. "All right, if it suits you, Captain, let's do it this way. Let's send Winnemac off with the message right away. I'll round up an escort of Miamis to follow as soon as possible. May take a few days, but I think we'll get there in time."

"Apekonit." It was Winnemac speaking up. He was frowning. "You should know this: it is said that Peesotum is now with Wapeme and that Wapeme is with Nescotnemeg. If trouble comes at Chicago, Peesotum may be there and you may meet."

Wells grinned mirthlessly. "Then one of us will come away and one of us will not. You just pass the word on to Captain Heald to be ready to leave immediately when I get there with the escort. We've got to do it fast before Black Partridge realizes it and can get organized. Captain?"

Rhea nodded. "All right, do it that way." He handed the sealed envelope addressed to Captain Heald to Winnemac. "Get this to Fort Dearborn as quickly as you can. Captain," he turned to Wells, using the honorary title Wells still carried, "I wish I had a military escort to send with you. I don't, but I can give you one man, at least. Corporal Jordan. Walter Jordan. Let me know as soon as you're ready. All right, let's get moving on it."

The Potawatomi chief and the Indian Agent started to leave but stopped as Captain Rhea spoke Wells's name. "I hope you'll get your niece back here safely, Captain."

Wells smiled faintly and nodded. Then they were gone.

[*August 3, 1812 — Monday*]

Captain Nathan Heald had been feeling much better about the state of affairs at Chicago until this morning. The Indians were friendlier and there had been no incidents of any kind that might cause alarm. To the contrary, several Potawatomi wigwams had already been erected just a few hundred yards southwest of the Agency House. They were positioned a little beyond the west bank of the little rivulet choked with weeds that sprang up in the prairie several hundred yards or so south of the river and flowed into it. A little wooden footbridge had been built across it about fifty yards up from its mouth so residents south and west of the fort, such as the Clarks, Mirandeaus, Beaubiens and others were able to get to the fort without having to detour all the way around its source. The little stream had always been a favorite place for the small boys in Chicago to catch frogs and so it was generally called Frog Creek. Not infrequently the area flooded after heavy rains.[241]

The Potawatomies who had already resettled there went about their activities casually, the children playing their games, the women doing their varied chores and cooking over open fires, the men talking in a pleasant, friendly manner and occasionally dropping by the U.S. Factory to barter with Dr. Van Voorhis for one item or another. On several occasions Black Partridge himself had visited the fort, once bringing a freshly killed deer and two different times going out of his way to spend time with little Mary Lee, the twelve-year-old who liked him so much and always called him "My own special chief."

It was all very peaceful and despite Ensign George Ronan's grumbling that he didn't like the smell of things, Captain Heald's little bubble of complacency was expanding. That is, it was until this morning when Chicago Militia Sergeant Tom Burns reported that during the night three of his half-breed militia privates had deserted. They were the LaFramboise brothers, Claude, Alexis and LaFortune, aged seventeen, sixteen and fifteen respectively. Not only were they gone, the whole LaFramboise family was gone as well, allegedly toward Milwaukee, and a dozen horses were missing from the fort's stable.[242]

Other citizens of Chicago — French or half-breeds or mixed-bloods without exception — were also preparing to leave and there was an ominous feeling in the air. While Captain Heald did not care to accede to Ensign Ronan about anything, he now had to admit to himself that perhaps things were not quite so peaceful as they seemed; that perhaps those who were beginning to leave the Chicago area knew something the other Chicago settlers and the garrison did not.

So, very quietly, Captain Nathan Heald once again tightened security at Fort Dearborn.

[*August 8, 1812 — Saturday*]

The American Army of the Northwest was beside itself with fury, coming almost to a man to the realization now of who their greatest enemy was on this campaign: not the British at Amherstburg, nor even the Indians under

Tecumseh. No, their most dangerous foe was the commander of their own army, General William Hull. The events of this past week had proved it.

At the end of July the American prisoners at Amherstburg, taken captive with the *Cuyahoga* nearly a month ago, had already lost hope. The initial strong belief they had nurtured that General Hull's army would march on Amherstburg within days to free them, had gradually diminished. At the end of the month, Quartermaster General William Beall, who had been writing letters of growing concern, wondering where Hull was and why he did not attack when he could do so very easily and with hardly any real risk, had plunged to the depths of despair by this time as he wrote:

> . . . *The British officers and soldiers begin to laugh at Hull. . . . He is now the object of their jest and ridicule instead of being, as he was formerly, their terror and greatest fear. . . . I can scarcely think that Gen. H. will be defeated, but appearances justify such a belief. I am confident that he will not take Malden, though 300 men could do it. . . . Why does he not, by taking Malden, silence and drive the Indians away who infest the Country and secure a safe Communication with the States, and safety to our Frontiers? Heaven only knows. I for a Harrison . . . !*

As badly as Beall viewed Hull from his peculiar vantage as prisoner of the British, the actuality was even worse. The American general, unable to shake the fear and depression that had descended upon him at news of the fall of Fort Mackinac, had allowed his strong pessimism to surface in the letters he had written to Washington; letters which outlined his plans for the future of this campaign. Those letters, in a packet, awaited only a messenger to carry them, but Hull was loath to send them by special courier. A regular mail packet had been bundled up, ready to go, carrying the letters of soldiers to their loved ones back home — letters now strongly critical of their commander — and Hull's plans and reports, filled with pessimism as they were, could accompany that packet, whenever it would leave.

That departure came sooner than expected. On August 4 the express from Captain Henry Brush arrived, announcing his need for an escort from Raisin River to Detroit. Hull's immediate reaction was rejection of the request, but his field officers became so vehement in their demands that an escort be sent, he gave in and authorized Major Thomas Van Horne to lead a detachment of one hundred eighty soldiers to the rendezvous at Frenchtown and bring Captain Brush and his supply convoy to Detroit. The mail packet would go with Van Horne and be relayed onward to its destination.

At almost the same moment, forty British and seventy Indians under

Major Adam Muir, aware of the advance of Brush's convoy from Ohio, crossed the river to set up an ambush to hit it near Brownstown.[243] But, during the night of August 4, Tecumseh's spies brought him word that the American detachment from Sandwich had crossed the Detroit River, marched some fourteen miles to the Ecorse River and was camped there, heading for the Brush convoy, and plans were changed.

Tecumseh split his force in three, sending forty-six of his men under Chaubenee and Roundhead to move southward and lay an ambush for Captain Brush's convoy, unaware that it had stopped its forward movement at Raisin River. Twelve warriors under Main Poche and Sauganash were ordered to remain with Major Muir's British to set up the ambush near Brownstown.[244] Tecumseh himself and Little Blue Jacket, son of his old Shawnee war chief friend, Blue Jacket, now long dead, moved north in a party of twelve to set up a small observation and ambush party to intercept Major Van Horne's detachment.

Early in the morning on August 5 the American force prepared to resume its march from the Ecorse River camp. Militia officers Robert Lucas and William McCullough set off in advance with a small guard. A short distance past Walk-in-the-Water's abandoned village of Maguaga, the road split around a cornfield. McCullough and his black slave, along with one guard, took the left path, closer to the river, while Lucas and his few men took the right. It was McCullough who was unfortunate, moving directly into the ambush set up by Tecumseh. All three men were shot simultaneously and fell. Immediately Tecumseh, Little Blue Jacket and the other ten Indians burst from cover, tomahawked and scalped the three downed men and melted away back toward the main force.

Lucas heard the shots and came at once to investigate, but he was too late. The bodies were hastily carried back the short distance to Maguaga and hidden under some bark and then Lucas and his men, fearing similar attack, themselves faded into nearby cover to take refuge, working their way back to Van Horne very carefully. They arrived just as a party of mounted civilians from the nearby area — mostly Frenchmen — joined the party and warned Van Horne of a force of three of four hundred British and Indians ahead of them. Van Horne refused to believe it, especially when Lucas related that the McCullough party had been hit by what, from all evidence, appeared to be no more than ten or twelve Indians. The detachment pressed on, alert and no little afraid.

Close to Brownstown, where the road passed through a narrow area at Brownstown Creek, the main ambush was sprung on them. Although the American force far outnumbered the attackers, the sudden burst of gunfire accompanied by the shrieks of the Indians so demoralized the Americans that many dropped their weapons, their packs and the small mail packet and fled in panic. The officers tried to hold their men in a rally, but three times they broke and ran. Early in the action a ball creased Tecumseh's side but did not stop him and he seemed to be everywhere at once. Little Blue Jacket leaped onto the back of a mounted officer and killed him with a tomahawk blow; an instant later another officer very nearly beheaded the Shawnee warrior with one stroke of his saber.

The Van Horne detachment fell back nearly four miles to the Ecorse River with seventy men missing, twenty wounded and seventeen left dead at the scene of the ambush. The wounded were sent by boat to Detroit and the remainder came back afoot, straggling in all the rest of the day. At the battleground, all the dead were scalped and then the corpses hung on poles as a warning to others who might pass. One young officer captured by Main Poche was being held, his fate in the balance, when four warriors came in carrying the nearly beheaded body of Little Blue Jacket. Immediately Main Poche gave a signal and two of his squaws drove their knives into the young officer, one in the neck, the other in the side. As he was falling, Main Poche buried his tomahawk in the young man's head.

When word of what had occurred reached the army at Sandwich, there was great excitement in Hull's camp. A council of field officers with the general was convened on August 6 — yesterday — and they demanded that he authorize the sending of another detachment — this one with five hundred men — to gather and bury the American dead and to bring Captain Brush's convoy safely to Detroit. Hull, more fearful than ever, refused at first but then finally said he would allow one hundred to go. Since the Van Horne detachment had met disaster with a force nearly twice that number, the project was canceled and General Hull seemed to care little, if at all, what the fate of Captain Henry Brush and his convoy would be.

Then, unexpectedly, there was a change in the general — what seemed to be a sudden resolve to finally *do* something. He agreed to make a full-scale assault on Fort Malden and issued a general order to the army:

Sandwich, August 7, 1812

Doctor Edwards will take charge of the medical and surgical departments until further orders, and will immediately make every preparation to take the field against the enemy. All the tents and baggage not necessary will be immediately sent to Detroit. The boats not necessary for the movement of the army will be sent to Detroit. An officer and 25 convalescents will be left at the fort at Gowies, with a boat sufficient to carry them across the river if necessary. All the artillery not taken by the army will be sent immediately to Detroit. The army will take seven days' provisions. Three days' provisions will be drawn tomorrow morning and will be cooked, the residue will be taken in wagons. Pork will be drawn for the meat part of the ration. One hundred axes, fifty spades and twenty pickaxes will be taken for the army; and a raft of timber and plank suitable for bridges, will be prepared and floated down with the batteries. Only one day's whiskey will be drawn each day, and twelve barrels will be taken in wagons. All the artificers, and all the men on any kind of extra duty, will immediately join their regiments.

— Wm. Hull, Brig. Gen., Com.

The elation of the troops was unparalleled. At last it was happening! They fell to the preparations with excitement and enthusiasm. And then, with everything loaded and ready for departure, came another order from the general which shocked the army beyond anything that had yet occurred. General Hull canceled the assault against Fort Malden and Amherstburg and ordered the army to get into the boats and retreat to a campground behind the fort at Detroit. The unbridled fury which swept through the army was frightening and never before had General Hull's men come so close to rebelling. Some threw down their weapons in disgust and others wept openly in their anger and frustration. Now it was clear to them that Hull never intended to assault Amherstburg, that his order in that respect was merely a smokescreen to get everything loaded and ready to transport to Detroit.

To maintain his hold on Canada, Hull changed his order of yesterday for leaving twenty-five convalescents at Fort Gowie in Sandwich to an order to Major Denny to take command there with one hundred thirty men, plus Lieutenant Anderson's corps of artillerists.[245] Ohio militiaman Sergeant James Foster recorded in his journal the emotional state of the army at this juncture:

. . . When, to our astonishment, we were ordered to strike our tents and cross over to Detroit! — To encamp in the rear of the fort, and to give up every pretention of a hostile nature. — Great God! what were our feelings now? A territory which we had invaded without opposition, we quit in disgrace. The laurels we had hoped to reap before the ramparts of Malden, were left ungathered — and we were doomed to bear the agonizing burden of dishonor.

And so now, almost to a man, the Army of the Northwest had altered its thinking about who was its greatest enemy — the dubious distinction now going without question to Brigadier General William Hull.

[*August 9, 1812 — Sunday*]

"Sir," the tall sergeant said, leaning into the doorway of his commanding officer's office, "there's an Indian out here with an express from General Hull. He says — the Indian says, I mean — we have to get out of here fast. Away from Chicago. He says there's going to be big trouble."

Captain Nathan Heald's brows pinched together and he pushed aside the report he'd been working on. "From General Hull? Who's the Indian, Sergeant?"

"Winnemac," Isaac Holt replied. "He's worked for us at Vincennes and Fort Wayne."

"All right, show him in. Is John Kinzie around?"

"Yes sir, just saw him outside."

"Good. Get him, too."

A moment later Winnemac entered and handed the sealed orders from Hull to the Fort Dearborn commander. By the time the officer had opened the envelope and read its contents, John Kinzie had arrived, curious at being called and even more at the expression on Nathan Heald's face. The officer told him of the evacuation order he had just received and that he wished to have the trader here as an adviser and, if necessary, as interpreter. Then he asked Winnemac how he had come to be delivering General Hull's order.

Winnemac shook his head. "Winnemac talk English not much. Talk own talk to Shawneeawkee?" He pointed at Kinzie.

Heald sighed. "All right, Mr. Kinzie, interpret if you will, please. However, just what he says, without any elaboration, understood?"

The trader grunted an affirmative, his lips tightening. Already his mind was awhirl with what the consequences might be to him personally if the fort were evacuated. He faced Winnemac, whom he had met on several occasions before on the Maumee, at Detroit, and at his former headquarters adjacent to Topenebe's village on the St. Joseph. He rattled off a string of Potawatomi phrases and then listened with narrowing eyes as Winnemac replied at some length. Then he turned back to Heald.

"He says, Captain, that he was dispatched to come here with the order by Captain Rhea at Fort Wayne, who received it from General Hull, along with instructions to relay it to you immediately. He says that what General Hull tells you in that letter is not all correct — that Mackinac and St. Joseph Island are not being evacuated; that the British from St. Joseph Island invaded Mackinac and forced the fort to capitulate without bloodshed. Says if you're going to evacuate, it has to be done at once, no later than tomorrow. He says —"

Heald interrupted with a finger held up. "Hold it, Mr. Kinzie. Ask how it is he happens to know what's in this order. The seal was unbroken when he handed it to me."

"He says," Kinzie replied, after questioning Winnemac, who had responded briefly and then shrugged, "that he thinks he heard it at Fort Wayne. He thinks from Captain Wells, but he's not sure." He paused a moment and then went on. "He says the Indians all know it here; that they all know you've been told to leave after a while and that the Indians from all over will be here in a few days when you leave. I should add something of my own here, Captain. I've seen considerable increase of the Indians here close to the fort in the last few days. There's something brewing and I smell trouble."

"We'll get into your observations a little later, Mr. Kinzie. Just ask him to continue, please. I want to know why Captain Wells did not deliver this order."

The trader's nostrils flaired at the rebuff but he turned back to Winnemac, spoke briefly and listened to the response, his expression becoming stony. Then he interpreted.

"Here's the story: William Wells is out gathering up a number of the Miamis to come along with him here to act as an escort back to Fort Wayne when you evacuate. He's hoping to bring fifty to a hundred Miamis with him. Winnemac doesn't think that's possible because of the conflicting position it would place them in. Anyway, according to Winnemac, Wells told him to relay to you the word that you should be all prepared to leave, with everyone — civilians included — as soon as he arrives, which will probably be in a few days. Winnemac says that's too long to wait. He says if you've got to leave, it should be first thing tomorrow."

Heald shook his head peremptorily. "No."

Winnemac understood that well enough and unleashed a string of talk, with John Kinzie interpreting almost simultaneously. "If you won't leave, Captain, then you must be prepared to stay here and hold your place in the fort, since you have plenty of ammunition and could do so."

Again Heald shook his head. "My orders are not discretionary except in the matter of distribution of goods in the government store. I can neither leave immediately, nor can I remain. Orders preclude that. We'll leave in a week or so, as soon as things are taken care of here."

"You cannot afford to do that, Captain!" Kinzie was continuing to interpret verbatim. "On my way here from Fort Wayne, the road leads through Mishshewakokind — the village of Chief Manguago.[246] I found his warriors ready to join others in moving here against you. But his warriors by themselves are not many. If you leave at once, they will try to stop you at Mishshewakokind, but you will be able to knock them out of your path and reach Fort Wayne with only a small fight. If you wait even a few days it will be too late. If you wait even a few days, then you must be prepared to stay here behind the walls of your fort."

"I cannot follow either of those alternatives, Winnemac. I have my orders."

"One who cannot think for himself and too closely follows the orders of a chief who is not present to know what should and should not be will soon be in big danger. Chief Monguago depends on your taking time to give away those things you will give away and he knows it will then be too late for you."

"Damn it all, Winnemac!" Heald said sharply, more than a little dis-

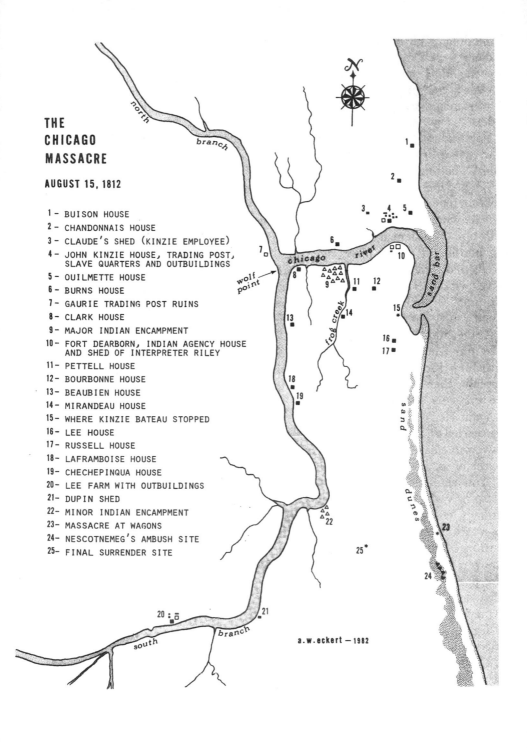

THE
CHICAGO
MASSACRE

AUGUST 15, 1812

 1- BUISON HOUSE
 2- CHANDONNAIS HOUSE
 3- CLAUDE'S SHED (KINZIE EMPLOYEE)
 4- JOHN KINZIE HOUSE, TRADING POST,
    SLAVE QUARTERS AND OUTBUILDINGS
 5- OUILMETTE HOUSE
 6- BURNS HOUSE
 7- GAURIE TRADING POST RUINS
 8- CLARK HOUSE
 9- MAJOR INDIAN ENCAMPMENT
10- FORT DEARBORN, INDIAN AGENCY HOUSE
    AND SHED OF INTERPRETER RILEY
11- PETTELL HOUSE
12- BOURBONNE HOUSE
13- BEAUBIEN HOUSE
14- MIRANDEAU HOUSE
15- WHERE KINZIE BATEAU STOPPED
16- LEE HOUSE
17- RUSSELL HOUSE
18- LAFRAMBOISE HOUSE
19- CHECHEPINQUA HOUSE
20- LEE FARM WITH OUTBUILDINGS
21- DUPIN SHED
22- MINOR INDIAN ENCAMPMENT
23- MASSACRE AT WAGONS
24- NESCOTNEMEG'S AMBUSH SITE
25- FINAL SURRENDER SITE

a.w. eckert — 1982

trustful of the Potawatomi. "How the hell does Monguago know what's in General Hull's order?" At Winnemac's shrug and veiled expression, he went on. "No, we're not leaving now. We'll wait for Captain Wells. After he arrives and we take care of matters, then we will go. It is necessary for me to collect the Indians of the neighborhood here for a council to distribute goods and learn from them their feelings and temper."

The tone of voice alone brought Winnemac up short and he frowned, turned his back to the commanding officer and spoke to John Kinzie rapidly and at length, with the trader nodding at intervals and occasionally interjecting a word or two. Finally, just as the officer was about to interrupt, Kinzie turned back to him, expression unreadable.

"He was appealing to me, Captain, to add my influence, such as he thinks it is, to what he was telling you. I'm doing that now. He says under no circumstances should you invite the Indians here to council and so you can distribute goods to them; that you should leave everything just as it is, take all the arms and ammunition away and move out. He says if you go by forced marches, you'll be able to get away unmolested while the Indians are busy ransacking this place and dividing the goods among themselves. I want you to know, Captain Heald, I agree with him completely. All the way. Either leave immediately or don't leave at all. I recommend the latter. I hope you'll reconsider."

"No! There will be no reconsideration of anything."

"You asked me here as an adviser, Captain." John Kinzie's voice was thick with controlled fury. "Obviously you do not wish to hear advice or take it, so it is pointless for me to remain." He spun about and strode toward the door.

"Mr. Kinzie!" When the trader stopped and turned around, Captain Heald went on. "I did not mean to offend you. Your advice is most appreciated and certainly it is considered. It's simply that I cannot disobey a direct order from my general." It was as near an apology as Kinzie had ever heard him come and his temper cooled a little as the commander continued. "Please tell Winnemac he's welcome to stay here as long as he likes. And I'd like you to wait here for a while. Sergeant!"

Isaac Holt entered immediately. "Sir?"

"Please show Winnemac out and provide him with food and lodging if he desires. On your way, have Lieutenant Helm and Ensign Ronan report here on the double."

"Yes sir!"

Less than a minute later, both subordinate officers were in the commander's office and he showed them the order from General Hull, then related what had passed between himself, Winnemac and John Kinzie. It was the trader's son-in-law who spoke first.

"I'd recommend we don't evacuate at all, Captain."

"And I agree with Lieutenant Helm, sir," Ronan put in immediately.

"We have plenty of guns and ammunition, as well as artillery. We have plenty of food, water, everything we need to hold out in case of siege by the Ind——"

"Ensign Ronan! That's enough, sir! This is not a debate and the matter is not open to recommendations from junior officers. That includes you, too, lieutenant! We have orders to evacuate and we *will* evacuate!"

"Captain." It was John Kinzie. "I'd like to say something."

"Then say it."

Kinzie pursed his lips. "I say this with no disrespect, implied or otherwise. You have not had a great deal of experience with the Indians. Almost none before you came here. I've lived with these people most of my life and I know them. Very well. I know a lot of them personally and I know the character of the Potawatomies in general, so I expect you to respect — and *consider* — my counsel. There's a very dangerous situation here. Enough clues have come my way that I'm convinced now they mean to attack. Desertion of three of the militia — half-breeds — is only one such indication. Our best chance lies in remaining right where we are, in spite of General Hull's order, and wait until the government sends a strong reinforcement. General Hull has sent that order without understanding the situation here. His ignorance of the situation places you in the position of moving into extreme jeopardy if you follow his orders. As I say, our best bet lies in holding on here and waiting for reinforcement. Indians are no great shakes at laying siege to anything. They haven't the patience or discipline for it. Now, you say you *must* evacuate, because of the general's order. All right, if that's the case, then do it now, immediately. Leave everything as is except for weapons and gunpowder and let them fight it out amongst themselves for it. It'd take two or three days of squabbling among them to agree on who gets what. By that time we can be far away."

Captain Heald made a tent of his fingers as he listened to the trader and now he smiled in a somewhat supercilious manner. "Let me ask you a question, Mr. Kinzie. What happens to you — to your post — when we leave here?"

The trader knew what he was leading up to. "Just about everything I have is here, Captain — everything I've worked for most of my life. If the garrison leaves and we're at war with the Indians, I'm wiped out. I don't think I or any member of my family would be harmed — though I'm not entirely sure of that, if we're at war — but where goods are concerned, that's different. I'd lose everything. Obviously, I don't want that to happen and it would definitely be to my benefit if the garrison stayed. But, before God, I tell you that my concern here and now is *lives!* What happens to the people of Chicago, apart from the military and their families, if you pull out?"

"Their protection is part of my responsibility here, Mr. Kinzie. They will be given the option of accompanying the garrison on its march to Fort Wayne, and I'm sure none will refuse. They'd have nothing to gain and everything to lose by staying behind."

Ensign Ronan spoke up, jaw jutting pugnaciously. "Captain Heald, if I may?" Heald's nod was grudging. "What Mr. Kinzie says makes sense. Since you are determined to obey General Hull's evacuation order, then we should do everything possible to retain whatever advantage we can. We can only do that by following Mr. Kinzie's advice to leave immediately."

Lieutenant Helm nodded in agreement, but said nothing. The two junior officers came to attention as Captain Heald stood up. He looked at them steadily for a long while, until they became uncomfortable at his gaze. "Gentlemen," he said at last, "you surprise me. Either your comprehension is faulty or else your military training is deplorable. Do they no longer, Ensign Ronan, insist on obedience to orders at West Point?" Ronan flushed but the commanding officer went on without pause. "The orders, which you have both read, gentlemen, state that not only must we evacuate, but that we *will* distribute the goods presently in the government store and destroy all excess guns and ammunition. Both matters will take time. I will have to notify the neighboring tribes to collect here for proper division of the goods. It will also be necessary to properly organize our evacuation which means, as well, organizing the civilian population who will accompany us. Our orders are quite clear, sirs. We will indeed leave here, but we will not do so until General Hull's orders are followed to the letter. I have nothing further to say on the matter. Dismissed."

[*August 12, 1812 — Wednesday morning*]

The skirmish at Brownstown had turned out to be only a prologue.

With the humiliating retreat across the Detroit River from Sandwich to the fort very nearly more than General Hull's field officers could bear, they finally convinced him to accede to their demands: another detachment — larger this time — would be sent to bury the American dead at Brownstown and make the rendezvous with Captain Henry Brush at Raisin River to escort the supply convoy to Detroit. Hull's second-in-command, Lieutenant Colonel James Miller, was ordered to lead the detachment.

It was precisely what the British and Indians had been waiting for in the area of Brownstown for four days. Instead of fleeing after the Brownstown affair and returning to Amherstburg as the Americans thought they had, the British under Major Muir and Indians under Tecumseh had remained concealed, hoping to strike just such a detachment. Tecumseh had been positive one would come and that they had only to wait.

Pleased with the results of the Brownstown affair, Tecumseh was also deeply saddened by the death of Little Blue Jacket. At the same time, it was good to have Chaubenee and Sauganash back again and he listened with interest as they reported on their meetings with the various Potawatomies and the fact that all were poised for attack. Nescotnemeg's plan was drawn, Siggenauk was prepared to carry it out and Black Partridge was already infiltrating the enemy's settlement under the guise of friendship. All were ready to strike there at the middle of the Heat Moon — August 15. They also told Tecumseh of their visit with Shawneeawkee and their fear for him and the rest of his family during the attack. The Indians who knew him would not harm him, but not all who were coming knew him. Would it be possible, they asked, for them to return to Chicago in time to be on hand for the attack — not to participate in it, but to protect the Kinzies? Tecumseh considered this, knowing well their liking for Shawneeawkee, which he shared.

"It would be a great sadness," he told them finally, "if Shawneeawkee or his family came to harm. On good horses, how long will you need to arrive at Chicago?"

Five days, they told him, which would allow them to arrive the evening before the center of the Heat Moon. Tecumseh had nodded. "Then you will leave here the evening of the fourth day from now, when there will be more good news to carry from here to the chiefs there." When they asked him what he meant by "more good news from here," Tecumseh only smiled.

During those four days that had followed, the British detachment remained hidden at Brownstown, their hope at being able to strike another American detachment gradually diminishing. Tecumseh's spies continued to hover near Detroit, watching for any activity in Hull's army. Finally, with rations all but depleted, Muir's men gave up and were just getting into their boats for the return to Amherstburg when Tecumseh galloped up and stopped them.

"It is as I told you it would be," he said. "Another detachment of Americans is coming from the fort. It is larger and better armed than the first, but I have a plan."

He outlined his strategy and Major Adam Muir readily agreed to it. The odds were great — six hundred American soldiers against Muir's forty soldiers and Tecumseh's seventy Indians — but the plan was so boldly conceived that they could not resist. There was no time to discuss it at length and they moved quickly to the point where Tecumseh had planned the ambush, three miles above Brownstown, close to Maguaga. Here the soldiers could hide in a ravine which the road crossed, and Tecumseh's warriors could hide in a cornfield flanking the road. At the prearranged signal a volley would be fired, followed by the immediate rush of the British soldiers with bayonets fixed and a simultaneous rush by warriors on both sides with tomahawks and war clubs.

It had occurred precisely as Tecumseh had said. At the abandoned Wyandot village of Maguaga, Lieutenant Colonel Miller's detachment filed past the spot where the bodies of Captain McCullough and his two companions lay bloated beneath covering bark which hid much of the sight but little of the stench. These, like the dead at Brownstown, would be buried on the return trip. They were within a few hundred yards of the same spot that McCullough had been ambushed — and certainly where no one among the Americans even conceived that an ambush could reoccur.

But it did.

The attack broke out about four in the afternoon and there was immediate chaos. American lines faltered and broke, reformed and faltered again. Men were falling all around and within minutes there was so much smoke in the breezeless air that it clung like a shroud, turning the battlefield into a phantasmagoric world of fearsome shadowy human shapes unidentifiable as friend or foe beyond twenty feet. Within minutes Major Muir took a bullet through the shoulder and then another through the leg, but he kept on fighting. Ensign John Whistler, Jr., son of the former Fort Dearborn commander, received a severe bullet wound low through the rib cage on the right.[247] A ball nipped the right earlobe of Chaubenee and another neatly clipped away an eagle feather being worn by Sauganash on the side of his head. Tecumseh was in the thick of the fighting at all times, swinging his war club with deadly energy, the slight wound in his side from the skirmish four days ago forgotten. He was not touched this time.

Even though strengthened by the arrival of sixty soldiers under the new Fort Malden commander, Lieutenant Colonel Henry Procter, the British and Indians under Muir and Tecumseh gradually gave way. They were followed for two miles by the Americans but, with evening approaching, the pursuers were finally recalled. Despite the much larger size of the American force, the battle statistics were interesting. Among the Indians there were two dead and six wounded.[248] Among the British, six were dead and twenty-one wounded. And among the Americans — who held the field at the end of the contest and therefore claimed victory in the battle — there were eighteen dead and fifty-seven wounded.

The British and Indians returned to Brownstown and from there to Amherstburg in their bateaux and canoes. Before crossing, Tecumseh called Chaubenee and Sauganash to him and embraced them both. "Go now," he said. "Keep our friend in Chicago from harm. Return to me as soon as you can."

An aftereffect of the battle was abortion of the mission to rendezvous with Captain Henry Brush and escort the supplies from Raisin River to Detroit. The majority of the Americans discarded their knapsacks as soon as the ambush was sprung and now they were without sufficient food to continue to their objective. They *might* have done so, but Lieutenant Colonel Miller had become very sick. Command could not devolve upon

Colonel Cass under the circumstances unless permission were received from General Hull. The lack of food was considered no insurmountable handicap by Cass. Obviously, there were plenty of supplies at the Raisin River camp of Captain Brush and that was only twenty-two miles away. Immediately he sent an express to General Hull:

Sir,
  Colonel Miller is sick. May I relieve him?

L. Cass

General Hull did not deign to respond. Instead, positive orders were received by Lieutenant Colonel Miller for the detachment to return to Detroit. There, General Hull was already busily writing letters — one of them a report of the Maguaga Battle in which, Hull expounded,

. . . the victory was complete in every part of the line.

He also wrote and dispatched an express by devious route to Captain Brush at Raisin River:

Sir — The state of the communication between this and the River Raison, is such that a sufficient detachment cannot be sent at present to bring on the provisions there with safety — you will therefore remain at the river Raisin, and in conjunction with the regiment, Le Croix's corps and your-selves until further orders. The detachment sent for the purpose of opening the communication are so fatigued after a severe and victorious battle that it will return here.
  I am, respectfully,

W. Hull, Gen Commanding.

Capt. Brush, or the commanding
  officer at the river Raisin.

The exuberance on Hull's part was strictly facade. He was a man almost beside himself with fear and indecision — a sullen, querulous, intemperate man who had become devoid of any sense of humor or decency. Part of this was due to a report that he had just received that General Isaac Brock was approaching Amherstburg with a very strong British reinforcement. Even more of it was due to his continued, almost petrifying fear of the Indians.

Because of Hull's correspondence having been captured at the August 5 ambush at Brownstown — in which he had expressed again to the Secretary of War his morbid fear of "hordes of Indians sweeping out of the north" — an interesting letter had now fallen into his own possession. A supposed courier from Amherstburg had been captured, presumably en route to Mackinac. He carried an express from Lieutenant Colonel Henry

Procter to Captain Charles Roberts — a letter specifically designed to fall into Hull's hands. It very seriously instructed Roberts that it was no longer necessary for him to send more than five thousand Indians to Amherstburg, since the British force there had just been augmented by a very substantial reinforcement of regulars. Hull swallowed it all.

For a considerable while William Hull's officers had considered him an incompetent, a fool and a coward. Virtually none had one iota of confidence left in him. And now, because of what had happened only a short while ago, they considered him traitorous as well. Robert Lucas, writing to a friend of his in Ohio, was very bitter, saying that never was there a more patriotic army than the one he was in, nor an army that had it more completely in its power to have accomplished every object of its desire; an army, he added furiously, that had now sunk into disgrace because of the lack of a real general to lead it. He termed Hull imbecilic and treacherous and opposed to his colonels, who were strongly united in their patriotism; and he yearned that one of these colonels could take command from Hull so that they could yet wipe away the foul stain that Hull had brought upon the army.

Those Ohio militia colonels — Lewis Cass, Duncan McArthur and James Findley — had been having secret meetings to discuss the deplorable situation; meetings which came to a head today. Obviously, Hull was incapable of commanding his army properly and therefore was it not their duty — ethically, if not officially — to remove him from power? A plan gelled and they carried it with some trepidation to Hull's second-in-command, Lieutenant Colonel James Miller, who they believed felt as strongly about the situation as they, even though he was not so vocal about it. If Cass, McArthur and Findley forcibly removed General Hull from command, would Miller then take command of the army? Miller, still weak from the illness that had smitten him three days before, weighed the consequences briefly and then shook his head. What they were suggesting was mutiny and it could result in the death penalty for him. He neatly turned the tables by offering to support the three colonels in the takeover, if Duncan McArthur would then assume command of the army. Now it was McArthur's turn to backwater, and he did so. They knew Hull was guilty of cowardice and incompetence and perhaps even treason; yet knowing it and proving was another matter, and the death penalty was as real a threat to McArthur as it was to Miller. He, too, declined.

The upshot was that they would write a letter immediately to Governor Return Jonathan Meigs of Ohio, a man in whom all had implicit faith, stating to him in couched terms what the conditions were here and giving him to believe that if he would come here immediately, command of the army would be placed in his hands. It was Cass who undertook the actual writing of the letter, but Miller — who gave his word to provide them verbal support — told them he simply would not append his signature to the letter. They agreed and Cass wrote swifty:

Detroit, August 12, 1812

Dear Sir:

From causes not fit to put upon paper, but which I trust I shall one day live to communicate to you, this army has been reduced to a critical and alarming situation. We have wholly left the Canadian shore, and have left the miserable inhabitants, who had depended upon our will and our power to protect them, to their fate. Unfortunately, the General and the principal officers could not view our situation and our prospects in the same light. That Malden might easily have been reduced, I have no doubt. That the army were in force and spirits enough to have done it, no one doubts. But the precious opportunity has fled, and instead of looking back, we must now look forward.

The letter from the Secretary of War to you, a copy of which I have seen, authorizes you to preserve and keep open the communication from the State of Ohio to Detroit. It is all important it should be kept open. Our very existence depends upon it. Our supplies must come from our State. This country does not furnish them. In the existing state of things, nothing but a large force of two thousand men at least, will effect the object. It is the unanimous wish of the army, that you should accompany them.

Every exertion that can, must be made. If this reaches you safely by Murray, he will tell you more than I can or ought here to insert.

Very respectfully,
I am yours, & c.
Lewis Cass

Hardly had the letter been finished when Quartermaster General James Taylor rushed to them with unbelievable news: a boat from the American side, bearing an officer, was heading toward the British under a white flag, crossing the river directly to Sandwich, now occupied by British troops. Instantly Cass, Findley and McArthur raced to General Hull's office and, their indignation very apparent, demanded to know what was going on.

Hull affected a look of surprise and incomprehension that fooled none of them. "Gentlemen," he said, "I have no idea what is going on. If a boat is going to the British from here under a flag, it is without my knowledge and I have no idea what its purpose may be. If you'll excuse me a moment, I'll go check on it."

The general left them standing there and went out, allegedly to query one of his aides, Captain Hickman. In a few moments he returned. He told them in a somewhat offhand way that Captain Hickman had had a conversation with Captain Rough on the matter of capitulation. Hickman, he said, did not wish Captain Rough to consider that he had permission to carry a flag to the enemy. "However," he added lamely, "evidently Captain Rough probably misunderstood and believed he had such permission. That's all I know, gentlemen."

It was a dismissal and, containing their fury only with the greatest of effort, the three colonels returned to their quarters and, with the added support of James Taylor and Major Elijah Brush of the Michigan Territorial Militia, a postscript was now added on the reverse side of the letter Cass had written a short while before:

Since the other side of this letter was written, new circumstances have arisen. The British force is opposite, and our situation has nearly reached its crisis. Believe all the bearer will tell you. Believe it, however it may astonish you, as much as if told you by one of us. Even a ———— is talked of by the ———— ————.[249] *The bearer will supply the vacancy. On you we depend.*

> *Lewis Cass,*
> *James Findley,*
> *Duncan M'Arthur,*
> *James Taylor,*
> *E. Brush.*

The message was entrusted to an Ohio soldier named Murray and, to help make sure Murray got safely through the enemy forces, he was provided with the best possible guide available — an Indian of proven ability, who had carried many important messages to their destinations under trying conditions; a Shawnee whose loyalty was to the Americans. They knew him as Johnny Logan. His Indian name was Spemica Lawba.[250]

[*August 12, 1812 — Wednesday afternoon*]

Captain Nathan Heald was beaming when he and John Kinzie entered the quarters where the officers and noncoms were gathered. It was the first time he had smiled in several days, but no one seemed to notice. Their own expressions were strained, sober. Eleven men were here, the only one missing being Sergeant Otho Hayes, who was Corporal-of-the-Guard today. Officers present included Second Lieutenant Linai T. Helm and Ensign George Ronan, along with Surgeon's Mate Isaac van Voorhis. Among the noncommissioned officers were Sergeants William Griffith and Isaac Holt — as well as Chicago Militia Sergeant Thomas Burns — and Corporals Rhodias Jones, Thomas Forth, Richard Garner and Joseph Bowen. John Kinzie stopped near the door and leaned against the wall with folded arms, but all eyes were on Captain Heald, who walked around his desk and sat down.

"Gentlemen," he said, "I think whatever fears we've been harboring can now by and large be laid to rest."

The men stirred and looked at one another, glancing between their commanding officer and John Kinzie, wondering what had happened at the Indian council to have justified this sudden optimism. But while Nathan Heald's expression was far more relaxed and cheerful, the trader's was unreadable. The commander didn't notice, or at least appeared not to.

"Mr. Kinzie and I spoke with quite a few of the more important chiefs," he went on, "including Black Partridge, of course. But also Mad Sturgeon and Blackbird were there, plus Sits Quietly," — Nescotnemeg, Siggenauk and Topenebe — "who're all very important, plus . . . I can't remember those names. Mr. Kinzie?"

"Naunongee," the trader said, "Peesotum, Winnemac, Waubansee, Sunawewone, all Potawatomies, and also Karamone, Sansamani and Mackraragah of the Winnebagoes. Some other minor chiefs."

"But by far the majority Potawatomi, is that correct?" He waited for Kinzie's nod and went on. "The point is, they were mainly Potawatomies, who are our greatest concern here and between here and Fort Wayne. With no dissenting voice, gentlemen, they've professed friendship for us and a willingness to escort us safely to Fort Wayne. That becomes very important, especially in light of the fact that Captain Wells has not yet arrived with the Miami escort he was to bring and there's no guarantee he will. My considered opinion is that we have merely to present an appearance of friendly strength from this point on and we'll have no real difficulty. Don't you agree, Mr. Kinzie?"

The trader remained leaning against the wall, arms folded across his chest. For a long moment he did not respond, as if considering the question. When he spoke, it was quietly, but the two words burst like bombs in the room.

"Hell no."

Ever since the arrival of Winnemac on Sunday, John Kinzie had become more convinced that everything that could possibly go wrong was doing so and in no way did he share the sense of assurance the Fort Dearborn commander was presently exhibiting. As soon as Captain Heald had called an assembly of his men on the parade Monday morning and read General Hull's order to them, a great fear had bloomed and the tension that existed between the commander and his subordinate officers increased. Everyone was aware of the marked increase of the Indian population in the immediate vicinity of the fort since Winnemac's arrival. The few wigwams that had sprung up close on the west shore of stagnant little Frog Creek west of the Agency House had abruptly bloomed until now there were scores of them covering an area of many acres and Indians were everywhere. No one knew for certain how many there were already, but estimates ran between two hundred and five hundred warriors, plus squaws and children.[251]

The settlers had become frightened and those who had moved back to their own homes returned to the Agency House for mutual protection. Dissatisfaction increased among the soldiers and their dependents with what General Hull's orders required. Their consternation grew as they began to realize how very vulnerable they would become if they simply marched out of the fort according to the present arrangment expressed to them by Captain Heald. A fair number of the garrison were super-annuated or invalids. Many of the women had babies or very small children. One woman was pregnant. There were nowhere nearly enough horses for everyone to ride and so their rate of travel would be excruciatingly slow.

As the assembly was dismissed, the murmur of voices raised until it was a veritable din, with everyone expressing his fears and comments and ideas. And the recurrent theme was, why didn't everyone just stay here inside the fort where there was protection and ample supplies for a considerable period? It was immediately after the dismissal that Ensign Ronan had presented himself to the commander and spoke up with reason and firmness, his carriage stiff, his manner unbending.

"Sir, if you'll permit me to make an observation?"

Captain Heald did not look pleased, but he nodded. "Go ahead."

"I do not believe, sir, that General Hull's order is either well thought out or binding. There is, as you may be aware, a War Department Special Order which *requires* that no American post be given up without battle having been given, unl———"

"Unless," the captain interrupted and finished for him, "it is the considered opinion of the commanding officer, with or without the agreement of his subordinate officers, that the post is untenable due to his military strength being inadequate to withstand the assault of a threatening enemy. It is my considered opinion," he added dryly, "that our force here is wholly inadequate to withstand an attack. I would remind you that there are in the neighborhood at this time some five hundred warriors, while our garrison has a total strength of only sixty-eight."

Ronan was not daunted. "Sixty-eight, sir, plus twelve militia remaining, plus the civilian population. We are also inside a stockade they could not breach. We have seventy rifles, four pieces of artillery, three thousand pounds of gunpowder and plenty of ammunition. Would it be more *adequate* to expose ourselves in the open, with women and children to protect? We have —"

"Mr. Ronan!" Heald's voice was sharper. "I could not remain even if I thought it best. I have only a small store of provisions."

"Begging your pardon, Captain," Ronan pressed on, "but you have a three months' supply of corn and two hundred head of horned cattle — enough meat to last the troops for six months!"

"But I have no salt to preserve it with."

"We have seventeen barrels of salt on hand, sir," the ensign pointed out doggedly, "and even if we didn't have enough to preserve the meat, we could jerk it as the Indians do their venison."[252]

Captain Heald shook his head as if trying to dislodge a bothersome fly. The agitation in his voice was clear as he spoke again. "I do not care to be censured for remaining here when there is the prospect of a safe march through to Fort Wayne. I will call the chiefs together and ask them to collect their people here to receive the goods in exchange for their providing us safe escort."

"And what's to prevent their taking the goods and still attacking?"

"I will promise them at least as many goods upon our safe arrival at Fort Wayne. Mr. Ronan, I do not intend to argue the point further with you."

"But —"

"Dismissed, sir!"

Enough men were within hearing at the parade that word of the exchange between Captain Heald and Ensign Ronan quickly swept the fort and from that point on the officers kept more or less aloof from their commander, while the attitude of the soldiers was one of dissatisfaction and fear as they began packing their things and preparing their families for the departure. The settlers became more frightened. If the garrison left, they would be at the mercy of the Indians and the incident at the Lee farm was still too fresh in their minds to countenance that. Most of the citizens decided that when the garrison left, they would have no choice but to accompany it.

There were those who felt sure Captain Heald would not go through with it, but their conviction did not last. Shortly after the assembly, accompanied by John Kinzie, Captain Heald visited Black Partridge in his new lodge several hundred yards from the fort and asked him to send runners to other chiefs to collect their people here for a distribution of the government stores "in a few days." Black Partridge masked the exultation he experienced at hearing this; he had been concerned over what the reaction of the Americans would be when, very soon now, Indians began converging on the Chicago area. Now there was justification for it, without any stigma of suspicion. It couldn't have been better.

Black Partridge, glancing at John Kinzie and speaking through him, promised he would send runners at once to the other villages, but gave no indication that a sizable number had already gathered and were waiting beyond sight of the fort. He told Heald, however, that a few chiefs were on hand and they would like to see the goods that would be given to them. Captain Heald told him to bring them to the fort tomorrow and they would be shown what was to be distributed. He also invited the chiefs to dine with the officers until the evacuation, since there was a superabundance of food in the fort.

By the next day — which was yesterday — the Indians had greatly expanded their encampment beyond Frog Creek and a large delegation of chiefs came to the fort, carrying rifles and wearing tomahawks and knives and war clubs in their waistbands. They entered the main gate arrogantly, brushing aside the guard who said they had to wait until the captain came, and strolled about at their leisure, almost with insolence, under the guns of the soldiers on the parapets, while the guard ran to fetch the commanding officer. Because they had come sooner than expected, there was not time to put out of sight the items that were *not* to be given to them — the excess arms and ammunition from the government store, as well as the large supply of whiskey, including the bulk of Kinzie's liquor, which had been brought inside the fort for safekeeping and which represented a great deal of money.[253]

The chiefs were surprised at the amount of goods to be given to them as Captain Heald showed them through the government store and they were especially excited about the guns, ammunition and whiskey. Captain Heald made a sweeping gesture, taking in everything, and smiled at the chiefs.

"All this will be yours," he told them, "as a partial payment for escorting us safely to Fort Wayne, and there will be a similar amount given to you when we arrive there safely."

John Kinzie was shocked and after the chiefs had filed out, his anger and despair became evident. "My god, Captain!" he whispered, "surely you are not going to give them the guns, powder and whiskey!"

"Of course not, Mr. Kinzie, but they'd've been angry if they thought they weren't getting them."

Kinzie cursed bitterly, then said, "Just what the hell do you think their reaction's going to be now that you've promised them and then don't follow through?"

"I have no intention of telling them that, Mr. Kinzie, until we're ready to leave the fort. I agree, they'll probably be upset, but I'll simply tell them the guns and liquor were not included. They'll all have been destroyed by then, so what matter?"

"God help us," Kinzie groaned. "You can't imagine how seriously you've compounded the problem. You say you're going to destroy all of the liquor. Am I to assume that includes mine?"

"It does."

John Kinzie expelled a loud sigh. "The greater amount of all my assets," he said quietly, "are tied up in that whiskey. I have used practically all of my cash reserves and have gone heavily into debt to purchase it. Since it is to be destroyed by your order, I will assume the government will make restitution when this is all over?"

"You have no grounds to make such an assumption, Mr. Kinzie. I cannot guarantee it. I would *hope* the government would reimburse you for your loss, but I cannot vouch for it."

"I'll be ruined if they don't."

"I'm truly sorry about that, Mr. Kinzie, but I can't help it. The whiskey will be destroyed. All of it."

The gloom and mistrust among the garrison and civilian population increased when what happened became known. Immediately there were several families who told Kinzie they were not going along when the fort was evacuated — the Ouilmettes, for example, and the Buisons — and they urged Kinzie not to go, telling him he'd be much safer staying put.

"I know it," he said. "I'd rather not go, but now I don't really have any choice. If I'm with them, the Indians just *may* hold off attacking. If I'm not, there's no way on earth that the group's going to get through."

Immediately the trader met with his principal clerk, the half-breed French-Potawatomi, Jean Baptiste Chandonnais, and explained to him what he wanted him to do: along with some of the Kinzie servants, he would see that Mrs. Kinzie and the four children — John H., Ellen, Maria and Robert — were safely aboard the large Kinzie bateau, to be taken by water along the Lake Michigan margin to the St. Joseph and there put into the care of trader William Burnett until Kinzie's arrival.

Tensions continued to rise all yesterday and today. Indians in hostile array came and went at the fort with contemptuous arrogance, clearly aware that the commanding officer in no way wished to offend them. They moved unhampered through the parade, peered into doorways and even entered the officers' quarters, where one discharged his rifle into the ceiling, causing momentary panic in the belief that a massacre had begun. Even the old chiefs and squaws camped outside had become excited at that, but the immediate raw fear of the whites died away when it became clear there was no real trouble.

Today, at Captain Heald's summons, relayed through Black Partridge, the supposedly newly arrived chiefs attended the major council. Somewhere near six hundred warriors were now at the encampment and John Kinzie recognized many of the chiefs who attended. All had been friendly to him in the past and most had been guests at his table, yet now they were cool in the extreme and seemed annoyed by his continued presence here, when he'd had ample warning and time enough to leave safely with his family, as the Mirandeaus had, and the Beaubiens. Even Topenebe, his old friend, had arrived, along with Wapeme — who was in turn shadowed by Peesotum — and though their eyes had met and Topenebe flashed him a warning, there was no immediate opportunity for them to talk. Siggenauk was here from Milwaukee, Waubansee from Fox River, Naunongee from the Calumet and Nescotnemeg from the Kankakee, along with many others, including Winnebagoes and a few Kickapoos. And though they all spoke politely enough at the council and professed their continuing friendship with Americans, Kinzie detected an undercurrent of hostility that was frightening.

The other officers at the fort had been invited by Captain Heald to the council being held on the esplanade close to the fort, but it was not an order and they refused to attend, on the grounds that they had heard a rumor that at a signal to be given during the council, all the officers were to be simultaneously killed. Captain Heald did not believe it but nonetheless ordered that the cannon in the northwest blockhouse be trained to cover the Indian encampment and the gunports opened.

Now, with John Kinzie's reply of "Hell no," to Captain Heald's query in regard to their safety, the Fort Dearborn commanding officer scowled. "What kind of an answer is that, sir?" he demanded. "You were at the council with me. Did or did not the Indians affirm their friendship and promise to escort us as we requested?"

"They did," Kinzie said tonelessly, "but if you believe that, you are a fool." Captain Heald colored, but the trader went on. "At this point, all we can hope for is that Captain Wells does, in fact, get here with his hundred Miamis. If he doesn't . . ."

He left the sentence unfinished and as everyone on hand completed it for himself the prevailing gloom deepened.

[August 13, 1812 — Thursday]

In the makeshift shelter they had set up for themselves at the mouth of the St. Joseph River, Chaubenee and Sauganash philosophically continued to sit out the storm. For over five hours already it had raged and they had had no alternative but to wait. Obviously, it was the will of Moneto and what would be, would be.

They had arrived at Topenebe's village on the St. Joseph greatly fatigued, having stopped only for brief intervals of rest since leaving Detroit, close to two hundred miles behind. So, since they had ample time to arrive at Chicago on August 14, they paused for a good rest and food. Topenebe, they learned, had already left for Chicago and had probably reached there by this time. However, when Chaubenee and Sauganash told of the defeat of the Americans at Brownstown, Hull's retreat from Canada back to Detroit and the subsequent Battle of Maguaga, where so many Americans were killed and wounded — along with word from Tecumseh himself that attack on Detroit itself was coming in a few days — this information was relayed to Chicago by a warrior astride a swift horse.

Because their own horses were so jaded, Chaubenee and Sauganash decided to continue the remainder of the way to Chicago by canoe and pick up their rested mounts on their return. They would still have ample time to reach Chicago before the attack came. So they had continued downriver in the canoe but then, just as they reached the mouth of the St. Joseph, the storm had risen out of the north. Howling winds quickly turned the vast blue lake into a churning gray maelstrom and it would have been suicide to attempt to paddle a canoe in those waters. So they had made their little temporary shelter and camp and here they sat now, smoking their pipes, occasionally conversing and awaiting the whim of Moneto to cause the storm to end.

But it looked as if it might be a very long wait.

[*August 14, 1812 — Friday*, 10:00 P.M.]

The events that had occurred at Fort Dearborn since the arrival yesterday of William Wells and his mounted escort of Miami warriors had been moving with an inexorability that was frightening.

Captain Wells had arrived at midday, clad in light buckskins and moccasins and almost indistinguishable from the Miami warriors who accompanied him. But the escort he brought was not a hundred warriors, as Winnemac had intimated it would be. There were twenty-seven of them, all young men, none of them chiefs, about a dozen wearing only breech-clout and moccasins, the rest in buckskin.[254] No influential chiefs were with them because these warriors represented only themselves, not the Miami tribe. Their leader was a good-looking young subchief named Keah Keakah, who was about twenty-five. For the Miamis, neutrality had been the official tribal position since they signed the Greenville Treaty in 1795. They meant to keep it that way. Had any chiefs accompanied the group of volunteer escorts, it could have been misconstrued by the Potawatomies and other tribes as officially sanctioning protection of the Americans and thereby caused the other tribes to regard the Miamis as enemies. All the Indians were mounted on rangy ponies, short-legged and tough, with great resistance against exhaustion and able to travel for endless hours through the forests and fields.

Also accompanying Wells was one uniformed man — Corporal Walter Jordan of the Fort Wayne garrison. Jordan was a lanky, genial individual who considered this whole affair a lark and certainly a welcome change from being so long cooped up at Fort Wayne. A high-spirited young man of about twenty-four, Jordan had always craved adventure and felt now that he was at last going to find it, so he would have wonderful tales to tell his wife when he returned home.

Wells had been mounted on an excellent thoroughbred gelding that had been a gift from his brother, Samuel, when he and Mary Geiger were married. He wore a floppy black hat and his long carrot-red hair was woven into a single queue at the back of his head and tied with a black ribbon. At his belt was his favorite weapon, a beautifully crafted tomahawk with fine engraving. Within his saddlebags were some sealed pots of black paint which it was possible, he realized, that he would be using to paint himself before beginning the journey back to Fort Wayne. It was a mark of death — the mark of a man who would kill or be killed, the mark of a man resigned to perish in whatever lay ahead, the mark of a man grieving a fallen relative, the mark of the *cut-ta-ho-tha* — the condemned man. Black paint had many meanings, depending on how it was worn and where and by whom and under what circumstances. Whether or not Wells would paint himself with it depended largely on the events that would transpire here.

They had left Fort Wayne on August 7 and six days later had reached Fort Dearborn and, though Wells had expected matters to be bad when he reached Chicago, he did not expect the situation to be so terrible as it was. His agitation over the stupidity of General Hull's order to Captain Heald, in view of the circumstances existing at Chicago, was not at all well hidden. That agitation grew as it was explained to him that the Indians who had gathered here had been shown the government stores that were to be given to them, and it reached a peak of white heat when he learned that Captain Heald had shown them the guns, ammunition and whiskey and had told them that they would be receiving those items, too, as part of the partial payment for safe escort.

The only bright spot of his arrival so far as he was concerned was his reunion with Rebekah Heald, his niece, who had rushed to meet him as he dismounted and allowed herself to be swung about by him in the unbounded enthusiasm of seeing one another again. The meeting he had with her husband was considerably less exuberant — a warm handshake and friendly, concerned smile. The Indian Agent's first query of the captain was why so many Indians were present. Then he learned that Winnemac, who had been conspicuously absent since Wells's arrival, had taken seven full days to reach here, when it had taken Wells and his Indians only five and a half. Wells liked Winnemac to a point, but he certainly did not trust him very much.

"Captain," he gritted to Heald, "that red rascal somehow or other was a long time getting here. I don't know how he got those sealed orders opened and then closed again, but evidently he did. I'm afraid he probably notified the Indians along the way that things would be distributed here and there may be even more of a crowd than you already have. I'm not positive it's anything serious yet, but I'd sure as hell a lot rather he'd've come right here. He had no right to know, unless he was told, what the orders contained. Rhea didn't tell him and neither did I. I don't like it. I don't like it at all. I smell something in the air."

Wells met privately almost immediately with Lieutenant Helm and Ensign Ronan, then a little later with John Kinzie. He agreed with them that it would be the worst possible mistake they could make to give up the supplies and evacuate the fort. Together they all went to the captain and discussed the whole matter anew, Wells backing the junior officers in their urgings to stay here.

"Gentlemen, no!" Captain Heald shook his head. "Believe me, I understand your reasoning and even sympathize with it, but I have no choice in the matter. My orders say we must evacuate and evacuate we will."

"Then, damn it," Wells growled, "do it if you must but, for God's sake, don't hand over the supplies, especially the whiskey, arms and ammunition, to the Indians. That's madness! Look, before *anything's* decided definitely, let me go to council with 'em and see what I can sniff out."

Captain Heald protested mildly, but gave in immediately when Wells persisted. And when the Indian Agent returned, two hours later, his face was set in hard lines. Not all the Indians had attended the council he called, but over five hundred had. He hadn't learned much from them insofar as admissions went, but Wells knew the Indians and their ways very well and he read them clearly enough to become assured they they meant to strike the Americans during the march. He had also encountered Peesotum and the two had stared at one another for a long hostile moment.

"One of us dies soon, Apekonit," Peesotum muttered, fingering the tomahawk in his waistband.

"That is true, Peesotum," Wells agreed, "but don't make the mistake of thinking we know which one, yet." He had deliberately turned his back to his enemy, tempting fate but once again having read correctly the cowardice inherent in Peesotum and once again shaming him before his fellows.

"You really believe," Captain Heald asked Wells after his return, "that they'll attempt to strike us? What about the escort of Miamis?"

"They're brave young men," Wells said, "but don't depend on them to stop anything once it's started. Chances are they'd just fade back and watch from out of the way. I understand they're being pressured right now to join in on the attack. All right, now what about the guns and ammunition? And the liquor?"

"My orders are to destroy the weapons and ammunition," Heald said. "The disposition of the whiskey is up to me." He shifted uneasily. "I regret now that they saw it but, since they did, it might be a good idea to leave it behind and just let them use up a lot of time drinking it while we get away."

"Worst possible thing you could do," John Kinzie broke in.

"He's right," Wells seconded. "These Indians go crazy when they've got a gutful of liquor. The whiskey'll have to be dumped."

"All right," Heald conceded. "I'll go along with that, but now what are we going to tell them, since they think they're going to get it when we distribute the goods tomorrow?"

"Jest tell them," Wells said, "that because of the trouble it causes, it'll be the last thing given to them. That and the guns and ammunition. They'll go along with that. Tell them those goods'll be left in the fort for them when we go."

"And what happens, then, when they look for it and don't find it? Won't they be mad?"

Wells shrugged. "Probably. But all you'll have to do is tell them that you reconsidered the matter and became concerned that they would hurt one another if they drank too much, so you thought it best to dump the whiskey. As for the guns and ammunition, they'll probably ask you for an explanation of that and you just show them Hull's order to you to destroy them. They know enough of the military to realize you have to obey your general's orders. They won't like any of it, but I don't know what else we can do. The main thing is, keep up a bold front. If we don't show fear, we might be able to pull it off."

Last night and today, then, had been a time of preparation. The three wagons were readied for the march, with necessary food supplies, water, baggage and personal goods placed in two of them. The third wagon, canvas covered as the others were, was fitted with bedding and was to be used to transport the infants and small children. Those soldiers who were too ill or lame to walk would ride with some of the baggage in the second wagon.

During the night the whiskey and rum barrels were rolled to the storehouse which covered the interior access to the sally port, carefully lowered into the tunnel and then rolled down the slight grade to where the subterranean emergency well was located. The same was true of the excess weapons, gunpowder, bags of flint, shot and gunscrews. Each man was issued twenty-five rounds of ammunition and one extra box of cartridges already made up was hidden in one of the wagons.[255]

Individuals involved themselves in the very personal matters of which of their possessions they would bring, being very strictly limited to what one person could carry, even though some of it might be stowed in the wagons. John Kinzie met again with his chief clerk, Chandonnais, and went over the details of him and the other servants transporting Eleanor and the four children — with Josette LaFramboise Beaubien as nursemaid — by bateau to St. Joseph.

In their private quarters, at her husband's instructions, Rebekah Heald was busily engaged in ripping apart the lining of a short inner jacket that Nathan would wear beneath his uniform. Into this she carefully sewed a sort of money-belt called a wamus, or roundabout. It held thin packets of paper money equally spread out so that they would not be visible at a cursory glance. This was the remainder of the military payroll through the end of September — fourteen hundred fifty dollars.[256] She did a very neat job of it and it was scarcely noticeable when she was finished. After completing that and setting it aside, she gathered up those items that were very personal and dear to them: the beautiful saber with the engraved silver guard that Nathan had received as a wedding gift; the exquisite eagle-head tortoiseshell comb decorated with silver that had been given to her; a silver shawl-pin sometimes worn by Nathan; a brooch she treasured which had been given to her by her father, containing a lock of that man's hair and his initials, S.W., engraved in the silver; her peridot ring engraved R.W. and the set of six fine sterling tablespoons and soup ladle, all engraved with the initials N.H. All were keepsakes with which she could not bear to part.

Similar packing of small personal treasures was going on among all the people clustered in the fort. Lieutenant Linai Helm and his wife, Margaret, carefully packed into the saddlebag of her horse the keepsakes that were dear to them; Ensign George Ronan selected several volumes of his own little library of books; the surgeon's mate, Isaac van Voorhis, carefully packed his medical instruments and the letters he had saved, stuffing them tightly into his saddlebags.

As prearranged, at noon today the goods to be distributed to the Indians from the government store were carried outside through the main gate and placed in a large pile. There were blankets and tools, salt and sugar and flour, dried meats and a variety of foodstuffs. Some six hundred Indians assembled and when the chiefs looked over the collection, their expressions turned sour. Where were the guns? Where was the gunpowder and shot? Where was the liquor? A delegation of the chiefs approached Captain Heald, who was flanked by Wells and Kinzie, and demanded answers to the questions. Boldly, even with a commendable touch of arrogance, the commanding officer told them, through Wells, that this was all that would be distributed now; whatever was missing would be available tomorrow morning at the time of their departure, left within the fort for them.

There was anger in the chiefs' mien but they controlled it, accepted with reasonably good grace the presents that had been provided and returned with them to the temporary village on the far side of Frog Creek. A crisis, it seemed, had been averted, yet everyone remained painfully aware that the greatest potential for danger remained ahead of them, when the entire body of whites would move out of the fort and begin the long march to Fort Wayne.

Late in the afternoon, Topenebe came alone to the fort and visited John Kinzie. They discussed the trader's safety and that of his family and Topenebe listened carefully as Kinzie told him of the preparations already made to send his wife and young children by boat to St. Joseph. The chief nodded, then strongly suggested that Shawneeawkee himself go along in the bateau. The trader shook his head.

"I thank you for your concern, Topenebe. You are a good friend. But we both know that many of the Indians here have been my friends. I have enjoyed a certain influence among them. Now I can do no less than try to help my own people. If I do not accompany the march, surely they will be attacked; if I am with them, my presence may have some degree of restraining influence on the Indians."

Topenebe grunted sourly. "Do not depend on that, Shawneeawkee. Even Black Partridge has been trying to make them give up the idea of attacking the whites and it does not look as if he will be successful. There is more danger than you know."

"I still have to try," Kinzie said simply.

Topenebe sighed. "Then Moneto be with you," he said. "I will send two of my most trusted warriors, Keepoteh and his younger brother, to go along in your boat to protect your family in my name if they are threatened."[257]

He left and, toward sunset, Black Partridge came to the gates, the gold ring in his nose and the brass medallion on his chest reflecting the final rays of the sun. He asked to see Captain Heald. In a few minutes he was facing the Fort Dearborn commander in his quarters. Lieutenant Helm was there, as was William Wells as interpreter, but no one else was present. The chief stood quietly for a long moment and then finally reached up and removed the large brass medallion from around his neck.

"Father," he said, placing the ornament on the desk and then stepping back, "I have come to deliver up to you the medal I have worn for seventeen summers. It was given to me at Fort Greenville by General Wayne as a token and reminder of friendship between the Americans and my people. Now I can no longer keep it. I have heard the singing of leaden birds among the Indians gathered here. My counsel is not heeded. Our young men are resolved to stain their hands with the blood of the whites and I can no longer restrain them. My heart will not let me wear a token of peace while I act as an enemy. Be wary as you leave this place in the morning."[258]

Again he looked at the commanding officer sorrowfully for a long interval, then turned and walked out without speaking further.[259]

A short time later, just after sunset, a delegation of three of the Miamis brought to Chicago by Wells entered the fort to see him. They were led by Keah Keakah. The twenty-seven Miamis had counciled with the Potawatomies several times since their arrival, but they had made their little camp just outside the main gate of the fort, either not invited to stay at the main Indian encampment or else holding themselves aloof to retain the aspect of neutrality. Now, however, they were concerned as they met with their brother, whom they knew as Apekonit, but whom they often called Epiconyare — The Brave One.

"An attack *will* occur tomorrow morning after the march begins," Keah

Keakah told him without equivocation. "It will be very bad. We have been warned to stay back and keep out of it. We replied to them that we cannot really believe that such an attack will occur and that we have given our word to act as escort, and this we will do. But *if* such attack does occur, we will draw ourselves away from it and neither defend the Americans against them, nor join them in their attack on the Americans. Our presence alone, as an escort, may have some effect in preventing the attack from occurring. This much we will provide, as we said we would, but no more."

William Wells thanked him and the Miamis began to go, but then Keah Keakah turned back and shook his hand. "Tomorrow morning you must ride not as Captain Wells and not as our brother Apekonit. Tomorrow you must ride only as Epiconyare. I tell you this because at this moment Peesotum is in his camp blackening his face, as you, too, must do. Whatever is to come, either your bones or his will be left to bleach in the sun here."

They left and the .fierce, humorless smile remained on the Indian Agent's lips as he returned to his quarters. He was very determined that the bones that would be left to bleach in the sun here would not be his.

With the gates of the fort shut and barred following the departure of the Miami delegation, there was a bustle of activity within the walls. The barrels and kegs of whiskey and gunpowder that had been hidden in the sally port tunnel near the well were pounded open with mallets. All the excess guns were broken apart and tossed in a pile. Soon everything was ready to be dumped into the river.

John Kinzie tossed a towel over his shoulder and then slipped out of the sally port and began walking toward the waterline about twenty feet away. Almost instantly two shadows moved swiftly up on him and he was grabbed by both arms.

"It is the Shawneeawkee!" said one of them. They released him at once, but the same individual spoke again. "What are you doing, Shawneeawkee? Why are you out here?"

Kinzie remained unruffled. He indicated the drying-cloth draped over his shoulder. "I have come out to wash myself. I have not," he added, a twinkle in his voice, "come out to attack the Potawatomi camp all by myself."

They grunted in an approximation of a chuckle, liking the effrontery of his response. One placed his hand on the trader's arm again, more in a gesture of friendship than to restrain. "We heard pounding inside. What is happening there? What are the soldiers doing?"

Kinzie's response was casual. "There are more barrels of pork and flour and salt being opened to be distributed tomorrow."

They accepted the explanation and began moving off into the gloom.

One paused and spoke soberly. "It is known, Shawneeawkee, that your family leaves here in the morning by boat. That is good. They will be safer. It would be good for you if you were on the boat with them."

"Perhaps I may be," the trader replied. "I thank you for your concern. Now I have a concern for you: there are soldiers up there on the walls." He made a gesture toward the top of the stockade pickets. "They have guns. The activities of the Indians have made them very nervous. If they see my friends, the Indians, slipping about below them in the shadows, they might become excited and begin to shoot and that would be most regretful. I would not wish to see any of my friends — Indian or white — be hurt."

They did not respond but simply disappeared into the darkness and immediately Kinzie returned to the sally port and was admitted. Several torches had been lighted and were held by privates standing well back along the walls, a safe distance away from the opened gunpowder kegs. One of the privates holding a torch was Daniel Daugherty, who had reenlisted on June 1 and who now looked as if he very much wished he were almost any place else but here. The three officers — Heald, Helm and Ronan — approached the trader at once and he shook his head.

"They're outside," he told them. "Only a few, I think, but we can't take the chance of letting them know what we're doing. They're already suspicious. If we try to dump all this in the river now, they're going to know it and there'll be hell to pay."

Evidently Captain Heald had been considering this and the alternatives and he was ready. "All right," he said, "let's get that cover off." He pointed to what appeared to be a platform of planks about six feet square. Four soldiers immediately lifted it by one end and leaned it against the wall, grunting with the effort. Beneath it was a large hole — the fort's emergency well. The water in it was only a foot or so below the lip, on a level with that of the nearby river. "Everything gets dumped in there," he ordered, pointing, "beginning with the weapons."

Working quickly and as quietly as possible, the men began. The broken firearms, heavy shot bags and bags filled with flints and gunscrews were dropped into the water. Next came the gunpowder, the heavy kegs rolled on their rims to the edge and then the contents poured into the well. By the time this was finished it seemed that the level of the water had raised several inches.

"I don't think it'd be a good idea if we poured the whiskey in there, Captain," John Kinzie said. "On two counts. First, we've got hundreds of gallons to dispose of here and if we dump it into the well, even with the water mixed with it, it'd be potent enough that they'll drink it. Second, if they start drinking it, they're going to find the lead, flints and everything else we've dumped."

"What do you suggest, Mr. Kinzie?"

Kinzie pointed to the sally port door. There was a gap of about an inch between the bottom of the door and the ground, with a decided slope toward the river. "Dump it right in front of the door and let it run down into the river by itself."

Captain Heald considered this and then nodded. "I agree. Let's get it done."

With considerable effort the heavy barrels, contents slopping with the movements, were moved to the portal and then one by one gently tipped and the contents poured onto the ground, gurgled beneath the doorway and flowed down to the sluggish river. By the time they were finished, the reek of liquor in the air was all but overpowering. For John Kinzie, the whiskey being destroyed here was money being lost that there was little likelihood of his ever being able to recover. He put the thought out of his mind. Lives were at stake here, which was far more important now than the small fortune being poured away.

But this was a night, John Kinzie knew, that he would never forget.

[*August 14, 1812 — Friday*, 11:00 P.M.]

Colonel James Findley, eyes still grainy with sleep, stared unbelievingly at the concerned young artillery officer standing before him in his Detroit quarters — an earnest regular army lieutenant named James Dalliba.[260] Quite obviously the younger man was nervous at being here, nervous at having awakened the militia colonel, and it seemed, now that he had spoken of what was troubling him, that he wished he hadn't come here at all. It was his desire to be a career officer in the United States Army and by his action tonight he might well have jeopardized that career.

"General Hull told you *what?*" Colonel Findley's eyes narrowed. He had heard well enough what Lieutenant Dalliba said, but his own questioning response had sprung from his lips automatically, so dismaying was the revelation. Now, more than ever, he wished Lewis Cass and Duncan McArthur were here. Or that he were with them. Or that he could be anywhere but here at Detroit with the British artillery looking down the American army's throat from across the river.

The tension that had bloomed in the army since confirmation of General Brock's arrival to command the British forces at Fort Malden had become almost palpable. Isaac Brock was nothing less than a formidable enemy and only top-notch leadership could thwart him. By no stretch of anyone's imagination could General William Hull be considered as possessing top-notch leadership capabilities.

The Detroit Frenchmen who were working as spies for the Americans had not only confirmed his arrival, but had faithfully reported his activities since then. Brock had met with the Indians soon after his arrival, during which meeting he had his initial encounter with Tecumseh. Brock was no political general and he rarely minced words.

"I have come," he announced to Tecumseh and his Indians, "to battle the Americans who invaded Canada, intent on taking lands belonging to the Indians and the British. I cannot and *will not* allow this."

Tecumseh, when his turn came to speak, held out a hand toward the general and said to his followers, "My brothers, *this* is a man! In him there is no falseness, only strength. With him we will succeed against the Americans. My brothers! Carry the memory of Tippecanoe into battle against the Americans." Though he spoke loudly enough for all to hear, he now directed his remarks to Brock. "They suddenly came against us with a great force while I was absent and destroyed our village and slew our warriors. They came to us hungry and then cut off the hands of our brothers who gave them corn. We gave them rivers of fish and they poisoned our springs.[261] We gave them forest-clad mountains and valleys full of game and in return, what did they give our warriors and our women? Rum! And trinkets! And a grave!"

Brock had immediately put the Fort Malden garrison into motion, along with the reinforcement that he had brought, moving them up the Detroit River on the Canadian side to Sandwich. And, apprised of his coming, Hull at Detroit became deeply apprehensive. Only too aware of the antipathy for him held by the three Ohio Militia colonels, what he wanted most was to get them and their suspicious natures away. McArthur and Cass were the two Hull was most concerned would cause trouble for him. So, quickly, before they could become aware of Brock's approach toward Sandwich, he sent them away. He did so by reversing his own earlier decision to send no more detachments to Captain Brush at Raisin River to escort the supplies to Detroit.

Colonels McArthur and Cass were given a detachment of three hundred fifty men to go by a roundabout route — fifty-eight miles as opposed to thirty by the direct route — and bring in the supply convoy.[262] He told them to leave immediately. When the colonels protested that there were no provisions ready for them to take, Hull ordered them to leave at once anyway, saying that he would send the supplies after them on packhorses. They left at once, but Hull made no arrangement to send the provisions. He had had no intention of doing so.

As soon as the detachment under the two colonels was gone, General Hull alerted Major Denny, across the river at Fort Gowies in Sandwich, that Brock was coming and they were to evacuate. Regretfully — because they had improved the works considerably and felt assured of putting up a good defense — the little force evacuated, burning the works as they left and accidentally burning down the Gowies house in the process. They returned without incident across the river to Detroit.

Only a short time later Brock's force arrived, trundling heavy artillery with it. Immediately they began erecting a battery at point-blank range to bombard Detroit. That was when James Dalliba had come into the picture. The artillery lieutenant had established a very strong American battery within Detroit — twenty-eight heavy cannon, including the devastating twenty-four-pounders. As soon as Lieutenant Dalliba had been able to deduce where the British batteries were being situated, he had ordered the American guns brought to bear on those positions. It was after 10:00 P.M. when he was finished and with that accomplished, the British battery under construction could easily be smashed to smithereens. That was when, a short time ago, he had approached General Hull and asked permission to commence firing.

"Sir," he had said, "if you will give me permission, I will clear the enemy on the opposite shore from the lower batteries."

And it was for a repetition of General Hull's response to that which Colonel Findley was now asking Lieutenant Dalliba. The artillerist swallowed and then repeated what he had said.

"General Hull's exact words to me were, 'Mr. Dalliba, I have made an agreement with the enemy that if they will never fire on me, I will never fire on them.[263] Those who live in glass houses must take care how they throw stones. The answer to your question, Mr. Dalliba, is no. Permission is denied.' "

[*August 14, 1812 — Friday midnight*]

The Indian council had begun at dusk and had all the earmarks of lasting for at least another hour or so. One huge fire and several smaller ones burned in the Frog Creek encampment and at intervals various groups of Indians had done their stilted war dance before them. Now, with the information that had come to them, they were infuriated and whatever remote possibility had existed that an attack would not take place was now eliminated. There was no longer the slightest element of doubt that these Indians would attack the Americans during their march tomorrow.

Earlier in the evening there had still been a few doubts. Some of the older, more reserved chiefs continued to advocate making no attack at all; that they should simply be content with the goods they had already gotten and with destruction of the fort, which would soon take place. These voices were, however, few and faltering. All lingering doubt as to whether or not the attack would occur as Nescotnemeg had planned it were put to rest permanently about half an hour after the council began, with the arrival of a Potawatomi runner from the St. Joseph.

Chaubenee and Sauganash were coming, he told them, and should arrive in the small hours of the morning by canoe. The messenger had been sent ahead while they rested and he had been entrusted with the large red war belt which he now held high for all to see. The news was stirring. Despite Hull's far superior strength in arms and manpower, the British and Tecumseh had forced him to retreat from Canada and go into hiding behind the walls of Fort Detroit. He was soon to be struck there by the combined forces of Tecumseh and General Brock and there was every reason to believe the attack would be a total success. Furthermore, a large detachment of the Americans had been struck at Maguaga in a move initiated by Tecumseh; an attack that stalled the detachment and sent it running back to Detroit leaving dead men all over the battleground.

The excitement this news aroused in the Potawatomies and other Indians in the Frog Creek encampment was extreme. Almost immediately personal preparations were begun. The fast had already commenced at midday, but now they prepared their war bundles, filled with magic powders and bits of bone, tokens and charms and personal items which they believed would bring them success. The war bundles were passed through an incense fire of smoke from dried tobacco, herbs and kinnikinnick to make the magic contents more potent. Weapons were sharpened and loaded and rechecked a half dozen times until no doubt whatever existed as to their readiness. And, finally, they smoked their pipes, applied their war paint and carefully went over the plans of attack which Nescotnemeg had devised and which Siggenauk would implement.

It was while they were so engaged a short while ago that two of the Potawatomies who had been sent out to keep the fort under surveillance came back to the camp with the report that so infuriated them. There had been pounding inside the fort and sounds as if guns were being broken. A little later the smell of liquor permeated the air. When they had crept close to the river side of the fort to investigate, they found fresh little gullies in the earth from the little tunnel door to the river; gullies caused by liquid in large quantity running down; liquid that had turned out to be whiskey. The smell from the river was very heavy and the warriors had tasted the river water and discovered that the sluggish stream tasted like strong grog. All the indications were that the Americans would give them neither the guns and ammunition nor the whiskey, as had been promised. The assembled Indians shrieked in rage and for that act of the Americans alone, they vowed a deadly vengeance.

Now, at the midpoint of night, Chief Black Partridge took a stance at the council fire before them and silenced them with upraised arms. Close behind him stood Chief Topenebe and Chief Siggenauk.

"Hear me well," he said loudly, "all you warriors who will strike them in the morning. You have heard me express my feelings about Shawnee-awkee and his family. They are my friends. They are the good friends of Chief Topenebe. They are close to Chaubenee and Sauganash and even to Tecumseh. And Shawneeawkee himself recently did a great favor that may have saved the life of Chief Siggenauk's son, and so Siggenauk, too, is of a heart with Topenebe and me with what I say to you now."

Black Partridge looked over the listening Indians for an uncomfortably long time and then continued in a voice that had become a little more brittle:

"Many of you know Shawneeawkee by sight. Those who do not must have him pointed out to them. His family will not march with the others; they will be in a boat and two of Topenebe's warriors will be with them. They are not to be harmed. The Shawneeawkee will be with the marchers, but he is not to be harmed. *Hear me well!* If one drop of blood is spilled from Shawneeawkee or any member of his family, we three here will personally kill those responsible, even should they turn out to be friends who have done it."

CHAPTER XII

[*August 15, 1812 — Saturday*]

THE scalp-prickling scream jerked Private James Corbin awake at
2:20 A.M. in the Fort Dearborn soldiers' barracks and he turned to see
his wife now making pitiful little moans and thrashing about in the throes
of a nightmare. He awakened her gently as possible and she sat erect with
a start, at first not comprehending where she was, then dissolving into his
embrace and clinging to him tightly, her whole body trembling. He felt the
damp warmth of her tears against his chest and he smoothed back her hair
and pressed his lips to the top of her head.

"Hush," he said softly, "hush now. It's all right. You're safe. It was just
a dream, Sukey. Just a bad dream, that's all. It's all over now."

"No," Susan countered, "it was more than that. It was a . . . a presentiment. It was . . . oh, Jim, it was just terrible." She glanced toward the
other little bedstead in their cramped cubicle and saw that both of their
children — three-year-old Wilma and Henry, nearly four — were still
soundly asleep, undisturbed by the cries she had made. She calmed a little
and nestled in her husband's arms, telling him of the terror just experienced. She had dreamed of the procession of soldiers and citizens filing
out of the fort and when they were all outside, the fort had abruptly
vanished and they were in the midst of an encircling throng of hideously
painted savages armed with tomahawks, knives, war clubs and guns, and
they were killing, killing, scalping and gruesomely cutting to bits the
women and children and soldiers whose guns were useless because they
were all empty. The black earth had become a sea of ankle-deep red muck
from the blood being spilled and then one enormous Indian had snatched
Henry and Wilma out of her grasp, holding each by an ankle and whirling
them in circles on either side of him, gradually bringing them closer until
at each revolution their heads were banging together. Their tiny screams

had quickly stopped and their heads had become bloody and then soft pulpy masses of lifeless flesh and Susan Corbin had screamed and screamed and . . .

"Shhh, shhh," he hushed as her terror grew again. "It's just a dream, Sukey, and it's all over now. The children are sleeping and they're fine. Everything's fine."

But Susan Corbin couldn't accept that. The march from Fort Dearborn was scheduled to begin at nine o'clock, only mere hours from now, and she was convinced that the dream was actually a premonition. She knew what she had to do and, though it took a while, she convinced him. Exactly an hour from the time of their awakening, they were at the outer sally port gate, having slipped through the darkness unseen from the barracks to the tunnel, accompanied now by Jim's brother, Phelim, also a private. Tiny Wilma, still asleep and swaddled in a blanket, was in Susan's arms; little Henry, blearily half-awake, was being carried by Jim.

"I still think it's stupid," Phelim Corbin muttered as he softly slid the bars and opened the portal, peering out carefully and seeing nothing to cause alarm.

"We've been over that," Jim whispered. "Just stay here and open it again when I get back. I won't be gone long; half hour, maybe less."

Then they had slipped out and crept as silent shadows to the small canoe beached at the river's edge nearby, beside the huge bateau moored there that belonged to John Kinzie. James Corbin helped Susan into the light bark craft. When she was seated and Wilma adjusted in one arm to make room, he handed her Henry, who snuggled against her comfortably. Then, just as silently, he launched the canoe and began paddling diagonally upstream, heading across toward the Burns house.

The plan was simple: Sukey would hide with the children at the house into the dawn and through the day and night following. By then the Americans would be well gone and the Indians would have dispersed. She had taken all their money, much of which she had earned as a washerwoman, and with it she could then approach one of the French families who were staying behind — the Ouilmettes, perhaps, or the Buisons — and pay them to escort her safely to Fort Wayne or Detroit with the children, where she would rejoin him. If the column were not attacked, all well and good; if it were, then Jim would have a much better chance of escaping by himself than if hampered by a wife and two tots.

At the Potawatomi encampment along the south shore of the Chicago River, beginning just west of where little Frog Creek emptied its contents, few people were any longer about. The frenetic dancing and face painting and weapon-preparation begun before midnight had continued until about 3:00 A.M., but now, some forty minutes later, most were asleep in their wigwams, whose dark conical shapes could be vaguely seen, silhouetted by numerous campfires.

Most were asleep, but not all. One who was not was the Indian known to the whites as White Elk, but whose Potawatomi name was Wabinsheway. His villages were located on the Elkhart River in the Indiana Territory and he was one of the most recognizable of all the Indians gathered here, because of his great height. At nearly seven feet tall, he towered over everyone — a long, lean warrior chief whose face and chest were now ghoulishly painted in white markings to approximate skull and skeletal bones. As with the others, he had lain down to sleep in his wigwam, but then awakened with a strong need to relieve himself. Sleepily, he had walked to the river's edge and was just finishing urinating into the water when he glimpsed the shape of a canoe being silently paddled. He thought at first there were two people in it but then a small shape momentarily straightened from the larger shape in the front and he deduced it was someone with a child, perhaps even more than one child. He remained rooted in place, unseen, and watched as the little craft touched shore near the Burns house and its occupants disembarked. He lost sight of them in the darkness but, intrigued, he continued to watch.

On the other side of the river, James and Susan Corbin carefully and quietly approached the dark Burns house. There was, Sukey knew, from having visited Mary Burns on occasion, a root-cellar below the floor of the house and it was here she planned to take refuge for the next thirty hours or so. But the house was not only dark, its shutters were barred from the inside and its single door was heavily padlocked. They walked around the house twice, seeking an entry. Finding none, they finally halted and the woman pointed.

"There," Sukey said. "We'll just hide in there and stay out of sight until it's safe. It's plenty roomy enough."

She was pointing at the oversized woodbox on the porch near the front door, its top covered with a heavy hinged lid of joined planking. Private Corbin didn't care much for the idea, but there was no alternative. He opened the box and they heard the scurry of tiny feet as a family of mice fled. Except for little bits of bark and a few splinters, the box was empty and, as Susan had said, there was more than room enough for her and the two children. With some misgivings he helped her and them inside, kissed all three and gently closed the lid over them. There was room enough for Sukey to sit up or, if she wished, to lie down with knees slightly bent.

"See you in Fort Wayne," Corbin whispered, with far more assurance than he felt. He melted away in the darkness and in a minute was back afloat, returning toward the fort.

Wabinsheway, still on the south bank of the river, heard the faint dippings of the paddle before he saw the craft. He blinked his eyes against the darkness and saw it — with only one shape aboard. For several minutes after the canoe had passed out of sight and hearing he thought about this and then he turned and retraced his steps to his wigwam.

5:00 A.M.

A bustle of activity was occurring on the parade ground within Fort Dearborn as frugal baggage and supplies were carefully loaded aboard the three wagons. Simultaneously, four oxen were being harnessed to each. The one that would be in the lead was merely a canvas-covered flatbed wagon with sides two feet high. Into this the majority of supplies and some baggage had been packed very tightly. Then the canvas tarpaulin had been lashed down securely. The other two wagons had higher sides and a squared superstructure forming a framework. Over the top of this was canvas, with sagging folds of the material at the upper edges, to be freed and laced to the wagon sides to form a protective covered conveyance. In those two the wagon beds would be covered with blankets over corn-husk mattressing. One was to be used to transport the women with children too young to walk; the other for soldiers on the garrison sick list, who were ill with fevers or other infirmities. In both of these wagons, as well, would be packed most of the victuals — fresh beef, salt pork, condiments, vegetables and bread baked earlier this week, plus some cooking gear and some baggage unable to fit into the first wagon.

As John Kinzie assisted, he was summoned to the gate to talk with a Potawatomi chief who had come and asked for him. In the space between the main gate and the outer pickets on the south side of the fort he approached the Indian in the dim light of dawn and saw that it was Topenebe. They shook hands warmly, but Topenebe wore a gravely troubled expression. He spoke in his own tongue and Kinzie listened closely, his smile quickly disappearing.

"I ask you one last time, Shawneeawkee," Topenebe said, "not to accompany the march. Go instead with your wife and children who will be in the boat. I promise you it will be allowed to pass unmolested to the St. Joseph." As the trader began shaking his head, the chief hurried on. "I tell you now that though the Potawatomi have promised to escort you, they plan mischief against the march. It will be very dangerous if you are with the marchers and I cannot guarantee that I can protect you under such circumstances."

"Thank you for your concern, my friend," Kinzie said, "but I have to answer no. The very fact that mischief *is* planned makes it all the more important that I accompany them. I still believe my presence with the column may help deter those who would otherwise cause trouble."

Topenebe sighed, but argued no further. "It is good your family will go by boat. My man Keepoteh and his brother have been given their instructions." He glanced at the rifle the trader held cradled in his left arm and motioned toward it. "You will be taking that?"

"I will."

"It would be better if you did not but, if you must, then I warn you, whatever you see happening about you and whatever the provocation, do not shoot except to save your own life. You have my protection and Siggenauk's, so long as you do not shoot."

Kinzie nodded, understanding. He accepted Topenebe's hand in a strong grip and, without speaking again, the Potawatomi chief turned and walked away in the gathering light of morning. Kinzie watched him go and returned to the parade ground where now well over one hundred people were milling about. The gate was carefully closed and barred behind him as soon as he reentered. The skies were cloudless and it was pleasantly warm. Obviously it was going to be a clear, bright day, but the promise did little to lift the aura of apprehension of those moving about here. They were silent as they listened to the commanding officer establishing their order of march.

"We will move at a steady brisk pace," he told them, "set to accommodate those women and children who will be afoot. No dallying, however, will be permitted. At some little distance ahead will be Captain Wells and about half of the mounted Miami escort he brought with him. Next will be the officers of the garrison, followed by the musicians and regular foot soldiers. Next will be the three wagons, accompanied by the women and children who are capable of walking. Sergeant Burns's militia squad will follow the wagons and the remainder of the Miami escort will bring up the rear. We will begin moving out precisely at nine o'clock."

"How long you reckon it'll take us to reach Fort Wayne, Captain?" called out one of the militiamen.

"Assuming we will be able to maintain a steady pace each day," Nathan Heald replied, "it will probably take at least three or four weeks. I'd say, at a guess, about twenty-five or twenty-six days." He let his glance pass over the crowd listening to him and nodded. "All regular military shall wear full uniform," he added. "Rifles, with bayonets fixed, will be carried loaded and primed at all times until such order is rescinded. All right, carry on."

6:45 A.M.

In his quarters in the officers' barracks against the west wall of the stockade, William Wells unhurriedly dressed himself in soft leathers — frilled buckskin moccasins and leggins and a soft doeskin shirt that buttoned up the front. His shoulder-length rusty-red hair had been hanging loose, but now he drew it back into an unbraided queue, the end of which he tied again with the strip of black ribbon. On his head he would wear his slouch-brimmed leather hat with a turkey feather projecting backward from the band. Over his left shoulder and hanging down his right side he donned a bullet pouch and on the opposite shoulder and side he hung his brass powder flask with a fully antlered elk head in relief on each side framed by a wreathwork of oak leaves and acorns. To his left hip he buckled his saber and from his belt at the right rear hung the fine tomahawk with his initials on the shank — a favorite weapon he had carried for many years — and a sheathed knife with razor edge. Into his belt front he thrust two long-barreled flintlock pistols. Finally, in his hands he would carry his specially modified rifle with shortened barrel and stock.

There was one last step to his preparations and, as he reached into a pouch for one of the little covered pots he had brought along from Fort Wayne, he again went over in his mind the conversation he had had a few minutes ago with Keah Keakah — a talk that had made this final step a necessity. The Miami warrior had told him that he and the rest of the Miamis had still been kept isolated from the Indian encampment and though he suspected that during the night war plans were made, the Miamis had not been taken into the confidence of the Potawatomies. A young Potawatomi warrior named Awbenabi had come to them several hours ago in the night and reassured them that if the Americans marched away without burning the fort and remaining goods and supplies left behind, they would be allowed to go unharmed. Yet, from the sounds in the Indian encampment until three o'clock this morning, there was every indication that they planned to attack the column.

There was now no doubt left in Wells's mind that attack was sure to come. He was also resigned to the fact that whatever else occurred, today's sunrise would be the last for him. He was a condemned man and even if he managed to kill Peesotum before that big young Potawatomi could find and kill him, he had no illusion that he would survive a general melee. He was an adopted Indian who had gone back to the whites and for that alone there was grave condemnation. And, being a condemned man — a *cut-ta-ho-tha* — he would mark himself as such, and so he uncovered the pot withdrawn from the pouch and thrust the fingers of his right hand into the viscous black mass within. The heavy, greaselike substance had been made by mixing a proper amount of water with pure chimney soot. This he smeared onto his cheeks, chin, forehead and neck, spreading it and rubbing it in until his entire exposed skin was black. What residue remained in the pot when he finished rubbing it into face and neck he now rubbed onto the backs of his hands and wrists. Then he carefully checked his weapons again.

Cut-ta-ho-tha he might be, but if indeed he must die, he was determined that he was going to take as many as possible along with him.

7:00 A.M.

Along the east wall of the Fort Dearborn stockade, in the commanding officer's barracks, Captain Nathan Heald and his wife were dressing in preparation for the departure. Rebekah's long hair rolled and held firmly to her head with the silvered tortoiseshell eagle-head comb and she had donned soft boots and a pale blue long-skirted dress which, as usual, she would tuck around her thighs and under her rump as she rode.

Refusing to walk along with the other women or to leave her beautiful thoroughbred mare behind, she had announced — quite without room for argument — that she planned to ride at the van of the column, pacing the officers and close to her husband. Unwilling either to argue at this point or to show favoritism, Heald announced that those who had horses to ride would be allowed to do so. Now, apart from the twenty-seven-man mounted Miami escort, there would be seven riders with the column: William Wells, riding along with the Miamis; John Kinzie, Rebekah Heald and Margaret Helm riding with the officers at the van of the column; and Dr. Isaac van Voorhis riding near the sick wagon. The other two horses — one an excellent thoroughbred and the other a cherished saddle horse — would be ridden by females. The former, owned by Sergeant Isaac Holt, would be ridden close to him at the rear of the regulars by his wife, Jane. The latter, owned by Charles Lee, would be ridden by his twelve-year-old daughter, Mary.

Now, placing on the bed the matching pale blue bonnet she would wear today, Rebekah helped her husband don the heavy vest jacket he would wear beneath his uniform jacket, its weight attesting to the over fourteen hundred dollars of Fort Dearborn payroll money in the wamus sewn into the lining. It fitted him snugly when he buttoned it and so cleverly was the money concealed and distributed that the vest gave the impression of being no more than the garment it purported to be. An additional sum of one hundred fifty dollars of his own personal funds was in the buttoned-down pocket of his outer garment, should a need of ready cash be occasioned for any reason along the way. She next helped him put on the fine blue, tailed uniform jacket and buttoned it as he stood waiting patiently, a faint smile on his lips. When she finished, she stood on tiptoe, placed her hand on his cheeks and kissed him full on the mouth.

"Well," he chuckled, "what does that commemorate?"

"My loving you," she said lightly. Abruptly her expression changed and she became serious. "What are our chances, Nathan?"

His own smile died. He buckled on his fine sword before answering. "It's hard to say," he told her. "They've taken the goods we gave them and have promised an escort in return. We can only hope they'll live up to their promise."

"Do you think they will?"

"To be entirely honest," he admitted, shaking his head slowly, "I'm worried."

7:15 A.M.

Corporal Walter Jordan grimaced as he looked at his own less than respectable uniform. He had brought along no extra uniform clothing when he left Fort Wayne with William Wells for Fort Dearborn and the uniform he wore had suffered on the journey, gouged and picked here and there by brambles and with a ragged tear down the length of his right sleeve. He looked across the room at Ensign George Ronan who was just completing his dressing and wondered if the time would ever come when he would be able to wear a fine uniform such as that.

As if reading his thoughts, Ronan glanced up and grinned. "I have three of these outfits," he said. "A second one's in my baggage. With the baggage limitations set by Captain Heald, there was no room for the third. Of course, if I had someone to wear it for me on the march, I guess I'd still have three when we reached Fort Wayne, wouldn't I?" His eyes twinkled.

"Me?" Jordan was surprised but immediately interested. "I know we're about the same size, but wouldn't Heald object?"

Ronan shrugged, unconcerned. "Don't think he'd make an issue of it," he commented. "After all, it'd certainly look better. Might lead the Indians to believe we have more officers than they thought, too, which couldn't hurt." He took the extra ensign's coat down from its hook and extended it toward the corporal. "I'd a lot rather see you wearing it than one of those Indians, who's sure to if we leave it behind."

Corporal Jordan stripped off his own ragged jacket and put on the ensign's, especially admiring the single large gold epaulet on the left shoulder. It fit him quite well and he smiled broadly. "I could get accustomed to a uniform like this."

Ronan laughed. "Needs to be a little more complete than that." He rummaged in the high narrow closet box and came up with a fine cockaded hat of boiled leather, so hard it was virtually a helmet, the plumes projecting from it long and white, sweeping toward the rear and then down in a graceful curve to the shoulder. Jordan tried it on and then laughed at his reflection in the small wall mirror. Ronan was rummaging again and this time he brought out a scabbarded saber, faintly tarnished on the haft but otherwise in good condition. The corporal accepted it with thanks and buckled it to his belt on the left, then strutted peacock proud before the glass.

"Well," he breathed at last, "don't I make a picture now!"

There was irony in George Ronan's reply. "Not only a picture," he pointed out, "but also a much better target."

7:25 A.M.

Sergeant Otho Hayes had been fighting his fever for almost a fortnight and now, though at last it was on the wane, he still felt very weak and took little comfort from the fact that the seven ailing privates were in worse condition than he.[264] He didn't feel sick enough to ride in the wagon with the other invalids, yet he wondered how he could possibly march all day. The dilemma was solved for him when Lieutenant Helm entered the second-floor hospital room in the west wing of the soldiers' barracks and inquired about his health. After the sergeant's succinct response, Helm nodded.

"All right, you'll do just fine. The first wagon will have the baggage in it. The second will carry these sick men who can't walk, plus some equipment. The third will have little children and a few women. The wagons are to move in single file. The two men least sick from among these," he indicated the fever-ridden privates who were listening closely, "will drive the second and third wagons. You'll drive the first and be in charge of the wagon contingent."

"Yes sir!" Sergeant Hayes replied. He was very pleased.

7:30 A.M.

Surgeon's Mate Isaac van Voorhis was more than a little disgruntled. To save time this morning, he had last night packed all his surgical apparatus and medicines, along with various texts and important papers in the saddle bags of his horse, deciding it wouldn't hurt to let the mare remain saddled and saddlebagged overnight. But a few minutes ago, when he'd gone to the horse compound just a few rods southwest of the fort, she was gone. One of the split-rails was knocked down and he presumed she had simply bounded over the lower rail and then strayed off.[265] The thought of the Indians perhaps finding her and taking all his professional equipment made the young doctor half sick.

He explained the situation to Captain Heald, stressing the possible great need for the equipment during their long march. The commanding officer had nodded, equally concerned about the ramifications. He had sent word immediately for the quartermaster sergeant to report to him on the double. Now, Sergeant William Griffith had just run up to them and listened as the commanding officer explained the situation.

"I really don't think it's too likely that the Indians took the doctor's mare," Captain Heald concluded. "Much more likely she's just strayed. Sergeant, I want you to go out immediately and see if you can locate the animal and bring her back here."

Sergeant Griffith, a large man with a huge black moustache, saluted smartly. "Yes sir!" He did an about-face and trotted out of sight toward the main gate.[266]

8:00 A.M.

As John Kinzie opened the sally port door and looked outside cautiously, he saw nothing to cause alarm. The huge Kinzie bateau was moored as it had been last night and the trader's boatman, a burly French-Canadian named Claude, had been expecting him and immediately signaled that it was safe to emerge.[267] On the broad deck with Claude were Topenebe's two men, Keepoteh and his younger brother, who waved greetings to the trader.

Kinzie acknowledged the salutation and immediately relayed the all-safe message to those behind him. They streamed out of the portal quickly and in single file walked up the long, insecure double-plank to board the boat. The large wooden craft was close to thirty feet in length and wide in the beam. A small shelter of wood and canvas had been constructed forward and a short-masted sail could be raised when conditions warranted. The gunwales were fitted with six oarlocks, three to the side, but only four oars were presently at ready. Most of the Kinzie goods to be taken had been stowed aboard the boat over the past several days, including even a mule being brought along in case a pack animal was needed. The mule was tied to the short mast amidships.

As much as was already stowed aboard in way of equipment, supplies and goods, John Kinzie had not been able to have loaded all he would have liked to take, because of the number of people to be accommodated. In addition to the three men already aboard, eleven others in the Kinzie party were to be included. Eleanor Kinzie and the Kinzie children — John H., Ellen, Maria and Robert — were there, as well as three of the Kinzie slaves, old Athena and Henry, along with the husky twenty-year-old called Black Jim, who would be helping with the rowing and other manual chores. Then there was the nursemaid for the Kinzie children, Josette Beaubien, who had remained behind in Kinzie employment when her husband went to Milwaukee. The final two were Kinzie's chief clerk and long-time friend, Jean Baptiste Chandonnais, fraternal nephew of Topenebe and therefore an added protection, and Chandonnais' assistant, a young French-Indian halfbreed.[268]

With everyone safely aboard, Kinzie gave the final instructions that he had coordinated with Topenebe: the boat was to remain at rest here until the last of the column left the fort's gates. In all matters, they were to do as directed by Keepoteh and Chandonnais. The boat would take them safely to the St. Joseph, where he would subsequently join them.

The trader kissed his children and embraced Eleanor with more tenderness than usual and her eyes filled with tears. "I wish you were coming with us," she said in a small voice.

He nodded, kissed her again and quickly strode back into the sally port, closing and barring it behind him.

8:05 A.M.

Sergeant William Griffith was still searching for the horse belonging to Dr. Van Voorhis, but thus far he had been unsuccessful. After leaving the fort he had walked to the mouth of the river, passing around behind the residences of Charles Lee and William Russell, then back along the river shore on the east and north sides of the fort. As he passed the sally port he glanced at the large bateau moored there and waved to the occupants, but did not stop. He circled the two-story Indian Agency House, now vacant, and then continued walking west. Now, approaching the rickety plank bridge that crossed the boggy little Frog Creek not far above its mouth, he was intending to continue his search in the Indian encampment on the other side. Well beyond the creek as he crossed the bridge he could see large numbers of warriors garishly painted and heavily armed. He was largely hidden from them by a screen of brush, but their demeanor seemed hostile and the mild apprehension that had been plaguing him increased sharply. He gasped when, as he began thrusting his way through the bushes, he was suddenly seized from behind, his arms pinned in a strong grip and his rifle, sword and bayonet taken from him.

There were three Potawatomies and he immediately recognized one of them as Topenebe. The chief indicated he should be silent and beckoned him to follow, then walked toward the mouth of Frog Creek, still hidden from the encampment by underbrush. Griffith hesitated, but Topenebe's two warriors took his arms and moved him after their chief. At the creek's mouth he was put into a canoe, sitting in the middle with Topenebe while the two warriors paddled. They took him nearly directly across the river to the little landing near the Burns house, where the lead paddler got out, followed by Topenebe and Griffith.

Topenebe stood before him and tapped him in the middle of the chest with a stiff forefinger, then pointed to the skirt of woodland north of the Burns cabin. "You go away now," the chief told him.

Griffith stood still, no little confused. He brushed nervously at his moustache. "What's going on?" he asked. "What am I supposed to do?"

Topenebe shook his head, not understanding, and the warrior with them stepped forward and spoke in passable English. "Bad time come very soon," he said. "Chief say you go to trees. Hide. If no hide, die. All others soon die. You go. *Now!*"

William Griffith was no fool. A trembling had begun in his legs and he bobbed his head once and set off at a lope, muscles tensed for the knife-blade or tomahawk he expected to strike him in the back. None came. He looked back once and saw that Topenebe and his warrior had gotten back into the canoe and were returning to the encampment where now, including women and children, some thirteen hundred Indians were gathered. His pace carried him past the front of the Burns cabin, which he noted was locked. He ran by without pause, unaware that the wife and children of Private James Corbin were hidden in the porch woodbox near the front door.

Within a few minutes, angling northeastward, he entered the woodland

and thought he had managed to do so unseen. His apprehension had grown to raw fear, fueled by his flight, and his only thought now was to find a haven. It was in this state of mind that he almost ran into the well-hidden little playhouse shed that John Kinzie had built for his son and where the trader had hidden after killing Jack Lalime. It seemed ideal as a hiding place and he scrambled inside on hands and knees and then cowered in a dim corner, his breathing ragged, his heart thudding dizzyingly and a great fear consuming him.[269]

8:20 A.M.

"Take this," said Private Phelim Corbin, extending the scabbarded sword toward his wife. When she accepted it, he went on. "Carry it with you on the march. God knows what's going to happen now, but if there's trouble, at least you'll be able to protect yourself."

Victoria Corbin, in the eighth month of her pregnancy, was an attractive young woman, but the strain of these last few hours had made her drawn and nervous. She was wearing a pale gray ankle-length dress loosely belted at the waist and trimmed in white, with matching bonnet. Her shoes were low-cut black slippers with dull silver buckles. She fumbled with the sword, attempting to attach it to her belt on the right, but Phelim shook his head and took it back from her and attached it to the belt over her left hip, haft forward. As he did so, he fervently wished that he had insisted on her going into hiding last night with his sister-in-law, niece and nephew at the Burns place. He tried to smile confidently when he stepped back from her, but the smile was a travesty. She stepped forward and placed her hand on his arm, touched by his concern, knowing how filled he was with stories of the unspeakable horrors perpetuated upon captives by the Indians, and sharing them. Phelim had been one of the soldiers in the squad that had recovered and buried the hideously mutilated remains of Liberty White at the Lee farm last April.

"Don't worry, Phelim," she murmured. "No matter what happens, I won't let them take me alive."

Twenty feet away, as part of the general confusion of packing, carrying and loading by men, women and children at the wagons, Margaret Helm paused, a small portmanteau in her grip, and glanced at the soldier and his obviously pregnant wife, who had a sword buckled to her belt. She had seen them about the fort before but did now know them on a personal level. What caught her attention was the fact that she and the private's wife were identically dressed and remarkably similar in physical appearance — their height, figure and features so alike that they might well have been sisters. The only significant difference between them, in fact, was the great swollen abdomen of the private's wife.

She's with child and I'm not, Margaret thought, and suddenly she found herself wishing fiercely that she and Linai would have a baby.

8:35 A.M.

The loading of the wagons with baggage, victuals, supplies and equipment was completed and now those who were to ride in the two canvas-covered wagons were taking their places. Sergeant Otho Hayes directed the operation, ordering five of the seven sick privates to be placed on the bed of the rear wagon and made as comfortable as possible amid the gear also packed within it. A sixth private, one less ailing, would drive this wagon.

Another private was on the driver's seat of the middle wagon, which was to carry the women and children who would not be walking. The cornhusk mattresses that had been carried from the barracks and lined the wagon bed, covered now with blankets, would make the jolting ride a little easier to bear. Food and water had been secured inside and now the passengers themselves took their places. Five adults and twelve children settled themselves inside. There was Mary Burns and her four-month-old daughter, Catherine, as well as her three-, six- and nine-year-old daughters from the previous marriage, Frances, Anne and Isabella Cooper. The latter, who could easily have walked, was to help her with the younger children. Mary's husband and son, Thomas Burns and Andrew Cooper, would march behind with the militia.

Rebekah Heald's slave, Cicely, holding her year-old Benjamin, was there, as was Private John Simmons's wife, Susan, and their two small children, David, two, and little Susan, who had been born last February 12. Sarah Neads was inside, with her four-year-old son, Johnny, who had been whimpering almost constantly since awakening this morning. Finally, there was Charles Lee's wife, Martha, and their two-year-old girl, Sally; plus three other children of settlers.[270]

The Lee's older daughter, twelve-year-old Mary, had volunteered to ride her father's saddle horse close to the wagon and, though at first Charles and Martha had been against it, there was really no other choice. Martha certainly couldn't ride the gelding, since she had to take care of Sally, and neither Charles nor his fifteen-year-old namesake son could, since they were required to march with the militia. Besides, Mary *wanted* to ride. She was confident she would have no trouble at all and looked forward to possibly seeing what she called "my own special chief," Black Partridge, as they rode off so she could call good-bye to him. Nevertheless, as a precaution Charles Lee very carefully tied her into the saddle so that if the horse broke and reared or bucked and ran off, she would not be thrown to the ground.

Surprisingly, Victoria Corbin, despite her advanced pregnancy, elected to march along with the other women, at least until she became too weary to do so any longer. Part of the reason was that her husband, Phelim, would be marching with the other regular privates directly ahead and she would be able to stay at least within sight of him and experience some degree of assurance from that.

8:42 A.M.

To the vast relief of Dr. Isaac van Voorhis, his saddled mare, saddlebags intact and all the medical equipment still safely contained, showed up at the main gate of the fort on her own and was led inside. This meant that instead of having to ride in the sick-wagon, as had begun to seem likely, the young surgeon would now be mounted on his own horse beside it. The mare had come back from the area of the dunes southeast of the fort along the lakeshore. Captain Heald was pleased at her return and that she had not been confiscated by the Indians — a possibility he had suspected — but he was vaguely concerned over the fact that William Griffith had not returned with her. He shrugged, certain that the quartermaster sergeant would be back within another five or ten minutes.

8:48 A.M.

Under orders from Captain Heald, a squad of a half-dozen privates led by Corporal Joseph Bowen, all armed with rifles, passed through the main gate and the outer pickets and went directly to the livestock compound several rods to the southwest. Here the thirty or forty milch cows and one hundred fifty or more beef cattle were hazed out into the open prairie to wander and graze as they wished. Since the animals were to be left behind anyway, it was Captain Heald's belief that they might serve as a diversion, with the Indians trying to capture them as the column moved away. Within three minutes the squad had returned to the safety of the fort.

8:51 A.M.

William Wells, whose blackened-face appearance had caused a considerable stir and no little increase of apprehension on the parade ground, was talking quietly with Ensign George Ronan near the main gate when a sentry ran up to them.

"Captain Wells," he said excitedly, "your Miamis have just come up from their camp by the lake shore. They're milling around on their horses out front, sir. Are we supposed to let 'em in?"

Wells shook his head. "No. Tell Captain Heald I've gone out to form them into front and rear guard. I'll be back inside as soon as I've placed them."

As the sentry nodded and raced off, Wells strode to the gate and was let out at his signal. By this time the twenty-seven mounted Miamis had entered the outer pickets and were sitting their horses quietly to left and right of the gate. The fact that he approached them wearing the black paint of the *cut-ta-ho-tha* caused them to murmur nervously among themselves. Beyond them and beyond the outer pickets, numerous other Indians had begun collecting, mainly squaws, children and older people, anticipatory of the moment when the last of the column would leave the fort and they would be free to rush in and begin plundering.

Wells conferred briefly with Keah Keakah and arranged it so the Miami subchief would move out a few hundred yards in advance of the American column with thirteen of his followers, while the other thirteen would remain in place until the last of the column left the fort and then fall in a few hundred yards behind. Wells himself would ride sometimes with the front escort and sometimes with the rear. When they were finished talking, Keah Keakah shook the Indian Agent's hand with more than usual warmth.

"I am sorry," he said simply, "to see that Apekonit is *cut-ta-ho-tha*. His brothers will miss him."

As Wells returned to the interior of the fort, he was keenly aware of the fact that not one of the French residents — DuPin, LeClerc, the Buisons, the Ouilmettes and others — who had elected to remain here in Chicago in their homes, had come out to say farewell to their erstwhile friends. It was a clear indication of just how strictly they were observing the directive received from the Potawatomies to remain neutral in their homes, for their own safety. It was also just one more omen to be added to the growing list of very grave signs. Once again William Wells muttered a curse at the insanity of their leaving this fort.

8:55 A.M.

Obeying the order of the commanding officer, Private Hugh McPherson beat his drum in the signal for assembly. Immediately, as prearranged, the sentries still at their posts on the parapets climbed down to take their places with the troops. Everyone else not yet in the loosely formed line hastened to get into place, the only exception being the two privates who stood at the front gate, ready to throw it open at the command and then fall in with the troops. William Wells sat his horse between them, no expression readable on his blackened face.

Already astride their horses close to the gate were John Kinzie and his stepdaughter, Margaret Helm, as well as Rebekah Heald on her superb bay mare. The saddle-blanket chosen by the commander's wife was her favorite — a brilliant scarlet fabric that gave a nice touch of color to the scene.

From back near the militia, who were wearing ordinary civilian clothing, Lieutenant Helm and Ensign Ronan came striding briskly toward the front of the line, passing Dr. Van Voorhis astride his horse at the wagons. Captain Heald moved to join them, his steps dogged by fourteen-year-old

Salienne, the half-breed French-Potawatomi whom he had hired as interpreter on several occasions since Lalime's death.

All the regulars were in proper military attire and Private John Suttenfield, in the van of the troops, held the standard upright which bore the American flag. He was flanked on his left by the two drummers, Privates Hugh McPherson and John Hamilton, and on the right by the two fifers, Privates George Burnett and John Smith. They were all somber and very pessimistic about what lay ahead. Smith, who was bandmaster, held a brief whispered conversation with the other musicians, glancing furtively at Captain Heald as they talked, and they agreed on what piece they would play as soon as the order to march was given.

"Sir," Lieutenant Helm came to a stop before the commander and saluted, "Sergeant Griffith still has not returned."

Heald's jaw set grimly and he presumed the noncommissioned officer had been waylaid and killed. He did not put the thought into words. "We can only assume," he said, "that the sergeant's search for Dr. Van Voorhis' horse carried him farther than he anticipated and that he will join us as we begin the march. Everyone else is in place?"

Lieutenant Helm nodded. "Awaiting your order, sir."

Heald reached into his pocket, took out his heavy gold watch and checked the time. It was exactly nine o'clock. A heavy silence had fallen over the assemblage and the snap of the watch case as he closed it was abnormally loud. All eyes were on him as he returned the watch to his pocket.

"All right, Lieutenant, let's move out."

9:00 A.M.

"Open the gates!" Lieutenant Helm called loudly.

The pair of large squared timbers that served as bars were slid in succession in opposite directions and the gates were swung open fully inward. The privates who opened them then snatched up their rifles which had been leaning against the wall nearby and ran to their place among the troops. Flanking the gate on the outside, between main gate and outer pickets, were the two groups of mounted Miamis. The horse of William Wells began prancing and circling in anticipation and he brought it under control. He made a hand signal to Keah Keakah, who was with the group east of the gate, and immediately the Miami subchief issued a guttural command and led the first contingent of thirteen warriors out. Wells moved his horse into a canter and joined them. The remaining thirteen, west of the gate, held their horses firmly, ready to fall in behind the procession.

Lieutenant Helm held up his hand and shouted loudly, "Forwarrr-r-rd . . ." he dropped his arm sharply and pointed out the gate, ". . . ho-o-o-o!"

Instantly the front portion of the line began to move — three officers and two officers' wives and John Kinzie first, with Salienne only a pace behind the commander, then the standard-bearer and four musicians — the drummers immediately beginning a cadenced tattoo — followed by the marching regulars, which included a sergeant, five corporals and forty-five privates. The sergeant was Isaac Holt, who marched at the rear of the regulars so his wife, Jane, could ride behind him.

The wagons were next, starting more slowly, the oxen reluctant to begin and, once started, disinclined to keep up with the pace set by the troops ahead. Sergeant Hayes, in the lead wagon, cracked his whip and swore but it was only with difficulty that he urged the oxen into a slow pace.

Behind him, the wagon carrying sixteen women and children, plus the feverish private who was driving, was still not moving. Finally, when Dr. Van Voorhis rode up and smacked the oxen sharply with his crop and shouted at them, the team began to walk. Inside, ensconced as comfortably as possible, were the women with infants: Susan Millhouse Simmons with her two-year-old David and six-month-old Susan; Mary Burns with four-month-old Catherine; Martha Lee with year-old Sally; and the Heald's slave, Cicely, with two-year-old Benjamin. The other seven children in the wagon were four-year-old Johnny Neads and three others,[271] who were all being cared for by Cicely, although one of them, twelve-year-old Isabella Cooper, daughter of Mary Burns, was helping in caring for her two younger sisters, Anne, six, and Frances, three.

Just behind this second wagon, now beginning to move, was twelve-year-old Mary Lee, tied into the saddle of her father's horse, and the four women who were walking — Emmaline Clark, Sarah Neads — mother of Johnny, who was in the wagon — Tess Russell and the heavily pregnant Victoria Corbin, sword buckled on her hip, who shrugged off the admonitions of the other women that she ought to be riding. Actually, what she felt she should be doing was remaining behind in hiding at the Burns house with her sister-in-law, Sukey, and her two little ones.

In the third wagon was more equipment and the sick men. That wagon lurched and the driver and five ailing privates inside groaned as each small bump caused painful jarrings.

Finally, at the rear and also awaiting their turn to begin marching were the twelve men of the Chicago Militia, including Sergeant Thomas Burns, plus two civilian men not connected with the militia — John Kinzie's slave named Pepper and the Frenchman named Francis Bourbonne.

The entire little force, its front already in motion, excluding the Miami escort of twenty-seven warriors, was comprised of exactly one hundred nine individuals as it moved out through the main gate of Fort Dearborn.[272]

First to pass the outer pickets was William Wells with Keah Keakah and the thirteen other Miamis. They looked unsmilingly at the Potawatomi women and children clustered outside the pickets, who returned their gaze in kind. There were no waves, no calls of farewell, only a peculiar chilling silence. The escort vanguard began following the main road which moved south along the bend of the river to where it joined the lake and the Miami subchief kneed his horse up close beside Wells.

"It is a bad sign, Apekonit," Keah Keakah muttered. "The escort the Potawatomi promised is not here."

Wells nodded and pointed to the right. Several hundred yards away, beyond the scattered cattle in the fields, was a long line of Indians stretching a quarter mile or more southward from the Potawatomi Frog Creek encampment. Even from this distance they could see that all were armed.

At the southernmost end of the Potawatomi line, Chief Nescotnemeg grunted as he saw the vanguard leaving the fort. He barked a sharp command and immediately began walking southward at a steady pace, his warriors following him in single file. At the midpoint of the line, Chief Siggenauk also called out an order and began moving southward followed by his warriors, though at a somewhat slower pace than the head of the line. Closer to the encampment, Chief Sunawewone also gave an order and part of his line remained in place while part moved south even more slowly than Siggenauk's. All the warriors in the entire line were armed, a few with rifles — especially near the front of the line — but most with tomahawks and war clubs.

Back near the fort, Wells watched the movement begin, the mid-portion of the Indian line pacing them. He nodded again. "It is a bad sign," he agreed.

By now the three officers afoot and the three accompanying riders — Rebekah Heald, Margaret Helm and John Kinzie — had passed the outer pickets and they, too, noticed the distant line of three hundred or more warriors.

"Well," Nathan Heald remarked, "look there — seems as if the Indians are living up to their promise. There's our escort." He appeared encouraged by the sight.

"Strangest escort I've ever seen," Ronan muttered to Helm. The lieutenant grimaced but did not reply. He smiled wryly, however, when the four musicians, now having passed through the outer pickets, broke into the cadenced dirge called *The Dead March*, a piece normally played only for funeral processions. It was their previously agreed-upon way of expressing their disapproval of leaving the fort in this manner.

The commanding officer's lips tightened and angry red patches appeared briefly on his cheeks, but he said nothing, ignoring the sidelong glances sent his way by Rebekah and Margaret. It was John Kinzie who smoothed the moment over. He stood high in the saddle and looked back to where the troops, in column, were now marching through the outer pickets, then let his eyes sweep over the fort and beyond, across the river to where his trading post stood abandoned. It was filled with supplies of all kinds — goods there was no way for him to transport.

"Soon as we get out of sight," he said ruefully, "everything I have back there will be plundered. I'm losing a little fortune today."

"But perhaps gaining your life, Mr. Kinzie," the commander pointed out, then hastily added, "as well as helping to save ours."

"Let's hope so." Kinzie shrugged. He wasn't convinced.

9:02 A.M.

Distant shots startled the marchers and all eyes jerked toward their source out in the prairie, but it wasn't an attack. A half-dozen or more Potawatomies had broken from the middle of their line and were now whooping and laughing as they ran after the cows and beef cattle in the deep grass, shooting them indiscriminately. Even from this distance they could see five or six animals already down, their legs kicking the air in death throes.

Ensign Ronan frowned and, when he saw that Margaret Helm was looking, he spoke bitterly. "That will be our fate — to be shot down like beasts."

Captain Heald overheard and his nostrils flared. "Well, sir," he said, "are you afraid?"

The frustration and anger that had plagued the ensign for so long boiled up in him and spewed out in heated retort. "No!" he snapped. "I can march up to the enemy where you wouldn't dare show your face!"

Sparks of anger flashed in the commander's eyes but he kept it under control, knowing it wouldn't take much at this point to disrupt the entire column. The ensign's insolence he would tend to later, he promised himself; at the moment, he only wanted the brazen young officer away from his proximity. He glanced toward the rear where the first of the wagons was just emerging from the outer pickets.

"Mr. Ronan," he said levelly, "it strikes me that our wagons are not sufficiently guarded. "You may return there now and help defend them if need be. Dismissed!"

George Ronan was stunned. It was the ultimate ignominy, to be removed from the van and sent back with the women and children and sick. Not trusting himself to reply, even to acknowledge the command, he spun about and jogged away, almost blinded by the rage that filled him.[273]

9:03 A.M.

In his haven within the little hidden woodland playhouse north of the Chicago River, Quartermaster Sergeant William Griffith held his breath and strained to hear better. Faintly, ever so faintly, he could hear the piping of the fifers and tapping of the drums and he found himself wishing he were with the column which was now evidently evacuating the fort. A moment later came the sound of distant shots and in his mind's eye he saw the column being attacked by swarms of Indians and he hunkered in a dark corner in a fetal ball, thankful he was here, not there.

Several hundred yards away, at the Burns house, Sukey Corbin peered through a crack in the planking of the woodbox and could just barely make out the column moving southward from the fort, mostly hidden by the bulk of the fort itself. Little Henry and Wilma had been crying softly a few minutes ago with a combination of fright and hunger and she had reached into a pocket and drew out little dry biscuits for them to gnaw on. She, too, heard the fifes and drums and then the shots and she fought to resist the panic threatening to overwhelm her. She gathered the two children to her in the darkness of the woodbox and held them close, answering the question she knew they would ask.

"It's nothing, nothing," she whispered. "The soldiers are just testing their guns to make sure the powder is dry. There's nothing to be afraid of. We're safe here."

9:04 A.M.

The three wagons were well clear of the outer pickets now and, in a column of twos led by Thomas Burns, the Chicago Militia detachment was beginning to emerge. Inside the center wagon, Martha Lee pulled the flap of canvas open a little and saw her house just ahead on the left, close to where the river emptied into the lake. Her eyes filled with tears as she saw her twelve-year-old daughter riding beside the wagon, looking so grown up now, and she saw that Mary, too, was looking at their house. Then the girl turned in the saddle and waved behind and Martha knew she was waving at her father and brother, marching with the militia. She sniffled and let the flap drop back into place, holding little Sally close as she nursed her, wishing desperately that the five of them were even closer together right now and anywhere but here.

In the militia line, Charlie Lee returned his sister's wave and smiled in a strained way. "Mary seems to be doing just fine, Father," he said to the man marching beside him. "She's a good rider. I don't think there's anything to worry about." But again, as had happened a half-dozen times already since the march began, he thought of that day four months ago when the Winnebagoes had entered the Lee farmhouse up the river; the day he and John Kelso had luckily gotten away and Liberty White and the others had not been lucky at all.

The senior Lee smiled in return and nodded. "Yes, she'll be all right," he said, wishing he could believe his own words, "and so will your mother and Sally. We'll all be just fine."

9:05 A.M.

As the last of the militia passed through the outer pickets, the waiting Miamis put their horses into motion and fell in behind the column, moving very slowly and gradually letting the distance widen between themselves and the rear of the column until it had opened to a gap of thirty yards. This was the interval they held. The front escort was already riding along the lake shore on the road paralleling the beach and the van of the column was just reaching the mouth of the river and turning to follow the Miami advance guard.[274]

Topenebe's man, Keepoteh, who had been hunkered at the outer corner of the southeast blockhouse of the fort, now came quickly to his feet and loped back north along the pickets, arriving quickly at the large bateau. He freed the rope which bound the ungainly craft to shore and leaped aboard.

"We go now," he said.

The men shoved against the shore with their oars and when the craft was floating clear they took their places and began to row — the boatman Claude, Black Jim, Jean Baptiste Chandonnais and his assistant — and the sluggish craft swung around properly and began moving downstream. And sitting near the protective cover, well forward, Eleanor Kinzie watched ahead intently as they rounded the low promontory, turning south. When she was able to glimpse the column stretching from fort to lake along this section of river, she felt suddenly weak with relief. They had heard the shots and there had been no way of knowing, until now, if the column had been fired upon. Evidently it hadn't been and everything seemed all right. Yet the sense of dread was still heavy in her.

At almost this same moment, far at the front, William Wells reined his horse around and trotted smartly back along the column toward the rear to make certain the other half of the Miami escort had properly fallen in behind. Troops and civilians waved at him as he passed and he nodded back in a distracted way. He was dismayed to see that the column was stretching out so much, which could only weaken it. He called to Sergeant Hayes and the two privates driving the wagons to pick up the pace if they could, since it was from this point that the column was beginning to lag.

Reaching the rear, Wells grunted his approval at the interval the escort was keeping from the column and he rode with them for a short time, turning to look back, as they were doing, at the horde of Potawatomi women and children now streaming through the outer pickets and into the fort to begin plundering. The sight infuriated him and it was just one more omen to add to the growing list: the plundering was a foregone conclusion, but Indian courtesy predicated that it not occur until the last of the former occupants had passed out of sight. That they were so brashly streaming in while the rear of the column was still only a short distance away showed a contempt that was ominous.

9:07 A.M.

The forward troops were now moving at a brisk pace along the beach road, the sandy shore of Lake Michigan only thirty feet to their left. Several hundred yards ahead the first low sand hills of a ridge of dunes were appearing on the right, running along the flank of the lake sixty or seventy yards from the water.[275]

John Kinzie glanced to the right and saw that the pacing line of Potawatomies, though it had moved closer to the column as it progressed, was moving in a line which would soon have the dunes between them and the column and his heart beat a little faster. He would have felt much more comfortable if they had angled in enough so they were flanking the column at the foot of the dunes on the lake side, so they were in sight.

9:08 A.M.

William Wells, too, was watching the Indian line closely and what he was seeing now, from his vantage point at the rear, was causing his stomach muscles to tighten and the hair at his nape prickled. Far, far ahead, the advance portion of the Indian file with two hundred or more men was not only becoming hidden from the front part of the column, it was picking up speed behind the intervening dunes. The warriors first walked more swiftly and then, as fewer and fewer of the marchers could see them, they broke into a trot. The middle portion of the Indian line, also comprised of about two hundred warriors, was maintaining a steady pace, equaling that of the column's head; but now the rear portion of the Indian line — over a hundred warriors — began to lag, slowing to such extent that the whole Indian file was beginning to take the aspect of three distinct files with the gaps between them consistently widening.

With a word to the Miamis to keep their eye on the rear of the Potawatomi file, the Indian Agent spurred forward in a fast trot, moving up the right side of the column, his attention riveted on the Indian file. He had begun to suspect that the faster-moving advance of the Indian line was getting itself into position to set up an ambush from behind the larger dunes still a quarter-mile ahead.

William Wells was blinking rapidly.

9:11 A.M.

The advance of the Indian file was now out of sight of John Kinzie and the officers, and the middle of that Indian line was still keeping pace and gradually disappearing from view behind the intervening dunes. But now the trader saw what Wells had seen — the rear portion of the Indian line slowing, falling back and even beginning to move in somewhat toward the road; moving in, he thought grimly, to a point from which they could quickly cut off the column's retreat, if it came to that.

The sound of the horse's hooves brought Kinzie's gaze around and he saw the Indian Agent coming on rapidly from the rear. Wells pulled up momentarily beside Kinzie and as their eyes met, a message passed between them that said more than words could convey. In that instant John Kinzie became convinced that an ambush was being prepared ahead.

"You've seen the Indian line splitting?" Wells murmured, his voice so low that none of the others could hear him. At the trader's nod, he went on. "Those in front, behind the hills," he motioned toward the much larger dunes ahead on their right, "are running far ahead. I think they mean to surround us and cut us off. Don't say anything yet. Let me move up and check it out. Question now is, if true, what's to be done?"

Kinzie's expression was bleak. "The only thing possible," he said. "Pull together and defend ourselves as best we can."[276]

9:12 A.M.

At the southern edge of the Frog Creek Indian encampment closer to Fort Dearborn, Black Partridge and Topenebe stood together watching the tableau being played out before them — the American column stretched out along the beach road, its head moving behind the dunes, no sign of alarm visible. The Indian file was splitting into three — those far ahead under Nescotnemeg, now hidden entirely from the Americans, sprinting ahead at full run, those under Siggenauk in the middle angling in more quickly now to the foot of the dunes between them and the Americans, and those under Sunawewone closing in behind.

"I had hoped," Black Partridge said resignedly to his friend, "that in the end wisdom would have prevailed; that our warriors would have reconsidered and been content with having the Americans gone and with the plunder that is already theirs." His voice became sadder. "I'm afraid it is not to be."

"No," Topenebe echoed, no less soberly, "it is not to be. Those who are our friends — Shawneeawkee, others — may now be hurt. Whatever we can do to help them, we must do now."

The two chiefs looked at one another and nodded, then separated. Black Partridge, with three of his warriors, moved off toward the rear of the Indian line, angling toward the distant wagons. Topenebe summoned two of his young men.

"Run to the mouth of the river," he told them. "If it is not too late, stop the boat that is leaving, which carries the family of Shawneeawkee. Tell

Keepoteh, who is with them, to hold the boat there and keep those aboard from harm until I send word what he is to do."

The runners nodded and raced off.

9:15 A.M.

"What have you seen ahead, Keah Keakah?" Wells asked as he pulled his horse up beside the subchief.

The Miami looked at him and shrugged. "Nothing to cause fear that the eyes see," he replied, "only that which the heart feels. Something is not right."

Wells grunted in agreement and explained what was happening with the Indian line. He did not need to spell it out for Keah Keakah. "I will ride with you here a few minutes longer," he told the Miami subchief. "It may be that I have become a little sparrow, afraid of the hawk's shadow. But if the danger is real, do you still mean to get yourself apart from it?"

Keah Keakah looked at him with level gaze. "Apekonit has never before feared shadows. I do not believe he does so now. What will we do? When you are carrying a pot of honey and you are accosted by a big bear, it is wisdom to set the honey down and quickly move away from it."

9:16 A.M.

Because of the large sandbar that blocked most of the river's mouth, the Kinzie bateau was forced to move within a few yards of the shore on their right to pass out into the lake. Along the beach road two hundred yards or more ahead of them they could see the rear Miami escort and a portion of the rear of the column moving steadily.

"The little wind," grunted the boatman, Claude, "is good for us. It blows from the north and west. When we are out there," he dipped his head toward the lake, "we can let our hungry little sail fill its belly with wind." He laughed.

Some of the others joined in the laughter, but not Eleanor. She sat well forward, holding the sleeping two-year-old Robert in her arms with Ellen, seven-and-a-half, beside her. On the small bench seat in front of her sat Josette Beaubien, her arm loosely around the waist of five-year-old Maria. Nine-year-old John H. was in the bow, staring down through the clear water at the sand bar passing just beneath the keel.

The oppressive apprehension still mantled Eleanor — a dread she could not shake off and, despite the word games she had begun playing with the children and the laughter in which she joined at the clever little rhymes Josette was reciting at intervals, she was worried. She remembered vividly her years living with the Senecas in the household of Cornplanter and she could read the signs well when the Indians were preparing to attack. These were the signs she had seen here in the past few days and once again, as she had a dozen times before, she mentally berated Captain Heald for the stupidity of giving away all excess provisions and supplies, of destroying arms and ammunition, of leaving a fortress in which the whole population would have been perfectly secure for weeks or even months against concerted attack. The military mind remained an enigma to her and she could not understand blind obedience to the command of an officer hundreds of miles away who had never been here and who could not know or understand the situation here.

Now, because of such an order, two of the dearest people in her life — her husband and her eldest daughter — could be in real jeopardy at this moment and she wished again that John and Margaret were aboard this bateau with them.

"Mother!" It was young John. "There are two Indians coming."

The two warriors were approaching them on shore at a hard run and immediately Keepoteh called to the rowers to halt and stood up. He recognized the Potawatomies from his own village.

"Keepoteh," one of them called as they reached the shore and came to a stop, "Chief Topenebe sends us. The boat is to come ashore here and stay until he sends further word. We will help in the protection of those aboard."

"They need more protection? There is trouble?"

"Not yet, but soon."

As the bateau ground ashore they leaped aboard and told Keepoteh of the movement of the Indians to surround and ambush and, though they spoke in the Potawatomi, Eleanor understood enough to become deeply afraid. She held Robert more tightly and put her arm around Ellen, pulling her close. Chandonnais, Claude and Josette, all of whom understood the language well, had paled. Black Jim, understanding only that fear had come aboard, unconsciously put his hand to the knife at his belt, ready to protect the Kinzies with his life, if need be.

When the warriors had finished, Keepoteh addressed Eleanor in English. "You need have no fear here. You are under our protection, which is Topenebe's, and none will harm you. As for the Shawneeawkee and your daughter, Topenebe and Black Partridge will try to help them if they can. All now rests in the hands of Moneto."

9:22 A.M.

Two minutes ago William Wells had left the vanguard Miami escort, angling ahead of them and to the right. Now, a quarter-mile in advance and at the foot of the dunes, he leaped from his horse, tied the reins to a branch and scrambled up the loose sand to the summit. Slowly, carefully, he raised his head to peer over the top and felt his pulse quicken as he saw scores of Indians moving quickly into position toward him, scrambling up the steep sides of the dunes, rifles in hand, to position themselves, as far as he could see to the rear, for ambushing the column at this ideal spot where the dunes pushed in close to the road.

Instantly Wells ducked down and plunged back to his horse. In a moment he was galloping toward the Miami escort.

9:24 A.M.

Nescotnemeg, lying in hiding with his warriors atop the dunes, was not pleased. Directly below them was the road, within easy and accurate rifle shot, where the Americans would pass, but now there was some question as to whether the column would ever reach this point. The chief had been among the first to reach the top and he had immediately seen the disturbed sand on the other side and the *cut-ta-ho-tha*, Apekonit, riding at full tilt back toward the column. He had continued to watch as the man whose face was painted black had stopped and talked with the escort of Miamis. Then he had left them and thundered back toward the distant column headed this way.

Now that Miami escort had come to this point, their eyes searching the tops of the dunes. As they came opposite his concealment, Nescotnemeg came to his feet and stepped into clear view. Twenty or thirty of his warriors did so, too, ready for whatever command he would give them. Keah Keakah saw them immediately, recognized Nescotnemeg and rode to the foot of the dune beneath him.

"Nescotnemeg!" His call was filled with anger. "I am much astonished at your conduct. You have been treacherous with these people. You promised to conduct them safely through. You have deceived them and us and now you are about to murder them in cold blood. Let me advise you to beware. You know not what evil the deed shall bring upon you. You may, by and by, hear your wives and children cry and you will not be able to assist them. Potawatomi, beware!"

Nescotnemeg was silent for a moment and then he spoke with harsh tone. "The Potawatomi do not take advice from the Miamis." He pointed toward the southeast. "Go. Consider yourselves lucky that what is in store for the Americans is not also in store for you. Do not be foolish enough to even think of raising your weapons against us. Be gone!"

Keah Keakah hesitated, then wheeled his horse around and returned to his men, who had heard the exchange. In a moment all fourteen were galloping down the road to the south, away from the column. Nescotnemeg smiled coldly and shouted an order. Immediately his ambush party began moving back to reach the Americans where Siggenauk was located. With the warning from Apekonit, the Americans would surely come no farther down the road and the conflict would take place at Siggenauk's line.

9:25 A.M.

The column had stretched out even more now, the gap between the rear of the marching regulars and the lead wagon driven by Sergeant Hayes having increased to four or five hundred yards.[277] The only change in its order involved the oldest person on the march — a seventy-year-old militiaman known by most simply as Henry.[278] A bit addled, he had fumed at the slow pace with the rest of the militia following the ox-drawn wagons, upset over the possibility that the regular troops would engage the Indians while the militia would be left with nothing to do. Despite his years, he had trotted ahead and finally fallen in with the rear of the regular troops.

Captain Heald, watching ahead, suddenly pointed and spoke to Rebekah. "Look. Your uncle has seen something ahead of him that has bothered him. There's something wrong."

Some six hundred yards in front of them, William Wells was in full gallop. He had yanked his hat off and was now waving it in a broad circle in the air over his head. Rebekah understood the signal he was making and she paled.

"Oh, my Lord," she said in a rising voice, "we're surrounded by Indians!"

Instantly the commander's hand went up and he called a halt, shouting back an order for the rear to close up.

9:26 A.M.

William Wells raced his horse at a flat-out gallop until it seemed he wouldn't be able to stop before colliding with the troops, but he did. Even as he was arriving, Rebekah caught a glimpse of the heads of several Indians popping up atop the dunes, then ducking back down out of sight.

"They're up there!" she cried, pointing. "Indians! I saw them!"

Wells, still astride the excitedly prancing horse, kept it turning in small circles as he reported to the commanding officer what he saw ahead. "They've got us locked in, front and back," he added. He pointed in the direction from which he had just come. "There's a more protected place a few hundred yards, there, much more suitable for making a stand. I advise we get there at once. There are some sand ridges we ought to get in behind where we can stand half up and not be seen."

His jaw dropped when he saw Captain Heald shake his head and then heard his reply.

"No. We're going to charge them."

9:27 A.M.

"All wagons right up against the lake!" Captain Heald thundered. "Militia into place between wagons and dunes!"

The orders were relayed swiftly, Sergeant Holt at the rear of the regulars bellowing the word to the wagons where the leading driver, Sergeant Hayes, waved in acknowledgment and relayed the order to the wagons and militia behind him. Immediately the whips were laid onto the oxen in cracking, painful blows and the animals bellowed and lurched toward the water's edge until becoming bogged down in loose sand and unable to move farther. The militiamen, under Sergeant Burns's direction, ran to place themselves as defenders between the wagons and the Indians. A great fear, almost panic, was rising and cries of the women and children were lifted.

The fear intensified as the thirteen mounted Miamis in the rear escort immediatey turned their horses and angled out into the prairie, away from the wagons and militia.

"*Bastards!*" someone among the militia shrieked after them, but the cry was lost in the rising tumult and the Miamis continued away, making no move of hostility toward the Potawatomies under Sunawewone, now creeping low through the deep prairie grasses toward the Americans.

The bunched rear and front of the column were now separated by at least two hundred yards, with a slight elevation between them. At the van, Nathan Heald was still barking out his orders: "Check bayonets! Prepare for charge. Spread out the line — two ranks. Charge on the order." He spun around and shoved Salienne, the young interpreter, out of his way. "Get away, boy! Get back to the wagons!"

The boy sprinted off and Heald ran to Rebekah's horse. "Get out of here," he said tightly. "You get back to the wagons, too. *Now!*"

Rebekah's beautifully muscled bay mare shied at the excitement and partially reared, but the rider kept her saddle and spurred away. Instead of galloping to the wagons, however, she headed for her uncle, now twenty yards distant, his legs gripping his horse tightly as he used both hands to ready his weapons. He saw her coming and waved her off.

"Go on!" he cried. "Back to the wagons! Go!"

She passed him, eyes wide and mouth grimly shut, heading in the direction ordered, her fear becoming a vile taste in her mouth. Vaguely she noted that the boy, Salienne, instead of running to the wagons, had now veered to the left and was running full tilt out onto the prairie to join the approaching Indians.[279]

Sergeant Isaac Holt, too, was trying to get his wife to turn her horse around and gallop back to the wagons. Jane refused, unless he accompanied her, pointing out that the wagons were going to need protection, too. In his fear for her safety he gave in and ran alongside the horse toward the wagons, certain in his own mind that in running back like this at the verge of a charge he was guilty of desertion.

Behind them, Lieutenant Helm was also giving urgent directions to his wife. "Margaret, you've got to get out of here!" He pointed to the fleeing commander's wife. "Follow her. Go on — you've *got* to get to the wagons."

Margaret nodded and pulled away a dozen yards or so, but then stopped. She looked for her stepfather, but John Kinzie, still astride his horse, was around at the front of the line talking urgently with Captain Heald, gesticulating and pointing toward the wagons, evidently urging that instead of a charge, the troops fall back to the wagons to reunite their entire force and form better protection for everyone. And Captain Heald was shaking his head with every word the trader spoke.

Wells spurred his horse up to them and found Captain Heald now ordering Kinzie to go back to the wagons to help the women and children. Wells joined the conversation, bringing it back to the matter of the proposed charge, backing Kinzie's idea, knowing that after an initial assault against a united force, the Indians would almost certainly fall back and eventually gather up their plunder and abandon the fight. It was not the Indians' way to win a fight through attrition — no warrior was considered expendable. The Indian Agent's stomach was churning at the thought of the captain and his lieutenant leading a direct charge of only a few over forty men into the teeth of an enemy at least three or four hundred strong right here and with more coming, and with cover to hide behind to begin with. That was insanity! The thought struck him then that the soldiers each had only twenty-five charges of ammunition — a pitifully inadequate amount with which to launch a charge. The commander's idea was to make the initial charge up one side of the dunes and down the other side. He hadn't got around to thinking yet what he would do then.

Matters seemed to be moving in slow motion, with startling, unreal clarity.

9:29 A.M.

"*Charge!*"

The word ripped out of Captain Heald's mouth explosively as he held his sword high in the air. Ten yards away Lieutenant Helm, also with sword raised, repeated the command and, following his commander's lead, sprinted forward, followed by the two ranks of troops. William Wells, still mounted and far to the left, jabbed his heels into his horse's flanks and started up the steep sandy slope. At the far right of the first rank was the septuagenarian militiaman close to John Kinzie who, rifle in hand but not held at ready, sat his horse not more than ten yards to the right of Helm and just beyond the outermost troops. He was alert but calm, watching what was occurring but not participating.

The troops shrieked incoherently as they floundered ankle-deep in sand up the dune. They had no more than reached the crest when the first shots broke out, fired from the Indians beyond them on the dune and from Siggenauk's principal position, hidden in a nearby skirt of pine woods. Immediately there was an American casualty — the seventy-year-old militiaman. He was slammed backward and rolled all the way down the slope to a stop at the bottom close to Kinzie. The trader could see the blood oozing from the small round hole in the left center of the old man's forehead.[280] Two or three other soldiers had fallen, too, of which at least one was trying to regain his feet.

Corporal Walter Jordan, brandishing his rifle and ready to fire instantly upon the command being given, paused momentarily at the crest as the enemy firing broke out. He felt a slight tug at the ensign's hat that had been given to him by George Ronan and the fine white plumes spun to the ground, neatly clipped from the hat by a ball. He jerked the hat from his head, tossed it aside and plunged on. Some Indians were now becoming visible, breaking from cover.

"Fire!"

The command was echoed and reechoed and a ragged barrage broke out. A couple of Indians fell, but none stayed down. The first rank of regulars paused to reload and the second swept past them, still in their charge, and now the hoarse voice of Siggenauk was heard barking a command and the line of Indians crouched in the sand before the troops rose and broke, split to one side or the other and then began immediately regrouping at the flanks of the little force.

Wells knew that there was nothing left to do now but press on. Far out on the prairie there was an isolated knoll. If they could get there, they could take cover in the tall grass and fire in all directions at approaching enemies. He knew they must get there if there was to be any hope of survival and he roared "Charge them!" over and again. Captain Heald looked at the knoll Wells was pointing to and instantly realized the imperative of getting there and he took up Wells's cry, echoed by Helm.

Another volley came from the troops and then the shooting became very general. Lieutenant Helm took careful aim at an Indian, fired and saw him fall and was confident he'd killed or badly wounded him. Soldier after soldier fell and still the charge continued, though slowed considerably, gradually moving down the west side of the sandy slope, plunging toward the prairie beyond.

Confused, frightened, not knowing what else to do, Margaret caught a glimpse of her stepfather riding up a lower portion of the sandy slope well to the right, a hundred yards distant or more, and she put her horse into motion after him. When she got to where he had been, he was gone, but she could see him slightly farther ahead over the crest of this low hill, still to the right of the fighting troops and within a dozen yards or so of her husband. At this instant a roar of gunfire and cries from behind and toward the lake reached her and she jerked around in her saddle. A horde of Indians was converging on the militia and wagons, having burst from cover in the long grasses at the first volley of the regular troops at the dune. And, seeing them, Margaret felt her fear fall away and a calmness settle in her. I will die today, she thought. All of us are going to die today. The thought did not particularly disturb her. She murmured a brief prayer, took a final look toward her stepfather and husband and then put her prancing horse into motion toward the wagons.

At the slight elevation that had separated the wagons from the van at the outbreak, Rebekah Heald also heard the shrieking and gunfire. Her horse began to buck and jerk about and it was only with difficulty that she was able to bring the bay mare under control.

The charge of the Indians toward the wagons was petrifying. Over a hundred war-painted savages, armed mostly with tomahawks, war clubs and knives and led by the garishly painted Sunawewone had, within moments of the first volley, effectively cut off any retreat to the fort, had such been contemplated. Other Indians — part from Nescotnemeg's group and part of Siggenauk's, broken and scattered by the charge — cut in from the other direction, south of the wagons. In a moment more the whole bunched group of wagons and militia had become the core of a great semicircle of advancing Indians.

The first faintly heard shots brought Eleanor Kinzie to her feet in the bateau. She handed two-year-old Robert to Josette and stood high on her seat to see what was occurring. She couldn't see much. The action was more than a mile away, but puffs of smoke were rising near the dunes and the faint shrieks from the Indians and screams from women and cries from injured men touched her ears. She froze, a chilling fear momentarily numbing her, and then she sank slowly to the seat and began shaking uncontrollably, certain she would never see her husband and eldest child again.[281]

At the Burns house across the river upstream from the fort, Sukey Corbin heard the firing, knew instantly what it was and held her two children close against her in the darkness of the woodbox, sobbing uncontrollably. Several hundred yards away, in the woodland playhouse, Sergeant Griffith heard the shots, too, and knew their significance. He was trembling and wished desperately he had a drink of whiskey.

9:30 A.M.

Captain Heald continued urging his men on down the slope on the west side of the dune, finally finding better footing as they neared the bottom where grass was growing. Less than two minutes had passed since the charge began, yet already about fifteen of his regulars had been killed. He felt a jolt in his lower left arm and glanced at it in time to see the first spurt of blood from where a ball had passed through. Strangely, it didn't hurt and though his arm felt logy, it was still functioning.

Corporal Walter Jordan, only a few yards away, heard the angry buzz of a ball as it struck the epaulet on the left shoulder of the ensign's coat he was wearing, neatly snipping it off without harming him. With the feathers on his hat earlier shot away, the weird thought struck him that the Indians were trying to get his uniform piece by piece and he laughed aloud, crazily. Then reaction struck him and he dropped to the ground, scrambling away with sword in hand and getting separated from the others.

Astride his horse forty yards away, William Wells watched as the little company of men reached the grasses and began following their commander out into the prairie toward the knoll. He doubted the Indians would expose themselves to follow and so now he wheeled his horse about and started toward the wagons, where he assumed Rebekah had gone. Even as he started a ball from somewhere grazed his horse's hip, causing it to leap wildly and scream in pain, but he brought the gelding under control and continued. All three of his weapons were empty and now he reloaded as he rode — a feat few men could do so well as he.

Lifting his head above the grass, Corporal Jordan saw his Fort Wayne companion moving away toward the wagons and decided he'd better stay with him as best he could. He began to follow, keeping himself hidden as much as possible and therefore traveling much slower than Wells.

9:31 A.M.

The militia could not reload so rapidly as Wells, even under conditions far more ideal for it. Thus, after their initial volley at the encircling Indians rushing in on them — during which only a few Indians were shot — the action became hand-to-hand in a desperate struggle, the Indians sweeping around the beach side, even wading in the water in an effort to get at the wagons.

Cicely, Rebekah's slave, thrust her little Benjamin into a corner of the wagon and leaped out the back with a sword in her hand. She turned and ran toward where the other women outside — Tess Russell, Victoria Corbin, Emmaline Clark and Sarah Neads — stood in a pitiful line, trying to shield the children's wagon with their bodies. Victoria, reaching across her vastly swollen belly, jerked from its sheath the sword her husband,

Phelim, had given her and stood ready with it. Cicely raced up and took a position near her. Close by, screaming in her panic, twelve-year-old Mary Lee had dropped the reins of her horse and gripped the pommel with one hand, the animal's mane with the other as the horse leaped and bounded this way and that, eyes bulging, mouth flecked with foam. Had she not been tied in, certainly she would have been thrown by now.

Sergeant Thomas Burns had given his men the order to fire and immediately after the volley had clashed with the rush of Indians. Rifle butts, tomahawks, bayonets, war clubs, knives — all were being swung in wild abandon, striking, parrying, thrusting. Burns felt his bayonet plunge through the upper arm of an Indian and he gloated in the scream that erupted from the man's mouth, but then the rifle was jerked from his grasp and he was weaponless. He looked around wildly, trying to find a rifle that had fallen. A bare arm gripped him about the neck and he reached up and grasped the hand, jerked a finger backwards and broke it, at the same time breaking the grip. Another Indian with upraised tomahawk lunged at him and he dove beneath the strike and grappled with him, but the weapon continued down behind him and slammed into his back just above the hip. He gasped, lost his hold and staggered away, the tomahawk still embedded in him. Another Indian surged by, striking at him with a war club in passing, catching him on the shoulder and crushing both shoulder joint and clavicle. He reeled and never even saw the source of the tomahawk blow that caught him on the right side of the stomach just below the rib cage and plunged deeply into his body. He fell then, writhing in his agony, and was passed over as the battle surged about him.

Indians from Nescotnemeg's contingent now raced up on the scene from the south, their rifles as yet unfired. They stopped and fired generally toward the wagons and Rebekah Heald, astride her horse, was in the line of fire. In less than ten seconds she was struck by three different balls, all in the arms and hands, painfully, but not too seriously, she thought, and she was still in control of one arm and hand. When her horse reared, she was able to hold on and remain seated until the mare settled down. Her left hand was useless, a ball having broken one of the bones of her lower arm. The other injuries were merely flesh wounds. Her mind was amazingly clear and she thought, It is my horse they are after and they are taking great care not to hit her. Almost automatically with the thought she crouched lower in the saddle and no more shots came her way.

One of the balls from the volley that struck her caught Tess Russell in the temple, killing her instantly. Emmaline Clark was seriously wounded in the stomach by another. Yet another also slammed into the stomach of Mary Lee and the twelve-year-old girl screamed and pitched forward and then hung down the side of her horse as it ran back and forth, dangling from the ropes that held her.

9:32 A.M.

Three or four hundred yards away, some twenty yards out into the prairie but still not safe from the firing, Nathan Heald and Linai Helm continued to urge their men toward the distant knoll. Private James Corbin, running along with them, thought of his wife and children in hiding at the Burns house and thanked the Providence that had led him to hide them there rather than let them accompany the wagons, wishing immediately after that thought that they were all safely home in Virginia. He was limping badly, a ball having gone through his heel, striking no bones but tearing away a large piece of flesh. A thrown tomahawk that had come out of nowhere as they had plunged down the west side of the dune had struck him in the shoulder, sticking there for a moment and then falling out as he continued running. Now two more balls caught him simultaneously as he ran, one in the fleshy part of the inner thigh, just barely missing his genitals, the other punching a hole through his right buttock. He fell and rolled over, losing his rifle, but regained his feet and staggered on with the troops.

Corporal Jordan, still a considerable distance from the wagons he was heading for and still squirming through the grass, thought he was probably safe enough now to come to crouch as he continued to follow William Wells. He no sooner raised himself, however, than a ball smashed into the hilt of the sword George Ronan had given him. It shattered the haft, knocking the weapon out of his grip and badly numbing his hand, but otherwise not hurting him. Now he was weaponless and he crouched even lower as he continued toward the wagons.

Some distance away, approaching the wagons at a run beside his wife's mount and appalled at the conflict occurring there, Sergeant Holt called to Jane to stop and she reined in her horse. He stood gasping beside the animal, trying to think of where to send her where she would be safe. He didn't have time. A rifle ball caught him in the neck and felled him. Instantly Jane leaped out of the saddle, having presence of mind enough to keep a tight grip on the reins. She kneeled over him, weeping, kissing his closed eyes, but then he stirred and the eyes opened.

"I'm gone," he told her. "You've got to get away, Jane. Take my sword. Use it. Don't let them take you." His eyes closed and he fell back.

Jane Holt thrust her horror aside, slid the sword from her husband's scabbard and remounted the horse with the weapon in her hand. Several Indians were racing toward her afoot and she kicked the horse into a run. One of the warriors cut her off and she slashed the sword at him, clipping off his queue as neatly as if she had tried to do just that. The warrior leaped back and his companions laughed aloud and continued to chase her. The horse had almost no place to go without running into more Indians and time after time hands reached out to pull her down and were snatched back quickly out of the whistling arc of her sword.

Fifty yards away Sergeant Holt's eyelids fluttered open again and he rolled over with a groan. Slowly he came to hands and knees and began to crawl toward the lake, only sixty feet away. He had covered a quarter the distance when a warrior rushed up, buried his tomahawk in the back of his head and expertly removed the scalp. This time Sergeant Isaac Holt was dead.

His wife, still slashing at the Indians, now had twenty or thirty of them chasing her, laughing uproariously at her antics to escape, grunting approvingly at her courage, calling to one another not to kill her, that she was Epiconyare — the Brave One. They struck at her only with the butt ends of their guns and she hacked furiously at the weapons as they were thrust at her. She managed to break loose and galloped out onto the prairie, but again she was cut off by others coming from that direction.

At last, as she thrust and chopped at three who were grasping at the reins and stirrups, another leaped high from behind and caught her around the neck, dragging her from the saddle. Several of the warriors had been cut rather severely by her slashings; yet, now that she was in their power, they only regarded her with admiration and took her away with them unharmed toward the Frog Creek encampment.[282]

9:33 A.M.

The fight was far from over.

At the wagons, the seven sick privates, two of them wagon drivers, staggered and fell out, trying to protect themselves. They were immediately overwhelmed by Indians, five of them killed within seconds and the remaining two badly wounded — John Fury and Thomas Poindexter.

Around them the hand-to-hand combat continued, interspersed with shots being fired, especially as more of Nescotnemeg's men reached the scene. One of these was Chief Naunongee of the Calumet River village. He arrived just in time to see a soldier with bayoneted rifle leap from the driver's seat of the baggage wagon. The Potawatomi chief threw his rifle to his shoulder and shot at him. The soldier staggered as the ball passed through his body but he did not fall. He stood, weaving, seemingly dazed. Naunongee rushed forward with a grating shriek, tossing his rifle aside and drawing his tomahawk to strike and scalp.

Sergeant Otho Hayes, grievously wounded by the ball that had passed through his lung, waited until the tomahawk wielding Indian was very close and then brought his rifle up in a strong jab. The bayonet caught Naunongee in the center of the chest and, with the chief's own momentum added to the thrust, plunged through his sternum, nicked his heart, tore through the edge of a vertebra and emerged from his back by two inches or more, the barrel of the gun flush against the chief's chest. Hayes tried to jerk the bayonet free but it was tightly wedged and, as he tried, the impaled Naunongee brought his tomahawk around and drove it well into the sergeant's head. They fell together. Some of Naunongee's warriors rushed up, scalped Hayes and only with difficulty managed to free the bayonet from their chief's chest. Unlike Hayes, Naunongee was still alive and they carried him to one side and lay him down.[283]

The furious action in the area of the wagons increased. Everyone, it seemed, was engaged simultaneously. The clash of swords, thuds of war clubs and tomahawks, screams and cries and shrieks of men, women, children and horses, punctuated by scattered shooting still occurring, created a din of hideous proportions. At the onset the horse of Isaac van Voorhis was shot out from under him and he fell with it, rolled free uninjured and was getting to his feet when a rifle ball passed through the calf of his leg and he fell again. The twenty-two-year-old surgeon struggled to his feet, staring fearfully at the incredible melee around him.

Not far from him, Ensign George Ronan was knocked to the ground with a ball in his shoulder. He came to his feet, drawing his sword, and stood crouched and ready as three Indians circled him, tomahawks in hand, looking for an opening. Twice they lunged in and twice he parried effectively, cutting one of them badly on the upper arm, driving his blade through the lower arm of another. A tomahawk blow from somewhere caught him in the upper right side of his back, plunging in deeply, and he fell, wrenching free and striking his assailant a minor wound in the leg in the process. In an instant he was back on his feet again, still holding his attackers at bay.

The black slave Cicely held her sword as if it were a club and swung it in great whistling sweeps that were impressive but not at all effective and in a moment one of the warriors leaped inside the arc of her swing and thrust his spear deeply into her breast. She staggered back, took another feeble swing with the sword and then dropped first to her knees, then sprawled dead on her side.[284]

Victoria Corbin was far more effective. Despite the fact that the Indians made motions to her to lay down her sword and she would not be harmed, she held them at bay, living up to her vow never to be taken alive, fighting with a demonical passion that was phenomenal considering her advanced pregnancy. Time after time she drew blood from the small ring of attackers around her, but time after time she, too, was wounded, cut and stabbed until she and her clothing and the ground about her was stained considerably with her blood. At one point she shrilled, "I won't let them take me, Phelim!" and fought with even greater fury. But the odds were too much and a well-swung tomahawk caught her from behind at the base of the neck, all but severing her spine, and she fell dead.

Close to the wagons, though not close to one another, the horses of Rebekah Heald and Margaret Helm became even harder to control and leaped and ran about violently. The lieutenant's wife managed to get hers under control first and the animal stopped, eyes bulging and sides heaving. A man staggered toward her, his face etched with terror, and she saw that it was young Doctor Van Voorhis.

"Do you . . ." he gasped and began again, ". . . do you think they'll kill us? I'm badly wounded, but I don't think it's mortal. Suppose we offered them money — a reward for not killing us. Do you think they'd accept?"

Margaret, who had already made up her mind to the fact that she was going to be killed, looked down at the young man and replied disparagingly. "Doctor Van Voorhis, let's not waste the few moments we have left with vain hopes. There is *no* hope! In a few minutes we'll all appear before the bar of God, so prepare for it!"

Van Voorhis stepped back, his fear increased by her fatalism. "I *can't* die! I'm not *fit* to die . . ." The words tumbled out, laced with panic. "I need time to prepare . . . death is awful!"

The contempt in Margaret's voice was clear as she pointed to one side where, not very far from them, George Ronan, still with bloodied sword in hand and still fighting with grim savagery, was down on one knee and obviously weakening rapidly. His back was coated with blood and he had suffered several other wounds in addition to the tomahawk blow.

"Look at *him!*" she said. "At least he's dying like a soldier!"

The young surgeon's lips trembled and he shook his head. "Yes, but . . . but he's not afraid of what's ahead. He's an unbeliever!"

Margaret's horse, strength recovered somewhat with the brief respite, abruptly plunged away and she clung to the saddle desperately as a flurry of shots broke out from more newly arrived Indians. She hardly felt the ball that nicked her ankle and did not even see that Dr. Van Voorhis had just fallen with a tomahawk in his brain.[285]

The horse carrying the dangling form of little Mary Lee was still plunging about violently, but now a large powerful Indian ran after it and finally managed to grasp the bit and bring the animal under control. It was Black Partridge and he swiftly used his knife to cut the cords that bound the girl to the saddle. He gently lay her on the ground.

"My . . . my own special chief," she murmured.

He had thought her dead from the terrible stomach wound from which she had bled profusely, but her eyes had fluttered open and she tried to smile as she repeated the phrase. Then her eyes closed again and her chest heaved and she groaned with the pain of breathing. There was no doubt that she was dying. Steeling himself, Black Partridge placed the tip of his knife against her chest and then thrust the blade deep into her heart. She stiffened and then relaxed in death.[286]

Rebekah Heald was momentarily motionless on her horse, the frenzied action swirling about her and filling her with the sense that this was all some peculiar dream, made more believable as a nightmare because even though she could see the blood seeping from her own wounds, there was no element of pain at all. In one small recess of her mind she was sure she was no longer being shot at because the Indians did not want to risk hitting her magnificent mare which they greatly coveted. She glanced to her right and saw Ensign Ronan down on both knees now, but still slashing dangerously with his sword and parrying blows coming his way. A war club collided with the sword and snapped the blade in two, sending the end piece spinning away, reflecting the sunlight in a glittering arc. Ronan looked at the short piece of blade in his grasp, barked out an ironic laughter and threw it at an Indian, who dodged out of the way. Another Indian closed behind him and buried his tomahawk in the back of the ensign's neck, entirely severing his spine. Seeing him fall, Rebekah wheeled her horse about in the other direction and caught a glimpse through the pall of smoke of John Kinzie approaching and she moved toward him.[287]

9:34 A.M.

Angling in toward the wagons from a different direction, William Wells had just completed reloading his rifle and both pistols, as he had done thrice before. So far as he could tell, he had already killed seven Indians. At least they had gone down with his shots and Wells knew his shots were seldom less than fatal. In the distance ahead he saw his niece, Rebekah, moving along with almost nonchalant slowness on her horse, picking her way through the incredible action that was occurring, and he moved to intercept her. He caught a glimpse of John Kinzie on his horse in the distance, beckoning him, and he raised his arm in acknowledgment. At that moment he was nearly knocked from the saddle by a tremendous blow to his breast. He managed to remain in his seat and looked down at his chest. His heavy shirt had a round hole in it, blood already staining the edges and running down inside. Almost immediately blood began seeping from his nose and mouth, slightly foamy and turning blackish as it channeled through the paint, and he knew the ball had gone through his lung.

9:35 A.M.

Moving with the surviving troops on the prairie toward the little knoll, Lieutenant Helm felt a jolt at his right side and found that a rifle ball had gone through his coat pocket, struck the pistol in his belt and then fell, spent, in the lining of his coat. Even as he counted his blessings for this fortunate turn of fate, another ball struck him in the right heel. The injury was quite painful, but not serious. He limped on, following the troops that had flowed past him. He caught a glimpse of Captain Heald, ten yards away, favoring his injured arm. Abruptly the commanding officer gave a cry and went down and Helm rushed to his side. A ball had struck the captain in his hip and he was holding his hand over the wound and grimacing. Helm helped him to his feet and they moved on toward the knoll.[288]

9:36 A.M.

John Kinzie had been approaching the wild affray at the wagon area on his horse, still holding his unfired rifle with one hand. In the midst of the melee he could see Rebekah Heald on her horse, moving slowly toward him and, far to the right and closer to the lake, his stepdaughter, Margaret, astride her horse, moving in confused little circles. Considerably beyond her, angling in from the left, was William Wells on his horse. Immediately Kinzie had stood high in his stirrups and waved an arm, beckoning Wells toward him so they could work together in whatever had to be done to help the people at the wagons. He had seen Wells wave in response and then suddenly jolt in the saddle and only barely manage to retain his seat and he knew the Indian Agent had been hit. As yet, Rebekah had not caught a glimpse of her uncle and was still riding toward Kinzie.

Wells had by this time recovered his balance and straightened. Supposing his wound was not too bad and that the Indian Agent would see to his niece, Kinzie moved toward his stepdaughter, his move taking him directly toward the pitched battle occurring at the wagons, closer to the lake. In the cacophony rising around him he heard nothing come close, but unexpectedly a body launched into him from behind, gripping him tightly about the chest, pinning both arms and dragging him from the horse to the ground. He struggled vigorously for a moment until he realized his assailant was not fighting him, but merely gripping him and growling, "Stop fighting me, Shawneeawkee! Stop fighting me!" He relaxed and saw that it was Siggenauk, the chief of the Milwaukee Potawatomies, his face painted fearsomely. Three warriors were with him, watching uneasily but not interfering. When a cluster of other warriors moved up, evidently intent on being in on the kill of Kinzie, Siggenauk's warriors warned them away. When they would not at first go, there was a bit of scuffling. Kinzie heard his name repeated a number of times and then Siggenauk's men prevailed and the intruders quickly left.

Now Siggenauk released Kinzie, took the rifle from his grip and sniffed the end of the barrel, nodding when his nose told him the weapon had not been fired. He helped the trader to his feet and returned the gun to him. "You have been wise not to fight, Shawneeawkee," he said. "None who know you will harm you if not harmed by you. But do not go there!" He pointed in the direction of the wagons, where Kinzie had been heading, and where the fighting was still heavy. "You might not be recognized in the excitement and you would be dead before they knew who you were. You stay here, out of that trouble."

Kinzie nodded, regarding him with level gaze. "Why are you helping me?" he asked in the Potawatomi tongue. "I have not known you much, Siggenauk, and have done little for you."

"You have been fair with us always," Siggenauk replied. "And do you remember a summer ago when you stopped the Frenchman who was drunk from killing the young warrior who had no weapon?" Kinzie remembered and nodded and Siggenauk gripped his shoulder with one hand and squeezed. "That," he said, "was my son."

Then Siggenauk wheeled and plunged back toward the fighting, followed closely by the three warriors.[289] The trader watched him go, at the same time seeing that now Rebekah was very near him. He walked toward her and took the horse's bridle. "You better stay with me," he said. He pointed to Wells, still sixty or seventy yards away. "I think your uncle's been wounded, but he should join us in a minute." Rebekah looked where he pointed, gave a little gasp and pulled her horse's head around out of his grasp. She began walking her mount in that direction, heedless of Kinzie's warning to her to wait here. He watched her a moment and then began moving toward Margaret.

The shrieks and screams erupting from the wagon area were awful. Not only had warriors attacked in force, but many squaws were running about among them, darting in to scalp those who had fallen and strip them of shoes, weapons, jewelry, anything of value. The handful of militia who had been under Sergeant Thomas Burns and had formed a weak semicircle to protect the wagon bearing the women and children had no real chance at all. Burns himself still lay writhing weakly on the ground and now a squaw rushed up and cut away his sandy-colored scalp. She left him supine and bleeding, but still alive.[290] Peeking through a slit in the wagon canvas, nine-year-old Isabella Cooper had seen her stepfather fall and now her horror was monumental, having just seen him scalped. Her brother, militia Private James Cooper, fifteen, rushed toward his stepfather to help and was himself downed by an arrow that struck him in the back, passed through his heart and projected from his shirtfront by seven or eight inches.

Militia Private William Russell fought with all the strength he could muster, but to no avail. Though he injured one Indian, he was almost simultaneously run through by a spear and received two different tomahawk blows and any one of these three injuries would have been fatal. He was dead before he sprawled to the ground, his body falling across that of fellow militiaman Samuel Clark, who had the broken shaft of an arrow protruding from the side of his neck.

In a little cluster into which they had drawn themselves, four other militiamen — Louis Pettell and his son, Michael, along with the two other Frenchmen — engaged in a brief mad tangle of arms and legs and bloody weapons. In less than half a minute, all four were dead. Nearby, Charles Lee and fifteen-year-old Charlie fought back to back. A rifle ball slammed through the elder Lee's chest, killing him, passed through and entered Charlie's back, felling him. His empty, bayoneted rifle was jerked from his grip and his throat was slashed.

Tess Russell and Victoria Corbin were already dead close together and the slave Cicely lay dead not far from them. Now, Emmaline Clark, wounded in the stomach, and Sarah Neads stood together trembling, weaponless, their arms about one another. Two warriors and a squaw were guarding them. An Indian youth of no more than fifteen rushed past them with fiendish screech and pulled at the canvas on the wagon bearing the women and children, moving a flap of it to one side. He reached in, felt long soft hair, gripped it and dragged screaming Isabella Cooper halfway out, swinging his tomahawk at her head as he did so. The blade glanced off the top of her skull and the Indian youth was left with her scalp still twisted around his hand as she fell to the ground. He turned to strike her again with his tomahawk but was restrained by one of the squaws, who gathered the moaning child up into her arms and carried her off.[291] Disinclined to argue about it, the youth spun away and vaulted into the wagon. Instantly the cries from inside became piercing shrieks. The youth, gripped by a murderous frenzy, swung his tomahawk with abandon, slamming it time and again into the children inside. Within moments he had plunged his weapon into the heads or bodies of seven children, killing them, his victims including the year-old black child, Benjamin, the three-year-old and six-year-old sisters of Isabella Cooper, Anne and Frances, as well as two-year-old David Simmons, whom he snatched out of the grasp of Susan Simmons as she attempted to leap from the wagon with her two children in her arms. She managed to get outside with six-month-old Susan. Similarly, Mary Burns, having just seen her daughters, Anne and Frances killed, scrambled out of the wagon with her four-month old Catherine, and Martha Lee leaped into the sand from the rear of the wagon with year-old Sally in her arms. All three women with infants were taken prisoner immediately. The blood-stained Indian youth still inside the wagon completed his grisly work by scalping the seven dead children and throwing their lifeless bodies outside, where they fell to the ground as if they were limp dolls.

Other than the scalped but still-living Isabella Cooper, the only child who had escaped on his own from the wagon was four-year-old Johnny Neads who, during the confusion, slipped under the canvas on one side of the wagon, fell to the ground and then ran to his captive mother and clung to her legs, wailing.

9:37 A.M.

Apart from the wagons by about a hundred yards but still approaching that area in a half crouch through the deep grass, Corporal Walter Jordan suddenly realized that four Indians, their leader carrying a long spear, were bearing down on him at a trot and his heart nearly stopped. Weaponless, he now considered himself as being good as dead. He came up out of the crouch and stood still, waiting, expecting to feel the impact of bullet or spear or arrow at any moment. It didn't happen. A slow smile came to his lips as he recognized one of the Potawatomies as White Raccoon, a casual acquaintance made at Fort Wayne. In addition to carrying the spear, the chief was wearing a scabbarded sword. Jordan held out his hand and White Raccoon gripped it.

"Well, you have me now, old friend," the corporal said calmly. His eyes flicked from sword to spear. "Are you going to kill me?"

White Raccoon shook his head. "Jordan, I know you. When I saw you from a distance, I thought it was you, so we came at once. You gave me tobacco at Fort Wayne. We won't kill you, but now you belong to me."

Jordan agreed without hesitation. There was a new flurry of shots and they all looked. William Wells and Rebecca Heald were being fired on. Wells and his horse went down and neither got up. White Raccoon broke into a short harsh laugh and took Jordan's arm.

"Come," he said. "You may see what we will do with your captain."

Pinned beneath his horse as he was, William Wells knew with utter finality that his last moments of life were at hand. This was the moment he had foreseen when early this morning he had painted his face black in representation of the *cut-ta-ho-tha* — the condemned man. As had happened all throughout this business, events had moved with an unreal slowness, as if his brain were functioning at such an accelerated pace that everything else took twenty times longer to occur than was actually the case.

The foamy blood was still oozing from his nostrils and the corner of his mouth and a faint wheezing sound was coming from the hole in his chest. When he had seen Rebekah reach Kinzie and the trader had pointed, she had wheeled and started her horse at a walk toward him. He continued toward her, weaving slightly in the saddle, wanting only to warn her to keep away from him, to go back to Kinzie who was being protected and in whose company she would be safer.

With the sound of the screaming at the wagons beginning to ease off, he and Rebekah converged on one another and stopped their horses, almost leaning against one another, facing in opposite directions. He reached out and took her hand, failing to notice her wounds.

"Farewell, my child," he said in a wheezing whisper.

She shook her head, frightened, but holding it in, her injured hand hurting in his grasp, weak though it was, her eyes locked on the small, faintly stained hole in the front of his blouse. "Why, Uncle William," she said with forced lightness, "I hope you'll get over this."

"No," he said, and the peculiar sound of his voice brought her eyes up to his blackened face. For the first time she saw the blood at his lips and nostrils and her eyes widened. "No, I'm shot through the lungs and I'm dying. I can't live over five minutes more. Tell Mary . . ." He coughed painfully. ". . . Tell my wife — if you live to get there, but I don't think a single one here will ever get there — tell her I died at my post doing the best I could." He made a slight motion toward the rear with his thumb. "There are seven over there that I have killed. Now, go from me. Go back to John Kinzie. He will protect you."

He released his grip on her hand, jerked his horses's reins and started off. Less than a hundred feet away from them, a huge Potawatomi with face painted black stared at them, recognizing Wells. It was Peesotum and he began to raise his rifle. But before he could shoot a flurry of shots suddenly broke out and he spun around. Considerably farther away to his left, a cluster of seven or eight warriors had sighted the riders, too, and were firing at them. Peesotum looked back in time to see his enemy's horse go down.

Wells was no more than fifteen feet from Rebekah when the shots came. Three of them struck her — one of them grazing her right breast, two others barely creasing her ribs on either side — none of them doing any serious damage.[292] Another shot struck Wells's horse in the chest and immediately the gelding went down. Weakening rapidly and unable to react quickly enough to throw himself out of the saddle, Wells went down with it and was pinned by one leg beneath the dead weight of the horse. The Indian Agent was on his back. He thought his leg was broken, but wasn't sure.

Immediately, ignoring the searing burn of her own fresh wounds, Rebekah moved her mare quickly over to him and started to dismount, but he stopped her. "No!" he gasped. "Don't get down."

"But I'll help you," she protested.

"You *can't* help me." Even as he spoke he was repriming his rifle. "It's hopeless. Just get away from here. Get back to Kinzie."

"I won't leave you!" she cried, fighting to control the mare who was shying from the smell of fresh blood and the dead gelding. When she got her horse stopped, she was a dozen feet away.

With some difficulty, Wells propped himself up on an elbow, took careful aim at a warrior among the group approaching and fired. One of the warriors was slammed off his feet and there was no doubt he was dead when he hit the ground. Not expecting this, the others scattered.

"Number eight," Wells murmured. He dropped the rifle, knowing he could not reload, and rolled onto his back again, his head turned toward Rebekah. Blood was coming in much greater volume from mouth and nostrils now. Abruptly he heard Rebekah gasp sharply.

"Uncle! There's an Indian aiming right at the back of your head!"

"Get away!" he said sharply. He put a hand behind his head and used the waning strength of his arm to lift and turn his head so he could see. It was Peesotum.

Wells gave a grunt of recognition at seeing the man who had for so long sworn to kill him. His eyes rolled toward his niece. "Good-bye, Rebekah," he said. He looked back at black-faced Peesotum, whose rifle was leveled at his head. With the hand that was propping up his head, Wells pointed at his own neck, smiled mockingly at his final enemy and said loudly, "Shoot away!"

Peesotum shot.

The lead ball struck Wells on the side of the neck toward the rear, a fraction of an inch from where his finger pointed, tore through the spinal column and killed him instantly.[293] The Potawatomi let out a whoop and ran to his dead enemy. He scalped Wells quickly and efficiently, shaking the blood free, the end of the queue tied with the black ribbon dancing a wild jig in the air as he did so. He stuffed the red scalp into his belt as the Indians who had initially shot regrouped and came up from one direction while White Raccoon, along with his four warriors and their prisoner, Jordan, arrived from another. Five or six, from the first group, at Peesotum's order, grasped the body and with some effort, pulled it out from under the horse. They stripped off his shirt, leggins and moccasins and then Peesotum waved them back and with the same knife he had used to scalp the Indian Agent, he now cut a very deep X across the chest. He reached into the great incision and cut the heart free and then held it high for all to see, screaming in triumph. They joined him in the yell as Rebekah looked on aghast and the shrieks became even louder when he jerked the ramrod from Wells's rifle nearby, impaled the heart on the end of it and lifted it high overhead.

More Indians came running at the victory cry as Peesotum whirled the grisly trophy round and round. Others of the Indians pranced about, many of them striking with knives and tomahawks at Wells's body as they passed, until it was a mass of mutilation. As a dozen or more Indians joined them, Peesotum lowered his trophy and began cutting the still-warm heart into pieces and distributing them. Two pieces he took for himself and stuffed one into his mouth and ate it in the traditional method of taking into himself the strength and courage of a powerful enemy who has been slain. The others, too, ate their pieces with gusto and continued their cries of triumph and approval.

Peesotum approached the bay mare, grasped the bridle and held up the extra piece of heart toward Rebekah.

"Eat!" he commanded.

Unable to speak, she shook her head and averted her face, but he grasped her and pulled until she leaned far toward him in the saddle and had to hold the pommel tightly with her uninjured hand to keep from being pulled off. Again he commanded her to eat and when she refused a second time, he smeared the bloody piece of meat on her face. Rebekah jerked out of his grasp and shook her fist at him, calling him a fiend. The Indians laughed then and pointed at her, calling out "Epiconyare! Epiconyare!"

Now it was White Raccoon who stepped forward. He dropped his spear, drew the sword from its scabbard and used it with both hands to sever the head of the corpse with several hard blows. He wiped off the blade on the dead man's arm and resheathed it, then picked up the head and thrust the blunt end of the spear up into it. Then he raised it aloft and thrust the point of the spear well into the soil. Again a chorus of cries erupted at the sight of the head high on the spear shaft.

Peesotum said a few more words to the others and then walked off toward the wagons with the carrot-colored scalp of Wells back in his hand again, its queue hanging nearly to the ground. Another Potawatomi — a young subchief named Kawbenaw — disengaged the reins from Rebekah's hand and began leading the horse and rider away, heading toward the wagons close to the lake. Not far from them he could see his chief, Black Partridge, with a small group of warriors, walking toward John Kinzie and Margaret Helm.

A little distance away from where Jordan was still standing with his captors near the impaled head of William Wells, Siggenauk and a small group of his men were leaving the wagon area and returning toward where the sound of a few shots was still coming from the prairie. White Raccoon nudged the corporal.

"Come. We will go with Siggenauk."

9:41 A.M.

The pitiful remainder of Captain Heald's company had finally reached the slight elevation southwestward in the prairie and the men, many of them wounded, threw themselves down. Though the Indians had not followed out into the open, shots still came occasionally from the distant trees and dunes. At a range of two hundred yards or more, they were ineffective. Close to half the men who had participated in the initial charge were no longer with them and lay dead, either among the dunes or in the grass between here and there.[294] The furor of sounds that had carried to them from the area of the wagons, now more than a quarter-mile distant,

had faded away for the most part and the occasional rifle shots had
become abnormally loud. Amid the groans of the wounded, the soldiers
now agreed among themselves in a hasty conference to stick together and
continue to fight so long as one of them remained to fire. Captain Heald,
however, shook his head.

"There is a chance that those of us left alive will survive if we surrender," he told them. "The only alternative to surrender is death for all of
us. Courage is one thing; foolhardiness is another. Our deaths at this point
would serve no useful end. If we surrender, we may ultimately expect to
be ransomed and eventually, perhaps, bring a terrible vengeance against
these savages."

Opposed to surrender, Lieutenant Helm found it difficult to keep the
sarcasm out of his voice now. "What does the captain propose we do at
this point?"

"We stay where we are and we wait," Nathan Heald replied, retaining
his calm with an effort. "One of two things will happen. Either they'll
charge us or they'll send an emissary under a flag to discuss our surrender.
If the first, then we will indeed go down to the last man. If the second
occurs, then I suggest we at least listen to what they offer. It's the only
thing that makes any sense. But for the time being, we wait."

The argument began to make sense to some of them.

9:43 A.M.

The carnage and looting at the wagons was over now, but the hideous
remains were apparent. The bodies of the children that had been tossed
from the wagon had been stripped and beheaded. All the dead among the
defenders, women as well as militia and soldiers, had been scalped. Some
had been stripped and further mutilated, though none worse than Victoria
Corbin. Her severed head lay face down two feet from her shoulders. Her
abdomen had been sliced open and the eight-month fetus removed, beheaded and flung away. Her body now lay on its stomach, the clothing too
bloodstained for the Indians to want.

Among the captive women, all but Emmaline Clark were holding children. Emmaline was rather badly wounded with a rifle ball in her stomach. Sarah Neads stood with Johnny, Mary Burns with Catherine, Martha
Lee with Sally and Susan Simmons with little Susan. They still stood
under guard, but now an old Potawatomi woman who could speak English
brokenly told them they must follow her back to the encampment. They
began doing so numbly, the face of Susan Simmons a mask of tearless
grief as they filed by the naked, decapitated body of her two-year-old
David, fearful that if she broke down both she and Susan would be killed
as well. Emmaline Clark, hands pressed to the wound in her stomach,
shuffled past the body of her husband, Samuel, in a daze of anguish and

pain. Martha Lee moaned faintly as they passed the desecrated bodies of her husband and fifteen-year-old son, wondering what had become of Mary, whom they had tied to the saddle of their horse. Silent tears blinded Mary Burns when she stumbled past the body of her fifteen-year-old, James Cooper, and she all but lost control when they were forced past her husband; scalped and grievously wounded, Thomas Burns was still alive and his pain-filled gaze met hers for just an instant, communicating a mute message of sorrow and bewilderment. For Mary Neads there was no horror on the ground here directly related to her, but she held the face of four-year-old Johnny against her breast so he would not see the remains, and she wondered what had happened to her husband, John, with the regular troops; were they all dead like this, too?

9:44 A.M.

"Keepoteh!"

The warrior who had come running up to the river's mouth scrambled down the bank, breathing hard, and Keepoteh and his younger brother and the other two Potawatomi warriors aboard the bateau became very alert.

"What is it?" he asked.

"It is nearly over. The soldiers who are left on the prairie are surrounded. Half are dead, the others have nowhere to go. They must surrender soon or all be dead. Topenebe has sent me to tell you to bring the boat back up the river, to where the little creek comes in at our camp. He will meet you there to instruct you further."

Eleanor Kinzie was listening closely, assimilating most of the dialogue. She reached out and touched Keepoteh's leg. "Please," she said, "ask if my husband is still alive."

Keepoteh grunted an affirmative and asked him. The warrior shook his head. "I do not know. The last I saw Shawneeawkee, he was near the wagons, where nearly all have been killed. But I do not think he was hurt. Black Partridge is protecting him."

"Thank God," she murmured. "Chandonnais, as soon as possible, you must go see what has happened. Mr. Kinzie may need help."

"No!" It was Keepoteh. "Not yet. We will do as Topenebe says. When we get back to the creek, then Chandonnais may leave if he wishes, but no one else. Not yet." He smiled briefly at the trader's wife. "Do not fear. No one will harm the Shawneeawkee, and you will soon be back in your own home, I think."

He turned around and gave an order to the oarsmen to shove off and return up the river.

9:45 A.M.

No more than seventy yards from the wagons and at the final fringe of grass where sandy beach began and sloped down to the waterline of Lake Michigan, John Kinzie stood with his stepdaughter, Margaret Helm, who was trembling badly. Almost all the gunfire had ceased by now and a pall of smoke hung low over the devastation. Incredibly, only a quarter-hour had passed since the initial charge and outbreak of the fighting.

Striding through the smoky air toward them now came seven Indians, their leader with a gold crescent dangling from his nostrils. It was the final straw for Margaret Helm and she screamed piercingly, plunged away from her stepfather's side despite his assurances and splashed into the water of the lake, not stopping until she was waist deep. There, face buried in her hands, she stood forlornly, her shoulders heaving as she wept.

The leader of the small group of warriors was Black Partridge and he made a little sign of peace with his hand as he approached, which Kinzie returned. They shook hands gravely and then Black Partridge relieved the trader of his rifle. "You should not be carrying this, Shawneeawkee," he admonished lightly. "Someone who knows you not might mistake your intentions. All steps possible have been taken to keep you and your wife and little children safe."

"Eleanor and the children — they're safe now?"

Black Partridge nodded. "Topenebe has seen to them. I have not heard of them for a little while, but the last I heard they were still in your boat."

"A great many have been killed, Black Partridge," Kinzie said grimly.

"Yes," he replied sadly, "and more will probably die yet. It is unpleasant, but we are at war and war is not pleasant. I came to your captain the night before and warned him; as Topenebe warned you. Yet, instead of staying safe where you were, you walked into the danger you knew was there. That was foolish. Foolish men die young."

Kinzie responded with a noncommittal grunt. A movement caught his eye and he saw it was Rebekah Heald on her horse, being led by an Indian. He pointed. "That is the wife of our captain. She is a friend. Will you have her brought here with us and protected?"

Black Partridge shrugged, then gave a sharp yelp and motioned to Kawbenaw — The Carrier — who acknowledged and headed more directly their way. "She will come here," he said. "How much protection she will have, I do not know. But since she is your friend, I will try. I will take you to a place of greater safety."

Out in the water, Margaret Helm's panic had subsided and, as she watched the men on shore and saw that they were speaking in a friendly manner, she began wading back in. As she regained the beach her soggy shoes filled with sand and became very uncomfortable and she stopped to remove them. No sooner had she taken them off than a young squaw darted to her, snatched them from her hand and made off with them. Angry and disgusted, Margaret watched the woman running away and then continued walking barefoot through the warm sand toward her stepfather, hiccoughing as an aftermath of her cry.[295]

By the time Margaret returned to the men, Kawbenaw had arrived at the little group with Rebekah on her horse. Black Partridge directed him to protect her and proceed with her to the encampment west of the fort. As they started away, a saddleless horse was brought up by Nescotnemeg's brother, Waubinema — White Sturgeon. Margaret was placed on it and they began following the Heald horse. Riding bareback was difficult for Margaret, however. She had to grip her heels to the animal's side to hold her balance and this caused some pain in her slightly wounded ankle, so in a few moments she slid off the horse, electing to walk. Waubinema left the horse behind with a warrior as they all moved past the scene of tragedy at the wagons and headed for the Frog Creek Indian encampment.

9:59 A.M.

With the horrible feeling of despair and frustration that only a commanding officer can feel at the moment that he surrenders his force to the enemy, Captain Nathan Heald unbuckled his sword and handed it to Chief Siggenauk.

It was precisely one-half hour since the beginning of the fight.

Captain Heald could not believe so much had happened so quickly. Nor was he at all sure what lay ahead at this point. Lives — his own included — might still be in grave jeopardy, despite the promises of the Indians. As yet he had no idea what had occurred among the wagons, but his own statistics were grim enough to give him little hope. Only thirty-five of his men here were still alive, including officers and noncommissioned officers as well as privates, of which twelve were wounded, with eight of those in serious condition.[296]

The commander knew now, from having talked with the interpreter-intermediary, Pierre LeClerc, that shortly after he and his men had reached the little knoll out in the prairie, the chiefs had held a meeting on the dunes to discuss what should be done. The three principal commanders, Siggenauk, Sunawewone and Nescotnemeg — the latter having taken a ball in the upper chest — weighed the alternatives. None wished to send any of his warriors into an exposed situation on the prairie after the soldiers ensconced on the knoll and so they had decided to send LeClerc under a white flag to demand their surrender.[297]

So Pierre LeClerc, a white cloth dangling from a stick he held aloft, hesitantly approached the prairie knoll and, at a distance of about one hundred feet, called to Captain Heald to come out and talk. The commanding officer did so, limping badly because of the lead ball lodged in his hip joint.

When the captain heard the relayed demand of the chiefs for the surrender of the company, he evinced an immediate willingness to do so. Pierre LeClerc nodded, as if expecting no other response, but then he cautioned the commander not to be too hasty.

"You must not simply agree to surrender," he said. "You must send me back to them with word that you will agree to surrender only if the lives of the prisoners are to be spared. You must demand their pledge on this."

Captain Heald concurred and sent LeClerc back with that message, himself returning to the knoll. LeClerc disappeared in the cluster of pine trees at the base of the dunes and in less than five minutes he reappeared marching out onto the prairie again with his flag, this time followed by Siggenauk. They approached to within about half the distance from the knoll and stopped, where LeClerc again called for Captain Heald to come out.

Once more the Fort Dearborn commander hobbled out to them. LeClerc formally introduced Siggenauk and Heald and the two enemies shook hands, suspicion heavy between them. With Le Clerc interpreting, Siggenauk said that he was speaking for all the chiefs and warriors and wished the Americans to surrender. Heald said the men under his command would surrender only if assurance were given that their lives would be spared when they became prisoners.

"Not only the men with me there," he added, pointing to the knoll, "but any others — women and children as well as men — who are still alive over by the wagons at the lake."

Siggenauk considered this. "For everyone, you must pay us one hundred American dollars."

Heald countered. "I will pay the one hundred dollars, but only if you guarantee not only to preserve the lives of the soldiers and remaining women and children, but to deliver them finally to some British post unless they are first ransomed by traders acting in behalf of Americans or British."

The Potawatomi chief digested this for a moment, then nodded. "If you pay the one hundred dollars now," he said, "all of your fighting men and your women and children still alive now will be distributed to various chiefs who will take them to their villages and keep them for a while. If no traders come to ransom them, then by and by they will be taken to British posts and turned over as prisoners to them."

The important addition of the term "fighting men" slipped past Captain Heald unquestioned. It was a grave slip. The Indians considered fighting men as being those who were capable of picking up weapons and fighting.

It did not include those who were gravely wounded. The commander chose his words carefully when Siggenauk finished.

"Were this my decision alone, I should accept here and now," he told the chief. "But since the lives of each of my men are involved in this, I will carry the offer back to them and confer with them on it. Should they agree as I do, what do you wish us to do?"

Siggenauk told him that a short time would be allowed for the discussion. If the men agreed to surrender, they were to rise, step out to where they could be plainly seen, put down their arms and move away from them, at which time the Indians would come and meet them and take them prisoner. Any prisoner found hiding a weapon would be killed. But if, in a short while, they did not agree to surrender, then the Indians would renew their attack and none of the Americans, including those from in and near the wagons, would be spared.

The meeting ended and they separated. Heald returned to his men and explained the situation. "I agreed to pay them the one hundred dollars they are asking," he said, "as I have one hundred fifty dollars in my pocket." He said nothing about the money sewn into his vest. "My considered advice is that we accept the terms."

There were some strong voices raised against this, notably that of Lieutenant Helm, but then they dwindled off and Captain Heald spoke again, convincingly. "As I see it, our situation is hopeless. Like many of you, I have little confidence in the Indians, but it is the best I could do. If we don't surrender, in fifteen minutes more we will all be killed. That includes our wives and children as well."

The final argument was a telling one and they agreed to give up. At Captain Heald's order they rose, spread apart so all could be seen well, put their weapons down and began walking toward the dunes, those who were badly injured being helped along by the others. In a moment the Indians emerged from hiding and began walking toward them.

Private Daniel Daugherty and two companions — Duncan McCarty and William Prickett — walked closely together. "I don't like it," Daugherty murmured so only they could hear. "Mark my words, there's gonna be trouble. If there is, I'm not going down like a sheep led to slaughter." He opened his jacket enough that they could see the hilt of the knife he had hidden in his belt. "You with me?" They told him they were and he grinned. "Just stick close to me. If we're going down, we're gonna take some of these red devils with us!"

As the Indians approached, Captain Heald saw that Corporal Walter Jordan was their prisoner. The chief who walked with him told him to move forward and join the soldiers coming toward them and Jordan did so, merging with a group of fourteen privates as the whole group came to a halt.

The Fort Dearborn commander stepped up to Siggenauk and surrendered his sword to the chief. At the same time he handed him the one hundred dollars in cash which he had taken from his pocket as they left the knoll and carried in his hands.[298] Siggenauk accepted both gravely.

"We will gather up the weapons," Siggenauk told him now, through LeClerc, "and when that is done we will take you and your men to our camp and there decide how you are to be divided among the chiefs who have fought here."

10:00 A.M.

Wabinsheway was disgruntled. The fierce action that had swirled around him this past half-hour had perversely eluded him, though he had been in its very midst in the area of the wagons. Three times he had raised his tomahawk and three times he had been thwarted as the intended victim had been killed in the instant before he could strike. Twice other warriors had darted in and struck first. Once, as he had grappled with one of the soldiers who had tumbled out of the sick wagon, a rifle ball had passed through the man's throat, causing a gout of blood that had sprayed out and splattered Wabinsheway's chest, adding an even more macabre effect to the white paint with which he had daubed himself in skeletal representation. He had taken that man's scalp, though the knowledge was in his heart that it was an unearned trophy.

That he had himself managed to avoid being shot or otherwise struck was something of a miracle, since his near seven-foot height caused him to tower above everyone else present and provide a significant target. Yet, he remained unscathed. Now, having brought some of the women prisoners carrying children to the encampment, he heard the word spreading that the soldiers were surrendering. Few shots were being fired and an eerie quiet was beginning to pervade. It was all but over and his tomahawk had not bitten into living flesh. When the time came tonight and in the nights to come that the warriors would stand and recount their exploits in this affair to the others, what could he say — that he had *almost* killed three?

Vaguely frustrated, he moved to the river bank and began urinating into the water. His sweeping gaze as he relieved himself fell upon the Burns house across the river and for the first time since it had occurred, he recalled standing here for the same purpose in the pre-dawn darkness over six hours ago; remembered the silent shape of the canoe passing with people in it, landing at the opposite shore and returning in a little while with only one person aboard. The memory gelled. Someone must be at the house! Abruptly his spirits soared and he finished quickly and then sprinted to a canoe beached nearby and swiftly paddled across the river.

Wabinsheway — White Elk — approached the Burns house carefully, in a half-crouch, darting from bush to bush, making his great bulk as small as possible, feeling and enjoying the automatic tightening of his stomach muscles in anticipation of the shot that would come from an unseen gun and send a ball into his flesh. But no shot came and now he was at the outer wall of the house, moving stealthily from corner to corner, finding the windows all tightly shuttered and no sign of life.

He slipped around the final corner, stepped up on the porch and moved past the large woodbox to the front door. It was padlocked from the outside; who then could possibly be inside? Had he been incorrect? Had whoever it was not come here after all, but instead merely slipped away to the north? In his rising frustration he gripped the latch and shook the door furiously, but it remained firm.

Then came the faint, stifled little cry of a child and he spun around, again instantly on the alert, his gaze zeroing in to the source of the sound — the woodbox. A grin split the death's head paint on his face and he stepped silently to the box. He paused, tomahawk in right hand, the overhanging edge of the woodbox lid in his left. The faintest whisper of movement came from within, the tiniest scuff of small foot against wood, and he jerked the lid open.

Sukey Corbin erupted from concealment as if she had been a jack-in-the-box, leaping with clawing hands at the neck of the giant Potawatomi chief. A wild shriek came from her mouth as she launched herself at him and gripped his throat, her fingers digging in, her nails puncturing his flesh. Caught by surprise despite his readiness, Wabinsheway jerked back, dragging her with him and falling backward off the porch with the screeching woman atop him. Her forehead butted his mouth with stunning impact, splitting his upper lip against his teeth. The lid of the woodbox slammed closed.

He rolled over and over with her, ripping the hands from his throat with his free hand, bringing the tomahawk around in a short chopping blow with the other. It struck her low in the spine, hurting her very badly and she gasped, but still she clawed for his eyes. He thrust her from him and even as she rolled over and came instantly to a catlike crouch, preparing to spring again, he buried the tomahawk to its shaft in the left side of her forehead. Susan Corbin died in that moment.

Wabinsheway tried to pull the tomahawk free but it was wedged tightly in her skull and he let it go for the moment. He leaped back onto the porch and again jerked open the lid of the woodbox. Little Henry and Wilma Corbin cowered in a back corner of the box, whimpering, their arms wrapped about each other.

Wabinsheway grasped an ankle and yanked, pulling four-year-old Henry free of his sister's grasp. A piercing wail came from the boy as the huge Indian whirled him twice around the head by one foot. The terrified cry ended abruptly as his head was slammed into the side of the house, crushing his skull. Wabinsheway tossed the body down in a heap and immediately snatched out the three-year-old, whirling Wilma around in the same way, ending it all the same way.

He returned to the dead woman and freed the tomahawk, then scalped all three of the dead and walked casually back to his canoe without a backward glance.

10:03 A.M.

The soldiers stood in little clusters, stunned, unable yet to comprehend fully the enormity of their present situation, beyond the fact that the fierce action was over. Fifteen men — fourteen privates and Corporal Jordan — stood in one cluster and there were three here, four there and a few individuals standing by themselves. Captain Heald and Lieutenant Helm stood close together, a little apart from the enlisted men.

They had watched as the Indians gathered up the weapons that had been discarded at the knoll and returned to form a loose ring of still-menacing forms all around them. Many of the Indians looked as if they wished nothing more than to be able to wade in with tomahawks flailing and cut down each and every survivor.

From what he had been able to learn from Pierre LeClerc, Captain Heald was aware that fifty-five of his party had been killed and the Indian loss was seventeen dead, with Chief Naunongee severely wounded and sure to die before long. There was a great sorrow among the Indians for their own losses and now five warriors abruptly raised their rifles and fired them into the air as a salute to their own dead.

Unaware that this was going to occur, their attention occupied in another direction, Privates Daugherty, Prickett and McCarty whirled at the sound of gunfire. They were certain, even as the crash of the reports hung in the air, that the Indians had begun to execute the prisoners. Daugherty jerked his knfe out of concealment and the three crouched, ready to spring in another instant. Immediately a dozen or more other rifles fired in ragged volley and all three privates were killed.[299]

10:14 A.M.

Her mare still being led by Kawbenaw, Rebekah sat her mount stiffly, gripping the pommel with her uninjured hand, her eyes locked straight ahead as they approached the Frog Creek encampment, riding as if this were all some terrible nightmare from which she would soon awaken. The wounds in hands and arms, the lesser wounds in breast and sides, had now begun to hurt considerably and a general pain filled her, causing her on occasion to sway in the saddle.

From one of the wigwams the wife of Kawbenaw emerged, laughing in delight at the prize her husband was bringing home. She ran toward them and her gaze fell upon the brilliant red blanket beneath Rebekah's saddle. She let out a little cry and immediately ran to the side of the horse and began tugging at the blanket, trying to pull it free. It was a final straw for Rebekah Heald. She reached down with the uninjured hand and pulled out the riding crop she had been carrying wedged in her low boot. She slashed furiously at the squaw, striking her time and again on face and shoulders, raising immediate angry white welts. The squaw screeched and fell back, fending off the blows with upraised arms, and the onlookers, warriors and squaws alike, laughed aloud at the sight — Kawbenaw loudest of all. Murmurs of "Epiconyare!" rose from the crowd.

The commanding officer's wife had won their admiration.

10:15 A.M.

The bateau bearing the Kinzie family and servants, still under temporary command of Keepoteh, had come to shore only a moment ago at the mouth of Frog Creek west of the fort, only a few score yards from the nearest edge of the Indian encampment. Keepoteh's younger brother leaped out and tied the boat to a large emergent root and then he and the other two Potawatomies who had joined him set off at a run toward the bridge crossing the creek to the encampment, to alert Topenebe of their arrival.

Within the boat, Eleanor Kinzie heard cries and laughter coming from the encampment and she stood on her seat in order to see what was happening. A woman astride a horse being held by an Indian was slashing at a squaw with her riding crop and even from here she could hear the grunts and small cries of pain from the Indian woman. Abruptly Eleanor recognized the rider.

"Why, that is Mrs. Heald!" she cried. She turned to her husband's chief clerk seated beside his assistant. "Chandonnais, go help her. That Indian might kill her. Get her away from him."

Jean Batiste Chandonnais hesitated. "The man who has her looks to be Kawbenaw," he said. "Whoever it is, it makes no difference. He will not give the woman up without getting something in return."

"Then give him something!" Her eyes swept the boat and fell on the mule tied to the mast. She pointed at it. "Take the mule. Trade the mule for her release. If he wants more than that, offer him whiskey. We don't have it now, but promise it to him. We'll make sure he gets it. Tell him it's on the word of Shawneeawkee."

Chandonnais nodded and immediately they began to position the planks lying on the deck of the boat to make a ramp in order to get the mule ashore.

More people were coming into the Frog Creek encampment now; little Isabella Cooper, her head bloody from where she had been scalped, being led gently to a wigwam by a squaw; the women captives with the children they were carrying, taken to different dwellings; Emmaline Clark, barely able to walk and still clutching her stomach with bloodied hands; a swelling trickle of warriors from the prairie to the southeast, many of them carrying scalps.

The horse that Margaret Helm had refused to ride was brought in from the direction of the wagons, the scalped but still living and severely wounded militia sergeant, Thomas Burns, draped across the horse's back on his stomach. They stopped as they entered the large clearing among the multitude of wigwams and he was roughly shoved off the horse, landing on his side on the ground with a dull thump, the broken bones in his crushed shoulder grating. He rolled over onto his back, groaning, the tomahawk wounds in lower back and stomach again bleeding.

Next to enter the encampment was Margaret Helm, still in the custody of Chief Waubinema, John Kinzie several paces behind. Waubinema was prepared to fend off the other Indians who might try snatching her away from him, but none did. He led her toward his wigwam, passing close to where Sergeant Burns lay on the ground. There was an angry shriek as a squaw brandishing a tomahawk ran into view. She had just learned that her husband was one of the warriors who had been killed and her grief manifested itself in a mad need for vengeance. Waubinema quickly stepped in front of his barefoot prisoner to protect her, but it was not the woman the squaw was intent upon. She swooped down upon the recumbent Burns and buried her tomahawk in his stomach, then again and again in legs, arms, chest and, finally, head. The militia sergeant writhed and cried out at the first few blows but then slumped back and was dead before she finished striking him.

Margaret Helm was shocked but her stepfather only looked on grimly. John Kinzie knew the Indians very well and he was sure there would be many others who would die before this day was finished.[300]

The sorry procession of soldiers, with Captain Heald and Lieutenant Helm in their lead, were herded past the scene of horror at the wagons and to a man they paled, some becoming violently ill at the sight of the dead men, women and children, most of them stripped, some beheaded.

It was Lieutenant Helm who became nearly overcome with grief. He saw the body of Victoria Corbin lying on its stomach, her dress — seeming to him to be the same dress Margaret had been wearing when they left the fort — soaked with blood and the face-down head a few yards away, with residue of hair that was quite similar to Margaret's. He was stunned with shock.

"Oh, my God," he whispered, "it's Margaret! Look what these monsters have done to my Margaret!"[301]

Other soldiers passed and recognized wife or child as their own and became all but hysterical. Among these was Phelim Corbin, who saw the same decapitated corpse Lieutenant Helm had seen but who was not in error when he knew it to be his wife, his horror confirmed when he saw, some distance away, the headless corpse of a tiny fetus. He almost collapsed at the sight and was helped along by his brother James, in the knowledge that anyone who fell behind was sure to be tomahawked.

As the survivors plodded on toward the encampment there were now many among them — Lieutenant Helm in particular — who regretted ever having surrendered. And there were some who were beginning to feel they would regret it even more before very long.

10:20 A.M.

At the Frog Creek encampment, some of the prisoners were being surprised at the kind treatment they were now receiving. Margaret was taken gently by the arm and led by Waubinema's wife into the interior of their wigwam. There she was allowed to lie on a blanket-covered mat while Waubinema's wife took a small kettle and ran to Frog Creek, scooped up some water and scurried back to the wigwam. There she threw several handfuls of maple sugar into the water, stirred it vigorously with her hand and gave it to Margaret to drink. The lieutenant's wife did so, touched by the act of kindness, and very quickly felt considerably revived. Then she was led outside again and bade to sit with a small group of squaws watching the approaching line of prisoners.

Isabella Cooper had been brought to a wigwam by a robust squaw who had saved her from the young savage after she had been pulled from the wagon and scalped. Though she had not even felt the wound at first, soon her head hurt horribly and she had sat moaning softly as the squaw mixed a muddy-colored poultice in a small bowl, sprinkling in a variety of dried herbs and powders. But when the squaw delicately daubed the mixture on Isabella's wound, the pain miraculously vanished. The nine-year-old girl sat quietly now, letting the ministrations continue, looking through the open tent flap at the people who were passing, mostly Indians. Abruptly she gave a little cry and then began to sob. A warrior had passed by with a sandy-colored scalp dangling from his hand and Isabella was positive it was the scalp of her stepfather, Thomas Burns.

A moment later another squaw entered with two other prisoners — a woman and child — in her charge and Isabella erupted with a sharp cry of joy. It was Mary Burns, still carrying four-month-old Catherine, neither of them hurt. Mary sat beside her eldest daughter and hugged her close, then began to nurse Catherine. As gently as possible she told Isabella that her brother and sisters, James, Anne and Frances were dead, as was her stepfather.

The little girl looked at her, eyes wide and lower lip trembling, and replied: "I didn't know about Anne and Frances but I was looking out of the wagon when the trouble all started and saw Jimmy and Poppa get killed." And Mary Burns had no heart to tell her that though her husband had fallen at the wagons, he had not died until only a few moments ago mere yards from where they sat.

Rebekah Heald, in the wigwam of Kawbenaw, was being similarly well treated. A compress of buzzard breastfeathers had been pressed into the hole in her arm where the ball had entered and broken the bone, and other dressings and medications were being rubbed gently on the other wounds to her hand and arm, breast and sides, all of them painful but none very serious. Just before entering the wigwam she had caught a glimpse of John Kinzie. For an instant their eyes met and she thought his glance had held the message of "Bear up, and I will help if I can," and she nodded just as he was told to move to another place by the cordon of warriors around him.

Only a moment or so later she heard a swell of voices and understood enough to realize the warriors were coming in with their prisoners. She moved to get up and go outside, but Kawbenaw restrained her with a tight clasp of her shoulder and she settled back, thinking it was just as well she didn't look, her heart heavy in the feeling that her husband had been killed and would not be with the prisoners anyway. She remained sitting in the dimness, not moving even when Kawbenaw's daughter and wife — the latter's face still marked with weals, now turned red, from Rebekah's riding crop — entered and, with Kawbenaw's permission, removed her ring, brooch and tortoiseshell-and-silver comb. She was not afraid of them, knowing that they would not harm her now without Kawbenaw's permission, but not caring. Not caring about anything at all at this moment.

With the swell of conversation still rising outside, there was a slight disturbance at the entry and a man entered whom she recognized as Chandonnais, an employee of the Kinzies. He shook hands with the chief, sat down beside him on a mat and immediately broke into a rapid dialogue in the Potawatomi tongue, which she could not follow. At one point the chief rose and looked outside at a mule being held by the halter by a Potawatomi boy of about ten. Then he returned and the conversation continued, but Rebekah had closed her eyes and her mind to everything occurring around her, retreating deep into some more peaceful place within her own soul.

10:26 A.M.

The surviving soldiers, many of them — including Captain Heald — limping very badly and some being helped by others, straggled into the encampment. Lieutenant Linai Helm, in the depths of depression over the death, beheading and scalping of what he took to be his wife, experienced an electric thrill when his glance fell upon a group of squaws sitting before a wigwam with a woman prisoner whose face was buried in her hands as she wept. Then the prisoner took her hands away and looked up and he saw that it was Margaret and his relief was immeasurable.

"Margaret!" he cried. "*Margaret!*"

She saw him then and she cried his name in return and tried to scramble up and rush to him, but she was held by the squaws. He, too, was restrained from running to her and forced to continue moving to the central clearing where the prisoners were being assembled.[302] Here they stopped and many of them gratefully slumped to the ground, their eyes haunted and an aura of fear surrounding them all.

John Kinzie, standing to one side, saw Captain Heald looking about anxiously and knew he was desperately hoping for a glimpse of Rebekah, not knowing whether she was alive or not, but fearing she was not. His expression was haggard, pain-filled. Kinzie spoke briefly to his guardians — he was more in protective custody than a prisoner — and, at their nods, walked over to the commanding officer.

"Kinzie!" Captain Heald said eagerly, when he saw the trader approaching. "Have you seen anything of Rebekah? Is she alive?"

"Yes, I've seen her. She's alive. She's right here."

"Oh, God!" Heald sighed. "Oh, thank God! She's all right, isn't she? She hasn't been hurt or anything?"

"She has a few wounds, Captain, but nothing really serious. She'll be all right. She's in one of the wigwams over there. Chief Kawbenaw's. She's his prisoner. My man, Chandonnais, is in with Kawbenaw right now, trying to rescue her. He said my wife sent him with a mule to try to ransom her into our care. We'll do whatever we can. For you, too, if possible."

"Thank you. Thank you!" Heald gripped his arm, close to tears.

Voices down the line of men caused them to turn and look. The soldiers were methodically being stripped of their outer clothing — hats, if they wore them, jackets, shirts, pouches, trousers, shoes. They were being left only with their undergarments. Captain Heald blanched and his grip on Kinzie's arm tightened.

"Listen!" he whispered urgently. "I have a vest on beneath this jacket. It's . . . it's . . . there's money in it. Sewn into the lining. A lot of money. You've got to help me keep them from getting it."

Kinzie thought about that a moment and nodded. "They'll be here any moment. Here's what you do. Take off your coat and the vest together and hand them to me as if it's just the coat. I'll put them on the same way. Anyone who sees us'll think I'm just trying it on. Then I'll take the coat off alone and hand it back to you, keeping the vest on me. I don't know if it'll work, but it's the only hope."

At once Heald pulled the two garments off as one and the trader donned them. Heald murmured to him to also take the evacuation orders, which were folded in an inside pocket of the coat. Kinzie nodded, transferred the papers to his own pocket, then pulled the coat tight around the waist as if trying it for size. He shook his head, took the coat alone off and held it out to the commander.

"Doesn't fit me," he said loudly.

A Potawatomi ran up and snatched the garment before the captain could take it back. Others converged and in a moment Heald, too, was reduced to his inner garments. Kinzie, wearing the vest, had moved away casually as this was occurring and now Heald saw him continuing toward where he said Rebekah was located, followed by the protectors that had been assigned to him. Heald closed his eyes and, for the first time in a very long time, prayed. When he opened them again he saw the trader had stopped and was deep in conversation with a chief whom Heald recognized as Topenebe.

Inside the wigwaw where Chandonnais had gone, negotiations were just being concluded. Kawbenaw, with Rebekah's pale blue bonnet perched ridiculously on his head and tied under his chin, had at first rejected the offer Chandonnais had made, but this was only part of the bargaining game and both knew it. Chandonnais had then offered him two bottles of whiskey, to be paid later, on the word of the Shawneeawkee, but Kawbenaw continued to shake his head.

The dickering continued: three bottles . . . five . . . seven! Still Kawbenaw refused to bend. Chandonnais shook his head and sighed. "As always," he groaned in mock agony, "Kawbenaw is a great trader. I have one offer left to make. You already have the beautiful horse the white chief's woman was riding. To that I add the mule. And to that I add ten — ten! — bottles of whiskey, to be paid as soon as possible at your village, on the word of the Shawneeawkee."

Behind them on the mat where she was now lying, Rebekah moaned with the pain filling her from her wounds and this seemed to do the trick.

"But she is badly wounded," Kawbenaw said. "If I let you buy her from me in this bargain and she dies, do I then still get the ten bottles of whiskey as well as keeping the horse and mule?"

Chandonnais assured him that he did and, with that, the bargain was struck. There was now the problem of getting her to the boat unseen by others, who might have objection to the premature deal. Kawbenaw directed his wife and daughter to remove Rebekah's dress, stockings and boots, rub her feet with earth to darken them and wrap her in a blanket. They did so gladly, appropriating the garments for themselves, and abruptly the prisoner could pass as a squaw if the inspection were not too close. Then, with a word to the boy holding the mule to stay where he was, Kawbenaw and Chandonnais, with Rebekah obeying the clerk's order to walk just behind them, left and walked toward the little bridge over Frog Creek. No one seemed to notice them, most eyes on the soldiers whose wounds were now being amateurishly doctored by Monsieur DuPin, the trader, who had been summoned for that purpose. He had often treated the minor wounds of Indians.

In a moment the trio crossed the little foot bridge and were walking down the east bank toward the river. As they approached the bateau, Keepoteh saw them coming and stood up, as did Eleanor. Black Jim began getting up, too, but Eleanor motioned the husky slave back with her hand. No one mentioned the blue bonnet being worn by Kawbenaw, nor did anyone smile. They helped the blanket-wrapped figure aboard and Rebekah Heald sank to her hands and knees on the floor of the bateau, grasped Eleanor's ankle and wept.

Chandonnais and Kawbenaw immediately turned away and retraced their steps to the encampment. Only then did Eleanor realize that she had neglected asking Chandonnais if he had learned anything of her husband. She thought to ask Rebekah, but the woman was in such pain, moaning and crying so steadily, that this was hardly the time.

"Indian coming, ma'am," Black Jim whispered.

Eleanor looked up and saw approaching them along the shore from the direction of the fort a warrior of about twenty-four, savagely painted, stained with droplets of blood and a dark scalp tucked in his waistband. He also carried a bloodstained tomahawk in his belt and a pistol in his right hand. Immediately Eleanor snatched a buffalo robe and tossed it over Rebekah. "Not a sound!" she hissed near the woman's covered head. "No sound, no movement, if you want to live!"

Keepoteh, standing in the front of the boat with his brother, dipped his head at the warrior but said nothing. The warrior stopped at the side of the boat, leaned both hands on the gunwale, still holding the pistol, and craned his neck to see who was inside. Nine-year-old John H. Kinzie stared back at him defiantly. Henry and Athena, the black house servants, sat motionless, expressionless. The boatman, Claude, along with Chandonnais' assistant and Josette Beaubien who was holding Robert, dipped their heads faintly in greeting. Eleanor, her arms about Ellen and Maria, said nothing but did smile faintly. Only Black Jim took the initiative.

"Stop!" he growled. He snatched up an axe lying nearby. "If you shoot," he threatened darkly, "I'll kill you. This is the Shawneeawkee's family, under protection of Topenebe and Black Partridge!"

In the bow, Keepoteh laughed and interpreted the gist of Black Jim's warning. The warrior, realizing now who these people were, backed off a step or two. "I am looking for a soldier named Burnett, who cheated me some time ago. I mean to kill him. I thought he might be here."

"There is no soldier named Burnett, or any other soldier aboard the Shawneeawkee's boat," Keepoteh said tonelessly, his laughter gone and his hand resting on the tomahawk in his belt.[303]

The warrior backed up even more. "I will find him somewhere else." He turned and walked swiftly away.

10:35 A.M.

The division of the prisoners among the Indians was accomplished with surprising speed. The soldiers were forced to sit in a circle in the midst of the clearing while the chiefs held a council and the distribution was made. Kawbenaw was asked if he wished to retain the white chief's wife, since it was known she was already prisoner in his wigwam. And Kawbenaw, having no desire to have it known he had already made a deal with the Kinzies whereby Rebekah had already been turned over to them, agreed.

Corporal Walter Jordan was awarded to his captor, White Raccoon, to be taken to that chief's village on the Iroquois River. Lieutenant Helm was awarded to Chief Mittatass, whose village was on Peoria Lake — a fact that gave the officer hope, since he knew that John Kinzie's half brother, Thomas Forsyth, was a trader there and might be able to ransom him. Margaret Helm had been awarded to Topenebe. Captain Heald, as chief of the whites, was initially offered to the architect of the massacre. Nescotnemeg, absent at the moment, since he was in his wigwam where his chest wound was being treated. A runner brought his refusal to accept, along with his recommendation that, as leader of the Americans, Heald should be put to death. For a moment that measure was put in abeyance as division of the prisoners continued.

Individually, sometimes in couples or threesomes, the remainder of the prisoners were parceled out. Siggenauk waived accepting prisoners in favor of a larger share of the spoils, as did several other chiefs. Privates James Corbin and Paul Grummo, along with Corporal Joseph Bowen, were awarded to Black Partridge's brother, Waubansee, whose village was on the Fox River. Six other privates were awarded to chiefs with villages in that same general area.

The women with infants were allowed to keep them and were awarded together to various chiefs, with Susan Simmons and her six-month-old Susan going to the Winnebagoes from Green Bay, who had participated in the fight. Black Partridge, whose due was no less than that of Nescotnemeg and Siggenauk, elected to accept a somewhat larger portion of the goods for his people and the only prisoners he accepted were Martha Lee and her year-old Sally.

During the midst of the apportioning, the warrior who had peered into the Kinzie boat began moving around the circle of men, staring at each intently. He was still looking for the man named Burnett and, though he had looked over the prisoners as they were being marched here and had not seen him, now he looked more closely.

Private George Burnett, not realizing he was being sought, was sitting in the circle with the others. He had been slightly wounded. A rifle ball had skimmed along his brow, neatly trimming away both eyebrows and a fair amount of skin at the same time. Though not serious, the wound had bled profusely and a handkerchief, now well blood-soaked, had been tied around his head, nearly hiding his eyes and somewhat masking his features. That was why the warrior had not recognized him earlier.

Now he did.

With a harsh cry he plunged his tomahawk with total unexpectedness into the crown of the man's head, killing him instantly. Even while his victim was still twitching at his feet in the sudden hush that had fallen over the assemblage, the warrior scalped him, held his trophy high and shouted that it had been his right to kill the man who had cheated him. The chiefs held a brief whispered conversation and then gave the act their unanimous approval.

And the fear that had dwindled somewhat among the prisoners came surging to the fore again.[304]

10:42 A.M.

In the bateau, Eleanor Kinzie could not restrain the cry of relief and excitement that sprang from her lips when she saw her husband, wearing a vest she had never seen before, approaching on the east shore of the little stream. She had learned, finally, from the whimpering Rebekah Heald, that John was still alive, but hearing about it and actually seeing him coming toward her unharmed were two very different matters.

Chandonnais was with him, as were Topenebe, Black Partridge and five warriors. John gave her a brief wave as he neared and, close to the boat, stopped and talked for a short while with the two chiefs in their own tongue, shaking hands with each warmly. "Without your help," he told them, "none of us would be here now. I am grateful."

Topenebe nodded, as did Black Partridge, but the latter remained very serious. "The danger is not yet over for you and your people here." He looked at the boat, then back at Kinzie. "When the others learn that Kawbenaw has sold the white chief's wife to you, they may be angry." Topenebe agreed, adding, "If they learn that tonight I will be returning to you the woman who is the wife of the second chief, this also may make them angry, even though she is the daughter of your wife. They may feel she is more a soldier's wife than a member of your family."

"My men," Black Partridge spoke again, indicating the five warriors with them, "will go with you now to your house. They will stay outside the house and guard you. You must stay inside. If they come, you must be sure to hide the woman."

Kinzie nodded. "Whatever I have," he said, "is yours and Topenebe's."

Topenebe spoke again. "My two, Keepoteh and his brother, will take you across in the big boat and they will stay with the boat to protect it from the others. Good-bye for now, my friend." He turned and started back toward the encampment with Black Partridge beside him.

Kinzie and Chandonnais boarded the boat and the trader was finally able to greet his family as the boatmen shoved off and began rowing toward the Kinzie landing. In a few minutes they touched the opposite shore there and within another ten minutes they were back in their own home again, Chandonnais and Josette with them, surprised to discover that as far as they could tell, it had not been plundered, although evidently most or all of the goods had already disappeared from the store, barn and other outbuildings.

An elderly chief from Black Partridge's village was in the house, having been placed there by Black Partridge to prevent its being entered and looted. John Kinzie recognized him as a medicine man of his tribe with some renown at surgical skills. He asked the old chief now if he would operate on Rebekah Heald's forearm, which was what was causing her so much pain now, the ball lodged near the bone it had broken.

The old man shook his head. "No, Father," he said, placing his hand over his heart. "It makes me sick here."

Kinzie understood. The man simply did not wish to become involved, and with justification. His standing as medicine man might be injured should it become known that he used his skills to help a woman who was, for all intents and purposes, a fugitive from his fellow tribesmen. The chief left and, with him gone, it was obvious that irrespective of whatever else occurred, the rifle ball had to be removed from Rebekah's arm. John Kinzie reluctantly elected to perform the operation himself, his scalpel to be his keenly honed penknife.

With Eleanor assisting him and Black Jim, Athena and Henry helping to hold her motionless, Kinzie began. Fortunately, Rebekah, though she tried to steel herself for it, fainted as he made his first incision. He worked swiftly and, probing with the point of the knife blade, quickly located the now badly misshapen ball. With some difficulty he removed it. The broken bone was set as well as possible under the circumstances and the incision sponged with water that had first been boiled. Then it was sewn shut with some of Eleanor's silk sewing thread and bandaged.

"What now?" Eleanor asked, as she and Athena began preparing something for them all to eat, including the five warriors sitting on the ground a few yards from the house, and the men still in the boat.

Kinzie thought about it and finally shook his head. "We're not finished with trouble yet. First we better try to somehow arrange the ransom of Captain Heald. If we can do that, then we've got to get him and Rebekah away from here — to St. Joseph, I suppose. Then, as soon as it's really safe for us to do so, we'll all go, too."

"Do you think it'll get really safe?" his wife asked.

"Maybe," he replied. After a moment he added, "Maybe not."

2:45 P.M.

The summons for John Kinzie and Jean Baptiste Chandonnais to attend a council of the Indians being held at the Frog Creek encampment across the river had come just an hour ago, brought by none other than Black Partridge. With him, the trader — no longer wearing the money vest — and his chief clerk recrossed the river and were led to one of the larger wigwams. There, a dozen or more chiefs were gathered, all the principal Potawatomi chiefs exclusive of Ncscotnemeg, and here also was Captain Nathan Heald, under guard and seated upon a mat, in pain and favoring his injured hip. His features were drawn, but his eyes lighted when he saw the trader and his half-breed employee.

The temper of the Indians in the confined quarters was not good. There were ugly murmurings at the entry of the men and, as was his due as resident chief, Black Partridge immediately addressed the trader.

"Shawneeawkee, the chiefs of the Potawatomi wish to know why they were deceived. They were told they would be given guns and ammunition and liquor; yet these things were not given, they were destroyed. Why? Further, we have been told, Brother, that the flour that was given to us by him," he pointed at Heald, "is poisoned and that if we eat of it, we will die."

Kinzie bristled at once. "Whatever bad bird has whispered to you that the flour you were given is poisoned has a tongue that is black with his lies. Had the white chief even thought of doing such a thing, which he did not, I myself would have told you of it and asked for his death as a consequence." He looked at Siggenauk, Waubansee, White Raccoon, Sunawewone, Nescotnoning, Mittatass and the others in a sweeping glance. "Bring this supposedly poisoned flour to me now," he said angrily, "and I will eat of it in your presence!"

Black Partridge waved off the suggestion. "I was sure that he who told us that, spoke falsely," he said, "but what of the other?"

Kinzie smiled frostily and reached into his pocket, extracting the folded order. "This," he said, holding it up for all to see, "is the order Captain Heald received from his chief, General Hull, at Detroit." Then he read it to them, translating the written English into the spoken Potawatomi. When he finished he pointed at the commanding officer. "This white chief was required to obey. If, at your battle, Siggenauk . . . Sunawewone . . . Mittatass . . . Black Partridge . . ." he looked at each in turn as he spoke their names, ". . . you send a runner to one of your lesser chiefs with instructions to do something, is he not obliged to obey? Would not his very life be forfeit if he refused to obey?" At their reluctant nods he went on. "Then how can you expect less of this white chief? He was ordered to destroy the extra guns and ammunition and this is what he did." As he spoke, he hoped no one would think to remind the listeners that Heald's offer to give them the guns and the ammunition was made *after* he had received the evacuation order. To forestall the possibility, he hurried on.

"As for the destruction of the liquor, Brothers, only a little of it belonged to the fort. Most of it was mine, to do with as I saw fit. You know, as do I, that when whiskey fills the belly, good sense flees the mind, leaving behind only anger and hatred and blood-lust, which in the end can only hurt those who have partaken of it. Often you chiefs have yourselves asked me to limit the amount of whiskey I sell to your warriors, and I have done as you asked. Can you hold me to account now for destroying that which would have turned them into beasts and ultimately led to their destruction? No! Too greatly do I value your friendship to do such a thing, for which you would then have been fully justified in holding me to account.

"No," he went on persuasively, "in all these matters there was not deception. But if we here are to speak of deception, what of yours — you who promised to escort the Americans in peace to Fort Wayne? Who were those who were deceived, the Indians or the Americans? You *know!*"

Now it was Siggenauk who rose from among the seated chiefs, who were obviously discomfited by the turn the talk had taken. "Our Brother, Shawneeawkee, speaks sharply," he said, "but with truth. We did deceive the Americans, but what we did was part of the warfare in which we are engaged, for we are tied to the British, who are our allies and who have provided our needs when the Americans would not; who have not used every means to take our lands from us, as the Americans have."

He paused, glanced at Nathan Heald, then back at Kinzie. "I would speak to the white chief and you will be my tongue and my ears. In many ways we now regret what we have done here. Will your President forgive us for what we have done? Will he pardon us if we were no more to raise our tomahawk against him?"

Kinzie interpreted and Heald tried to stand, gasped with the pain the effort cost him, then sank back and replied without rising. "My President is a very kind and generous man. It is well known that he has always been disposed toward peace where the Indians are concerned. Yet, with what has happened here, which is very bad, I do not know what his reponse would be to such a question."

The trader repeated what he said to Siggenauk and then added his own comment. "If you are truly repentant in the matter, I offer myself in your service. If some of your principal chiefs will go with me to speak to the great white father, and bring along others who may be left as hostages to insure the return of those who have been taken here today, then the President might smile favorably upon you."

The chiefs began to discuss this among themselves in undertones and Kinzie seated himself beside Chandonnais, who looked at him approvingly. To the trader's left was Black Partridge's man, Awbenabi, a warrior with whom Kinzie had developed a friendship over the years. Now Awbenabi leaned close and whispered in his ear.

"Shawneeawkee, they will not do what you ask. Before you returned here, they had already reached their decision about what to do with the white chief, since Nescotnemeg refused to accept him. It is their decision that he is to be burned at the stake tomorrow night. Not all of the chiefs want this. Not Black Partridge. Not Waubansee. Not Topenebe. But enough that their way will be done. He is a dead man."

Kinzie's expression did not change and he sat quietly a few minutes more, knowing the crucial moment was now, if he was going to do anything at all. He came to his feet saying, "I would speak." The chiefs looked at him, surprised at being interrupted, which was in poor grace on the trader's part.

"I do not break in to hasten your decision," he went on, "for you should think well on it, to whatever length is necessary to do what you believe to be right. But this man," he pointed at the captain, "has wounds and is in great pain. I ask that while you deliberate, you give me leave to take him, with the help of Chandonnais, across the river to my house, where I may treat his wounds. Such an act of kindness," he added with quiet emphasis, "would do much to make the President believe you are honest in your desire for peace and be an aid in encouraging him to grant you pardon."

He had boxed them in neatly. Almost certainly they would not decide to ask pardon of the President, yet they were not ready to admit this; just as they were not prepared to have it known that Captain Heald was to be executed tomorrow. Now it was Sunawewone, a chief of medium height but heavy build, who came to his feet and responded.

"We do not wish him to be in pain," he said, "but he is still a prisoner and we would be foolish to let him from our hands without some guarantee of his return when you have finished treating his wounds."

"What sort of guarantee?" Kinzie asked, immediately suspicious.

"Two persons from your household," Sunawewone replied.

Kinzie hesitated only a moment. "It shall be done," he said. "Send some of your men across with us when we take him and they will be returned with two persons from my household."

The die had been cast. Now there was no way either side could back down and permission was granted. Immediately Kinzie and Chandonnais helped Captain Heald to his feet, Kinzie muttering to him to say nothing, and led him back to their canoe. Topenebe and four Potawatomi warriors Kinzie did not know ran after them and entered their own canoe and paced them as they crossed, then followed them to the house.

"Wait here," Kinzie told the warriors at the doorway, as he and Chandonnais helped the officer into the house. The warriors did not like it, but they waited. Inside they could hear a woman's voice raised in a joyful cry, followed by low conversation and, after a little while, the voices of men raised in protest. In a few minutes more Kinzie and Topenebe returned to the doorway. With them, their features a mixture of anger and fear, were his house slaves of so many years, Henry, along with Black Jim. Inside the house Athena was sobbing audibly. The trader, assuring his slaves that he would secure their release very soon and that there was nothing to worry about, turned them over to the warriors. One of the four Potawatomies scowled, saying the hostages were supposed to be members of Shawneeawkee's family. Topenebe shook his head and replied that the stipulation was that the hostages be persons from the Shawneeawkee's household — and these two slaves had been in his household for years. With misgivings, the warriors gave in and led the hostages back to their canoe.

Topenebe walked with them and when they were in the canoe, told them to wait a moment and then strode to the bateau where Keepoteh and his younger brother were still on guard. He spoke to them a few minutes and then returned to the canoe and was paddled back across the river with the two black hostages.

As soon as they were well gone, Kinzie returned inside and immediately made arrangements for the departure of the Healds. If they did not escape now, within the hour, chances are they would never get away at all. Kinzie had asked Topenebe's help and Topenebe had promised to send Chechepinqua — whom they all knew as Alexander Robinson — and three other warriors he could trust, to take the Healds away by canoe to St. Joseph. Keepoteh and his brother would not interfere. The men in the canoe carrying the Healds would be expert paddlers. As soon as they were moving along rapidly, Keepoteh and his brother would raise an alarm that the white chief and his woman were escaping. Obviously, they would be pursued, but Topenebe's paddlers were so good that the chief had no doubt they could keep ahead of pursuers at least until after nightfall. After that, escape would be easy. It was a risky plan, but the best possible under the circumstances.

4:00 P.M.

The plan worked with surprising ease.

Immediately after the departure of Topenebe and the four Potawatomi warriors with the two blacks as hostage, Rebekah and Nathan were prepared for departure. Kinzie returned Captain Heald's money vest to him and Heald donned it at once. Their wounds were cleaned and medicated with a healing salve and bandaged as best possible under existing conditions — though there was no possibility of Kinzie operating on the captain's hip to remove the lead ball, as he had done with the one in Rebekah's arm. They were given clothing that belonged to the Kinzies and a few supplies — flour and salt in leather pouches, a few pieces of jerky, a small amount of pemmican. By this time a fairly large canoe had arrived at the Kinzie landing, with the fifty-one-year-old Chechepinqua and three other warriors from Topenebe, all of them disguised in the garb of French voyageurs.[305]

At a surreptitious signal from Keepoteh on the bateau, who had waited for a time when none of the Indians across the river were in sight, the Healds, carrying their meager provisions, left the house as nonchalantly as possible and, Rebekah helping to support her husband, walked to the canoe and got in. Within moments the paddlers were thrusting it along at a remarkably swift pace. As soon as it reached the point where the river turned southeast to enter the lake in another hundred yards or so, John and Eleanor Kinzie and Chandonnais burst from the house and ran to the landing yelling and waving their arms. Keepoteh and his younger brother took up the cry and soon some Indians began gathering near the mouth of Frog Creek, drawn by the ruckus.

Keepoteh and his brother leaped from their bateau and ran to a canoe nearby and started paddling across. Halfway there, Keepoteh called to those who gathered that the white chief and his woman were escaping in a canoe. Instantly there was consternation on the shore. Some of the Indians ran for the encampment and others raced toward the mouth of the river. Four men ran to where the canoes were beached, leaped into two of them and, with both men paddling in each little craft, surged in pursuit.

It was too late. By the time the runners reached the mouth of the river, the canoe bearing the Healds was well out into Lake Michigan, beyond effective rifle shot and paddling swiftly to the south and east. The two canoes in pursuit soon appeared and shot out into the lake, continuing to follow, but there seemed little likelihood they could overtake the one manned by what appeared to be four French voyageurs ahead of them.

"Now," Kinzie said, "we have only four things to worry about."

Eleanor and Chandonnais looked at him expectantly.

"Convincing them," he explained, pointing at the two canoes now com-

ing across the river toward them from the encampment, "that Captain
Heald escaped on his own without any help from us; getting Margaret
back into this house tonight; seeing if we can get Henry and Black Jim
back here safely; and getting away safely ourselves."[306]

4:30 P.M.

With a strong guard of his own men left behind to watch over the
Kinzies' house, Black Partridge and the several chiefs who had accompanied him returned to the encampment in their canoes. They had listened
in angry silence as Shawneeawkee explained how he had treated the
wound of the captain and then had left him, seemingly asleep, in a bedroom while he saw to his own family. A little later, checking the room, he
found the window open and the captain gone. Immediately he and his wife
had rushed to the door, had seen the canoe just turning the bend toward
the mouth of the river and had immediately raised the alarm, which had
been echoed by Keepoteh and his brother. No, Shawneeawkee said, he
had no idea who the French voyageurs were that Heald had somehow
managed to hire to get him safely away.

Had it not been for Black Partridge's reserved acceptance of the story
and the corroboration, so far as they knew, by Keepoteh and his brother,
the delegation would not have believed them. But, swayed in particular by
Black Partridge, they grudgingly accepted the explanation and left, darkly
warning the Shawneeawkee that he probably had not heard the last of this.
No mention had been made of Rebekah Heald and Kinzie had breathed a
sign of relief since evidently it was not widespread knowledge that she was
no longer a prisoner in Kawbenaw's wigwam.

The important thing now was to await Margaret's return here after dark
tonight and then make plans for getting away.

12:00 MIDNIGHT

"Thank God the children are asleep at least," Eleanor said, her voice
strained. "Those cries will be in our dreams — our nightmares! — for the
rest of our lives."

Her husband, standing with his arm around her on their porch facing
the river, tightened his grip around her and agreed. "The children and
Margaret, too," he said. "There would've been no way to convince her
that Linai wasn't a part of it."

"Maybe he was." The words had a hollow ring.

"Maybe," he echoed. "We can only hope not. Somehow, some time
we'll find out for sure."

But he wondered if they really would. Nothing was certain now, including the possibility of their own escape. The successful flight of the
Healds — still just the captain, so far as the Indians knew — had set the

Potawatomi encampment into an uproar. The pursuit had continued for fifteen miles, following the Lake Michigan coastline toward the Indiana and Michigan territories. The anger of the Indians was terrible and word had filtered to the Kinzies through Black Partridge's men that there was a good possibility that some sort of vengeance on Shawneeawkee and his family was being contemplated for the morrow, as retaliation for letting the white chief escape, whether or not with the trader's knowledge.

Two hours ago Black Partridge had returned, bringing with him Margaret Helm. Her fear was still immense. Unable to speak the Potawatomi tongue with any degree of proficiency, she had no idea of why Topenebe had turned her over to Black Partridge nor why the Chicago Potawatomi chief had taken her quietly out into the night. She had expected only the worst. Instead, he had brought her here and now she was under her parents' roof again, safe . . . to a point. Her fears for her husband remained unabated and she begged Black Partridge, through her stepfather, to find out where he was now and what would be done with him. Not until then did she learn that he had been awarded to Chief Mittatass of the Peoria Lake area.

"Tom," her stepfather told her gently, referring to his half brother, "knows Mittatass very well. I'll get word to him as soon as possible and see if we can effect a ransom. Just don't give up hope. Things have a way of working out."

Not unexpectedly, an enormous exhaustion had settled over Margaret and immediately after her mother had doctored her slightly injured ankle, she fell into a sleep that approached unconsciousness. And, as Eleanor and John had agreed, it was well that she had and that the four smaller children were also sound asleep. Only a short while later the screaming had begun from across the river and it was terrible — agonizing, drawn-out screams of terror and anguish and pain; cries of men being tortured. Cries of death.

Now, at last, the screaming had ended and a terrible silence had settled over Chicago. The long, long day of August 15, 1812, had finally come to an end.[307]

CHAPTER XIII

[*August 16, 1812 — Sunday, sunrise*]

WHEN Black Partridge and his brother, Waubansee, crossed the river at this time to relieve the warriors who had stood guard at the Kinzie house all night, they brought three warriors with them. They did not remain outside, as the previous guard had done, but came into the house and maintained their vigil there. That two important chiefs and three warriors should come personally to protect him and his family was a considerable honor to him, Kinzie knew, but it also created a sense of foreboding. And what Black Partridge told them now alleviated their apprehension not at all.

"Their anger over the white chief's escape still burns," the Potawatomi told him, his gold nose-ornament dancing slightly as he spoke. "New logs were heaped on that fire this morning when it was learned that I had given over to you last night the wife of the second white chief."

"Lieutenant Helm's wife is my stepdaughter," Kinzie said. "My wife's daughter. A part of my family."

"I know, but that is not how they consider her," Black Partridge said patiently. "To them she is the woman of an American officer and so she should be a prisoner and meet whatever fate it is agreed she should meet. During the night Kawbenaw left as well and everyone believes he took the first white chief's woman with him, for fear he would have to give her back for torture because of the escape of her husband. No one is very happy about what is happening. They are very suspicious of you because Captain Heald escaped yesterday. They are even beginning to get suspicious of me in that matter, and of Topenebe, yet we have continued to tell them that if any harm comes to you or your wife or children, those responsible will die. It is all that holds them back. Yet, as I have just said, they do not consider the Helm woman as part of your family and I am sure they will come looking for her here today. That is why I am here with Waubansee. Our presence will protect you, but it is doubtful that it will protect the officer's woman, your wife's first daughter. When they come here, they will want to search and I will not be able to stop them from doing so. You must get her away from here now."

They had discussed how best to accomplish this and finally came up with a plan: they would dress Margaret in the clothes of a Frenchwoman, borrowed from Josette Beaubien, and then she and Josette would calmly walk the short distance to the house of Antoine Ouilmette, whose wife, Archange, was the daughter of the French-Potawatomi half-breed François Chevalier. There she would pose as a French servant and return to the Kinzie house only after the Indians who were making the search had left the premises.

That was what they did now, as the Indians across the river were otherwise occupied. What they were occupied *with* was now becoming only too apparent. Distant shrieks rent the air as plumes of smoke began rising from the fort across the river. In a very short time the entire fort was a vast conflagration sending an immense billow of smoke into the sky.

Even from this distance the Indians could be seen prancing wildly about, many of them wearing shawls, bonnets, uniform coats, military hats and other items of clothing from amid the plunder taken from the fort before it was fired. Very soon the Indian Agency House just west of the fort was also being consumed by fire. These, however, were the only structures burned.[308]

As soon as the fire was over, Black Partridge said, some of the different tribal factions would begin leaving for home with their plunder and prisoners. Some, in fact, had left already, well before the dawn. But until all were gone, he warned, the possibility remained strong that they would send out a party in search of Margaret Helm.

But now she was at the Ouilmette house and, they thought, quite safe.

8:00 A.M.

Sergeant William Griffith crept out of his hiding place in the little playhouse in the woods north of the river. His eyes were haunted and his hands shook, though he clenched them into fists. He had heard the far-distant firing yesterday and was frightened by it, planning to remain in his hideaway throughout the whole day, but then the silence became just as unnerving and finally he had crept out, moving slowly and cautiously to the edge of the woods to peer out toward the south. He had been just in time to see the tallest Indian he had ever beheld tomahawk Sukey Corbin and smash out the brains of her two children against the side of the Burns house. He didn't think it possible to vomit silently, but somehow he man-

aged to do just that as he sped swiftly — and silently — back to his tiny
haven.

Now, having eaten nothing for close to thirty hours, he had analyzed
his situation carefully and the options open to him. Obviously, he could
not stay in the little playhouse, since hunger and thirst alone would drive
him out. But where could he go? His first thought was the Kinzie place, but
he rejected that idea out of hand. The Kinzie family had fled — or tried
to — with the departing garrison. Whatever had happened to the garrison
had very likely happened to them as well and it only stood to reason the
Indians would soon come to the trader's house and trading post to pillage,
assuming they were not already there.

The only answer seemed to be Ouilmette. Antoine Ouilmette was a
friend of the Americans, but he was also a friend of the Indians. His wife
was part Indian, wasn't she? The attackers would have no reason to
bother him, would they? So what better place to seek sanctuary than
there? With the decision made he felt better, much better. Nevertheless, as
he cautiously crept from his little haven, he was trembling violently.

8:20 A.M.

Nescotnemeg was in considerable pain from his wound. He had no
doubt he would survive it, but he was extremely uncomfortable. Shortly
after midnight, unable to sleep, he had ordered his party to mount their
horses and take him back to his village on the Kankakee. Now, having
crossed the Chicago Portage, they had reached the Des Plaines River,
which they would follow to where it met the Kankakee River to form the
Illinois. Then they would go upstream on the Kankakee to Nescotnemeg's
village at the mouth of the Iroquois. But here, where the Des Plaines
changed direction from running distinctly southwest to almost due south,
they paused to rest and eat.[309]

It was here that they were hailed and approached by a dozen horsemen.
They were Potawatomies from Tecumseh's village on the Mississinewa
and they had been moving very rapidly to be on hand for the attack at
Chicago. They were extremely disgruntled when they learned it was all
over, that the Americans had been defeated, a great portion of them killed
and scalped and a very large amount of the plunder already distributed to
the various Indian factions that had participated.

They listened gloomily to the details, but when they heard that the
Kinzie family had been spared, their interest sharpened. They knew of
the Shawneeawkee, but none knew him well and none owed him
any particular devotion. They immediately announced their intention to
ride on there and kill all the Kinzies and their friends and any Indians who
tried to stop them. Nescotnemeg warned that Shawneeawkee and his family were under the protection of Black Partridge and Topenebe, but they
scoffed at this.

"We are from Tecumseh!" they said boldly. "And Tecumseh is at war with the Americans. They will not stop us, lest they wish to face the wrath of Tecumseh!"

At this, Nescotnemeg was forced to admit they were probably correct. As the Mississinewa Potawatomies prepared to continue to Chicago and even hastily blackened their faces as a sign that they were coming in a matter of death, Nescotnemeg had no doubt that the Kinzie family would now be destroyed and nothing his protectors could do would any longer be of avail. They were now as good as dead. He sighed and shrugged as the black-faced party remounted and rode off.

It was sad, but it was war.

10:00 A.M.

The huge pillar of smoke that marked the final fate of Fort Dearborn and the Indian Agency House had begun trailing off considerably now, with only the crumbling brick magazine remaining standing and nothing but a few smoldering, blackened timbers left as evidence of what had been the fort. Many of the Indians, laden with the spoils that had been their share, were beginning to move away, a sudden haste upon them to leave this place, as if the ghosts of those who died would rise to wreak a terrible vengeance upon them should they linger too long.

As heavily laden as the Indians were, their prisoners were forced to carry even more, staggering under the weight of goods that had been forced upon them and made to understand that if they did not keep up, they would be dispatched. The bodies of those dead, stripped of clothing, universally scalped, some beheaded and most mutilated in various ways, were left lying where they had fallen.

But not all the Indians left and those who remained were still very angry over the escape of Captain Heald. They continued to believe that somehow John Kinzie was responsible for that and they also believed that the second officer's wife was hiding across the river. And so now they came to search. At the Kinzie house, Black Partridge was first to see them as half-a-dozen freshly painted warriors, armed with rifles, tomahawks and knives, put out from the far shore and came paddling swiftly across. At the Ouilmette house, Margaret Helm was watching, too, under protection of the Ouilmette family, who were presently being visited by Archange Ouilmette's sister, Sheshi Buison, wife of French trader Pierre Buison, whose house was a little farther up the north shore of the lake. And, in the cluster of currant bushes behind the Ouilmette house, Sergeant William Griffith watched from concealment, the fear heavy in him and the vision of the blackened remains of Fort Dearborn etched in his mind. All expected the approaching Indians to go immediately to the Kinzie house, but they did not.

The canoe scraped ashore and the six Indians set off at a lope, heading directly for the Ouilmette house. Immediately there was great concern inside. Even though Margaret was disguised as a French servant woman wearing a short gown and petticoat and a blue cotton handkerchief wrapped turbanlike about her head, there was fear she would be recognized. Hurriedly, she was concealed beneath a large featherbed against a wall. Madame Buison snatched up some sewing from a basket and sat down on the floor in front of the bed, spreading out some quiltwork in front of her. It was already a very hot day and Margaret felt nearly suffocated beneath the featherbedding, her discomfort so much increased by fear and excitement that she found it all but intolerable. Her voice was greatly muffled coming from beneath the bedding.

"Madame Buison! I can't stand this. I want to come out. I don't care if they see me. I can only die once. Let them put an end to my misery if they want to."

"*Silence!*" hissed the trader's wife. "If you have no thought for yourself, have thought for others! Your death would be the destruction of us all. Black Partridge has said that if one drop of the blood of your family is spilled, he will take the lives of all concerned in it, even his nearest friends. Once such murders begin, there will be no end to it so long as there remains one white person or half-breed in this country. So be still!"

From her hiding place, Margaret heard the Indians come to the door where they were greeted by Antoine Ouilmette in a friendly manner and invited to come in. The voices were muffled and speaking in the Potawatomi tongue, so she did not follow all they were saying, but her heart beat so rapidly she thought she would die. The Indians were not making a concerted search, but it was obvious they were moving about the house from room to room, looking casually at everything and everybody. Several times she saw the legs and feet of Indians pass by her hiding place and at one point Sheshi Buison got up from the floor and sat on the side of the featherbed, almost stifling her, talking calmly all the while to the Indians in the room.

At last they left and began walking toward the Kinzie house. Shaken and breathing heavily, Margaret emerged from beneath the bedding. Then the whole family experienced another great scare when someone was heard climbing stealthily into the house through a back window. It turned out to be Sergeant Griffith who, as soon as he saw the Indians leave, left his hiding place in the bushes, sprinted to the house and climbed in.

The American sergeant's presence did nothing to ease the fears of the Ouilmettes, but he begged them to protect him and they did. His heavy black moustache and swarthy features made him look like the French-Canadian voyageurs, so they provided him with the clothing of such a workman. His uniform was taken away and he was clad in old dirt-stained and greasy buckskins, with the moccasins and belt and red kerchief for his head of the type the French engagees customarily wore. An old battered pipe clenched between his teeth made the disguise complete and very effective. The entire family was ordered to address him in French and though he did not understand the language, he passed very well as a *Weemteegosh* — which is what the Indians called the French-Canadian voyageur in the fur trade.

At the Kinzie house, the Indians arrived at the front porch and were met by Black Partridge, Waubansee, Keepoteh and his younger brother and another warrior. Three other warriors — Topenebe's men — were aboard the bateau, protecting it and its contents.

"What do you wish here?" Black Partridge asked.

"We seek the woman of the second white chief," one of them replied. "We have been told she is here."

Black Partridge shook his head, the gold nose-crescent bobbing. "Why then did you go first to the house of Ouilmette?"

"We were told she might be there, too."

"Then you really do not know where she is and are only hoping to find her."

"Yes, that is true. But we believe she is here. We wish to see inside the Shawneeawkee's house."

Black Partridge and his fellow protectors, at a signal he gave, stepped back to let them pass. The chief had his hand on the tomahawk in his belt. "Do not think to hurt any member of this family as you look," he said coldly. "Any who harm them will die."

The expressions of the warriors darkened but they made no response. They entered the house and walked from room to room. When they filed into the parlor where the Kinzie family was seated, Black Partridge and his people followed them into the room and sat down on the floor between the family and the intruders. There they remained while the warriors looked about until the searchers finally left without a word, returned to their canoe and recrossed the river.

"Now what?" said Kinzie.

"Now we wait more," Black Partridge said, "until word comes from Topenebe that it is safe for you to leave. That may not be for two or three days. Then you and your family will be taken to St. Joseph."

4:00 P.M.

Having withstood the search by the Potawatomies at midday, the Kinzie family became a bit less apprehensive. Under the mantle of protection given by Black Partridge and Topenebe, they began to feel that all would be well. A few hours later a French-Canadian voyageur and a French house servant came to the Kinzie house from the Ouilmette house and turned out to be Margaret Helm and Sergeant William Griffith. The latter was immediately included in the plans for getting away from the area as soon as possible. For the first time the prospects actually looked bright.

That was when the dozen Potawatomi horsemen, their faces blackened, arrived at the Frog Creek encampment, left their horses there and immediately prepared to cross the river toward the Kinzie place in several canoes. Still on watch over the Kinzies and seeing the warriors' approach, Black Partridge became very alarmed. Their demeanor, the weapons with which they were armed and their blackened faces broadcasting their deathly intent permitted him to deduce with surprising accuracy what had occurred and why they were heading this way.

"Shawneeawkee," he murmured, "you and your family have escaped until now, but now I fear that time is past. Warriors are coming and I think this time, though we will try, I and my brother and the others here will not be able to stop them. Prepare yourselves." He turned and walked out, followed by Waubansee, moving toward the river and speaking in a low tone to his younger brother as they walked. "We have tried to save our friends, but it has all been in vain. There is nothing will save them now."

Inside the house, the trader put his arm about his wife's waist and told her what Black Partridge had said. She paled and looked immediately to the children, being watched over at the moment by Margaret. Kinzie could see a pulse beginning to beat rapidly in her throat and he tightened his grip around her. "We have been very fortunate so far, and our friends have done all they can to keep us safe. Now, for whatever lies ahead, we must meet it with courage."

Outside at the river's edge, Black Partridge and Waubansee met the approaching Indians, helped them beach their canoes and then questioned them. They told him of their meeting this morning with Nescotnemeg, of their disappointment at arriving too late for the actual attack and of their determination now to find what measure of satisfaction they could in the destruction of the Kinzies. And, anticipating Black Partridge's possible interference, they warned him to stay clear lest he and his people be hurt, and repeated to him what they had told Nescotnemeg about being Tecumseh's men. To attempt to balk them in their aim now would be to bring the wrath of Tecumseh and his forces down on them and, hearing them advise him of this in all seriousness, Black Partridge believed it. With a motion to his brother to do likewise, he stepped aside to let them pass and then fell in behind as they walked to the house. They pulled their tomahawks from their waistbands as they approached the structure. They were only twenty feet from the house when a loud halloo came from across the river. They all stopped and looked back. Two Indians stood there, their arms upraised for attention.

"Who are you?" Black Partridge called.

"I am a man!" came the arrogant answer from one of them. "Who are you?"

"I am Black Partridge," he called back. "Again I ask, who are you?"

"I am Sauganash!"

"And I," called the man beside him through cupped hands, "am Chaubenee."

A thrill shot through Black Partridge as a nervous muttering broke out among the black-faced warriors. Sauganash! And Chaubenee! These were two of Tecumseh's most powerful lieutenants. Immediately he cupped his own mouth and called back to them. "Come across. There are men here you should meet."

The pair waved in return and began moving up the shoreline toward a beached canoe. Black Partridge turned to the warriors who now stood looking at one another uncertainly. "Go inside the house if you must," he told them, adding, "but those with wise heads will not to be too swift to bring harm to those who are here until they learn the will of Chaubenee and Sauganash."

The warriors hesitated a moment more and then stepped inside. Waubansee entered after them, but Black Partridge and Keepoteh moved back to the river's edge to meet the pair now paddling toward them. When their canoe scraped ashore, Black Partridge shook their hands warmly and then swiftly outlined the situation for them. "Our friend, the Shawneeawkee," he concluded, "is in grave danger. You two alone can save him."

He followed them inside. Chaubenee's expression was grim as he entered, but Sauganash wore a pleasant smile and immediately removed his powderhorn and shot pouch and placed them, along with his rifle and tomahawk, on the floor behind the door. He was still smiling when he straightened, but there was no reflection of that smile in his eyes.

"Well, my friends," he said, addressing the warriors who stood with tomahawks in hand, facing the Americans who stood clustered together against one wall, "a good day to you. I was told there were enemies here, but I am glad to find only friends." His voice was buttery smooth and he went on easily, adroitly providing them a means of backing out of this touchy situation without losing face.

"Why," he asked, "have you blackened your faces? Is it that you are mourning the friends you have lost in battle? Or is it that you are fasting? If so, ask our friend here," he indicated Kinzie, "and he will give you food to eat. Perhaps you have never met him before, and it is good that now you have at last. The Shawneeawkee is the Indians' friend and never yet refused them what they had need of."

"Friends such as that," spoke up Chaubenee meaningfully, "always deserve the utmost of protection from those who have benefited from such kindness. It is a policy that our chief — and close friend — Tecumseh has always observed."

There was a long pregnant silence and then the warrior who was spokesman sighed heavily. "We have come here with our faces black in mourning for our friends," he said, the little speech delivered in a constrained voice. "We came to beg of the Shawneeawkee some white cotton cloth in which to wrap our dead before we bury them."

The tension relaxed. Kinzie immediately provided them with a full bolt of white cloth which was in a closet. He also gave them food and other presents — some clothing, a little gunpowder, several knives and a supply of lead. They accepted it without comment and left, returning to their canoes and then crossing the river.

"We are sorry to have arrived here so late," Chaubenee said, speaking to both Black Partridge and Kinzie. He added, without elaboration, "We were delayed."

Sauganash agreed with him. "You will be safe while we are here," he told the trader. "But we will not stay long and it would be well for you to leave."

"We are waiting," Kinzie said, "for Topenebe to tell us when we should leave to go to his village at St. Joseph."

Chaubenee nodded. "That is good. It will be safe for you there under his protection. It will not," he added, "be safe for you at this time in Detroit or at Fort Wayne. We will speak with Topenebe and he will get you away soon."

And for the first time since the arrival of General Hull's order for the evacuation of Fort Dearborn, John Kinzie's deep fear for his family began to abate.

5:00 P.M.

Hardly a few miles from Detroit, the American detachment under Colonels Duncan McArthur and Lewis Cass stood watching quietly and with deep suspicion as the three British officers approached on horseback under a white flag. They stopped some thirty paces away and one — Captain Elliott — dismounted and strode to where McArthur and Cass were standing. He stopped and saluted and then courteously handed Colonel McArthur a folded piece of paper.

"From your commanding officer in Detroit, sir," he said.

Duncan McArthur held the note for a moment without looking at it, then bent his head faintly. "Thank you, Captain," he said. He opened the paper, found he was holding it upside down, turned it over and read, the blood draining from his face as he did so.

> Head-Quarters, at Detroit
> 16th August, 1812
>
> SIR —
>
> *I have signed articles of capitulation for the surrender of this garrison, in which you and your detachment are prisoners of war. Such part of the*

Ohio militia as have not joined the army, will be permitted to return to their homes, on condition that they will not serve during the war — their arms, however, will be delivered up if belonging to the public.

I am, very respectfully, your most obedient servant.

W. HULL, *Brig. Gen.*
Commanding the N.W. Army

COL. DUNCAN M'ARTHUR.

His expression frozen in a tight-lipped grimace, McArthur silently handed the letter to Cass, who read it swiftly. Never noted for an ability to control his temper, he could not do so now. Tears sprang into the eyes of the detachment's second-in-command and were dribbling down his cheeks when he finished.

"Traitor!" he cried in a voice that was breaking. "He has disgraced our country!" He jerked his sword from its scabbard, causing the British captain to take a hasty step or two backward in alarm, but he needn't have feared. The Ohio Militia colonel snapped the sword in two across his knee and flung the pieces savagely from him. Then his shoulders heaved and he buried his face in his hands.

Without option in the matter, the colonels surrendered their detachment and marched the remaining distance to the fort. Most of their companions were gone by the time they arrived, but from the few who remained they learned what had occurred to result in so incomprehensible a situation.

When the three militia colonels — McArthur, Cass and James Findley — had said their farewells on Friday, none could even have conceived of today's development. All three were nervous at the haste with which General Hull had sent them off, especially without provisions, yet they did not even entertain the possibility that Hull would not send the follow-up supplies as he promised; and in a few days they would be returning with the supply convoy which had waited so long at Raisin River. Colonel Findley was remaining at the fort and that alone eased the minds of McArthur and Cass, since their faith in Hull had plummeted.

The galling matters of the past few weeks — the failure to march upon Amherstburg, the failure to meet the British at Fort Malden in all-out battle when the advantage was so clearly and overwhelmingly with the Americans, the ignominious retreat from the Canadian side of the river at Sandwich back over to Detroit — all were enough to shake their faith to the very foundations. Despite that, and despite the fact that their spies had reported the arrival of General Isaac Brock with some three hundred fifty troops at Amherstburg, it was inconceivable that Detroit should fall. The statistics alone where amazingly in favor of the Americans.

Brock's force was hardly to be considered a real threat — thirty artillerists, three hundred regulars, four hundred largely undependable Canadian militia, six hundred Indians under Tecumseh. A total force, counting the Indians, of only thirteen hundred thirty men. Hull, on the other hand, not only had the Detroit fortifications for protection, he had over two thousand men. True, it was important to escort in the supply convoy with the beeves and foodstuffs and equipment being brought by Captain Brush, but those supplies were not yet absolutely essential for survival.

At the time the American detachment under McArthur and Cass left, the army's strength at Detroit was impressive. In addition to the two thousand men, General Hull had thirty-three pieces of artillery — twenty-five iron and eight brass pieces, with cannon up to the twenty-four-pounder class. Nor was ammunition for the big guns wanting. For the monstrous twenty-four-pounders alone there were six hundred rounds of shot, of which two hundred were the grapeshot that was so devastating and demoralizing to infantry troops. A similar number of rounds was on hand for the six-pounders and there were two hundred rounds for the four-pounders. Above and beyond that, seventy-five thousand cartridges were all made up and ready to be fired in the rifles, plus the fact that every soldier had twenty-four cartridges in his belt-box. If, for some inconceivable reason, that ammunition ran short, more cartridges could easily be made up, since there were sixty barrels of gunpowder and one hundred fifty tons of lead. Finally, although they were admittedly on short rations, there was food enough in the fort to support the garrison fully for twenty-five days if need be.

On the morning after McArthur and Cass left with their detachment — the very morning that Fort Dearborn's occupants at Chicago were marching out of the main gates and straight into total disaster — the Detroit garrison was astonished to find that General Hull had erected his huge red-and-blue marquee tent in sight of the enemy across the river. There were those who murmured darkly that it was some kind of prearranged signal being sent to the British by the American general. A short while later, Major Jessup, who had been reconnoitering downstream from the fort in the area of Spring Wells with Captain Josiah Snelling, returned and asked the general for permission to take a twenty-four-pounder down there, believing they would have no difficulty using it to sink the principal warship of their enemy here, the *Queen Charlotte*, but General Hull denied the request.

When next both Jessup and Snelling asked permission to take a one-hundred-man detachment across the river to spike the enemy's cannon, which were now positioned to bombard Detroit, General Hull merely sent them on their way again with the vague comment that "I will think on it." The matter was never brought up again.

At ten o'clock yesterday morning, the fifteenth, a court of inquiry had convened under General Hull's second-in-command, Lieutenant Colonel Miller, to inquire into the fall of Fort Mackinac. The inquiry had been called at the request of Porter Hanks, erstwhile commander of the post, who wished to clear his name of any wrongdoing in Fort Mackinac's capitulation. That official inquiry was abruptly adjourned and postponed when it was learned that two British officers were coming across the river under a white flag.

The two officers were Major J. B. Glegg and Lieutenant Colonel John McDonnell. Incredibly, they carried with them a surrender demand from General Brock to General Hull. It read:

H.Q., Sandwich, August 15th, 1812

Sir —

The force at my disposal authorizes me to require of you the surrender of Fort Detroit. It is far from my inclination to join in a war of extermination; but you must be aware, that the numerous body of Indians, who have attached themselves to my troops, will be beyond my control the moment the contest commences. You will find me disposed to enter into such conditions as will satisfy the most scrupulous sense of honor. Lieut. Col. M'Donnell, and Major Glegg are fully authorized to conclude any arrangement that may prevent the unnecessary effusion of blood.

I have the honor to be your most obedient servant,

Isaac Brock, Maj. Gen.

His excellency, Brig. Gen. Hull,
Commanding at Detroit.

Initially flabbergasted at the unmitigated gall of the inferior force demanding the surrender of a superior force safe within its fortification, the American troops finally burst into laughter. It was the most classic example of insolence they had ever encountered. But then, when Hull remained closeted with the two British officers for what seemed an unconscionable length of time, the laughter dwindled away and was replaced by a faint but growing apprehension. Surely the general couldn't possibly even *consider* such a demand!

The tenor of his troops evidently had much to do with the way William Hull, after deliberating for over three hours, finally answered Brock's demand. He seemed almost ingratiating in his response and clearly eager to absolve himself of anything that might cause his opposite number irritation.

Head Quarters, Detroit, Aug. 15

SIR —

I have received your letter of this date. I have no other reply to make, than to inform you that I am ready to meet any force which may be at

your disposal, and any consequences which may result from any exertion
of it you may think proper to make.

I avail myself of this opportunity to inform you, that the flag of truce,
under the direction of captain Brown, proceeded contrary to my orders,
and without the knowledge of Colonel Cass, who commanded the troops
who attacked your picket, near the river Canard bridge.

Adroitly, it seemed, General Hull had laid the blame for the attack on
Colonel Cass and seemed to absolve himself of knowledge of the offer to
surrender which he had sent earlier to the British when, in fact, it was only
Cass who was ignorant of it. Hull went on:

I likewise take this occasion to inform you, that Gowie's house was set
on fire contrary to my orders and did not take place until after the evacu-
ation of the fort. From the best information I have been able to obtain on
the subject, it was set on fire by some of the inhabitants on the other side
of the river.

I am, very respectfully,

> *Your excellency's most obdt. servt.*
> *W. HULL, Brig. Gen.*
> *Com. the N.W. army of the U.S.*

His excellency maj. gen. Brock,
commanding H.B. Majesty's
forces, Sandwich, U. Canada

As soon as the British officers had left the fort with his reply, General
Hull, appearing very distraught, vanished into his quarters within the fort.
A short while later a rider left, carrying a message to Colonel McArthur,
ordering him to abort his mission to escort the supply train from Raisin
River and return immediately to Detroit. Ironically, at this very moment,
McArthur and Cass, twenty-five miles away and having been without food since their departure the day before, had decided to camp where
they were to await the supplies Hull had promised to send after them. If
the supplies didn't come by tomorrow morning, they had decided on their
own to turn back. Captain Brush's supply train was still forty-seven miles
from them and without food to sustain them, they could not possibly
make it.

At three-thirty in the afternoon, the bombardment of Detroit had begun
from the British batteries across the river — the batteries that Hull had
steadfastly refused to fire upon. There was still no American return fire,
by order of General Hull, and the American troops tried as best they
could to protect themselves from the cannonballs striking and exploding
about them. The bombardment lasted for six and a half hours and when it

ended, at 10:00 P.M., it was followed by an ominous silence for an hour, and then that silence broken by a full-scale war dance of the six hundred warriors under Tecumseh.

Long after midnight, and still hours before dawn this morning, Tecumseh and his warriors crossed the river and silently surrounded the fort. At dawn the bombardment recommenced, during which the majority of General Brock's army crossed the river from Sandwich to Spring Wells uncontested.

By seven o'clock this morning, General Hull was near a state of collapse, uncontrollably shoving wads of chewing tobacco into his mouth and chewing it automatically, while drools and dribbles of browned saliva dripped from his mouth corners and stained his uniform. He did not even notice. When his officers addressed him, he replied not at all or with answers so garbled that they were beyond comprehension. Captain Abraham Hull, his son and aide, had gotten himself so thoroughly intoxicated and became so belligerent that he accosted a superior officer and even challenged him to a duel. He was taken to his quarters and immediately passed out across his bed.

General Hull became even more out of control when a sixteen-pounder cannonball screamed across the river, smashed into the fort and caught Lieutenant Porter Hanks in the middle and tore him in half, then ripped the legs off of Dr. James Reynolds, surgeon's mate of Cass's company, killing him as well. Another officer, Captain Robert Blood, was badly injured at the same time.

It was not long after that when Brock began moving his army up the main road from Spring Wells to Detroit, advancing directly on the fort, expecting at any moment to be met by a devastating barrage of grapeshot. Instead, he was astounded to be met by an officer from General Hull under a white flag. Could it be possible that Hull was going to give up without a fight? In his message to the British commander, Hull asked for three days of truce in order to consider the advisability of surrendering. Brock's curt reply left him little room for dilly-dallying. He would give Hull three hours. If Detroit was not surrendered by then, full attack would begin.

The American artillerists had their cannons pointed directly at the approaching enemy, but the senior artillery officer, Captain Dyson, acting under direct orders from General Hull, ran up to them, whipped out his sword and threatened to cut down the first artillerist to fire.

Major Jessup stumbled over his own feet in his haste to reach General Hull in the commander's quarters. Was the general actually preparing to surrender? Hull's reply was jibberish and Jessup finally went away, to be replaced only a few minutes later by Ohio Militia Colonel James Findley rushing into the general's quarters.

"What in the hell is going on?" he demanded, his sharp words cutting through the fog blanketing the general's mind.

"We can get better terms if we surrender now," Hull replied.

Stunned, appalled and angrier than he could ever remember being, Findley spun away and sought out the general's second and suggested they arrest Hull, whereupon Lieutenant Colonel Miller could assume command and they could fight the enemy. Miller, in full sympathy with Findley, could only shake his head. "I am," he said, "a soldier; I shall obey my superior officer."

At 10:30 A.M., Abraham Hull, still reeling a bit from his indulgence, was sent out to the British under a white flag. Half an hour later he returned with Lieutenant Colonel McDonnell and Major Glegg again. They repaired to the general's quarters and Hull sent word out asking that several officers assist in drawing up the articles of capitulation. All refused, at first, but finally, being ordered to appear, Lieutenant Colonel Miller of the regulars and Captain Elijah Brush of the Michigan Militia presented themselves for that distasteful task.

By 11:30 A.M. the capitulation had been drawn up and signed, by which General Hull surrendered not only the Northwestern Army of the United States at Detroit, but the supply train at Raisin River, the detachment under Colonels McArthur and Cass, and the entire Michigan Territory:

> Camp at Detroit, August 16, 1812
>
> Capitulation for the surrender of Fort Detroit, entered into between Major General Brock, commanding His Britannic Majesty's forces on the one part, and Brigadier General Hull, commanding the northwestern army of the United States, on the other part:
>
> 1. Fort Detroit with all the troops, regulars as well as militia, will be immediately surrendered to the British forces under the command of Major General Brock, and will be considered prisoners of war, with the exception of such of the militia of the Michigan Territory as have not joined the army.
>
> 2. All public stores, arms, and all public documents, including everything else of a public nature, will be immediately given up.
>
> 3. Private persons and property of every description will be respected.
>
> 4. His excellency, Brigadier General Hull, having expressed a desire that a detachment from the State of Ohio, on its way to join the army, as well as one sent from Detroit, under the command of Colonel M'Arthur shall be included in the above capitulation, it is accordingly agreed to; it is, however, to be understood, that such part of the Ohio militia as have not joined the army will be permitted to return to their homes, on condition that they will not serve during the war. Their arms, however, will be delivered up, if belonging to the public.

5. *The garrison will march out at the hour of 12 o'clock this day, and the British forces will take immediate possession of the fort.*

J. M'Donnell, Lt. Col. Mil. P.A.D.C.
J. B. Glegg, Maj. A.D.C.
J. Miller, Lt. Col. 4th Regt. U.S. Inft.
E. Brush, Col. 1st Regt. Mich. Mil.

Approved:
Wm. Hull, Brig. Gen. Com. N. W. Army
Isaac Brock, Maj. Gen.[310]

As soon as the American soldiers — regulars and militia alike — learned that their general had actually signed a capitulation without even firing a shot in defense, they reacted as men who had been betrayed in the worst possible way, which many felt to be the case. Numbers of the men wept openly and others smashed their guns or swords. Vile names rent the air as General Hull was roundly castigated. And now the men were more certain than ever that Hull's sending out the detachment under McArthur and Cass had been no more than a ploy to get them out of the way so he could surrender without interference. Not a man there believed other than that if the two Ohio Militia colonels had been on hand, they would never have allowed the capitulation to take place, had they had to resort to mutiny in order to prevent it.

By the middle of the afternoon, the Americans, having surrendered their weapons, had filed out of the fort and been loaded aboard British vessels, which took them to the landing at Spring Wells. One of the officers, in the cramped quarters of the vessel he was on, composed a bitter verse on a scrap of paper, which effectively reflected the temper of the entire army at this time:

> *Our hopes were fixed — our honor safe —*
> *Fancy had shown us victory won,*
> *Full blooded valour fill'd each breast —*
> *Courage and country made us one.*
> *Yet one there was, whose dastard soul,*
> *Ne'er felt a pulse, but beat to fear —*
> *Yes, Hull was there, he had controul,*
> *And drew from bravery's eye the tear.*
> *Curst be this wretch — forever curst,*
> *Who has his country's trust betrayed,*
> *May Hell with all its horrors burst,*
> *And hurl destruction o'er his head!*

General Brock had quickly composed a proclamation which was publicly posted in Detroit:

Whereas, the Territory of Michigan was this day ceded by capitulation to the arms of His Britannic Majesty, without any other condition than the protection of private property, and wishing to give an early proof of the moderation and justice of the government, I do hereby announce to all the inhabitants of the said Territory, that the laws heretofore in existence shall continue in force, until His Majesty's pleasure be known or so long as the peace and safety of the said territory will admit thereof. And I do hereby also declare and make known to the inhabitants, that they shall be protected in the full exercise and enjoyment of their religion, of which all persons both civil and military will take notice, and govern themselves accordingly. All persons having in their possession, or having any knowledge of any public property, shall forthwith deliver in the same. Officers of the militia will be held responsible that all arms in the possession of the militiamen, be immediately delivered up, and all individuals whatever, who have in their possession arms of any kind, will deliver them up without delay. Given under my hand at Detroit, 16th of August 1812, and in the 52nd year of His Majesty's reign.

Isaac Brock, G.C.[311]

That left only the matter of the detachment under McArthur and Cass. True to their plan agreed upon yesterday, when no supplies had reached them by this morning, they abandoned their mission to reach the supply train and began to return to Detroit.[312] They had been without food of any kind, except a few green pumpkins and raw potatoes that they found growing in a field, since Friday morning. They were within a mile of the fort when they were intercepted by a messenger informing them of the surrender. Refusing to believe it, McArthur ordered his men back to the Rouge River. They found a steer en route which the colonel ordered killed as food and, though it was put over a fire to cook, most of it was eaten raw or partially so.

They deliberated on what to do and finally sent Captain Mansfield in under a flag of truce. Along the way he was accosted by Indians and his horse, arms and everything of value that he had was taken. Nevertheless, he made it back to the fort and shortly afterwards was with the three British officers who returned with him to the encampment at the River Rouge.

Now the detachment stood and stared aghast at the British colors flying over Fort Detroit and they knew that they were a part of perhaps the worst military disgrace to Americans since the nation was established with its Declaration of Independence.

[*August 18, 1812 — Tuesday*]

John Kinzie stood at the bow of the large bateau that was ready to be shoved off at his order. All his family was in the boat, including Margaret

Helm. Sergeant Griffith was, of course, going with them.[313] They were still at rest along the northern bank of the Chicago River at his landing and he felt a pervading sadness well up within him as he looked across at the remains of Fort Dearborn and the Indian Agency House. Some fifty hours or more had passed since the installation was fired and yet, from here and there among the charred remains, tiny tendrils of smoke still wafted into the air. Except for those in the bateau awaiting him, and those whose bodies still lay where they had fallen, all the Americans were gone. A hundred or more Indians remained, but most of these were from Black Partridge's village, the others having gone back to their own villages with plunder and prisoners, or else gone on with the main body of warriors for the purpose of attacking Fort Wayne.

The trader's expression was bleak as he gazed upstream. Such a shame . . . such a waste. Most of what he had here was gone now and what little remained would disappear soon after his departure, he knew. Yet, he was no less convinced than Jean Baptiste Point du Sable had been during his years at this place, that Chicago and its portage was a gateway to empire. The setback it had suffered now was severe. But he knew that eventually the war would end, eventually there would be another peace with the Indians, and eventually, come what may, so long as he remained alive, he would return here one day and begin again. His future and Chicago's were inextricably interlocked.

"Let's go," he said quietly.

EPILOGUE

[*October 15, 1816 — Tuesday*]

CHICAGO had a history now.

Lifeblood had seeped into its soil and would forever remain as a heritage. Lives had been permanently altered by the events of August 15, 1812. And there were those who survived the initial massacre, only to die in captivity in the days and weeks and months to come. They were small, insignificant deaths, hardly noticed in the swirling maelstrom of the continuing war, but there were some who cared and noted the passing.

Private John Neads, his wife, Sarah, and their four-year-old son, Johnny, were among the remaining unfortunates. Led into captivity, John and Sarah were forced to carry heavy burdens of plunder and thus were unable to carry their son when he tired of walking. His whining and crying grated on the nerves of his captors and he so slowed their progress that they finally solved the situation by binding him to a tree. Forcing his parents to move on, they left him there to die of exposure. The private was next to go, surviving extreme rigors during a bitterly cold winter until mid-January before finally falling in his tracks and dying of starvation and exhaustion. The same fate struck Sarah Neads less than a month later.

Private Hugh Logan, cherubic, rotund, out-of-shape; a little man who quickly became exhausted when his captors marched him toward the villages on the Elkhart River. They had little patience with his lagging. Twelve miles south of Chicago they tomahawked him and took his scalp.

Privates Michael Lynch and John Suttenfield fared little better, though for a different reason. Both had been wounded badly enough that they, too, were unable to keep up as their captors marched them toward the villages on the Illinois River. In less than twenty-five miles they, too, had been tomahawked and scalped.

Private William Nelson Hunt did not quite last out the year. He managed to reach the Indians' village on the Rock River in northern Illinois — a tiny place of no more than a dozen wigwams — but, worn down by fatigue and privation and with insufficient clothing to adequately protect him, he froze to death during the last week of December.

The last of the immediate survivors to die was Private August Mortt. Unable to stand the rigors of the intensely cold January while traveling with his captors from one village to another, he sat down on a snow-covered log and wept uncontrollably. The Indians had no patience with this sort of behavior. They tomahawked him.[314]

Only eleven out of the total of fifty-seven privates survived, only two of the five corporals and only one of the three sergeants. Corporal Walter Jordan was one of the fortunate ones. At first his captor, White Raccoon, tied him up at night as they headed for the Wabash River, but Jordan acted so convincingly enthusiastic about being adopted as an Indian that on the fourth night of their march — August 20 — he was not bound. During the night he stole one of his captor's horses and fled, wandered generally eastward through the unfamiliar territory for a week and finally reached Fort Wayne on August 27, just in time to undergo the brief siege laid against that fortification by the Indians — including some who had been at the Chicago massacre — beginning September 1.

One of the greatest odysseys by the survivors was undergone by Susan Simmons, carrying her little daughter, Susan. Awarded to the Winnebagoes, she was forced to walk almost thirteen hundred fifty miles before reaching her home again. In addition to carrying Susan, she had to carry heavy packs, gather firewood, build camp fires and do other chores, as well as having to run a gauntlet with Susan in her arms. She was marched first to Green Bay and then, after a few weeks there, back to Chicago en route to Detroit. But then plans were changed by her captors after passing through Chicago again and instead of going to Detroit, they followed the east shore of Lake Michigan all the way up to the Mackinac Strait. Finally, from there she went to Detroit and then to Ohio. Still carrying Susan, she eventually arrived at her parents' home in Piqua.

Martha Lee's lot was considerably better. She and her daughter, Sally, had been awarded to Black Partridge and taken to his nearby village. He treated her with kindness and respect and it soon became clear he wished her to become his wife. She managed to put him off. In the midst of the following March, when Sally became ill, she prevailed upon Black Partridge to carry her daughter to Chicago to be treated by the limited medical skills of the trader, DuPin. Black Partridge found DuPin living in the Kinzie house and confessed to DuPin, as the trader treated the little girl, his desire for Martha Lee. DuPin suggested he go back to his village, get Mrs. Lee and return to Chicago with her. Black Partridge did so and, ultimately, when Martha made it clear as gently as possible that she did not wish to become Mrs. Black Partridge, allowed DuPin to ransom her. Monsieur DuPin and Martha, living in John Kinzie's house, soon married.

Mary Burns, with her youngest daughter, Catherine, in her arms and her eldest, Isabella Cooper, beside her, underwent a similar situation, though with a different outcome. The chief she was awarded to became enamored of her and wanted to have her as his wife, notwithstanding the fact that he already had an Indian wife who was not overly pleased at such a prospect. She vented her wrath by striking the baby with a tomahawk. Although the squaw missed killing Catherine, she did leave her with a scar on her forehead, not too unlike the scar Isabella had from being scalped by the young warrior at the wagon.

One of the corporals and eight of the privates who survived remained in captivity nearly two years before ultimately being released. They included Corporal Joseph Bowen and Privates James Corbin, Phelim Corbin, Dyson Dyer, Nathan Edson, Paul Grummo, Elias Mills, Joseph Noles and James Van Horne. These captives had been taken to villages along the Fox River and tributary streams in Illinois where they remained until the following summer, when they were ransomed by trader Michael Buison — son of Pierre and Sheshi Buison — in Chicago. Early in August of 1813 they were relayed to Mackinac and from there to Detroit in early September. There the British commander, Colonel Henry Procter, questioned them and then sent them on to Montreal as prisoners. They arrived there late in September and were questioned again before being sent on, still as prisoners of war, to Quebec, where they arrived on November 8. Finally, during the general prisoner exchange of April 18, 1814, they were released to American authorities at Plattsburg, New York.

The paths of the Kinzies, Healds and Helms remained intertwined for a while longer. Rebekah and Nathan Heald arrived safely at St. Joseph on August 18, resided temporarily with the trader William Burnett, and had their wounds quite adequately treated by the medicine man of Topenebe's village. Four days after their arrival, the Kinzies got there, accompanied by Margaret Helm, Sergeant William Griffith, Athena, Jean Baptiste Chandonnais and Topenebe's trusted warriors, Keepoteh and his younger brother. The Kinzies took up temporary residence with Topenebe's sister, Madame Bertrand, wife of a trader.

Not long after that, news of the fall of Detroit to the British came to them and immediate plans to go there were put in abeyance. The Kinzies were safe enough, but the Healds remained in distinct jeopardy; Indians were reported en route to St. Joseph, having heard the Healds were there. Dipping into the fund of money sewn into his vest, Captain Heald hired Chechepinqua — Alexander Robinson — for a fee of one hundred dollars to take him and his wife and Sergeant Griffith by canoe to Fort Mackinac, three hundred miles north, where they could turn themselves in to the British authorities. Heald reasoned, with some justification, that being a prisoner of war by the British was certainly better than being a captive of the Indians.

Far to the south, at Louisville, Rebekah Heald's father, Samuel Wells, received a package on September 5, sent by an old friend, Colonel O'Fallon. The colonel had seen, recognized and redeemed at St. Louis a number of the personal items that had been taken from Rebekah and Nathan — his monogrammed sword, her tortoiseshell-and-silver eagle's-head comb, their silver flatware, the monogrammed ring and brooch — and sent them on to Samuel Wells. News had reached Louisville only a few days before of the Chicago massacre and so, at receiving the mementos, the Wells family was certain both Rebekah and Nathan had been killed and they mourned the loss deeply.

Those two, however, along with Griffith, arrived at Mackinac on September 8 and Captain Heald immediately surrendered himself and the sergeant to the British commander, Captain Charles Roberts, who had captured Mackinac seven weeks before. Roberts treated them very well and a camaraderie was struck up between the two captains when it was discovered both were Freemasons. Roberts paroled Heald and offered him money to help him on his way — an offer that Heald politely refused with the explanation that he had ample funds to see him through, as well he did. On the next day, in a little open sailboat hired by Captain Heald through the help of Captain Roberts, the three set out for Detroit.[315]

Back at St. Joseph, still a bit concerned for his family, John Kinzie sent them on to Detroit, despite its being in British hands, on September 15. He, however, remained behind to do some business, moving about in the territory dressed as an Indian.[316] Eleanor Kinzie and her four younger Kinzie children, along with her elder daughter, Margaret Helm, arrived in Detroit on September 21. They turned themselves in to the Indian Agent, Thomas McKee.[317] In turn they were delivered up to the British commandant at Detroit, Colonel Henry Procter. That officer paroled them at once and allowed them to resume occupancy at the old Kinzie mansion close to the fort.[318] The two older Kinzie children, John H. and Ellen, were immediately enrolled in school nearby.

Ironically, the day after their arrival, the little open sailboat bearing the Healds and Sergeant Griffith arrived at Detroit and Captain Heald reported to the Detroit commander. Procter treated him with courtesy and allowed him to buy passage for all three of them on board the British ship-of-war, *Detroit*, upon which quite a number of American prisoners from Hull's surrender were to be transported on September 28 to Fort Erie on the Niagara River across from Buffalo.[319] Until that time the Healds and Griffith rested and recuperated at the Kinzie house and frequently visited with Judge Augustus Woodward, a prominent Detroit citizen, who was most interested in their story and greatly concerned for possible survivors of the Chicago massacre.

The three left on the scheduled date and reached Fort Erie on October 8. They were immediately taken across the river to Buffalo and released to American authorities.[320] The following day, Nathan and Rebekah left Buffalo aboard a small boat he had hired, heading for Fort Presque Isle.[321] They arrived there on October 11 and immediately hired a guide to take them southward across country to the old Fort Venango area on the Allegheny River.[322]

Four days later — on October 15 — they reached that destination, purchased a fairly good boat from an inhabitant there and began floating downstream to Pittsburgh.[323] On October 21, Nathan and Rebekah Heald arrived at Fort Pitt and here, two days later, Captain Heald wrote his official report of the Chicago Massacre to Adjutant General Thomas H. Cushing. It was a reasonably accurate but, at best, a rather sketchy report, recording the deaths of twenty-six regulars, twelve militia, two women and twelve children.[324] In his report, Captain Heald — who, unbeknownst to him, had been promoted to major on August 26, while he was still at St. Joseph — did not mention the money he carried away from Chicago with him and with which he had thus far purchased passage from St. Joseph to Mackinac, Mackinac to Detroit, Detroit to Buffalo, Buffalo to Presque Isle, guide service from Presque Isle to the Allegheny, a boat at the Allegheny for passage to Pittsburgh, and the passage he would still be purchasing for Rebekah and himself for the downriver trip he was planning to Louisville, nor for food, clothing and accommodations along the way.[325]

On November 8 the Healds left Pittsburgh, having bought passage to Louisville on a vessel heading for New Orleans. They reached their destination on November 19 and immediately went to Samuel Wells's house. Rebekah's family had been quite convinced of the demise of both of them and so the reunion was a startling, tear-filled, joyous occasion.

Unknown to Captain Heald, at just about the time he was arriving at Louisville, another survivor of the massacre was passing on his way upstream toward Pittsburgh with barely a pause — Heald's second-in-command, Lieutenant Linai T. Helm. He had been taken away from Chicago by Chief Mittatass, to whom he had been awarded, and wound up in that chief's village on the shore of Peoria Lake.[326] Nearby, at his trading post, Thomas Forsyth was alerted to the fact that Helm was a prisoner at the village. At this time Black Partridge was visiting and the Chicago chief volunteered to act as intermediary in an attempt to ransom Helm and gain his freedom. Forsyth authorized Black Partridge to offer Mittatass two mares and a keg of whiskey, which Helm did. Mittatass was not entirely pleased with the offer and held out until Black Partridge, on his own, offered in addition the gold nose-crescent he had worn for so many years, his rifle and his horse. Mittatass accepted and Helm was ransomed.

Second Lieutenant Helm remained with Forsyth for a while, giving his wounded heel an opportunity to mend completely before starting on a long journey. Then he floated down the Illinois to the Mississippi and arrived at St. Louis on November 2. Within a few days he managed to find passage aboard a bateau heading downstream on the Mississippi to the mouth of the Ohio, then upstream to Pittsburgh, paying for his transportation by performing the labors of an oarsman.

At Detroit, Margaret Helm, convinced now that Linai was quite probably dead, decided she should go to New York and inform her husband's parents of the loss. She left Detroit on December 15 and arrived at Fort George on Christmas Day. She was taken across the river on a smaller boat and then made her way from Buffalo to New York by going overland to Niagara, securing passage to Fort Oswego and traveling the portage route to the upper Mohawk River at Fort Stanwix. From there she traveled down the Mohawk to its mouth at the Hudson at Albany, then down the Hudson to New York City. She arrived at the Helm house in late February and delivered the tragic news to Linai's parents. She was still there a week later when, in early March, Linai Helm showed up at the door.[327]

For John Kinzie, just when it seemed that the worst had been weathered, unexpected problems developed. He rejoined his family at Detroit early in January, 1813, reported to Colonel Procter and received a parole. He then took up residence with his family in his old home and spent a good bit of time moving about the town, listening to conversations, observing things and occasionally visiting the British garrison at Amherstburg. And he wrote a good many letters. On February 4 he told Eleanor he was going out for a short while and was promptly arrested by Procter's men and taken to headquarters. There he was charged with spying and sending reports of his observations to William Henry Harrison. Before he could be imprisoned, however, a group of Indians arrived, led by Chaubenee and Sauganash. They had been alerted by Eleanor when John hadn't returned after a reasonable time, and so they took him out of the hands of the military and escorted him back home.

Eight days later — February 12 — he was arrested again and once more the Indians took over and freed him before he could be incarcerated. The third time, Henry Procter moved more swiftly. On February 22 he had Kinzie arrested again, immediately manacled and taken to a cell at Fort Malden, where he received very bad treatment. Here he remained for seven months.

After initial successes at Detroit and Raisin River, the war in the Northwest had started going very badly for the British, especially since William Henry Harrison had become commander of the Northwestern Army. Two sieges by the British and Indians at Fort Meigs failed and they had been dealt a signal defeat at Fort Stephenson. Time after time Henry Procter, now a general, retreated until the frustrated Tecumseh eventually confronted him, calling him a fat dog running away with his tail between his legs. He demanded that Procter stand and fight.

Much hinged on the naval battle shaping up on Lake Erie — the British fleet under Commodore Barclay against the American fleet under the much less experienced Oliver Hazard Perry. Permitted these days to take walks under guard along the riverbank at Fort Malden, John Kinzie heard the distant battle being fought on the lake on September 10 and then felt the thrill of excitement when, contrary to all expectations, it became known that the Americans had won.

Now John Kinzie was sure he would be liberated at last. He was wrong. The next morning he was tied to a horse and taken under guard on the long ride to Quebec, with the threat ringing in his ears that if he attempted to speak to anyone, he would be shot in the head. And so he was not in the vicinity when Procter abandoned Amherstburg and Detroit, hotly pursued by General Harrison, and when Tecumseh was killed at the Battle of the Thames on October 5.[328] The night before that battle, Tecumseh had predicted his own death on the morrow, divested himself of his personal effects to his closest friends, including Chaubenee and Sauganash, and then met privately with those two.

"What I have tried to do," he said sadly, "in uniting all Indians to stop the whites who have been pushing us back, has failed. Chaubenee . . . Sauganash . . . you have been my brothers and I have loved you. Now I speak from that love and ask that you obey in how I will now direct you. Our cause is done. After tomorrow, when I am gone, return to your own people at once. No longer raise your weapons against the Americans; it can only end in disaster for you and all your people. Make peace with them and in all ways possible, live in harmony with them. Help them in any way you can; be loyal to them in all ways; defend them against their enemies if need be, even should those enemies be other Indians, for, hear me, my brothers, the Indians can *never* win against the Americans. Join them, that you and your people may survive."

And because they believed him implicitly, both Chaubenee and Sauganash gave solemn oaths that they would do as Tecumseh directed. The sorrow in their hearts was immense the next day when, as he had predicted would occur, Tecumseh was killed. They had crept back into the battlefield that night and took the body away and buried it in a secret place. Then they left together immediately and returned to the area of Chicago, determined hereafter to adhere to the Americans as close friends and help them in any way possible.

Three weeks after that — on October 28 — John Kinzie, having undergone extensive questioning at Quebec, was placed in irons aboard a vessel bound for London. There, almost certainly, he would be put to death as a traitor and spy. But the vessel was only a few days out when it was pursued by an American frigate and forced to put in to Halifax for protection. On November 5 it tried again and this time sprang a leak so severe that they were forced to limp back to Quebec. There, Kinzie was removed from the ship and returned to his prison cell in the citadel, where he remained for the winter.

The shape of things was changing and the Indians were very clearly discouraged at supporting an ally who, ever more apparently, could not win. Chaubenee and Sauganash, back in the area of Chicago, met with Black Partridge and convinced him, too, to adopt the precept that Tecumseh had outlined for them. It was not difficult, since Black Partridge was inclined in that direction anyway. He was one of the few powerful chiefs who had always known in his heart the futility of trying to stand against the Americans. On January 2, 1814, he signed a major treaty of peace with the Americans at St. Louis.

The following day saw the commencement of the court-martial of General William Hull on charges of treason and cowardice. Whispers of its progress reached even to John Kinzie in his Quebec cell — along with another whisper of far more interest to him: someone — he didn't know who — had intervened on his behalf and he was to be released.[329]

With hardly more than the clothing on his back, John Kinzie was released on March 6 and began the long walk back to Detroit. Reasonably enough, he chose a route along the southern shore of Lake Ontario and Lake Erie, so that he would remain in American territory and run no further risk of being arrested by the British. It was on the twentieth day of his walk — March 26 — when the verdict was announced in the Hull court-martial. William S. Hull was acquitted of the charge of treason, but he was found guilty of cowardice and sentenced to death before a firing squad.

On April 18, John Kinzie, with a single shilling in his trouser pocket, stepped up to the door of his own house in Detroit, knocked gently, and a moment later was being smothered with hugs and kisses from an almost overcome Eleanor Kinzie and his four children.

Exactly one week later, President James Madison remitted the death sentence of William Hull. That same day a brief general order was issued in Washington, D.C.:

Washington City, April 25th, 1814
The rolls of the army are to be no longer disgraced by having upon them the name of Brigadier General William Hull. The general court martial, of which General Dearborn is president, is hereby dissolved.
　　　　　　　　　　　　　　By order of
　　　　　　　　　　　　　　J. B. Walbach, Adjt. Gen.

Perhaps the grandest development of all came when the Treaty of Ghent was signed on the day before Christmas, formally ending the War of 1812.[330]

Now, nearly two years after that, eyes were once again turning to the West. Treaties had been made with the Indians and they were no longer a problem. People were saying, in fact, that they'd never be a problem again. The last of the strongly anti-American chiefs among the Potawatomi, Main Poche, had died on a hunting trip last March in Michigan, while smashingly drunk. Indiana was now a state and, with that accomplished, could Illinois be far behind?

Last July 4, Captain Hezekiah Bradley, with a detachment of one hundred twelve men, arrived at the mouth of the Chicago River and began construction of a new United States fort there, directly on the ashes of the first. And, as the first had been, its name was Fort Dearborn.

And on this fifteenth day of October 1816, a small ship dropped anchor in the lake just off the mouth of the Chicago River. At its rail stood a fifty-two-year-old trader, his forty-seven-year-old wife and their four children, aged thirteen, eleven, nine and six. He put his arm around her and smiled, then pointed toward his trading post, still standing on the north side of the river.

"Welcome to Chicago, Eleanor," John Kinzie said. "It's going to be a great city. I promise you."

AMPLIFICATION NOTES

The amplification notes which follow here are numerically keyed directly to the text, without segment or chapter separation.

* * *

1. There have been a variety of spellings of John MacKinzie's surname, including MacKenzie, Mackenzie, McKinzie and McKenzie, but the correct spelling is MacKinzie.
2. Details of the French and Indian War, including the Battle of Quebec, may be found in *The Winning of America* series volume entitled *Wilderness Empire*.
3. The village of Cahokia was located in present St. Clair County, Illinois, just north of the present town of Cahokia and about two miles south of the city of East St. Louis, Illinois.
4. Full details of the siege of Detroit will be found in *The Winning of America* series volume entitled *The Conquerors*, along with details of the fall of the nine British forts: Fort Sandusky (Sandusky, Ohio), Fort St. Joseph (Niles, Michigan), Fort Miami (Perrysburg, Ohio), Fort Ouiatenon (Lafayette, Indiana), Fort Mackinac (Mackinac City, Michigan), Fort Venango (Franklin, Pennsylvania), Fort Presque Isle (Erie, Pennsylvania), Fort Le Boeuf (Waterford, Pennsylvania) and Fort Edward Augustus (Green Bay, Wisconsin).
5. Pontiac was buried by his friend and former commander of Fort de Chartres, Illinois, Captain Louis St. Ange de Bellerive, whom Pontiac had visited only a short time before his death. The burial is believed to have taken place on the site of the old Southern Hotel in St. Louis, Missouri, where a tablet was later erected in honor of the fallen chief.
6. Path Valley lost its identity after a few years, when the growth of Carlisle enveloped it. Located in Cumberland County, Pennsylvania, the Carlisle settlement was the genesis of the present city of Carlisle, Pennsylvania.
7. The Miami Indian villages along the Lake Michigan shoreline were located at the site of the present cities of South Milwaukee, Racine and Kenosha, Wisconsin; Waukegan, Evanston and downtown Chicago, Illinois; and Whiting, Indiana.
8. In years to come this great outcropping of rock overlooking the Illinois River eight miles southwest of Ottawa, Illinois, came to be known as Starved Rock and it is today the focal point of one of the Illinois state parks. It is probably the state's most recognizable natural landmark.
9. It has been estimated that the total population of the six tribes and seven sub-tribes of the Illinois Confederation was some two thousand four hundred fifty warriors and about three thousand women, children and elderly. A small handful

of women and children escaped the general slaughter which all but annihilated the tribes and took refuge under the French. A generation later, in 1800, their numbers had increased to a total of one hundred fifty individuals, but thereafter they gradually declined. In 1837 the remnant survivors sold whatever remaining rights they had to Illinois lands and removed to a reservation in Kansas. In 1867 they removed again, this time to Oklahoma, and became consolidated with the remainder of the Wea and Piankeshaw branches of the Miami tribe.

10. Tecumapese was also known as Menewaulakoosee.

11. Chiksika was also known by the name of Papquannake, meaning Gunshot.

12. Details of the birth of Tecumseh at the site of present Old Town, near Xenia, Ohio, may be found in *The Winning of America* series volume entitled *The Frontiersmen*.

13. The other four Shawnee septs were the Chalahgawtha and Thawegila (who were in charge of all things political and all matters affecting the tribe as a whole), the Maykujay (in charge of matters pertaining to health, food and medicine), and the Peckuwe (in charge of the maintenance of order and duty and Shawnee religion). The Kispokotha sept was in charge of all circumstances of warfare, including the preparation and training of warriors.

14. Burnett's trading post was located at the site of present Niles, Michigan.

15. The confluence of the two rivers was at the site of present Fort Wayne, Indiana. The Maumee at that time was also known as the Miami-of-the-Lake, differentiating it from the other two Miami rivers not too far to the south and east, the Great Miami River and the Little Miami River of western and southwestern Ohio.

16. France had ceded the vast Louisiana Territory to Spain in 1762.

17. Fort de Chartres, originally established by the French in 1722, was located on the east bank of the Mississippi River halfway between the mouths of the Missouri and Kaskaskia Rivers five miles upstream from the site of present Prairie du Rocher, Illinois. It was renamed Fort Cavendish in 1765 when the French commander, Captain Louis St. Ange de Bellerive, surrendered it to British Captain James Sterling and withdrew to St. Louis. The original name was preferred, however, and the name Fort Cavendish fell into disuse and gradually died away.

18. A case in point occurred as recently as the previous June, when William Murray, settler of Kaskaskia, purchased without government sanction a vast stretch of country from the mouth of the Illinois River just above St. Louis all the way upstream to the Des Plaines River and then up that stream to the mile-long portage to the Checagou River, then down that latter stream to its mouth at Lake Michigan, the site of present Chicago. Millions of acres were involved in the so-called purchase, for which Murray paid the magnificent sum of five shillings "and certain goods and merchandise." Murray, associated with several other Englishmen, formed themselves into the Illinois Land Company and prepared to sell it to would-be settlers from the East. The Potawatomies were only dimly aware of the transaction and they were not pleased. It was only the beginning. Similar organizations were in the formative stages under the names of the Ohio Company, the Ouabache (Wabash) Company and the Scioto Company.

19. Kispoko Town, principal village of the Kispokotha Shawnees, was located on the west bank of the Scioto River, across that river from the Pickaway Plains, approximately two miles southwest of present Circleville, Ohio, and fifteen miles north of present Chillicothe, Ohio.

20. According to Juliette Kinzie in her book, *Wau-Bun* (page 193) there were four other younger half-brothers to John Kinzie, but since they are never again mentioned anywhere else, it is reasonable to assume she referred to John Kinzie's four older stepbrothers, the Forsyth boys — George, William, Jr., Philip and Robert.

21. The present Hudson River.

22. Chalahgawtha was located three miles north of present Xenia, Ohio, at the small community called Old Town. This expansive Shawnee village was situated less than half a mile from the point where Massie Creek enters the Little Miami River from the east.

23. Site of present Point Pleasant, West Virginia.

24. In some accounts Spemica Lawba's name has been translated as meaning Bright Horn, but Big Horn is correct.
25. The McKenzie homestead being abandoned had been occupied by the family since early December, 1768. It was located on the east bank of the New River at the site of present Thurmond, West Virginia, approximately twenty miles northeast of Berkeley, West Virginia.
26. Henry Hay later became a prominent British trader among the Indians of the Ohio and Michigan areas.
27. That area in question was the whole region westward of what is now Fort Street in Detroit.
28. The fears were fully justified. The skeletal remains of George Forsyth were found by an Ottawa Indian fourteen months later, on October 2, 1776, in a heavily overgrown area rather close in to Detroit; so close in that he was evidently unable to hear the searchers, who were much farther out, calling to him. The rather extensive tract where his remains were found was known at the time as The Prairie Ronde. The remains were identified by lingering bits of auburn hair on the skull and the boots still covering the bones of his feet.
29. Full details of the Battle of Oriskany and related events will be found in *The Winning of America* series volume entitled *The Wilderness War*.
30. This was the stream presently known as Raccoon Creek, which empties into the Ohio River about ten miles downstream from present Gallipolis, Ohio.
31. The present Scioto River, which empties into the Ohio River at the western edge of Portsmouth, Ohio.
32. Formerly Kispoko Town.
33. In most accounts Jean Baptiste Point du Sable is credited with being the first permanent resident of Chicago. Gaurie, however, resided here at least two years before Du Sable and his "permanency" was of about fourteen years' duration, as opposed to Du Sable's permanency of about twenty-one years. Vague references indicate that even Gaurie was far from being first to settle in the Chicago area with any degree of permanency. Gaurie's home and trading post were located on the west bank of the North Branch of the Chicago River at approximately the point where present Fulton Street meets the river. The designation Gaurie River for the North Branch was short-lived and such reference vanished almost immediately following Gaurie's departure from the area.
34. In some sources the spelling of Topenebe's name is given as Topinebe, Topinebi or Topineby. The English meaning of his name is He-Who-Sits-Quietly, often shortened to merely Sits-Quietly.
35. The name has also been spelled Sigenak, Siggenaak, Suggenunk and Saganaynubee. In earlier years, the French traders had called Siggenauk by the name Le Tourneau.
36. The Potawatomi name of Black Partridge has variously been recorded as Mkede-poke, Muk-ay-tay-wu-zuk, and Muck-otey-pokee. Due to the difficulty of pronunciation, the English translation — Black Partridge — will be used in this volume.
37. The Potawatomi name of Main Poche has evidently been lost. In various documents of the British and Americans, Main Poche's name has been presented as Main Poc, Man Pock, Main Pock, Mar Pock, Marpoc, Mar Poc and other variations. However, the greatest accuracy occurs with Main Poche, which is directly of French origin and means "Puckered Hand" or "Withered Hand," referring to the congenitally deformed left hand of Main Poche, which rendered it clubbed, though not wholly useless.
38. Chechepinqua's name also appears in some accounts, alternatively, as Shishibinkwa.
39. The silver nuggets brought to John Kinzie by the Potawatomi and other tribesmen were very likely obtained by them from the Shawnees, who reportedly had a highly productive silver mine in Clifton Gorge near present Yellow Springs, Ohio. For further details on this and other matters of Indian silver in the Ohio area, see *The Winning of America* series volume entitled *The Frontiersmen*.
40. The Shawnee term *Shemanese* is literally translated as "Long Knives," referring to the swords carried by American officers, usually officers mounted on horseback and most specifically referring to the officers from Virginia generally and Kentucky

in particular. The Potawatomies also had a term for the whites of this ilk, though not particularly confined to those of Kentucky and Virginia, calling them *Chemokemon.*

41. Windigo's Indian name has been variously written as Wandaygo, We-en-dee-go and Wyndeego. His English designation was The Cannibal or, more loosely translated, Man-Eater. The Indian name of Chief Nakewoin has appeared in such spellings as Naakewoin, Nakiyowin, Nakewoin and Naukwin.

42. In some documents, official and otherwise, his name is presented as Pointe du Saible; occasionally as Pointe au Saible.

43. The land at the point of this confluence was for many years in Chicago's history known as Wolf Point, where one of the first and best known of Chicago's early liquor and hostelry establishments was built — the Wolf Tavern.

44. The Des Plaines River, named by early French traders in the area as "the River of the Plains," has also frequently been referred to in the earlier documents as "Riviere aux Plaines."

45. In some accounts, Du Sable's mother is said to have been a slave. The author has been unable to find any verification of this claim.

46. The post was located just above high water mark of the lake approximately one mile southwest of present Michigan City, Indiana.

47. This post was located on the west bank, less than one mile south of the city limits of present Port Huron, Michigan.

48. At the time when Du Sable arrived here, the area was referred to under a variety of similar names: Checagou, Chikagou, Checagoo, Eschecagou, and Chicago. Trader William Burnett, in his letters and records, referred to it principally as Chicago. There is, however, no clear-cut date recorded when the present spelling of Chicago came into general usage. However, to avoid confusion and further use of unfamiliar spellings, from this point forward in this narrative, the present form — Chicago — will be utilized. Although some rather extensive writings have been done on the etymology of the name and a number of interesting and perhaps accurate theories advanced, the most prevalently accepted basis is a derivation from the word Checagou or Eschikagou in the Potawatomi, meaning "onion" or "onion smell," referring to the great numbers of wild onions which grew in the swampy lowlands where Chicago was located. This tends to be borne out by many early references, especially among the French, to Garlic Creek when referring to the Chicago River.

49. Site of the present city of Olean in Cattaraugus County, New York.

50. Cornplanter here alludes to a common practice among the Seneca and many other tribes of adopting into the tribe a captive to fill the place of a relative slain in battle. The person so adopted did not have to be the same age as the slain relative, nor even of the same sex. The belief was that the Great Spirit would imbue the captive, after adoption, with the spirit of the slain relative.

51. What was then called Plum Creek is now known as Crooked Creek, though the name of Plum Creek is still used as a designation for one of its tributaries about fifteen miles upstream. The then Plum Creek emptied into the Allegheny approximately five miles downstream from present Kittanning, Pennsylvania.

52. Present Ford City, Pennsylvania.

53. The present city of Kittanning is the county seat of Armstrong County, Pennsylvania.

54. In subsequent years, Thomas Lytle moved with his parents to Detroit. During late May 1798, when he was twenty-five, he traveled on horseback to the Thames River, in Ontario, en route to see the young woman he had been courting for some time. At this time he found the river badly swollen from recent rains. He attempted to swim his horse across in spite of this and was drowned.

55. This junction of trails was along the Mahoning River at or near the site of present Punxsutawney, Pennsylvania, generally following the course of present U.S. Route 119.

56. The north trail was encountered in the area of present Du Bois, Pennsylvania, and the course it took is largely the course of present U.S. 219 through Brockway, Ridgeway, Johnsonburg, and Bradford, all in Pennsylvania.

57. The mouth of the Tunungwant is at the eastern border of Allegheny State Park, about two miles south of present Carrollton, New York.
58. Colonel John Johnson was the British Indian agent to the Iroquois at this time.
59. The name Mackinac was initially Michilimackinac, but this was gradually shortened to Mackinac or, phonetically, Mackinaw. To avoid confusion here, the presently correct form of Mackinac will be used throughout the narrative, even though many people at this time were still referring to it as Michilimackinac.
60. The French Store was located on the site of present Fort Wayne, Indiana.
61. Site of present Defiance, Ohio.
62. The name Shawneeawkee, bestowed by the Potawatomi and soon used by other tribes as a name for John Kinzie, has an interesting origin. The only tribe of the area with native silver was the Shawnee, who were alleged to have mines in Clifton Gorge near Yellow Springs, Ohio, and along Kentucky's Red River. Though early settlers sought these mines, they were never discovered. Geologists claim the local formations preclude the existence of silver; yet despite this, traces of silver-bearing ore have been found in Clifton Gorge. For further information on this, see Amplification Note no. 15, Chapter X, in *The Frontiersmen*. At any rate, the Shawnee being the purveyors of silver in the area, other tribes, including the Potawatomi, associated the name Shawnee with silver, often referring to the Shawnee as Shawneeawkeemi, meaning People-with-the-Silver. Ergo, John Kinzie's Potawatomi-bestowed name, Shawneeawkee — Silver Man.
63. Full details of the incident and the death and burial of Chief Black Fish are found in *The Frontiersmen*.
64. The name Stand Firm, which was the literal translation of the name Wasegoboah, had nothing to do with courage. It referred to the male genitalia.
65. These were the Stillwater River from the northwest and the Mad River from the northeast, which converge on the Great Miami River within the city limits of present Dayton, Ohio.
66. Located in the vicinity of Lair, Kentucky.
67. Because of the events which followed, even though Chalahgawtha was subsequently rebuilt, the silver and other goods were never recovered from the marsh. Years later this marsh was drained and became farmland. Extensive searches have been carried out by various individuals and groups, including modern Shawnees, but this lost treasure has never been recovered. Greater details of the amount of silver and other goods and the circumstances involved in the hiding of it, as well as a closer pinpointing of the area where this occurred, are found in *The Frontiersmen*.
68. Mackachack was located two miles east of present West Liberty, Ohio, along a stream known now as Mac-o-chee Creek, which is a tributary of the Mad River. Peckuwe was located on a flat fertile ground five miles west of present Springfield, Ohio, between the present George Rogers Clark Memorial and the Mad River, in George Rogers Clark State Park. The site is now bisected by Interstate 70.
69. Onondaga was on the site of present Syracuse, New York.
70. Milo Milton Quaife in *Checagou*, pp. 94–95, attributes the Lytle family move from Pennsylvania to the Detroit area as being predicated on the harassment Lytle was allegedly receiving from Pennsylvania neighbors because of supposed British leanings on Lytle's part; that Lytle was branded a Tory and, fearing for home and family, sold out to remain a British subject at Detroit. Juliette Kinzie, on the other hand, in *Wau-Bun*, pp. 287–288, attributes the move to fear of Cornplanter's change of mind where Eleanor Lytle was concerned. Both issues were undoubtedly matters of consideration. Be that as it may, Eleanor never again encountered Cornplanter or Old Queen.
71. Fort Stanwix was located on the upper waters of the Mohawk River at the site of present Rome, New York.
72. Present Maysville, Kentucky.
73. The man who was killed was Willis Chadley, a gawky, serious newcomer to Kentucky, who deserted from Logan's Army at Todd's Fork, sixty miles from Mackachack.
74. "Bahd-ler," as the Shawnees called him, was Simon Kenton, the noted frontiers-

man who, at the time he was captured by the Shawnees, was known under the alias of Simon Butler, which the Shawnees distorted to Bahd-ler. Because of his great courage and strength, Kenton was considered by the Shawnees as being one of the greatest warriors of the whites. It was justified praise; Kenton was outstanding throughout his life as a frontiersman. The story of his life, including his capture, torture, gauntlet runnings and subsequent escape can be found in *The Frontiersmen*.

75. Although by this time the practice of polygamy among the Shawnees had begun to disappear, some of the older chiefs, such as Moluntha, still had two or more wives.

76. Hugh McGary was court-martialed in Kentucky on November 11, 1786, on four indictments, as follows: One — Murder of a Shawnee Indian, Chief Moluntha, who was unarmed and under protection of General Benjamin Logan at the time; Two — Disobedience of Orders; Three — Disorderly conduct as an officer, in that the accused made threats to kill Colonel James Trotter, his superior in rank and who did not approve Captain McGary's act; Four — Abuse of other field officers for the same reason. McGary was found guilty of Indictments One and Three, innocent of Indictment Two, and part-guilty of Indictment Four. The sum total of his sentence was suspension from command for a period of one year.

77. The prohibition of slavery in the Ordinance of 1787 represented an ideal and hardly an overnight achievement. Slavery continued to prevail in the Northwest Territory for sixty-three years after enactment of the Ordinance, although in diminishing numbers as the years passed.

78. Pimitoui is, on some older maps, located at about the site of present Utica, Illinois, but that is an error; actually its situation was upstream on the Illinois River from there, at about the site of present Ottawa, Illinois.

79. A few accounts have stated that Chaubenee was "fully six feet tall," but he was not. His great bulk tended to make him look taller than he actually was. One of his names, Built-Like-a-Bear, was bestowed on him when he was still just a young man, due to his huge bulk.

80. In some accounts, the mother of Chaubenee has been stated as being a Mohawk. However, since she was purportedly from a village on the Genesee River of western New York, and that is the territory of the Senecas, it is more likely that her tribe was Seneca. Chaubenee's name presents a number of complications. Quite often the spellings of Indian names are given in a variety of ways, especially in the Indian language rendition, but the author has rarely encountered an individual with more different spellings of his Indian name or more different interpretations of that name into English. Just a few of the spellings of the Indian name include Shaw-bo-nee, Shabonee, Chaboner, Shab-eh-nay, Shab-eh-nah, Sha-be-nai, Chamblee, Chab-o-neh, Shobonier, Co-wa-bee-nai, Shabbone, Chamblie and Chambly. The English translation of his name has been given as follows: Field-of-Wheat, Built-Like-a-Bear, Burly-Shoulders, Fighter, He-Has-Pawed-Through, and Coal-Burner. Even on the occasions when he signed his own name, Chaubenee did it differently — often differently on different pages of the same document. In the treaty signed at Prairie du Chien in 1825, he signed it Chaboner; at another treaty there four years later, he signed it Shab-eh-nay; in the Chicago Treaty of 1833 he signed with two different spellings, Shab-ehnah and Sha-be-nai. Tecumseh wrote and spoke of him as Chaubenee and called him The Coal-Burner. In DeKalb County, Illinois, there are two towns allegedly named after him, called Shabbona and Shabbona Grove. The author, after considerable study of this matter, has elected to use the forms Chaubenee and The Coal-Burner, since these two have been the most frequently encountered in the documents of the period.

81. The village was located near the site of present Wabasha, Minnesota.

82. Siggenauk (the elder) was one of the few Indian chiefs east of the Mississippi who saw clearly the power that the Americans would one day have in this region. Few believed him and when he died, his own son, Siggenauk (the younger) was very anti-American.

83. Rhode Island became the thirteenth state on May 29, 1790.

84. Site of present Cincinnati, Ohio.

85. "A draught of milk" was an Indian euphemism often used for brandy.

86. Among the chiefs involved in this land cession of about half the Ontario Peninsula to the British were Sko-neque (also known as Mskwaneke or Red Goose), Penash (also known as Pinase, Pinesi, Little Turkey or Little Partridge), Ke-Wey-Te-Nan (also known as Kiwaytin or North Wind) and She-Bense (also known as Shebinse, or The Shaker).

87. Antoine Ouilmette's house was located on the site presently occupied by the Encyclopedia Britannica Building at 425 N. Michigan Avenue. From his name comes the name of the present suburb, Wilmette.

88. Named after Secretary of War Henry Knox.

89. A more fully detailed account of the Harmar defeat may be found in *The Frontiersmen*.

90. Her Indian name was pronounced Puh-SKIP-ah-kah Whiskey-LO-tha.

91. Blue Jacket, whose Shawnee name was Weh-yeh-pih-ehr-sehn-wah, was indeed a white. A Virginian, he had been captured as a youth by the Shawnees and adopted by them. So thoroughly did he become an Indian that he rose to become War Chief of the Shawnees, as well as chief of the Maykujay sept of that tribe. The story of his captivity and subsequent events may be found in *The Frontiersmen*, and in the author's more expanded biographical novel, *Blue Jacket: War Chief of the Shawnees*.

92. Present Windsor, Ontario, Canada.

93. In the family Bible of the Healds (the family into which Rebekah Wells wed) her Christian name is spelled Rebecca. However, in all other accounts and documents, her name is spelled Rebekah, which is believed to be the correct spelling and the one that will be followed here.

94. His Indian name, Apekonit, translates literally into Wild Carrot and was used for him as being descriptive of his carrot-colored red hair.

95. William Wells was born in the vicinity of Jacob's Creek, Pennsylvania, in 1770, the son of Samuel Wells, Sr., and Elizabeth Wells. He had four brothers and a sister, he being the youngest child. In 1775 his eldest brothers, Samuel Jr. and Hayden, explored the region called Beargrass, in the area of present Louisville, Kentucky. Four years later the entire Wells family moved there, migrating down the Ohio River on flatboats with the families of William Pope and William Oldham. William Wells's mother died early and in 1781, two years after their arrival in Kentucky, the senior Samuel Wells was ambushed by Indians near Louisville and killed. William Wells, now an eleven-year-old orphan, was taken into the home of the family friend, Colonel William Pope. In 1784, while hunting close to Pope's house with three boys his age, William was surprised and captured by Miami Indians. He was first taken to Eel River where he was adopted into the family of Gaviahatte — The Porcupine — and swiftly adapted to the Indian life.

96. Fort Miami is sometimes incorrectly identified as Fort Miamis.

97. Site of present Hamilton, Ohio.

98. The fort was built on the site of present Fort Jefferson in Darke County, Ohio, five miles south of present Greenville. The two streams in question are today known as Mud Creek and Prairie Outlet.

99. Present site of Fort Recovery in Mercer County, Ohio, twenty-three miles northwest of Greenville and three miles east of the Ohio-Indiana border.

100. Included in this figure are the estimated two hundred children, wives and prostitutes who were killed. The official American tally was 632 officers and men killed and 264 wounded. Only twenty-four men of St. Clair's force returned uninjured out of a total of 920 American officers and men who took part in the battle. St. Clair's defeat was then, and remains today, the greatest Indian victory over an American military force.

101. The John Kinzie mansion, so-called, was a large, well-appointed two-story house located at what is now the corner of Jefferson Avenue and Wayne Street in Detroit.

102. Another effort at warless peace was made about this time by Brigadier General Rufus Putnam at Vincennes, who met with a delegation of Miamis and Potawatomies who portrayed themselves as being principal chiefs of their nations. Among

these were Le Gesse — The Quail — and Gomo, both relatively minor chiefs of the Potawatomi at this time, and Wawiyezhi — Something Round — who passed himself off as "son of the first King of the Nation." Another was a Miami warrior, Masemo — Resting Fish. Putnam told them that the United States wanted peace and that "the great Chief General Washington wanted to establish a good and lasting Friendship" with his red brothers. The Indians signed the treaty and two of them, Gomo and Le Gesse even went under a government escort to meet George Washington (during which journey Le Gesse died of natural causes). Putnam distributed gifts to the Indians who were on hand and only much later discovered that none of them had any right to treat for their nations and that the tribes, when they learned of it, denounced the treaty and said they would indeed sign a fully authorized treaty of peace with the United States the next spring at Sandusky if the United States would destroy all its forts in Ohio, relinquish claims to lands east of the Muskingum River and abandon all land north of the Ohio River. The demands would never have been met, of course, but it was all academic anyway; later in the year the United States Congress failed to ratify the treaty made by General Rufus Putnam at Vincennes.

103. Kinnikinnick was a form of pipe tobacco prepared by the Indians of indigenous dried leaves, often without the presence of the plant we know today as tobacco. The mixture differed in its ingredients from one locality to another and from tribe to tribe. However, some ingredients remained consistent in almost all concoctions of kinnikinnick and these included osier (dried willow leaves), dried sumac, dried and shredded or pulverized dogwood bark and, especially among the southeastern tribes, actual tobacco. When smoked, it was slow-burning and pungent, ranging from acrid to very aromatic, but said always to have been distinctly harsh to the membranes of the smoker's mouth.

104. In 1798, while talking about this with the French philosopher Constantin François Volney, William Wells admitted that he very quickly readapted to the comforts of civilized life and very soon "could find no comfort with a people who lived almost wholly to the present, with little or no remembrance to the past and hope of nothing for the future."

105. Located at present Eaton, Ohio, twenty-four miles west of Dayton, in Montgomery County, Ohio.

106. Site of present Greenville in Darke County, Ohio. Named in honor of the Revolutionary War officer General Nathaniel Greene. Why the final e in Greene was eventually omitted remains unexplained.

107. Fort Recovery was built on the site of present Fort Recovery, Ohio.

108. Among the men Wells selected for his spy company were William Polke and Nicholas Miller, who had both been captured by Indians as boys and raised by them. Miller's younger brother, Christopher, was still voluntarily with the Shawnees at this time. Another of the handpicked spies was William May, who had lived with the Shawnees and, more recently, had served as a spy for General James Wilkinson. The huge, amazingly powerful young Pennsylvania frontiersman named Robert McClellan was named by Captain Wells as his lieutenant and second-in-command of the spy company. Other members of the spy company included Paschal Hickman, William Ramsey, William England, David Reed, Joseph Young, Fielding Pilcher, Charles Evans, George Casterson, Dodson Thorp, Tabor Washburn, David Thomas, Thomas Stratton, Benjamin Davis, Chatin Dogged, James Elliott, and, later on, Christopher Miller, brother of Nicholas.

109. From which Defiance, Ohio, at the same site presently, got its name.

110. The author has been unable to locate in any of the many sources that have been closely checked, any record of the name of the Potawatomi woman married by Captain William Caldwell.

111. In the Ottawa tongue the name is Sagonas.

112. Alexander McKee, in his official report, claimed that only nineteen Indians were killed and about the same number injured. Wayne reported that he believed the Indian losses were about double his own. The figures shown in the text represent the closest figures available for actual losses.

113. Later, Wayne learned how very close matters had come to actual warfare with the British. While he was overseeing the burning of the buildings outside Fort Miami, a British soldier within the fort, angry at Wayne's gall in so doing, attempted to fire a cannon that was pointed at Wayne. By Campbell's order, the soldier was forcibly subdued and placed under arrest.

114. Almost six years later, late in the summer of 1800, close to five hundred Indians, including over two hundred Shawnees, along with such British agents as Simon Girty, Matthew Elliott and McKee's son, Thomas, gathered near Amherstburg and held a belated death dance for Alexander McKee. It was a lavish spectacle and the first time in anyone's memory that the Indians had so honored a white man. The two-day dance of death was traditionally held only for chiefs of great distinction.

115. At this time the Potawatomi were by far the most widespread and populous tribe in the area comprised of the Illinois, Indiana and Ohio territories, and the southern portions of Michigan and Wisconsin. Chippewas were more populous in the north, but much of their population extended into the Canadian territory. The Potawatomi at the time of the Greenville Treaty were situated most abundantly in the following areas: in northwestern Ohio on the Auglaize, Maumee, St. Marys and St. Joseph Rivers and their tributaries; in southern Michigan along the St. Joseph-of-the-Lake, the Huron, Raisin and Rouge Rivers and their tributaries; in Indiana along the Lake Michigan shoreline and on the rivers St. Joseph, Elkhart, Little Elkhart, Mississinewa, Tippecanoe, upper Wabash and their tributaries; in Illinois along the Lake Michigan shoreline and on the rivers Chicago, Calumet, Des Plaines, Iroquois, Kankakee, Salt, Fox, Rock and their tributaries; and in Wisconsin on the Lake Michigan shoreline to north of Milwaukee and along the Milwaukee River for some distance upstream and along the shores of Lake Geneva. Each such group or sometimes individual villages had to be negotiated with on an individual basis, due to the lack of tribal political structure binding upon the tribe as a whole. This, of course, greatly complicated matters.

116. However, in its written form, the Greenville Treaty calls for the Indians to turn over to white authorities any Indian guilty of killing a white person unjustly, but there is no mention whatever of whites turning over to the Indians any white person guilty of unjustly killing an Indian.

117. Among the chiefs who spoke at the negotiations and/or signed the Greenville Treaty were the following: *Delaware Tribe:* Buckangehela (Deer Chaser), Peketelemund (One-Who-Hops-About), Teteboxti (Spirit Man); *Ottawa Tribe:* Augooshaway; *Piankeshaw Tribe:* Reyntwoco; *Wea Tribe:* Tebui; *Kickapoo Tribe:* Keeahah; *Wyandot Tribe:* Tarhe (The Crane); *Miami Tribe:* Michikiniqua (Little Turtle); *Eel River Tribe:* LeGris; *Chippewa Tribe:* Massas, Michimang (Chamung), Bad Bird; *Shawnee Tribe:* Catahecassa (Black Hoof), Shemeneto (Black Snake), Weh-yeh-pih-ehr-sehn-wah (Blue Jacket); *Potawatomi Tribe:* Mtamins (New Corn, LePetit Bled), Asimethe, Keesas (Gizes, Sun), Windigo, Cashkoa (Fast Walker), Oukia (Wakaya, Bay), Skoneque (Red Goose), Pinase (Penash, Little Turkey), Chaubenee (Coal-Burner, Burley Shoulders), Main Poche (Puckered Hand, Withered Hand, Little Chief), Black Partridge (Muck-otey-pokee), Topenebe (Topinebi, He-Who-Sits-Quietly), Nawak (Nawac, Noon), Nenanseka (Nanameski, Rumbling Earth), Siggenauk (Blackbird), Wapeme (White Pigeon), Padekoshek (Pedagoshok, Pile of Lead); LaChasse (The Huntsman), Meshegethenogh (Mzhikteno, Thunder-Coming-Down, Barren, Childless), Wawasek (Distant-Flash-of-Lightning), Matchiwokama (Missennogomaw, Big Chief), Wawiyezhi (Waweegshe, Something Round), LeBlanc (The White), Shebinse (Shewinse, Shebense, The Shaker), Ksanadjiwan (Segagewan, Senatchewine, Cold River), Senajawan (Senatchawin, Rocks-Splashed-in-Stream), Marchand (The Peddlar), Winamek (Winnemac, Wenameak, Catfish), Gomo (Okama, Leader, Great Chief), Pinesi (Partridge), Kiwaytin (Keweytenan, North Wind). It should be noted that while most of the names are, with some variations, Indian, in some cases only the French or English name of the individual is known. Also, since some signed the treaty more than once under different names, the names above may in some

cases indicate the same individual with different spellings. Where possible, variations of individual names are shown.

118. The six-miles-square tract at Chicago took in the area which is today roughly bounded by the Lake Michigan shoreline on the east, Fullerton Avenue on the north, 31st Street on the south, and Cicero Avenue on the west.

119. William Wells was very well paid for his services to the United States in the preliminaries to the Battle of Fallen Timbers, and for his efforts in rounding up army deserters, acting as Wayne's emissary to the tribes, and acting as interpreter and adviser during the Greenville Treaty negotiations. His pay for the period of twenty-three months — September, 1793, through August, 1795, totaled almost $2,000, which was an extremely high salary at the time. He was also, in 1808, granted by Congress for his services a preemption of 320 acres of land in the vicinity of Fort Wayne.

120. The flagpole in question was located at the foot of present Griswold Street in what is now the center of the Detroit Civic Center area. The Kinzie home was located four blocks distant, at present Jefferson and Wayne (First) Street in the southwestern corner of this same Civic Center area.

121. Fort Mackinac — which was still being referred to occasionally at this time as Michilimackinac — had been moved by the British in 1780 from the mainland on the northern tip of the Southern Peninsula near present Mackinaw City to Mackinac Island in the Mackinac Strait.

122. Roche de Bout — or Roche de Boeuf — was an earlier designation of the Maumee River Rapids by the French during their possession of it, which ended in 1760.

123. James Wilkinson was general-in-chief of the American Army, 1796–1798.

124. At the entrance to the Detroit Main Post Office there is a bronze tablet that states that at that spot, at 12 o'clock noon on July 11, 1796, the final act of the War of Independence was performed.

125. Eulalie Marie Pelletier was eventually baptized by Father Badin when her parents took her to Cahokia, but not until three years later, on October 7, 1799. As a young woman she ultimately inherited much of the estate of her grandfather, Jean Baptiste Point du Sable.

126. Wayne County embraced almost all of Michigan and large portions of Indiana, Illinois and Wisconsin, including the sites of the present cities of Cleveland, Toledo, Fort Wayne, Detroit, Milwaukee and Chicago. A nebulous claim by Quebec of the territory which included Chicago was for all time negated at the British evacuation of Fort Mackinac on September 1, 1796.

127. William Wells had continued in his duties as U.S. interpreter. When Major John Francis Hamtramck came to Detroit to assume command for the United States late in July 1796, Wells accompanied him. A month later, when General Anthony Wayne arrived in Detroit, the commanding general appointed Wells and Miller to accompany the Indian delegation on their visit to the President in Philadelphia.

128. Following the surrender of Detroit to the Americans on July 11, 1796, the British garrison moved across the Detroit River to the Canadian side and downstream to within five miles of the mouth of the Detroit River, above Lake Erie, where they occupied Fort Amherstburg, site of present Amherstburg, Ontario, named after Sir Jeffrey Amherst. This fort was often referred to by the Americans as Fort Malden.

129. Named after General Moses Cleaveland, the city somehow lost the first letter a in its name after its foundation.

130. General Anthony Wayne, en route from Detroit to Philadelphia, died of an aggravated case of gout at Fort Presque Isle, at what is presently Erie, Pennsylvania, on December 15, 1796.

131. Although some accounts have stated that Margaret and John Kinzie were legally divorced at this time, the author has been unable to discover any documentation substantiating this claim. More likely, the couple merely agreed between themselves to irrevocably separate — a form of self-imposed divorce not uncommon at the time. Margaret Kinzie subsequently married Benjamin Hall and Elizabeth Clark subsequently married Jonas Clybourne, both men of Giles County, Virginia.

132. The Kinzie Trading Post complex was located in an area known for many years as

Bertrand, Michigan, but which eventually become a part of the site of present Niles, Michigan. The small stream in the area is presently known as Kinzie Creek.

133. There is some dispute over whether or not Jean Lalime was yet employed by John Kinzie at this time. Bills of lading indicate that Kinzie did indeed have a clerk at his St. Joseph post, but there is no recorded data regarding his identity. Since Lalime is mentioned later in the records as Kinzie's clerk at this post for some time past, the assumption is made that the resident clerk employed by Kinzie at this time was, in fact, Lalime.

134. The four children of William Burnett and Kawkeeme were named James, Abraham, Nancy and John. Abraham (in some accounts referred to incorrectly as Abram) was described as being ". . . extremely, grossly corpulent."

135. Many of the accounts of Du Sable's sale of his Chicago property state that he sold it to a French trader named Le Mai, Le Mail or Le Maile. There is some evidence that supports the existence of a French trader named Le Mai living in Chicago at this time in a cabin not far from the home of Antoine Ouilmette. It is also possible, if such is the case, that the said Le Mai was an employee of Du Sable, since Du Sable often hired numerous engagees from among the voyageurs who passed through en route between Mackinac and St. Louis. Whether or not there was a Le Mai there at the time, no known record exists substantiating the claim that an individual named Le Mai purchased the Du Sable property, although records do exist that it was sold to Lalime. It is also rather interesting to note that the names of Le Main, Le Mail or Le Maile are anagrams or near-anagrams of Lalime, the actual purchaser of record. Oddly enough, three years later, Captain John Whistler reported there was a French trader named Pierre Lemay residing occasionally at Chicago in a decrepit cabin. He was still there when the troops arrived in Chicago in August of that year to begin construction of Fort Dearborn. The similarity of names indicates this Lemay could have been the same individual referred to as Le Mai, Le Mail or Le Maile, erroneously identified as the purchaser, in 1800, of the Du Sable property.

136. The six major Indian trails converging at Chicago are still surprisingly traceable today, since they gradually evolved into significant thoroughfares. The Portage Trail is presently followed by Cicero Avenue and 34th Street to Madison and Stewart Streets and runs relatively parallel to Ogden Avenue. The Green Bay Trail is presently followed from Chicago's center northward along Clark Street (which formerly was called Green Bay Road) to Foster Avenue, then northwest to Howard Street and Robey Avenue and from there northward along the present Green Bay Road through the suburbs. The major east-west trail, called Lake Trail, is presently followed closely by the course of present Lake Street, from Lake Michigan westward through Elmhurst, Addison and Elgin, then up the east shoreline of the Fox River. The Cottage Grove Trail is followed by present Cottage Grove Avenue but has lost some of its clearly traceable characteristics due to the construction of housing complexes over the years, its route being essentially along the Lake Michigan shoreline from the Chicago River into Indiana. The Archer Trail meandered considerably and was eventually followed by equally meandering Archer Avenue. Finally, the Berry Point Trail is followed northward from present Roosevelt Road and Cicero Avenue to the Lake Trail, at the point where present Lake Street and Western Avenue intersect. In addition to these six major hard-packed trails, a dozen or more similar but smaller trails came in from the north, northwest, west, southwest and south to converge at the point where Du Sable's post was located.

137. Many accounts of Du Sable's departure relate that after leaving Chicago he returned to Peoria Lake where he took up residence in the home of "his good friend, Glamorgan," who was alleged to be a fellow San Domingan. Evidently this is an error. It is possible, even likely, that Du Sable did know him and did join him after leaving Chicago, but if such were the case, it was in St. Louis rather than Peoria. Glamorgan was a rich merchant and landowner of St. Louis who had many years previously received a large Spanish land grant. So far as the records indicate, he never resided in Peoria or elsewhere in Illinois.

138. Chicago was at this time in the expansive Wayne County of the Northwest Ter-

ritory, the county seat of which was Detroit. The bill of sale he carried to Detroit is still on file in the Wayne County Building there.

139. The meeting was held in a small Delaware Indian village located on the north bank of the West Fork White River, less than one mile north of the center of the present city of Winchester, seat of Randolph County, Indiana.

140. Located at the site of present Toledo, Ohio.

141. George Washington Whistler had been born at Fort Wayne. At the age of fourteen he entered West Point and emerged five years later with a commission as second lieutenant. However, enamored of railroading, he resigned his commission after fourteen years and, at the age of thirty-three, began building railroads. So well did he do that he achieved considerable fame in his field and was later chosen by the Czar of Russia to take on construction of the railroads there. One of his achievements was building the railroad from St. Petersburg to Moscow. He died in 1849. His son, James Abbott McNeill Whistler, also entered West Point but was dismissed in his third year there. Later he became an artist; his most famous work a painting of his mother entitled "Study in Black and White" but which has become more popularly known as "Whistler's Mother."

142. William Whistler remained in the United States Army for over sixty years, until his retirement in 1861, one of the longest individual military services on record. His son, J. N. G. Whistler, graduated from West Point in 1842, was several times brevetted for gallantry and distinguished conduct in battles of both the Mexican War and Civil War. He retired, due to his age, with the rank of colonel and died in 1899 at Fort Wadsworth, New York. His son, George Washington Whistler, also graduated from West Point, became major of artillery and represented the fourth successive generation of the Whistler family to serve as an officer in the army of the United States.

143. This tract ran from the area of present Mount Carmel, Illinois, up the Wabash to near the point where the present line of Knox and Sullivan counties meets the Wabash.

144. Keesas' town was located on the Wabash a few miles south of the mouth of the Tippecanoe River, about eight or ten miles upstream from present Lafayette, Indiana.

145. Caroline Whistler was indeed the last of the children born to John and Ann Whistler. She was married in 1836 to William Wood at the home of her sister, Sarah, then Mrs. James Abbott, in Sandwich, Ontario — now Windsor. Their only child was named James Whistler Wood. He entered the military before age twenty, was successively lieutenant, adjutant and captain of his company and, during the Civil War, was a member of Major General James B. Steedman's staff.

146. Captain Zebulon Pike's son, Zebulon Montgomery Pike, was the officer who led the United States exploratory expeditions to the headwaters of the Mississippi River and to the Rocky Mountains in Colorado — during which he was discoverer of Pike's Peak.

147. General Henry Dearborn had been appointed Secretary of War in 1801.

148. Early in the year, President Jefferson had sent James Monroe to Paris to join the United States minister there, Robert R. Livingston, in a United States offer of up to $10 million for the Isle of Orleans — New Orleans — and West Florida. Napoleon, who had reacquired the whole Louisiana Territory from Spain in a secret deal, countered by offering all of Louisiana, up the Mississippi to Canada and westward along the Canadian border on the north and generally up the Red River on the south, all the way to the Continental Divide in the Rocky Mountains. The price was $11.25 million in bonds, plus $3.75 million indemnities to American citizens with claims against France. Provisional acceptance was made at once and actual title passed to the United States on December 20, 1803.

149. General James Wilkinson was, in fact, appointed first governor of the Louisiana Territory, largely because of his familiarity with it when the territory was under Spanish control. He died in 1825 and it was not until eighty years later that evidence was uncovered showing that Wilkinson had received large amounts of money from the Spanish government as payment for acting as a spy for Spain against his own government.

150. Only three of the eight Potawatomies who signed this first of six such treaties involving territory in central and northern Indiana are identifiable from their marks. These are Mogawh — The Bear — also known as Mko; Nenewas — Little Man; and Wapmimi, or Wapeme — White Pigeon. Other recognizable signatories of the Potawatomies on the subsequent five treaties included Skesh, also known as Oshkesh; Tokwish, whose villages were in Canada; Topenebe — Sits-Quietly; the brother of Topenebe, Shissahecon — Standing Bear — also known as Shisamko; Onoxa — Five Medals — also known as Nyanenseya, Onaksa and Onangizes, meaning He-Flies-Away; Osmet, the brother of Onoxa; Nanoseka; Winnemac — Catfish; Sigenashet — Blackbird Flying; and Gizes — Sun. With the possible exception of Topenebe, Onoxa, and perhaps even Gizes, all were minor village chiefs without tribal authority and with no right to sign away lands occupied by the Potawatomies or any other tribes.

151. A son named Leonard was born to David Bacon and his wife in Detroit near the time of this marriage. Leonard later acquired considerable renown as a leader of social reform. He was a Yale professor and was recognized as the most noted and influential Congregational clergyman of his generation.

152. The distance is somewhat less than this on modern roads that are more direct than the Sac Trail, Potawatomi Trail and St. Joseph River Trail that had been followed by Swearingen's detachment.

153. Captain Whistler's description of Ouilmette appearing to be "little more than a half-starved Indian" was unfortunate, since he is on this basis considered by many to have been either Indian or half-breed. He was neither. He was French-Canadian

154. The burn suffered by John Harris Kinzie left an oval-shaped mass of scar tissue on the side of his neck which he carried the rest of his life.

155. The *Tracy* was subsequently lost when she struck a reef in Lake Erie and sank in the spring of 1809.

156. Fort Dearborn was constructed on the high bank above the south edge of the Chicago River, at the site now occupied by the southern end of the Michigan Avenue Bridge.

157. The fur brigades out of Mackinac that Kinzie and his men helped to cross the Chicago Portage included such well-known traders of the time as Hugh Patterson, Ramsay Crooks, James Aird, August Choteau, Pierre Sangenette and Edward Creich.

158. Chaubenee's village was located just a little southeast of the site of the present village of Shabbona Grove, on Indian Creek, in the southern portion of DeKalb County, twenty-nine miles due north of Ottawa, Illinois, and twenty-six miles due west of present Aurora, Illinois.

159. Beaubien's wife was an Ottawa woman named Mahnawbunnoquah. At this time they had two sons — Charles Henry and Madore.

160. The Lee farm was established on the west side of the South Branch in the area of Chicago that became known as Bridgeport. While the buildings were on the west side, the property was bisected by the river. In later years, this property came to be known as "Hardscrabble."

161. The five chiefs included Pashepaho (also called The Stabber); Layowvois (Laiyuva); Quashquame (also called Jumping Fish); Outchequaha (also called Sunfish); and Hashequarhiqua (also called The Bear). Quashquame was the most influential of the five but in no way authorized to cede any Sac or Fox lands or commit the tribes to any treaty.

162. The chief in question was Quashquame, whose relative, believed to be either a brother or nephew, was at this time confined in a St. Louis jail on the charge of having murdered a settler the previous June. Quashquame stated: "Mr. Pierre Chouteau (Harrison's Agent) came several times to my camp, offering that if I would sell the lands on the east side of the Mississippi River, Governor Harrison would liberate my relation, to which I at last agreed. . . ." It is interesting to note that Harrison applied to President Jefferson for a full pardon of the imprisoned Sac Indian. The pardon was granted but before it could be enacted, the

Indian was killed by being shot in the back of the head with a shotgun. The official report stated that he had been killed while attempting to escape.

163. Three of the signers were never heard of again after leaving the treaty chambers in St. Louis. Whether they ever left the city is not definitely known.

164. Oshkesh, a Potawatomi, should not be mistaken for Oshkosh, the Menominee chief of Wisconsin, who came into prominence later.

165. In this, Harrison was seriously mistaken, as he was confusing the Delawares with the Wyandots. It was the latter tribe, an offshoot of the Hurons, that was so particularly venerated by the other Great Lakes tribes. This error alone in Harrison's letter greatly undermined its effectiveness.

166. Lieutenant William Whistler and his wife, Julia Fearson Whistler, had a son born to them in Chicago in the autumn of 1805. This was the first white male child and the second white child (Ellen Kinzie being first) born in Chicago. This grandson of the Fort Dearborn commander, Captain John Whistler, was named Meriwether Lewis Whistler.

167. Charles Jouett married Eliza Dodemead of Detroit in the spring of 1803. In spring, 1804, they had a daughter. A year later, Eliza Jouett died.

168. Ebenezer Belknap's salary was $1,000 annually, plus $365 in lieu of subsistence. Belknap was authorized to have an assistant, whose salary was not to exceed $500 annually. The records do not indicate that he ever had any such assistant.

169. Although the land upon which the Kinzie post was situated had been ceded to the United States in 1795 as part of the Greenville Treaty, the Chicago area Potawatomies considered the land as still being theirs. Since they had never sold it to either Du Sable or Lalime, the Chicago Potawatomies on November 4, 1806, gave to John Kinzie as a gift the land upon which the Chicago trading post was located.

170. The 150-ton brig *Adams* had been built in 1799 at the River Rouge shipyard at Detroit. Major Brevoort had been in command of her since 1802.

171. A great favorite of the Indians, Elliott, after long service to the British government as Indian Agent, had been dismissed early in 1798 for misappropriation of Indian goods. The charges had been brought by his nemesis, British Captain Hector McLean, commander of Fort Malden.

172. Gomo was born of Potawatomi parents in 1765 at or near Peoria Lake. He had an older sister and younger brother. The latter, who became a noted warrior, was named Senajiwan (sometimes spelled Senatchewine) and was also called Petcha'o. When their parents were killed, about 1773, the three children were taken into the home of French trader Louis Chattelrou of that area, taught religion by Jesuits and learned French.

173. William Clark, following his expedition to the mouth of the Columbia River with Meriwether Lewis, had been named Indian supervisor at St. Louis, overseeing western Indian tribes.

174. Philip Ostrander (spelled O'Strander in some accounts, but that is erroneous) was born in Maryland in 1784 and joined the army as a private in 1801. In 1806, while stationed at Fort Mackinac, he was commissioned an ensign. He remained at Fort Mackinac until January 1808, when he was transferred to Fort Wayne to serve as second-in-command under Captain Nathan Heald.

175. A well-done monograph on the life and career of William Wells, including his troubles with John Johnston, has been written by Dr. Paul A. Hutton, assistant editor of *The Western Historical Quarterly*, Utah State University, Logan, Utah, under the title "William Wells: Frontier Scout and Indian Agent" in *The Indiana Magazine of History*, LXXIV, No. 3 (September, 1978), pp. 183–222.

176. It was essentially through the maneuvering of William Wells that the reaffirmation of friendship by Michikiniqua — Little Turtle — came about. Michikiniqua was the first chief of any significance to inform Governor Harrison of the perfidy of British agents in the Northwest. In his message to Harrison, Michikiniqua said: *Brother: — At the time we were making bright the chain of friendship at Canandaigua, the commissioner on you part told us that the time might come when your enemies might endeavor to disturb our minds and do away with the friend-*

ship we had then formed with you. That time, Brother, has already arrived. Since you have had some disputes with the British Government, their agents in Canada have not only endeavored to make the Indians at the westward your enemies, but they have sent a war belt among our warriors to poison their minds and make them break the faith with you. This belt we exhibited to your agents in council and then sent it to the place from which it came, never more to seen among us. At the same time we had information that the British had circulated war belts among the western Indians and within your territory. We rested not, but called a general council of the six nations [meaning not the Iroquois League, formally known as the Six Nations, but rather the Miami, Ottawa, Kickapoo, Shawnee, Potawatomi and Delaware] *and resolved to let our voices be heard among our western brethren and destroy the effects of the poison scattered among them. We have twice sent large deputations to the council fire for the purpose of making their minds strong in their friendship with your nation and, in the event of war between the white people, to sit on their seats and take no part on either side. So far as our voice has been heard, they have agreed to harken to our counsel and remain at peace with your nation. Brother, if war should take place, we hope you will inform us of it through your agents and we will continue to raise our influence with all the Indians with whom we are acquainted, that they will sit still in their seats and cultivate friendship with your people.*

177. This was the last treaty completed and ratified by the United States Senate before the War of 1812.

178. The Cooper (later Burns) house was located at the site of the present Merchandise Mart. Wolf Point was on the west shore where the east-west flowing Chicago River formed from branches flowing from north and south.

179. Alexander Robinson became one of the better known Indians of the Chicago area and was noted as being a very loyal and devoted friend of the whites. His Indian name, which also has been translated as meaning "The Squinter," has variously been spelled Chee-chee-neen-guay, Cheecheebingway, Chechepinquay, and Tshee-tshee-beenguay. He was born at Mackinac in 1762, son of a Scots trader who had previously served as a British officer, and an Ottawa mother. He married a Potawatomi woman and moved with her first to St. Joseph, where he worked in the Indian trade as an associate of Joseph Bailly, and then near the Chicago area, where he took up residence in the village of Chief Nescotnemeg on the Iroquois River. He was a friend of Topenebe, Chaubenee and Sauganash. He consistently befriended the whites and served as interpreter at the Chicago Indian Agency in 1823 and 1826. He rose to prominence and chieftainship among the Potawatomies during the removal period. He did not, however, move beyond the Mississippi with the Potawatomies, but settled on the Des Plaines River with his family and lived there until his death on April 22, 1872, at the age of 110 years.

180. On April 28, 1809, the new Illinois Territory was divided into two counties — Randolph in the south and St. Clair in the north. President Madison appointed Ninian Edwards as governor of the territory and Nathaniel Pope as secretary, to also serve as acting governor until Edwards assumed his office.

181. Blue Jacket is believed to have died of cholera.

182. At this point in his speech, Tecumseh said what has been recorded as "It was me." It is very difficult to say exactly what Tecumseh meant by that brief sentence. Possibly he was thinking of something else entirely. Possibly, too, the interpretation of his speech at this point was faulty, or that the subsequent transcription was either in error or inadvertently omitted something which gave this line significance.

183. Grasshopper's Potawatomi name was Peesotum, which means "Big Fighter," a name he had adopted when he became a village chief a few years before. Prior to that his name, which he had always disliked, was Quaquanese which, translated literally, means "Little Flying Creature."

184. This volume is the oldest literary relic of the City of Chicago and is now in the collection of the Chicago Historical Society.

185. It is alleged that in later years Heald went back to the area to get what he left behind on this occasion, but though he had marked the area well in his mind at

the time, he was unable to find the log that hid his treasures and supplies left behind.

186. Jean Baptiste Mirandeau was the first permanent white settler of Milwaukee. The name of his Ottawa wife has not been recorded. Their first two children were Jean Baptiste Jr. (1796) and Madaline (1797); the former died of poisoning at age three; the latter died of drowning at age one; two children born later were given the same names. The children in 1811 included Madaline (1798), Joseph (1799), Victoire (1800), Louis (1809), Jean Baptiste Jr. (1811). Three other children — Rosanne, Genevieve and Thomas — were born to the Mirandeaus after 1811.

187. There is little information regarding the activities of Lieutenant Philip Ostrander subsequent to his arrival back at Fort Wayne, where he resumed his duties as second-in-command under Captain Oscar James Rhea. It is believed he was reassigned after a few more months, but no further definitive data is available until he is reported on the army list of 1813 as "Deceased — July 30."

188. The Jouetts reached Kentucky safely and took up residence on a farm just outside the city of Harrodsburg. Susan Jouett bore three daughters and Charles Jouett, in 1812, became a judge. However, late in 1815 Charles returned to the Indian service and was reassigned as Indian Agent at Fort Dearborn in Chicago. His wife and children accompanied him there.

189. The younger brother of Black Partridge, Mkedepoke, who had come to Tippecanoe from Fox River, had slipped away with a party from Tippecanoe as soon as it was learned that William Henry Harrison was moving against them. Moving down the Wabash, this party intercepted a supply boat en route to Harrison. Seeing that all but one boatman was on the opposite shore pulling the boat with a rope, Mkedepoke left his companions, slipped into the water, swam silently to the boat, climbed in and slew the one man aboard, dumped supplies overboard and then rejoined his companions. For this feat he acquired much renown and thereupon changed his name to Waubansee (Wabansi) meaning "He Causes Paleness."

190. De Charmes' Trading Post was located at the site of the present city of Ypsilanti, Michigan.

191. Present Reelfoot Lake on the Kentucky-Tennessee line.

192. This earthquake, often referred to as the New Madrid Earthquake, was among the most severe ever recorded in America. Though no such device as the Richter Scale existed at the time, the power of the quake has been estimated from a very conservative low of 7.2 on the Richter Scale to well above 9.5. For comparison purposes, the most powerful earthquake for which figures are available was that which struck Japan on March 2, 1933, registering 8.9 on the Richter Scale. The Alaskan Quake of March 27, 1964, registered 8.5, and the San Francisco Quake of April 18–19, 1906, registered 8.3. This earthquake predicted by Tecumseh lasted intermittently for two days. It was followed by three others in the same area; one the succeeding January 23, another on January 27 and a final tremendous shock, said to have caused as much damage as the other three combined, on February 13 and lasting for an hour.

193. Francis LaFramboise was the son of a father of the same name. The elder Francis and his brother, Alexander, were traders of Mackinac and Milwaukee. In 1795, Alexander established a house at the mouth of the Milwaukee River and after returning to Mackinac, sent brother Francis to manage it. Francis had trouble with Potawatomi Chief Siggenauk — Blackbird — whose hostility, added to the mismanagement by Francis, brought the post and his brother Alexander to ruin. After a stay in Chicago following that, Francis established a post among the Winnebagoes in central Wisconsin. There he was murdered and his wife, Madeline, took over the business, moved her headquarters to Mackinac and ran it prudently and with great success.

194. In some accounts his name is spelled Kelsoe. Kelso is correct.

195. Fort Harrison was located on the east bank of the Wabash River, two miles from the center of present Terre Haute, Indiana. Construction was begun October 5, 1811, and the fort was completed on October 28, 1811.

196. Because he happened to be on the parapet, Lieutenant Helm is, in at least one

account, stated as being officer of the day; actually, he was there merely taking some air on the warm late March afternoon, while the Officer of the Day, Ensign George Ronan, was at this moment inspecting the artillery in one of the blockhouses.

197. In one account — HC-I-73 — it is stated that John Kinzie was wounded in the side, but this is an error. The wound was in the side of his neck (although one account states it was in his shoulder — an error undoubtedly caused by the fact that his shoulder became heavily bloodstained from the neck wound.) Kinzie bore the scar of this wound on the side and back of his neck for the remainder of his life.

198. The ruse of John Kinzie having gone to Milwaukee worked so well that it was accepted as fact by practically everyone at Chicago. Many subsequent written accounts have perpetuated this error. Actually, throughout the time of his absence, John Kinzie was never more than a mile from his house.

199. Seventy-nine years and five weeks later, on April 29, 1891, a cellar was being dug at the southwest corner of Illinois and Cass Streets (Cass Street is now Rush Street) when workmen encountered a human skeleton. Authorities were summoned and an investigation made. The age of the skeleton and the determination that it had belonged to a white man who was five feet four inches tall resulted in the official conclusion that these were the remains of Jean Baptiste "Jack" Lalime.

200. John Kinzie lived up to his word. So long as he was alive — and Eleanor Kinzie after him — the Lalime grave was carefully tended, the ground kept free of weeds, flowers planted and the little white picket fence which was ultimately erected, freshly painted every spring on or near the anniversary of Lalime's death.

201. This incident occurred in what is now southeastern Jefferson County, Illinois, a few miles north of the present hamlet of Frisco and eight miles west of the large impoundment presently called Rend Lake. The area where the men were killed is now known locally by the name of Moore's Prairie.

202. Present Lake Geneva, Wisconsin, just north of the present Illinois-Wisconsin border. The village was built on the south shore of the lake, about a mile west of the site of present Big Foot Beach State Park.

203. Battledore, also called Battlecock, was a popular outdoor game of the period, which had its origin in the Orient many centuries before. As time passed, it gradually evolved into the present game called shuttlecock in England and badminton in the United States.

204. It is stated in most accounts that Naunongee addressed this comment "to the Fort Dearborn Indian interpreter." However, the fort was at this time without an interpreter due to the death of Jack Lalime, and Margaret McKillip Helm was enough conversant in the Potawatomi language that she would not have required the aid of an interpreter to know what Naunongee said.

205. The little campsite was located on the grounds of the present Elmhurst Country Club at Addison, Illinois, just west of present Wooddale Road. The minor Indian trail leading toward Chicago eventually became present Grand Avenue in Chicago and the suburbs.

206. Upstream only a few hundred yards from the site of present Fox River Grove, Illinois.

207. Lake Geneva, Wisconsin.

208. Nescotnemeg's village was situated less than one half mile from the present town of Aroma, Illinois; located four miles up the Kankakee River from the present city of Kankakee, Illinois.

209. The Potawatomi word *Chemokemon* means the whites, specifically the Americans, and was similar in meaning to the Shawnee word for them, *Shemanese*.

210. Just north of the present north boundary of the Palwaukee Airport in Chicago's present northwestern suburb of Prospect Heights, two miles south of Wheeling, Illinois.

211. The man named DuBou was never seen nor heard of again. It is surmised that DuBou somehow managed to escape. Had the Winnebagoes killed him, there would have been no reason for them to hide the body or take it with them. The possibility exists that he escaped, wounded, and died somewhere in the surrounding

woods or prairies, although no trace of his body was ever discovered. One further and much more disturbing possibility exists: that DuBou, who was known to have spent some time in Wisconsin before coming to Chicago, worked in concert with the Winnebago attackers, either as a result of preplanning, which is unlikely, or because of recognition of him by the Winnebagoes and their taking him back to Wisconsin with them as either prisoner or friend.

212. The question has never been answered. Dolly was never seen again.

213. The following list includes those civilians known to be members of that militia force, by name or designation:

> Sergeant Thomas Burns, noncommissioned officer in charge.
> Private James Cooper, fifteen-year-old stepson of Sergeant Burns.
> Charles Lee, Sr., co-owner, with William Russell, of the Lee farm.
> Charles Lee, Jr., fifteen-year-old son of Charles Sr.
> William Russell, co-owner, with Charles Lee, Sr., of the Lee farm.
> Samuel Clark.
> Louis Pettell, French (or half-breed) settler.
> Michael Pettell, son of Louis Pettell.
> A "Seventy-year-old man" formerly a revolutionary soldier.
> Unidentified French settler # 1
> Unidentified French settler # 2
> A man whose surname was "Henry."
> Claude LaFramboise, seventeen, son of Francis LaFramboise.
> Alexis LaFramboise, sixteen, son of Francis LaFramboise.
> LaFortune LaFramboise, fifteen, son of Francis LaFramboise.

(John Kelso, shown in some accounts as having been a member of the militia, was not. Upon the outbreak of troubles, he reenlisted in the regular army at Fort Dearborn, not in the militia.)

214. Crozier and Hurtt were shown on the May 31, 1812, Muster List as having deserted, but no formal charges are known to have been lodged against them. Never heard of again, the deserters were most likely captured by the Indians and killed.

215. Fort McArthur was located in Hardin County, three miles southwest of present Kenton, Ohio.

216. Found guilty of drunkenness and dereliction of duty, Vassar suffered having both his ears chopped off short and the letter M branded on each cheek.

217. The Mirandeau family did, in fact, return to take up residence in Chicago again, in 1816. ♦

218. The Chicago garrison continued to be plagued with a fever that was generally called a swamp fever, miasmic fever or ague. Some accounts have stated it was malarial in origin, although this was not correct. Malaria did occur occasionally in the Chicago area, but this was not the source of the fever that so regularly afflicted the garrison. Attributed to organisms from the marshlands throughout much of the area of the south shore of Lake Michigan, the fever was characterized by moderately high temperature, diarrhea, general weakness and vertigo, lasting anywhere from a minimum of about ten days to as long as several months. That it stemmed from the marshes was evident, for in later years when the marshes were drained, the fever generally disappeared.

219. Until this time, United States Army privates were often called "Dime-a-Day Soldiers" because they received only $3.00 per month in pay.

220. Prior to the April 1812 increase in pay, ordinary privates received $3.00 per month; musicians were paid $3.60 per month; corporals $5.00; sergeants, $10.00; ensigns, $35.00; second lieutenants $50.00; surgeon's mates, $60.00; and captains commanding, $100.00. With an authorized garrison strength at Fort Dearborn of fifty-eight privates, four musicians, two corporals, four sergeants, one ensign, one second lieutenant, one surgeon's mate, and one captain commanding, this amounted to a monthly payroll of $483.40 and an annual payroll of $5,800.80. With the pay increase of April 1812, the monthly payroll for the full strength Fort Dearborn garrison was $985.00, and an annual payroll of $11,820.00.

221. Site of present Monroe, Michigan.

222. Toronto, Ontario, Canada.

223. This bridge was erected one-half mile up the Huron River from its mouth at Lake Erie and seven miles below present Flat Rock, Michigan.
224. Brownstown is the site of present Wyandot, Michigan, and Maguaga was located on the site of present Ecorse, Michigan.
225. Site of present Three Rivers, Michigan, in St. Joseph County.
226. Hog Island, so-called then, is present Belle Isle.
227. Brigadier General William Hull's proclamation to the Canadian was as follows:

by WILLIAM HULL, Brigadier General, Commanding the American North-western Army.

Inhabitants of Canada! After thirty years of peace and prosperity, the United States have been driven to arms. The injuries and aggression, the insults and in-dignities of Great Britain, have once more left them no alternative but manly resistance or unconditional submission. The army under my command has invaded your country, and the standard of the union now waves over the Territory of Canada. To the peaceable, unoffending inhabitants, it brings neither danger nor difficulty. I come to find enemies, not make them. I come to protect, not injure you — separated by an immense ocean and an extensive wilderness from Great Britain, you have no participation in her councils, no interest in her conduct. You have felt her tyranny; you have seen her injustice; but I do not ask you to avenge the one or redress the other. The United States are sufficiently powerful to afford every security, consistent with their rights or your expectations. I tender you the invaluable blessings of civil, political and religious liberty which gave decision to our counsels, and energy to our conduct, in a struggle for independence; and which conducted us safely and triumphantly through the stormy period of the Revolution — that liberty which has raised us to an elevated rank among the nations of the world; and which has afforded us a greater measure of peace and security, of wealth and improvement, than ever fell to the lot of any other people.

In the name of my country, and by the authority of my government, I promise you protection to your persons, property and rights. Remain at your homes; pursue your peaceful and customary avocations; raise not your hands against your brethren. Many of your fathers fought for the freedom and independence we now enjoy. Being children, therefore, of the same family with us, and heirs to the same heri-tage, the arrival of an army of friends, must be hailed by you with cordial welcome. You will be emancipated from tyranny and oppression, and restored to the dig-nified station of freedmen. Had I any doubt of eventual success, I might ask your assistance; but I do not; I come prepared for any contigency. I have a force which will look down all opposition; and that force is but the vanguard of a much greater! If contrary to your own interests and the just epectation [sic] of my country, you should take part in the approaching contest, you will be considered and treated as enemies, and the horrors and calamities of war will stalk before you. If the barbarous and savage policy of Great Britian be pursued, and the savages are let loose to murder our citizens, and butcher our women and children, this war will be a war of extermination. The first stroke of the tomahawk, the first attempt with the scalping knife, will be the signal for one indiscriminate scene of desolation. No white man found fighting by the side of an Indian will be taken prisoner. Instant destruction will be his lot. If the dictates of reason, duty, justice, and humanity cannot prevent the employment of a force which respects no rights or knows no wrongs, it will be prevented by a severe and relentless sys-tem of retaliation. I doubt not your courage and firmness; I will not doubt your attachment to liberty. If you tender your services voluntarily, they will be ac-cepted readily. The United States offers you peace, liberty, and security; your choice lies between these and war. Choose, then, but choose wisely — and may He who knows the justice of our cause, and who holds in His hands the fate of na-tions, guide you to a result the most compatible with your rights and your interests.

WILLIAM HULL

By the General,
A. F. Hull, Captain, 13th U.S. Regiment and aide.
Sandwich, July 12, 1812.

228. The McArthur detachment followed the Indians upstream on the east shore of the Detroit River, then eastward along the south shore of Lake St. Clair to the Thames, then up the Thames as far as present Chatham. The nephew of General Hull, Isaac Hull, lived on the Thames River not far above its mouth. He was found being guarded by a British corporal and six militia privates, who were captured by McArthur's men, relieved of their weapons and paroled.

229. One hundred thirty-five of these were Indians brought from Wisconsin and Minnesota by British agent Robert Dickson. The rest were Chippewa and Ottawa of the area of the Sault Ste. Marie and Straits of Mackinac.

230. That beach is now known by the name of British Landing.

231. Both the *Erie* and *Friends' Good Will* were seized by the British when they reached Detroit and became part of the British lake fleet. The *Friends' Good Will* was thereupon named *Little Belt* and armed with two cannon. It participated in the Battle of Lake Erie, September 10, 1813, when Oliver Hazard Perry destroyed the British fleet.

232. The name Mascotapah was bestowed upon Robert Dickson by the Sioux of the upper Mississippi River. It meant "The Red Head" or, more literally, "The Red-Haired Man."

233. Matthew Irwin was paroled by the British along with the United States officers and soldiers of Fort Mackinac. He later was appointed as the United States Army's Assistant Commissary of Purchases, in which position he served until disbandment of the United States Army in June 1815.

234. In at least one account it is stated that both Rebekah Wells Heald and Samuel Wells (niece and brother of William Wells) were on hand for the funeral of Michikiniqua (Little Turtle) but this is wholly without foundation. Rebekah Heald was in Chicago and Samuel Wells was in Louisville, Kentucky, at the time.

235. In later years, Josiah Snelling established an American outpost on the upper Mississippi River at the mouth of the St. Peter (or Pierre) River where it empties into the Falls of St. Anthony. The fort was at first named Fort St. Anthony, but later was renamed Fort Snelling. The smaller river's name was eventually changed to the Minnesota River and the settlement which grew up around the fort subsequently became Minneapolis, Minnesota.

236. In General Hull's subsequent court-martial on charges of cowardice and treason, it was charged that Captain Brown had gone to Amherstburg under secret orders from General Hull, for the purpose of arranging the details of a surrender by Hull of his army to the British. Events which followed Brown's secret meeting with the British tended to support this contention and later comments by Hull himself appeared to authenticate the allegation. Hull, however, at the trial, emphatically denied the allegation and the charge was not proved.

237. Because of reports being circulated injurious to the honor and reputation of Major Denny following this affair, Colonel McArthur, at Major Denny's request, ordered a court of inquiry to sit in the matter at 10 P.M. September 25. President of the court was Colonel Findley and the other two members were Colonel Cass and Major Van Horne. The court interviewed witnesses and participants and after weighing the testimony, unanimously acquitted Major Denny with honor.

238. In the original letter, presently in the collection of the Wisconsin Historical Library at Madison, the last four words of the paragraph are obliterated. Milo Milton Quaife in "Some Notes on the Fort Dearborn Massacre," which was published in the 1910–1911 *Proceedings of the Mississippi Valley Historical Association*, interprets the obliterated portion as being the single word "Detroit." However, the author feels certain that the obliterated passage contained the words as shown in the text, not only because the single word "Detroit" would make the sentence incomprehensible and incomplete, but because bits of the sentence remaining indicate it was completed in the manner shown here. In addition, it is more in keeping with Hull's initial attitude of blaming Lieutenant Porter Hanks for the fall of Fort Mackinac and the interruption of the Fort Dearborn supply line.

239. There remains an unanswered question as to why Hull would have implied that

Fort Mackinac was still in American hands, or why he should have stated that *both* Fort Mackinac and the British post on St. Joseph Island would be evacuated. The most logical explanation seems to be that should this letter fall into the wrong hands, the seriousness of the American position would be camouflaged. Yet, even that *is* questionable, since Hull must have realized that the enemy, both British and Indian, undoubtedly received confirmation of Fort Mackinac's capitulation long before he. There are also some historians who say this letter was not written in General Hull's hand, yet a comparison of the handwriting with his letter of the same date to Secretary of War Eustis shows them to be the same hand, which *is* somewhat unlike Hull's normal writing, but which may be put down to his extremely agitated state of mind at the time of the writing. In later writings, both Lieutenant Linai T. Helm, Heald's second-in-command, in his account of the massacre, and Juliette Kinzie, daughter-in-law of John Kinzie and wife of John Harris Kinzie (who was only a small boy at the time of the massacre) in her book *Wau-Bun*, written half a century after the massacre on hearsay information, state unequivocally that Hull, in his order, gave Captain Heald a choice of whether or not to evacuate the post, through use of the words "if practicable." The original order shows no such condition being given, even though in his letter to Eustis, Hull stated that he was ordering the evacuation of Fort Dearborn "provided it can be effected with a greater prospect of safety than to remain." In light of what subsequently occurred, the fact that Heald received an unconditional order to evacuate becomes very important. Mrs. Kinzie also claimed in *Wau-Bun* that Hull's order directed Captain Heald to give *everything* to the Indians, making no mention that he was also instructed to give goods to "the poor and needy" of his post.

240. In some accounts it is stated that General Hull gave the letter to the Potawatomi Chief Winnemac to take to Fort Wayne, but this is not correct. Winnemac was already at Fort Wayne at this time and it was from there that he carried the order to Fort Dearborn at the instructions of Captain Rhea and William Wells.

241. The stream then known as Frog Creek no longer exists, but at that time it originated from a spring located at approximately the site of the present Richard J. Daly Center in downtown Chicago and emptied into the Chicago River at about where the south end of the State Street Bridge is presently located.

242. That the missing militiamen were the LaFramboise brothers is based upon a close analysis of what individuals were in the militia, those subsequently killed, and the sketchy description of the individuals who deserted. They are described as having been half-breeds who, in company with a Frenchman, took the horses and went to Milwaukee. The LaFramboise family left Chicago at this precise time and since the three sons, who were sons of Frenchman Francis LaFramboise and his wife, accompanied them, mere deduction seems to indicate the obvious. Shortly afterwards the eldest daughter of the LaFramboise family, Josette Beaubien, remained in Chicago as nursemaid to the Kinzie children when her husband, Jean Baptiste Beaubien, left Chicago for Milwaukee with his children. It is stated in *Wau-Bun* that Josette LaFramboise was in the Kinzie boat with Eleanor Kinzie and the Kinzie children as nursemaid. Actually, she was at that time Josette Beaubien.

243. Included with the Indians and clad in Indian garb like them was Alexander Elliott, son of British Indian agent Matthew Elliott.

244. Chaubenee and Sauganash had returned to Tecumseh on the night of August 2, 1812, following their visit to Chicago.

245. The actual order was as follows:

> *Sandwich, August 8, 1812*
> *Major Denny, You will take command of the stockade work at Gowies — the detachment consists of one hundred and thirty non-commissioned officers and privates, with the addition of lieutenant Anderson's corps of artillerists.*
> *The object of your command is, to hold possession of this part of Upper Canada, and afford all possible protection, to the well disposed inhabitants — you will defend your post to the last extremity, against musketry — if cannon should be*

brought against it, and the state of the army at Detroit should be such, that no relief can be afforded to the post, and the enemy should be so powerful, that you cannot dislodge them by your cannon and musketry in the fort, or by a sally out of it, you will be authorised to retreat, for which purpose boats will be provided, and you will keep them in constant readiness — you will complete the stockade as soon as possible, and put in the best state of defence — you will not suffer your men, on any account to straggle from the fort, or do any injury to the inhabitants. Confiding in your discretion, and good conduct, I am satisfied you will defend your post, in a manner, honorable to yourself and your country.

W. Hull
Brig. Gen. commanding

Because of the advance of the British to Sandwich with heavy artillery beginning on August 12, Major Denny was forced to evacuate his force to Detroit.

246. Site of the present city of Mishawaka, Indiana, seventy-five miles from Fort Wayne on the Indian Trail (presently the route of U.S. 33) and ninety miles from Chicago on the Indian Trail, now followed by U.S. 20 to Michigan City and U.S. 12 from there to downtown Chicago.

247. John Whistler, Jr., survived the wound, though only with difficulty and after a long convalescence. Just a little over a year later, in the autumn of 1813, he contracted a disease, probably cholera, and died.

248. Some accounts say sixty Indians were killed, which is ridiculous and wholly a fabrication.

249. The missing words in this addenda, which were to be filled in verbally to Governor Meigs by the bearer of the message, were "Capitulation" and "Commanding Officer."

250. One hundred and one days later, on November 21, 1812, Spemica Lawba, nephew of Tecumseh and son of Tecumapese, was dispatched by William Henry Harrison on a spying mission to the Maumee Rapids. With two companions, Bright Horn and Otter, he went there and found British and enemy Indians in large numbers. Immediately they returned to Fort Winchester at the mouth of the Auglaize and reported their discovery to General Winchester. The fort's second-in-command, a Major Samuel Price of Kentucky, who knew nothing of Spemica Lawba's long-time dedicated service to the United States, and who despised Indians generally, said without any foundation for his allegation, that the report was a lie. He accused Spemica Lawba of treachery. Deeply stung, Spemica Lawba decided to prove his loyalty. The next day he returned toward the Rapids with his two friends, encountered and subsequently killed and scalped the Potawatomi Indian named Winnemeg and British Indian Agent Alexander Elliott, eldest son of Matthew Elliott. In the process, however, Spemica Lawba was shot through the body. He was brought back to Fort Winchester where he lingered until November 25, then died. Though he was a full-blooded Shawnee Indian, he was buried with full military honors.

251. The Indian encampment had grown to such extent that the area of wigwams covered what is presently the area of from State Street on the east to the south branch of the Chicago River on the west, and from Wacker Drive on the north to about Madison Street to the south.

252. "Jerking" meat, which permitted it to be kept for long periods of time without spoiling, was accomplished by cutting the meat into thin strips and stretching it out onto a scaffolding of sorts beneath which a small, smoky fire was built which simultaneously dried and smoked the meat. Thus cured, it could be stored for many weeks, even months. Lieutenant Helm in his account exaggerates the supplies on hand, saying there were two hundred stands of arms, six thousand pounds of gunpowder and twenty-seven barrels of salt.

253. In the *Wau-Bun* account, Juliette Kinzie states that the trader's large supply of liquor had been collected "in a warehouse across the river opposite Fort Dearborn." That is an error. John Kinzie himself recorded that his liquor supply had been moved inside the fort for safekeeping; also, there was no such "warehouse" across the river from the fort at this time.

254. Juliette Kinzie, fifty years later in *Wau-Bun*, stated that the Miami warrior escort numbered fifteen. Sergeant William Griffith, in his account at the time, said there were fifty. Most historical accounts give the number as thirty. However, both John Kinzie and Lieutenant Linai Helm said there were twenty-seven Miami warriors in the escort, and this seems to be the most accurate figure to be found.

255. At least one account states that all but twenty-five rounds of ammunition, in total, was destroyed, which is ridiculous, since that amount would provide only one shot each for less than half the garrison. The correct figure is as stated.

256. By Captain Heald's own admission to the United States Auditor, later, no payment was made to the men after the June 30 payment. A single payment for July, August and September was scheduled to be made at the end of September.

257. No record of the name of Keepoteh's younger brother is known to exist.

258. One account states that Captain Heald concealed the occurrence of the warning from his subordinate officers and the only other person to know of it was William Wells.

259. Some historians have disputed the reality of this incident having occurred as later reported by Linai T. Helm. Yet, considering the nature of Black Partridge and his respect of — if not friendship for — Captain Heald, along with his own strong personal code of morals, the incident very probably occurred. On numerous occasions in history, the author has discovered, meetings of this same tenor occurred between whites and Indians who had shared some degree of amity and who were soon to be pitted against one another. In many such meetings, the Indian(s) in question returned personal gifts received from the white(s); it is fully in keeping with the Indian character and a not infrequent occurrence. The author is fully convinced this incident actually did occur, just as Lieutenant Helm recorded it.

260. In some accounts, the lieutenant's name is incorrectly spelled Dalaby.

261. In some versions of this speech by Tecumseh, "springs" is translated as "fountains."

262. The direct route from Detroit to Frenchtown (present Monroe, Michigan) where Captain Brush was waiting was along the road presently followed by Michigan State Route 56; the paths Hull sent the two colonels and their detachment to follow to reach Brush are generally traced today by Michigan State Route 112 westward to Ypsilanti, U.S. Route 23 southward to Dundee, and State Route 50 eastward to Monroe.

263. Another version of this comment has the words "will make" substituted for "have made," which makes a considerable difference. The latter clearly indicates that Hull had made arrangements with the British previously, either through Captain Brown or, more likely, through Captain Rough. All the evidence, even though circumstantial, indicates that this is precisely what General Hull did.

264. The eight soldiers who were more or less incapacitated by illness at this time included Sergeant Otho Hayes and Privates Asa Campbell, John Fury, Samuel Kilpatrick, Peter Miller, Thomas Poindexter, James Starr, and an individual identified only as Private Burman.

265. Some sources have stated that the surgeon's "horses" rather than "horse" had strayed. It was actually only one horse — a mediocre saddle mare which Dr. Van Voorhis had bought from Charles Lee some months earlier.

266. Several accounts transfer the illness of Sergeant Otho Hayes to Quartermaster Sergeant William Griffith, which is incorrect. It may be that the association of Sergeant Griffith with the post doctor at this time led to the confusion. Griffith was not ailing at this time; Hayes was, and had been on the sick list for the preceding twelve days.

267. No surname has been found to have been recorded for Claude, the French-Canadian (sometimes described as a French-Indian half-breed). However, he is not to be confused with the French-Canadian Claude LaFramboise, who earlier deserted the Chicago Militia with his two brothers, Alexis and LaFortune, and fled to Milwaukee with some of the garrison's horses.

268. The young clerk is never named in any of the existing accounts, though he is definitely not the clerk known simply as François; neither is it Pierre LeClerc or Peresh.

269. In one or two accounts it is stated that Griffith was alarmed by the sound of shots breaking out at the Indian encampment and that he had deferred his search for the horse to investigate and see what was wrong, at which time he was captured and disarmed by Topenebe and his warriors. However, no other accounts give any indication whatever of shots being fired by anyone at this time, so the story is believed to have been fabricated, probably by Griffith himself, who fabricated so much in his account.

270. Considerable research has been done in an effort to indisputably identify the three remaining children, but in vain. By logic and deduction it appears that these three were possibly the children of Samuel and Emmaline Clark, but this is only a possibility and in no manner verified.

271. The possibility that the three unidentified children were children of the Clarks — Emmaline and Samuel — is enhanced by the fact that they were under care of Cicely in the wagon. Cicely, slave of Rebekah Heald, is said to have worked on occasion for the Clarks and therefore had become familiar to the family. The three children were evidently not infants, though they were small enough to be unable to keep up with the march if on foot. It would be logical for them to be left in Cicely's care by Emmaline Clark so she could walk outside the wagon, just as Sarah Neads left her son, Johnny, in Cicely's care so she could walk outside.

272. Most accounts state that there were 96 individuals involved in the march out of Fort Dearborn, but that is incorrect. There were 109, broken down as follows:

    68 Regular army officers and soldiers

        (1 captain, Nathan Heald; 1 lieutenant, Linai Helm; 1 ensign, George Ronan; 1 surgeon's mate, Isaac van Voorhis; 2 sergeants, Isaac Holt with marchers and Otho Hayes driving first wagon, but excluding William Griffith, in hiding across the river; 5 corporals, Joseph Bowen, Thomas Forth, Richard Garner, Rhodias Jones, and including Walter Jordan on detached duty from Fort Wayne; 57 privates, including 1 flag-bearer, 4 musicians, 2 wagon-drivers, 5 sick, 45 marchers.) [Note: The Simmons account, accurate in some respects, inaccurate in others, lists Prv. John Simmons as a corporal, though on all muster lists known, including that of May 30, 1812, he is shown as a private. Also, Simmons indicates there was a Private Bell and his wife and six-year-old son, Peter; allegedly the parents were killed and the boy survived. There is no record anywhere else of any of these three individuals and the author believes the Simmons account — a hearsay narrative — to be in error.]

    13 Children below teen-age

        (Including 12 in wagon and one riding behind on horse, but excluding the Victoria Corbin fetus and excluding Wilma and Henry Corbin hiding at the Burns house; and also excluding the four Kinzie children.)

    11 Women

        (Including 3 on horses — Rebekah Heald, Margaret Helm, Jane Holt; 4 in wagon and 4 walking; but excluding 3 in boat — Eleanor Kinzie, Josette LaFramboise Beaubien and Athena.)

    4 Civilian males

        (Including John Kinzie, Francis Bourbonne, the slave Pepper, and boy-interpreter, Salienne; but not including those in boat — Claude, slaves Henry and Black Jim, and clerk Jean Baptiste Chandonnais.)

    12 Chicago Militia members

        (Including Sgt. Thomas Burns and 11 privates.)

    1 Indian Agent

        (William Wells, on detached duty from Fort Wayne.)

More confusion seems to exist among the historical accounts in the matter of identification of the Chicago Massacre participants than anything else — who the people were and where they were at the time of the massacre and the final disposition of each. In an effort to clarify the situation for once and all, two listings have been prepared which follow here, one a statistical listing for quick reference, the other a more detailed listing of individuals involved (or sometimes erroneously reported as being involved) in the Chicago massacre.

BASIC STATISTICS ON THE CHICAGO MASSACRE
CHICAGO, ILLINOIS — AUGUST 15, 1812

People on Hand	Type	Total Number	Survived	Killed
Captains	U.S. Army	1	1	0
2nd Lieutenants	U.S. Army	1	1	0
Ensigns	U.S. Army	1	0	1
Surgeon's Mates	U.S. Government	1	0	1
Indian Agents	U.S. Government	1	0	1
Sergeants	U.S. Army	3	1	2
Corporals	U.S. Army	5	2	3
Privates	U.S. Army	57	11	46
Sergeants	Chicago Militia	1	0	1
Privates	Chicago Militia	11	0	11
Women	Civilian and Military	20	14	6
Children	Civilian and Military	20	8	12
Men	Civilian	26	24	2
		148	62	86

A COMPLETE LISTING OF THE INDIVIDUAL PARTICIPANTS INVOLVED IN THE CHICAGO MASSACRE
CHICAGO, ILLINOIS
AUGUST 15, 1812

* * *

The following listing includes the individual whites, Indians, French, blacks, half-breeds, mixed-bloods and any others known to have been involved in the massacre, along with information germane to that connection, including final disposition.

In those cases where (?) follows the individual's given name or surname, there is some question regarding the accuracy of the name provided.

Names which appear in brackets — i.e., [Caldwell, Billy] — are other names for individuals whose actual name(s) can be seen as indicated.

Italicized entries represent individuals erroneously shown in some accounts as being on hand at the massacre but who were *not* there at the time; some of these being individuals who left shortly before the massacre or returned shortly afterward.

Adams, George	U.S. Army private; enlisted on August 21, 1806; first enlistment expired August 21, 1811, at which time he reenlisted; enlistment to expire August 21, 1816. Killed in initial battle.
Allin, John	U.S. Army private; in some accounts, surname is erroneously spelled Allen; enlisted on November 27, 1810; enlistment to expire on November 27, 1815. Seriously wounded during the initial battle; executed later in the evening.
Andrews, Prestly	U.S. Army private; given name incorrectly shown in some accounts as Presly or Pressley; enlisted on July 11, 1806; enlistment expired on July 11, 1811; reenlisted on July 11, 1811; enlistment to expire July 11, 1816. Wounded in initial battle; taken captive; executed later in the evening.
Ashbrook, Thomas	*U.S. Army private; enlisted on December 29, 1805; enlistment expired December 29, 1810; departed from Chicago immediately upon termination of enlistment.*
Athena	Negro slave belonging to John Kinzie, who serves a⌐

cook and housemaid; wife of slave known by the name of Henry. Is in the Kinzie boat at time of massacre. Survives.

Awbenabi — Potawatomi warrior; also known as He-Looks-Black; believed to have survived.

Beaubien, Charles Henry — *Half-breed son (born in 1803) of Jean Baptiste Beaubien and Ottawa wife, Mahnawbunnoquah; brother of Madore Beaubien; stepson of Josette LaFramboise Beaubien. Leaves Chicago for Milwaukee shortly before massacre, with family; returns to Chicago residency in autumn, 1818.*

Beaubien, Jean Baptiste — *Milwaukee trader and settler, who moved to Chicago about a year prior to the massacre; after natural death of his Ottawa wife, Mahnawbunnoquah, he marries Josette LaFramboise. He leaves Chicago with his sons for Milwaukee shortly before the massacre; returns to Chicago residency in the autumn of 1818.*

Beaubien, Josette LaFramboise — Second wife of Jean Baptiste Beaubien; stepmother of Charles Henry and Madore Beaubien; daughter of Francis and Madaline LaFramboise; sister of Alexis, Claude and LaFortune LaFramboise; employed as nursemaid to Kinzie children and remains in such employment when her husband and stepsons leave for Milwaukee shortly before the massacre; is with the Kinzie family in the boat at the time of the massacre. Survives.

Beaubien, Madore — *Half-breed son (born 1810) of Jean Baptiste Beaubien and his Ottawa wife, Mahnawbunnoquah; stepson of Josette LaFramboise Beaubien; brother of Charles Henry Beaubien. Leaves Chicago for Milwaukee with father and brother shortly before the massacre; returns to Chicago residency in autumn, 1818.*

Beaubien, Mahnawbunnoquah — *Full-blooded Ottawa; wife of Jean Baptiste Beaubien; mother of Charles Henry and Madore Beaubien. Dies of natural causes over a year prior to the massacre.*

Benjamin(?) — Negro boy (born 1811); son of slave woman named Cicely, who belongs to Rebekah Heald. Killed in wagon by tomahawk blow; beheaded.

Berry, Redmond — U.S. Army private; enlisted on July 2, 1806; enlistment expired July 2, 1811; reenlisted on July 2, 1811; enlistment to expire July 2, 1816. Killed in the initial battle.

Best, William — *U.S. Army private; enlisted on April 22, 1806; declared unfit for duty and discharged in December(?) 1810; left Chicago area immediately.*

[Big Man] — See Peesotum.

Black Jim — Negro slave belonging to John Kinzie; is aboard Kinzie boat as rower at time of massacre. Survives; traded to Indians, along with Henry ——, by John Kinzie to effect release of Captain Nathan Heald. Final disposition unknown.

Black Partridge — Potawatomi chief of Chicago area villages; elder brother of Waubansee; also known as Mkedepoke, Muck-otey-pokee and Nanaloibi. Protector of the Kinzie family during massacre. Survives.

[Blackbird] — See Siggenauk.

Bourbonne, Francis — Chicago settler and possibly merchant; probably on hand at massacre as civilian; believed to have been killed during battle.

Bowen, James

U.S. Army private; believed to be brother of Corporal Joseph Bowen; enlisted January 30, 1808; enlistment to expire on January 30, 1813. Killed during initial battle.

Bowen, Joseph

U.S. Army corporal; listed erroneously in some accounts as a private; enlisted April 22, 1806; enlistment expired April 22, 1811; reenlisted and promoted to corporal, April 22, 1811; enlistment to expire April 22, 1816. Taken captive during massacre. Survives.

Buison, Jean Baptiste

Son of Pierre Buison, Sr. and Susanne(?) Chevalier Buison (who is daughter of French-Potawatomi half-breed, Francis Chevalier); brother of Nicholas, Michael and Pierre Buison, Jr. Remains inside home at time of massacre. Survives.

Buison, Michael

Adult son of Pierre Buison, Sr., and Susanne(?) Chevalier Buison (who is daughter of French-Potawatomi half-breed Francis Chevalier); brother of Jean Baptiste, Nicholas and Pierre Buison, Jr. Remains inside home at time of massacre. Survives.

Buison, Nicholas

Adult son of Pierre Buison, Sr., and Susanne (?) Chevalier Buison (who is daughter of French-Potawatomi half-breed, Francis Chevalier); brother of Jean Baptiste, Michael and Nicholas Buison, Jr. Remains inside home at time of massacre. Survives.

Buison, Pierre, Jr.

Adult son of Pierre Buison, Sr., and Susanne(?) Chevalier Buison (who is daughter of French-Potawatomi half-breed, Francis Chevalier); brother of Jean Baptiste, Michael and Pierre Buison, Jr. Remains inside home at time of massacre. Survives.

Buison, Pierre, Sr.

Trader and settler; husband of Susanne(?) Chevalier Buison; father of Jean Baptiste, Michael, Nicholas and Pierre Buison, Jr. Remains inside home at time of massacre. Survives.

Buison, Susanne(?) Chevalier

Wife of Pierre Buison, Sr.; mother of Jean Baptiste, Michael, Nicholas and Pierre Buison, Jr.; daughter of French-Potawatomi half-breed, Francis Chevalier and his French wife. Her Indian name is Sheshi. Remains inside home at time of massacre. Survives.

Burke, Patrick

U.S. Army private; enlisted on May 27, 1806; enlistment expired on May 27, 1811; reenlisted on May 27, 1811; enlistment to expire on May 27, 1816. Killed in initial battle.

[Burly Shoulders]

See Chaubenee.

Burman, ——

U.S. Army private; enlisted on August 26, 1811; enlistment to expire on August 26, 1816; believed to have been killed in or near the wagon carrying sick soldiers.

Burnett, George

U.S. Army private; in some accounts his name is erroneously spelled Burnet; fifer for the Fort Dearborn band. Enlisted on October 1, 1806; enlistment scheduled to expire on October 1, 1811, but he reenlisted on July 1, 1811; enlistment to expire on July 1, 1816. Was slightly wounded during battle; specifically hunted down and slain after the surrender by a warrior he had previously offended.

Burns, Catherine

Four-month-old daughter of Thomas and Mary Burns; stepsister of James, Anne(?), Frances(?) and Isabella Cooper. Survives.

Burns, Mary

Widow of Ezekiel Cooper; remarried to Thomas Burns; mother of James, Anne(?), Frances(?) and Isabella

Cooper with first husband, and Catherine Burns with second. Survives.

Burns, Thomas   Chicago Militia sergeant; settler; former soldier at Fort Dearborn; husband of widow Mary Cooper Burns; father of Catherine Burns; stepfather of James, Anne(?), Frances(?) and Isabella Cooper. Severely wounded during battle; executed after surrender by Potawatomi woman.

[Caldwell, Billy]   See Sauganash.

Campbell, Asa   U.S. Army private; listed erroneously in some accounts as a corporal; enlisted January 26, 1805; enlistment expired on January 26, 1810; reenlisted January 26, 1810; enlistment to expire on January 26, 1815. Believed to have been one of the sick soldiers killed at or near the sick wagon.

Cardin, Jean Baptiste   *French-Canadian employee at the Lee farm (later called Hardscrabble) as a field hand, on South Branch Chicago River; killed at that farm on April 6, 1812, by band of marauding Winnebagoes.*

[Carrier]   See Kawbenaw.

[Catfish]   See Winnemac.

Chandonnais, Jean Baptiste   French-Potawatomi half-breed; employed as chief clerk in the Kinzie store; fraternal nephew of Potawatomi Chief Topenebe; is in boat with Kinzie family at time of massacre; aids in escape of the Kinzies and the Healds. Survives.

Chapman, James   *U.S. Army private; enlisted on December 1, 1805; enlistment expired on December 1, 1810; left Chicago immediately following discharge.*

Chaubenee   *Potawatomi chief of village(s) at present Shabbona and Shabbona Grove, Illinois; close associate and lieutenant of Tecumseh; also known as Shabbona, Chamblee, Burly Shoulders, Coal-Burner and many other variations. Not on hand for massacre but arrives following day with Sauganash and helps save Kinzie family.*

Chechepinqua   Potawatomi-English half-breed; later a significant chief of the United Potawatomi bands; also known as Alexander Robinson; helps save the Healds and William Griffith. Survives.

Cicely   Negro slave belonging to Rebekah Heald; mother of year-old son, Benjamin; killed by blow of tomahawk; later beheaded.

Clark, Emmaline   Wife of settler Samuel Clark; lives near the fork of the Chicago River; taken captive during the massacre; believed to have died in captivity.

Clark, James   *U.S. Army private; enlisted on December 4, 1805; enlistment expired on December 4, 1810; left Chicago immediately.*

Clark, Samuel   Chicago Militia private; settler; husband of Emmaline Clark. Killed at wagons.

Clark, Silas   *U.S. Army private; enlisted on August 15, 1806; enlistment to expire on August 15, 1811. Reassigned to Fort Wayne on December 10, 1810.*

Claude ——   French or Indian-French half-breed; boatman in employ of John Kinzie; *not* the Claude LaFramboise who deserted from Chicago Militia; operator of the Kinzie boat at time of massacre. Survives.

[Clear Day]   See Wasachek.

Clerk	Unnamed clerk of Kinzie Store; *not* Pierre LeClaire, Francois, Peresh, or Jean Baptiste Chandonnais; believed to be French or French-Indian half-breed. Survives.
[Coal Burner]	See Chaubenee.
Cooper, Anne(?)	Daughter (born 1806) of Mary and Ezekiel Cooper; stepdaughter of Thomas Burns; sister of James, Frances(?) and Isabella Cooper; half sister of Catherine Burns. Killed by tomahawk blow in wagon.
Cooper, Ezekiel	*Chicago settler; husband of Mary Cooper (who later marries Thomas Burns); father of James, Anne(?), Frances(?) and Isabella Cooper. Dies over a year prior to massacre.*
Cooper, Frances(?)	Daughter (born 1809) of Mary and Ezekiel Cooper; stepdaughter of Thomas Burns; sister of Anne(?), Isabella and James Cooper; half sister of Catherine Burns. Killed by tomahawk blow in wagon.
Cooper, Isabella	Daughter (born 1800) of Mary and Ezekiel Cooper; stepdaughter of Thomas Burns; sister of Anne(?), Frances(?) and James Cooper; half sister of Catherine Burns. Struck by tomahawk at wagon and scalped, but survives.
Cooper, James Andrew(?)	Chicago Militia private; son (born 1797) of Mary and Ezekiel Cooper; stepson of Thomas Burns; brother of Anne(?), Frances(?) and Isabella Cooper; half brother of Catherine Burns. Killed while defending wagons.
Cooper, John	U.S. Army private; *not* the same as Dr. John Cooper, former Fort Dearborn post surgeon, who left Chicago many months before massacre; enlisted May 28, 1808; enlistment to expire on May 28, 1813. Killed in initial battle.
[Cooper, Mary]	See Mary Burns.
Corbin, Fielding	U.S. Army private; often mistaken in accounts for the unrelated Private Phelim Corbin, but not the same; enlisted on October 25, 1811; enlistment to expire on October 25, 1816. Believed killed in initial battle.
Corbin, Henry(?)	Son (born c. 1808) of Susan (Sukey) and James Corbin; brother of Wilma(?) Corbin; nephew of Phelim Corbin. Killed after battle when skull crushed against side of house by Wabinsheway.
Corbin, James	U.S. Army private; husband of Susan (Sukey) Corbin; father of Henry(?) and Wilma(?) Corbin; brother of Phelim Corbin; enlisted on October 2, 1810; enlistment to expire October 2, 1815. Wounded in heel, hip, thigh and shoulder, but survives.
Corbin, Phelim	U.S. Army private; husband of Victoria Corbin; brother of James Corbin; enlisted on December 7, 1805; enlistment expired December 7, 1810; reenlisted on December 7, 1810; enlistment to expire on December 7, 1815. Captured. Survives.
Corbin, Susan	Nicknamed Sukey; wife of Private James Corbin; mother of Henry(?) and Wilma(?) Corbin; hides with her children from Indians at Burns house; discovered; killed by tomahawk blow.
Corbin, Victoria	Wife of Phelim Corbin; eight months pregnant; refuses to surrender to Indians; fights with sword; cut down and killed; beheaded.
Corbin, Wilma(?)	Daughter (born c. 1809) of James and Susan (Sukey)

Corbin, ——

Corbin; sister of Henry(?) Corbin; niece of Phelim Corbin. Killed after battle when skull is crushed against side of house by Wabinsheway.

Unnamed eight-month fetus of Victoria and Phelim Corbin. When mother killed, her stomach cut open; fetus removed, scalped, beheaded.

Crozier, John

U.S. Army sergeant; enlisted July 2, 1803; enlistment expired July 2, 1808; reenlisted and promoted to corporal on July 2, 1808; enlistment to expire July 2, 1813; promoted to sergeant on December 4, 1810; deserted from Fort Dearborn just prior to massacre; captured by Indians; ultimately freed; never known to have been charged with desertion.

Daugherty, Daniel

U.S. Army private; enlisted on August 13, 1807; enlistment was scheduled to expire on August 13, 1812; however, he reenlisted on June 1, 1812; enlistment to expire June 1, 1817; name in some accounts has erroneously been spelled Dougherty. Killed in volley immediately following surrender.

Denison, Micahjah

U.S. Army private; given name has occurred erroneously as Michael; surname has been mistakenly spelled Dennison in some accounts; enlisted on April 28, 1806; enlistment to have expired on April 28, 1811, but reenlisted early, on January 23, 1811; enlistment to expire on January 23, 1816. Badly wounded in the initial battle; taken captive; executed later same evening.

Draper, Stephen

U.S. Army private; enlisted on April 19, 1806; enlistment expired on April 19, 1811; reenlisted April 19, 1811; enlistment to expire April 19, 1816; (one account says he enlisted July 19, 1811, with enlistment due to expire July 19, 1816); severely wounded during battle; captured; executed the night of the battle.

DuBou, ——

Frenchman employed as field hand at the Lee farm (later Hardscrabble) on South Branch Chicago River; missing and never heard of again following attack by Winnebagoes on Lee farm on April 6, 1812.

DuPin, ——

French trader; settler; in some accounts the name is written as DuPain; probably in Chicago at time of massacre. Survives. Occupies abandoned Kinzie house the subsequent winter.

Dyer, Dyson

U.S. Army private; in some accounts, first and last names are mistakenly reversed; enlisted on October 1, 1810; enlistment to expire on April 6, 1815. Survived.

Edson, Nathan

U.S. Army private; enlisted on April 6, 1810; enlistment to expire April 6, 1815. Survives.

Forth, Thomas

U.S. Army corporal; enlisted July 6, 1807; enlistment expired July 6, 1812; enlistment extended due to emergency. Killed in initial battle.

François ——

Surname unknown; French-Potawatomi half-breed who is interpreter at times and employee of John Kinzie at times. Survives.

Frenchman # 1

Chicago Militia private; name unknown; killed near wagons.

Frenchman # 2

Chicago militia private; name unknown; killed near wagons.

Fury, John

U.S. Army private; enlisted on March 19, 1808; enlistment to expire on March 19, 1813. He is one of the sick soldiers riding in the sick-wagon at time of massacre. Captured. Killed later same night.

Garner, Richard
U.S. Army corporal; enlisted on October 2, 1805; enlistment expired on October 2, 1810; reenlisted on October 2, 1810; enlistment to expire October 2, 1815; promoted to corporal on March 4, 1812, though still shown, erroneously, as private on muster list of May 31, 1812. Severely wounded during battle; executed later in evening.

Glass, Joseph
U.S. Army sergeant; enlistment dates unknown; reassigned from Fort Dearborn to Fort Washington at Cincinnati, Ohio, late in 1811.

Griffith, William
U.S. Army quartermaster sergeant; enlisted at Chicago as sergeant on May 1, 1812; enlistment to expire on May 1, 1817; saved by Topenebe before battle; hides; helped by Buisons; escapes with Healds. Survives.

Grummo, Paul
U.S. Army private; enlisted on October 1, 1810; enlistment to expire October 1, 1815. Surname has also been incorrectly shown as Grummond, Grumow, Gromit and Grummon. Captured. Survives.

Hamilton, John
U.S. Army private; drummer in the Fort Dearborn band; enlisted on July 5, 1808; enlistment to expire on July 5, 1813. Killed in initial battle.

Hayes, Otho
U.S. Army sergeant. Surname appears incorrectly spelled Hays on May 31, 1812, muster list. Promoted to sergeant on April 23, 1811; enlistment to expire on April 23, 1816. Engages in hand-to-hand combat with Naunongee; thrusts bayonet through Naunongee's chest, who then kills him with tomahawk blow to head. See Awbenabi.

[He-Looks-Black]
Heald, Nathan
See Awbenabi.
U.S. Army captain; promoted to captain of the 1st Infantry Regiment on January 31, 1807; becomes commander of Fort Dearborn in June, 1810; husband of Rebekah Heald; wounded in arm and hip. Survives.

Heald, Rebekah
Wife of Nathan Heald, Fort Dearborn commander; daughter of Colonel Samuel Wells of Louisville, Kentucky; niece of William Wells who was killed at massacre; wounded six times (not all six in arms and hands as most accounts contend); left arm broken by ball; three wounds in one arm, one in other arm; both sides and breast creased by balls; rescued through efforts of Kinzies, aided by Topenebe. Survives.

Helm, Linai T.
U.S. Army second lieutenant; promoted to second lieutenant on December 15, 1808; second-in-command at Fort Dearborn; husband of Margaret McKillip Helm, who is stepdaughter of John Kinzie; some accounts say, incorrectly, that he was wounded in shoulder; only wound was slight, in heel. Captured. Ransomed by Thomas Forsyth. Survives.

Helm, Margaret McKillip
Daughter of Eleanor and Daniel McKillip; stepdaughter of John Kinzie; stepsister of John H., Ellen, Maria and Robert Kinzie; slightly wounded in ankle. Captured. Survives.

Henry, ——
Chicago Militia private; settler; fights to protect the wagons. He is killed in initial battle.

Henry
Negro slave of John Kinzie; husband of slave named Athena in same household; in Kinzie boat at time of massacre. Survives massacre but traded by John Kinzie to Indians to effect release of Captain Heald; disposition thereafter unknown.

Holt, Isaac
U.S. Army sergeant; listed as Edward Holt in some

accounts; promoted to sergeant on April 22, 1811; enlistment to expire on April 22, 1816; husband of Jane(?) Holt; shot in neck; tomahawked to death while trying to crawl to safety.

Holt, Jane(?)
Wife of Isaac Holt; on horseback, pursued by Indians whom she holds off with sword. Captured. Survives.

Hunt, William Nelson
U.S. Army private; enlisted on October 8, 1810; enlistment to expire October 8, 1815 (though shown incorrectly in one account as having enlisted on October 10, 1810. Captured. Freezes to death during ensuing winter, while captive.

Hurtt, Nathan A.
U.S. Army private; deserted from Fort Dearborn with Sergeant Crozier just prior to massacre; surname incorrectly spelled Hurt in some accounts; enlisted December 29, 1811; enlistment to expire on December 29, 1816; captured by Indians while deserter; shown in some accounts as having been killed at massacre; was killed by captors, but not at massacre.

Irwin, Matthew
U.S. Government Factor at Fort Dearborn; just prior to massacre, while at Fort Mackinac to locate new interpreter for Fort Dearborn, captured by British and Indians at capitulation of Fort Mackinac. Survived.

Jones, Rhodias
U.S. Army corporal; enlisted as private on December 9, 1807; enlistment to expire on December 9, 1812; promoted to corporal on November 1, 1811, but still shown, erroneously, as private on the May 31, 1812, muster list. Killed in initial battle.

Jordan, Walter
U.S. Army corporal; on detached duty (with William Wells) from Fort Wayne to Fort Dearborn. Captured by White Raccoon; escapes; survives.

Karamone
Winnebago chief. Survives.

Kawbenaw
Young Potawatomi chief who saves Rebekah Heald; also known as The Carrier. Survives.

Kawbenaw's Wife
Wife of Potawatomi Chief Kawbenaw, who tries to steal saddle blanket of Rebekah Heald and is beaten off with riding crop.

Keamble, ———
U.S. Army private; first name not known to be recorded; surname sometimes appears erroneously as Kimble. Believed to have been killed in the initial battle.

Keah Keakah
Subchief of Miamis, who is leader of Miami escort of twenty-seven warriors, including himself. Survives.

Keepoteh
Potawatomi warrior from village of Chief Topenebe on St. Joseph River; at direction of Topenebe, boards Kinzie boat; helps save Kinzie family. Survives.

Kelso, John
U.S. Army private at Fort Dearborn; enlisted as private on December 17, 1805; enlistment expired on December 17, 1810; accepted discharge, remained in Chicago; worked for a while as tutor to Kinzie children; then became field hand at Lee farm on South Branch Chicago River where, with Charles Lee, Jr., he escaped Winnebagoes who struck on April 6, 1812; rejoined the U.S. Army as private on May 3, 1812, at Chicago; enlistment to expire on May 3, 1817; erroneously shown as member of Chicago Militia in some accounts; also erroneously shown as sergeant in some accounts. Killed in initial battle. Surname incorrectly shown as Kelsoe in some accounts.

Kennison, David
U.S. Army private; surname erroneously spelled Kini-

son in some accounts, including May 31, 1812, muster list; enlisted on March 14, 1808; enlistment to expire on March 14, 1813. Captured. Survives. Returns to residency at Chicago and dies there in 1852.

Kilpatrick, Samuel
U.S. Army private; surname erroneously appears as Kirkpatrick in some accounts; enlisted on December 20, 1805; enlistment expired December 20, 1810; re-enlisted on December 20, 1810; enlistment to expire on December 20, 1815. Killed at sick-wagon.

Kinzie, Eleanor
Wife of trader John Kinzie; mother of John H., Ellen M., Maria I., and Robert A. Kinzie, and Margaret McKillip Helm (with first husband, Daniel McKillip); in boat with the four Kinzie children at time of massacre; saved by Topenebe. Survives.

Kinzie, Ellen Marion
Daughter (born December 1805) of Eleanor and John Kinzie; sister of John H., Maria I., and Robert A. Kinzie; half sister of Margaret McKillip Helm; in Kinzie boat at time of massacre. Survives.

Kinzie, John
Chicago trader, settler; second husband of Eleanor; father of John H., Ellen M., Maria I., and Robert A. Kinzie; stepfather of Margaret McKillip Helm; step-father-in-law of Second Lieutenant Linai T. Helm; saved by Topenebe, Chaubenee, Sauganash and others. Survives.

Kinzie, John Harris
Son (born July 1803) of Eleanor and John Kinzie; brother of Ellen M., Maria I., and Robert A. Kinzie; half brother of Margaret McKillip Helm; in Kinzie boat at time of massacre. Survives.

Kinzie, Maria Indiana
Daughter (born September 1807) of Eleanor and John Kinzie; sister of John H., Ellen M., and Robert A. Kinzie; half sister of Margaret McKillip Helm. In Kinzie boat at time of massacre. Survives.

Kinzie, Robert Allen
Son (born February 1810) of Eleanor and John Kinzie; brother of John H., Ellen M., and Maria I. Kinzie; half brother of Margaret McKillip Helm; in Kinzie boat at time of massacre. Survives.

[Knowles, Joseph]
See Joseph Noles.

LaFramboise, Alexis
Chicago Militia private who, with brothers Claude and LaFortune, deserts just prior to massacre and goes to Milwaukee with parents; son (born 1794) of Francis and Madaline LaFramboise; brother, also, of Josette LaFramboise Beaubien. Survives.

LaFramboise, Claude
Chicago Militia private who, with brothers Alexis and LaFortune, deserts just prior to massacre and goes to Milwaukee with parents; son (1795) of Francis and Madaline LaFramboise; brother, also, of Josette La-Framboise Beaubien. Survives.

LaFramboise, Francis
Husband of Madaline LaFramboise; trader, settler; accompanies (with wife) his militia-deserting sons to Milwaukee just prior to massacre; father of Alexis, Claude and LaFortune LaFramboise, and Josette LaFramboise Beaubien. Survives.

[LaFramboise, Josette]
See Josette LaFramboise Beaubien.

LaFramboise, LaFortune
Chicago Militia private who, with brothers Alexis and Claude, deserts just prior to massacre and goes to Milwaukee with parents; son (born 1797) of Francis and Madaline LaFramboise; brother, also, of Josette La-Framboise Beaubien. Survives.

LaFramboise, Madaline
Wife of trader and settler, Francis LaFramboise;

mother of Alexis, Claude and LaFortune LaFramboise, and Josette LaFramboise Beaubien; goes to Milwaukee just prior to massacre with husband and the three militia-deserting sons. Survives.

Landon, Jacob | U.S. Army private; enlisted November 28, 1807; enlistment to expire November 28, 1812. Wounded; captured; executed later in evening.

Latta, James | U.S. Army private; surname also incorrectly recorded as Lata, Latte and Lutta; enlisted on April 10, 1810; enlistment to expire on April 10, 1815. Captured; executed later in evening.

[LeClaire, Pierre] | See Pierre LeClerc.

[LeClerc, Peresh] | See Peresh.

LeClerc, Pierre | Potawatomi-French half-breed; also known as Pierre LeClaire; raised in trading business by John Kinzie; lives near fort; sometimes confused with Indian called Peresh LeClerc (or Peresh, the Clerk) who also worked for Kinzie at times; has been listed (probably erroneously) as interpreter for John Kinzie, though may have served in that capacity at times for Fort Dearborn; acts as negotiator between Americans and Indians at surrender. Survives.

Lee, Charles, Jr. | Chicago Militia private; son (born 1797) of Martha and Charles Lee, Sr.; brother of Mary and Sally Lee. Killed in defense of wagons.

Lee, Charles, Sr. | Chicago Militia private; settler; husband of Martha Lee; father of Mary, Sally and Charles Lee, Jr. Killed in defense of wagons.

Lee, Martha | Wife of Charles Lee, Sr.; mother of Mary, Sally and Charles Lee, Jr. Captured. Survives. Subsequently marries Frenchman trader, DuPin, in Chicago.

Lee, Mary | Daughter (born 1800) of Martha and Charles Lee, Sr.; sister of Sally and Charles Lee, Jr. Severely wounded; mercy-killed by Black Partridge.

Lee, Sally | Daughter (born 1811) of Martha and Charles Lee, Sr.; sister of Mary and Charles Lee, Jr. Survives.

Leonard, Michael | U.S. Army private; enlisted on April 13, 1810; enlistment to expire on April 13, 1815. Believed to have been killed in initial battle.

Locker, Frederick | U.S. Army private; enlisted on April 13, 1810; enlistment to expire on April 13, 1815. Killed in initial battle.

Logan, Hugh | U.S. Army private; enlisted on May 5, 1806; enlistment was to have expired on May 5, 1811, but he reenlisted early, on February 5, 1811; enlistment to expire on February 5, 1816. Captured; executed later in evening.

Loy, Andrew | U.S. Army private; enlisted on July 6, 1807; enlistment was due to expire on July 6, 1812, but was deferred for one month, to August 6, 1812, due to emergency situation; enlistment extended a second time on August 6, 1812, for one month, due to continuing emergency situation, to September 6, 1812. Believed to have been killed in initial battle.

Lynch, Michael | U.S. Army private; enlisted on December 20, 1805; enlistment expired on December 20, 1810; reenlisted on December 23, 1810; enlistment to expire on December 23, 1815. Captured; executed while en route to Illinois River, for inability to keep up.

Mabury, James   U.S. Army private; enlisted on April 14, 1806; enlistment expired on April 14, 1811; reenlisted on April 14, 1811; enlistment to expire on April 14, 1816. Believed killed in initial battle.

Mackraragah   Winnebago chief. Survives.

[Mad Sturgeon]   See Nescotnemeg.

[*Mahnawbunnoquah*]   *See Mahnawbunnoquah Beaubien.*

McCarty, Duncan   U.S. Army private; enlisted on August 31, 1807; enlistment to expire on August 31, 1812. Killed, along with two others, in volley following surrender.

McGowan, Patrick   U.S. Army private; enlisted on April 30, 1806; enlistment expired on April 30, 1811; reenlisted on April 30, 1811; enlistment to expire on April 30, 1816. Captured. Survives.

McPherson, Hugh   U.S. Army private; drummer in Fort Dearborn band; enlisted on October 20, 1807; enlistment to expire on October 20, 1812. Believed killed in the initial battle.

[Mdpoke]   See Waubansee.

Miller, Peter   U.S. Army private; enlisted on June 13, 1806; enlistment supposed to have expired on June 13, 1811; however, was declared "unfit for service" early in 1811; remained in Chicago and reenlisted on July 24, 1811; enlistment to expire on July 24, 1816. One of the sick soldiers killed at or near the sick-wagon.

Miller, Ralph   *U.S. Army private; enlisted on December 19, 1805; enlistment expired on December 19, 1810; left Chicago at once.*

Mills, Elias   U.S. Army private; enlisted on October 26, 1811; enlistment to expire on October 26, 1816. Captured. Survives.

Mirandeau, Jean Baptiste, Jr.   *Son of Jean Baptiste Mirandeau, Sr. and Ottawa woman, name not known; brother of Joseph, Louis, Madeline and Victoire Mirandeau; returns with family to Milwaukee prior to massacre.*

Mirandeau, Jean Baptiste, Sr.   *Chicago settler, trader; husband of Ottawa woman whose name is not known; father of Jean Jr., Joseph, Louis, Madeline and Victoire Mirandeau; returns with family to Milwaukee prior to massacre.*

Mirandeau, Joseph   *Son of Jean Baptiste Mirandeau, Sr., and Ottawa woman, name not known; brother of Jean Baptiste Jr., Louis, Madeline and Victoire Mirandeau; returns with family to Milwaukee prior to massacre.*

Mirandeau, Louis   *Son of Jean Baptiste Mirandeau, Sr., and Ottawa woman, name not known; brother of Jean Baptiste Jr., Joseph, Madeline and Victoire Mirandeau; returns with family to Milwaukee prior to massacre.*

Mirandeau, Madeline   *Daughter of Jean Baptiste Mirandeau, Sr., and Ottawa woman, name not known; sister of Jean Baptiste Jr., Joseph, Louis and Madeline Mirandeau; returns with family to Milwaukee prior to massacre.*

Mirandeau, Victoire   *Daughter of Jean Baptiste Mirandeau, Sr., and Ottawa woman, name not known; sister of Jean Baptiste Jr., Joseph, Louis and Madeline Mirandeau; returns with family to Milwaukee prior to massacre.*

Mittatass   Potawatomi chief from the area of Peoria, Illinois; is awarded possession of Lt. Linai T. Helm. Survives.

[Mkedepoke]   See Black Partridge.

Moffett, William   U.S. Army private; surname has erroneously been spelled Moffitt and Morfitt in various accounts; enlisted on April 23, 1806; enlistment was to have expired on April 23, 1811; however, reenlisted on January 23, 1811; enlistment to expire January 23, 1816. Believed killed in initial battle.

[Moran, Pierre]   See Peresh.

Mortt, August   U.S. Army private; surname in some accounts appears erroneously as Mott; enlisted on July 9, 1806; enlistment to have expired on July 9, 1811; however, reenlisted on April 9, 1811; enlistment to expire on April 9, 1816; in many accounts is said to have been killed in captivity after having gone insane; this is erroneous; he was killed because in going from one village to another during captivity, he was unable to keep up due to exhaustion.

Moyan, John   U.S. Army private; enlisted on June 28, 1806; enlistment expired June 28, 1811; reenlisted on June 28, 1811; enlistment to expire June 28, 1816. Believed to have been killed in initial battle.

[Muck-otey-pokee]   See Black Partridge.

[Nanaloibi]   See Black Partridge.

Naunongee   Potawatomi chief of village(s) at mouth of the Calumet River; name also recorded as Nan-non-gee; severely wounded with bayonet through chest by Sgt. Otho Hayes, whom he kills; carried to own village and dies several days later; only Indian chief known to have died in massacre.

Neads, John   U.S. Army private; erroneously spelled Needs on May 31, 1812 muster list; enlisted on July 5, 1808; enlistment to expire on July 5, 1813; husband of Sarah Neads; father of Johnny(?) Neads. Captured; dies in captivity of starvation and exposure.

Neads, Johnny(?)   Son (about four years old) of Sarah and John Neads; tied to tree and left behind to die of exposure.

Neads, Sarah   Wife of John Neads; mother of Johnny(?) Neads. Captured; dies of starvation and exposure in captivity.

Nelson, ——   U.S. Army private; enlisted May 21, 1809; enlistment due to expire on May 21, 1814. Captured; dies in captivity of freezing.

Nescotnemeg   Potawatomi chief from village(s) at junction of Iroquois River with Kankakee River in Illinois; one of the principal chiefs of the massacre; planner of the Chicago massacre; also known as Mad Sturgeon; brother of Wasachek and Waubinema ("White Sturgeon"); badly wounded in upper chest during massacre. Survives.

Nescotnoning   Potawatomi subchief from Des Plaines River village; often confused with Nescotnemeg because of the similarity of names. Survives.

Noles, Joseph   U.S. Army private; surname has erroneously appeared in several accounts spelled Knowles; enlisted on September 8, 1810; enlistment to expire on September 8, 1815. Captured. Survives.

Ouilmette, Antoine   Chicago settler and trader; French; husband of Potawatomi woman named Archange; father of Archange, Elizabeth, François, Joseph, Josette, Michel, and Sophie Ouilmette. Remains neutral at home during massacre. Survives.

Ouilmette, Archange (elder)	Wife of Antoine Ouilmette; known also as Okra; Potawatomi woman; mother of Archange (younger), Elizabeth, François, Joseph, Josette, Michel, Louis and Sophie Ouilmette. Remains neutral at home during massacre. Survives.
Ouilmette, Archange (younger)	Daughter of Antoine and Archange Ouilmette; sister of Elizabeth, François, Joseph, Josette, Louis, Michel and Sophie Ouilmette. Remains neutral at home during massacre. Survives.
Ouilmette, Elizabeth	Daughter of Antoine and Archange Ouilmette; sister of Archange (younger), François, Joseph, Josette, Louis, Michel and Sophie Ouilmette. Remains neutral at home during massacre. Survives.
Ouilmette, François	Son of Antoine and Archange Ouilmette; brother of Archange (younger), Elizabeth, Joseph, Josette, Louis, Michel and Sophie Ouilmette. Remains neutral at home during massacre. Survives.
Ouilmette, Joseph	Son of Antoine and Archange Ouilmette; brother of Archange (younger), Elizabeth, François, Josette, Louis, Michel and Sophie Ouilmette. Remains neutral at home during massacre. Survives.
Ouilmette, Josette	*Daughter of Antoine and Archange Ouilmette; sister of Archange (younger), Elizabeth, François, Joseph, Josette, Louis, Michel and Sophie Ouilmette. Sometimes erroneously placed in boat with Kinzies at time of massacre (being mistaken for Josette LaFramboise Beaubien); not born until 1813.*
Ouilmette, Louis	Son of Antoine and Archange Ouilmette; brother of Archange (younger), Elizabeth, François, Joseph, Josette, Michel and Sophie Ouilmette. Remains neutral at home during massacre. Survives.
Ouilmette, Michel	Son of Antoine and Archange Ouilmette; brother of Archange (younger), Elizabeth, François. Joseph, Josette, Louis and Sophie Ouilmette. Remans neutral at home during massacre. Survives.
Ouilmette, Sophie	Daughter of Antoine and Archange Ouilmette; sister of Archange (younger), Elizabeth, François, Joseph, Josette, Louis and Michel Ouilmette. Remains neutral at home during massacre. Survives.
Peesotum	Potawatomi subchief; also known as Big Man; kills William Wells during massacre and eats his heart. Survives.
Pepper	Negro slave owned by John Kinzie; serves Kinzie at different labors; with marchers, but not part of militia. Believed to have been killed defending the wagons.
Peresh	Potawatomi-Kickapoo mixed-blood chief; also known as Perish, Peresh LeClerc, the Stutterer, and Pierre Moran; employed by John Kinzie on occasion; in some accounts erroneously shown as being the negotiator between Indians and whites for the surrender, but that job was done by Pierre LeClerc. Survives.
[Perish]	See Peresh
Peterson, Frederick	U.S. Army private; enlisted on June 7, 1808; enlistment to expire on June 7, 1813; shown, probably erroneously, in one account as having enlisted on June 1, 1808. Believed to have been killed in the initial attack.
Pettell, Louis	Chicago Militia private; settler; father of the younger trader, Michael Pettell; surname sometimes erroneously

recorded as Pettill or Le Pettell. Killed in defense of the wagons.

Pettell, Michael
Chicago Militia private; trader; son of Louis Pettell. Killed in defense of wagons.

Poindexter, Thomas
U.S. Army private; surname in some accounts appears erroneously as Point Dexter; enlisted on September 3, 1810; enlistment to expire of September 3, 1815. One of the sick soldiers at the sick-wagon. Captured. Executed later in the evening.

Prickett, William
U.S. Army private; surname in some accounts is erroneously spelled Pickett; enlisted on June 6, 1806; enlistment was to have expired on June 6, 1811, but reenlisted on March 7, 1811; enlistment to expire March 7, 1816. One of three privates killed in volley following surrender.

Rickman, Richard
U.S. Army sergeant; enlisted on May 10, 1806; promoted to corporal in 1809; reenlisted and promoted to sergeant on May 10, 1811; reassigned to Washington, D.C., in August 1811.

Riley, James
Half-breed son of Ottawa woman and Judge Riley of Schenectady when he was a trader at Saginaw Bay; brother of Peter and John Riley; occasional interpreter at Fort Dearborn; presence at time of massacre uncertain, but probability strong. Believed to have survived.

Riley, John
Half-breed son of Ottawa woman and Judge Riley of Schenectady when he was a trader at Saginaw Bay; brother of James and Peter Riley; purported to have been a ne'er-do-well; presence at time of massacre uncertain, but probability strong. Believed to have survived.

Riley, Peter
Half-breed son of Ottawa woman and Judge Riley of Schenectady when he was a trader at Saginaw Bay; brother of James and John Riley; purported to have been a ne'er-do-well; presence at time of massacre uncertain, but probability strong. Believed to have survived.

[Robinson, Alexander]
See Chechepinqua.

Ronan, George
U.S. Army ensign; graduated from West Point and appointed ensign on March 1, 1811; junior officer at Fort Dearborn. Killed after valiant fight in defense of wagons.

Russell, Tess(?)
Wife of William Russell, settler; killed at the wagons.

Russell, William
Chicago Militia private; settler; partner, with Charles Lee, Sr., in the Lee farm (later Hardscrabble) on South Branch Chicago River; husband of Tess(?). Killed in defense of wagons.

Salienne
French/Potawatomi half-breed youth of about fourteen; occasional interpreter at Fort Dearborn; may have lived in the Riley cabin with the three brothers; not, as erroneously reported in some accounts, the half-breed interpreter who helps negotiate the surrender (that was Pierre LeClerc); leaves Fort Dearborn with procession at beginning of march; immediately runs off to Indians as the trouble begins. Survives.

Sansamani
Winnebago chief. Survives.

Sauganash
Potawatomi-English half-breed; also known as Billy Caldwell; son of Captain William Caldwell (British)

and Potawatomi woman, name unknown; later becomes a chief of the United Potawatomi bands; aide and secretary to Tecumseh; close friend of both Tecumseh and Chaubenee; arrives at Chicago the day following the massacre; helps to save the Kinzies.

Seventy-year-old Man — Chicago Militia private. Killed at dunes.

[Shabbona] — See Chaubenee.

Sherror, David — U.S. Army private; enlisted October 1, 1810; enlistment to expire October 1, 1815. Believed to have been killed in initial battle.

Siggenauk — Potawatomi chief of village(s) at Milwaukee; also known as Blackbird; commands the Indian forces at the massacre, following the battle plan made by Nescotnemeg. Survives.

Simmons, David — Son (born 1810) of Susan and John Simmons; brother of Susan Simmons. Killed in wagon by tomahawk blow; later beheaded.

Simmons, John — U.S. Army private; in some accounts erroneously listed as Simmonds; husband of Susan Simmons; father of David and Susan Simmons. Enlisted on March 14, 1810; enlistment to expire on March 14, 1815. Killed in initial battle.

Simmons, Susan — Daughter (6 months old) of Susan and John Simmons; sister of David Simmons. Captured. Survives.

Simmons, Susan Millhouse — Wife of John Simmons; mother of Susan and David Simmons. Captured. Survives.

[Sits-Quietly] — See Topenebe.

Smith, John, Jr. — U.S. Army private; son of John Smith, Sr.; fifer and probably bandmaster of Fort Dearborn band; enlisted June 27, 1806; enlistment to have expired on June 27, 1811, but he reenlisted on April 22, 1811; enlistment to expire April 22, 1816. Captured. Survived.

Smith, John, Sr. — U.S. Army private; father of John Smith, Jr.; enlisted on April 2, 1808; enlistment to expire on April 2, 1813. Severely wounded. Captured. Executed later in evening.

Smith, Philip — U.S. Army private; enlisted on April 30, 1806; enlistment expired April 30, 1811; reenlisted on April 30, 1811; enlistment to expire on April 30, 1816. Believed to have been killed during the initial battle.

Starr, James — U.S. Army private; enlisted on November 18, 1809; enlistment to expire on November 18, 1814. Killed in initial battle at sick-wagon.

[Stutterer] — See Peresh.

Sunawewonee — Potawatomi chief of Prairie Potawatomies of the area of Peoria; one of the principal chiefs during the massacre. Survives.

Suttenfield, John — U.S. Army private; surname in some accounts is erroneously shown as Suttonfield; enlisted on September 8, 1807; enlistment to expire on September 8, 1812. Captured. Executed for inability to keep up during march to Illinois River.

Topenebe — Potawatomi chief of village(s) at St. Joseph River; also known as Topinebi and Sits-Quietly; brother of Kawkemee, who is the wife of trader William Burnett at St. Joseph; fraternal uncle of Jean Baptiste Chandonnais; good friend of the Kinzies, whom he helps to save. Survives.

[Topinebi] — See Topenebe.

Unidentified Child # 1	Child killed in wagon during massacre.
Unidentified Child # 2	Child killed in wagon during massacre.
Unidentified Child # 3	Child killed in wagon during massacre.
van Horne, James	U.S. Army private; name erroneously shown on May 31, 1812 muster lists as Vanhorn; enlisted May 2, 1810; enlistment to expire May 2, 1815. Captured. Survives.
van Voorhis, Isaac N.	U.S. Army surgeon's mate; graduated from Fishkill Academy, N.Y.; appointed surgeon's mate March 11, 1811; unjustly accused of cowardice in many accounts. Wounded, then killed at wagons.
[Wabansi]	See Waubansee.
Wabinsheway	Potawatomi chief of village(s) at Elkhart River; also known as White Elk. Survives.
Waggoner, Anthony L.	U.S. Army private; enlisted January 9, 1811; enlistment to expire January 9, 1816. Badly wounded. Executed later in evening.
Wasachek	Potawatomi warrior; brother of Nescotnemeg and Waubinema; also known as Clear Day. Wounded. Survives.
Waubansee	Potawatomi chief at Fox River, Illinois; also known as Mdpoke and Wabansi; name means "A-Little-Eastern-Light"; younger brother of Black Partridge. Survives.
[Waubeeneemah]	See Waubinema.
Waubinema	Potawatomi chief from Illinois River; name means "White Sturgeon" and appears also as Waubeeneemah; brother of Nescotnemeg and Wasachek; saves Margaret Helm. Survives.
Waubinema's Wife	With husband, Waubinema, has wigwam at Indian encampment at State Street Creek. Survives.
Wells, William	Indian Agent and interpreter from Fort Wayne on detached service from Fort Wayne; fraternal uncle of Rebekah Heald; adopted son of Michikiniqua (Little Turtle), Miami chief; also known as Apekonit and Epiconyare; title of captain not official at time of death. Wounded; killed by Peesotum and his heart removed and eaten.
[White Elk]	See Wabinsheway.
White, Liberty	*Settler; manager of the Lee farm (later Hardscrabble Farm) where he is killed by marauding Winnebagoes and body mutilated, April 6, 1812.*
White Raccoon	Potawatomi chief from village(s) of the Iroquois River, Illinois, area. Survives.
Winnemac	Potawatomi chief of village(s) of the Mississinewa River, Indiana, area; also known as Catfish; ally of the United States; former U.S. spy for William Henry Harrison; brings General Hull's evacuation order to Captain Heald; noncombatant in the massacre. Survives.
Winnemeg	Potawatomi warrior from Illinois River near Peoria Lake; often confused with Winnemac, but not the same. Very hostile to the United States. Participant in the massacre. Survives.

273. Some historians have chosen to discount the incident between Captain Heald and Ensign Ronan as a fanciful tale created by Margaret Helm in her account. She is, indeed, guilty of some outright fabrications in other parts of her account. Nevertheless, despite the fact that John Kinzie gives no hint of any friction existing between the two officers, judicious digging has indicated that a certain amount of antipathy did exist, evidently because Ronan believed (with some justification) that Captain Heald was deliberately withholding his recommendation for Ronan's

promotion to second lieutenant. Much later, Rebekah Heald flatly stated that there was never any quarrel between· Ensign George Ronan and her husband, offering as proof of this the fact that Ronan had given Captain Heald a large dictionary with both their names on the fly-leaf, though why this should constitute proof of her contention is rather a mystery. Be that as it may, Ronan left Fort Dearborn in the van of the column and a short time later, when the massacre began, he was with neither the officers nor the troops but was, in fact, defending the wagons.

274. In modern perspective, the rear of the line was at this time at approximately the northeast corner of Michigan Avenue and South Water Street; the head of the line at East Madison Street, a few hundred yards east of Michigan Avenue. Some accounts say the column had by this time stretched out some five blocks in length, but actually the distance along the old road was about three modern blocks in length.

275. The dunes have been reported in various accounts as being as far west of the road as one hundred yards or more, to as near as ten yards. Though the distance varied at different points, it averaged between sixty and seventy yards to the right of the column, making them seventy or eighty yards from the lake shore.

276. Most earlier accounts had placed Wells with the vanguard Miami escort at all times since departure from the fort, but the recently discovered John Kinzie account shows without doubt that Wells, after the departure from the fort, had ridden from front to rear, then back to front again, and having the discussion with Kinzie as shown.

277. At this point the front of the column was at approximately 18th Street, while the rear was at about 14th Street.

278. No surname is known to have been recorded for this septuagenarian of the Chicago Militia.

279. Sergeant William Griffith, whose account was recorded in later years by Robert McAfee, was the genesis of much misinformation in regard to the Chicago Massacre. Griffith, of course, hidden north of the river at this time, was not with the march and did not engage in the fighting at any time. It is Griffith who stated that the Frenchman he called Pierre LeClair, whom he characterized as a militiaman, ran off at the beginning of the fight, for which Griffith was allegedly going to kill him, but that LeClair begged Griffith for mercy. Actually, the man's name was Pierre LeClerc, not LeClair, he was not a militiaman and he did not desert either the militia or the march, since he was not a member of neither. Evidently Griffith based his erroneous report on a misinterpretation of a report that subsequently reached him of the young Salienne running to join the enemy.

280. Some accounts claim the Americans fired first, but this is almost surely incorrect, since the Indians were initially hidden from view of the Americans and because white soldiers — first the seventy-year-old militiaman, and then others, fell in the first volley. Also, some accounts contend that it was the Indians who charged the Americans, but this is entirely incorrect; the Indians fired upon the charging Americans from behind the protection of dunes and scattered pines. This first attack occurred at present 18th Street between Prairie Avenue and Lake Shore Drive.

281. At least one account, misinterpreting the Juliette Kinzie account and especially the line that Eleanor Kinzie "was certain she would never see her husband and eldest child again," has asserted that nine-year-old John H. Kinzie was at the van of the column with his father, mistaking him to be Eleanor Kinzie's "eldest child." The reference is, of course, to Margaret McKillip Helm, wife of Lieutenant Helm, Eleanor Kinzie's daughter by Daniel McKillip and, of course, her eldest child and John Kinzie's stepchild. Nine-year-old John H. Kinzie was beyond doubt in the boat with his mother and three younger siblings at all times, as described here.

282. Jane Holt was well treated by her captors and subsequently ransomed at Peoria by Thomas Forsyth, half brother of John Kinzie.

283. Naunongee was subsequently carried back to his village at the mouth of the Calumet River where he lingered for three days before dying. Some accounts have erroneously stated that both Hayes and Naunongee fell dead together. So far as is known, Naunongee is the only chief to have been killed in this affair.

284. Forty years later, in 1852, Rebekah Heald made an appeal to Congress for re-compense in the loss of her slave, Cicely, in this action. She claimed a $1,000 loss. The Congress, however, denied her claim.

285. Some historians have discounted this incident reported by Margaret Helm but that may be a hasty presumption. Some, who accept the account, interpret it as craven cowardice on the part of Isaac van Voorhis. This, too, is a hasty presump-tion. Van Voorhis was obviously — and quite justifiably — afraid, but fear and cowardice are hardly the same. The incident and conversation has all the earmarks of being factual and the author is inclined to accept it at reasonably face value. It is interesting to note the reaction of the friend and classmate of Van Voorhis, John Cooper, who was his predecessor at Fort Dearborn. After publication of Wau-Bun, Cooper made a public statement affirming the courage of Van Voorhis and his personal worth and Cooper continued protesting throughout the rest of his life that the depiction of Van Voorhis as a coward was "a cruel slander and grave injustice."

286. In speaking of this incident later, Black Partridge became quite emotional about the mercy killing, saying it was one of the hardest things he had ever had to do, since he liked her very much. In Wau-Bun it is stated that he killed her with his tomahawk, but Black Partridge himself said he had killed her with the same knife he had used to cut her free from the saddle.

287. At least one account has stated that Rebekah Heald, seeing this "fine young officer fall" thought it was her husband and remained under this impression until some time after the massacre. However, since she had only minutes before left him as he led the charge up the dunes, such a conclusion is entirely unjustified.

288. The one-ounce ball lodged in Captain Heald's hip joint, where it remained for the rest of his life, continually causing him pain until the day he died, some twenty years later.

289. In some accounts it is Black Partridge who is depicted as being the chief involved here, but that is not correct; it was Siggenauk — Blackbird.

290. Years afterward, in a letter to Nathan Heald, Sergeant William Griffith com-mented on "the soldierlike conduct of Burns on the battlefield while engaged with an unequal number of savages," but he spoke from hearsay alone, since Griffith was in hiding on the north side of the Chicago River and nowhere near the con-flict at this time.

291. For the rest of her life, Isabella Cooper carried a bald spot of scar tissue on the top of her head as a result of this incident.

292. In most accounts it is stated that Rebekah Heald was wounded six times, in arms and hands. She *was* wounded six times, but only three of these in the arms and hands — one of them breaking the smaller bone in her left arm. It was a little later that she received the other three wounds, as stated here, which, according to her son, Darius, struck her slightly in the right breast and both sides.

293. A total fabrication of the death of William Wells is given in the account written later by Margaret Helm. She said that Wells had come up to where the massacre at the wagons was occurring and: "When Captain Wells, who was fighting near it, beheld it, he exclaimed, 'Is that your game, butchering women and children? Then I will kill, too!' So saying, he turned his horse's head and started for the Indian camp near the fort, where had been left their squaws and children. Several Indians pursued him as he galloped along. He laid himself flat on the neck of his horse, loading and firing in that position as he would occasionally turn on his pursuers. At length their balls took effect, killing his horse and severely wounding himself. At this moment he was met by Winnemeg and Waubansee who en-deavored to save him from the savages who had now overtaken him. As they sup-ported him along, after having disengaged him from his horse, he received his death-blow from another Indian, Peesotum, who stabbed him in the back." All that, of course, is complete balderdash, akin to the fanciful story Mrs. Helm con-cocted about her struggle with a warrior and rescue by Black Partridge.

294. Those killed in the initial action at the dunes and out onto the prairie beyond included twenty-three men out of a total, including officers and noncoms, of

fifty-six. Dead included Corporals Thomas Forth and Rhodias Jones; Privates George Adams, Redmond Berry, James Bowen, John Cooper, Fielding Corbin, John Hamilton, —— Keamble, John Kelso, Michael Leonard, Frederick Locker, Andrew Loy, James Mabury, Hugh McPherson, William Moffett, Frederick Peterson, David Sherror, John Simmons, Philip Smith, and the unidentified seventy-year-old militiaman.

295. In her account, Margaret Helm in this matter invented a whole incident that never occurred; one which provided her with a mantle of courage and added unnecessary drama to an occasion already more than filled with it. She wrote that after concluding her talk with Dr. Van Voorhis just before his death (and forgetting that she was still mounted on her horse at this time). "At this moment a young Indian raised his tomahawk at me. By springing aside, I avoided the blow which was intended for my skull, but which alighted on my shoulder. I seized him around the neck, and while exerting my utmost to get possession of his scalping knife, which hung in a scabbard over his breast, I was dragged from his grasp by another and an older Indian. The latter bore me struggling and resisting toward the lake. Notwithstanding the rapidity with which I was hurried along, I recognized, as I passed them, the remains of the unfortunate surgeon. Some murderous tomahawk had stretched him upon the very spot where I had last seen him. I was immediately plunged into the water and held there with a forcible hand, notwithstanding my resistance. I soon perceived, however, that the object of my captor was not to drown me, for he held me in such a position as to place my head above water. This reassured me, and regarding him attentively I soon recognized, in spite of the paint with which he was disguised, the Black Partridge. When the firing had nearly subsided, my preserver bore me from the water and conducted me up the sand-banks. It was a burning August morning, and walking through the sand in my drenched condition was inexpressibly painful and fatiguing. I stooped, took off my shoes to free them from the sand with which they were nearly filled, when a squaw seized and bore them off, and I was obliged to proceed without them." Although the account was pure fiction, in lieu of any other eyewitness account, the Margaret Helm version was accepted as truth. Later, historians began finding so many distortions and untruths in the entire account that they began to suspect this whole incident was fabricated. Fully a century later, John Kinzie's account was discovered, was found to be very accurate and debunked this particular incident quite succinctly as follows: "A Potawatomi [Black Partridge] now came forward & after taking my gun offered to take us to a place of safety but my daughter thinking his intentions hostile ran at first into the lake but soon returned." It is indeed ironic that when a statue was proposed commemorating the Chicago Massacre, it was a recreation of Margaret Helm's fictionalized struggle with the warrior and her being saved by Black Partridge that was eventually sculpted in bronze, to become one of Chicago's most famous pieces of statuary. The statue is presently in the lobby of the Chicago Historical Society.

296. Survivors at the prairie knoll at the time they were surrendered by Captain Heald included: Captain Nathan Heald (wounded); Second Lieutenant Linai Helm (slightly wounded); Corporals Joseph Bowen, Richard Garner (badly wounded) and Walter Jordan; and Privates John Allin (badly wounded), Prestly Andrews (badly wounded), George Burnett (slightly wounded), James Corbin (wounded), Phelim Corbin, Daniel Daugherty, Micahjah Denison (badly wounded), Stephen Draper (badly wounded), Dyson Dyer, Nathan Edson, Paul Grummo, William Hunt, David Kennison, Jacob Landon (badly wounded), James Latta, Hugh Logan, Michael Lynch, Duncan McCarty, Patrick McGowan, Elias Mills, August Mortt, John Neads, —— Nelson, Joseph Noles, William Prickett, John Smith, Jr., John Smith, Sr. (badly wounded), John Suttenfield, James Van Horne, and Anthony Waggoner (badly wounded).

297. There has been much needless confusion in this respect in past accounts. Some contend the emissary was Peresh, also referred to as Perish, Peresh LeClerc and Pierre Moran, a Potawatomi-Kickapoo mixed-blood chief, who is described in some accounts as a half-breed. Others contend it was the fourteen-year-old interpreter

Salienne, who had deserted from the march at the onset of hostilities. Foremost originators of such misinformation were Lieutenant Helm (whose account of the surrender is considerably in error and written with the intent to cast Captain Heald in a very bad light and to exalt himself) and Sergeant William Griffith, who was not even on hand at the surrender (being hidden on the north side of the river at this time) but who later, when serving in the Thames Campaign with Robert B. McAfee, dictated to that historian an account of the Chicago massacre that had Griffith in the thick of things throughout, which had Griffith wounded in the battle, and which had Griffith intending to kill the boy-interpreter Salienne, when he came with a surrender demand, and which was all pure hokum. McAfee had no way of knowing that Griffith was lying and so he wrote the account as Griffith gave it to him. In point of fact, the intermediary was Pierre LeClerc, a genial French-Potawatomi half-breed in his middle or late twenties, who had been indoctrinated at a young age into the fur trade by John Kinzie, who worked for Kinzie for many years and who, at the time of the massacre, was still working for Kinzie on occasion and also occasionally served the fort as interpreter. To further muddy the situation, Pierre LeClerc has also been referred to as Pierre LeClaire. LeClerc lived in his own home (some say with a Potawatomi wife, though this is not verified, but likely) just southwest of the fort in, or adjacent to, the area where the temporary Indian encampment was made west of Frog Creek.

298. In some accounts it is erroneously stated that Captain Heald paid a fee of $100 per prisoner still alive at this time, but that is incorrect. It was a single payment of $100 for the safety of everyone. Also, it was to Siggenauk that Captain Heald surrendered his sword, not to Black Partridge, as some accounts have erroneously contended.

299. Several accounts have stated that immediately following the surrender, "every other prisoner was immediately put to death." That statement is wholly without foundation.

300. Again, Margaret Helm let her imagination run away with her in describing this incident, stating that the man was killed by a squaw wielding a stable fork which she repeatedly jabbed into him until his writhing and cries ceased and he was dead, bolstering her tale by stating that Waubinema, "with a delicacy of feeling scarcely to have been expected under the circumstances," stretched a mat across two poles to shield her eyes from the grisly sight. John Kinzie, who was also there, simply stated that Burns, badly wounded, was brought to the camp and there tomahawked to death by a squaw.

301. Some accounts have attributed the misidentification to Captain Heald, thinking it to be Rebekah Heald's beheaded form on the ground, but it was actually Helm who made the error.

302. In some accounts it is Captain Heald who is credited with sighting his wife, Rebekah, sitting among the squaws, weeping. That is not correct. It was Lieutenant Helm and his wife, Margaret. Also in one account it is stated that Margaret Helm went to her husband and dressed his wound with a handkerchief. This is probably untrue for at least two reasons: Mrs. Helm was still a prisoner herself and not free to go to the prisoners; also, Lieutenant Helm's wound, a bullet nick in the heel, was very minor and scarcely needed any urgent attention.

303. Some accounts have misidentified the Burnett that the warrior was looking for as William Burnett, trader at St. Joseph and brother-in-law of Topenebe. That is incorrect. William Burnett was at St. Joseph at this time and the Burnett the warrior was seeking and subsequently found was Private George Burnett, one of the two fifers of the Fort Dearborn band, who had been slightly wounded during the initial battle. Burnett had evidently cheated or otherwise wronged the warrior in some sort of encounter months before.

304. In at least one account it is stated, apparently without basis, that the prisoners were herded into the fort and held at guard on the parade ground all night. Actually, the prisoners, already divided among the chiefs, spent the night in the wigwams of those to whom they had been assigned.

305. In some accounts it is stated that Kinzie's man, Jean Baptiste Chandonnais, con-

veyed the Healds to St. Joseph and that Chechepinqua conveyed them from there to Mackinac. Actually, Chechepinqua conveyed them to St. Joseph and, two days later, Chandonnais conveyed the Kinzies, Margaret Helm and Sergeant William Griffith to St. Joseph. On August 29 Chechepinqua was paid by Heald to convey him and Rebekah and Sergeant Griffith to Mackinac.

306. No further mention is ever made concerning Henry and Black Jim, so far as the author has been able to determine. Athena, Henry's wife, is believed to have accompanied the Kinzies to St. Joseph, but no mention of either male slave is made, leading to the probability that neither escaped. Their ultimate fate remains a mystery.

307. One severely wounded woman, Emmaline Clark, and twelve soldiers were killed by various means, primarily tortures of different sorts, by the Indians this night. Exact details are not known, although later evidence showed some had been burned at the stake. Of the twelve soldiers, eight were known to have been so severely wounded in the fighting that they would have been unable to march away with their captors to the respective villages and so they were executed. The same was true of two privates who had been captured at the sick wagon and were too ill to march. The final two were neither injured nor sick, but no reason is known for why these two were singled out to be executed, although the probability is that they had in some way, prior to the massacre, offended the Indians and the execution was a form of revenge. Whatever the case, the identity of those killed this night is as follows:

Severely wounded, unable to march:	Mrs. Emmaline Clark
	Corporal Richard Carner
	Private John Allin
	Private Prestly Andrews
	Private Micahjah Denison
	Private Stephen Draper
	Private Jacob Landon
	Private John Smith, Sr.
	Private Anthony L. Waggoner
Sick, too ill to march:	Private Thomas Poindexter
	Private John Fury
Neither sick nor wounded:	Private James Latta
	Private Hugh Logan

Thus, the total number of dead at the conclusion of the day of the massacre, including not only those killed in the actual fighting, but those killed afterwards — Privates Daniel Daugherty, Duncan McCarty and William Prickett, who were killed in the volley at the surrender; Private Burnett and Militia Sergeant Burns, killed at the encampment; and Susan Corbin and her two children, Henry and Wilma, killed at the Burns house — was eighty. That total of eighty dead at the end of this day was augmented by another seven who were known to die in captivity, plus the Corbin eight-month fetus, removed from the mother and beheaded after the massacre at the wagons. Therefore, the final total (including the fetus) was eighty-eight dead out of a total of one hundred forty-eight men, women and children involved.

308. Some accounts have stated that every structure owned by Americans in Chicago — whether military or civilian — were burned, but that is erroneous. Only the fort, with its interior buildings, and the Indian Agency were burned.

309. This was approximately fifteen miles upstream from present Joliet, Illinois, about thirty miles above the point where the Kankakee and Des Plaines River meet to form the Illinois. The place they stopped was within a few miles of where Cook, DuPage and Will County now meet, near a woods that is now appropriately named Black Partridge Woods, several miles northeast of Romeoville, Illinois.

310. Evidently, subsequent to the sailing of the American troops from Detroit in the British ships, Generals Brock and Hull added two supplemental articles to the capitulation, the content of these articles unknown to the troops. General Brock

related that "certain considerations afterwards induced me to agree to" the supplemental articles, which were as follows:

> An article supplemental to the articles of capitulation concluded at Detroit, 16th August.
>
> It is agreed that the officers and soldiers of the Ohio militia and volunteers shall be permitted to proceed to their respective homes on this condition, that they are not to serve during the present war unless they are exchanged.
>
> W. Hull, brig. gen.
Commanding N.W. Army U.S.
Isaac Brock, maj. gen.
>
> An Article in addition to the supplemental article of Capitulation, concluded at Detroit, 16th August.
>
> It is further agreed that the officers and soldiers of the Michigan militia and volunteers, under the command of maj. Wetherell, shall be placed on the same principles as the Ohio volunteers and militia are placed by the supplemental article of the 16th inst.
>
> W. Hull, brig. gen.
Commanding N.W. Army U.S.
Isaac Brock, maj. gen.

311. Just fifty-eight days later, on October 13, 1812, Major General Isaac Brock was killed by a bullet through his heart at the Battle of Queenston on the Niagara River.

312. The supply train under Captain Henry Brush was ultimately jeopardized by the approach of a war party led by Tecumseh. Abandoning the supplies and cattle, Brush led his men in a forced march to escape. He was pursued by Tecumseh's men for some time, but ultimately escaped unharmed and returned to Chillicothe, Ohio.

313. Sergeant Griffith later told how he had located a canoe in which he and Captain Heald and Rebekah Heald escaped. That, of course, did not occur either at this time or when the Healds and Griffith subsequently went by canoe from St. Joseph to Mackinac.

314. Several accounts have stated that Private Mortt was executed when he went insane. However, that was not true; he was simply overwrought with emotion. The Potawatomies, as did many other Indian tribes, considered people who were truly insane to be "touched" by the Great Spirit and therefore under the special protection of that deity. As a result, they very studiously avoided doing harm of any sort to anyone who was insane. Some captives in early accounts (though none of the Chicago captives) realized this and were successful in saving their own lives by feigning insanity.

315. This hire is believed to have cost Captain Heald about $150 to $200.

316. In view of subsequent events, it is possible that Kinzie at this time went to William Henry Harrison to report the Chicago events to him and was at that time enlisted to act as a spy for Harrison in Detroit and send him reasonably regular reports concerning the British and Indians.

317. Son of the deceased Alexander McKee.

318. At the corner of Jefferson and Wayne Streets in present Detroit.

319. Formerly the American ship Adams. What the cost of this passage was is not definitely known, but it was believed to be about $100.

320. At this point, evidently, Sergeant Griffith left the Healds and next appears as a member of Colonel Richard M. Johnson's Regiment in the Battle of the Thames during William Henry Harrison's Detroit Campaign, and it was at this time that Griffith related his largely fanciful and self-aggrandizing account of the Chicago Massacre to Captain Robert B. McAfee.

321. Present Erie, Pennsylvania.

322. Site of present Franklin, Pennsylvania.

323. During this stretch of their journey, the Healds passed the area where Eleanor Kinzie, as a girl named Nelly Lytle, was captured by Chief Cornplanter of the Senecas and taken into captivity thirty-three years before.

324. The actual death toll, which of course Captain Heald could not have known at this time, was one ensign, one surgeon's mate, one Indian Agent, two sergeants, three corporals, forty-five privates, twelve militia, six women, twelve children, four civilian men, and one fetus, for a total of eighty-eight.

325. The evidence seems fairly conclusive that Captain Nathan Heald embezzled the U.S. Army payroll money that had been left in his trust at the end of June 1812 by First Lieutenant Jonathan Eastman, District Paymaster. In a deposition given under oath by Sergeant William Griffith to Justice of the Peace Thomas Rowland at Detroit on July 22, 1818, Griffith states that Eastman, in addition to giving Heald the garrison's back pay for nine months, left in his care for ultimate distribution three months' advance pay for the garrison. Not knowing that Heald had sewn the funds into his garment, Griffith was under the impression that the funds had been confiscated by the Indians. Eighteen months after the Griffith deposition had been taken, Major Heald was queried about the loss of the funds, by Peter Hagner, Third Auditor's Office, Treasury Department, Washington, D.C., that query dated March 30, 1820. Heald replied to that letter in a letter dated May 18, 1820, from St. Charles, Missouri Territory, in which he stated: "After making the payment [of June 30, 1812, to his garrison] there was a small balance remaining in my hands in favor of Mr. Eastman, but I can not say what the amount was. Every paper relative to that transaction was soon after lost. I am, however, confident there was no deposit with me to pay the garrison for the three months subsequent to the 30th of June, 1812.

"The receipt-rolls which I had taken for Mr. Eastman, together with the balance of money in my hands, fell into the hands of the Indians on the 15th of August, 1812, when the troops under my command were defeated near Chicago; what become of them afterwards, I know not." By his own account of having the money sewn into his garment, of purchasing passage, guide service, a boat, food and clothing, as well as his refusal to accept money from Captain Roberts at Mackinac because he didn't need it as he had funds with him, and also in light of John Kinzie's account of helping to save the money when Heald admitted he had it, then later returning the money to Heald, it seems quite apparent that Captain Heald lied in his letter to U.S. Auditor Peter Hagner and that he had, in fact, embezzled the funds in question. However, so far as is known, no further investigation was ever made after this time.

326. Some accounts say he was taken to the Kankakee River and remained there for two months, but those reports do not hold true in the light of close analysis. The village of Mittatass was located on Peoria Lake, not on the Kankakee, and Helm was ransomed by Thomas Forsyth (with Chief Black Partridge as intermediary) on August 30, which was only fifteen days following the massacre.

327. Although the account has all the earmarks of an exciting romance of enduring love, it did not quite work out that way. They were later divorced.

328. The full account of the battle of the Thames and Tecumseh's death is found in *The Winning of America* series volume entitled *The Frontiersmen*.

329. It is clear from what is known that indeed some high-placed person did exert considerable pressure to effect the release of John Kinzie and the dismissal of all charges against him. However, no record is known to exist of who this benefactor was. Kinzie himself remained forever in the dark in this matter.

330. During the treaty negotiations at Ghent, the British negotiators argued with great earnestness in an attempt to make the United States agree to renounce its ownership over all of the Northwest beyond the lines of the original Treaty of Greenville in 1795. Their intent was to create an Indian State — a reserve set aside for the Indians which would provide a buffer state and permanent barrier between the United States and Canada, westward of Niagara. The proposition, had it been accepted, would have given the Indians, in absolute ownership, an area comprised of roughly half the present state of Ohio, all of Indiana, Illinois, Michigan, Wisconsin and part of Minnesota. However, the Americans would not even agree to consider the proposal. The Duke of Wellington himself advised the British negotiators that the course of the war had provided no basis whatsoever for the British

to demand a cession of territory by the United States in order to terminate the war. The treaty ultimately provided for a better-defined boundary between Canada and the United States, but no surrender of territory by either party. But what might have occurred if such a proposition had been agreed to? For a marvelous, very sensitive portrayal of just such a supposition, the author recommends the short novel by Kenan Heise entitled *The Journey of Silas P. Bigelow* (Collage, Inc., Publishers, Wheeling, Illinois, 1981.)

SPECIFIC SOURCES

Note: The specific sources listed below, chapter by chapter, are keyed by the author or publication given here to the Bibliography of Principal Sources which follows this section.

CHAPTER I

Andreas, I, 33–35, 69–70, 72–72f, 73–73n, 74–75, 97, 639. Berton, *Invasion*, 191. *Bulletin of the Chicago Historical Society*, I, 1934–1935, 106. Clifton, 139, 162–163, 165. Cotterill, 38f. Cuneo, 135, 137–138, 195. Draper Papers, D₁G₁2²³⁻²⁴. Drimmer, 74. Edmunds, 96, 98–100, 222. Flexner, 236–240, 261. Galloway, 40, 106, 114–115, 284, 289. Gibson, 19, 31, 33–34, 91. Hagan, 5, 9–10, 51. Hatcher, *Great Lakes*, 145, 156. Hatcher, *Lake Erie*, 52. Henry, *Travels*, 52–53, 59–64, 80. Hough, *Diary*, vi–ix, xviii, 6n16, 42–43, 50–52, 70, 89. Howe, I, 310, 371, 391, 679, 961; II, 144, 405–410. Hudleston, 186, 195. *Indiana Magazine of History*, LII (Dec. 1956), 383–396. Kenton, 21, 32–33, 40, 45, 137–139, 240. Kinietz, 310. Kinzie, *Wau-Bun*, 191–195. Kirkland, 157, 173. Francis Parkman Papers, XXII, 413–414; XXVII, 441, in Massachusetts Historical Collections. McAfee, 144. *Michigan Historical Collections*, IX, 347–348; X, 277. Mitchell, 11. Moore, 41, 612, 612n, 613–615, 630, 634–639, 654–669. O'Callaghan, VIII, 955. Parkman, *Montcalm*, II, 374–377, 407. Parkman, *Pontiac*, I, 20, 209–211, 256, 265–266, 266f, 273, 285–286, 317–318; II, 11–13, 20–21, 46, 77–78, 257, 271, 307–308, 329–331. Peckham, 30–74, 77–82, 88, 90–97, 107, 112–117, 147, 154–155, 165, 186–187, 193, 196–199, 224–225, 232, 237–238, 306–308, 310n, 311, 311n, 313, 315–316, 316n. Pierce, I, 409. Quaife, *Checagou*, 90–93. Quaife, *Lake Michigan*, 100–101, 105, 178–179, 319. Quaife, *War*, 36–37, 37f13. Seelye, 25. Sterling, 5, 37, 62, 70–71, 95. Stevens, 17, 22, 24. Swanton, 241–243, 249, 251, 253, 256. Wainwright, 175–180, 182, 196. *Wisconsin Historical Collections*, XII, 7–13, 38–48. Wissler, 31–32, 91. Wood, N., 122, 126–128, 131–136, 166–168.

CHAPTER II

Andreas, I, 70–75, 77–79, 82, 92, 108–109, 639. *Bulletin of the Chicago Historical Society*, I, 108. Clifton, 156–163, 165–166, 462. Draper Papers, D₁G₁8²⁴⁶. Edmunds, 101–108. Flexner, II, 329. Galloway, 13–14, 41, 56, 61–62. Gibson, 34–

39. *Illinois Historical Collections*, I, 233, 393; II, 169–174; VIII, 72, 140–147, 311–313. Kenton, 96–97. Kinzie, "Chicago Indian Chiefs," 108. Kinzie, *Wau-Bun*, 270, 272–279, 289–291. *Michigan Historical Collections*, IX, 374–376, 466; X, 275; XIX, 353. Parkman, *Pontiac*, I, 317–318. Pierce, I, 409. de Peyster, 10n4. Quaife, *Checagou*, 36–37, 42, 63. Ward, 639. *Wisconsin Historical Collections*, XVIII, xix, 40–421.

CHAPTER III

Andreas, I, 34, 69, 72–75, 93, 97, 639. Bowers, 15. Clifton, 110–112, 114–116, 140–141, 163, 166–167. Cotterill, 65f, 72n. Coues, 303–304. de Peyster, II, 12–14. Horsman, *Expansion*, 181–183. *Journals of the Continental Congress, 1774–1779*, XXV, 680–695. Draper Papers, D5BB113, D1f98K–L–M, D1F111B, D10F160, D10F168, D11F11–13, D2G5. Edmunds, 107–110, 115–117, 156, 163. Galloway, 31, 49–52, 66–70, 72–79, 79n, 85–86, 90–94, 122, 128–134, 299. Gibson, 39. Great Lakes Indian Archives, Potawatomi File, Montgomery to Clark, May 30, 1780. Hagan, 8. Hatcher, *Great Lakes*, 198–200. Hatcher, *Lake Erie*, 55. Hodge, II, 46, 49, 55, 475. Howe, I, 108–109, 245, 293, 310, 325, 387, 389, 467–480, 502–504, 543, 594, 746; II, 98–99, 175–176, 244, 682, 684–685, 732, 778, 796, 888–890. *Illinois Historical Collections*, I, 456–457. *Journal of the Illinois State Historical Society*, XXIII (Jan. 1931), 676–677. Kenton, 148, 152–156, 179. Kinzie, *Wau-Bun*, 279–285, 287–288. McAfee, 194. *Michigan Historical Collections*, IX, 558, 563, 582–583, 617, 629; X, 380–381, 391–393, 395–396, 406, 424, 435–437, 450–451, 453–455; XIX, 519–520, 529–530, 540; XX, 174–187; XXIV, 24–25. *Mississippi Valley Historical Review*, II, 195–210; V, 214–228. Pierce, I, 12–13, 409–410. *Proceedings of the Mississippi Valley Historical Association*, II, 205–206, 209–210. Quaife, *Checagou*, 37–38, 50–51, 90–91, 94–100, 127. Quaife, *Lake Michigan*, 105–111, 173–175. Quaife, *War*, 131n43, 156n54. Seelye, 29–31, 53, 55–56. Stevens, 21. Swanton, 257. *Transactions of the Illinois State Historical Society*, 1904, 62–62n, 63. *Wisconsin State Historical Society Collections*, VII, 182; IX, 282–283, 286, 290–291; XI, 151, 170n2, 180n; XII, 49–76, 133–136, 219–220, 283.

CHAPTER IV

American State Papers, Indian Affairs, I, 8–9, 72, 92–93, 131–135. Andreas, I, 36n, 73n, 78–80, 82, 97, 109–110, 204, 268. Appleton's Journal, VI (1871), 544. Berton, *Invasion*, 54, 191. *Bulletin of the Chicago Historical Society*, I (1934–1935), 109–110. Butterfield, 249–255. Carter, II, 31–35, 78–79, 89–90, 119–120; III, 300–301, 320–321. Clifton, 99, 117, 122–123, 142, 166–167. *Collections of the Massachusetts Historical Society*, 3rd Ser., V., 159–163. Cotterill, 80. Coues, 215n. Cruikshank, *Correspondence*, I, 55, 369. *Documents Illustrating the History of Missouri, 1785–1804*, I, 167–168. Drake, B., 40–44. Edmunds, 57n, 117–125, 142, 154, 156. *Filson Club Quarterly*, XLVI (July 1972), 247–249. Galloway, 95–96, 98–100, 114, 131–132, 310. Gibson, 39–40, 42–43, 45–47. Great Lakes Indian Archives, Potawatomi File, "Fort Wayne Manuscript" by Hiram Beckwith. Hagan, 4, 10–12. Harmar Papers, Clements Library, Hamtramck to Harmar, Aug. 2, 1790. Hatcher, *Great Lakes*, 200. Hatcher, *Lake Erie*, 58–59. Howe, I, 217, 300, 669–671, 747, 854, 876; II, 144, 223, 559, 777–778, 807. *Journal of the Illinois State Historical Society*, XVII, No. 3 (Oct. 1924), 378–388. Kappler, II, 18–25. Kinzie, *Wau-Bun*, 265. Kirkland, 174–175. Marmar Papers, Clements Library, Harmar to Knox, Dec. 13, 1788. McAfee, 144, 194. *Memoirs of the Historical Society of Pennsylvania*, VII, 331–334. *Michigan Historical Collections*, XII, 10–11; XXIV, 101–102, 108–109, 187–197, 200–222, 306–307. *Michigan Pioneer Historical Col-*

lections, XI, 499–501; XXIV, 261–262. Mitchell, 9–11. Nasatir, I, 167–168. Northwest Territory Papers, 348–350. *Ohio Archaeological and Historical Quarterly*, XX (Jan. 1911), 83–84. *Pennsylvania Archives*, 1st Ser., XI, 72–73. Pierce, I, 13, 92, 410. *Proceedings of the State Historical Society of Wisconsin, 62nd Annual Meeting*, 251. Quaife, *Checagou*, 38–39, 42, 52–56, 67–68, 91, 98. Quaife, *Lake Michigan*, 208–210, 316–317. Seelye, 32, 56–61, 135. Smith, William, II, 106. Stevens, 24. Thornbrough, *Outpost*, 159. Webb, 1. *Wisconsin State Historical Society Collections*, XII, 83–96, 136. Wissler, 91–92.

CHAPTER V

American State Papers, Indian Affairs, I, 36–38, 136–138, 227, 241, 338, 340–342, 352–353, 491, 559–560, 564–582. Andreas, I, 34–34, 52, 70–75, 80–84, 91, 96–97, 105, 109–111, 144, 543, 640; II, 452. Berton, *Invasion*, 58, 61, 191–192, 204. Buell, 335–362. *Bulletin of the Chicago Historical Society*, I (1934–1935), 106–110. Butterfield, 261, 265. Carter, II, 297, 335, 447–449, 454–455; VII, 71–72, 433–434. Clifton, 123, 126, 142–148, 153–155, 158, 162–169, 171–172, 180–181, 190, 195, 461. Cotterill, 80, 97, 100–102, 102n, 103–104, 111. Cruikshank, *Correspondence*, II, 344. Draper, D4BB55, D1F27, D11F2, D1G1^{10}, D4U145, D2YY120, D11YY11, D12YY1821. Edmunds, 123–127, 130–136, 147–156, 158, 170–172, 186, 222. *Filson Club Quarterly*, XXII (July 1953), 268. Galloway, 41–42, 125, 217, 315–317. Gibson, 47–50. Graham, 72. Great Lakes Indian Archives, Potawatomi File, "Hamtramck to Wayne, Sept. 24, 1795 and Oct. 10, 1795." Hagan, 4, 10–12, 27. Hatcher, *Great Lakes*, 200. Hatcher, *Lake Erie*, 58–62. Heward, *Journal* Manuscript in Chicago Historical Society (transcript). Horsman, *Matthew Elliott*, 103. Houck, II, 528. Howe, I, 52, 72–75, 294, 300–301, 342–344, 374, 391, 411, 426, 502, 529–532, 543–546, 673, 751–755, 814, 876, 907; II, 137–145, 172, 222–223, 229, 232–234, 300, 420, 452–454, 559, 594, 742, 807, 859–860. *Indiana Magazine of History*, L (Sept. 1954), 287–289; LVI (Sept. 1960), 217–226. *Journal of the Illinois State Historical Society*, XVII, No. 3, (Oct. 1924), 386; XLII, 272. Kenton, 217, 230–231. Kinnard, III, 102, 107. Kinzie, *Wau-Bun*, 288. Kirkland, 20–21, 35, 175. *Massachusetts Historical Collections*, 3rd. Ser., V, 137–142. Matthews, 265–282. McAfee, 12–15, 125, 143–144, 194. McDermott, 287–318. *Michigan Historical Collections*, XII, 143–144; XIX, 545; XX, 370–372; XXIII, 39–42; XXIV, 43–44, 108, 167, 329–330, 414–416, 518–519, 551–554, 571–572, 587–593, 659–660, 734; XXV, 14, 40–46; XXXIV, 640. *Mississippi Valley Historical Review*, I (Dec. 1914), 425; XVI (June 1929), 86n5. Nasatir, I, 173–174, 322; II, 528. National Archives, Record Group 94, "Muster Roles of Volunteer Organizations: War with Northwest Indians, 1790–1795; Records of Adjutant General's Office." *Northwest Ohio Quarterly*, XXXV (Spring 1963), 54–68. Northwest Territory Papers, "Subsistence Account of William Wells from 13 September 1793 to 30 June 1794," and "The United States Account with William Wells." *Ohio Archaeological and Historical Quarterly*, XXXII (July 1924), 238–252, 257–262; LIX (July 1950), 244; LXVI (April 1957), 168–171; LXX (July 1961), 202–203. *Pennsylvania Magazine of History and Biography*, XII, No. 2 (1888), 173–184. Pierce, I, 12–15, 92, 410. *Pioneer History of Illinois*, 280. *Proceedings of the American Antiquarian Society*, LXIV (Oct. 1954), 279–287. Quaife, *Checagou*, 56–58, 60, 62, 66–68, 91–92, 95–96, 105, 108, 123. Quaife, *War*, 197, 197n6. Sargent Papers, "Sargent to St. Clair, Feb. 5, 1792," "Francis Vigo to Winthrop Sargent, April 1, 1792." Seelye, 60–62, 69–81, 85–87, 90–94, 96–97, 135, 155. Smith, D.L., 281n9z. Swanton, 243, 263. *Transactions of the Illinois· State Historical Society*, 1904, 63, 88, 104; 1907, 289–290. Thornbrough, *Outpost*, 159. University of Ky., 40. Van der Beets, 213–413, 313n47. Volney, 363, 372–374, 378–379. Walters, 386. Webb, 1. Wentworth, 21. *Wisconsin Historical Collections*, II, 96–97; X, 90; XII, 97–100, 106, 133–135; XVIII, 45, 442–443. Woehrmann, 44–48.

CHAPTER VI

Andreas, I, 34, 70, 72–73, 73n, 74–75, 82, 84, 92, 97, 101, 109–110, 204, 288, 640. Berton, *Invasion*, 112, 192. *Bulletin of the Chicago Historical Society*, I (1934–1935), 106, 106n1, 107, 110. Butterfield, 262–268. Carroll, 420. Clifton, 127–128, 155, 171–172, 185, 187, 462. Cotterill, 117n. Cunningham, 70, 112, 143. Edmunds, 153, 156, 158–159, 172. Graham, 72–73. Hagan, 3, 18. Hatcher, *Great Lakes*, 159. Hatcher, *Lake Erie*, 63–64. Howe, I, 41, 283, 391, 486, 495, 503, 753, 814; II, 276, 491, 501, 807, 831–839. Hurlbut, 66–67. *Indiana Magazine of History*, LXXIV, No. 3 (Sept. 1978), 183–222. *Journal of the Illinois State Historical Society*, XVII, No. 3 (Oct. 1924), 388, 395. Kinzie, *Wau-Bun*, 195. Kirkland, 35. McAfee, 14, 143–144. Pierce, I, 13, 410. Poinsatte, M.A. Thesis. Quaife, *Checagou*, 42, 60, 63–65, 68, 88, 92–93, 95, 98–99, 123, 145–148. Quaife, *Lake Michigan*, 111–113, 121n3, 210. Quaife, *War*, 156. Seelye, 98, 135–136, 138–139. Swanton, 239–240, 249. *Transactions of the Illinois State Historical Society*, 1904, 62, 62n, 63–64. *Wisconsin Historical Collections*, XII, 100–104, 138.

CHAPTER VII

American State Papers, Military Affairs, I, 175. Andreas, I, 35, 72–75, 80, 84, 87, 97, 239, 240, 640. Berthrong Collection, "Meigs to Wayne, Aug. 30, 1796." Berton, *Invasion*, 40–43. Clifton, 179, 185, 187–189. Coues, xx–xxii, xxiin4, xxiii–xxvi, 98. Dawson, 36. Drake, B., 62. Draper Papers, D9T2–3. Edmunds, 155–156, 159–165. Esarey, I, 41–46, 52–54, 56–57, 76–84. Gibson, 53, 55, 92. Hagan, 3–5, 7, 12–13, 16–19, 26. Hamtramck Papers, "Dearborn to Hamtramck, Nov. 4, 1801." Harrison Papers, Indiana, "William H. Harrison to Charles Jouett, Jan. 15, 1803." Howe, I, 42, 148, 310, 342, 435, 609, 688, 754, 814, 854; II, 270, 408, 420, 501, 557, 573, 587, 657, 692, 740, 758. *Journal of James Strode Swearingen*, Chicago Historical Society manuscript. Kappler, II, 64–66. Kingsbury Papers, Chicago, "K. to Whistler, July 12, 1804," "Whistler to K., July 26, 1804." Fort Dearborn Papers, "Return of Military Agents' Stores on Hand at Fort Dearborn, 31st December 1809." Kinzie, John, *Account Books*, July 1804. Kinzie, *Wau-Bun*, 492. Kirkland, 57, 173. McAfee, 194. *Mississippi Valley Historical Review*, XV (June 1928), 89–92. *Missouri Historical Review*, IX (Jan. 1915), 97. National Archives, M–15 (Microfilm) Roll 1, 118–121, 135–137, 142–143, 328–331; Roll 2, 126–128. Northwest Territory Papers, "A Brief Account of the Proceedings of the Committee Appointed by the Yearly Meeting of Friends, Held in Baltimore, for the Improvement and Civilization of the Indian Natives," 25; *ibid.*, "A Mission to the Indians from the Indian Committee of Baltimore Meeting to Fort Wayne in 1804," 167–173. Pierce, I, 12–16, 20, 71–72, 77n, 410–411, 639–640. Quaife, *Chicago and the Old Northwest*, 127–129. Quaife, *Checagou*, 39–44, 63, 65–66, 69, 70–72, 74–75, 83–84, 86, 88–90, 97, 103, 145, 163–164. Quaife, *Lake Michigan*, 113–114, 131n4, 201, 206. Sargent Papers, "W. H. Harrison to Secy. of War, Nov. 17, 1797 and July 15, 1801." Seelye, 150–154. Shapiro, M.A. Thesis, 1929. Sheehan, 171. Stevens, 23–24, 26. Swanton, 242, 251. U.S. War Dept. Papers, "Insp. Gen. Cushing to Col. Hamtramck, March 14, 1803," "Insp. Gen. Cushing to Burbeck, July 12, 1803." Washington, IV, 472. Wentworth, 12–13. Williams, K., 31–32. Wilson, 4–16.

CHAPTER VIII

American State Papers, Indian Affairs, I, 695; II, 27, 40, 45, 65. Andreas, I, 8, 35, 72–76, 84–92, 97, 233, 507, 640. Berton, *Invasion*, 41–42, 48, 62, 92. Buck, 58. Burt, 114–119. Carter, II, 496–499; XIII, 76–80. Clifton, 186–187, 190, 192–193, 195. Coues, 242. Edwards Papers, "Manuscript Report on Rivers and Indian Villages in Northern Illinois and Southern Wisconsin (ca. 1810)." Edmunds, 67–89, 158–

166. Esarey, I, 184–186. Galloway, 140–142, 149–150. Gibson, 48, 56–58, 98. Hagan, 6, 19–22, 24–27, 31–33, 37–41, 92. Harrison Papers, Indiana, "Jefferson to Harrison, Jan. 16, 1806." Harrison Papers, Library of Congress, I, 183–184, 235, 239, 251. Hodge, II, 476, 729–730. Horsman, *Matthew Elliott*, 157–158. Howe, I, 43, 391; II, 640. Hurlbut, 106. *Journal of the Illinois State Historical Society*, XVII, No. 3 (Oct. 1924) 386, 388. Kappler, II, 67–89. Keating, I, 171–172. Kenton, 62, 268. Kingsbury Papers, Chicago, "Whistler to Kingsbury, Aug. 14, 1804," and "Kingsbury to Whistler, Sept. 10, 1804." Kinzie, John, *Account Book*, entry of June 14, 1806. Kinzie, *Wau-Bun*, 491, 493. Kirkland, 62, 67–69. *Michigan Historical Collections*, XL, 77–78, 247–252. *Mississippi Valley Historical Review*, XLV, 53–55, "British Indian Policy in the Northwest, 1807–1812" by Reginald Horsman. *Missouri Historical Review*, IX (Jan. 1915), 97. National Archives, RG 94, M–15 (Microfilm), Roll 2, 233, 248. Pierce, I, 16–20, 411. Pike, 46. Quaife, *Checagou*, 64, 75–80, 82, 84, 88–89, 96–97, 99–101, 104–105, 117–118, 164. Quaife, *Chicago and the Old Northwest*, 158, 193, 296–299, 301–302. Quaife, *Lake Michigan*, 114–119, 210. Quaife, *Life of Black Hawk*, 89. Seelye, 106, 111–120, 161. Stevens, 21, 26–35, 38. Swanton, 240, 256–257, 259. *Transactions of the Illinois State Historical Society*, 1904, 65; 1916, 57. *Treaties Between . . .* , 109. Wentworth, 9–10, 12–13. Wesley, 31–54. Wilson, Ms. *Wisconsin State Historical Collections*, III, 134; IX, 136–137, 158–161; XI, 344–345; XII, 218–219.

CHAPTER IX

American State Papers, Indian Affairs, I, 760–763, 776–779; Andreas, 72–73, 73n, 74–80, 84, 87, 87n, 88, 90, 97, 99, 104–105, 109–110, 166, 204, 240, 457, 599, 640. Ayer, Ms., "McHenry to St. Clair, April 30, 1799." Berthrong Historical Collection, "Wells to Dearborn, April 2, 1808," "Statement of John Connor, June 18, 1808," and "Harrison to Eustis, July 5, 1809." Berton, *Invasion*, 24–39, 51–52, 63–76, 99–100. Blair, II, 203n76. Bradbury, 17n. Brice, 170. *Bulletin of the Chicago Historical Society*, I (1934–1935), 109–111. Caldwell, "Deposition of Billy Caldwell, Aug. 1, 1816." Carter, VII, 465–466, 472, 555–558; XVI, 162–163. Cleaves, 100–101. Clifton, 61, 168–169, 187, 193–194, 196–199, 201–209. Dillon, 426. Drake, B., 16–163. Draper Papers, D12YY1821. Edmunds, 165–177. Edwards, 38–55, 285–286. Esarey, I, 211–215, 284, 290–291, 337–343, 363–367, 417, 420–430, 438–440, 447, 511, 548–551, 576–584, 591–592, 614–615, 620–624, 691–692, 702–703. Galloway, 139, 146–148, 150–152. Gibson, 56, 58–62n22, 63, 67, 96, 98. Gilpin, 18–20. Goebel, 117, 119–120. Graham, 233. Great Lakes Indian Archives, Potawatomi File, "Wells to Secretary of War, April 19, 1807," and "A Correct Statement of the Numbers of Indians that Attended at the Treats of Fort Wayne in June, 1803, and September, 1809." Hagan, 15, 38–42, 43–44, 89. Harrison Papers, Library of Congress, I, 365–368, 389. Havighurst, 25–26. Henry, *New Light . . .* , II, 529. Hodge, II, 408, 517–518. Howe, I, 261, 391–393, 400, 466, 611, 814–815, 941; II, 529, 607, 809. Hutton, 183–222. *Illinois State Archives*, Governor's Correspondence, May 25, 1809. *Indiana Magazine of History*, LVI (Sept. 1960), 212–216; LXXIV (Sept. 1978), 183–222. Jarrot, June 28, 1809, affidavit. *Journal of the Illinois State Historical Society*, XVII (Oct. 1924), 386, 389; LXII (Jan. 1970), 341–362. Keating, I, 171–172. Kinzie, *Wau-Bun*, 154, 213. Kirkland, 62–63, 69–70, 175–177, 186–188, Appendix E. Lossing, 205. Louisiana *Gazette*, June 6, 1812. Matson, 17–20. McAfee, 20–21, 24, 30–45, 49, 115, 118, 406–407. *Michigan Historical Collections*, XV, 44, 136–137; XIX, 42. *Missouri Historical Review*, XXXIII, No. 8 (1939), "The War of 1812 on the Missouri Frontier," by Kate L. Gregg; Forsyth Papers, "Forsyth to Clark, Nov. 1, 1811," and "Harrison to Esitis, Nov. 18, 1811." National Archives, RG–94, (Microfilm), Ratified Indian Treaties, M–668, Roll 3, 384–392; M–15, Roll 2, 324, 362, 389; M–15, Roll 3, 25–26; M–16, Roll 1, 231–235, 295–299; RG–107 "Secretary of War — Letters Received." Neill, 279. Parsons, 212–216. Pierce, I, 20, 411. Pratt,

51, 140. Public Archives of Canada, RG–10, XI, "Gore's Speech and Gore to Craig, 27 July 1808," and "Tecumseh's Speech, Nov. 15, 1810," CO, 42/351/42. Reynolds, 204. Quaife, *Checagou*, 76, 79, 80–81, 84, 99–101, 105–106, 108–112, 114, 134, 156. Quaife, *Chicago and the Old Northwest*, 193. Quaife, *Lake Michigan*, 113, 116, 118–119, 122–123, 135. Quaife, *War on the Detroit*, 232–233. Seelye, 122–124, 136, 143–146, 149–150, 159–170, 175–176, 193–196, 199, 201, 204–205, 207–209, 211, 233. Stevens, 37–38, 44–45. Swanton, 253, 257. Thornbrough, *Correspondence* . . . , 151. Thornbrough, *Letter Book* . . . , 66–69. Thwaites, *Early Western Travels*, V, 48–49; *Transactions of the Illinois State Historical Society*, 1904, 64–66, 68–96, 108, 165–168. Tucker, 77–78, 111–114, 124. Tupper, 94–96. Vogel, 132–135. Washington, Vll, 232–239. Webb, 2. Weld, 192–196. Wentworth, 12. *Western Sun* of Vincennes, Sept. 19, 1807, June 5, 1808, and July 14, 1810. Williams, K., 46. *Wisconsin State Historical Collection*, IX, 174, 178–182; XII, 135–136, 138–139, 169, 218–221. Wissler, 67–68. Woehrmann, 119, 141, 190–192, 197–198.

CHAPTER X

American State Papers, I, 805–806, 808. Andreas, 72–75, 80–84, 88, 97, 105, 164, 264, 640. Berton, *Invasion*, 23, 65, 69, 75–76, 81–86, 88–90, 97–100, 103, 106–107, 269. *Bulletin of the Chicago Historical Society*, I (1934–1935), 107. Carter, XVI, 159–160, 193–195. Clifton, 175, 177–179, 184, 201–202. Cruikshank, *Documents* . . . , 6, 22. Cruikshank, *General Hull's Invasion*, 247. Edmunds, 178–179, 184, 201–203. Edwards, 39, 292, 300–302. Esarey, II, 21–22, 41–44. Forsyth Papers, Missouri, Nov. 1, 1811. Gibson, 63–65, 97. Gilpin, 16–18. Hagan, 42–47. *House Executive Document No. 38*, 5–7. Howe, I, 393; II, 199, 277. *Indiana Magazine of History*, XVII (Dec. 1921), 353–363. Kentucky *Gazette*, Sept. 3, 1811. Kinzie, *Wau-Bun*, 202–203, 205–209, 212, 217, 244. Kirkland, 69–70, 75, 77–80, 146, 188–189, 194, 194n. Knopf, Pt. I, 11, 37, 73–75, 127, 134. McAfee, 26, 45–46, 48–51, 108–109, 122. McCullough, Almeda. *Michigan Historical Collections*, VIII, 601. National Archives, RG–94, M 221/43. Pierce, I, 21–22. Quaife, *Checagou*, 81, 97–98, 106, 111–112, 117–119, 136. Quaife, *Lake Michigan*, 119, 123, 206. Quaife, *War on the Detroit*, 6n3, 266n31. Seelye, 233–235, 239. Stevens, 41. Thornbrough, *Correspondence* . . . , 226–228. Thornbrough, *Letter Book* . . . , 100–101, 116–117. *Transactions of the Illinois State Historical Society*, 1904, 96, 98–100, 112. Tucker, 230. Tupper, 151–153. Wentworth, 49–50. Whickar, 353–363. *Wisconsin State Historical Collections*, IX, 182–183; XII, 139.

CHAPTER XI

Adams, VI, 308. Andreas, 72–76, 78–84, 88, 90, 92n, 105, 109–110, 640. Beall, 786–791, 795, 799. Berthrong Historical Collections, "Clark to Eustis, April 12, 1812." Berton, *Invasion*, 24, 33, 77, 99–100, 106–112, 117–124, 134–141, 146–171, 183–184, 192–193, 203–205, 210, 267, 269, 282–284, 312. Bonney, 209–211. Burton Historical Collections, Leaflet IV, 77. Carter, XIV, 570–571, XVI, 238–240, 248, 253–255, 261–265. Clark Papers, "Forsyth to Clark, July 20, 1812." Clifton, 202–206. Cramer, 128–130. Cruikshank, *Documents*, 28, 32–33, 40–41, 47–49, 51, 55, 58–61, 74, 76, 78, 130–131, 136–142, 157, 185–186, 193, 214, 216, 219, 242. Dobbins, 303. Draper Papers, D1F116, 116n; D26S37, 50. Drennan Papers, "Hull to Eustis, July 29, 1812," and "Heald to Cushing, Oct. 23, 1812." Edmunds, 179–185, 188. Edwards, 54–55, 316, 321, 325–326. Esarey, I, 444; II, 41–45, 48–49, 50–53, 77. Forsyth Papers, Missouri, "Forsyth to Edwards, June 8, 1812." Foster, 360. Gibson, 49, 61–62, 65–67, 71. Gilpin, 79. Green, 56. Grignon, 268–269. Hagan, 47–49, 51–52. Hatch, 35. Hatcher, *Lake Erie*, 73–75. Howe, I, 373, 393, 876. II, 35, 319–321, 861. Hull, *Memoirs*, 35, 61–64, 76, 208–209. Hull, *Report*, 57–58, 82, 107–108, 135–136. Irwin, 148. *Journal of the Illinois State Historical*

Society, XLVI (Winter 1953), 347–362. Kellogg, The British Regime . . . , 135–136, 138–139, 281–285. Kinzie, John Kinzie's Narrative, 347–362. Kinzie, Wau-Bun, 165, 210–222, 227, 235–237, 245–257. Kirkland, 75, 79–80, 82–83, 93–94, 175, 182–183. Lossing, 258, 262. Lucas, 27, 37, 42–43, 46–52, 59–60, 105, 174. McAfee, 16–17, 51–52, 61–98, 101–118, 122, 125–127, 194, 340. Michigan Historical Collections, XV, 129–130. Michigan Historical Collections, XL, 413–415. Montreal Herald, July 4, 1812. National Archives, RG–107, "Secretary of War, Letters Received, Edwards to Secretary of War, May 12, 1812", M–221/43; M–221/47; M–341. National Intelligencer, July 11, August 14, September 3, 1812. Nursey, 118–119. Parish, v–vi, 37, 43, 174. Pearkes, 459. Perkins, 427–433. Pierce, I, 20–22, 403, Appendix III. Quaife, Askin Papers, 730. Quaife, Brownstown, 74–75, 77. Quaife, Checagou, 81–83, 87–106, 119–125, 148, 165–167, 279–290, 429. Quaife, Chicago and the Old Northwest, 215–216, 216n, 217–227, 393, 583. Quaife, Lake Michigan, 119–120, 123–125, 206. Quaife, War on the Detroit, 6n3, 77–81, 84–93, 187, 187n, 188–195, 195n, 196, 209, 222, 225, 233–266, 266n31, 267–279, 291–313, Appendices A, B, C, E. Reynolds, 131–132. Richardson, Richardson's War, 32, 34, 37, 49–51. Seelye, 235, 238, 241–245, 254. Smith, W., 83. Stevens, 41. Thornbrough, Correspondence . . . , 230–232. Thornbrough, Letter Book, 80, 102–110, 114–115, 120–121, 124–125, 130–133, 140–143, 158–159, 170n. Thwaits, Early Western Travels, XXVII, 71. Transactions of the Illinois State Historical Society, 1904, 100–122, 138–139. Tucker, 235–238, 243, 245, 252–259, 264–265. Tupper, 200–201, 243–245, 259, 262. Webb, 2. Wentworth, 49, 89. Williams, K., 12–14, 43–45, 51–52. Wisconsin State Historical Society Collections, IX, 182–183, X, 113, XII, 139–141, 221. Wochrmann, 216. Wood, C., I, 430, 432–434, 436–437, 442, 488, 533–535. III, Pt. 1, 7. Woodford, 59.

CHAPTER XII

Andreas, I, 31, 35, 72–75, 78n, 80–83, 90, 94–95, 95n, 97, 99, 100, 108–110, 457, 640. Askin, II (1931), 719–730. Berton, Invasion, 74n, 162–163, 165–171, 190–191, 193–195, 197–198. Carter, XVI, 261–265, 727–728. Clarke, 450, 453, 455–456. Clifton, 205–207. Cruikshank, 139–141. Dowd, 30. Drennan Papers, "Heald to Cushing, Oct. 23, 1812." Earle, 312–317. Edmunds, 138, 185–188. Fort Dearborn Papers, "Lt. Helm Narrative of the Massacre (ca. July 1814)." Hatch, 42. Hatcher, Great Lakes, 163. Hatcher, Lake Erie, 74. Howe, II, 144. Hull, Report, 82. Hurlbut, 105. Indiana Magazine of History, XLIV (Dec. 1948), 414. Journal of the Illinois State Historical Society, XVIII, No. 3 (Oct. 1924), 386–387. Kinzie, John Kinzie's Narrative, 346–362. Kinzie, Chicago Indian Chiefs, 107–110. Kinzie, Wau-Bun, 148, 178, 181, 212–237, 239–240, 242, 244–245, 247. Kirkland, 19–22, 22n, 23–38, 40–41, 43–44, 48, 69, 82–84, 93–94, 99–100, 178, 180–181. Lossing, 258–289. McAfee, 95–98, 101, 113–116, 194. Simmons, 1–75. National Intelligencer, August 14, September 3, 1812. Norris, J., A Business Advertiser and General Directory of the City of Chicago for the Year 1845-6. Nursey, 118–119. Pierce, I, 17, 22–24. Quaife, Checagou, 36–103, 107, 111, 121–137, 141–145, 147–151. Quaife, Chicago and the Old Northwest, 215–216, 216n, 220–223, 225–226, 229–261, 393, 407, 409–413, 417–420. Quaife, Lake Michigan, 120, 126–128. Quaife, War on the Detroit, 106–107, 111n, 290–291. Richardson, Richardson's War, 49–51. Seelye, 246. Transactions of the Illinois State Historical Society, 1904, 118–124. Tucker, 252–258, 264–265. Tupper, 244–245, 260–262. Walters, 385–389. Webb, 2. Wentworth, 19–20. Williams, K., 44–46. Wisconsin State Historical Society Collections, X, 113–113n. Wood, C., I, 534–535, 548.

CHAPTER XIII AND EPILOGUE

American State Papers, Indian Affairs, II, 12, 64, 208, 361–362, 365. Andreas, I, 72–77, 80–85, 87–89, 90, 92–93, 97–100, 105, 109–110, 166, 192–193, 204, 264,

524, 640. Berton, *Invasion*, 130, 164, 170–184, 187, 194–198, 201–202, 213, 216–217, 222–225, 282–284, 312. Blair, 278n103. Brice, 214–215, 269. Buck, 12. Varnum, *Incidents*, 1809–1823, Ms., Chicago Historical Society. *Bulletin of the Chicago Historical Society*, I (1934–1935), 107–110. Clifton, 205–207. Cruikshank, *Documents*, I, 144, 158, 187, 214, 219–220; III, 272; IV, 36–37, 41–42, 79. Cruikshank, *General Hull's Invasion*, 284–285. Drennan Papers, "Bradley to Parker, August 3, 1816." Edmunds, 187–189. Esarey, 438–440, 506–507, 514–516. Galloway, 126, 152–153, 159–162, 204–205, 215, 264–266, 271, 307–308, 310–317. Gibson, 72, 77–78. Hahan, 51, 60–61, 80–81, 84. Hatcher, *Lake Erie*, 74, 87–88, 90. Horsman, *Matthew Elliott*, 195–196, 201–202, 213. Howe, I, 394, 579, 815; II, 861. Hull, *Report*, 35–40, 46, 89–93, 99, 103, 109, 150, 163. James, 291–292. *Journal of the Illinois State Historical Society*, XVIII, No. 3 (Oct. 1924), 385–389. Kinzie, *John Kinzie's Narrative*, 346, 350–351, 359–360. Kinzie, *Wau-Bun*, 229, 234–239, 240–253, 258–259. Kirkland, 14, 37, 44, 49n, 98–99, 178, 186, 189, 197. Kosche, 56–58. Lossing, 30. Lucas, 62–71. *Magazine of History*, XV (March 1912), 89. McAfee, 42, 61–113, 116, 143–144, 192–195, 244, 323, 331, 369, 374, 400–404, 406, 409–410, 412–414, 417–431, 438. *Michigan Historical Collections*, XV, 151–154, 293–296, 347–350, 535–536. Simmons, 1–75. *National Intelligence*, Sept. 3, 1812. *New York History*, XXV (July 1937), 312–317. *Northwest Ohio Quarterly Bulletin*, II (Oct. 1930), 11. Pierce, I, 19, 23–31, 411. Quaife, *Checagou*, 73, 81, 84, 101, 109, 133–154, 158–159, 161. Quaife, *Chicago and the Old Northwest*, 235–236, 254–255, 407–408, 413, 419–420. Quaife, *Lake Michigan*, 120, 123, 128–129, 132–133. Quaife, *War on the Detroit*, 74n, 104–106, 106n, 107–112, 137–139, 144–152, 157n55, 188n1, 266n31–267n31, 291–292, 294–304, 435–436, 305–309, 315–317. Read, 158. Richardson, *Richardson's War*, 55, 57–58. Richardson, *Wau-Nan-Gee*, 126. Seelye, 246. *Transactions of the Illinois State Historical Society*, 1904, 117, 121–127, 165, 168. Tupper, 260, 262, 290–292. Webb, 2–3. Wentworth, 14, 20, 89. *Wisconsin State Historical Collections*, IX, 299n; X, 71, 94–98, 113n; XII, 146–148, 221. Witherell, 303–304. Wood, C., I, 536–538, 550, 596. Woodford, 70–71.

BIBLIOGRAPHY OF PRINCIPAL SOURCES

Adams, Henry. *A History of the United States of America during the Administrations of Thomas Jefferson and James Madison.* New York: Scribner's, 1889–1891.

American State Papers. Indian Affairs, 2 vols., 1832–34, and Military Affairs, 7 vols., 1832–61. Washington, D.C.: Gales & Seaton.

Andreas, A. T. *History of Chicago, from the Earliest Periods to the Present Time.* 3 vols. Chicago: A. T. Andreas, publ., 1884.

Armstrong, John. *Notices of the War of 1812.* 2 vols. New York: G. Dearborn, 1836.

Ashe, Thomas. *Travels in America Performed in 1806.* London: Foxe, 1808.

Atherton, William. *Narrative of the Suffering and Defeat of the North-Western Army under General Winchester.* Frankfort, Ky., 1842.

Auburey, Thomas. *Travels through the Interior Parts of America.* London, 1789.

Ayer, Edward E. Ayer Manuscript. Chicago: Newberry Library.

Beall, William K. "Journal of William K. Beall," in *American Historical Review,* XVII (1912).

Berthrong, Donald J. Berthrong Collection. Bizzell Memorial Library, University of Oklahoma, Norman.

———. *Indians of Northern Indiana and Southwestern Michigan.* New York: Garland, 1974.

Berton, Pierre. *Flames Across the Border — 1813–1814.* Toronto: McClelland & Stewart, 1981.

———. *The Invasion of Canada — 1812–1813.* Boston: Little, Brown, 1980.

Blackbird, Andrew J. *Complete History of the Ottawa and Chippewa Indians of Michigan.* Ypsilanti: Babcock & Darling, 1887.

Blair, Emma H. *Indian Tribes of the Upper Mississippi Valley and the Region of the Great Lakes.* 2 vols. Cleveland: Arthur H. Clarke Co., 1911.

Bonney, Catharina V. R. *A Legacy of Historical Gleanings . . .* 2 vols. 2nd ed. Albany, 1875.

Bowers, Leo. *A History of the Sac and Fox Indians until after the Opening of their Reservation in Oklahoma.* Unpublished M.A. thesis, College Library, Oklahoma A & M College, Stillwater, 1940.

Bradbury, John. *Travels in the Interior of America in the Years 1809, 1810 and 1811.* Liverpool, 1817.

Brannan, John. *Official Letters of the Military and Naval Officers of the United States, during the War with Great Britain in the Years 1812, 13, 14 & 15.* Washington, D.C., 1838.

Brice, Wallace A. *History of Fort Wayne.* Fort Wayne: D. W. Jones & Son, 1868.

Brownell, Charles D. *The History of the Indian Races of North and South America*. Hartford: University of Connecticut Press, 1865.
Buck, Solon J. *Illinois in 1812*. Fergus Historical Series. Chicago: Fergus Printing Co., 1918. (2nd edition reprint by University of Illinois Press, Urbana, 1967.)
Buell, Rowena. *Memoirs of Rufus Putnam*. Boston: Houghton, Mifflin & Co., 1903.
Bulletin of the Chicago Historical Society.
Burnet, Jacob. *Notes on the Settlement of the Northwest Territory*. Cincinnati: Derby, Bradley & Co., 1847.
[Burnett, William]. William Burnett Papers. Burton Historical Collection. Detroit Public Library, Detroit.
Burt, Alfred L. *The United States, Great Britain and British North America from the Revolution to the Establishment of Peace after the War of 1812*. New Haven: Yale University Press, 1940.
Burton, Clarence M. *The City of Detroit, Michigan, 1701–1922*. 2 vols. Chicago, 1922.
Burton Historical Collections.
Butterfield, Consul Willshire — *History of the Girtys*. Cincinnati: Robert H. Clarke Co., 1890.
[Caldwell, William]. Billy Caldwell File. Chicago Historical Society.
Carter, Clarence Edwin. *The Territorial Papers of the United States*. 27 vols. Washington, D.C.: U.S. Government Printing Office, 1934– .
Carver, Jonathan. *Travels through the Interior Parts of North America*. London, 1778.
[Cass, Lewis]. Lewis Cass Papers. Burton Historical Collection. Detroit Public Library, Detroit.
[Clark, William]. William Clark Papers. Kansas Historical Society.
———. William Clark Papers, Missouri Historical Society.
Clarke, James F. "History of the Campaign of 1812, and Surrender of the Post of Detroit," in *Revolutionary Services and Civil Life of General William Hull . . . by Maria Campbell*. New York: D. Appleton, 1848.
Claus, William. "Diary of William Claus," in *Michigan Pioneer and Historical Collections*, XXIII (1895).
[Claus, William]. William Claus File. Chicago Historical Society.
Cleaves, Freeman. *Old Tippecanoe: William Henry Harrison and his Time*. New York: Scribner's, 1939.
Clifton, James A. *The Prairie People*. Lawrence, Kans.: Regents Press, 1977.
Colden, Cadwallader. *History of the Five Nations*. 2 vols. New York: Cornell University Press, 1922.
Collections of the Massachusetts Historical Society.
Collins, Lewis and Richard. *History of Kentucky*. Louisville, 1874.
Cotterill, R. S. *The Southern Indians: The Story of the Civilized Tribes Before Removal*. Norman: University of Oklahoma Press, 1954.
Coues, Elliott. *The Expeditions of Zebulon Montgomery Pike*. 2 vols. Minneapolis: Ross & Haines, Inc., 1965.
Cramer, C. H. "Duncan McArthur: The Military Phase," in *Ohio State Archaeological and Historical Quarterly*, XLVI (1937).
Crew, Harvey W. *History of Dayton*. Dayton, Ohio, 1889.
Croil, James. *Dundas: or, A Sketch of Canadian History*. Montreal, 1861.
Crooks, James. *Recollections of the War of 1812*. Transaction No. 13, Women's Canadian Historical Society of Toronto, 1913/14.
Cruikshank, Ernest A. *Correspondence of Lieutenant Governor John Graves Simcoe*. 5 vols. Ontario Historical Society. Toronto. 1923–1931.
———. *General Hull's Invasion*. Series 3, Section 2, Vol. 1, Royal Society of Canada Transactions. Toronto, 1907.
Cuneo, John R. *Robert Rogers of the Rangers*. New York: Oxford University Press, 1959.
Cunningham, Wilbur M. *Letter Book of William Burnett*. Fort Miami Heritage Society of Michigan, 1967.
Dawson, Moses. *A Historical Narrative of the Civil and Military Services of Major General William Henry Harrison and a Vindication of his Character and Conduct as a Statesman, a Citizen, and a Soldier*. Cincinnati, 1834.

de Peyster, Arent. *Miscellanies by an Officer, 1774–1813*. 2 vols. New York: A. E. Chasmar & Co., 1888.

Dobbins, Daniel and William. "The Dobbins Papers," in *Buffalo Historical Society Publications*, VIII (1905).

Dowd, James. *Built Like a Bear*. Fairfield, Wash.: Ye Galleon Press, 1979.

Downes, Randolph C. *Council Fires on the Upper Ohio*. Pittsburgh: University of Pittsburgh Press, 1940.

Drake, Benjamin. *Life of Tecumseh and His Brother, the Prophet, with a Historical Sketch of the Shawanoe Indians*. Cincinnati: E. Morgan Co., 1841.

Drake, Samuel. *Indian Biography*. Boston, 1832.

[Draper, Lyman C.] The Lyman Copeland Draper Papers. State Historical Society of Wisconsin. Madison. (Microfilm)

[Drennan, William]. William Drennan Papers. Transcript, Chicago Historical Society.

Drimmer, Frederick. *Scalps and Tomahawks*. New York, 1957.

Earle, J. P. "The Bennington Cannon," in *New York History*, XXXV (July 1937).

Eccles, William J. *The Canadian Frontier*. New York: Holt, Rinehart and Winston, 1969.

Eckert, Allan W. *The Conquerors*. Boston: Little, Brown, 1970.

———. *The Frontiersmen*. Boston: Little, Brown, 1967.

———. *Wilderness Empire*. Boston: Little, Brown, 1969.

———. *The Wilderness War*. Boston: Little, Brown, 1978.

Edmunds, R. David. *The Potawatomis: Keepers of the Fire*. Norman: University of Oklahoma Press, 1980.

Edwards, Ninian W. *The Edwards Papers*. Fergus Historical Series. III. Chicago Historical Society Collection. Chicago: Fergus Printing Co., 1884.

[Edwards, Ninian W.]. Ninian Edwards Papers. Chicago Historical Society.

Edwards, Ninian W. *The History of Illinois from 1778 to 1833; Life and Times of Ninian Edwards*. Springfield: Illinois State Journal, 1870.

Ellet, Elizabeth E. *Pioneer Women of the West*. New York, 1852.

Ellis, G. E. *The Red Man and White Man in North America*. Boston, 1882.

Esarey, Logan. *Messages and Letters of William Henry Harrison*. 2 vols. Indianapolis: Indiana Historical Commission, 1922.

Ferris, Robert G. *Explorers and Settlers*. Vol. V of *National Survey of Historic Sites and Buildings*. U.S. Department of Interior, National Parks Service, Washington, D.C., 1968.

Filson Club Quarterly.

Fitzpatrick, John C. *The Writings of George Washington*. 39 vols. Washington, D.C.: U.S. Government Printing Office, 1931–1944.

Flexner, Thomas. *George Washington in the American Revolution — 1775–1783*. Boston: Little, Brown, 1967.

[Forsyth, Thomas]. Thomas Forsyth Papers. Missouri Historical Society.

———. Thomas Forsyth Papers. State Historical Society of Wisconsin.

Fort Dearborn Papers. Chicago Historical Society.

Foster, Vere. *The Two Duchesses*. London: Blackie, 1898.

Frost, John. *Border Wars of the West*. Cincinnati, 1853.

Galloway, William A. *Old Chillicothe*. Xenia, Ohio: Buckeye Press, 1934.

Gibson, A. M. *The Kickapoos: Lords of the Middle Border*. Norman: University of Oklahoma Press, 1963.

Gilpin, Alec R. *The War of 1812 in the Old Northwest*. East Lansing: Michigan State University Press, 1958.

Gipson, L. H. *The British Empire before the American Revolution*. 15 vols. New York: Alfred A. Knopf, 1939–1970.

Goebel, Dorothy B. "William Henry Harrison: A Political Biography," in *Indiana Historical Society Collections*, XIV (1918).

Goodrich, Calvin. *The First Michigan Frontier*. Ann Arbor: University of Michigan Press, 1940.

Goodrich, Samuel G. *Lives of Celebrated American Indians*. New York, 1844.

Gookin, Daniel. *Historical Collections of the Indians in New England*. 2 vols. Massachusetts Historical Society Collections.

Graham, Lloyd. *Niagara Country*. New York: Duell, Sloan and Pearce, 1949.

Great Lakes — Ohio Valley Indian Archives: Potawatomi File, in Glenn A. Black Laboratory of Archaeology. University of Indiana, Bloomington.

Green, Constance M. *Washington — Village and Capital: 1800–1878*. Princeton, N.J.: Princeton University Press, 1962.

Grignon, Augustin. *Seventy-two Years' Recollections of Wisconsin*. Vol. III in State Historical Society of Wisconsin Collections, Madison, 1856.

Hagan, William T. *The Sac and Fox Indians*. Norman: University of Oklahoma Press, 1958.

Hamilton, Henry R. *The Epic of Chicago*. Chicago: Willett, Clark & Co., 1932.

[Hamtramck, John]. John Hamtramck Papers. The Burton Collection. Detroit Public Library, Detroit.

[Harmar, Josiah]. Josiah Harmar Papers. Clements Library. University of Michigan, Ann Arbor.

———. Josiah Harmar Papers. State Historical Society of Wisconsin, Madison.

[Harrison, William Henry]. William Henry Harrison Papers. Indiana Historical Society Library, Indianapolis.

———. William Henry Harrison Papers. United States Library of Congress. Washington, D.C.

Harvey, Henry. *History of the Shawnee Indians from the Year 1681 to 1854 Inclusive*. Cincinnati, 1855.

Hatch, William S. *A Chapter in the History of the War of 1812 in the Northwest*. Cincinnati: Miami Printing and Publishing, 1872.

Hatcher, Harlan. *The Great Lakes*. New York: Scribner's, 1944.

———. *Lake Erie*. New York: Greenwood, 1945.

Havighurst, Walter. *Wilderness for Sale: The Story of the First Western Land Rush*. New York: Hastings House, 1956.

Hayden, William. *The Conquest of the Country North West of the River Ohio*. Indianapolis, 1896.

Henry, Alexander. *Travels and Adventures in Canada between the Years 1760 and 1776*. New York: I. Ripley, 1809.

——— (with David Thompson). *New Light on the Early History of the Greater Northwest*. New York, 1897.

[Heward, Hugh]. *Journal of a Voyage Made by Hugh Heward to the Illinois Country, 1790*. Transcript in Chicago Historical Society.

Hitchcock, Ripley. *The Louisiana Purchase and the Exploration, Early History and Building of the West*. Boston: Athenaeum Press, 1903.

Hodge, Frederick W. *Handbook of American Indians North of Mexico*. 2 vols. Bulletin XXX, Bureau of American Ethnology. U.S. Government Printing Office, Washington, D.C.: 1910.

Horsman, Reginald. *Expansion and the American Indian Policy, 1783–1812*. East Lansing: Michigan State University Press, 1967.

Houck, Louise. *The Spanish Regime in Missouri*. 2 vols. R. R. Donnelly and Sons. Chicago: Lakeside Press, 1911.

Hough, Franklin B. *Diary of the Siege of Detroit in the War with Pontiac*. Albany: J. Munsell, 1860.

———. *Papers Relating to the Indian Wars of 1763 and 1764*. Albany: J. Munsell, 1860.

House Executive Document No. 38, United States 22nd Congress.

Howe, Henry. *Historical Collections of Ohio*. 2 vols. Cincinnati: C. J. Krehbiel & Co., 1888.

[Hubbard, Gurdon S.] Gurdon Saltenstall Hubbard Papers. Chicago Historical Society.

Hudleston, F. J. *Gentleman Johnny Burgoyne: Misadventures of an English General in the Revolution*. Garden City, N.Y.: Garden City Publishing Co., 1927.

Hughes, Rupert. *George Washington*. 4 vols. New York: Alfred A. Knopf, 1927.

Hull, William. *Memoirs of the Campaign of the North Western Army of the United States, A.D. 1812*. Boston: True & Greene, 1824.

[Hull, William]. *Report of the Trial of Brigadier-General William Hull . . .* New York: Eastburn, Kirk, 1814.

Hurlbut, Henry H. *Chicago Antiquities*. Privately printed in 1881. Reprinted by Eastman & Bartlett. Chicago, 1890.

Hutton, Paul A. "William Wells: Frontier Scout and Indian Agent," in *Indiana Magazine of History*, LXXIV, No. 3 (Sept. 1978).

Illinois Historical Collections.

Illinois State Archives. Governor's Correspondence: Nathaniel Pope to Indian Agents, May 25, 1809. Springfield, Ill.

Illinois State Historical Society Journal.

Indian Documents. Chicago Historical Society.

Indian Papers. Missouri Historical Society, St. Louis.

Indiana Magazine of History. Indiana University, Bloomington.

Irwin, Ray. *Daniel D. Tompkins, Governor of New York and Vice President of the United States.* New York: New-York Historical Society, 1968.

Jackson, Donald. *The Journals of Zebulon Montgomery Pike.* 2 vols. Norman: University of Oklahoma Press, 1966.

James, William. *A Full and Correct Account of the Military Occurrences of the Late War between Great Britain and the United States of America.* Vol. I. London, 1818.

Jarrot, Nicholas. Affidavit of Nicholas Jarrot given at Cahokia, Illinois. June 28, 1809.

Journal of the Illinois State Historical Society.

Journals of the Continental Congress.

Kappler, Charles J. *Indian Affairs, Laws and Treaties, 1778–1783.* 2 vols. Senate Documents, 58th Congress, 2nd Session. Document No. 319. U.S. Government Printing Office, Washington, D.C., 1904.

Keating, William H. *Narrative of an Expedition to the Source of the St. Peter's River.* 2 vols. Philadelphia: George B. Whittaker, 1824.

Kellogg, Louise Phelps. "The Capture of Mackinac in 1812," in *State Historical Society of Wisconsin Proceedings.* 1912.

———. *The British Regime in Wisconsin and the Northwest.* Madison: State Historical Society of Wisconsin, 1935.

———. *The French Regime in Wisconsin and the Northwest.* Madison: State Historical Society of Wisconsin, 1925.

Kelsey, D. M. *Our Pioneer Heroes and their Daring Deeds.* St. Louis, 1884.

Kenton, Edna. *Simon Kenton: His Life and Period, 1755–1836.* Garden City, N.Y., 1930.

Kentucky Gazette Newspaper.

[Kingsbury, Jacob]. Jacob Kingsbury Papers. Burton Historical Collection. Detroit Public Library, Detroit.

———. Jacob Kingsbury Papers. Chicago Historical Society.

Kinietz, W. Vernon. *The Indians of the Western Great Lakes, 1615–1760.* Occasional Contributions from the Museum of Anthropology of the Univ. of Michigan, No. 10. Ann Arbor: University of Michigan Press, 1940.

Kinnard, Lawrence. *Spain in the Mississippi Valley, 1765–1794: Annual Report of the American Historical Association for 1945.* 3 vols. Washington, D.C.: American Historical Association, 1949.

Kinzie Family File. Chicago Historical Society.

[Kinzie, John]. The John Kinzie Account Books; Barry Transcript. Chicago Historical Society.

———. "John Kinzie's Narrative of the Fort Dearborn Massacre," by Mentor Williams in *Journal of the Illinois State Historical Society*, XLVI, No. 4 (Winter 1953), 343–362.

Kinzie, Mrs. John H. (Juliette A. Magill Kinzie). *Wau-Bun, The "Early-Day" in the North-West.* New York: Derby & Jackson, 1856.

Kinzie, Juliette. "Chicago Indian Chiefs," in *Bulletin of the Chicago Historical Society*, Vol. I (1935–1936), 107–110.

———. *Massacre at Chicago*, Fergus Historical Series No. 30. 2nd Ed. Chicago: Fergus Printing Co., 1914.

Kirkland, Joseph. *The Chicago Massacre of 1812.* Chicago: Dibble, 1893.

Knopf, Richard C. *Letters to the Secretary of War, 1812, Relating to the War of 1812 in the Northwest*. Vol. IV in *Document Transcriptions of the War of 1812 in the Northwest*. Historical Society, Columbus, Ohio, 1959.

Loeb, Edwin Mayer. *Cannibalism*. Unpublished M.A. Thesis. Yale University. May 14, 1921. Yale University Library Collections, New Haven.

Lossing, Benson J. *The Pictorial Field-Book of the War of 1812* . . . New York: Harper and Brothers, 1868.

Louisiana *Gazette* Newspaper.

[Lucas, Robert]. *The Robert Lucas Journal of the War of 1812 during the Campaign under General William Hull*. Edited by John C. Parish. Iowa City: Iowa State Historical Society, 1906.

Magazine of History.

Marshall, Humphrey. *History of Kentucky*. Frankfort, 1824.

Mason, Edward G. *Early Chicago and Illinois*. Fergus Historical Series. IV Chicago Historical Society's Collection. Chicago: Fergus Printing, 1890.

Matson, Nehemiah. "Memories of Shaubena," in *Bulletin of the Chicago Historical Society*. August 1935. Chicago: D.B. Cook & Co., 1878.

Matthews, John J. *The Osages: Children of the Middle Waters*. Norman: University of Oklahoma Press, 1961.

McAfee, Robert B. *History of the Late War in the Western Country*. Lexington, Ky.: Worsley & Smith, 1816.

[McArthur, Duncan]. Duncan McArthur Papers. Burton Historical Collection. Detroit Public Library, Detroit.

McBride, James. *Pioneer Biography*. Cincinnati, 1869.

McClung, John A. *Sketches of Western Adventure*. Covington, Ky., 1832.

McCullough, Almeda. *The Battle of Tippecanoe: Conflict of Cultures*. Tippecanoe County Historical Association, Lafayette, Ind., 1973.

McDermott, John. *The Spanish in the Mississippi Valley*. St. Louis, 1926.

Michigan Historical Collections.

Michigan Pioneer and Historical Collections.

Mississippi Valley Historical Review.

Missouri Historical Review.

Mitchell, Harley B. *Historical Fragments on Early Chicagoland*. Privately printed. Chicago, 1928.

Montreal Herald Newspaper.

Moore, Charles. *The Gladwin Manuscripts and the Bouquet Papers*. Lansing: Robert Smith Printing Co., 1897.

Nasatir, A. P. *Before Lewis and Clark: Documents Illustrating the History of the Missouri, 1785–1804*. 2 vols. St. Louis: Historical Documents Foundation, 1952.

National Archives. General Records of the U.S. Government (Record Group 11).

———. Ratified Indian Treaties (M668) 1772–1848. (Microfilm)

———. Letters Received by the Office of Indian Affairs (M234).

National Intelligencer Newspaper. Washington, D.C.

Neill, Edward A. *History of Minnesota*. Minneapolis, 1882.

New York History.

Nicholas Boilvin Letters (1811–1823), in State Historical Society of Wisconsin.

Northwest Ohio Quarterly.

Northwest Territory Papers. Indiana Historical Society Library, Indianapolis.

Notes on a Tour from Fort Wayne to Chicago, 1809. Chicago Historical Society.

Nursey, Walter R. *The Story of Sir Isaac Brock*. Toronto: McClelland & Stewart, 1923.

O'Callaghan, Edward B. (with B. Fernow). *Documents Relative to the Colonial History of the State of New York*. 15 vols. Albany: Weed, Parsons & Co., 1853–1887.

Ohio Archaeological and Historical Quarterly.

Ourada, Patricia K. *The Menominee Indians: A History*. Norman: University of Oklahoma Press, 1979.

Palmer, Frederick. *Clark of the Ohio*. New York: Dodd, Mead, 1929.

Parish, John. *See Robert Lucas Journal*.

Parkman, Francis. *The Conspiracy of Pontiac and the Indian War After the Conquest of Canada*. 2 vols. Boston: Little, Brown, 1894.

————. *Montcalm and Wolfe.* 2 vols. Boston: Little, Brown, 1894.
————. *The Pioneers of France in the New World.* Boston: Little, Brown, 1894.
Parsons, Joseph. "Civilizing the Indians of the Old Northwest, 1800–1810," in *Indiana Magazine of History*, LVI (Sept. 1960), 212–216.
Peckham, Howard A. *Pontiac and the Indian Uprising.* Princeton, N.J.: Princeton University Press, 1947.
Pennsylvania Archives.
Pennsylvania Magazine of History and Biography.
Perkins, Bradford. *Prologue to War: England and the United States, 1805–1812.* Berkeley: University of California Press, 1961.
Phillips, Paul C. *The Fur Trade.* 2 vols. Norman: University of Oklahoma Press, 1961.
Pierce, Bessie L. *A History of Chicago.* 3 vols. Chicago: University of Chicago Press, 1937.
Pioneer History of Illinois.
Poinsatte, Charles A. *A History of Fort Wayne, Indiana, from 1716–1829: A Study of its Early Development as a Frontier Settlement.* M.A. Thesis. Department of History. Notre Dame University, 1951.
Potawatomi Chiefs. Whitney Collection. Illinois State Historical Society.
Potawatomi Chronology. Whitney Collection, Illinois State Historical Society.
Pratt, Julius. *Expansionists of 1812.* New York: Macmillan, 1925.
Proceedings of the American Antiquarian Society.
Proceedings of the Mississippi Valley Historical Society.
Proceedings of the State Historical Society of Wisconsin.
Public Archives of Canada (RG).
Public Archives of Canada. Military Series C, Manuscript Collections.
————. National Map Collections.
————. Record Group 10 — Indian Affairs, Ottawa, Ontario.
Quaife, Milo Milton. *The John Askin Papers, 1796–1820.* 2 vols. Detroit: Detroit Library Commission, 1931.
————. "The Story of Brownstown," in *Burton Historical Collection Leaflets*, vol. IV (1926).
————. *Checagou: From Indian Wigwam to Modern City, 1673–1835.* Chicago: University of Chicago Press, 1933.
————. *Chicago and the Old Northwest, 1673–1835.* Chicago: University of Chicago Press, 1913.
————. *Lake Michigan.* New York: Bobbs-Merrill, 1944.
————. *War on the Detroit: The Chronicles of Thomas Vercheres de Boucherville and The Capitulation, by an Ohio Volunteer.* Chicago: Lakeside Press, 1940.
Read, David B. *Life and Times of Major-General Sir Isaac Brock, K.B.* Toronto: W. Briggs, 1894.
Reynolds, John. *My Own Times, Embracing Also the History of My Life.* Fergus Historical Series. Chicago: Fergus Printing Co., 1887.
[Richardson, John]. *Richardson's War of 1812 . . .* edited by Alexander C. Casselman. Toronto: Historical Publishing, 1902.
Richardson, John. *Wau-Nan-Gee, or the Massacre at Chicago.* New York: H. Long, 1852.
Rupp, Israel D. *The Early History of Western Pennsylvania.* Pittsburgh, 1846.
[Sargent, Winthrop]. Winthrop Sargent Papers. Massachusetts Historical Society.
Schoolcraft, Henry Rowe. *History of the Indian Tribes.* 6 vols. Philadelphia, 1853.
————. *Historical and Statistical Information Respecting the History, Conditions and Prospects of the Indian Tribes of the United States.* 6 vols. Philadelphia: Lippincott, Grambo & Co., 1851.
Seelye, Elizabeth E. *Tecumseh and the Shawnee Prophet.* Chicago, 1878.
Shabbona File in the Chicago Historical Society.
Shapiro, Dena. *Indian Tribes and Trails of the Chicago Region.* Unpublished M.A. Thesis. University of Chicago, 1929.
Sheehan, Barnard. *Seeds of Extinction: Jefferson Philanthropy and the American Indian.* Chapel Hill: University of North Carolina Press, 1973.

Simmons, N. *Heroes and Heroines of the Fort Dearborn Massacre.* Lawrence, Kan.: Journal Publishing Co., 1896.

Shetrone, H. C. "The Indian of Ohio," in *Ohio Archaeological and Historical Journal,* XXVII (1918).

Skaggs, David C. *The Old Northwest in the American Revolution.* Madison: The State Historical Society of Wisconsin, 1977.

Smith, Dwight L. *From Greenville to Fallen Timbers: A Journal of the Wayne Campaign.* Indianapolis: Indiana Historical Society, 1952.

Smith, William H. *The St. Clair Papers.* 2 vols. Cincinnati: Robert Clarke & Co., 1882.

[Starling, James]. James Sterling Letterbook. William Clements Library. University of Michigan, Ann Arbor.

Stevens, Frank E. *The Black Hawk War.* Chicago, 1903.

Swanton, John R. *Indian Tribes of North America.* Smithsonian Institution Bureau of Ethnology Bulletin 145. Washington, D.C.: U.S. Government Printing Office, 1953.

[Swearingen, James Strode]. *Journal of James Strode Swearingen.* Typescript in Chicago Historical Society.

Tecumseh Papers (Microfilm). State Historical Society of Wisconsin. Madison.

Thornbrough, Gayle. *The Correspondence of John Badollet and Albert Gallatin,* 1804–1836. Indianapolis: Indiana Historical Society, 1963.

———. *Letter Book of the Indian Agency at Fort Wayne,* 1809–1815. Indianapolis: Indiana Historical Society, 1961.

———. *Outpost on the Wabash,* 1787–1791. Indiana Historical Society Publications No. 19. Indianapolis, 1957.

Thwaites, Reuben Gold. *Early Western Travels.* 32 vols. Cleveland: Arthur H. Clark Co., 1904–1907.

———. *How George Rogers Clark Won the Northwest and Other Essays in Western History.* Chicago: A. C. McClurg & Co., 1904.

Transactions of the Illinois State Historical Society.

Treaties Between the United States of America and the Several Tribes of Indians. Washington, D.C., 1837.

Tucker, Glenn. *Tecumseh: Vision of Glory.* New York: Bobbs-Merrill Co., 1956.

Tupper, Ferdinand B. *The Life and Correspondence of Major General Sir Isaac Brock,* K.B. London: Simpkin, Marshall, 1847.

Turner, F. J. *The Frontier in American History.* New York, 1920.

United States War Department Papers

Varnum, Jacob B. *Incidents in the Life of Jacob Butler Varnum,* 1809–1823. Manuscript. Chicago Historical Society.

[Varnum, Jacob B.] Jacob Varnum Papers. Burton Historical Collection. Detroit Public Library.

Volney, C. F. *A View of the Soil and Climate of the United States of America.* New York: Brown & Co., 1968.

Volwiler, A. T. *George Croghan and the Westward Movement,* 1741–1782. Cleveland: Arthur H. Clark Co., 1926.

Wainwright, Nicholas B. *George Croghan, Wilderness Diplomat.* Chapel Hill: University of North Carolina Press, 1959.

Walters, Alta P. "Shabonee," in *Journal of the Illinois State Historical Society* XVII, No. 3 (Oct. 1924).

Ward, Christopher. *War of the Revolution.* 2 vols. New York: Macmillan, 1952.

Washington, H. A. *Collected Writings of Thomas Jefferson.* 9 vols. New York: Taylor & Maury, 1853–54.

Webb, George. *Chronological List of Engagements Between the Regular Army of the United States and Various Tribes of Hostile Indians which Occurred during the Years 1790 to 1898 Inclusive.* New York: AMS Press, 1976.

Weld, Isaac. *Travels through the States of North America and the Provinces of Upper and Lower Canada during the Years 1795, 1796 and 1797.* 3rd. ed. London, 1800.

Wentworth, John. *Fort Dearborn.* Fergus Historical Series No. 16. Chicago: Fergus Printing Co., 1881.

Wesley, Edgar B. *Guarding the Frontier*. Minneapolis: Ross & Haines, 1935.

Western Sun Newspaper of Vincennes, Indiana.

Whickar, J. Wesley. "Shabonee's Account of Tippecanoe," in *Indiana Magazine of History* XVII (Dec. 1921): 353–363.

Williams, Kenny J. *Prairie Voices: A Literary History of Chicago from the Frontier to 1893*. Nashville: Townsend Press, 1980.

Williams, Mentor. *See* John Kinzie Narrative.

Williams, Samuel. "Expedition of Captain Henry Brush with Supplies for General Hull, 1812," in *Ohio Valley Historical Series*, No. 2. 1870.

Wilson, James G. *Chicago from 1803–1812*. Manuscript. Chicago Historical Society.

Wisconsin State Historical Society Collections.

Wissler, Clark. *Indians of the United States*. Garden City, N.Y.: Garden City Publishing Co., 1966.

Witherell, B. F. *Reminiscences of the North-West*. State Historical Society of Wisconsin Collections. Vol. III. Madison. 1856.

Woehrmann, Paul. *At the Headwaters of the Maumee: A History of the Forts of Fort Wayne*. Indiana Historical Society. Indianapolis. 1971.

Wood, C. H. *Select British Documents of the Canadian War of 1812*. 17 vols. Toronto: Champlain Society, 1920–1928.

Wood, Norman B. *Lives of Famous Indian Chiefs*. Aurora, Ill., 1906.

Woodford, Frank B. *Lewis Cass, the Last Jeffersonian*. New York: Octagon Books reprint of 1950 edition, 1973.

INDEX